RACE AND REPARATIONS:

A BLACK PERSPECTIVE FOR THE 21ST CENTURY

RACE AND REPARATIONS:

A BLACK PERSPECTIVE FOR THE 21ST CENTURY

Clarence J. Munford

Africa World Press, Inc.

P.O. Box 1892

Trenton, NJ 08607

P.O. Box 48

Asmara, ERITREA

Africa World Press, Inc.

P.O. Box 1892 P.O. Box 48
Trenton, NJ 08607 Asmara, ERITREA

Book and Cover design: Jonathan Gullery

Library of Congress Cataloging-in-Publication Data

Munford, Clarence J.
    Race and reparations : a Black perspective for the twenty-first century / Clarence J. Munford.
      p.   cm.
    Includes bibliographical references and index.
    ISBN 0-86543-510-3 (cloth : alk. paper). -- ISBN 0-86543-511-1 (pbk. : alk. paper)
    1. Blacks--Social conditions. 2. Race relations. 3. Racism. 4. Afro-Americans--Social conditions. 5. United States--Race relations. 6. Reparations. I. Title.
HT1581.M86 1996
305.896'073--dc20   96-10811
                                          CIP

TABLE OF CONTENTS

PART ONE:
WHITE SUPREMACY

WHITE SUPREMACY

Chapter 1

WHITE CIVILIZATION—WHAT IS IT?

There is a worm lying coiled in the heart of Western civilization— the worm of white racism. Like the DNA which governs the genetic features of each individual human being, racism has controlled the evolutionary development of white civilization. While interacting with many other factors of social life, it has ultimate control of societies that have been created or dominated by people of European ancestry. The study of the history of society reveals a genocidal instinct embedded in white civilization. Since the mid-fifteenth century this trait—enthroned as white world supremacy—has inflicted catastrophic damage on people of color around the globe. Dominating all the complex systems which drive Western societies, white racism singled out Africa and Africans of the Diaspora for a holocaust of five hundred years and more—one which shows no signs of letting up. On the eve of the twenty-first century, white racism threatens Black people with continued exploitation, degradation, social confinement, and marginalization—and, failing that, extermination.

My fundamental argument is that white civilization—and its global economic, political and cultural expression, white supremacy—is inherently racist and incompatible with the liberation and humanity of African and African-descended people. Western racist society is the root cause—without exception—of all the multiple forms of oppression Black people endure.

*

My primary concern is with the United States and Canada. However, since the *global* system of white supremacy is most at home in North America, we cannot afford to skip a theoretical analysis of white civilization per se. The totality of the cultural,technological, military, and economic phenomena evolved by human collectives through the ages is the proper referent of the term *civilization*. A civilization entails organized human industry, science, art, and environmental manipulation. I am convinced that this greater whole is one of the most intelligible units of historical study. If, as Malcolm X taught, history should be our favorite inquiry, civilization is a most rewarding object of study. This conviction is based on the postulate that each distinct civilization possesses a specific unity which sets it apart, regardless of whether the unit in question is an independent original creation free of outside influence or the offspring of cultural diffusion. In either event, civilization is a social whole whose historical evolution is primarily *self*-determined.

Civilizations differ. They have been as different from one another as African civilization is from European, or as, say, the Chinese is from the civilization of pre-Columbian America. Civilizations are vast, encompassing phenomena. At any given moment, one and the same civilization may consist of many distinct *"socio-economic formations,"* as unlike one another as Nigeria is unlike Mozambique, or as white America is unlike Russia. Usually, socio-economic formations which are the building blocks of each distinct civilization vary over historical time. Medieval France functioned very differently from the way present-day France functions, for instance, and the economic processes of contemporary hypercapitalist Japan do not resemble the samurai Japan of the Tokugawa Shogunate (1603–1867). Each socio-economic formation bears the indelible stamp of its own generating civilization. Yet each specific formation is also a living social organism in its own right, running according to its own clock and functioning according to rules peculiar to it alone. The rules which govern a socio-economic formation are essential, stable, repetitive, internal connections between phenomena. They are an expression of necessity, in that any one change in the system must—necessarily—evoke changes in other aspects of social life. And each socio-economic formation sports its own peculiar style of family relations, class structures, leisure activity, culture, science and religion. These are expressed in a political, legal, aesthetic, and ideological superstructure unique unto itself. This "way of life" changes over time. Nevertheless, despite dissimilarity and unique features, a given set of socio-economic formations display *common* elements which reveal all to be the "children," as it were, of a single, determining parent—the offspring of one specific civilization. For example, Britain and Germany, white America and Canada, Italy and Poland are unmistakeable manifestations of a single unitary civilization—white European civilization.

A civilization is an all-encompassing marvel. Certain civilizations in history have been racially and ethnically homogeneous communities (e.g., Black pharaonic Egypt). However, most of the time the notion is used to describe a linguistically and ethnically diverse, but racially homogeneous, traditional cultural area like Europe or Black Africa.

*

U.S. social arrangements are determined by the character of *white* civilization. Billions of dollars and innumerable buckets of blood were squandered in an attempt to subjugate or eradicate the Vietnamese—a small, brave, Brown people—while small, needy Black children in American ghettoes starved, were devoured by rats, plied with drugs, and taught to turn their rage against themselves and against their own kind. Racial discrimination creates waves of racist neo-conservatism, "Reagan Revolutions," police brutalities against Blacks, and the daily judicial outrages of the "justice system." Illusions about democracy, freedom, equality, and Martin Luther King's ideal of reciprocal love between the Black and the white community, are still prevalent in Black America. But in real-life America the nightmare predicted by the prophet Malcolm has swamped the idealistic dream of the prophet Martin. The country that triggered the world's scientific and technical revolution, "won the Cold War," and assumed the mantle of a "lone super-power," now claims to have but dwindling resources to spend on rescuing the inner cities and clearing away the slums where Blacks and dark-skinned Latinos live. Meanwhile, it digs down, deepening its deficits, to bail out well-off *white* S & L tricksters to the tune of $400 billion. At the same time the underfunded education of Black children falls further and further behind the requirements and rate of technological change. Official ideology condones the criminalization of the entire Black community, while policy constructs an elaborate political economy of Black male penal incarceration.

*

According to the standard wisdom of Black scholars, the enslavement of Africans fuelled commercial capitalism, developed the wealth of Europe, and helped create industrial capitalism. The four and a half centuries of Atlantic slave trading and subsequent expropriation of African surplus lent muscle to Western technology and military. The dialectic between Black slavery and the installation of the capitalist mode of production in the western hemisphere enabled the accumulation of wealth by American white people—another name for which is capitalism—and confirmed its indelible white racist coloration (Munford 1991; Rodney 1972; 1966; and 1985; and E. Williams 1944).

I agree with this classical wisdom that much of the contemporary ideology and practice of racism is a product of the development of capitalism. Yet that is not enough. We must undertake another task if we are to unravel white supremacy and deal with the white man in the twenty-first century. We must probe the *racist predisposition* which is the basic substratum of white civilization.

*

By *racist predisposition* I mean something which explains the propensity that the *majority* of white people have shown for ages— the propensity to act in a manner detrimental to Blacks and other people of color. The predisposed person is one who is ready without specific cause or grounds to evaluate any relevant situation in racist terms, and to act in conformance with the principles of racism. The racist predisposition is *stable*. It consists of value orientations and a hierarchy of perceived interests which assure that white people will continue to act in inter-racial situations as they have before. The empirical evidence of history leads us to search for this predisposing substratum, for this kind of genetic code or master program, as it were, is located in the depths of white civilization and culture. Even certain white scholars have admitted with unease that this predisposition probably exists. For instance, in his *White Over Black*, Winthrop Jordan, a white researcher, exposed an anti-Black xenophobia in Anglo-Saxon society as far back as the Elizabethan era. Others have evoked an "herrenvolk democracy." That which we must seek, however, is a pre-cognitive substratum in the grass-roots civilization which limits the thought of white people, and forces their thinking into the racist mould.

Like the *a priori* concepts of space and time, cause and necessity which the German philosopher Immanuel Kant (1724–1804) claimed as the foundations and preconditions for all reason and science, white civilization has always contained *a priori* forms of racist impulses and purposes. *A priori* is here understood not in any fixed, absolute, a-historical sense. It refers to antecedent, pre-determining qualities which themselves have been—and will continue to be— subject to historical transformation and development. In this instance, *"a priori"* identifies white mind-sets which are obtained prior to and independent of any brush with reality. These are inclinations inherent in the European *"collective mind"* from the beginning. These proclivities exist prior to and independent of actual social experience on the part of the individual. They were inherent in the European consciousness from the birth of the civilization, caused by events at the birth of European civilization. *A priori* forms disposed the quality of subsequent white historical development beforehand. As explained by Charles Simon, Black expert on Amilcar Cabral, white racism must thus be comprehended as a deep "primal urge."

The white racist predisposition can be shown to have taken concrete form in the course of historical events and processes, epitomized in the genocide of the Amerindians, the Atlantic slave trade, Black slavery in the Americas, and the imperialist colonization of the African continent. The seemingly natural tendency of people in white dominated societies to "form" groups along racial lines, as an expression of voluntary choice, is thus not as it seems. People do not actually form, but rather are formed *into* racial groups by the operation of social laws emanating from the racist predisposition as mediated by historical development (Van den Berghe 1967; Frederickson 1971; Huggins, Kilson and Fox 1971, I: 240-254; and Huggins 1989). There is a "civilization-level" determination at work.

In this connection, the explanatory propositions of Black psychiatrist Frances Cress-Welsing are suggestive. She says it is melanin deprivation which drives the savage behaviour of whites towards people with sufficient melanin—the people of color. The Cress-Welsing theory seeks the source of white supremacy in a deep-seated psychological color-deprivation syndrome. The symptoms of the disease are grouped in a morbid fear of genetic annihilation that has led whites to lash out in jealousy against people of color throughout the history of civilization. For Cress-Welsing, racism is thus a primal determination which precedes the economic structure as the ordaining factor in white society. According to this hypothesis, the origin of racism entails an instinctual psychic quality or behavioral reflex innate in white folk. Although one may harbor doubts about the scientific value of ascribing historical events mainly to a biological factor, the Cress-Welsing theory is an indication that serious-minded Black scholars have begun to wrinkle the brow seriously over the derivation of racism in white civilization. Among them few have done so with more impact than Derrick Bell (see Bell 1987 and 1992).

There are many contradictory elements in the history of white civilization, none more radical than the contrast between the philosophical and rhetorical tradition of democracy, belief in human rights, race-neutral strivings for equality and the dignity of Man, on the one hand, and five hundred years of ruthless genocide against non-white human beings, on the other. The racial goals of white civilization have never been diverted by humanitarian means, no matter how enlightened and "idealistic" individuals have been. Like the proverbial roosting chickens, the racist character of white civilization always seems to come home. "Whether Europeans are discussing world peace, writing history and theology, or organizing for the next revolution," observed James Cone, "they often act as if other peoples' viewpoints do not have to be taken seriously" (Cone 1991).

This can be seen in problems relating to the theoretical connection between capitalism and racism. Not many analysts have wanted to deal with the notion that racism can be embedded at the civilization level. There has been the tendency, therefore, to regard white racism merely as a kind of supplement, a corollary and addendum, at best a consolidation-and-replenishment factor. Racism has been viewed as a means to "divide the working class along color lines." Never was it seen as the kernel or germ cell of capitalism. White thinkers shied away from asking the ominous question—is racism a fundamental political-economy category of the white-dominated capitalist mode of production? There was an unwillingness to look for a racist *context* in white social development. That would have meant distinguishing what is objectively *necessary* in white racist civilization from that which is merely *possible*. Of course, we are not talking about any rigid determinism like that based on belief in divine predestination, and which leads to fatalism. Meant instead is recognition that every cause has its effect, that the racism inherent in white civilization must affect all social phenomena. Racism needs to be scrutinized as something more than merely a specification of Black slavery, as more than a mode of slavery's existence. It is not enough to view it merely as a means of perpetuating and consolidating and intensifying the exploitation of slave labor, and, after Emancipation, merely as a tool to set Black and white wage-earners at each others' throats. Racism has served those purposes, yet it is much more. The status of racist ideology as a rationalization and implementer of slave-and-segregation practices, need not blind us to the *pre-existence* of racial prejudices in the minds of the very first white slavers to appear on the African coast in the fifteenth century.

*

Most social scientists are familiar with the explanatory model which distinguishes between two levels of social reality. There is a *socio-economic foundation*, the level at which human beings enter into social relations with one another. No one can escape this web of ties, for productive activity is required to sustain life. To this socio-economic level is credited the ultimate, dominant causal determination. It is said that we must look to the socio-economic foundation for the final, conclusive cause for all the phenomena and events that occur in society. On top of this basic structure sits a secondary, derivative level. This is the famed *"superstructure."* This level of determination is a force to be reckoned with. For the superstructure contains the entire political, legal, military, and ideological aspects of society—the power components. Emanating from it are powerful reverberating and rebounding "overdeterminations" that condition the way concrete men and women behave from day to day. Despite their extreme potency, superstructural causes are nevertheless secondary and derivative, caused ultimately by events taking place deep within the socio-economic foundation. Many feel that this two-part explanatory model solves the mystery of human behavior.

Now there is something wrong with this. I contend that this analysis is *incomplete*. This tableau lacks a very real *third* level of determination—one that overrides the other two, one that is *senior* to both the superstructure and the socio-economic foundation. I hold that there exists a level that is even more deep-rooted, more primal and pristine. There is a third level from which flows original, initial causation "upwards" through the socio-economic foundation and the superstructure — from the "bottom up" in the sense of the metaphor which conceives society as an edifice consisting of a socio-economic basement, topped by a political-intellectual superstructure. The third level is the site of progenitive *underdetermination*, as it were.

This rock-bottom underdetermination should be what is meant by the term *civilization*. I propose the notion of civilization as synonymous with third-level causation. The explanatory model has now been expanded to three levels of causation: a) civilization; b) socio-economic foundation; c) superstructure. Propensities, proclivities, ends, and goals run from a to c, in terms of primary and ultimate determination. Just as socio-economic relations determine superstructural phenomena, so both the socio-economic foundation and the superstructure are governed by the civilization. The latter projects *a priori* causations. Civilization underdetermination sets *limits* for social behavior, it draws configurations, it creates the "paradigm". Functioning as a touchstone, the third level is the cultural stem from which individualized social formations spring. Procrustean civilization underdetermination commands, ultimately, the social relations 'above', thus flavoring the whole society all the way 'upwards' through the superstructure.

There should be no mystery about this, for there is nothing metaphysical or supernatural about the effects of civilization. Like socio-economic relations of production and superstructural activity, civilization underdetermination is tangible and can be traced. Only it is more fundamental than the former, situated, if we continue the metaphor of the edifice, down in the bedrock below the basement. The civilization layers are the soil from which the tree sprouts. Civilization is the acorn of the social oak. It is the silent nurturing soil which invigorates the shrub. As bedrock, its underdetermining tremors can bring the whole construction crashing down, should discordance arise between its quality and goals and the policies of political decision-makers.

Dominating all secondary and derivative determinations, civilization-level causation can appear arbitrary and violent. For a long time we have been aware of being tied to the economic sphere. Periodically depressions (recessions) rattle the economy with unemployment, poverty swells and homelessness soars. There are various reciprocal, rebounding determinations. We have seen how the Reagan cutbacks—a policy decision of the political superstructure—shrank solvent economic demand. There is the tricky situation in which religion, art, ideas, and other cultural manifestations seem to go their own way, uncontrolled by political and economic trends. Although I have chosen *underdetermination* to characterize the theory I propose, perhaps the terms *super-determination, ultimate* or *primal determination* are equally apt. They indicate a profound level of impulses that, in a pinch, can override contradicting influences. As an analogy, civilization-level determination can be said to be felt in a manner similar to the way the surrounding soil conditions the seed, and nurtures its product as it approaches fruition. In an alternative view, it might be compared to the inherent, genetic information code which determines a living organism's pattern and development through life.

As a general rule, disharmony between civilization-level values on the one hand, and socio-economic and superstructural tendencies on the other, is temporary, apparent rather than real, and socially disruptive. The contradiction is usually overcome in one of several ways. There can occur a decline and fall of a civilization's key social formations (e.g., the fall of the Roman Empire), and even the eventual expiration of the whole civilization as such, one example of which appears to be the disappearance of the Harappa culture of ancient India, ca. 2500–1700 BC. Often the outcome is victory for the original civilization values in their pristine form. Another possibility is a hybrid synthesis of contradictory influences and principles, like the current United States of America, giving rise to an equilibrium that will prove unstable in the historical long run.

That which I designate as "ultimate civilization determination" can be likened in a sense to that which some anthropologists call "style of life," when they seek to shed light on values and virtues. There are life-style features which run throughout European society, for instance, like the diversity of languages, national customs, traditional institutions and the Judeo-Christian legacy which epitomize its ideal values and virtues. The sum-total of these "style of life" features is the germ-molecule of the civilization, and they are what differentiates Europeans culturally from, say, Africans.

11

Spiritually and intellectually, a civilization is a worldview in process. It dictates certain modes of hospitality, ways of looking at the world, and other unrehearsed cultural expressions that, at first sight, give the appearance of being throwbacks—reversions to remote and outdated opinions and behaviour. But these are authentic cultural manifestations. It turns out that these "reversions" are not throwbacks at all, and should be expected. This is the ultimate source of the racist "throwback" that is the leitmotif of white civilization. It is in racism that European tribalism acquires substance, takes on form and flesh, so to speak. Navel-gazing selfishness, hatred of foreigners, and morbid dread of strange folkways—the lifeblood of European culture—converge in a do-or-die devotion to the principle of white supremacy. White supremacy springs from a gut-deep feeling that is more primal than the influences which arise from economic relations. Some critics have cast doubt on the economic rationality of white racism. Nevertheless, they must admit its stubborn persistence and lasting modernity. The reason is that racism is the objective backdrop to economic and superstructural relations in all European-derived societies.

By way of contrast, it is this same analytical principle—i.e., the primacy of civilization-level causation—that enables us to understand the basic *African* heritage of the Black people in the Western hemisphere, descendants of the slave populations. This principle alone justifies our insistence on the consequences of the *Africanness* of the men and women who survived the Middle Passage and the "seasoning." In the slave environment, much of their specific ancestral cultural "baggage" was lost, along with the bulk of their linguistic heritage, as the captives were forced to learn the white man's tongues. Holding out against this cultural rape, however, was a special world view, a stubbornly African civilization substratum which could not be stripped away. It resisted and in time provided the seedbed from which has sprung the distinctive Black communities of the western hemisphere. As Molefi Asante has shown through his studies on the persistence of African syntax and grammatical rules in contemporary U.S. Black speech patterns (Asante 1980), African civilization traits could not be bleached out. The African worldview interacted with chattel slavery and oppression in a transforming process. It interacted with the cruel material reality of white supremacy to create the unique African-American perspective. The Diaspora survived and regenerated because its taproots reached into the African civilization bedrock.

*

Along the way, however, history has played some cruel tricks on the world's unsuspecting peoples of color. For instance, take the situation in the thirteenth century, a period termed the "High Middle Ages" by white historians. Actually, the first half of the century brewed a crisis that threatened the life of white civilization. In 1206, Temujin (1162–1227), crowned Ghenghis Khan, established a mighty Mongol empire that seemed destined to rule over all of Asia and Europe from the China coast to the Atlantic Ocean. By 1223 the Mongols had scythed Russia, and western Europe trembled helplessly, awaiting the bite of the conqueror's sword. However, before the blow descended, the Mongols surprisingly relented and returned to Asia. In 1237 they renewed the assault, this time under the command of Batu. His general-in-chief was Subutai, a military genius superior to the likes of Napoleon Bonaparte. By 1241 the horsemen from the Gobi desert had sliced through Russia, Poland, Hungary, and Bohemia like a hot knife through butter. Subutai's copper-skinned cavalry was poised on the Danube river. The Mongols were invincible still. Suddenly, like a bolt from the blue, news from home caught up with the frontline armies. Were the white man's gods working overtime to protect him? The urge to deal with political complications at home took precedence over the westward surge. Batu withdrew from western Europe in 1242 and white civilization was spared again. In all probability, had the Mongols not voluntarily halted their advance, the conquest would have carried to the Atlantic. Certainly no white army could have beaten them. The Mongol yoke would have fastened on Christian Europe. The white folks would have been the ones subjugated and downtrodden, instead of themselves going out to become world conquerors. The imminent Mongol conquest would have crushed white supremacy in its cradle. These events occurred in the mid-thirteenth century, a mere two hundred years before the first Portuguese slave hunters appeared on the coast of Mauritania to kidnap Africans. This was also a mere 250 years before Columbus set out on the dreadful voyage that would culminate in the extermination of Native Americans and in the enslavement and attempted dehumanization of the children of Africa. Had the Great Khan not died when he did, had Batu's warriors continued their occupation of Europe, we the peoples of color might have been spared the white plague which began its march in the fifteenth century! We mourn a great chance lost. We lament a great tragedy and irony of history.

By the sixteenth century racist ideology was embedded as a cultural factor not only in Tudor England (Jordan 1968), but also throughout white Christian Europe. It was the guiding principle for the white plunderers who by then were rampaging through Africa, Asia and the Americas. In dealing with racism we are dealing with a universal feature present in all European slaving enterprises and not, as some white scholars have claimed, an aberration peculiar only to Anglo-Saxons and other northern European Protestants. As the record of atrocities in Brazil and Spanish America proves, white racism was just as much at home in the Latin branch of European civilization. The variation is merely in degrees of severity, and in ingenuity of ideological rationalizations.

The belief in a pervasive anti-racism among whites, inspired mainly by the deeds of eighteenth and nineteenth century Abolitionists, would appear to contradict the theory that white civilization is racist by nature. Some writers allege that ancient white society was devoid of racism—most likely meaning the Near East, the Hellenistic Mediterranean, and Rome. Others point to a muted sympathy, and even solidarity, between Black and white indentured servants in colonial Virginia until about 1670. White indentured women were a special case. When permitted the choice, they evinced a preference for mating with Black males.

The universality of racist opinions among white *individuals* is not the issue, however. Despite the evidence of some anti-racism in early America, we must not exaggerate either its extent or its historical significance (Aptheker 1992). Anti-racist activism in early America was restricted to a small minority of white people. Today their legatees are the ones who, among other activities, join with Black voters to form the slight majorities which occasionally elect Black officials in districts where Black voters are not a majority and sometimes turn back overt racists like the David Dukes. But no civilization is a featureless monolith without countervailing influences, and the very principle of bedrock determination allows for non-characteristic trends and influences which do not fit with the basic features of the civilization. Some white upper- and middle-class representatives, along with a few lower-class whites, may not have been racists at one juncture or another in history. Some may even have *actively* rejected racism for reasons ranging from affection to religious scruple to enlightened calculation of personal interests.

The point is that these elements were *never* decisive in determining the character of white society. From the ideological perspective, the essence of white culture was fixed by the attitudes of the ruling elite, and those ruling ideas were racist. Ideological hegemony in social formations based on a civilization like the European could hardly be anything but racist.

*

The generality of racism in Western civilization, the fact that it was not restricted to antipathy towards Blacks, is strikingly evidenced in the annihilation of the Native American peoples. Columbus and his posterity "encountered" "Indian" tribes who had developed distinctive economies and cultures—all sophisticated and complex. These farmers domesticated potatoes, beans, cotton, pumpkins, maize, peppers, tomatoes, sunflowers, tobacco, agave, and cocoa. Artificial irrigation and terracing were common. In the Caribbean the peoples ranged from the Taino to the Caribs and Arawaks. Dominant cultures on the South American mainland were the Uzo-Aztecan, Mayan, Inca, Tupi-Guarani, and Araucan. In North America were to be found the Algonquins and the Athabascans, the Sioux and the Iroquois, the Cherokee and the Seminoles, and many others. Some used stone implements, while others mastered metallurgy, worked silver, tin, lead and gold. Some tribes were skilled in making an alloy of gold and copper. Native American weavers and potters had developed craft and trade networks. The Mayan, Inca, and Aztec were urban cultures whose architects, stone masons, and builders had raised magnificent towns and cities, including soaring palaces, temples, fortresses, stadiums, and mansions. Science flourished. Like the Egyptians before them—and perhaps under African influence—the Mayans calculated the solar year accurately and wrote subtle hieroglyphic texts. Aztec surgeons used anaesthetics. Central and South American Indians were similar to West Africans in possessing a vast lore of pharmacology and the medicinal properties of plants. Native Americans could calculate the advent of solar eclipses and knew the times of the orbits of the moon and the planets. Again like the ancient Egyptians, Inca doctors knew how to open the human skull (art of trepanation). The pictorial arts, drama, and sculpture were highly developed. In 1491 there were some 120 million people all told in the western hemisphere.

The political scene presented a great contrast between socially egalitarian, loosely-organized tribal societies on one hand, and powerful, class-stratified, hierarchical states on the other. Communalism was the way of life among the overwhelming majority of native peoples throughout what later became Canada and the United States, in the Caribbean and in the eastern expanses of South America. In this system the land—the chief resource—belonged to everyone. These societies contrasted starkly with the empire-building states. Peru was the site of the famed Inca empire. On the eve of Columbus' arrival, the mighty Aztecs had subjugated the lesser peoples of Mexico. In Central America the Yucatan peninsula hosted the Mayans, creators of one of the greatest civilizations of Pre-Columbian America. The problem was political passions and disunity in the face of the pale invaders. The Mayan city-states were ripped by inscrutable feuds and bloody vendettas. The Inca emperors had their hands full putting down the rebellions of subject tribes. Civil wars had brought the Aztec empire to the brink of collapse even before Cortes and his Spaniards. As in Africa, in the final analysis it was disunity and gullibility which enabled the white conquest.

Delayed in places for decades and even centuries, the Spaniards tramped westward towards the Pacific shoreline in the quest for gold. Along the way they slaughtered "Indians" like cattle, particularly women and children. Spanish colonial domination was firmly in place by the early sixteenth century, not to be shaken in South America until the nineteenth century.

Just as lethal for the native Americans, but also mournfully fateful for Africans, was the Portuguese colonization of Brazil. It began in a dithering fashion. Portuguese mariners accidentally ran upon the boundless country jutting eastward into the Atlantic towards Africa. The year was 1500. Though it was to become the greatest concentration of Black people outside Africa and a bulwark of slavery, Brazil was not what the Portuguese were searching for. At that point in time they were interested primarily in Africa which they had been exploiting for more than half a century already, and where they had established a string of trading posts and slaving forts along the west coast. Preoccupied with Africa and Asia, and thinking that Brazil lacked gold, the Portuguese left the country alone until 1534. Furthermore, Portugal was stretched thin and lacked the manpower for colonization. Thus it was not until the 1540s and onwards that the native Indians were enslaved, slaughtered and wiped out. Canting Jesuit missionaries and scalp-hunting Portuguese *bandeiras* fanned out in the interior, and African slaves were imported to replace the annihilated Amerindians. From 1630 to 1654 the Dutch seized huge areas of northeast Brazil to develop sugar plantations, marking the advent in the "New World" of the Northern European Aryan-Nordic-Gallo-Frankish predators—the Dutch, British, French, *et al.* The most virulent white 'germs' had arrived on the scene.

Along the Pacific coast, on a line running from Mexico to Peru and Columbia, the former Aztec, Mayan, and Inca empires were replaced by a system of white colonial feudalism which subjected the indigenous population to merciless exploitation. The communalist tribes faced total holocaust. Not only was their organic, independent development cut short; over vast stretches they were annihilated. The white intruders were bent on enslaving and manipulating the labor of these tribes. The communalist Indians died by the thousands, fled into the remote hinterland, were pursued, hunted down, and massacred. Malaria, smallpox, and venereal diseases introduced by the Europeans sped the extermination. None suffered more awfully than the Arawaks, Caribs, and Taino in the West Indies. Mercilessly, the whites pressed the native peoples westward, stepping up the offensive during the seventeenth and eighteenth centuries.

The genocide practiced by the white man against the Native Americans ranks second in history only to the annihilation visited upon Black Africa, which lost upwards of 100 millions. In Canada and the United States the Indians have been reduced to the sad remnants that one now finds on reservations or wandering big city streets. In Cuba, Haiti and other West Indian islands the Arawaks, Taino, and Caribs disappeared from the face of the earth. Slave labor at the notorious Potosí silver mines took the lives of 150 Mexican Indians a day for a period of 150 years—a total of eight million. Before the white conquest, Central Mexico was the home of 25 million people. In 1519 Hernando Cortés and his butchers began the slaughter. In thirteen years they killed 8.2 million people. Between 1532 and 1568 the Spaniards killed another 14.2 million. In 1580 there were 1.9 million indigenes left in Central Mexico, a number which by 1605 had shrunk to a little over a million. Virtually speaking, a nation almost as numerous as present-day Canada was obliterated. Ten and a half million of the 12 million Inca empire population were destroyed in thirty-eight short years (1532–1570) (Galeano 1984, 1991).

This capsule history of white violence in the conquest of the western hemisphere is instructive. It highlights the savage treatment of the Native Americans and the subsequent enslavement of Africans. It proves that in the Americas the wealth possessed by whites is not the outcome of any natural development of productive forces, as usually claimed. Rather, violence was the key factor in undermining the foundations of native American modes of production and replacing them with European ones. Thereafter, white violence branded the whole history of the Black man in the white-run economy. We know that the white colonizers extended the new capitalist economy to America by means of the blood, sweat, and tears of Black slaves. In the wake of the genocide against the Indians, four hundred years of slave trading and Black enslavement was an act of collective violence unparalleled in modern history.

It is an old chestnut that at the beginning, before it becomes dominant, each new mode of production must utilize the productive forces created by the preceding mode of production. The history of the Americas, however, provides at best negative proof of this principle. Upon arrival in the New World, Europeans were confronted with Amerindian civilization based on productive forces suited to the environment, and skilfully refined. Following the victory of the conquistadores, the productive forces in Mexico and Peru were diverted from their original purpose and forced to serve white men, while the indigenous peoples were subjugated and exploited unceasingly. In the West Indies, in Brazil, and on the mainland north of Mexico the native peoples were brutally eradicated and the vestiges of their productive forces simply became extinct. Little was left but the land and its resources. That was the purpose of the genocide—to clear the land for white settlement. Once he had completed the annihilation, the white predator in the Caribbean, in Brazil, and in the future United States had to start from scratch, so to speak. The new social relations could not spring from the wombs of preceding Amerindian formations, for those formations had been destroyed. To fill the vacuum, Africa was immolated and millions of Africans were imported in foul slave vessels. Only the crudest form of human exploitation—slavery—was considered economically feasible and ideologically consistent with the racist presumptions of European civilization. As the sometime Black novelist Frank Yerby remarked: "For white people...are maybe the only race in history born without shame. The only race stupid enough and arrogant enough to assume God made them in His image.... They assume that they're handsome, their women are beautiful, what they think and believe is so, and that no other race of people has any rights whatsoever.... Look at what they've done to the poor Indians—I mean the folks *they* call Indians because Christopher Columbus was so damned dumb he didn't know where th'hell he was even after he'd got here—and the real Indians of India and the Chinese and every other race in the world what looks even a little different from them. Tha's why one day th'darker races have got to get together and push the white race right off the edge of the world" (Yerby 1979: 642-643).

In short, the white man's destruction of the civilizations created by the Amerindians opened the way for the enslavement of Black people in colonial America. White racism made it morally easy. The torment of the African had begun. The early accumulation of capital (wealth) by whites was, in reality, the accumulation of Black laborers.

*

By the time of Columbus' endeavor the white-run slave trade in Africans was already some fifty years old, feeding markets in Portugal, Spain, and islands located off the West African coast. The 1492 voyage put the seal on the downfall of Africa, for it opened an inexhaustible greed for captive African labor along the whole western shore of the Atlantic Ocean. One hundred million Africans dead was Columbus' legacy. So too were 400 years of Black slavery, followed over the last hundred years by grinding poverty, degradation, and racial discrimination, enforced by white supremacy everywhere from New York City to Rio de Janeiro.

Whites gloat in the conquest of the western hemisphere as the triumph and expansion of "Western Civilization." In 1992 they rejoiced and celebrated the quincentennial of 1492. For them the Americas represented the "land of opportunity", to which in its northern tier they could import the "gift" of civic arrangements dubbed "political democracy". Their pundits allege that the latter had been invented by ancient Greeks—white men from the eastern Mediterranean. Never mind the fact that ancient Black Ethiopia—a civilization that *owned* Black pharaonic Egypt (Kemet) as its northern region—had developed a refined system of social democracy long before the Greeks had even cottoned to the notion that they would have to "go to school" in Egypt in order to learn civilized behavior (Williams 1987; and Diop 1978 and 1981). Never mind the fact that an African-American interchange predated Columbus' "discovery" by many centuries, a peaceful connection that had enriched Native American society through authentic solidarity between African and American indigenous peoples (Nascimento 1985: 179-180). Whites did not know and did not care that Black men from the Nubian-Kemetic sphere (i.e. ancient Ethiopia) established the Olmec civilization in Mexico some 3,200 years ago. Or that the African-founded Olmec civilization flourished for some 800 years (Van Sertima 1976). Or that Mande-speaking merchant explorers from West Africa sailed the Atlantic more than fifty times during the span from 1310 to 1491, dropping anchor at Panama, Honduras, Haiti, and other Caribbean and mainland sites. Or that during the great age of African trans-Atlantic exploration, between 1305 and 1312 emperor Bakari III of Mali mounted two massive expeditions to the Americas, a hundred and eighty years before Columbus. Instead the media inundated the public with paeans to "European legacies" and white racial Judeo-Christian values. The quincentennial resounded with refrains about Columbus' "triumphs" and Columbus' "tragedies"! It ignored the 500-year tradition of resistance and survival that has been the story of Diaspora Blacks and Amerindians since 1492. It had no time in the celebration for that ceaseless struggle by the peoples of color against white racist world supremacy.

*

As early as 1620/1621, the brand new Plymouth colony recorded its opposition to race mixing. Arriving from England with abhorrence for African blood firmly fixed in their opinions, the Puritans scourged white women known to consort with non-white males. From Day One, New England's courts were determined to impose rigid separation of the races. Stunned by the relative lack of prejudice among some white female indentured servants, the colonial ruling class turned sex into politics, insisting that racial hatred was essential for western values. They knew already that racial preference was the best way to nip in the bud political challenges from the less powerful within their own white community. In order for European Christian civilization to take root in the New World, white supremacy must reign. In the late seventeenth century, once both

England's southern colonies (directly) and the northern maritime colonies (indirectly) became economically dependent on the enslavement of "Black-skins," white women were banned from miscegenating, and race-mixing was proclaimed immoral, in theory. Of course, in practice the ban did not extend to white males, for as long as slavery existed the wholesale rape of Black women—in itself a classic act of war—served the sexual, economic, and "managerial"interests of white supremacy. Class interests and economic advantage generated sexual racism in colonial America, and sexual racism conditioned class interests and economic advantage.

Puritan moralists, European clergy, and sixteenth-century white theorists condemned the "degradation of Man." By degradation they meant the corruption of "God's creation" by mixing its blood with the blood of the children of Africa. It was a fundamental principle of European civilization that divine creation was *white*, and that racial mixing created nothing but mongrelized, degraded mulattoes. In *White Over Black*, Winthrop Jordan confessed that white Christian Europe harbored a racist agenda as far back as the Crusades (1095–1270). Paranoic fear fuelled the medieval anti-Muslim war in the Levant (Middle East) and along the fringes of the Mediterranean. But xenophobia reached even further into the European past. While slavery in classical Roman antiquity may *seem* to have been non-racial, marking *all* eligible for enslavement—whites (the vast majority of Roman slaves) as well as Blacks—the Roman elite—who *were* white—was a prey to superiority complexes which contrasted the "civilized" (themselves) to "Barbarians" (everyone else).

By the nineteenth century, the salient principles of Western civilization were firmly fixed. In fact, "Western" civilization had become an encodement for the notion of global white supremacy. In the United States, "Judeo-Christian values" and European social patterns were synonymous with capitalistic political economy. Whites revered the profit motive as the supreme motivator and expected everyone else to agree with them. The doctrine of white supremacy sprouted from rock-hard racial preference. Despite Sermon-on-the-Mount rhetoric, might was prized over morality. Western civilization is hierarchical in the Social Darwinistic sense that extols the law of merciless struggle between the "superior race" of white people (termed "supermen" by the more frank racists) and the hordes of the "second rate" (i.e., people of color). Only the fittest must be allowed to set the rules for society. To permit those classified as inferior to rise to equal status is to condone social evil. To let the "colored" races swamp the "master race" with superior numbers is to court disaster. It follows that white society is relentlessly militaristic, and that it extols individualism.

Dynamism has been the strong suit of European civilization for the past several centuries. Its vigor and energy pushed it to the cutting edge of scientific-technological development and made it supreme in mass production—a dominance that is only now beginning to be challenged successfully by Asians, notably by the Japanese. Of course, Western mass production achievements were not without the indispensable aid, first of Black slave labor, and then of superexploited Black industrial workers. Western civilization's dynamism has also been expressed in a complexity and pluralism that have sheltered counter-cultural tendencies. This explains the oppositional trends in European-derived social formations. At various junctures, since the sixteenth century religious protest, humanitarian and revolutionary movements have arisen. In form, if not in substance, and at least in original intent, they have mounted apparent challenges to the dominant, racist, and hierarchical, principles upon which the civilization is built. Though never successful in the long term, secular and anti-racist trends—liberal, collectivistic, socialist, democratic, rationalist, abolitionist—have punctuated and spiced white political history for some 475 years. It is this "progressive" tradition that white revolutionaries from Rousseau and Robespierre to Marx and Lenin have extolled.

We pay homage to white civlization's enlightened contributions. None but the tone deaf would spurn Mozart and Beethoven (in whose veins coursed the African Moorish blood of his forefathers). The art works of Leonardo Da Vinci and Michelango, of the Impressionists and Picasso have a beauty and symmetry that is universal in its appeal. The architects who designed and the sculptors who decorated Europe's great Gothic cathedrals were masters within their own cultural tradition. Only a fool, or a total obscurantist, would not appreciate the secrets of the physical universe revealed by Newton and Einstein. For decades now, Third World activists, questing for social change, have sought inspiration in the writings of Marx and Lenin. No right-thinking person wants to "trash" these or other cultural treasures of European creation. The breakthroughs in the treatment of heart disease and cancer pioneered by Western medicine, and in immunization against epidemical infections are a priceless benefit to all humanity. The first leaps into the cosmos from planet Earth have been made from Caucasian societies.

Unfortunately, this progressive tendency is nullified historically by a counter-tradition that has always been the stronger, because it is more in tune with the true values of white civilization. The counter-trend is the reactionary one—mass-based and powerful. It is the hateful, egoistic current of *white populism*—and, yes, it is *democratic*. Populism owes its mass appeal to its democratic character. Even the rabidly "anti-democratic" regimes of Nazi Germany and apartheid South Africa enjoyed *mass* white popular support. Reactionary white populism is staunchly "democratic"— in terms of democracy for *white* people.

Populism, a term coined by an obscure white politician (David Overmyer) in 1892, is premised, in white society, on the conviction that virtue resides in the white common people. It nourishes their collective traditions, including their racist folklore. Political power, according to democratic populist thought, must benefit white people as a *whole,* not just one small clique of white people. Sovereignty—i.e., government authority—should be popular, exercized by ordinary (white) folks, either directly or through representatives, or by means of community-based organs. Simple and traditional forms and values—foremost among them the idea of white supremacy—take pride of place with populism. Phrases like "will of the people," "the average American," "home and family," "family values," and "rising expectations," are common coinage for the spokesmen of white populist democracy. This tendency is aggressively democratic and egalitarian, insisting that one *white* man is no better than any other *white* man, and equally, one *white* man is no less than any other *white* man. This is what Thomas Jefferson and his "Founding Father" colleagues meant when they proclaimed democracy and the rights of "man." This is what Andrew Jackson— Indian-killer and hero-democrat—was all about. This is why contemporary populists, the Newt Gingrichs and Phil Gramms, the Bob Grants and Patrick Buchanans, find such favor among today's white males. This insistence upon human rights and equal opportunity *for whites* has evoked fierce loyalty among the great mass of ordinary white folk since 1776 and 1789. And they understand that, no matter how much their political leaders may pretend that these rights extend to *all* mankind, *full* enjoyment of democracy is restricted to

23

themselves alone, to whites solely. Thus, far from being a protective umbrella, democratic political forms are extremely *dangerous* for non-white minorities. Under white rule, democracy is a mindless redneckism parading in the garb of super-patriotism, according to the principle that the *white* majority rules. Populist democracy umpires the game of presidential elections every four years, during which a majority of the white voters who choose to cast ballots elect a paramount leader against the wishes of a minority of white voters —an arrangement that is perceived as "fair" and sporting. Equally fair and democratic in the eyes of the white majority is a "justice" system which regularly stages events like the legal lynching of boxer Mike Tyson by an all-white jury of his non-peers, and the acquittal of brutal white racist police by white jurors in Southern California's Simi Valley. White populism is a great material force.

On the world scale, this evolution has molded "race relations" as the essential problem of international exploitation and oppression. Throughout the first half of the twenty-first century, if not longer, there will be no avoiding serious "racial conflicts." They are inevitable because white racist supremacy has relegated people of color to an oppressed status, with human entitlements far below those enjoyed by whites. The most severe "racial conflicts" in the future will continue to pit Blacks against whites, because both continental and Diaspora Africans are singled out for the worst treatment in the racist world system. We must prepare ourselves for a titanic, decades-long contest of strength and will between the so-called "North" and the "South" hemispheres. The future, it seems, demands that Black people persevere in a struggle between an international "lower class" of Black, Brown, and Yellow peoples, and a global "upper class" of whites. If it means anything in today's world, the concept of *world revolution* means the eventual triumph of the downtrodden peoples of color in Africa, the Americas, and Asia, over the emerging great white league now stretching from North America right across Europe, uniting white folks from Russia to Australia, NATO with the former Warsaw Pact countries. Five centuries of white supremacy have given world history a racist character. The North-South contradiction has become implacable. It is the inescapable political contradiction on earth today. The once vaunted class contradictions have been subsumed under the racial contradiction, swallowed up in race conflict. While the question of power *within* most African states may well have to be sorted out on the basis of *class* struggle, we are concerned here with the fundamental *international* racial-color contradiction between white supremacy and Black empowerment. The fight against white racism—not class struggle—now functions as the driving force of the development of society. Third World peoples are the only remaining global revolutionary force.

Chapter 2

WHITE RACISM DEFINED

Let us expose the heart of white racism, as we encounter it today. Actually, the notion of *"race"* has a double meaning. As a neutral scientific idea, it is a useful ethnographic and biological concept. As a key to the understanding of white supremacy, in contrast, we must deal *not* with any truly scientific concept of race, but rather with the notion of *racial identity*. The science of ethnography analyzes individual cultures. At root source, it describes how tribes of people evolved an ethnic consciousness and consolidated on the basis of economic and cultural ties, common territory, and language. Race as a general scientific notion is derived from the study of such superficial human biological characteristics as skin pigmentation, nose and lip configuration, hair texture, etc. Grafted to the techniques of ethnography, race highlights differences in the external physical appearance of tribal-cultural groups which consolidated ethnically in regions relatively isolated from one another.

Hence the concept of race, properly used, has nothing to do with measuring historical similarities or differences, nor with any inferiority-superiority criteria, nor with political and legal allegiance, nor with endorsing or invalidating any particular civilization. European civilization has misused the notion of race, however, as a means to assign unequal social fates to groups of people according to external physical features like skin color. The most that can be said of the "racial identity" often discussed by white sociologists, is that it is the feeling of "being different," based, in turn, on individual consciousness of membership of a group who share certain physical characteristics, and who are called a "race" because of those characteristics. In the last analysis, racial identity is caused by being regarded as a member of a specific race, and being *treated* as such by others—it is a social-historical circumstance rather than an ethnographic-biological fact.

There is nothing quite so nebulous about plain old white racism: a collection of mainly anti-Black beliefs and actions, it has a solid, practical purpose—to establish and perpetuate white supremacy. It sanctions discrimination against people of color, justified on biological grounds, in order to secure the objective material interest that white people have in keeping social relations the way they are, permanently. The racists are obsessed with psychological and cultural values innate in Western civilization, regarded as somehow superior to the "immutable" psychological and cultural characteristics of Africans and other peoples of color. Even during periods when such utterances are politically inexpedient, the presumption remains. Either directly as persons, or indirectly through institutions, racism entitles white people to dominate others as the natural consequence of their alleged superiority. Where this domination is challenged, racism implies that the master race is entitled to eliminate unmanageable "troublemakers," even if this means going as far as genocide.

In 1967, and again in 1978, UNESCO tried to come to grips with the notion and reality of racism. It catalogued racist ideologies, prejudiced attitudes, structural arrangements, and institutionalized practices resulting in racial inequality, without, however, in any way stigmatizing Western civilization. In a way, the UNESCO effort was a little like allowing a serial rapist to help frame the felony statute defining and prohibiting rape. The victims of racism are tired of this. We have less and less patience with definitions which restrict racism to proved intent while ignoring the *results* of racial discrimination.

28

Nowadays Blacks more and more insist that there is only *one* kind of racism operational in the world today—global white supremacy (Cress-Welsing 1991; Madhubuti 1994).

While one may argue that this equation oversimplifies the complex evolution of white racism from the fifteenth through the nineteenth century, it fixes firmly on 1) the everyday racial prejudices and practices of whites; 2) the fact that the ruling elites in Canada, the United States, and Europe are lily white; 3) the objective material solidity of racism as the political-economic *system* of white supremacy, and 4) Black oppresson and super-exploitation.

Equating racism with white supremacy peels away the belief that racism is nothing more than the innermost attitudes and "prejudices" of individuals wrapped in themselves. Discarded also is the tendency to view racism as the product of some other-world consciousness beyond the control of man, as the workings of some "absolute spirit" or "universal reason," or as the manifestation of the "Evil" that religions tell us about. To see racism as contemporary white supremacy returns it from the realm of a thought-world which allegedly determines reality, to the real world of social and group relations which, in fact, determines the way we think and feel. It shields us from propaganda crafted to drown our understanding of American racism in a sea of non-racial, national, religious, regional and cultural strife. It keeps us from being bedazzled and diverted from our struggle against white racism by the constant media hype of ethnic, environmental, Gay-Lesbian, labor and gender troubles and prejudices.

Of course, white racism also has a linguistic dimension. Many have remarked on the fact that merely to learn to speak the English language is to be infected with the thought patterns, attitudes, customs, emotional inclinations, and behavior code of a culture that reaches back at least to Chaucer's fourteenth century. This is equally true of other European languages. In other words, racist ideology and the English language came wrapped neatly together. The 1983 edition of *Webster's Encyclopedic Unabridged Dictionary of the English Language* lists 28 negative definitions for the word '*black*', and 14 positive ones for the word '*white*'. In the Warner Books' 1978 edition of J.I. Rodale's *The Synonym Finder, black* has 170 negative synonyms, while *white* has 11 good ones; not to mention the uniformly negative connotations of the many synonyms for the words: *blackball, blacken, blackguard, blacklist, blackmail,* and *black sheep.*

Thus the very process of learning to speak the dominant tongue of the United States and Canada initiates one into a select racist ideology. In the "collective unconscious" of American whites not only is death black, but dirt, darkness, shadow, shades, abysmal depths, malice, viciousness, knavishness, criminality, corruption, depravity, the earth's bowels, as well as Satan and evil itself, are all associated with the color black. To the white mind, the vision of chaste womanhood is embodied in blonde, pale-skinned, blue eyed forms. Black womanhood reeks of lasciviousness, sensuality, and lust (Davis 1981). Black symbolizes wretchedness, bereavement, famine, pestilence, and war. For thirty years, the only images of starvation the white-owned media have shown us are the emaciated *Black* children of Biafra, Ethiopia, Somalia, Rwanda. In the proverbial white suburbia, now that "carjacking" has threatened its immunity, the dread of crime has become synonymous with a visceral fear of young Black men.

The linguistic and language pattern of racism which courses through society is inherent and unavoidable, for it is injected from the civilization level. There is no Black child in America who has not suffered emotional damage by the time (s)he has learned to speak the white supremacist English language. There is no Black youngster anywhere in the Americas who has been able to avoid this injury, for all the dominant tongues of the western hemisphere come from Europe. There is no white person anywhere whose childhood has not been one of linguistic racism. This despite half-hearted attempts since the 1960s to "clean up" the vocabulary. The very nurturing by which the Caucasian child comes to be a "white" social personage, involves not only learning how to think and feel about non-white people, but also—and first of all—how to speak the language of white supremacy. For instance, Bavaria is a German province far removed from the main scenes of Black-white encounter. Yet it is an age-old custom there to threaten misbehaved small children with the unspecified but terrible punishments to be inflicted by the *"Schwarze Mann"* (Black Man). Should anyone have been surprised, therefore, when a young Bavarian schoolgirl fled in utter terror to her grandmother's inn, when in 1945 for the first time in her life she spied real living Black men pass through her village— a unit of Black U.S. GIs? Ironically this same woman later married an African American and bore and raised two Black sons.

Nevertheless, this should not blind us to the extremely complex relationship between racist ideology and racist practice. Racist ideology constantly reacts (back) upon the material practice of racism, both before the event and after the event, conditioning economic action, imposing its own rhythms on the motion of the whole system of racism. Think of how the "supply-side" speculations and anti-welfare rhetoric of the so-called "Reagan Revolution" incited concrete federal policies, policies which savaged the civil rights gains that had been won by Black people. Think of how white middle-class paranoia enabled George Bush to "Willy Hortonize" the 1988 presidential campaign.

Knowledge of the history of American racism is the key to the relationship between the practice and the ideology of the present-day system. These two components of America as we know it—namely, racist ideology and racist practice—are rooted historically in the slave system, and in the ideological rationalization of slavery, refined from the seventeenth to the nineteenth century. Both aspects are merely the realization of that which white civilization is in itself, i.e., its racist essence made specific and concrete in modern history. There is a single, unbroken history of economic racism from the inception of colonial conquest and the Atlantic slave trade. This was a continuous development over centuries, through several stages, to the present one of global white supremacy. There is also an accompanying and intervening system of racist ideas, notions, feelings, and urges, embedded as an irreplaceable cog in the machinery of white supremacy.

In overlapping sequences, racist practice always entails some form and degree of apartheid, tyranny, and disregard for the rights of the oppressed. Its standard operating procedure includes police brutality, penitentiary discipline, and partial political castration of its victims. White racism has always been bent on conquering people of color in order to use them as a tool to secure the well-being of whites, accumulate wealth for themselves and enhance their own life chances. Racist ideology in turn socializes ordinary whites to view this situation as *normal* while linking their expectations for personal happiness to it.

Racist ideology also does a job on the victims. It instills self-hatred, a sense of inferiority and powerlessness in Black people and other people of color, inducing them to rationalize their abject condition as the inevitable outcome of their own degenerate traits and worthlessness, as the outcome, for instance, of the problem of crime within their own communities. Ian Haney-Lopez puts this one way by remarking that "in much of the world, as in the United States, racism is driven by notions of white supremacy over non-white peoples" (Haney-Lopez 1991:59). Haki Madhubuti, a pace-setting Black moralist, puts it another way, insisting that contemporary racism is neither more nor less than "white world supremacy."

This zeroes in on the *power* aspect of racism. It implies that defeating racism is a matter and consequence of Black empowerment. The top priority is not to change white attitudes, nor to soften prejudices that lurk in the heart of white folks. Implicit in the definition of racism as white world supremacy, instead, is the conviction that white racism cannot be overcome simply by eliminating "petty apartheid." Only Black power (in alliance with people of color around the world) can smash white world supremacy. This is the proposition put forward throughout this volume. It differs from the tack taken by, say, St. Clair Drake, who implicitly denies the racist nature of white civilization from its birth, by defining white racism narrowly as a "special type of nineteenth-century pseudo-scientific racism," which issued from the deterioration in Black-white relations that occurred when the Atlantic slave trade began the Black Diaspora into the western hemisphere (Drake 1987). Oliver Cromwell Cox, the famed Black sociologist, thought somewhat along the same lines (Cox 1976). Both thinkers were wrong.

*

THE POPULIST ROOTS OF WHITE RACISM

Rudy Fichtenbaum, white commentator, differentiates between ideology and social psychology, marking the latter as the lower form of social consciousness. Actually, he seems to want to shift the blame for the "spontaneous" anti-Black racism exhibited so often by white workers from the workers themselves to an impersonal, "traditional racist psychology", alleged to drive them willy nilly, and beyond their control. Nevertheless, some of Fichtenbaum's remarks are useful. In his equation, racist ideology is conscious in nature and leads to purposeful and organized political action. For example, KKK and Aryan Nations atrocities, the White Citizens Councils' moves to block school desegregation, Richard Nixon's Republican Party electoral "Southern Strategy," the tirades of David Duke and Patrick Buchanan, are concrete political manifestations of conscious racist ideology. Racist social psychology, in contrast, is an unorderly concoction of feelings, prejudices, and ideas transmitted from past generations. Racist social psychology equals spontaneity. It is a mish-mash of sentiments, aspirations, customs, traditions, and habits. Skinhead attacks, as well as the Howard Beach and Bensonhurst lynchings, for example, would fall under this heading. Fichtenbaum does specify, however, that while racist ideas are transmitted through individuals, "these ideas are a reflection of institutional processes which are racist" (Fichtenbaum 1989: 39).

In any case, it should be clear that race prejudice against Blacks is too deeply rooted in the cultural instincts of the white masses to die a swift death. Even in the face of the incontrovertible *visual* evidence of merciless flagellation of a Black person—viz. the Los Angeles police scourging of Rodney King in 1991—a jury of fairly typical white suburbanites—try as they might—simply could not bring themselves to a verdict that would punish white men for brutalizing an African American. White racism is implanted too securely in the populace. Racist responses are visceral, gut-level things, among the vast white popular masses. By *popular masses* I mean the lower and upper middle classes, as well as the blue collar working class. The *popularity* of white racism is such that it would be certain to live on in some form, even long after the economic soil which nourishes it were destroyed. Even once deprived of its economic fangs—without which most of its capacity to do actual harm to Black people would disappear—the racist predisposition would survive among ordinary whites in the guise of perverted sexual lusts, sick fantasies, aversions to "Negroid" racial features, and genocidal urges. It is too firmly seated in white cultural patterns and languages to enable European civilization-conditioned Caucasians to encounter large numbers of Africa-derived people without hostility and contempt. The process by which a white-skinned individual learns the superstitious rites entailed in identification with white civilization (e.g., learning to conform to "mainstream" clothing styles and food preferences unlike minority preferences; assuming that first class citizens are automatically "free, *white,* and twenty-one") by and large condemns each one to act out the racist drama of Western psycho-history in the course of his/her own lifespan (Kovel 1971). This is true of all but a small minority of dedicated non-racist whites. We have long observed the proverbial "salt-of-the-earth" white "Joe Six-Pack"—acting out his instinctive fears—react to Black people as if they were diseased aliens to be shunned like the plague as soon as one leaves the workplace, stadium, or theater.

From the moment the African was brought in chains to the New World, white men have seen him as excess, redundant, as another species suited at best to work for and entertain white folks, tolerated only as long as he fulfils those functions. Should those functions no longer be fulfilled, then it becomes the duty of white political culture to marginalize and contain the African as redundant and unwanted, and to see to his gradual extermination should he prove unruly and a danger!

Bastardized scholarship backed the white multitude's inherited prejudices. It endowed them with the "prestige" of junk science. Pre–Civil War white Americans invented the pseudoscience of craniology. Craniologists measured skulls in order to claim that the Negro brain is smaller in size and lighter in weight than the Caucasian brain. Black people were smaller brained, bellowed craniology, hence were mentally inferior. The Anglo-Saxon cranium was alleged to be some 12 cubic inches larger than that of descendants of Africans. The African's brain "strongly resembled" the monkey's brain! Nazi *Rassenwissenschaft* ("racial science") was based on American craniology. This was only one of the prostitutions of science on the bed of white racist populism. The 1930s U.S. Public Health Service's use of Black men as syphillis guinea pigs set the precedent for Nazi SS medical experiments on concentration camp inmates.

White mythmakers have even tried to "compensate" Blacks for being "less cerebral than whites." The lack of brain power is made up for in Blacks by sharper instincts—we can run faster than white people, jump higher, have more powerful muscles and quicker reactions, says the 'Good Book' of white popular myth. How often have we heard TV sports commentators extol the "instinctive" reactions and the speed of Black football players, in contrast to the "courage" and "leadership" qualities of "cerebral" white quarterbacks? It does not require genius to realize that the other side of this "coin of praise" signifies Black inability to control emotions. The white masses are firmly convinced that we Black people are slaves to our own passions, and that left alone— i.e., without white tutelage—we are lazy, imitative, craven, clownish, and addicted to welfare handouts. The assertion that, "it is in the nature of white folks to cherish and enhance their neighbourhood, while it is in the nature of Black people to destroy their own neighborhood," gets little argument from white "mainstreamers."

*

The vigilante mode has been one of the main procedures of white racist democracy, historically. White America owns considerable disposable income. As confirmed by the rush to purchase guns and ammunition in the white bedroom communities surrounding Los Angeles during the rebellion in Spring 1992, many white civilians continue to regard themselves as "Minutemen". They hold themselves ready to act as police auxiliaries at a moment's notice. They see themselves called upon to "protect" their homes and families, and "family values", from rampaging Blacks, from minorities bent on crime, from *"them,"* in general. This on-one's-toes wariness is bolstered by the longstanding sexual racism which, as a 1932 press report from Harlem indicates, has always been as much at home in the urban North and West as in the cracker South: "The white man foams at the mouth to see even in 'civilized' New York a white-skinned woman smiling into the face of a dark man. Call it outraged instincts, race pride if you will, but those who know the real feelings of the objectors recognize this emotion for what it is ... pure and simple sex jealousy" (*Claude A. Barnett Papers*, 3 May 1932).

Racism is as much a *pan-white* phenomenon in North America as it is in the rest of the world. "Poor whites have always systematically attacked poor blacks," notes political economist Theodore Cross, "while middle-class whites continue to threaten and feel threatened by middle-and-upper-class blacks" (Cross 1984:115). White racism cuts through class barriers, ignores class lines. Pan-white and supra-class, it propels whites, regardless of class, to disdain and ostracize Blacks, regardless of class. During the Second World War, Gunnar Myrdal from Sweden formulated his anti-amalgamation thesis. He observed that ordinary American whites could be relied upon to shun persistent or intimate dealings with Blacks, at times even against their own political and economic interests (Myrdal 1964 edition). A half century later, garden-variety white folks are still more likely to shrink from sexual intercourse and intermarriage with Blacks than from employment affirmative action for African-Americans, even when such programs are perceived as involving "quotas" disadvantageous to whites. There has been so little real movement in attitudes that plain and simple white folks have less against Black voter participation, even if it should threaten to cut into white power monopoly, than they have against integrated neighborhoods and social events. As bizarre as it seems, they would relinquish the practice of all-white juries which keeps white supremacy in the court system, before they would give up their predominantly white schools and churches. Pedestrian whites hold Blacks at arm's length, uncomfortable with anything more than polite acquaintance, detached and random association. For homespun white folks, the greatest bugaboo remains intimate contact on *equal* terms, a prejudice rooted in the values of a civilization which allows for friendly contact between the races only in the form of white superiority, condescension and charity. They live, therefore, by a kind of critical-mass rule, whereby when Black people appear in *significant* numbers in their schools and neighborhoods, whites are "spooked" in droves. The larger the metropolitan area, the greater the *de facto* residential segregation, as any trip around Chicago, Cleveland, or Detroit will confirm.

With the depth of the devotion to workaday and trivial forms of racial standoffishness, it should come as no surprise that even the most outlandish and disgusting of political organizations can win popularity when they sing the right racist refrain. Throughout most of its history, the Ku Klux Klan has had heavy populist anchors. In 1925 its nationwide membership numbered between three million and six million "card-carrying" adult whites. That was about one quarter of the white male Protestant population in America at the time. Imagine the hysteria in white communities should even as bland an organization as the NAACP enroll anywhere near as many as 25 percent of the Black men in this country. Not only did the Klan dictate the law in the state of Alabama during the 1920s, it was a political power in the midwestern state of Indiana as late as the early 1970s. Indiana had not belonged to the slave Confederacy, nor had Oklahoma, where the Klan dominated sheriffs' offices for most of the twentieth century. In the 1980s and early 1990s, it was still a force to be reckoned with in small, predominantly white prison towns like Attica, N.Y., everywhere a rabid corps of mostly white prison guards rides herd over an overwhelmingly Black and Hispanic convict population. In places like these, Klan activists and other radical white supremacists still act as spokesmen and organizers for the community at large, because they articulate local sentiment. Klan sentiment is rampant in the Los Angeles and San Diego police departments. The Aryan Nations, an organization hell-bent on transforming the Pacific Northwest into a lily-white enclave, "cleansed" of Blacks, Hispanics and Asians, is making headway with the idea among certain white youth.

The *social morality* of white racism is a primitive in-group ethic. The five-hundred-year history of "close association" between Africans and Europeans is premised on enduring white denial of Black humanity. The primitive in-group ethics of racist ideology has kept this five hundred year "state of war" against Black humanity a fresh and vibrant impulse in the minds of whites. It instructs their behavior in moments of racial stress. It is a reflex of the basic civilization. In respect to Black people, here and abroad, this has meant permanent suspension or eclipse of most of conventional (Christian) morality's prescriptions in matters of property, freedom, civil rights, personal integrity, and life itself.

Thus one may logically and scientifically "disprove" the allegations of racism to the brink of apoplexy, but racist ideology cannot be invalidated by scientific reasoning. The whys and wherefores are that white racism is a solid *social* phenomenon, germinating from European civilization, from the events of modern history, and from current power relations. When I cast the argument presented in this volume solidly in terms of race, therefore, a case is not being made for the reliability of skin color (or any other physical racial characteristic) as marking absolute frontiers between the *biological* races. On the contrary, I am pointing to a real historical fact—the *color bar* against people of color, against Black people absolutely, in order to facilitate and perpetuate our super-exploitation and oppression. And to sanction our annihilation, if necessary. Genes are invisible, but skin color is not, and one has to be blind to the whole history of western civilization not to recognize that the racist powers-that-be apportion different social destinies to people according to visible racial traits. The fact that a minority of whites burst through the narrow bonds of inherited race-caste prejudice to reject white skin privilege, alters little.

*

SOCIAL ASPECTS OF WHITE RACISM

Culture and heritage may be defined as the sum total of the behavior, ideas, and objects which constitute a society's common legacy to successive generations. The components in the heritage package are determined, above all, by the nature of the civilization and, secondarily, are the result of a specific mode of production and its corresponding social relations. In the western hemisphere the most influential of the sets of production and social relations which have conditioned whites and Blacks culturally is not, in fact, the corporate capitalism of today, but rather the slavery mode of exploitation imposed on Diaspora Africans several centuries ago. Each member of the two primary groups—Black and white—in the course of his/her education, informal and formal, maternal and subsequent, internalizes the whole. This ensemble enacted by the ancestors becomes a part of oneself. The individual is condemned, as it were, to make this legacy his own. No white man or woman has ever completely escaped the enveloping umbrella of racist ideas and attitudes, for its unconscious, reflex, linguistic, and folkloric aspects are imprinted in children, even if indirectly, absentmindedly and unintentionally. In certain homogeneous European locales, far removed from non-white populations, it is done as if by remote control. In the case of the small minority of whites who are genuinely free of racial prejudice, it either is the outcome of unceasing, life-long, militant struggle against racism, or entails the sharp break with the white community that comes from marriage with a Black person and integration in a Black family.

When it comes to being white in the United States, the *social* substance is derived not from any anthropological (racial) features, nor from any "preference for one's own appearance" and awareness that people of color "look different," as one white sociologist claimed (Hoetink 1967). It is a matter of a peculiar inheritance from white civilization. But not that alone. Being white in America also consists in benefitting from (if not actively participating in) the oppression of the Black man. At the very least, the social significance of "whiteness" is that bottom-line factor that from birth spares one from the social disregard, cultural disabilities, and political disempowerment which torment the vast majority of the western hemisphere's people of color. This, by the way, is how "whiteness" expresses itself in a place like Canada where, according to official propaganda, "racism is less virulent."

An acceleration seemed to take hold in the social history of racism from about the simultaneous overthrow of Black Reconstruction and the onset of the imperialist partition of Africa. In the United States, Plessy vs. Ferguson in 1896 put the finishing legal touches on the system of segregation and discrimination enforced at the grass roots by rampant Klan terror and lynch law. Land grabs in the Philippines and the Caribbean, in the aftermath of the Spanish-American War, gave imperialist reality to the Anglo-

Saxon chauvinism preached by the likes of Theodore Roosevelt and his fellow Manifest Destiny pluggers. Cecil Rhodes and other "theorists of empire" sounded the starting bell for the horde of white settlers who trampled Africans and carved up the continent in the imperialist carnival from the mid-1880s to World War I. At the same time, culminating in D.W. Griffith's obscene film, *Birth of a Nation,* the most extreme ideological formulations of racist doctrine were being published in the United States, Britain, France, Germany and elsewhere. Blacks were depicted as beasts, definitely not created in the same "image of God," as Judeo-Christian myth alleged white humanity to be. Some denied that people of African origin belonged to the human race at all, or argued that they were a collateral primate species, inferior to *homo sapiens.* Others, disciples of the German philosopher Hegel, who pretended to reason from history rather than biology, claimed that Blacks were incapable of creating civilization, that Africans were "historyless." Sub-Saharan African communities had been anthropological artifacts, frozen in time, unchanging before the fifteenth century advent of the white man, according to this refrain. Supposedly Africans were unable to contribute to the store of civilized lore. African places were places that had never been subject to the law of progress. Rival national interests did not prevent the French politico Jules Ferry (1885) and his English counterpart Joseph Chamberlain (1888) from agreeing that exploitation of African resources and labor was "a question of life and death," in order to relieve the "crowded" condition of their respective countries. While the likes of French marshal Lyautey, British administrator Lord Lugard, and Belgian King Leopold II were "civilizing" Africa with fire, sword and the Bible, Social Darwinists were lauding the annihilation of dark-skinned "heathens and savages" as the law of nature. White missionaries justified the scramble for Africa in the name of holy salvation of morally degenerate "natives" (Yeboah 1988).

The rhythm of racist practices harmonized with racist ideology. From the 1880s to 1914, the outpouring of racist doctrinal filth crested more or less simultaneously with the practical outrages perpetrated by white supremacists. The likelihood that such correspondence is a general rule is supported by evidence from other, more recent periods of history. Coincidental with the career of Adolf Hitler, discussions about Nietzsche's famous concept of the "Superman"—*Der Übermensch*—and fascist pseudo-scientific speculations swirled about Europe, not to wane until the Nazi defeat in 1945. White backlash following the assassination of Martin Luther King, and during the Reagan Administration of the 1980s, went hand in glove with "blaming the victim" and "reverse discrimination" theories, and also with academic updates by Cyril Burt, Arthur Jensen, William Shockley, Richard Herrnstein, Charles Murray, and Hans Eysenck of the old doctrine that whites are intellectually superior. Canadian psychology professor Philippe Rushton argued that Blacks, whites, and yellows are completely different species.

Each flare-up in racist doings is matched with a flurry of racist writings and pronouncements. Increased racist activity, in turn, is linked to socio-economic stress, e.g., business-cycle downturns and reduced job opportunities.

Nevertheless, as an *ideological* phenomenon, racism—i.e., white world supremacy—can float free from its grounding in the exploitative economic system. Racist ideology often appears autonomously as one trait of a collective mentality, as popular tradition built into white society. It can appear as a "vestige" in the form of ideas and urges from the long criminal history of slave trading, plantation slavery, and the genocide of whole peoples, seemingly out of phase with "tolerant" modern white ideals.

Religious sanction of Black slavery and racism has ranked high in the social history of racist ideology. The Judaeo-Christian tradition has never accepted the African tradition as an equal. At bitter odds on most other issues, Catholics, Protestants, and Jews alike, at one time or another, found common ground in humiliating black people. Dutch Jewish slaveholders figured prominently among those who developed sugar plantations in seventeenth-century Brazil. In *The Black Ordeal of Slavery,* I have detailed the roles of Jews as slave traders and owners of Black slaves in the French and Dutch West Indies during the seventeenth and early eighteenth centuries. Jewish merchant capital based in Bordeaux invested heavily in France's eighteenth-century Atlantic slave delivery. Jewish capital also had its hand in the New England slave trade. Judah Benjamin, a leading light in the government of the Confederacy, was Jewish.

For balance, it must be noted that the record of Islam, as far as Africans are concerned, is not any better. For though Muslim Arabs were not involved substantially in shipping Black Africans to the western hemisphere, for more than a thousand years Arabic Islam engineered a trans-Saharan traffic that spread Black slaves from Arabia to Iraq, from Persia to India. During the first half of the nineteenth century Arab traders ravaged East Africa in an orgy of slave hunts.

With respect to Christian belief, the myth of Noah's humiliation by his black-skinned son is well known, and New Testament passages like Ephesians 6: 5—enjoining Christian "Servants [to] be obedient to them that are *your* masters according to the flesh, with fear and trembling, in singleness of your heart, as unto Christ"—were cited *ad nauseam* by white priests and preachers in defense of the enslavement of Black people. Protestant Reformers and the Catholic Counter-Reformation both found divine sanction for the chattel enslavement of Africans. The Atlantic slave trade and Black slavery dovetailed with the dynastic and economic interests of Europe's crowned heads, as well as with the profits of merchant capital and colonial slaveholders. So ecclesiastical hierarchs and theologians from the Papacy to Luther and Calvin ganged up to defend and justify those practices. They remained at each others' throats over every other doctrinal question. Enslaving Black people was the one thing they could agree upon. White theologians argued that in practicing their ancestral religions, Africans were refusing to acknowledge Jesus the Savior's blood sacrifice to redeem mankind. Hence they were ingrates, sinners against freedom who deserved to be enslaved. They forfeited the right to freedom. They had to be deported to the Americas for their own good, for only foreign enslavement would break the bond between Africans and their ancestral divinities, allowing Christianity to "save" their immortal souls.

Fact and logic were disregarded. Church leaders knew full well that West Africans, living remote from the historical cradle of Christianity, would have had no opportunity to sample Christian doctrine—assuming that any would have wanted anything to do with Christianity—prior to the arrival of the white slavers. They also knew that Black slaves, baptized as Christians on the plantations and thus entitled to freedom as members of the "free commune of the people of God," were nevertheless held in lifelong bondage. However, white men of the cloth were not about to let a few facts and a little logic dampen their religious enthusiasm for the enslavement of Black people.

The Catholic Church was particularly stubborn. As late as 1815, at the Congress of Vienna, at a time when the traffic in human beings was attracting concentrated abolitionist fire even in prominent white circles, Cardinal Gonsalvi, the Papal representative, resisted all pressure to condemn the slave trade. Not until 1839 did Pope Gregory XV deign to reject the practice. Still he hedged, approving the abolition of merely the Atlantic slave trade, saying that the institution of slavery itself was alright for Blacks as long as it was "kind." Gregory proclaimed that "kindly" slaveholders would be welcomed in heaven with open arms. As late as the mid-nineteenth century it was no sin in the eyes of the Catholic church to hold African human beings in bondage. Even in 1888, at the very dusk of slavery, reactionary Pope Leo XIII was still condemning slave insurrections. The Catholic Church, he reminded the faithful, had always required slaves to accept their lot in life. Leo opposed emancipation as a "radical" measure lethal to the interests of the slaveholding class so dear to him. Not until the 1960s did the Catholic hierarchy finally condemn racism —and then only formally, and then also only under the hammer blows of the national liberation movement which threatened its African missionary strongholds (See paragraphs 29, 42 and 73 of the constitution of the Second Vatican Council [1962-1965], as well as the encyclical of John XXIII *Pacem in Terris* [1963], and the encyclicals of Paul VI *Populorum progressio* and *Africa terrarum* [1967]). The U.S. hierarchy's hysterical censure of Father Lucas' attempt to make the Catholic liturgy relevant to African Americans throws light on the Catholic church's ongoing commitment to racism. Pope John Paul II's true aims in Africa remain to be seen.

For years the "Moral Majority" and the "Religious Right", especially far-right Protestant fundamentalists, have provided the populist core of scores of vicious anti-Black gangs and sects. As one travels southward and westward in the U.S., the more leather-bound the racism of white churchmen. In 1976, the *U.S. News and World Report* announced that the churches were the most segregated institutions in the land. Subsequent surveys have indicated that there has been little anti-racist movement in American ecclesia since then.

*

We have made an excursion through the strange history of white racism, tugging at its civilization roots, examining and testing its social aspects and populist character. A chilling story it is indeed. Not the least because of the *time lags* entailed by the uneven, unequal rates of development of the two nations that make up the United States.

In the latter decades of the eighteenth century, even though not yet stabilized as a fully-formed nation, the thirteen colonies established the independent *State* form. It was destined to be the world's greatest predator, and immediately began a continental expansion which trampled the Native Americans and paired that expansion with an accumulation of wealth sweated from the backs of imported Africans. For white America, the *State*—i.e., the government of the United States consolidated in the Constitution of 1787—definitely preceded and molded the *nation*. *White* America, as a community with the distinctive features now known the world over, did not take on *final* character and stability until the flood of white immigration was capped in 1924.

Meanwhile, *within* the confines of the State-formation, a separate, distinct national entity was taking form—*Black* America. It is this extraordinary process to which Black Nationalists refer and from which they draw strength. The U.S. Black community was a natural growth, a national folk, a commonweal very different from—and counterposed to—white America. Its development was dominated by the need to survive and resist white tyranny. It had its own rhythm of historical growth. The fight against slavery, intervals of migration, and recurring waves of liberation and civil rights struggle have puncuated its political history. Black America is a nation within a broader, antipathetic, nation-state. It may come as a surprise to some, but as a *stable* community it predates the stabilization of the U.S. white community, that is, Black America is *older* than white America, for its main accretions of population from Africa halted at the end of the slave trade to the United States at the outbreak of the Civil War. Immigration from the Caribbean—quite substantial at times—plus the trickles from Africa since World War II, have merely strengthened an already stable community of Black people. Reckoning in this manner, Black America is senior to white America by about a half century.

The evolution of Black America as an entity with its own identity resulted in "two nations," the Black one oppressed, defiant, and demanding. This circumstance impacted greatly on the "peculiar" social history of white racism. For it stoked a "great white fear" of just Black retribution. From the very birth of the Republic, everywhere he glanced, the jittery white oppressor saw hatred staring at him in the eyes of Black people. Everywhere he peered, he saw potential Nat Turners and Harriet Tubmans. In the mind of the white man, even the smallest transgression by a Black man, the slightest hint of dislike for a white police officer, conjured up the spectre of full-scale

Black national revolt. Real or imagined, each such act symbolized a bloody Black insurrection, cities in a flame of destruction, white property looted wholesale. The southern slaveholder had trembled in his boots at the thought of a Black "night of the long knives." Knowing that the oppression and super-exploitation of Black citizens have not ended, and uneasy of conscience, today's slumberers in white suburbia are troubled by the same nightmare. Inevitably, for the protagonists on both sides of the racial barrier, each "ghetto riot", and every police murder of a Black youth, assumes the character of the suppression of an uprising against white domination. Humdrum whites are quick to mumble that the victim got his just deserts, applauding energetic enforcement of "law and order", while disclaiming, Pontius Pilate–like, any personal responsibility for injustice and violence against Blacks. The Jim Crow of yesteryear and the "riot-control" of today—two forms of the same obnoxious regime—caused neuroses in many of the racists themselves.

The "Great White Fear" has its psychotic side. There has always been a white male dread and hatred of the Black penis, coupled with a simultaneous possessive paternalism towards the Black vagina. As Dr. Cress-Welsing has explained, the same white man who trembled historically at the likelihood that white women might succumb to the pleasure and genetic power of the Black penis, sought psychological solace in the image of the Black mammy, suckling little blonde boy-babies at her breast, lavishing affection and loyalty, while neglecting her own Black children. Young attractive Black women were visualized as crazed for sexual intercourse with white males. Racist lore taught that Black men were dangerous, Black women were not. This attitude echoed in the job market. The employment ratio for Black women in North America has consistently approximated the employment proportion of white females. Racists cherished the myth of the harmless but promiscuous Black female, ironically, even when it undermined white supremacy. Judge Bruce Wright gives eloquent voice to this paradox:

> ...Only when the NAACP began to employ female lawyers did the public become aware that black women were practitioners. They served the NAACP well during the hazardous work in the South. Because they were not burdened by the mythological black penis, they were less likely to be lynched or run out of southern towns, where many cases had to be tried. White society has always seemed some-

44

what kinder to the black female and less fearful than it is
of the black male (Wright 1990:84).

The fear of Black males can still nowadays prove counterproductive
for white power. It has shown up in the 1990s in the apparant willingness, for instance, of white voters in certain Congressional and
state elections to vote for Black women candidates where they would
refuse to elect a Black man. This occurs where no acceptable white
candidate is available, and where it is deemed expedient to placate
seething Black discontent. Ballots cast in favor of a Black woman
are taken as a means of defusing an explosive situation. Here the
white intent clearly is tokenism masked by support for "women's
liberation," but the payoff for the Black community is another Black
elected official. Black male candidates frighten white voters; Black
female candidates do not make white voters as nervous. This attitude facilitated the election of Carol Moscley Braun as a Senator for
the state of Illinois.

*

This chapter has exposed white racism's social and ideological roots.
As a set of ideas and attitudes, racism is a theory that justifies social
inequality, super-exploitation, and mass annihilation. The current
enlivenment and "respectability" of neo-Klan politicians (e.g., David
Duke), of neo-fascists (e.g., Oliver North), of terrorist gangs like
the Aryan Nations and Posse Comitatus, of racist police and skinhead outrages, are merely surface manifestations of the vast popularity and deep roots of racism in this white settler's country.
Nourished on the "win-the-West" frontier tradition of mass murder
of "Redskins," pedestrian conservative whites identify spontaneously
with the armed forces, police courts, prisons, injunctions, and mar-
tial law which protect their racial interests. For example, the alleged
"slowness to act" and initial "mildness" of the "overwhelmed" LAPD
during the first stages of the 1992 Los Angeles rebellion aroused
much conservative political ire. Racist presumptions encourage
young white layabouts to murder the Blacks who wander on to their
"turf" indiscriminately, as recent outrages in New York City's
Bensonhurst and Howard Beach sections have shown. White down-
and-outers, the dregs of society, skinheads, gangsters, convicts, rednecks, poor white trash, "good-old-boys," loutish descendants of
"ethnic" immigrants—all the rabble and anti-social dross of white

America—are emboldened when the volume of coded racist discourse goes up in exalted political circles, as happened during the Reagan-Bush years, and as is the likely outcome of Republican Party control of both Houses of Congress (1995–1996). Suddenly white political commentators rediscover the "intractability of race." Suddenly "pessimistic" white journalists begin once again to predict (i.e., dream) race war.

James Baldwin pilloried white America's acute "bad conscience" as an intricate, distilled, rarified, extremely *fetishized* form of false consciousness. Fetishism is a distorted, false and illusory notion held by people in respect to things which they come to worship and even endow with supernatural powers. The white middle class's "bad conscience" about its complicity in the crime of white supremacy is a phenomenal form so widely removed from its origins that its source is lost from sight. The nervous section of the middle class tries to take its mind off deteriorating "race relations," Baldwin said, by deliberately stupefying itself with the "feel-good" hogwash served up by government officials and the mass media, pretending (or pretending not to pretend) day after day that the trash they know to be trash is not rubbish and is taken seriously. White Americans are very much like white South Africans. They too are passionately devoted to sporting events, mostly as frenzied spectators rather than participants. Usually at events in which the contestants are Black. Breathless "yellow-ribbon" campaigns for troops returning from foreign military interventions are embraced with the same ultra-nationalistic, super-patriotic fervor as the 1984 Los Angeles Olympics, Superbowl Sunday, "America's Team," the "national pastime," football fascism, redneck car demolition derbies, NCAA's "Final Four," and the World Wrestling Federation. Psychiatrist Frances Cress-Welsing has some striking observations about white businessmen's fascination with little white balls in the game of golf (Cress-Welsing 1991). For a whole decade, the "Eighties generation" stroked its anxieties with the Bill Cosby show, misinterpreting what they saw as proof that Black folk were well off and happy-go-lucky.

These psychological components compound the social history of racism. They render its analysis messy, raising a confusing veil of illusion and false consciousness. Nevertheless, I have maintained that racism is inherent in Western civilization as such, and that racism's ultimate (under-) determination springs from that civilization, a unit that is intelligible to the social historian. Despite the curtain of false notions and unreal dreams hung by racist ideology, we must also insist that *global white supremacy* is the indispensable condition for the continued existence of Western civilization in its present form. And despite the red herrings and false clues of conventional American political science, we can ferret out the truth that racism is a *populist* phenomenon, firmly cemented in the "democratic" rule of the white majority.

The pressure of historical events in the years ahead, the militant struggles of peoples of color, may dictate to global white supremacy versions of racist ideology and usage which are more indirect, more sophisticated, purportedly more "refined" than, say, the crude lynching bees and outright segregation of the pre–World War II years. But the essence is unchanged, only the packaging is glossier and perhaps more insidiously subliminal in its ability to penetrate and be assimilated in mass consciousness. In order to battle our enemy effectively, we must constantly remind ourselves that this is what we must expect from white civilization, from people spawned by the European historical tradition.

The *racist predisposition* is the product of past events. It is inherited as the legacy of the genocide of the Native Americans, of slave trading and Black racial slavery, of the rape of Africa and the imperialist colonization of Asia, Africa, and Latin America. It was boosted by the Confederate victory-in-defeat, more than a century and a quarter ago. The beaten slavocracy survived on the morrow of Appomatox and transformed itself on a new class basis. It coalesced with and merged with its vanquisher—Northern capitalism. On all major social fronts the white South succeeded in nullifying the victory of the anti-slavery forces. With emancipation practically null and void, the Freedmen and -women were yoked, relegated for a century to a legally-mandated social inferiority. This was the social reality which in turn revived and solidified the belief in white supremacy in the climate of opinion among whites. Seeing that Black people were, in fact, *treated as inferiors* day in day out, whites felt their age-old beliefs confirmed. The conviction, handed down from their ancestors, that Blacks were genetically inferior, was vindicated, they felt. It was alright to discriminate against them, as their parents had done; to oppress Black people was the *normal* order of things. The demand for social equality was the thing that seemed abnormal, weird, socially bizarre to ordinary white folks.

Do not get me wrong. The majority of white folks do not gath-

47

er in Klaverns to plot ways to wipe Black people from the face of the earth. Yet that selfsame majority does not like us and would like to have nothing to do with us. They would count themselves fortunate if they could live their entire life without ever encountering a Black person.

Chapter 3

THE POLITICAL ECONOMY OF RACIST IMPERIALISM: THE WORLD IMPERIALIST SYSTEM

Now let us come down to earth. Let us shift from comprehension-enabling theory to actual practice. This chapter will examine political economy. By *political economy* we mean the precepts which govern legal arrangements through which the economy is managed. This chapter seeks to understand how racial groups, social classes, and the various strata of the population justify and protect economic policies which correspond to their interests. Political economy has to do with the macroeconomy, and entails viewing income, investments, and power relations as a whole. Since the times of Adam Smith (1723–1790), David Ricardo (1772–1823), and Karl Marx (1808–1865), a *social class* has been defined—most usefully—as a large group of people whose key connections with other people have evolved in the process of producing the material goods necessary for life, and in distributing, exchanging, and consuming these material benefits. Hence class and political economy are about who controls what, who owns what, and who gets what, in economic life. We will scrutinize American political economy and class structure through the microscope of *race*. For in this part of the world one's place in the historically derived system of social production is ascribed at birth by race.

*

We widened the focus in the previous chapter from socio-economic formations, nation-states and social classes to *civilizations*. We argued that the latter are a more comprehensive unit of intelligible human social behavior. We preferred the history of civilizations, not class struggle, as the stage for the conflict and interaction among people. Instead of feudal lords versus serfs, or the bourgeoisie versus the proletariat, we made the major historical components something African, European, Pre-Columbian American, Chinese, Indian subcontinental, and such like. We insisted that this new focus would enable us to concentrate more fruitfully on the total packages presented by the European-derived and African-derived sub-civilizations (i.e., white America and Diaspora Black America) that are our main concern. In other words, the new approach allows us to deal with the socio-economic, cultural, philosophical, political, and ideological traditions of the white Americas since Columbus, as well as with America of the Black Diaspora—our America. Keeping the civilization foundations (underdeterminations) foremost in our minds makes it easier, I believe, to investigate the interactions between the Black and white Americas, their compound mixtures and hybrid conglomerates. Only with this approach, it is argued, can we unravel the tangled cultural assimilations, interblendings, and patterns of adopting the cultural traits of other groups, that pass for racial acculturation in countries like Brazil and the United States. The civilization-procedure is adopted as the one that best enables analysis of the development, evolution, revolutions, and rules which govern these societies.

From the fifteenth century through the twentieth, white civilization forged ahead in science and technology. Prodded by the bourgeoisie (the capitalist class) it scored triumphs in medicine, internal combustion, engineering, aerodynamics, nuclear energy, computer science, electronics, communications, and cybernetics (i.e., robot systems). White capitalism perfected mass serial production. The unmanned exploration of the solar system and beyond, carried out by the Voyager project, for instance, has yielded spectacular discoveries, remote controlling sophisticated mechanical objects billions of miles from the earth. These accomplishments tend to confirm the principle that the dominance, radiance, hegemony, and exemplary attraction of a mode of production will not dissipate until all realizable achievements have been exhausted in the course of history. In simpler terms, we must not expect the capitalist bourgeoisie and white supremacy to be overthrown until they have played out all their inherent traits and possibilities. That leaves us with cold comfort.

However, there is another way of evaluating the world racist political economy. We can apply the insights which come from the civilization explanatory model. Then we see that white civilization displays real talent, applicable to all human beings, solely in the conquest of the physical universe. It is adept only at unearthing laws of nature and nurturing science. Certainly no paltry feat. Otherwise, however, white civilization is steeped in a cult of violence and perversions traceable to its racist predisposition. Its humanistic failure is crushing. Claims to the contrary raised in some of its religious and philosophical prescriptions should not blind us to that fact. Mired chest-deep in racist doings and gospels, daily social life in the U.S. and the rest of the West is predicated on militarism, dog-eat-dog Social Darwinism, crass materialism, and devil-take-the-hindmost individualism. Anyone Black knows this, although many of our timid brothers and sisters and those grasping accommodationists desperate to make the "get-ahead deal with the system," pretend they do not. White society swings from cold-blooded, war-time mass murder of "enemy" nations to peacetime obliteration of "backward" tribes in the way of "progress." It jumps from ego-inflating spasms of "feed-the-world's-hungry" concerts to arrogant campaigns to "save-the-children." Its most "respectable" and "presentable" political endeavors in the modern era have ranged from absolute monarchy to constitutional liberalism, from authoritarian conservatism to pluralistic (white) democracy, to white working class socialist regimes. Each one of these "Isms" has proven a disaster for the vast majority of earth's inhabitants—the people of color. Our lot has been deprivation and degradation, starvation and lethal new epidemics, dehumanization and oppression, super-exploitation and genocide—and incessant warfare (which for most of the first half of the twentieth century did not spare even Europoid lands).

These dire circumstances have prompted a growing fraternity of Third World commentators to view race as the basic contradiction in the world today, as a North-South one. There is growing awareness of the racist character of that vaunted "World History" which white racist political economy had brought to life by the early nineteenth century. From 1880, the white man's colonizing stranglehold on the earth's people of color grew firmer with each passing year. Imperialism flourished, while a process that had begun with captured Amerindian wealth and surpluses sweated from Black slave labor came to fruition, enabling the enrichment and industrialization of the white northern hemisphere. Military-industrial might fastened white supremacy on the world, and the impoverishment of the Black, Brown, and Yellow continents proceeded apace.

In colonizing the world at large, white imperialism—by subjecting all the separate racial and national components of the globe to the iron political-economic laws of the world capitalist system—for the first time in the record of human affairs created that which arrogant white scholars dubbed "World History." White imperialism gave birth to international race-class relations globally. Due entirely to the misdeeds of the white race over centuries, a situation was brought about wherein antagonistic social conflicts—often misunderstood as "class" conflicts—were marked across the globe by racial differences. White nations sat on top, people of color on the bottom, with Africa and Diaspora Blacks chosen for super-impoverishment and hyper-exploitation. Meanwhile, internal class antagonisms within the Westernmost white societies were lessening, losing their sting, or at least were being channelled into manageable forms that did not threaten the integrity of the system. This domestication continued to the point where now entire white "proletariats" in eastern Europe have spurned the socialist ideal and embraced the white supremacist creed. As white proletarians in Western Europe, North America, and Australasia gradually approximated lower-middle-class standards of material consumption, they renewed their devotion to the traditional values of western civilization and behaved like all other white folks toward Black people. In the United States all participants in the white class hierarchy endorsed the "two nations sharing one territory" dichotomy: one white, rich and dominant; the other Black, poverty-stricken, and abused.

Nineteenth century imperialism fastened the racism causal chain on the globe. Now we stand on the threshold of the twenty-first century. Contemporary imperialism has transcended the empire-building and empire-tending of the nineteenth and early twentieth centuries. It has been transformed in essence from the colonial administration of the times when Britain, France, Holland, Portugal, Belgium, and Spain were still "Great Powers" into a universal system of oppression weighing with special crudity on the Third World. It has learned to rip off the earth's people of color without the trappings of imperial flags and white expatriate colonial governors. The International Monetary Fund (IMF), the World Bank, the UN Security Council and other expressions of the political economy of white supremacy do the job just as nicely—thank you! For some fifty years now the system has been groomed and constantly revitalized by the activity of the United States—supreme imperialist power, captain of a "Free World" victorious in the Cold War, sole remaining military superpower, and chief enemy of the Third World.

Along with its sophisticated modern devices, today's imperialism includes many of the forms of old "classical" colonialism. (Despite the collapse of the socialist "Second World" in the Soviet Union and Eastern Europe, in order to facilitate matters for the reader I will continue to employ the conventional term—Third World— to indicate Africa, Latin America, and most of Asia). Imperialism feeds on the repercussions of past and present oppression of "racial minorities" at home -the classic example being the African American minority in the U.S.—while it draws lifeblood from the exploitation of "backward" or "underdeveloped" "natives" abroad. But the main thrusts now are the "refined" political manipulations and "modernized" "free market" mechanisms of neo-colonialism.

Racism is a global element of contemporary imperialist political economy, and it is double-edged. On one side it constitutes the historical foundation upon which the imbalance of power between the nations of the world was raised. This can be seen most obviously in the case of the United States—currently imperialism's gatekeeper—where the constitutional framework and early history of the Republic entailed the racist Three-Fifths Rule, Fugitive Slave Laws, segregation legislation and jurisprudence, and the Homestead Act. On the other side, it fills an essential ideological function for imperial domination. It is the cement for the effort that seeks to make the Whites-on-top-/Blacks-at-the-bottom hierarchy a permanent and "natural" feature of planet Earth. Across America, and from one end of Europe to the other, stereotypes of people of color, Blacks foremost, have become the building blocks of pathological white ego-structures. Looking down on and pitying "backward," "inferior" "colored folks" in the "developing nations," is a social drug for white egos sick with a disease engendered by selfishness and mass white complicity in hogging and squandering the planet's unrenewable resources. Here the term racism describes the peculiar manner in which the non-white multitudes of Africa, Latin America, and Asia are subjected to systematic material exploitation by the white North. At the same time racism is a causal link in imperialism's belief and opinion superstructure. In whatever psycho-social guise it may appear, racism is imperialism's only authentic ideology. Wherever the white North deals with the Third World South, be it in the United Nations or in bilateral diplomacy or in "aid" projects, racial discrimination justifies the post–Cold War brand of neocolonialism. It provides subtle arguments to explain that the super-exploitation of the Third World is not really what it appears to be—unlimited.

By super- or unlimited exploitation we mean the utilization for profit of people and resources in a manner not subject to the ordinary, historically-derived restraints that govern economic relations between white capitalists and white workers in Western countries, and which make up the complex bonds and customs which lend a degree of cordiality to white management-labor negotiations. These "gentleman's agreement" restraints are confined, overwhelmingly, to relations between the international white corporate elite and the international white "proletariat." When it comes to Third World people, all bets are off, and exploitation and oppression are unlimited. For example, take the attitude of G-7 leaders when they met in South America to discuss trade and the environment. G-7 officialdom turned a collective blind eye to the cold-blooded slaughter nightly in Rio de Janeiro of Black street children by Brazilian police death squads. The "New World Order" imperialists would not have tolerated the atrocity for an instant if the children being murdered had been Nordic white.

Of late the economic and technological-scientific superiority of the United States is being challenged by Japan, Germany, and the new United Europe—its imperialist rivals. U.S. military-political dominance remains unmatched, however. Political hegemony belongs to the United States. A hegemon is one (or a State) who maintains domination in a bloc of cooperating rivals through sheer power, moral and intellectual leadership, and compromise, on the basis of limited consent among the partners in order to secure common interests. U.S. political hegemony in the imperialist camp rests on twin pillars.

One pillar is the American military-industrial machine. U.S. industry emerged from the Second World War unscathed. The Cold War provided the excuse to transform this colossus into a monster. Since then, the military-industrial complex has battened on one military adventure after another, Vietnam followed Korea, Grenada followed Santo Domingo, Iraq followed Panama. Those invasions were aimed at Third World people, never at white Europeans, but were foisted on the public as "police actions," "counter-insurgency," "joint United Nations peacekeeping," or "anti-sedition," in aid of the "containment of communism" and/or "defense of freedom." In the case of Iraq the excuse was restoration of Kuwaiti independence. Tax-derived "defense" spending created a pork barrel of profits for military-industrial corporations.

The other pillar is the manipulation of the resources and labor of the non-white world as a source of wealth. This is the very stuff of which the United States was made. The Republic would never have risen to prominence, not to mention Great Power status, without the centuries of wealth-creating forced labor sweated from Black slaves. When chattel slavery ended, we were degraded as sharecroppers, convict lease laborers, and brutalized farm workers, KKK-terrorized beasts of burden worked to the point of collapse in a "late industrializing New South." Then, once we had fulfilled that purpose, since the 1950s and 1960s more and more of us are being thrown away. Rendered superfluous by the very technological progress created with our blood, sweat, and tears, growing multitudes of Black men have been condemned to unrelieved poverty, unemployment, and beggary, an eternal "underclass" for whom jail is sometimes an escape. The United States put this domestic "experience" in dealing with Black people to good stead when it went on its imperialist quest abroad. Beginning with the Spanish-American War in 1898, and the conquest of Cuba, Puerto Rico, and the Philippine Islands, U.S. imperialism eventually won champion laurels at prying strategic raw materials, oil and other natural resources, cheap labor, and other forms of wealth from the entire Third World.

With defiant accuracy, an Oakland-based group of Black activists has described the global system as an integrated world "parasitical capitalism" in which a minority of the people on the planet Earth live at the expense of the vast majority. The minority is white, the vast majority are people of color. This is the "pedestal on which all of fat, rich, 'free' white America rests." Not only were subsequent white achievements in science, technology, culture, and the art of warfare bought with the lives and misery of at least 120 million Africans, swept up in the Atlantic slave trade and chattel slavery, but the very culture of Europe and America in which an advanced level of science and industry has been reached, is the fruit of capital stolen from Africa and the rest of the Third World.

The causal chain runs from the sixteenth-century planting of slave communities in the western hemisphere to white capital accumulation throughout the twentieth century. That is why the white folks of Orange County, California, by themselves alone consume more goods and services annually than the entire population of the Indian subcontinent, a billion souls. The normal functioning of the world imperialist system assures these shocking disparities between North and South.

It is what, for instance, gives the Caribbean vacation syndrome its place in global white supremacy. Canadian and American white folks have a lemming-like fascination with cloudless, tropical, poverty-stricken Caribbean "islands in the sun." The Caribbean is esteemed as warm and cheap. More to the point, the white folks, Canadians in particular, like to think that the West Indies are jammed with rhythmic, laughing, happy-go-lucky, loveable Black people, "so friendly, hospitable and knowledgeable about how to have a good time." Not "cold," uptight, tight-assed, and serious like whites. And not at all like the sassy, sullen, dangerous Black folks back home in, say, Toronto or Detroit. Of course, the Caribbean is A-OK, as long as the locals behave like "help" who serve in every way from making beds to sweeping up, from playing music to sexual favors. The moment any of these Black islanders move to control their island and its resources, as in Maurice Bishop's Grenada, the freeze is immediate. The mass media begin to bad-mouth the island as a holiday spot, and lo-and-behold, the erstwhile worshipful tourists stay away in droves. Tourist-Mecca Jamaica was shunned like the plague when the Manley government entered its short-lived, mildly reformist phase. Not until the IMF had cleaned up the scene did white tourists again flock to the "good old" island for some swinging "fun-in-the-sun," attended by once-again "friendly" Black folks, flashing toothy white grins. And after all, "backwardness is good for these people," and if it is not, then at least it is picturesque, photogenic, and makes for a great vacation!

*

When we look back to the fifteenth and sixteenth centuries, we see that the disparity derived from certain military-political retardations in African development vis-à-vis Europeans. At that critical juncture West Africa suffered from a lack of powerful nation-states steadfastly opposed to the slave trade and able to compete militarily with European powers. There were too many Cayors, Dahomeys, and Kongos thirsting to do business with the white slavers. Political disunity conspired with a lack of will in the face of the white predators' steely determination. The Four Hundred Years' War disingenuously called the "Atlantic Slave Trade" accelerated the breakdown of traditional African communalist society, while simultaneously preventing the rise of the kind of hierarchical society suited to swift economic development and military modernization, comparable to those emerging in western Europe from 1492 to 1789. The Four Hundred Years' War bequeathed Africa stagnation and regression. By the nineteenth century the ravages of the Atlantic slaving holocaust had triggered industrial-technological disabilities which, combined with tropical Africa's cultural habit of not accumulating wealth for investment purposes, set the continent up for imperialist colonization.

Nonetheless, the concept of poverty in regard to Africans and African Americans should be properly delimited, for there are really no poor countries. There are only countries where the resources are badly used, where centuries of white domination have turned priorities upside down. In these countries and communities where policies are badly determined and poorly chosen because white power preys upon them, it is only the people who are poor. African, Latin American, and Asian resources are misused due to alien exploitation. Black people in America are "poor" only in the same relative sense. Rather we are degraded, exploited, manipulated, and brutalized by racism. The quality of Black life suffers because it is subject to white rule. Today's covert institutionalized racism perpetuates an inferior status that was first fastened upon us in the bygone overt racism of slavery and legal segregation (Carmichael and Hamilton 1967).

The physical and culturally-conditioned configuration of Black people—once generalized in the abstract social notion of race—greatly facilitated above-normal exploitation and oppression, both in Africa and the New World. European and American capitalism and imperialism had acquired a special category of people who could be treated as the perfect embodiment of an economic anomaly, i.e. as a people whose labor could be exacted under strange, merciless conditions, deviating from the common rule. Any way you cut it, for the past five hundred years Blacks have been subjected to a degree of exploitation far above and beyond the ordinary greed of modern capitalism. They have been oppressed much more methodically, continually, and mercilessly than "poor whites." In contrast to the Jews and other erstwhile, sporadic, or occasional victims of Aryan white supremacy, Black people were condemned to a perpetual servitude and sub-humanity, facilitated by pigmentation. Easily recognized by skin color, we could not escape our persecutors as easily as Jews or other supposedly "disadvantaged" white immigrants to North America. To "get over" they need only change religion, cultural habits, language, nationality, or name. They did not have to fight biology.

In the new post–Cold War scenario, world white supremacy is rejuventated in a grand alliance of white powers around the globe, free at last of ideological conflict and class hatred. A great white league cooperating in trade, science, technology, and weaponry is coming into being, anchoring North America to the European Union. In the long haul, the ethnic strife unleashed by the destruction of Yugoslavia and the Soviet Union is merely a speed bump. The "New World Order" will cooperate in ignoring Black protest against famine, disease, and death inflicted in the Third World. The iron laws of political economy will ensure continued Western access to Third World resources, human and mineral. Neocolonial cunning will see to it that enough corrupt Black and Brown puppets remain in office to keep Third World nations in line. Failing that, multinational "peacekeeping" forces would always be available. The streamlining of combat units and the reductions in military outlays made possible by the end of the Cold War—misnamed the "peace dividend"—are designed to enhance the capacity of NATO rapid deployment forces to strike at Third World adversaries (e.g., Iraq), while freeing up monies previously earmarked for the overblown "defense establishment."

In fact, post–Cold War solidarity is merely the latest episode in a crusade to heal international rifts between white supremacists that is nearly as old as the twentieth century. Instances of white inter-governmental mutual aid along racial lines dot the historical record. Uncle Sam has always been free-handed in doling out debt relief to European nations, including even erstwhile enemies. On several occasions, the United States has cancelled the unpaid bilateral debts owed it. At the end of World War I, as a case in point, the Allies—mainly Britain and France—owed the U.S. over $12 billion, a sum many times greater in value than $12 billion in our present deval-ued currency. These debts were first rescheduled, then the princi-pal sums were reduced or cancelled, and the interest rate reduced. By 1931, when the whole slate was wiped clean, White America's European "cousins" had anteed up less than a quarter of the origi-nal debt. More of the same after the Second World War, but now on a grander scale. Playing rich uncle, Uncle Sam reduced former Nazi Germany's debt by two-thirds and rescheduled the remainder for repayment over 35 years at the paltry interest rate of three per-cent. The early 1990s reverberated to schemes to shower Yeltsinist Russia with largesse, while Western politicians quibble about whether aid pittances to famine-stricken Africa should be "freed" or "tied," and while minority-dense U.S. inner cities suffocate for lack of transfer payments from "cash-strapped" federal and state governments. The twentieth century has also witnessed notable emu-lation among the great powers, whereby white imperialists sought to equal and excel each other in laying down the law to non-white peoples. White Anglo-Saxon "kith-and-kin" consideration styled the settlement which the British imposed on South Africa in 1909, for instance. From 1899–1902, the British Empire grappled bloodily with racist, Dutch-descended Boer settlers for the status of domi-nant exploiters of Black South Africans (Boer War). Britain won the war. Imitating U.S. Southern customs, the British decreed a consti-tution explicitly patterned on Jim Crow terrorism. Britain sought a "compromise," a gentlemen's agreement among white men, which would allow the defeated Boers to share in the savage oppression of the native African majority. Hammered together in this way in 1909 and later to evolve into the apartheid Republic of South Africa, the Union of South Africa expressed the British conviction that their American "cousins'" way of dealing with the Black folks in the United States was the best possible pattern also for white-ruled Africa.

Several decades later, when the ballyhooed Atlantic Charter was handcrafted in 1942, the Anglo-American alliance was locked in life-and-death struggle against Germany and Japan, and Winston Churchill and Franklin D. Roosevelt needed a propaganda piece to rally support worldwide. Nevertheless, the framers of the Charter seriously considered limiting the democratic principles expressed therein solely to Caucasians. They pondered the exclusion of all peoples of color. The latter were regarded as unfit for democratic liberties, or "not yet ready for them." By nature, such privileges were meant only for white folks. Churchill and Roosevelt, the pilots of the dual squadrons of Anglo-Saxon imperialism, were like-minded in the conviction that the pursuit of happiness did not entail any right to self-determination in the case of non-whites. Despite the now prevailing custom of "flag independence" in Africa, Asia, and Latin America, contemporary imperialism's attitude has not really budged from the days of Churchill and Roosevelt, which is perhaps why Black activist Don Rojas prefers the term "Semi-Colonial World" to Third World, as a more exact description.

Since "Africa Year" 1960, Third World subjugation to Western imperialism has evolved in the direction of dependency that is first and foremost financial. At the top of the heap in 1960 stood between 25 and 30 percent of the people in the world, all white, except for the Japanese. These are the ones who led the "good life," and whose resource consumption depended upon radical underconsumption among some 46.6 percent of the world's population, jammed together in the southern hemisphere. Over the next thirty years, the gap between the top and the bottom widened even further. By'any reckoning, the countries enjoying the highest material living standard, i.e., the West and Japan, are now home to barely more than 20 percent of the world population. For more than half of humanity, impoverishment worsens day by day. One fourth of the world's population in 1990, were dying of hunger, thirst and preventable disease. All of these were people of color, Africans the worst off. The political economy of today's global market is moving the top one-quarter closer and closer to resource monopolization, condemning the remaining three-quarters of humankind to unimaginable poverty.

The World Bank assessed the foreign debt "owing" in 1990 by the poverty-wracked South to the rich North at $1.34 trillion. In five years, 1985–1990, major Western countries sucked $45 billion in interest payments from the Third World. Yet in all, Third World arrears in 1990 were said to total $85 billion. This after herculean IMF-imposed efforts during those five years to raise money for debt payments that caused severe suffering and dislocations, above all in Africa and Latin America. Foreign "aid" disbursements to the Third World in fiscal year 1990-1991 totalled $6.3 billion, while developing countries watched $7.86 billion flow out as interest payment on debts, leaving a shortfall of $1.56 billion—typical of the annual South-North debit relationship. The West Indies were among the hardest hit, and Africa, struggling to service a cumulative debt of $270 billion, stood to lose some $21 billion a year, i.e., over 30 percent of its export earnings.

Africa labors under a foreign debt total that is 500 percent of the continent's exports and equivalent to 100 percent of its annual gross product. After straining to pay upwards of $30 billion in interest during the 1980s, the total outstanding debt in Africa's lower income countries nevertheless swelled more than 160 percent. Late in spring 1991 came the news that in per capita terms the people of thirteen African nations were poorer than they had been a generation before (ca. 1960), prompting Ghana's Foreign Secretary, Obed Asamoah, to warn the imperialist camp that the suffering imposed on Africa and other regions of the Third World is "a fundamental threat to international peace and security." Fifteen percent of the world population—whites and Japanese—could not continue to hog 70 percent of world income, leaving the remaining 85 percent to compete for the crumbs, without grave consequences. As the 1990s began, the average per capita income in the 41 least developed countries stood at $300 per annum, a mere two percent of the per capita income in the industrial countries.

On the whole, North-South disparity runs along the color line dividing white imperialists and people of color. We must be careful, however, not to carry the theme of solidarity between peoples of color against white racist supremacy too far. Solidarity is strained in the case of the Japanese. Japan was admitted to the inner circle of imperialist rivalry early in the twentieth century, on the strength of its military success. Though defeated in World War II, its economic acumen has given Japan current trade and financial preeminence in the world capitalist system. Japanese leaders have expressed contempt for African Americans. The attitude spills over into economic decisions. Japanese investment patterns in the United States, job-hiring practices, and related activities discriminate against Blacks. A report in January 1992 exposed the anti-Black prejudice of California's five largest Japanese-owned banks, for example. Those agencies routinely violated the federal Community Reinvestment Act (CRA). They denied home mortage and home improvement loans to Blacks and Hispanics. Even the Bank of America, a pillar of white finance, had a better record vis-à-vis Blacks. Though the color line is likely to remain the fundamental problem in world affairs during the twenty-first century, the hostility of Japanese finance capital towards African Americans shows no sign of lessening. Japan's economic forays into Africa are motivated solely by selfish lust for the continent's resources and labor. Many Japanese-Americans (Nisei) and other Asian-Americans act similarly. During the Second World War the Nisei were victims of white racism. They were oppressed, torn from their West Coast homes, locked in concentration camps for the duration, their property confiscated in many instances. The only Americans to assist and sympathize with the Nisei were Black Americans. But once the war and internment were over, the Nisei went out of their way to show contempt for Black people. Today, in San Franciso and elsewhere along the U.S. Pacific coast, miscegenation is much more likely to occur between Blacks and whites, and between whites and Asians, than between Blacks and Asians. Chinese Americans and Japanese Americans are happy to marry whites, but disdain marital ties with Blacks. The disrespect shown by Korean merchants to Black customers has resulted in violent clashes in New York and Los Angeles.

The prejudice and privilege inherent in membership in the club of imperialism tends to obliterate anti-racist solidarity among people of color, breeding hateful antagonisms among the minorities.

Chapter 4

THE DOMESTIC SCENE—
POLITICAL ECONOMY
IN THE UNITED STATES AND CANADA

Racism functions according to its own specific laws of motion. White civilization consists of distinct nation-states, each one outfitted with its own set of national and cultural traditions, its own peculiar temperament. Throughout history, these building blocks of white civilization have usually been caught up in one form or another of internecine rivalry. For the study of political economy, each distinct building block is best comprehended as a separate socio-economic formation, for this spotlights the racist procedures which operate in one state rather than in another. This means that the laws of racism peculiar to, say, the United States will, in detail, manifest themselves in different ways from racist exploitation in, say, Canada, France, England, or South Africa, although the general principle will be the same. British economic racism may bet its survival on London's role as the financial capital of a neo-imperialist Commonwealth centered on influence-peddling in its Third World components, while France may play military and currency master over an obedient Francophone Africa. While Paris, Lyon, and Marseilles traumatize Arab and Black cheap-labor minorities with skinhead and National Front assaults, Berlin, Hamburg ,and Leipzig may feature neo-Nazis on the march. South African racism may express itself in elaborate apartheid, while Canada may seek to hide systemic racism under the sugared cloak of official "multiculturalism." Dependency theorists may ponder white world supremacy as manipulation of a "Third World periphery." Racism may manifest itself as the "global outreach" of multinational corporations. White supremacy exhibits unique political-economic features in each separate socio-economic formation.

Perennial racist discrimination against African American citizens is not a "moral dilemma", nor is it the "shadow of history." It is an essential component of U.S. political economy. Until very recently, Black labor has always been the foundation of the "American standard of living." Since the sixteenth century the unpaid and underpaid labor of sweating Blacks has been transformed in the western hemisphere into investment capital of one form or another. Above-average profits gouged from Black slaves, sharecroppers, convict lease laborers, semi-skilled and unskilled industrial workers, enabled the U.S. economy to expand at an unprecedented rate. Even white economists are beginning to realize this. As a key component in U.S. economic history, Robert Cherry cites "the capital-labor accord," most noticeable in the heavily unionized durable goods industries, which "provided the institutional stability allowing both white male labor and capital to prosper" (Cherry, p. 60). Profits boomed following World War I. Much of the bonanza came from discriminatory wage differentials governing a racially divided southern workforce. While the surplus wage factor favored mainly white male unionized workers in core industries, benefits spilled over to non-unionized white men, noted Cherry. White skin privilege is not a myth in this country. And if it is not a myth, then white workers too must be receiving their share of its benefits. Their portion may not be the greatest, but it will nonetheless be substantial.

The unpaid (slave) or abnormally cheap wage labor of our people since 1865 produced a higher yield of surplus value on monetary capital outlay than that garnered from the employment of white workers—even though U.S. capital profited for decades from the "brain-[and-brawn]-drain" from Europe of cheap immigrant workers. *Surplus value* is the value created by a laborer for his employer (or slave master) over and above the cost of his labor for his employer (or slave master), i.e., value in excess of wages, or in excess of the cost of the means of subsistence consumed by the slave. In the capitalist economy surplus value assumes the form of *profit*.

Since there were no stops put on the degree to which Black labor was exploited—certainly not during slavery, and demonstrably not for a long time after slavery—piles of wealth were extracted from Black workers and accumulated as *capital*. This wealth enabled the American ruling class to pay key fractions of the white working class *surplus wages*. If not bought off outright, the domestic white "proletariat" was at least domesticated and neutralized as a political threat. Wages are a converted form of the value of a man's ability to work. Wages are the price the employer pays for the right to dispose of that capacity for a set period of time.

In as much as white supremacy made possible, first, unlimited exploitation of slaves, and then, after slavery, wage differentials on grounds of race, a *third* form of wages was added to time wages and piece wages (the normal forms of wages). The third form was *surplus wages,* a kind of wage bonus or supplement made possible because of the above-normal value extracted from Black labor and disbursed to white workers in order to buy "social peace." Not every white worker got surplus wages. Moreover, surplus wages fluctuated over time and in accordance with the business cycle. Yet enough surplus wages were added to the real wages of significant fractions of the white working class to enlist key leaders of organized white labor in the business of racist exploitation. From the era of Samuel Gompers (1886–1924) to George Meany and Lane Kirkland in our time, surplus wages swelled the goods and services white workers could actually buy with their money income at a given level of prices, after taxation and other deductions. When not paid to them in actual money form, the surplus came to many white workers in the form of job security, a lower rate of unemployment than Black workers, better, easier, safer jobs than Black workers, faster, surer promotion than Black workers, and seniority rights that made them the last fired after being the first hired. And recently it has come in the form of jobs located preferentially in white neighborhoods, miles from Black inner city job-seekers. All these perks were possible because victimized Black laborers were ready to hand.

Historically, surplus wages have nourished racism among "Middle America's" blue and white collar employees. It is the economic footing for the gut appeal of racist code-words and anti-Civil Rights politicians. The spur behind many of David Duke's and Jesse Helms' voters, for instance, is the belief that ordinary white people, especially blue collar families, live better in a material sense *because* Blacks live worse. Many suspect their well-being to be tied to Black social inferiority, and many fear that if the victimization of Black and Brown communities were to stop, their own living standards would suffer. The fear rampant in California's Ventura County, that the well-tended suburban homes, Volvos and BMW's, saunas and backyard swimming pools, decent schools and gentrified condos, might be jeopardized were it not for the kind of "justice" meted out to Rodney King, is a fear that pervades all of white America.

Not all the benefits are of the material kind. Some are psychological in nature. Along with the sense of superiority goes the advantage of having a despised scapegoat to blame for society's ills. The schools in Black communities are staffed with uncaring, racist teachers, are neglected, crummy and underfunded. Yet for the fearful white folks in, say, Irvine, Orange County, California, Black youth do poorly in school because they are not as smart as Asian-American children who, though also a minority, perform well. To their way of thinking, systemic discrimination and the bigotry of employers are merely a matter of misunderstanding, and Blacks have no one to blame but themselves for high unemployment. For the beneficiaries of the "capital-labor accord," such problems as family breakdown, poor quality of life in minority housing projects, AIDS, female-headed single families, the lack of appropriate role models for Black youth, and the "absence" of family values, are all self-inflicted scourges caused by promiscuity, indiscipline and laziness, and we Blacks are merely getting what we deserve. The disproportionate numbers of Black males behind bars are not there because of any discriminatory treatment by white police and judges, but because they are criminal-minded n'er-do-wells, say white workers as they smugly pocket the surplus wages that the system of racial discrimination showers on them.

*

This economy is *ruled* by a small oligarchy of almost anonymous white male financiers, corporate industrialists, lobbyists, investment consultants, and mega-asset owners, whose "right" to do business undisturbed by dissident "colored people" is divinely sanctioned in white America's "free enterprise" ideology. In basic economic structure, the United States and Canada are similar to other capitalist countries. And there are many capitalist economies in existence; in fact, with the collapse of the Soviet Union and other white socialist economies, capitalism has the world pretty much to itself nowadays. Nevertheless, there is a qualitative difference between U.S. capitalism and all others: the United States still dominates the entire imperialist camp–if only because of its overwhelming military superiority. Although the economic influence of resurgent Japan and the potential military-economic clout of the European Union are causing Washington to reevaluate these allies' positions, most foreign economies are either satellites or "junior partners" of the U.S., none more so than its northern neighbor, Canada.

The ruling "class" in America, as in other "advanced" industrialized countries, is the group which, by virtue of its economic position, controls both social life (including the judicial system) and the notions in ordinary people's heads. This circumstance is much denied. Yet in all, the dominant class does manage to rule politically, by hook or by crook, aided by its general cultural influence. History has created two peculiarities in our national situation. First, the constitutional setup does not translate the ruling class' domination into State power automatically, but instead requires detours and elaborate camouflage (mostly sops to white average-citizen populism). Secondly, since the birth of the Republic, the ruling elite has always been *white*.

America's rulers have been christened many names. They have been called, variously, an "imperialist bourgeoisie," "monopoly capital," "military-industrial complex," "the establishment," "the power structure," the "ruling elite," the "corporate conglomerate".... "What's in a name? That which we call a rose, By any other name would smell as sweet." More to the point are the fractions that can be distinguished within the ruling class as a whole. It can be said to consist of the following social categories in rough descending order of influence: 1) the directors of great industrial, financial, communications, and commercial corporations and institutions; 2) the major activist owners of the main means of production and finance (e.g., Ross Perot); 3) the top military commanders; 4) the paramount professional politicians; 5) top-level civilian and police officials; 6) coupon-clipping, but politically and economically inactive individuals and families possessing large private fortunes; 7) the traditional Southern racist aristocracy; 8) the high judiciary and leading corporate lawyers; 9) a growing "brain trust"—comprised of preeminent personalities of the sciences and liberal professions, universities and private foundations—that advances in step with the "technological and organizational revolution"; and 10) the dominant political leaders. The lines dividing one group from another are fluid. These elements relate to one another in interlocking, overlapping, changing networks.

These people are the core of America's billionaire capitalist class. They are white. On estimate, there are three million or so white men and women camped in the *second* ranks of the corporate and government bureaucracy that runs the country. In 1990, the top one percent of the economic ruling class hogged nearly as much after-tax income as the 100 million citizens in the bottom 40 percent of the social ladder. About a fifth of the super-rich are Jewish, but these are *white* Jews of European Ashkenazim descent, not Asian Sephardim or African Falashas. In fact, if there is anything remotely "pure" about the U.S. ruling elite, it is its racial "purity." The ruling class is still lily white.

Dispensing surplus wages, the white ruling elite projects a clear racist model for ordinary whites to emulate. In an economy where racial discrimination arbitrarily excluded or reduced the access of Black and other workers of color, reserving positions mainly for whites—especially in today's robotized and computerized branches of industry—class solidarity is usually either fragile or stillborn. For more than a century, this stubborn fact has been the undoing of generations of class-struggle Marxists and has frustrated any meaningful socialist initiative in America. Not only did he pocket surplus wages, but the white worker traditionally was given the opportunity to share more in the knowledge and skills that governed industrial production. Until the labor shortages created by two world wars, and 1930's CIO industrial unionization, there were few or no jobs for Black men in American industry. When we finally were admitted, it was on the customary second-class terms. While his Black counterpart faced daily speedups, compulsory overtime, hazardous working conditions, and racist abuse from bigoted foremen, the white worker, safe in his white skin cocoon, was allowed to integrate himself more fully in a technical unit, and gradually approximate the status of a technician. Of course, the white American blue collar employee had no control over political, economic, administrative, or cultural life—control was preserved for the ruling elite. He was subordinate to his employer. But, due to the racist buffer, his own subservience was not perceived with the same dissatisfaction, nor did it produce the same intense agony of estrangement, as that suffered by his Black fellow worker.

Thus at all junctures in modern history, white lower classes rejoiced at the opportunity to trample "colored inferiors," to prosper at the expense of the "Niggers." Many white "hard hat" workers believe that they too have a stake in distrusting and policing Black inner-city residents whose job competition they dread. The vast majority of whites—poor whites as well as wealthy ones—oppose government use of tax power to create parity and redress the grave disadvantages burdening Afro-Americans and Native Americans in this country. White racism is ingrained and cuts across class. It is an arresting effect of the ideology secreted by white civilization.

＊

Beyond racial, social, and psychological control, *Jim Crow* served a political-economic purpose. In one aspect, it separated Blacks from whites and *excluded* them from civil society. That is, it barred us from the economic competition, political bonds, and social civilities which make for "civilized" dealings between separate and private individuals in a modern community. In the other aspect, it set the terms for the *inclusion* of the Black labor force in material production and services. Jim Crow separation and exclusion of Blacks facilitated our subordination and set us up for unlimited economic exploitation which generated fine profits. North and south of the Mason-Dixon Line, organized white labor went right along with this. With an eye on surplus wage privileges, white workers went on strike to bar Black workers from unions and skilled jobs. They insisted on all-white union locals. They resorted to mob violence to keep us out of the skilled trades. White union leaders collaborated with management in erecting a racist social division of labor which enshrined job classification by race and a dual wage system. Stripped to bare bones, the shunting of Black male and female labor into low-paying, inferior jobs, coupled with the requirement that we accept lower wages for equal work, *was* the post–Civil War economic settlement. It did not even begin to loosen until well into the 20th century.

Racial quotas in favor of whites stretch all the way back to the seventeenth century and explain in large measure just how white people in America became wealthy. The English colonies of Massachusetts, Maryland and Virginia ceded free land grants to white settlers, but declared Blacks—free or slave—ineligible for the distribution. The land was stolen from the Indians, and Virginia and Maryland had the gall to pretend that Blacks were excluded merely because, as slaves, they had not paid for their passage across the Atlantic! Between 1800 and 1850 a series of preemption acts empowered the federal government to hand white settlers huge chunks of Indian land for purely nominal fees as low as a dollar an acre. The vast majority of Blacks were themselves chattels. Race laws and lynch mobs made sure that free Black claimants were turned away empty-handed, while federal, state, and local governments were creating a large class of white landowners. The Homestead Act of 1862—the centerpiece of Civil War legislation—deeded more than 250 million acres of government-held real estate to white "pioneers," many of them foreign immigrants fresh from Europe. It was the biggest land give-away in American history. Affirmative action for white entrepreneurs escalated with the advent of the railways, as Washington D.C. awarded some 130 million acres of "right-of-way" to private railroad companies for free. Often extending for 20 miles on either side of the roadbed, many of these plots were later mined for oil and minerals—a bonanza from which Black businessmen were excluded. Some of the first oil fortunes originated in the notorious Oklahoma Land Rush at the end of the 1880s, during which hordes of savage white Klansmen descended upon the Territory. In *The Black Power Imperative* (Cross 1984: 515-517), Theodore Cross chronicles the steps taken by the federal government between 1920 and 1941 to permit whites alone to prospect for oil, gas and other minerals on public lands. The government established white ownership of commercial airlines and assured that none but white pilots were seated in the cockpits. Lucrative radio broadcast licenses were denied to Black applicants. A thoroughly racist Federal Communication Commission was vested with the authority to refuse television broadcast licenses to Blacks (a policy not relinquished until the late 1970s). All government defense contracts were channelled to white-owned firms. Government contracting is the single greatest fountain of gold known to American business. These measures capped more than 260 years of proactive government designed to construct a political economy capable of sustaining white supremacy, both during and after slavery.

As the years passed, the U.S. took up its international imperialist expansion, while the home economy harmonized mechanization and greater productivity with refinement of the means to extort bigger and bigger profits from the labor of more and more Black, Brown and Yellow people. From the end of Black Reconstruction to the mid-1950s, Black labor and Indian lands were the chief targets of racist greed. After World War II, the military-industrial elite spearheaded the drive, replacing the cotton planters and frontiersmen of the generation following the Civil War. Blacks and Native Americans were subjected to racist terror, induced migration or incarceration in reservations. Systematic indoctrination and undereducation went hand-in-glove with cultural devaluation, racial discrimination and ridicule. From Wounded Knee to the Tuskegee syphillis experimentation, we were the victims of genocide parcelled out in doses. The economic object of this tyranny was to guarantee the super-profits which, in fact, enabled American capital to outstrip Great Britain, Germany and other imperialist rivals by the end of the First World War. The U.S. rode to super-power status on the backs of non-white producers. U.S. imperialism was breast-fed, as it were, by wealth sucked from the labor of Black men and women. The Black community was "bled white," at the same time as white America "developed" the fabulous resources stolen from Indian lands. Abroad, U.S. colonizers were moving into the Caribbean, the Pacific, the Far East and its South and Central American "private reserves." Throughout it all, the main thrust of American white supremacy in economic matters remained inward, at least until 1945.

Next came the advent of mass consumerism in "mainstream" America. It altered the flavor of the racist psychosis which conditions North American political economy. There was ever-widening distribution of high-tech electronic consumer goods and annually-renewed automobile models, among white consumers. Middle class incomes were inflated by surplus value extorted from the colonized Third World and from underpaid domestic minorities. The process gave birth to a consumption-crazed public, fascinated by unnecessary gadgets. It was during the 1950s that the mass white public really came to feel the pressure of false and artificial needs. Newly-sprung white suburbia was TV-commercialized. The psycho-conditioning caused by runaway advertising and strong pressures to conform, to resemble one another in taste, carriage, gestures, appearance, temperament, spirit, and values strengthened the tendency. The upper middle class set the popular social and cultural tone in white America, imposing the phoney values of the "American Way of Life" on a neurotic blue collar herd. Archie Bunker was no aberration; he faithfully reflected blue collar values.

In all, about seventy percent and more of the total white population, including the working and lower middle class, now clings to social mores that are narrowly and unimaginatively conformist. This is the segment of white America that has historically been most subject to those uncontrollable spasms of racist psychosis that more resemble mass rabies than anything else. Folks from these classes ran amok in the streets earlier in the century, massacring Afro-Americans in Wilmington, N.C. and Phoenix, S.C. in 1898, in New York City in 1900, in Atlanta in 1906, in Springfield, Ill. in 1908, in East St. Louis in 1917, in Elaine, Arkansas., Washington, D.C. and Chicago in 1919, and in Tulsa in 1921 (Shapiro 1988).

Today there is a renewed drive to finger Black and other Third World people as the "common enemy"—race baiting is its name. The malice is poorly concealed in recurrent discussions of "population explosions in underdeveloped countries," of "haves" against "have-nots," and of North versus South [see June 1992 World Earth Conference in Rio de Janeiro]. It is evident in white responses claiming that Rodney King was "in control" and "got what he deserved," and vilifying the freedom insurgents in Los Angeles South Central district as "criminals" and "looters."

It is a mistake to dismiss racial hatred of Blacks, and white racism in general, as mere "irrational atavisms," throwbacks preventing "the reign of good will and harmony between Black and white Americans," or as a roadblock to be overcome on the highway to the "beloved community," or as "societal racism" amenable to reform, unlike the allegedly more stubborn, intentional "ideological racism" (Frederickson 1981). All these are components in the edifice of the U.S. economic system. Despite the ongoing Black freedom struggle and a bewildering array of remedial legislation, from the Civil and Voting Rights bills of the 1960s to the Civil Rights Act of 1991, racial discrimination is still the criterion by which American Blacks are excluded from equal competition with whites for employment. An Urban Institute survey announced in May 1991 used undercover testers to demonstrate far-reaching racial discrimination in employment, 27 years after such practices were formally outlawed in the 1964 Civil Rights legislation. The misery borne by Blacks spares the white lower classes from the graver effects of the flaws inherent in the economy. The national rate of unemployment remaining constant, it is obvious that racial parity in joblessness would not only reduce Black unemployment from its usual rate of two to two and a half times that of the white rate, but would also necessarily imply an *increase* in the white rate of unemployment. The American system reclines on the pillar of white supremacy as one of the fundamental guarantees for its continued existence. Hence an attack on white racism is really an attack on America's whole social structure.

*

Since World War II, cyclical depressions have gripped the U.S. economy in 1948–1949, 1953–1954, 1957–1958, 1960–1961, 1969–1971, 1974–1975, 1980–1982 and 1990–1992. Combined with the effects of long-term structural changes in the economy, these "business cycles" have at long last reversed the direction of Black migration away from the Midwestern inner cities, "back South" to the "Sun Belt." The African American population is gradually reducing in such former industrial giants as Cleveland and Detroit, and even Chicago, leaving behind blighted streets, abandoned dwellings and garbage-strewn vacant lots. Uprooted Black folks abandon their wintery homes not in search of the sun, but in search of jobs. For in this latest phase of our oppression, the mass production industrial jobs at union wages, for which we and our fathers fought so hard, have vanished from the Northern industrial quadrangle. The infusion of cheapened Black labor from the North has oiled "Sun Belt industrialization." The jobs offered by the "industrial boom" in states like North Carolina, South Carolina and Mississippi are the precarious, non-unionized right-to-work, sweatshop and service sort, under the foremanship of rednecked "good old boys." Black women, for instance, hazard their lives for minimum wages in poultry and catfish processing plants. The only

employment available is in low-wage medium-level and light industries (e.g., tobacco and textiles), unlike the well-paid jobs many of
us had grown used to in the now-closed "smoke-stack" industries.
Very rarely has Sun Belt industrialization opened "high-tech" computer, aerospace, and microelectronics industries to Blacks. And
nowadays, corporate capital prefers to export much of its micro-
electronic, automotive, and durable consumer assembly production
completely out of the United States, seeking the cheap, docile, skilled
female labor of East and South Asia and El Salvador, as well as the
cheaper male labor of Mexico. Flight abroad provides the added
benefit of avoiding the Black citizens of the United States, renowned
for their union militancy and for combating racial discrimination in
the work place. It also enables the removal of traditional, environ-
ment-damaging heavy industries to places like South Korea, Latin
America, and South Africa, avoiding costly outlays for pollution
control. That does not leave a whole lot left over within the confines of the U.S. for Black workers. Increasingly, the only employment we can find are service jobs and medium-level and light
industry employment, devoid of health-care insurance and other
vital fringe benefits. That, and of course—at least until recent military downsizing—employment in the armed forces, where Black,
Puerto Rican, Chicano and Native American youth have been welcome to risk their life on foreign missions on behalf of white world
supremacy.

The 1980s brought the restructuring of *racist relations of production* to a head. The "new" "post-industrial" political economy
imposed wage "give-backs" on unions, "clawed-back" fringe benefits, cut-back social insurance, and increased the use of scab and
child labor. Astronomical Black youth unemployment made it easier to enforce below-minimum wages. Undocumented "illegal" immigrant workers, growing part-time employment, and the discrediting
of public education in favor of de facto segregated private schools
rounded the program out. This offensive has run on the wheels of
a strategy designed to set white workers and the white middle class
against racial minorities, but mainly against Afro-Americans. Its
political epitome was the Reagan Administration, prolonged under
the presidency of George Bush and revived in the mid-1990s by the
Robert Doles and Newt Gingrichs. The concentration of military
production, aerospace, and other high-tech industries in the Pacific
Northwest, California, and Texas, coupled with the military bases

scattered around former Confederate states like Mississippi, accentuated regional inequality. Swelling the voters' lists in the more hawkish, racist populist sections of the country, these structural tendencies strengthened the political hand of the ultra-conservatives.

The effect of Rust Bowl deindustrialization on Black poverty was most dramatic in the Midwest. For the first time in history, that region during the 1980s became the one with the most intensive Black poverty, outstripping the traditionally poverty-stricken South. It is also the region of the most rigid residential segregation. During the decade, the Midwest had the lowest Black income and the highest degree of inequality between Blacks and whites. Nowhere could one find greater polarization of income between Blacks and whites than in the greater metropolitan areas of, say, Cleveland, Chicago, and Detroit.

*

In summary, racial discrimination at home and abroad are still the pivotal production relations in U.S. political economy. The situation is much the same in neighboring Canada, taking into account the vast difference in population and scale of the economy, and given Canada's junior partnership in imperialism. This mode of operation has persisted throughout history, changing gears to match the speed of successive restructurings of the economy. Economic "prosperity" derived from slave labor before the Civil War. During the 1880s and 1890s it derived from the labor of Black sharecroppers and convict lease laborers. Through the middle years of the twentieth century, Black, Puerto Rican, and Chicano wage earners encamped in urban ghettoes and barrios were a major factor. Exploitation of the ghettoes was the yeast which swelled the white middle class to its legendary proportions. It helped that racist beliefs had the force of religion.

The ruling elite views the white "middle class," including its vast blue collar component, as a vital element of social equilibrium, compensating for and neutralizing the hostility of the Black inner-city "underclass" toward the inequities of the "American Way of Life." The middle class is a cherished ally. A vital source of social conservatism and inertia. As the typical lower middle class racist sees things, social inequality between white and Black communities is a natural fact. Tinkering can only bring "reverse discrimination" against white folk. Suburbia thrives on the images of successful, non-demanding Negroes like television's Julia and the Huxtables.

The proper Negro respects the property of others (even if he has no property of his own) and remains in one's proper "race-caste."

More than anything, U.S. political economy is a structure which dictates "law and order" to its Black minority.

Chapter 5

THE SWUNG PENDULUM: LIFE ON THE MARGIN

1992 marked the quincentennial of the conquest of the western hemisphere begun by Columbus in 1492—an event endorsed with festivities throughout the white world. Black bondage has lasted these 500 years and more. As the twentieth century ends, Black people are not yet truly free anywhere on earth. Whether on the African continent or in the Diaspora, Blacks are still poor, oppressed, and subordinate. We have never yet experienced any real liberation. What we have suffered through for the past 500 years is a series of *modernizations of enslavement*, disguised as "emancipations" in the span from 1792 to 1888. Each modernization has occurred at a crucial turning point in history when the system of Black servitude was in crisis and seemed threatened with collapse. Each modernization has involved some great political confrontation like the Civil War, or like the Civil Rights movement of the 1950s and 1960s. Each modernization has saved the day for the white man by discarding the unnecessary frills of white domination (i.e., the "petty apartheids"), while rescuing the essentials of Black subjugation. Each modernization has revealed that liberation can never be accomplished without breaking the back of white supremacy.

The need for these modernizations springs not alone from our ceaseless struggle for liberation, but also from economic relations and from the fact that history has made *race* an essential feature of those relations. In most Western countries economics of race are as natural as the ecological environment. Race is a relation of production and distribution—and a decisive one.

Now the key to the latest modernization of Black enslavement is the current transformation of the economy. Across the continent, large scale machine-based industries—pinnacles of the century-old second stage of the Industrial Revolution—are exiting in favor of production rooted in electronics and robotics. Fixed asset-intensive techniques oust human labor.

North America's answers to this transformation are several. One is the tendency to create massive permanent unemployment and maintain it in the form of a huge, mostly Black, "underclass." These are the *redundant* persons whose labor potential is considered superfluous, excess, without value, persons who can be dispensed with and whose earning power is virtually nil. These are people to be controlled and contained, not catered to. These are fodder for the debate over how to "change welfare as we know it." This strategy confines redundancy as much as possible to the non-white, racially-oppressed segment of the labor force, making sure that it has a rate of unemployment double or triple that of white workers. Another answer since the Second World War has been an insane-seeming militarization of the economy that on closer examination turns out to be not so loco after all. It enabled the federal government to give a significant proportion of the redundant work force—often the "best," brightest and most ambitious young Blacks—"military jobs" as soldiers. They became quasi-mercenaries hired to protect the interests of U.S. corporate capital, formerly against the now-defunct "Communist threat," at all times against the Third World.

Both schemes make it easier to remind white workers, periodically restless when the economy tailspins, that the "free market" system has inherent features which foster the interests of *white* people

78

as such, including white workers. White-skin privilege is thus construed as a *natural* fact of life shielding ordinary white folks from the most negative effects of economic change, much in the same way a sunscreen has the physical properties to protect skin from the sun's damaging ultra-violet rays. This is how the racist dimension of economic relations breeds callousness in white people. African historian Ali Mazrui reflects pointedly:

> The most generous things White Americans have done have been to fellow White people. The meanest things White Americans have done have been to non-whites. American generosity reached its apex with the Marshall Plan. American meanness has ranged from genocide against the native Americans to the dropping of the atomic bombs on Hiroshima and Nagasaki, from lynching 'Niggers" to the war in Vietnam. To this, one can ... add the bombardment of Baghdad. (Ali Mazrui 1990)

To this register can also be added the callous cruelty of a Bush Administration intent on "keeping America white" by keeping Haitian boat-people out at the cost of many Black lives.

These brutal reflexes are rooted in white civilization. Ali Mazrui calls them cultural imperatives and observes almost naively that they even outweigh hard-headed practical considerations. They certainly smother any humanitarian urges. Whether termed civilization reflexes or cultural imperatives, these are racist economic structures of domestic as well as international cultural conflict. Debate rages among political economists as to the actual rate of exploitation of the free white labor power sold as a commodity in the international market, i.e., controversy as to the actual amount of profit created by white workers and appropriated by capitalist owners (e.g., see Victor Perlo 1988). Regardless of the points scored in the debate, there is growing perception among Africans and African Americans that the exploitation of people of color has benefited and continues to benefit the majority of white persons in one manner or another; that the white population throughout the earth enjoys wealth created by Blacks who are victimized whether in Africa or in the Diaspora— although not every white beneficiary benefits to the same degree.

This is the key to the pattern of the modernizations of enslavement. At first, at the start of white appropriation of the western hemisphere, the labor of the Black slave could not be exacted apart from making the worker (the chattel slave) as well as his labor a condition of production. In other words, without him no white wealth; without his labor the riches of the Americas would have remained untapped for Europeans. The way the event actually happened, the prerequisite for the existence of present-day "post-industrial," "computerized" society was the existence in the Americas of a form of capital that functioned before the Civil War only on the basis of slave labor. Following that came a form that functioned from Reconstruciton through the 1950s only on the basis of segregationist exploitation of Black Freedmen and -women. The enslavement modernization we have to deal with today functions mainly on the basis of undervalued, sometime employment for the majority of Black wage and salary earners, and permanent redundancy for fully one-third of Black Americans.

For more than a generation, "normal" unemployment for Blacks in the U.S. political economy has always been twice that of whites and more, according to the Federal Bureau of Labor Statistics. Even this is a gross underestimation, the real rate of black unemployment always running about double the rate admitted by the government. Canada displays a similar pattern. Nowadays nobody even blinks at these grim statistics, now merely accepted as an unavoidable consequence of economic reality in "post-industrial" North America.

Yet this situation is of fairly recent date, and the history of Black unemployment is complicated. The two-to-one jobless ratio set in only with the change in the basic social makeup of Black America, a process which reached fruition some time between 1930 and 1940. Prior to then, roughly from Reconstruction to the Great Depression, the capitalist economy felt little need to impose different unemployment rates on the two races, in respect to white males as compared to Black men. This "equality" was grounded in the structure of the national economy. From the Civil War to the Second World War, the Northeast and Midwest formed the country's economic heartland. Europe orbited the great American "industrial quadrangle" as a labor satellite. American industry drew hordes of cheap white immigrants from an apparently inexhaustible European reserve. Most of them were completely unlettered and unskilled. Some of the newcomers had benefited from apprentice training at the cost of European taxpayers. These white "ethnics"—wave after wave were absorbed as industry expanded—kept wages down and profits up.

During all these years, racist exclusion kept Blacks locked in the South, away from the nation's industries. It followed as a matter of course that Northern industry would be the most sensitive to the boom-bust cycle. With the onset of each depression the unemployment rate would soar among urban white males, for they were the ones with jobs in industry. Each industrial slump would push white unemployment up higher than the jobless rate in the Black community. Black people were, in the vast majority, still confined in the agrarian South, picking cotton and planting vegetables. There was no break in the cloud of Jim Crow until war ignited Europe in 1914, choked white immigration and created a labor shortage in northern industry. These events induced the 20th century's first wave of Black mass migration northward. This initial exodus was renewed by a second wave of migrants in the mid-1920s and subsequent waves during and after World War II (Lemann 1991). However, as long as the majority of Black workers were the Southland's sharecropping, tenant farming, convict-lease laboring and debt peonage "neo-slaves," the incidence of unemployment in Black America remained less sensitive to the business cycle, and even during the depths of the Great Depression a few northern Blacks "escaped joblessness" because racist social custom dictated that shining shoes, for instance, was so lowly an occupation it had to be restricted to Blacks.

The two world wars opened jobs in the industrial North and changed the picture—radically. Brusque layoffs following the 1918 Armistice sent Black unemployment spiralling. During the Great Depression (1929–1933), Blacks endured the misery disproportionately (Foner 1976). It was not until about 1940, however, that Blacks in America were overwhelmingly urbanized and dependent on industrial employment. But once that transformation was complete and once nearly half of the Black population had migrated away from the Old South, the racist differential clicked in, cementing the last-hired, first-fired syndrome. From then on, a two-to-one jobless rate became the fixture with which we are familiar today.

The racist character of business has had far wider reach than just employment discrimination. On behalf of the capitalist economy, federal, state, and local governments have intervened vigorously over the years to foster Black inequality. There is an entire history of measures designed to establish color as a prime disqualifier in industry, banking, and commerce. Trade associations, chambers of commerce, manufacturers' associations and service clubs slammed the door on Black businessmen and professionals. The whole "old boy" networking combination so vital to successful business participation was closed to Afro-Americans. Government agencies countenanced and excused KKK-style violence to evict Blacks from jobs craved by white men, and sat calmly by while racist union bosses crafted the charters and by-laws of lily-white unions which excluded Black workers. Real estate brokers were encouraged to adopt "codes of ethics" sworn to sell land, commercial property, houses and apartments only to white buyers. Bankers cabaled to invest only in white-owned businesses and grant mortgages solely to white home buyers. Black entrepreneurs were denied business loans and contract performance bonds, and Black families could not get life, house and fire insurance from white companies. Throughout the first half of the twentieth century, public utilities unashamedly collected the fees paid by Black consumers, but systematically discriminated against Black job applicants.

Some time between the First and Second World Wars, the sharecropping system ceased to be a reliable source of profits. It had outlived its usefulness. Now the best way for white big landowners to accumulate capital was to dispense with the system their grandfathers had fabricated after defeat in the Civil War and do away with Black farming once and for all. The disruption reached its apex during the World War II period and has continued until there are almost no Black farmers left in America. In 1940, 80 percent of Black America was rural and agrarian. Most of us lived in the old Confederacy's "Black Belt" stretching from the Carolinas through Georgia, Alabama, and Mississippi to Louisiana. During the 1940s, three million Black people, mostly sharecropping families, were driven off the land and pushed north. Some ended up on the Pacific Coast. The lure of new jobs and the seductive lifestyles in the big cities were only half of the picture. The other half was the concerted effort of white land barons to clear southern fields of Blacks in order to make way for mechanical cotton pickers. By 1950 nearly twice as many Blacks were employed as unskilled or semi-skilled workers in industry, compared with those still in the rural sector. In the year 1940, 41 percent of southern Black males worked in agriculture. Ten years later, only 14.8 percent were left. Meanwhile in industry a racial income gap between Black and white workers averaging around $2,000 a year had taken firm hold.

Hiring procedures in industry made it clear that the commitment to Black labor was merely temporary, made necessary by a war-time emergency that could not be met with white labor alone. For instance, in 1944 the War Manpower Commission, a federal agency designed to provide the war industries with untapped sources of labor, congratulated itself that 75 percent of a cross-section of Chicago industry had put Blacks on the production line, where only 15 percent had employed us in 1939, two years before America's entry into the war. Some 55,400 Blacks were toiling in the Chicago area's 700 largest manufacturing establishments, constituting 8.6 percent of the total work force, i.e., one out of twelve. Many of the new faces on the assembly lines were Black women who until then had been restricted to cotton garment sweatshops at near slave wages (*Claude Barnett Papers*, Industrial Information Service of the Chicago YWCA, Bulletin, January 1944, Negroes in War Industry). But now, as the President's "Committee on Fair Employment Practices" [FEPC] announced, "Negroes" were needed. We were courted, sought after, persuaded, and encouraged. Black women were enticed from their kitchens (and from white women's kitchens) and into the plants. There were even some perks of sorts. The Office of Defense Transportation offered to transport Black workers to and from the job. The National Housing Authority (NHA) was pressured to come up with additional housing. The federal government twisted the arm of discriminating firms. City authorities guilty of under-utilizing Black labor were told to expect a cutback in war housing and transportation facilities in their jurisdiction. The War Production Board poised to revoke government contracts with firms which fell behind schedule in war production because they refused to hire Blacks. Factories importing white workers from out of town were told to stop and bring in local Blacks—a cheaper and more efficient solution. "Race relations" were hyped, as the War Manpower commission set out to instruct both employers and white trade unions how to utilize Blacks. Owners, employment managers, foremen, and union officials were interviewed in the interest of "racial harmony," while assembly line white workers were primed to work alongside Blacks without friction. Much time and effort were spent smoothing ruffled racist sensitivities.

Yet in all, even at the height of the war effort, state laws pursuant to the FEPC Executive Order 8802, forbidding racial discrimination in hiring or training on the part of war contractors, remained dead letters. No white offenders were prosecuted. Not even the direst national emergency could overcome, or even suspend, the civilization-derived racist instinct in white employers and employees. Decades after these events throughout her career on Capitol Hill, pioneering Congresswoman Shirley Chisholm of New York always insisted that racism was inherent in the bloodstream of America. World War II civilian factories, i.e., the ones without a government contract, were free to go on turning Blacks away on the basis of color, as of old. War plants engaged Black workers, but discriminated against them in training, promotion, transfers, wages, and work permits. We were barred from unions. Despite lip-service to Black-white worker solidarity, AFL and CIO both permitted their locals to keep lily-white clauses. In 1944, with the outcome of the war still at issue, the AFL Boilermakers Union relegated Black workers to a segregated auxiliary in the San Francisco and Los Angeles shipyards. Railways were essential for the movement of men and material, and there was an intense labor shortage. Yet throughout the war, the white Brotherhood of Firemen and Enginemen vetoed the hiring of Blacks as firemen, for fear they might be promoted to supervisory posts! As far north as Detroit, white workers, women in particular, objected against sharing toilet facilities with Black women workers. In one Chicago area plant, twelve white women quit their job rather than work beside a member of the "Negro race."

But still Black people came, slotted for humiliation in America's racist industrial relations. We had no choice. We needed work. From 1939 to 1969 Black male and female employment in construction, manufacturing, and mining soared from 21.8 percent to 41.3 percent, and from 3.7 percent to 16.1 percent, respectively. Meanwhile, during the same 30-year span, Black female employment in domestic service shrank from 60 percent to 17.5 percent, as Black male participation in agriculture dropped from 42.5 percent to 5.3 percent. Net emigration from the South to the North from 1940 to 1960 eventually totalled more than one-quarter of the national Black population, as it stood in 1940.

Through all the changes racism churned out above-average profits. The profit boom which extended from 1948 to 1968, said economist Robert Cherry, was caused by wage differentials to the disadvantage of Black workers (Cherry 1991:60-70). Super-profits also came from dirt-cheap female labor. A disproportionate number of these women workers were Black. In the ten years from 1949 to 1959, southern white workers' annual earnings averaged merely 75 to 76 percent of the average earnings of their northern industrial counterparts. But that hardly tells the story, for the most lucrative source of profits was the wage differential between Black and white workers in every section of the country. In 1949, the dollar value of the annual wage gap between Black and white men in the Jim Crow South was $1,052. Over the next ten years the disparity widened to $1,900. In 1949 Black workers in the South were held to less than half (49 percent) of the earnings of white men. And in 1959, despite the upsurge in the Black Liberation Movement ignited by the Montgomery bus boycott, the Black percentage of white income had fallen to 46 percent. North of the Mason-Dixon line the inequality between Black and white earnings was less—78 cents to each dollar in 1949, and 73.4 cents to each dollar in 1959—but still a substantial source of above-average profits for business. And, as in the South, in the North too the cleavage widened during the 1950s. In 1949 and 1959 the amounts in actual dollars of the annual income gap between Black and white men in the North were $605 [in 1949] and $1,227 [in 1959], respectively (Batchelder 1964:515 ff). As of 1994, U.S. businesses were raking in additional profits exceeding $100 billion a year from the racist wage differential.

*

Thus in every section of the country the post-war boom rode on the white businessman's ability to squeeze the same (if not more) value from the labor of a Black employee, but pay him less than the equivalent white employee, and pocket the difference. This was a key reproduction of racial domination in labor markets. Meanwhile the Black working class itself was splitting into hard-core industrial producers, and a growing body of service workers whose labor was very profitable to their employers, although not *directly* involved in the manufacture of value-bearing commodities. In 1968, towards the end of the postwar profit boom, the Black work force in the United States was roughly underestimated at more than eight million. By then 86 percent were confined in low paid, super-exploited, and often service-type jobs, many of the latter misleadingly classified as "white collar." The split which has subsequently come to fruition was then beginning, i.e., division between a diminishing core of unionized industrial workers who manufacture commodities like, say, automobiles, embodying tremendous amounts of profits for their employers on one side, and on the other a growing redundant underclass whose social labor is regarded as relatively worthless. The trend was clearly noticeable by the early 1970s.

But this was preceded as early as the 1950s by the notorious "niggermation" of Black semi-skilled workers on the non-automated sections of the production line. Desperate Black workers faced the alternative of life-shortening jobs or abandoning their families to welfare. In Michigan, for instance, Black auto workers were literally run ragged, sprinting up and down stairs trying to keep pace with accelerated sections of the asembly line, an outrage that elicited a flurry of protest from revolutionary Black workers in the late 1960s and early 1970s. This process cemented the racial division of labor between Black and white workers, but intensified the "profit valorization" problems that were emerging in American political economy. More and more businessmen argued that the growing high tech component of production made it possible for the first time in U.S. history to do without Black unskilled and semi-skilled labor, i.e., since a lot of it was no longer needed as a source of profit, Black labor was "de-valorized." Then along came computers as an agent of mass production to make traditional forms of Black manual labor obsolete. Automation, computerization, and robotization intervened to wipe even the obscene "niggermation" jobs from industry. Most damaged were the job hopes of young Black males just entering the work force. This latest "modernization" has culminated in the shift of state-of-the-art, high-tech production facilities to "right-to-work" states, and the present migration to "off-shore" locations. By 1984 this had happened in every branch from steel to auto to meat packing.

In short, the scientific and technological revolution (STR), in combination with the traditional racial division of labor, transformed the status of Black labor in a very ominous way. It has made questionable whether much profit can be made from hiring Black unskilled and semi-skilled job seekers, throwing hundreds of thousands of youthful Black males on the redundancy heap. It has strengthened white racist prejudice against Blacks, providing ammunition for media hate campaigns against an allegedly "shiftless underclass fit only to freeload on taxpayers." Although there is evidence that the ratio of discrimination has now been nearly equalized in the main regions of the country (Perlo 1988) with the Midwest for the first time even edging out the Old South as the worst locale, all the other traditional elements of racist production relations have survived. The environment of bitter competition for jobs between

Blacks and whites, seniority and apprentice privileges for whites, wage differentials, the location of industries in easy access of white workers and remote from our workers, inferior housing for Blacks, school funding inequalities, deteriorating sewage and water supply facilities in minority neighborhoods, etc., all are still firmly in place, as handed down from the past.

Economic marginalization means unfathomable and mysterious forms of exploitation of the urban ghettoes. Corporate capital has packed up and moved scarce employment to white areas away from the inner cities, all the while claiming that the jobs available are still open to Black applicants. Economic circumstances dictate that the inner city must buy necessary goods and services that are owned and operated by whites, or increasingly by immigrant surrogates, like the Korean and Arab retailers who have invaded Black turf. The appointment of a few, carefully screened Blacks as much-publicized members of boards of directors does not alter the fact that the commanding heights in the American economy remain in the steely grip of "lily white" hands. In any large corporation, a Black vice president, no matter what his alleged jurisdiction, is always really in charge mainly of polishing the firm's affirmative action image, pacifying liberal critics, and instilling confidence in Black customers. The glamour of one or two Black executives does not scratch the "glass ceiling," any more than the appointment of General Colin Powell to head the Joint Chiefs of Staff meant that the U.S. armed forces had escaped the control of a small group of white men. Robust profits are obtained from the ghetto owing to exorbitant retail prices and high rents. In large measure, these funds are *exported* from the Black community, very rarely reinvested in local improvements or industrial and commercial enterprises beneficial to inner cities. The removal is excused on the plea that investment on the spot would be unprofitable and locating expensive new high-tech assets in the volatile ghetto too risky.

One of the more intriguing twists is the Free Enterprise Zone concept (EPZ). Although the exact paternity of the scheme is doubtful, EPZs are usually touted as the pet political project of Republican Party populist Jack Kemp. Certain Black critics suspect that what he really has in mind is the economic Sowetoization of Black America. For a decade, New Right populists have boosted the "benefits" of tax free enterprise zones in urban ghettoes and barrios, usually coupled with alleged job-creating, non-unionized, below-minimum wages for

Black youth. EPZs are advertised as the only way to lure back big white corporations which have run away from the inner cities. The concept is lauded as a device to entice corporate capital to install manufacturing facilities in Black and Afro-Latino residential districts, generating jobs and incomes for minorities. Some envisage it as a domestic answer to the threat of the North America Free Trade Area (NAFTA), enabling our inner cities to compete with Mexico in offering cheap, unprotected labor. Its boosters carefully avoid comparison with South Africa's estwhile apartheid Homelands which functioned as the infrastructure for cheap Black migrant labor and segregated dormitory-encampments, epitomized by Soweto. There is no thought to the possibility that the spread of EPZs could bring the U.S. a step closer to its own apartheid nightmare (see Munford 1978, for early speculation along these lines). Ignored also is the parallel with the Export Processing Zones, now emerging in neo-colonized Africa. Export Processing Zones are special areas in African and other Third World countries where local government legislation has created a haven for foreign multinational corporations. Within these enclaves, some local but mainly foreign enterprises produce goods exclusively for international markets. These areas are exempted from normal tax codes, custom duty, and labor and environmental restrictions. These immunities guarantee foreign firms handsome profits, but the African host is mired deeper in the swamp of white imperialist dependency. In a striking sense, Export Processing Zones seem a modernization of the old seventeenth and eighteenth century ancillary export enclave which emerged along the coast of West Africa to service the Atlantic slave trade (see Munford 1991, Vol. I, chapters 2 and 7).

In the U.S., domestic EPZs would dovetail with Japanese auto makers' fondness for racist division of labor. In a move to further segregate the U.S. work force along the color line, the Japanese have opted to build their American assembly plants in rural areas, far removed from where we live. This discrimination is excused by leading Japanese officials on the plea that this is a "business decision" required by the need to avoid Blacks and other "lesser breeds" who, it is alleged, have been transforming America into a declining nation of racial mongrels.

Figures released in 1993 pegged 59 percent of African Americans as residents of 30 metropolitan areas. Courting Black voters, the Clinton Administration renamed the old Republican

Enterprise Zones "Empowerment Zones." Sixty-five urban communities were designated as such zones, as against 30 rural ones. Since the summer of 1994 the Empowerment Zones are funded by the federal government, unlike the Republican EPZ's which depended on state and local jurisdictions for money.

*

The United States has moved inescapably, if not smoothly, through a series of use-forms of Black labor. We have gone, men and women, from chattel slavery to the neo-slavery of sharecropping, tenant farming, debt peonage, convict-lease laboring, and humiliating domestic service. We have suffered through the heaviest, dirtiest and most dangerous kinds of unskilled and semi-skilled industrial labor. We have been urbanized well above the national norm in grim "smokestack" cities. We have undergone waves of migration, and now reverse-direction migration, all to satisfy the needs of white-owned big capital. We have had to put up with government-sanctioned wage differentials and discriminatory job classifications. Unemployment among us has escalated to two and a half times the white rate. Now, combined with continuing super-exploitation of the numerically declining core of Black industrial workers, we face a burgeoning services sector, offering the enticing lifetime career prospective of dead-end, minimum wage employment in fried chicken and hamburger emporiums.

The new buzzword is *redundancy*. A large segment of Black America is simply counted out of the work force, both youths who have never had a job and never will get one, and discouraged mature workers. For forty years and more now, we Blacks, shoulder to shoulder with Filipino and other Asian immigrants and with Latinos (often undocumented) have been expected to staff the nation's hospitals and fill other low-paid positions in a health-care system which deliberately neglects people of color. Black citizens people federal, state, and local government bureaucracies and fill the Volunteer Armed Forces (VAF), but we as a people get little payback and less thanks. Blacks lucky enough to have a job are stuffed increasingly into those sectors which do not turn out high-value, durable commodities, but which are nonetheless productive of money profit for their employers and which are of great "social profit" in bolstering the status quo. The misery of structural, periodical, and cyclical crises hits us disproportionately. We shoulder the main burden of the long term factors of economic dislocation. In fact, these, our specific woes, are the manner in which the racial division of labor and racist relations of production are realized in the course of history. This is the way economic racism works to realize its fullest potential.

The financial costs and profits of American racism are precise and can be estimated. A National Urban League study calculated that racist-generated economic inequality cost African Americans $129 billion in 1980, rising to $179 billion in 1988. It pegged the overall income differential between Blacks and whites at $178 billion. Dr. Billy J. Tidwell, the Urban League Research Director, argued that American white people as a whole are the beneficiaries of racist policies. In his words, "discrimination and its supporting prejudice persists mainly because the majority [of] people gain from them." Tidwell concluded that racism operates most effectively on the aggregate level. Racism affords whites control over economic resources and access to economic opportunities. It is the outcome of a process of national production governed by the principle of racial preference, a code of ethics that has instructed Western civilization for centuries. At the end of 1990 the differentials against Black blue collar and other wage- and salary-earners comprised the largest single source of superprofits for the corporate elite. Additional profits were extracted from Hispanics, Native Americans, and Somoans, and from the Third World millions employed at U.S.-owned facilities abroad, at wages far below the U.S. minimum.

But the rip-off is not merely about money profits. The racism embedded in labor-selection and employment-distribution procedures compounds the swindle. Take the practices of the New York International Brotherhood of Electrical Workers (IBEW) union Local 3, for example. For many years Blacks and Latinos were barred from membership. The employers acquiesced. The law now forbids such blatant discrimination. Nevertheless, the racist predisposition is such that, as of 1990, in a city where more than half of the work force is Black and Latino, fewer than 20 percent of the electricians' apprentices were Black and Latino. And even fewer will ever become full electricians. White workers manage not only to hog present positions, but also to reserve most of the future jobs in this relatively high-paying, skilled occupation for their own sons, nephews, sons-in-law, and friends' children. That is how U.S. and Canadian political economy functions. Any way the national economic pie is sliced, lucrative rewards accrue to those able to milk the income disparity between Black and white. Early in 1992 the annual value for U.S.

business of extra profits from the racism-imposed cheap wages of Black blue collar workers was running about $60 billion. This was without taking into account the much larger sum derived from over-all income differential between Blacks and whites.

*

The peculiar history of capital accumulation sealed our fate in many ways. It describes our experience in macro-economic terms. As capital accumulated in white hands, originally through the slave trade and conquest and colonization of Africa, "underdevelopment" accumulated in Africa. Degradation and demoralization accumulated in the Diaspora. The processes proceeded simultaneously—white wealth, Black poverty—and one engendered the other. Mighty America is a land in which white wealth was nursed initially by Black slavery and in which racial discrimination persists as a distinct mode of production. It is the land in which—some time between 1890 and 1919—capital found it wise to spare white workers from the extor- tion of *excess* profits, instead targetting Black and other workers of color as the source of enormous super-profits. America is the country in which the white middle and working classes joined hands with the lords of capital in exploiting and represssing the Black commu- nity—represssion manifested of late in the "prisonization" of the Black male. America is the country in which dirt-poor whites smoth- ered any sense of hostility toward rich whites under a blanket of hatred of Black people. America became a great white corporation whose main business for a long time was the exploitation of Black people, and whose chief product is still racism. Even if we set aside all of white racism's psychological implications of sexual jealousy, social prestige, and status, we are still left with its elephantine role in political economy. It bore down on a group whose physical appear- ance made it easy to set aside from the majority of the population. The "final solution" invented for African Americans by U.S. white supremacy proved much more useful to the long-range interests of white civilization than Nazi Germany's lethal "final solution" for Jews. For in America, racism created a system which enabled it to sweat and milk Black labor for wealth, generation after generation, seemingly with no end in sight.

This tradition of never running short of ways of manipulating Black labor to make money for white folks is, by the way, what will make the next 50–60 years such a perilous time for Black America.

For there are signs that the procedure may not be renewable. There are two circumstances at work—one economic, the other demographic. It appears that for the first time in the history of the Republic technology is repositioning the economy to do without the non-college-trained Black males under the age of 30. The fact that the majority of people entering the work force by the year 2000 will be white women, the disabled, and racial minorities, only means that these will be job-*seekers*, not necessarily job-*obtainers*. Should white capital find it can no longer profit from male Black labor, it may challenge these men's right to exist as human beings. The ultra-Right already growls that "America should rid itself of non-white drones who handicap it in the competition with Germany and Japan." Furthermore, white supremacy faces a prospect which it considers scary. Should it not be able to devise some population control scheme soon, then at the very latest by the year 2050 people of color are sure to outnumber whites as citizens of the United States. In other words, if unaltered, the demographic trend will create a non-white voter majority, changing national politics beyond description. Now, as historical time is measured, this is a short-run prospect. White supremacy must then either cede power to the New Majority of Blacks and other people of color, or scrap our current white-serving majoritarian democracy as obsolete, in favor of white minority rule along the model of, say, South African apartheid. The latter option would require outright fascist dictatorship, quarantine of non-white communities and wholesale slaughter of Black resisters. The White Aryan Resistance (WAR) movement, born in California, has been saying for years that such is the only solution that will allow white supremacy to survive in the America of the future.

*

OBSOLESCENCE AND REDUNDANCY

The organic development of racist capitalism has generated Black redundancy. Inner-city youth, mostly Black and Latino males, have been doomed to exclusion from the productive process by the very evolution of the American economy in the last decades of the twentieth century. The racial barrier prevents most of our young males from acquiring the technological expertise required for even middle level employment in a "high-tech," computerized environment. The organic process of restructuring U.S. domestic production, often termed "deindustrialization," has marginalized the huge third of

Black America called the "underclass." Thus, after the creation of big-city concentrations of Black industrial workers from Southern rural raw material in the first half of the twentieth century, the process reversed in the second half of the century. In its worst scenario, the process has resulted in many of the victims succumbing to drugs, criminal behavior and Black-against-Black violence.

Some analysts object, however, that this is not in fact the first wave of Black redundancy. They see today's rejection of Black labor as occurring for the second time in U.S. history. The first occasion was the expulsion of Black sharecroppers and tenant farmers from Southern agriculture as superfluous early in the century, an economic "push" which heightened the Great Migration to newly forming Northern ghettoes in the years from 1915 to 1920. The South was suffering from a cotton crisis. "Black Belt" sharecroppers could not compete with the superior efficiency of cotton plantations in New Mexico and Arizona. Big landowners were beginning the mechanization of agriculture in the Old South that would sweep Black labor from the fields by 1945. Bollweevils and disastrous floods accelerated the "economic slaughter" of the Black sharecropping system -mechanized cotton plantations required only one-fourth of the manual labor previously employed. Cotton's wage labor expenses dropped radically. By the mid-1940s the mechanical cotton picker had taken over the Deep South cotton fields, spelling the end for sharecropping. This was the definitive "push" for the final wave of Black migration northward. At least five million Black people invaded the North between 1940 and 1970.

The Black press was among the first to notice Black economic redundancy. On the eve of the U.S. entry into World War II an American Negro Exposition was planned in Detroit to celebrate the seventy-fifth anniversary of the Emancipation Proclamation and the end of the Civil War. On that occasion the Associated Negro Press (ANP) expressed keen awareness of the special role of Black workers under American capitalism, but noted that it was a *negative* one, as far as Blacks themselves were concerned. An ANP document dated 12 March 1940 scanned the problem of joblessness and referred to Southern "technological unemployment" as the road to the economic dustheap for thousands of Black persons (*Claude Barnett Papers*, 12 March 1940).

Since 1940 the long-term unemployment of Black males has soared in comparison with white males. In 1940 Black and white men spent about the same time unemployed during a 45-year work career. But after holding steady during the 1950s and 1960s at about 8.6 years of unemployment in 45 years of able-bodied labor potential, by 1980 the average Black man had to endure 13.3 years of utter joblessness in a 45-year work career. By 1985 the years spent without a job had climbed to 15.6, more than a third of one's working career, as compared with only 9.4 years for white males. The 1985 lifetime long-term unemployment expectancy was merely 1.2 years greater for Black women than for white women, a much smaller disparity reflecting the special history of female participation in the wage-earning work force.

Worsening this trend was the development of machinery operated by automatic appliances, limiting human workers to merely supervising, controlling, adjusting, and repairing the mechanisms. This was automation. Automation can be described as the degree to which the creation of real wealth comes to depend less on human labor and more on the power of instruments. The progress of technology either developed to the point where it began to render many categories of Black industrial labor economically superfluous, or took the peculiar, aforementioned "niggermation" form, in which increased productivity derived from doubling or tripling the workload of Black laborers. It showed up clearly also in the impoverishment and expulsion from the workforce of Black male youth. Theodore Cross remarked that during the early 1950s young Black men 18 to 19 years of age were much more active workforce participants than their white peers, but thirty years later they had fallen nearly 17 percentage points behind in the race to find jobs (Cross 1984:246).

Meanwhile the international environment changed radically. American imperialism outgrew domestic raw materials and now wanted to control markets abroad as well as at home. Computerized industrial production and data processing created a gigantic capacity to extort above-average profits around the globe, while making it easier to manipulate more and more Third World countries politically. Neo-colonialism came into being. These events occurred in the 1950s. By the end of the Korean War the pace of U.S. military aggression quickened as the British, French, Dutch, and Portuguese overseas empires were dismantled, taken into tow by the U.S., and compelled to pour streams of riches into the white American maw. The prizes were the Third World's raw materials, markets and cheap labor. This drive was temporarily derailed by defeat in Vietnam. The Reagan inauguration put it back on track. The "new era," the "American century" had dawned, and Washington vaunted the *"Pax Americana,"* rebaptized the "New World Order" by the Bush Administration. New management techniques, tailored to suit the "New Imperialism," targeted African, Latin American, and Asian "natives."

At home the very same technological and managerial advances were gradually expelling Black industrial workers from productive activity. By 1980, if not earlier, key fractions of corporate capital began to regard Black America more as a headache than as an indispensable source of profit. The Heritage Foundation and other right-wing think-tanks saw us as an "economic liability" and "threat to public order." Certain strategists suggested that U.S. Black folks be dispensed with as much as possible, instead concentrating on the Third World abroad as the source of profit. From corners come gleeful whispers that the disappearance overnight of 30 to 35 million Black U.S. citizens would cause no more than a "hiccup" in the national economy. A whiff of genocide? The marginalization of Black labor accelerated as droves of young whites, no longer needed on manufacturing assembly lines, invaded the services industries, ousting Blacks even from such low-prestige occupations as waiters and bellhops.

Lerone Bennett is right that the fundamental problem is racism compounded by technological changes. "As a consequence," he wrote, "the black share of the labor market was growing smaller and the number of permanently unemployed blacks was growing larger" (Bennett 1984:382). White supremacy combined with the scientific and technological revolution (STR) is an ominous mixture for Blacks. The STR reduced jobs but elevated the productivity of labor, particularly in the steel industry, until then a major employer of Black workers. Black steelworkers were bitten by "technological unemployment," a euphemism for the latest dose of last-hired-first-fired, subsequently worsened by runaway-shops, union-busting, and deindustrialization. Earlier in the century Blacks had fought hard and long to break through the Jim Crow barrier and win employment in steel and other basic industries. From the Great Migration (1915–1918) through World War II to the Civil Rights movement of the 1950s and 1960s, the growing concentration of Afro-Americans in the key basic industries had been a major accomplishment of the Black Liberation Movement.

"Technological unemployment," plant closings, and relocations and restructuring are striking this advantage from our hands. The STR in agriculture has driven more and more Blacks from the ranks of the nation's farmers, leaving no alternative to migration to the cities, there to face either perpetual unemployment or rock-bottom service industry wages. Blacks are by far the most urbanized contingent of the American population.

During the 1970s and 1980s Black STR redundancy was a chief cause of inner-city crime and the cocaine scourge. In less than 20 years Blacks lost nearly 30 percent of the decent-paying industrial jobs we previously held. The Equal Employment Opportunity Commission (EEOC) is a federal agency established by Congress to ensure equality of rights in employment. It was gutted by the Reagan Administration. Nevertheless, it did a very instructive survey of automobile manufacturing. In 1978, some 181,000 Black workers were employed in the U.S. auto industry, alongside 41,375 other Third World workers, mostly Arabs, Chicanos and other Hispanics, for a total of 223,375 minority workers. Of the Black workers, 135,723 were listed in the "operative" job category, including the semi-skilled; 11,000 were skilled; the rest were "laborers." All told, the EEOC reported that Blacks made up 19.2 percent of auto workers in 1979. Then the STR crisis hit. From August 1980 to August 1983, two dozen auto plants closed for good across the United States. Most of these were located in cities with heavy concentrations of Black and other oppressed minority workers. The plants had been the mainstay of the local Black communities. By 1983, 48,000 African-Americans had been laid off, leaving 133,000 still on the job. The number of Blacks in the "operative" category fell to 91,283 as 44,441 were thrown out of work, most of them permanently. Of the skilled category, 1,120 had been let go also, reducing the Black proportion of the skilled and semi-skilled classifications to a mere 6.7 percent. The flight of major sections of industry to foreign shores, coupled with domestic plant relocation in white suburbs and rural areas, badly damaged Black, Latino, and Native American job chances generally.

Large numbers of our folks have traditionally found employment as postal service workers, cleaners, transit workers, and packers and wrappers. Not any longer. By 1995 nearly a quarter of Black transit workers lost their jobs to automatic transportation systems. Packers and wrappers were diminished some 19 percent by mechanical sorting and packaging, while mechanized commercial cleaning brought Black cleaners down a whopping 53 percent. Since the early 1950s, street wisdom in the Black community assured folks that there would always be a job for a Black man in the post office. That prospect too has disappeared into thin air. By the mid-1990s, nearly a quarter of Black postal workers will have been shown the door, chased out by electronic mail and optical scanners. When ATT sought to tap the reservoir of cheap Black female labor, a lot of Black women went to work as telephone operators during the Civil Rights' Sixties, while supermarkets and other chain stores hired Black cashiers. These women too are succumbing to technological obsolescence. Universal product code scanners have eliminated much of the live labor from the nation's checkout counters. Automatic switching devices are doing away with Black telephone operators. All told, in some 24 other occupations Black workers stand to lose between 10 and 40 percent of the positions they held in, say, 1985. It is not surprising, therefore, that many fear that STR redundancy will mean the complete extinction of the Black industrial working class. Many fell behind in rent or mortgage payments, were evicted, or changed residence, many were forced to desert the industrialized Midwest completely, thousands seeking refuge in the non-unionized, low-wage Sun Belt.

The Black industrial working class is coming apart at the seams as veteran workers are thrown out of work and are unable to procure decent paying jobs comparable to the ones lost. Their sons are even worse off. Never to be gainfully employed at all, the next generation is destined for the *underclass*. Sons of fathers who once operated the assembly line in the giant auto, steel, and machinery industry, these youth have, figuratively, been "told" by the national economy that they will never be permitted to bring home an adequate, legally acquired pay check. This passage from industrial employment to the aimless desperation of permanent joblessness and the dole have bred a keen awareness among the young of institutionalized repression, perhaps best voiced in Rap music's assault against white supremacy. Illegal gainful employment is seized upon as a rational alternative. The migratory trend back to the Deep South, as well as to southwestern Sun Belt regions, only goes to strengthen the sense of uprootedness and estrangement. Economic restructuring has resulted moreover in the displacement of Black males by white females. Hitherto-inactive white women have been turned loose from their domestic hideaways to flood the market in search of jobs that could otherwise be filled by Black men needful of employment to support families.

Today, the U.S. political economy stands in indecision at a cross-roads, seemingly unable to decide whether there is any further use to which the labor of a huge portion of Black America can be put that is compatible with white profit maximization. Much Black labor is now marginalized and surplus in U.S. political economy, and young Black males have become an "endangered species," so to speak. Blacks face a similar situation in metropolitan Toronto, Nova Scotia, and Montreal. This malaise is bound to worsen in coming years as renewed contradictions build up between North America and its Japanese and European antagonists. Among the present-day effects of racist relations of production are growing marginalization, economic exclusion, denial of access to "high-tech" training, life-long unemployment for some, and relegation to an illegal parallel economy of drug-dealing and such like for others. The main victims are young Black males. Increasingly, they are left with the bleak options of jail, treadmill-like containment in the inner city, or a specious so-called "volunteer service" in the armed forces, where they get the "golden opportunity" to shed their blood stomping Third World people. As the misadventures in Panama and Iraq of recent memory indicate, this is what the armed forces mean politically for Black enlisted men and women, now that the white European former Warsaw Pact countries have joined the Racist International.

*

THE BLOOD SURTAX: MILITARISM AND MILITARIZATION OF THE ECONOMY

"You may not be able to get a job in the post office anymore, but you sure can in Uncle Sam's 'volunteer' armed forces." "Be all that you can be, although that may be being dead." "Be a G.I., it's either that or jail; one takes one's choice." The relationship between African Americans and the U.S. military is tragic and complex. There is no more ironic situation in the entire history of the Republic.

The twentieth century witnessed the militarization of America. Militarization means having the entire country prepared for war at all times—its economy, its mass media, its education and transportation systems. A militarized nation is one on a constant war footing. A militarized economy makes the production of weapons its number one priority. The United States has been on a war footing permanently since 1941 and the Lend-Lease Act. In 1949 it harnessed the NATO allies to its war chariot. By the end of his administration, even President Dwight D. Eisenhower, no friend of Black folk, had grown leery of the military-industrial complex. Since the Korean War, Black youth have been used as mercenaries.

This is tantamount to a *blood surtax* on Black youth, levied by the military industrial complex. The militarization of the U.S. economy appears in several guises. One is the transformation by economic means of Black and other minority youth—male and female—into a reserve pool of "volunteer" cannon fodder, soldiers whose only hope of "employment" is doing dirty jobs abroad. These youth serve, in effect, as mercenaries who protect American foreign capital and export counter-revolution to stifle anti-imperialist trends in the Third World. The economic goad is measurable in the simple statistic that since 1974 the unemployment rate for Black youth has never been less than 40 percent! Economic need herds non-white youth into the armed forces, and once there the same economic whip regulates them in a way which supplements and reinforces the normal discipline of the military. The lack of any civilian economic alternative often makes Black and other minority recruits the most ambitious, and therefore the most loyal, brave, and eager soldiers. This is the proverbial economic discipline of capitalism at its most efficient. Once a part of the military machine, otherwise dangerous, potentially radical anger is defused or channeled. The discontent generated by the deprived, aimless, jobless existence of the ghetto streets is effectively neutralized. Now hedged about by the controls of military rank and discipline, young Blacks are buffered against the political dangers inherent in the "radical rhetoric" they might have heard as civilians from militants on city streets. Instead their thoughts are dosed. Reactionary indoctrination poisons them against any Third World leader who dares to defy the U.S. State Department. Short of the disillusionment of unpopular military adventures and defeat in battle (e.g., Vietnam), enlistment in the armed forces reduces the likelihood of political radicalization for Black ghetto youth. Propaganda ballyhoos a few Black colonels and generals. The Pentagon has become an effective means for depriving the Black Liberation Movement of both rank and file militants and bright young leaders. It operates its own peculiar brain drain, stripping the Black community of its most stable and ambitious youth. Once again, the political needs of white supremacy are met.

The United States is the most thoroughly militarized structure on earth. Whole regions of the country in the West and Southwest feed on war production. That is why the modest downsizing under the Clinton Administration caused such economic hardship, laying off thousands of defense industry workers, particularly in California. That is why no sooner than they had taken control of both houses of Congress in 1994, the Republicans began to talk of restoring military spending. The Korean War, the occupation of Taiwan since 1949, the interventions in the Dominican Republic and Zaire, the attack on Cuba at the Bay of Pigs, the criminal aggression against the peoples of Indochina, the permanent alert on the sea and in the air, the network of nuclear missiles, the worldwide deployment of the Navy, the assaults during the 1980s and 1990s on Grenada, Panama, and Iraq—all are components in an elastic and permanent state of mobilization against Third World nations. A logistics feat which guarantees the clique of white rulers continued domination over people of color everywhere on earth.

More than a hundred years ago, social critics began to see a link between the European imperialist tradition and international capitalist competition. But they seemed to overlook its essentially white racist character. To their credit, these commentators did not miss the tendency in social life to glorify the ideals of the military caste, and they censured the "Manifest Destiny" domination of Black and Brown peoples in the Caribbean and the Philippines. The hard-riding frontiersman thesis, glorifying the image of the outdoorsy, hunting, sharpshooting, rugged individual, helped to fuel a militarism whose political role is two-sided. The armed forces are white supremacy's chief instrument for the conquest and pillage of foreign peoples of color as illustrated by the long drawn-out invasion of Vietnam and more recently by forays in the Caribbean and the Middle East. In addition, the armed forces are the government's bludgeon when domestic repression is called for. We saw the army at work in 1992 in South Central Los Angeles. Military might accomplished the political goal—terminating the rebellion.

Moreover, racism assigns *specific* military functions to the oppressed. White supremacy not only isolates, *de facto* segregates, and ignores Blacks and people of color, it sets aside specially onerous tasks for its victims. Despite humiliating discrimination throughout the history of the American armed forces, Black soldiers have always been used to fight the battles of the United States. We have fulfilled the task, but not without ambiguity. On the one hand, we have struggled for the right to be treated as equals in all branches of the service, to avoid insult and enjoy deserved promotions. On the other hand, the irony of bleeding to protect white rulers must at times have been extremely bitter. Good examples of the special surtax in blood levied on Afro-Americans are the 25 percent casualty rate suffered in Vietnam, and the heavy overrepresentation of Blacks in Desert Storm. The rank of sacrificial shock troops is enforced economically by the enormous disparity between white and minority youth unemployment, and by the inferior civilian career prospects open to young Blacks. When the concrete alternative is between homelessness, hustling and prison, on one side, and "volunteer" enlistment on the other, the choice is easy. Three meals a day, board, petty cash and veterans' benefits for otherwise destitute minority youths, offer one variant of the economic whip which disciplines all wage labor. In this case, racism says to Black youth: Sell combat capabilities at the risk of life and limb or join the underclass.

The Second World War taught this lesson with a vengeance. Some have lauded the anti-Hitler coalition of World War II as "progressive," because of the extreme racist character of the German Nazis. But Allied anti-racism was mainly for propaganda purposes. Black GIs did experience a kind of vicarious enjoyment. Their natural though suppressed desire for revenge against white American racists was diverted through the opportunity to kill some white German surrogates and feel extra good about it because the Germans were said to be ultra-racists. The use of Black troops in the Pacific, on the other hand, fit more exactly in the traditional imperialist pattern. Though Japan was an imperialist power, the United States was the direct oppressor of African Americans, and what pitted Washington against Tokyo was nothing more than conflicting predatory interests. Black men fell to killing yellow Japanese, and fell to dying at the hands of yellow Japanese. On the eve of World War II, the Bureau of Navigation of the U.S Navy Department voiced the feelings of the entire military command when it admitted that, on the presumption that Black men were incapable of disciplining white men, it opposed the "experiment" of appointing Black naval officers over white enlisted men. "For that reason," announced the Navy brass, "Negroes are not permitted to enlist in the Navy other than in the messman branch....Their work is similar to that of waiters in hotels and better class cafes" (*Claude A. Barnett Papers*, 5 May 1937).

Since then the role of the armed forces has changed in accordance with the changes in the financial and industrial setup. Banks no longer dominate the international economy to the extent they did during the epoch from ca. 1890 to the Second World War. For a good generation now, the typical and determining element is the giant transnational (or multinational) corporation which generates a lot of its expansion funds from profits gathered "offshore." "Self-financing" keynotes transnational wheeling and dealing, along with leveraged buyouts, junk bonds, and loans from the enormous pension and mutual funds administered by investment firms. These changes were reflected in the U.S. armed forces. Since the moment of its creation, the Pentagon has been run like a multinational corporation. Intimate personal ties bond ruling business circles to the top military men. Retired Pentagon chiefs regularly reappear as board members or as high-priced consultants of private military-industrial firms. And both the top brass and the corporation overlords are plugged into the "business" of controlling two-party politics and manipulating the lives of Black and Brown people.

Like the high technology industries, the U.S. armed services are constructed from prototypes. Throughout the Cold War, the Pentagon sought to build original models on which subsequent forms were based. And since racist imperialism felt threatened most of all by Third World wars of national liberation, the standard to which all other armed forces units were required to conform were the counter-insurgency troops, such as the Rangers, Special Operations, Green Berets and Rapid Deployment Units. The contemporary U.S. armed forces revolve around such combat units, considered the most capable of dealing with "emergencies" like Panama and Iraq, and heavily staffed with Black and Afro-Latino enlisted men and women.

The realization awakened in Vietnam among some Black troops that they were being hoodwinked and that they had been singled out for a special surtax in blood, was unfortunately shortlived and circumstantial. Civil rights militancy and anti-war sentiment in 1969–1971 among Black troops stationed in Vietnam spurred Richard Nixon's "change-the-color-of-the-corpses" retreat from that country. Fear of potentially disloyal forces encouraged the Nixon-Ford administration to cut its losses, speeding up the withdrawal of American troops. A *New York Times* service report in 1971 called the polarization of white and Black soldiers into hostile groups the most dangerous trend in the American military at the time, as reflected in group assaults by Black GIs against white military police. The uprising in the Long Binh stockade outside Saigon in September

1968 was an indication of Black GI retaliation against white racism. A white soldier was killed and several others seriously wounded. In 1971 Black GIs in South Korea locked in a bloody battle resulting in many injuries to racist white soldiers.

But the retirement of the Vietnam veterans, the shift from conscription to volunteer recruitment, and the allure of enlistment for the next generation of jobless minority youth, effectively snuffed out any substantial dissent among Black GIs. From 1976 to 1985 the proportion of Black male high school seniors planning to enter the armed forces climbed from less than 30 to almost 40 percent As the Reagan cutbacks gutted welfare checks and the food stamp system, minority youths fled to recruiting stations. Some joined up to avoid jail or to escape being mowed down in the street by trigger-happy cops or by some crack-happy dope fiend. Graduating high school seniors saw even the prospect of a job pumping gas go up in smoke, as the restructuring 1980s transformed gas stations into automatic self-serves, with the only employee being the cashier hunkered down behind bullet-proof glass. A lucky handful landed military-industrial jobs at the likes of Boeing, manufacturing items like helicopter blades for the police gunships that patrol the night skies of the inner cities. Many simply gave up on the civilian economy. Wanting to earn a bit more than they could get from serving fried chicken, Black and Latino high school graduates invaded recruitment offices. The Pentagon has established whole Spanish-speaking units with an eye for future invasions of Central and South America. Based on the racist assumption that Black and Afro-Latino recruits are a tad less intelligent than white ones, the army's recruitment and training techniques have been recast to accord with the presumed educational standards of ghetto and barrio residents. The traditional army training manuals, which required minimal language skills, were being phased out in favor of pictorial instructions on display screens.

Meanwhile, at the top of the hierarchy, the Pentagon has made propaganda hay of its status as the "number one equal opportunity agency" in society. Its public relations spokesmen broadcast the fact that the ratio of Black commissioned officers grew from less than one percent in 1949 to six-and-a-half percent in 1986, while in the army the percentage of Black officers in that year was 10 percent. Whereas there were no Black generals in the U.S. Army in 1962, by the 1980s, seven percent were Black. Until his retirement, the Army's top luminary was Colin Powell. The fact that this is mainly symbolic representation is quietly passed over. Some 38 percent of the troops in the Gulf in 1991 were Black, and 13 percent were Latino and Asian. Blacks remain significantly underrepresented as commissioned officers in the American armed services, with only six percent of the entire officer corps, and the majority of these representing mainly the lower echelons of the military command.

*

The military machine is an integral part of the racist imperialist state. Among its missions it fulfils two socio-economic functions. The recruitment of thousands of young Black and Latino youths artificially withdraws a large corps from the national work force, preventing it from seeking civilian employment for a number of years. The number of new job seekers annually—many of whom could not be accommodated in the private sector in any case—is reduced accordingly. Keeping potential job seekers out of the labor force gives the appearance of lessening unemployment. It relieves some of the social heat that would otherwise be generated by many of the most able and most vocal Black and Latino high school graduates, milling about demanding jobs. It is politically imperative for Washington to create the false impression that minority youth unemployment is being held within reasonably "tolerable limits." Armed forces recruitment helps prevent the radicalization of a potentially volatile segment of an inner city population already made jittery by poverty, police brutality, and the family stresses unavoidable under white racism. In other words, the volunteer army serves as an *escape valve* releasing some of the social pressure on the white supremacist economy, partially rectifying its tendency to expel Blacks as redundant. Equally important is the related street control function. Enlistment removes thousands of dissatisfied, potentially rebellious Black, Puerto Rican, Native American, and Chicano youths from the streets, making things much easier for white cops in patrol cars. It puts these youths in "cold storage," precisely during those years of their life when they would be most likely to cause "trouble" for the racist police. Armed forces enlistment does for the ambitious, able, minority high school graduate what the courts and prisons do for the "gangbanger" youth.

*

As always, the military machine remains a major source of profit for the military-industrial complex, foremost its aerospace component. The peripheral reductions arising from the end of the Cold War have not altered the fact. The maintenance of America's military-industrial complex still generates much economic activity. For example, the entire economy of the San Francisco Bay area and Silicon Valley is dependent on federal defense contracts. War production generates income and jobs for certain segments of the citizenry and increases the consumption of capital goods. This activity may be socially unproductive, but the rewards are handsome. By means of defense contracts, a large portion of the national income is redistributed by the government to the benefit of high-tech corporations. Huge piles of wealth are at issue. Fantastic cost overruns continue as a permanent feature of life for corporations engaged in weapons research and development. In the course of the Reagan-Bush 1980s, the federal government spent over two trillion dollars on the military.

At the outset of the 1990s, the deconstruction of the Soviet Union, the new diplomatic environment, and the desire to make the military a more effective weapon against the Third World elicited defense expenditure reductions and combat unit restructuring. This too took place according to the rules of white supremacy. Black GIs were overrepresented in demobilization unemployment. African Americans were the hardest hit by the troop cutbacks. After having sought refuge in the armed forces to escape discrimination in the civilian work place and unemployment rates twice as high as whites, Black GIs found themselves to be the most displaced as the army downsized. Between January 1991 and February 1992, attrition and "early retirement" push-outs removed 70,000 troops from the army. In the absence of any more Third World "police actions" like those in Vietnam and Iraq, it was anticipated that "reshaping" would cut another 171,000 personnel from the army by 1995. The Under Secretary of the Army sought to allay Black concern, announcing that despite reshaping he did not expect the 30 percent ratio Blacks had maintained in the Army since Vietnam to change. To be exact, 28.7 percent of the Army's personnel were Black as of 1992. Since African Americans were bunched in the lower ranks, the cuts in the military budget were decidedly anti-Black, as the first to be let go were in the services of support, supply, and administration, heavily staffed by minorities.

*

In December 1990, elder statesman Ramsey Clark, U.S. Attorney General in the Johnson Administration, accused the White House of planning to use the U.S. armed services as a "regional military force" to "dominate the poor of the planet and the resources where they live" (*The New York Amsterdam News,* 22 December 1990). At a moment's notice Black and Brown youth are shipped halfway around the world to wreak mayhem and risk maiming and death, all in order to protect "Mr. Charlie's" privileges. From Korea to Vietnam, from Grenada to the Persian Gulf, the list is long. There is an ancient adage that the worst that can be done to slaves is to make them fight and die for their masters. This ultimate humiliation prompted film director Spike Lee to question the integrity of General Colin Powell, Black Chairman of the Joint Chiefs of Staff. Citing Powell's exalted post, he quipped, "So what? So we've got a Black general that's going to be head of the Army that kills Black people in Panama [and] people of color in the Middle East? How come every war now is against people of color in Third World countries?" (*Peoples Weekly World,* 20 July 1991). Reflecting on the mood of Black folk as it was on the eve of Pearl Harbor, Gunnar Myrdal in his *American Dilemma* quoted a Black man as saying, "Just carve on my tombstone, here lies a Black man died fighting a yellow man for the protection of a white man." In the case of Grenada, the refrain would read: here lies a Black man died fighting a Black man for the protection of a white man; and in the case of Panama: here lies a Black man killed fighting an African-Latino for the protection of a white man! Since the days of Theodore Roosevelt, the surtax in blood exacted from Afro-Americans has remained the same.

Chapter 6

RACISM IN PRACTICE—THEN AND NOW

It **was one of those bone-brittling mornings** in January that can grip North America even during mild winters. The year was 1992. The radio droned on as I worked at my desk. The music program gave way to a news broadcast. My attention was snatched by the smugness sounding in the announcer's voice as he reported the prospect for the coming twenty-first century. The broadcaster compared the outlook for the white North with what is anticipated for people of color, extrapolations drawn presumably from one of the innumerable United Nations surveys.

The only people of value to human society in the twenty-first century, this white man predicted, able to "compete," and the only ones judged "competitive," are the 800 million *white* inhabitants of North America, Europe, and Australia, along with the Japanese (always the "honorary Aryans"). Lagging behind will be the losers, some six to seven billion people of color, useless souls concentrated in Africa, Asia, and Latin America, with many scattered as "minorities" throughout North America—i.e. the "rest of us." These are the vast majority, "uncompetitive" throwaways, marked, according to the broadcaster, for "slow death." The people of Black Africa, he said, have the mark of the grim reaper upon them. They will be singled out for mega-extinction, mainly through the ravages of AIDS! This is the prospect that white world supremacy has in store for us. Complacency resonated in the white announcer's voice, as he predicted a human disaster that should make any civilized human person shudder.

This projection is a logical outcome of the ideology and practice of white world supremacy—of racism in practice. It agrees, in substance, with current science fiction, a literary genre dominated by the writings of white Americans and Russians. With a few exceptions the pictures drawn by science fiction writers of the far-distant future in which humanity has spread to the stars and throughout the galaxy and beyond, describe mankind as either completely white, with the Black race having disappeared from the universe, or show space ships with a few token 'Browns', picturesque residuals of today's people of color, or conjure up suspiciously familiar scenaria in which blue-eyed, blond, white space heroes wander the galaxy rescuing, dominating and mentoring various savage and benighted dark-hided species that curiously resemble today's Afro-Americans. The anti-Africanism that is found throughout "European-American culture" reflects a deep-seated, racial hatred which cannot be expunged from white civilization, Dr. Leonard Jeffries has explained, despite attempts to silence him. White initiative is frozen in the complex ideological edifice of white racism. All elements of social existence are tainted with the brush of racism, economic, religious and social, as well as humdrum affairs.

As explained in the analysis of institutionalized racism and racist ideology presented above, racism is a set of practices shored up by an ideological rationale which defends the right of one group of human beings to exploit and oppress another. It presents itself as an elaborate code of behavior which censures or rewards Black folk according to the interests of white people. Thus racism's main content is social and practical, despite some very labored theorizing and emoting. It is grounded in the "iron facts" of history. Racism is different from caste bias, say like that of Indian Hinduism, in that it requires a minimum of social mobility. It is true that for a long time American racism imitated caste bias in insisting upon segregated occupational and professional specialization, prohibition of inter-marriage, and rigid etiquette in all Black-white relations. Yet its essence remained fluid. Social tensions and struggle between Blacks and whites cause constant historical change, throwing the future up for grabs, making it impossible for the racists to keep things the way they were, no matter how hard they try. Alleged "reverse Black racism" is nothing more than the invention of fevered white minds, a figment of the imagination of persons embittered and frightened at the prospect of competing with Blacks on parity terms. "Reverse Black racism" is non-existent for the simple reason that nowhere on earth do Black men exploit, oppress, and dehumanize whites, or members of any other race, for that matter. "Reverse racism" is merely another invention of white racist ideology—a defense mechanism designed to conceal and justify white supremacy.

Common persecution, felt to some degree sooner or later by each and every person of African descent, from the first to the last of us, is what more than anything else binds us together as one people, despite temperamental, philosophical, religious, and "class" differ-ences. White individuals oppress Black individuals, while the cor-porate entity that is racist North America exploits the entire Black community. Blacks are not in a position to reverse the tables. This inequity is the cardinal link in the oppression-exploitation-institu-tionalization chain.

To date "race relations" have always been regulated to the advan-tage of whites. In fact, social superiority of whites over Blacks has always been the precondition for that which passes for "civilized life" in the United States. From the "Founding Fathers" to current-day Heritage Foundation pundits, white thinkers have known this. White supremacy is neither accidental nor unintentional; it is fully in the interests of white people. So long as those interests remain vital, the institutions of our society, from exalted constitutional jurisprudence to humble county sheriff, from university to primary school, will remain racist.

Social phenomena which do not conform to this rule are indi-gestible and are spewed out as subversive. This principle explains, for instance, the easy "Willy Hortonization" of the 1988 presiden-tial campaign. As in other realms of social endeavour, the principle of racist reproduction holds firm in national politics, merely chang-ing its discourse, coded signals and style (body language and "rap") from one election to the next, and in accordance with current issues.

The domestication of Black music—in order to make money from it, as another example—has left firmly anchored in the white (and partially also in the Black) mentality the racist idea that African-derived rhythms and cadences are more "natural," closer to Nature, and, of course, savage. Black superiority in sports is twisted to reinforce the myth that Black people possess animal-like traits—i.e., "abnormal" speed, strength, agility, and reflexes, like, say, panthers or apes; abilities contrasted with the alleged "Caucasian qualities," including leadership, reflection, courage, intelligence, steely determination, and cool calculation.

The anatomy of racism reveals astonishing moral sanctimony. In both Canada and the U.S., racism-in-practice is a jumble of hypocritical piety and righteousness, a compound of white jealousy of Black sexuality and athletic prowess, with sheer racial animosity conditioned by tradition—an untidy mess of historical experience and illogical, incoherent propaganda and hearsay. But the clutter has an ordered underpinning—the political economy analyzed above. "Mainstream" white America prefers to ignore these underpinnings. It likes to pretend that everyone outside the mainstream is "marginal," "the incapable and the incurably lazy," the "socially pathological." These can be ignored. At most, they are an embarrassment to America, "which after all would be a very impressive country but for all the negative statistics created by the minorities." From time to time white society glances at these misfortunates to remind itself of its own "unprecedented success," betokening the moral righteousness and racial superiority of the white Anglo-Saxon.

One can say, then, that white supremacy in action needs constant reaffirmation and reinvention. The violence of the original enslavement of Black people must be constantly maintained and reinvented in daily conduct—even if only passively in the non-opposition to discrimination; even if only pettily in the refusal to, say, admit a Black applicant to post-graduate study because he/she wishes to pursue an Afrocentric program of History. The original crimes were committed many generations ago by the ancestors of today's whites, that bloody-minded horde which poured from Europe. Thereafter, each new generation of white children grown adult has had to internalize the decision to treat Black people as a lesser breed. They must make that decision their own. That which distinguishes the white conservative of today from the liberal, is that the former owns up to the knowledge that the represssion of Black freedom has to be ruthless if he himself is to survive as parasite and master, i.e., if he is to continue as social white man. The half-heartedness, hypocrisy, and fearful trepidations with which the white high court justices grudgingly extended Fourteenth Amendment protection to Black appellants during the 1960s and early 1970s is a fine illustration of this fact (Bell 1980).

Professor Ali Mazrui has his own way of distinguishing between the three types of modern white racism which he thinks are current in the world today. While not adequately descriptive of the hellishly complex racism Diaspora Blacks must contend with, his typology is nonetheless suggestive. According to him, the most unadorned, physical danger to us is *malignant racism*, a force hostile and contemptuous toward people of color. It is cruel, exploitative and always genocidal in potential, occasionally in actuality. Second, there is so-called *"benign racism"* which is a non-aggressive, patronizing racial ethnocentrism which permits the "superior" white person to voluntarily act with gracious equality towards "inferior," darker races. The third form, termed *"benevolent racism"* by Mazrui, seeks to "serve" "lower creatures" from motives of altruism and the "white man's burden" (Mazrui 1991:97).

While the malignant category would appear to account for hard-core bigots (the favorites of print and broadcast media in the United States and Canada) much more numerous is the great mass of white people who float on the fringes of the morass—Mazrui's second- and third-category racists. One is tempted to call these the "fellow travellers" of racism, persons whose racist utterances are sporadic and occasional, or in the case of category two: shamefaced and only behind closed doors. These are persons whose racist witticisms are intended mainly to win social approval. These are persons whose chief antagonisms toward persons of color are confined largely to employment-related competition, friction caused by efforts to keep Blacks from occupying housing in white neighborhoods, and sexual fear-derived hostility. These are the grassroots applauders for the law-and-order utterances of reactionary politicians. These are staunch Republican voters, or if Democrats, they are the kind who abhor "Jessecrats" and oppose concessions to "special interest" minorities. In Canada they span the political spectrum from the Reform Party to the New Democrats.

Political scientist and nationally syndicated journalist Manning Marable distinguishes between white supremacy's shock force—

111

"mass conservatism"—and nebulous "centrist social liberalism" which he says has in tow the Congressional Black Caucus and other established Civil Rights leaders (Marable 1984:182-183). To my mind, there is much that binds mass conservatism and centrist social liberalism together. Both trends share a common folk experience, a super-patriotic folk culture which gives two-party politics its flavor and moxie. Neither conservative nor centrist repudiates the tradition of families proud of "Billy-Budd" Marine Corps volunteers, of suburban target practice sessions to prepare for the "future race war" that Simi Valley types believe is imminent.

How else to explain the euphoria in white America in 1991 at the outcome of the Persian Gulf war, in utter disregard of the 70,000 Iraqi civilians killed in the bombing—mostly women and children? How else to explain the deep satisfaction with which white America greeted the "success" of Ronald Reagan's "mission" against tiny Black-inhabited Grenada, victim of a full-scale invasion? How else to explain white America's studied disregard of mayhem, disease, and starvation in Africa in the aftermath of the Cold War?

*

PAST PRACTICE—RACISM AND THE NATIONAL ECONOMY

For the moment let us go back to the beginning. In order to function profitably for whites, slavery, the "peculiar institution," needed a large force of skilled peasants, wise in the ways of agriculture. The slavers found exactly what they were looking for in the expert farmers of western and central Africa. The white man enslaved the African peasant with his long experience with agriculture and talent for creating advanced forms of civilization. The selection of Africans for bondage in the western hemisphere was deliberate and not by chance—the slavers wanted to tap the labor skills and genius of Black people; the Amerindians were decimated and the planters were not long interested in what white indentured servants had to offer. It was in the nature of the institution of slavery in general for the slave to receive nothing from his master but minimal food, clothing, and shelter. It was in the *racial* nature of slavery in the western hemisphere for the slave to be raped, brutalized, mutilated, and the object of bloody armed repression. It was the *peculiar* nature of American slavery for the Black slave to be the victim of the racist hatred of nearly *all* whites, owners and non-owners.

This general condition prevailed from 1619 to 1865. As we have seen, the 250 years of chattel slavery in the United States produced the original source of capital which watered both the plantation colonial economy and the first sprigs of manufacture. Our demand for reparations for losses suffered and injuries endured rests on this fact. We were a conquered people held against our will in foreign captivity, under the boot of a cruel alien army. This condition was evidenced in the hundreds of slave insurrections and conspiracies, in the Underground Railroad and mass escape, and in labor resistance and sabotage. These efforts undoubtedly hastened the abolition of slavery, bearing fruit once the maturation of white America's young industrial capitalism had made civil war between Northern capitalists and Southern slavocrats unavoidable.

But before the armed conflict that would break the Southern shackles on the developing white national market took place, the slave society erected with such solidity in the southern part of the country could only establish itself by means of a *racist unification* within the broader society. In practice, this meant steadfast solidarity linking white slaveholders with white non-slaveholders, Southerners, Northerners and Westerners. This white union withstood all strains as long as there was a community of interests. The concord flourished because it shunted most of the burden of the accumulation of wealth off on enslaved African labor forced to develop America's natural resources for the benefit of white people. Catastrophe struck the old planter South when the relationship between the slave states and the North changed. Abraham Lincoln squeaked into the presidency and the slaveocracy collapsed. With the Civil War came a *temporary* breakdown in white solidarity and, as a result, Abolition. However, it quickly became obvious that the Black man had not really been set free, and by no stretch of the imagination was he to be integrated into the white man's society.

So it should be no surprise that when industrialization came to the South its pattern was racist. The states of the former Confederacy remained the home for 90 percent of African-Americans. Limited to the northern states before the Civil War, large-scale industrial capitalism spread to the South only after Appomatox (1865). Invading the Piedmont and down through the Carolinas, Yankee industrialists built a string of textile factories, mostly cotton mills. At the turn of the century Pittsburgh steel magnates moved southward to exploit the iron mines of Tennessee and Alabama. Birmingham was transformed into one of the great metallurgical beehives of the world, attracting a string of immigrant workers from Europe, notably Italians. Next in line came cigar and cigarette manufacturers, in a hurry to use the Jim Crow terrorism of the post-Bellum South to ensure profitable exploitation of local Black labor. The powerful American Tobacco Company whose factories dominated North Carolina, capped this development. Strengthening racist oppression, industrial capitalism reinforced segregation. Meanwhile, loath to let the bulk of Black folk escape the Southern farm scene even after the collapse of chattel slavery, White America made it national policy to lock us in the area south of the Mason-Dixon Line for as long as possible. The Homestead Act of 1862 allotted 160 acres of free land to any husbandman willing to undertake their cultivation. However, the giveaway was deliberately designed to exclude Black farmers. In essence, the Homestead Act was at once federal Jim Crow legislation and a gigantic government-sponsored welfare scheme for Caucasian farmers, native and foreign born. Targeted for free land, in particular, were white immigrants born outside the continental United States. Though experienced and hardy farmers, long used to American conditions, American Blacks were, in practice, excluded from the Great Plains states and other western and midwestern farm settlements in favor of "lily-white" immigrant foreigners. The restriction of the benefits of the Homestead Act to whites went a long way towards keeping Blacks imprisoned in the South after Emancipation. This left the door open for whites to settle the farmlands of the Great Plains and further west by themselves alone, free from Black competitors. The "Great White Father" was not about to jeopardize the precious land he had so cunningly stolen from the "Indians."

The legal web of enforced racial segregation and statutory inferiority was woven between 1890 and 1910 (Bell 1980:83). Isolated, refused education, without firearms to defend himself, the rural Black man was abandoned to contend with a foe who had all the financial and military might, and the overall numerical majority as well.

The same theme played on through the first half of the twentieth century. Even during the vaunted "liberal" New Deal of the 1930s there was little real improvement. Racism flourished during the New Deal in the Detroit Post Office, for example. Postmaster Roscoe Hueston was a Democratic Party patronage appointee. This Roosevelt Democrat considered it a point of white honor to snub the Black press. He thumbed his nose at the NAACP and Walter White, its national executive secretary, when they came seeking to investigate racism in Detroit postal branches. Confident that everyone in the Administration from FDR himself to the Postmaster General shared his prejudice, Hueston flatly refused to instruct his departmental supervisors to alter their hiring practices in fairness to Black applicants. Despite Detroit's location in the far North, despite the Post Office's status as a federal agency, and despite New Deal rhetoric about "improved race relations," he stood firm. And he did not have to budge for he knew full well that here as elsewhere the overriding needs of segregation excused employment discrimination.

In San Francisco, in 1944, despite wartime demand for female workers, transcontinental bus companies refused to hire Black women on the plea that the need to construct special toilet facilities for the "colored" women, segregated from white facilities, would cost too much. In 1950, Honolulu reported strong residential restrictions against Black houseseekers, despite a Supreme Court decision nullifying restrictive covenants. Whole neighborhoods were being restricted to whites, although whites were less than a third of the total island population. A forthright correspondent quipped: "Anyway you figure it, it's still white supremacy ... what else can you expect? Hawaii is yet a part of America, isn't it?" (*Claude Barnett Papers*, 25 January 1950). The state of Virginia distinguished itself in the struggle against school desegregation, ordered by the *Brown Decision* of 1954. As one of many Virginian school districts, Alexandria insisted until 1963 on questions identifying race in the employment application form for prospective teachers. And for all that time a photograph was required, to make sure that no African American slipped through the strainer.

For more than a century Black economic needs were scorned as narrow "special" interests, white economic demands genuflected to as "national" interests. Political rights for Afro-Americans were deemed a grave threat to "national unity," certain to stifle the economy and undermine good government. Today, on the eve of the twenty-first century, civil rights and economic empowerment for Black people are still being scorned as an in-group "special interest," distinct from and damaging to the "national interest."

PAST PRACTICE—POLITICAL RACISM

Democracy is a key weapon in white supremacy's arsenal. International celebration of American political democracy started with Alexis de Tocqueville's *Democracy in America* (1835–1840). He mused about the system which kept Blacks enslaved, isolated, and confused by indoctrination with alien, white-crafted loyalties, values, and aspirations. Political democracy fulfils the same function today. Unconditional loyalty to the United States, the white "American way of life," and the doctrine that Black men owe good faith and good will to their white antagonists, are stock ingredients in political discourse. White man's "democracy" subtly diverts the attention of Blacks away from their own identity, and away from interests peculiar to themselves alone. Throughout history it has hindered the growth of a Black consciousness.

Hardly out of its cradle, American democracy led the way in ostracizing newly independent Haiti, because it was a Black state, and because it was revolutionary and had dared to overthrow white slaveholders. Applying pressure foreshadowing that later used against Castro's Cuba, U.S. diplomats screamed curses at Haiti from 1804 to the 1920s. The international boycott imposed by the white powers against the island after the successful slave revolution caused widespread poverty and destabilization. The resulting chaos and misery were then cited as evidence that Blacks were incapable of maintaining civilized society, that political independence was bad for ex-slaves and that the Haitian revolution was a wasteful "error" of history. Early State Department spokesmen contrasted the "prosperity" of white American democracy with Haitian poverty, claiming this as proof of Black inferiority. They suppressed the news that the Haitian Freedmen had defeated in combat the expeditionary army sent by Napoleon's military machine, then the white world's mightiest power. They concealed the fact that white racist paranoia had quarantined Haiti for decades, choking positive development. It was allowed to "emerge" from its isolation only once it had been made the poorest country in the Americas, and then only to be occupied by racist U.S. marines for some twenty years. It was U.S. foreign policy which transformed Haiti into what it is today: the downtrodden, prototypical semi-colony of U.S. imperialism. White American democracy could not have afforded the spectacle of an independent and prosperous Black state so near to its borders.

Compromise is said to lie at the heart of American democracy. However, the "compromises" which dot the history of the Republic have usually been to the detriment of Black people. It is a bitter irony of history that the South's defeat in the Civil War actually turned

116

out to be the prelude to a *historic accommodation*, a political reconciliation between southern planters and northern businessman
that proved distressingly durable, lasting from 1877 to 1964. The
1877 deal, in the tradition of "democratic" compromise, handed the
South over to the segregationist and terrorist rule of a coalition of
planters and industrializing businessmen. Only now the *balance of
power* between the two groups had shifted from what it had been
before the Civil War. The rising industrial-financial magnates now
held the upper hand. However, ample room was left for the emerging Southern merchant bankers, mine owners, and railway bosses.
"New South" planters had to be satisfied with a junior partnership
in the white ruling bloc. It was a "democratic" accommodation, a
white "gentlement's agreement." But the point of concern for African
Americans is that even though the planters were now the "liege vas-
sals" of Wall Street, they got a very sweet deal—their holdings were
lucrative; they were ceded undivided political sway within their
region; and most important, they were empowered to do as they
pleased with the Black folk living in the rural back counties. And
they were solidly backed by the racism of southern white lower class
democracy in general and, by the mid-1890s, by the racism of the
Populist Movement in particular. The "New South's" white middle
classes and small farmers took advantage of the restructuring of
some of the former slave plantations to increase their own holdings.
After 1872 they deserted their Reconstruction political "alliance"
with the former slaves to become wildly rabid racists.

*

This is a suitable spot at which to glance at the huge collection of
white people known to social scientists as the *"American middle
class."* Roughly about ten million lawyers, physicians, dentists and
other economically independent professionals, merchants and working farmers, formed the heart of the true middle class in the mid-
1980s. Some of these people had high incomes. Most were around
the national average (and mean) for white annual incomes. A few
fared little or no better than hired workers. The only constant with
the class is constant turnover, as some go bankrupt and others rise
to join its ranks. Most *true* middle class people own small capital,
and many employ a few wage-earners, a typical example being a dentist. Politically, the middle class tends to identify with full-scale capitalists and is influenced by big business evangelism. Nevertheless,

the core of the middle class is pushed and squeezed by the banks and the large corporations, and heavily taxed by government. The racist political economy of the country has positioned it as a junior partner of the ruling elite.

That which has confused the analysis of its role in "race relations" has been the national tendency—fostered by the mass media, education, political discourse and personal aspirations—to view the middle class as identical with the *entire* white population. Only the tiny, exalted clique of the super-rich at one extreme, and "drop-outs," poverty-stricken marginals, and other white social derelicts at the other extreme, are exempt from inclusion—according to popular myth. It is this arbitrary, yet effective universalization of the middle class that induces the vast majority of whites to come across as one and the same in attitude toward Blacks and other "unfavored" people of color. Though millions may not in fact belong to the *economic* core of the middle class, those same millions believe they do, and assume its compulsions and prejudices. We all know that the newly arrived immigrant from Europe soon considers himself "middle class." He also becomes quickly aware of the causes of his relative well-being in this "land of opportunity." As soon as a white man sets foot in America, especially if back in his homeland he comes from the lower end of society, he is made conscious of the relationship between the privileges he now enjoys in comparison with his status on his native soil, and the inferior ranking of Blacks, Native Americans, Afro-Latinos and other non-whites. However limited, there are still advantages to being white in North America. Without the oppressed minorities for a shield, much of the middle class would fall victim to the ills plaguing the national economy. A few understand this fully, the majority perceive it only instinctively. Without an "underclass" held down in Black ghettoes, Brown barrios, and Red reservations, the United States would soon possess a downtrodden white proletariat of many millions.

Racism was roused further by the cynical manoeuvre which pitted Blacks and Native Americans against each other. The move to make Afro-Americans hate Native Americans dates from the eighteenth century, when chattel slavery was the norm for Black people. Southeastern planters used Indians to track and capture runaway slaves. Later, following the Civil War, Washington D.C. stoked the resentment of Blacks among Native Americans by pitting Black Union army soldiers against Indians on behalf of the "Great White

Father." Black "Buffalo Soldiers" of the Ninth and Tenth Regiments were loosed on the Great Plains during the 1870s and 1880s. This cold-blooded incitement of hostility between two racially oppressed peoples not only foreshadowed the twentieth-century deployment of Black GIs against Vietnam, Iraq, and other parts of the Third World. It was an early white application of the political tactic known as "Lets-You-and-Him-Fight" which has surfaced in the 1990s antagonism between Blacks and Koreans in a number of urban centres. The conflict instigated between Buffalo Soldiers and Plains tribes was designed to counter the natural affinity between the two peoples, noticeable in such joint Black-Indian struggles as the Seminole Wars (1817–1819 and 1835–1843).

For a while during the 1870s it looked as though a second civil war was going to break out in the United States. Our sorely pressed Black people felt it was sorely needed. Unfortunately the day was saved for white supremacy, as the reflex of white solidarity kicked in. Northern and Southern politicians got together and hammered out the Hayes-Tilden "compromise" cited above. Suppression of Black rights was the political cement which held the Union together after Reconstruction and kept whites from tearing at each other's throats. Doing as one pleased with Black people was a kind of therapy which prevented the American polity from collapsing, kept it from exploding and tearing itself apart. From Reconstruction to the Second World War millions of European "ethnic" immigrants flooded the country. They saw eye-to-eye with the white South in despising Black people and in rock-hard determination to keep them "in their place." I contend that it was the presence of scapegoated Blacks that spared twentieth century America from the kind of class war among whites that rocked Russia in 1917 and Germany from 1919 to 1933, saving the U.S. from social revolution or fascist dictatorship. Most notably, the obsession with holding Blacks down united whites across class lines. Mainstream America regarded it as practically treasonable and certainly blasphemous to challenge the social setup. The few whites who dared were ostracized. "Wobblies," Communists, and other radical leftists were stigmatized as pariahs, ingrates, foreign agents, traitors to their race, godless demons—and worst of all: "Nigger lovers!" The "Negro problem" during the Great Depression decade shored up white supremacy during a very bad economic time. Preoccupation with keeping us down checked the rise of any massive native nazi-fascist movement attuned to anti-

Semitism. For Jim-Crowed Blacks served as a protective buffer for Jews in the United States. The fact that white Americans had Blacks to "pick on" enabled U.S. Jews to squat down and survive until World War II destroyed Jewry's arch-enemy, the Third Reich. America's Jews thrived in the safe haven while America's Blacks were crucified in their stead.

Racism retained its clout after V-E and V-J Day. Jim Crow raised its head as far away from the Confederate heartland as Hawaii. In 1949, four years after the war had ended, the islands' main city, Honolulu, was awash in anti-Black feelings. Whites backlashed against a 1947 Fair Employment Practices committee attempt to end job discrimination. Both the Honolulu NAACP Chapter and the Hawaii Civil Liberties Committee were put out of business, and white Catholics and Republicans moved to block civil rights legislation in the territorial assembly. White-owned bars refused to serve Black GIs and civilians. The Hawaii Restaurant and Dispensers' association defended racial segregation. The Commission on Subversive Activities, the Hawaiian counterpart of the House Un-American Activities Committee, applauded the executions of the Martinsville Seven, Willie McGhee and the Trenton Six–all victims of Southern legal lynching–in "inflammatory racial propaganda" that epitomized the "white supremacy mind" (*Claude Barnett Papers*, 5 January 1949, 3 May 1950 and 13 June–November 1951).

From Woodrow Wilson to Dwight Eisenhower, white politicos—municipal, county, state and federal—played the game of nullifying or diluting what there was left of the Black vote. It was poll taxes, literacy tests, and white primaries "at the South," and gerrymanders and a maze of disenfranchising registration hurdles "at the North." The southern specialities have since disappeared, but since the Voting Rights Act of 1965 state legislatures and election officials have "nationalized" the northern ruses. In some instances concentrations of Black voters were manipulated, in others they were dispersed in white majority districts. Only fairly recently have the courts declared illegal the system of at-large elections, a practice whereby for decades Black candidates were excluded from office by being forced to run in predominantly white voting districts, instead of in their own Black majority wards. There were runoff ballots designed to weed out Black candidates who enjoyed the support of a plurality of voters. Municipalities "threatened" with a potential Black voter majority were arbitrarily "engrossed" with lily-white suburbs. Polling stations in Black precincts mysteriously disappeared on the eve of elections, while posts that had always been subject to election suddenly became appointive, when it looked like Black candidates might win them. Blacks who wanted to run for office were fired from their jobs, faced mortgage foreclosure, and were denied loans. Black voters were bribed to vote for white candidates. Year in, year out, thousands of Blacks were purged from the list of registered voters, a dodge that continues today. Those too resolute to be discouraged by sleazy tricks were simply threatened with physical injury, and even death.

And since 1973 there has been a racist counter-offensive to emasculate Black mayors. In Detroit, for instance, white flight to the suburbs beyond the mayor's jurisdiction, leaving the inner city to its shrinking tax base and shrinking finances effectively reduced the authority of Coleman Young. In Birmingham Mayor Richard Arrington was driven to near desperation by constant FBI harassment, Justice Department snipings and attempted frameups. In 1994 the Susan Smith child-murder case in South Carolina showed once again just how alive and well the national pastime of scapegoating Black males as criminals is on the eve of the twenty-first century. And the backlash against the acquittal verdict in the O.J. Simpson trial showed just how irate whites become when one of us gets away.

Chapter 7

THE RACIST MENTALITY: DREAMS, URGES, AND DISPOSITIONS

s a more or less *formalized,* self-conscious *system* of thought,
racist ideology can be said to have begun its run about 1860.
The liberal academic version of American history says that racist
ideological production of all sorts peaked from the Civil War to
1920. That is a long time for something to peak, two full generations for the wave to crest. However, the output of formal racist ideology has always been uneven and episodic.

If we were to broaden our scope geographically and extend it in
historical time, we should find hot spots around the middle of the
nineteenth century in France with Count Artur de Gobineau (1853),
and later in England with the Germanophile, Houston Stewart
Chamberlain (1899) (Yeboah 1988). This European outpouring
occurred to rationalize the colonial system of imperialism in Africa

and Asia, the atrocities of which were rhapsodized by Social Darwinism, in Rudyard Kipling's "white man's burden" and in Cecil Rhodes' empire-building "civilizing mission." Later, in the 1930s and 1940s, there was a new spate of racist writings inspired by the Nazi whirlwind. From 1948 on apartheid South Africa generated racist literature by the ton. During the 1960s racist thought in America was on the defensive, but recovered strongly in the 1970s with the blaming-the-victim syndrome, and in the 1980s with Reagan racism. "Scientific" racism never took a break in the nation's universities, and the fulminations of professorial characters like Charles Murray and Phillipe Rushton are merely some of its more recent and well-publicized expressions. Since the late 1980s people of color have been the victims of an orgy of white racism that is sweeping across Europe from Great Britain to the former Soviet Union.

Scanning the history of white political philosophy in the USA, we can hardly fail to notice that non-Abolitionist thought in white America was racist before the Civil War, and that even a good many white Abolitionists themselves were unable to escape their paternalist shadow. Since the main social contradiction pitted *races* (in the social sense) against one another, political ideas put forward by different groups of whites often conflicted, but were rarely fundamentally antagonistic. In fact, it can be argued that only once in the more than 200 year history of the Republic has the basic political consensus among white Americans been shattered, and that debate led to the Civil War. With the exception of that bloody episode, white political solidarity has held firm, the word battles between liberals and conservatives, like the partisan falderal between Democrats and Republicans, generating much smoke but little fire. At all junctures Black political theorists have been ignored or dismissed as either mad anarchists or utopian revolutionaries.

Through it all, the so-called "ethnological defense of slavery" remained a standout in the stable of racist ideas. Widely propagated while chattel slavery was the norm for Black people, the concept proved to be one of the most *selectable features* of planter ideology (see Munford 1976) once slavery had been overthrown. The "ethnological defense" had what it took to go on serving the needs of white supremacy through the twentieth century. The alleged ethnological (or genetic) "inferiority" of Blacks became the blanket rationale for blanket discrimination. No matter how often refuted, it has survived as a main plank of current racist philosophy, constantly reiterated. Nineteenth century positivist racism masqueraded as a logic of science, completely neutral and non-partisan, allegedly limited to a pure description of facts. Twentieth century "neo-positivist" racists continue the tradition, insisting that in proclaiming the mental inferiority of the African race, they are merely letting the scientific chips fall where they may.

As demonstrated above, a second rationale was the deep-seated fear that inter-racial sexual intercourse, once having begun, would not forever remain a privilege restricted to white males, compelling the submission of Black females. The myth of the Black rapist was born in the white mind. Racism-in-practice learned to manipulate white male dread of Black male sexual prowess. The "unthinkable" became part and parcel of white folklore—the "ghastly" prospect of supine white females, thighs spread to super-potent Black men. The daydream terrified white men (A.Y. Davis 1981; Staples 1982; and Hernton 1965). They sought refuge in castration and lynching. "Moderates" made do with a campaign of "social non-acceptance of mixed marriages." They enlisted the legislature and the courts to prohibit miscegenation, and the school and the pulpit to preach against the "abomination" of race-mixture. Neither the lynchers nor the "non-violent" racists trusted white women not to lust after Black men.

Until very recently, there was an additional concern that large scale amalgamation would erase the African's distinguishing trait—his skin color and other physical features that make Africans look different from Caucasians. The chief feature which had made it relatively easy to spot the victim would be lost. Frances Cress-Welsing thinks there is more to it than that. As she sees it, the white male is anxious and frightened. He fears not only for his imperial domination over the earth, but he also fears "genetic annihilation"—extinction of the white community, and obliteration of its cultural values in the historical long run. The fear is rational, according to Cress-Welsing. For the white man recognizes that three-quarters of humanity is non-white, that white people are a minority world-wide. They are the majority only in Europe and North America. The only way for the white man to survive as a racial type is for white females to be impregnated by none but white males. When impregnated by non-white men, white women have children who are not white. This is a matter of fact. Even when the white male impregnates a non-white woman he loses, observes Cress-Welsing, for again the offspring is not white. The result, according to the genetic annihilation thesis, is an uneradicable feeling of genetic inferiority on the part of white males. Thus a *Great White Fear* nourishes racist ideology. It causes white men to dread Black men and triggers violent white overreaction to assertive, confident Black males.

Explaining the tragic drop in school performance of Black lads after the fourth grade, she observes that in the mind-set of white America, Black boys are regarded as cute and cuddly as long as they are tiny. But as soon as they begin to grow large physically, with the onset of puberty, usually after the fourth grade, they are perceived as a threat. Suddenly there is nothing cute about them. White teachers grow nervous and react negatively to Black male teens. First the school and then society at large opens the spout of repression. Enter police brutality. Once adult, for the rest of his life the Black male must contend with harassment, joblessness, incarceration. White America correctly perceives the Black male as *male*, explains Cress-Welsing, i.e., as aggressive in the nature of things, especially sexually. After all, it is the historically socialized male role to initiate and impose sexual intercourse, she says, to pursue and "capture" the female.

This brings us full circle to the myth of the Black rapist. Suburbia lives in mortal terror of the Black man ultimately out-competing white males in the rivalry for white, as well as Black and Brown women. Cress-Welsing's genetic annihilation thesis sees white supremacy threatened globally by a swelling non-white population against dwindling white birth rates. To stem the tide, the Black community must be curtailed, Black male elected officials harassed, national politics permanently Willy-Hortonized, and backlashing white conservatives mobilized.

●

Despite different emphases, styles, and "family disputes," academic racists agree on one fundamental issue. They insist that no matter how educated, acculturated in white ways, pampered and treated as an equal, stroked and rewarded for faithful service to white interests, the "animalistic" personality of the "Negro" will always peek through in the majority of Black folk. Because it is inherent, innate in the African's "nature." "Bestiality" will show through in dilapidated neighborhoods, neglected homes, broken families, laziness or poor quality work, sensuality and general indiscipline. It is no surprise, they claim, that many a Black is born a promiscuous athlete.

Depend on it, say the "bell curve" scholars, that all he will care about are dancing, partying and having fun; just about every one will sport an "attitude"; he is sure to "rap" and "style-out." What the Black man is *never,* says the racist theorist, is a self-controlled intellect, dedicated to cool-headed scientific analysis and forward planning. He may be devious but never cerebral. Thus the poverty in which Black people live is not the fault of any systemic bias; the unemployment we endure is the consequence of our own "bestial" urges. Action-oriented skinheads, Aryan Nations, Nazis, and KKK seize the hint that the final solution is genocide. Some take action off this cue, like Alabama skinhead Malcolm Driskill, for example, who went out and randomly murdered a homeless Black man.

Christian racists bob and weave and back off from the genocide conclusion, begging dispensation on religious grounds. God created humanity and it would be blasphemy to destroy any part of divine creation, no matter how "inferior" to the white part it may be. Most Christian racists argue in terms of the traditional tale of Adam and Eve—implausibly depicted as Caucasians—as the forebearers of all human beings. Mankind was one until the time of Noah, Adam's direct descendant. There was a firm connection between "Bible Belt" fundamentalism and the Ku Klux Klan. Integrated Christian worship was scorned as infringing racial barriers. Integration was "immoral" because it contravened God's "creation of separate races." Egalitarian aspects of the Christian doctrine were ignored for fear of encouraging the Black struggle for civil rights. The man who first headed the KKK upon its revival in 1915 was a congregation member in good standing of the Missionary Baptist Church—a fundamentalist outfit. It was not by chance that Martin Luther King saw fit in his historic "Letter from Birmingham City Jail" (1963) to castigate white ministers, priests, and rabbis for their refusal to recognize the equality of Black human beings and their stubborn support for the racist status quo (Washington 1991:289-302).

There is a secular conservative racism which is widespread among lay people in the U.S. and Canada. It appeals to moral law without alluding to religion. Its spokesmen mouth sermons about civics. Conservative racism postulates a general moral law which is supposed to make Black people love the country "right or wrong" and of course obey its white rulers. Since many inner city dwellers respond rudely to any such suggestion, the problem, say conservative racists, is that Blacks are irresponsible and amoral, if not immoral. Patriotic love for the United States is demanded of African Americans, regardless of how badly we are treated. Having no stake in the country's material wealth should not exempt one from civic duty, bellow conservatives. Moral decency and good citizenship mean willingness to work hard and honestly for one's employers. A deaf ear is turned to the complaint that for many Blacks employers are rarer than hen's teeth.

White conservatives grow uncomfortable when Blacks are not irrepressibly cheerful. A classic example of conservative devotion to the myth of "happy Negroes"—one example among many—was the "Monument to Mammies" in Sardinia County, South Carolina, erected in 1941 by the McFaddin's, an aristocratic white family clan. Billed as a contribution to the preservation of the history and traditions of South Carolina and the Old South, the memorial to the "Old Black Mammy" was paid for by subscriptions from members of the McFaddin family association, spread throughout the country from the Atlantic to the Pacific and from New York to Texas. The inscription proclaimed that "Mammy's fondest dream was...of having her grave near that of her beloved 'white folks'."

Protection of private property being, to conservatives, the ultimate moral purpose of society, and Afro-Americans being disproportionately propertyless, it becomes the sacred duty of government —local, state and federal—to police, control, and suppress this danger. The people in the ghettoes must never be allowed to realize their "evil," "immoral," socially disruptive potential. Neighborhood perimeters must be "secured," and "they" [Black folk] must be contained. Hence the exoneration of police brutality by jurors in conservative Simi Valley; hence the shrill "Cops-are-Tops" outcry in defense of Toronto police. Secular conservatives view racial stratification of society as not only unavoidable, but ethically acceptable. The yammer about "meritocracy" which pours from conservative circles is mere window dressing and propaganda. Instead, what conservative racism is really trying to get across, is that strict social differentiation along color lines is necessary for the "harmonious" interaction of races and diverse ethnic groups. Too much integration and homogenization will only "breed trouble among the races" (read: weaken white supremacy). Black subordination and white supremacy are the two sides of one coin. Second fiddle status for Black citizens, as regulated by the "free market," is the watchword of conservative philosophy in the U.S. and Canada.

Libertarianism, according to political folklore, comes from the opposite ideological direction from conservatism, yet it too is tainted with racism. Who is not familiar with the American Civil Liberties Union's (ACLU) "principled" defense of freedom of speech for the KKK? The ACLU has long been libertarian philosophy's flagship institution. Behind the anti-authoritarian refrain, one can spy deep-down acceptance of the status quo. Amnesty International—libertarianism's flagship on the international scene—refuses to classify rights violations against Afro-Americans under the human rights umbrella. It insists that the outrages we experience in the U.S. are merely civil rights matters. Libertarianism ignores the concrete social environment. It does not confront discrimination, poverty, fear of racists, unemployment and poor education. It is not communities, not large collectives of people that matter to the libertarians, but the *individual*, sovereign, separate, and supreme. The rights of the individual override all else. Hence the popularity of libertarian doctrine among Black neo-conservatives, anxious to cut ties with our community and "make peace with the system" as individuals. At the very most, libertarians will admit that luck may favor some more than most. Blacks of the strain of Clarence Thomas, Shelby Steele, Henry Louis Gates, Glen Loury, Armstrong Williams, Thomas Sowell, Stephen Carter, and Stanley Crouch—cited by conservatives and libertarians alike for having escaped the ghetto and "done well"—are lauded for their "solitary" climb up the social ladder. No mention is made of how precarious the perch. Libertarianism acknowledges accomplishments owing only to individual commitment, only to strength of character. It makes little headway in making sense of *collective* historical movements like Abolitionism and the Civil Rights struggle. It is unable to see that even the most time-serving Black "Oreo," blind to his debt to his people, owes individual "success" to the selfless sacrifice and struggle of bygone generations of anonymous Black folks. In 1993 a federal lawsuit charged Amnesty International with racist discrimination in its hiring and promotion practices.

Hard-core libertarianism wastes no sympathy on the millions of Black people who remain the poverty-stricken victims of racial discrimination—after all, "it's their own fault." The libertarian refrain goes like this: There is no discrimination, the significance of race is "declining," "society has grown color blind," and even if there is some bias still around somewhere, it is residual, and "it is divisive to dwell on it." If there are social problems remaining, they are problems with the environment and animal protection, problems connected with women's freedom of choice, with the "gender gap," and with the human spirit as such. Yes, there are social ills, but these are evils like drugs, child abuse, and "breakdown" in family values; no longer racist exploitation. Or, if there is still exploitation in North America, then it is the exploitation of prostitutes by pimps; it is sexual or "emotional" exploitation. Above all, according to libertarian doctrine, racist discrimination must not be legislated against and suppressed in practice by the government, for this would infringe the precious rights of the (white) individual. The Bill of Rights guarantees the Ku Klux Klan the right of free speech, the right to burn crosses, the right to march and demonstrate! Ideally, we should pass no further laws than the "Big Ten" originals, lugged down from the proverbial mountain by Moses and dubbed "Commandments." Libertarian "democracy" is that "greatest of all systems," in which a Strom Thurmond is free to flummox "nigger voters," conjure them into forgetting his racist past—acceptable doings as long as he adheres to the rules of the "democratic free for all." After all, sings this chorus of late, "the real racists are the Blacks": "Remember Idi Amin," and "I mean now that they have the vote, don't they all vote just for their own color—look at Chicago and Detroit and New York," and "I mean don't they all think that looting is just recovering goods stolen from them by white folks—look at Los Angeles, will you!"

One need not believe that North American Black people are poor because they are Black, or because society insists on white supremacy, for Blacks are naturally more "prone to poverty" because they are on the average younger than whites, and younger people proverbially earn less than older ones. One need not worry one's head that Blacks are kept down and powerless, for Blacks are poorly educated and less skilled than whites because their skills are concentrated in non-essential, outdated or unwanted pursuits like education and social work, rather than in computers and engineering. One need not feel guilty that wage differentials and other forms of racial discrimination benefit white folk, for Blacks are heavily into crime, due to "cultural pathology," and due to the fact that more than half of their families are headed by single females.

In 1991 a University of Delaware study found that liberal whites were addicted to "aversive racism." The latter was described as the subtle, subconscious anti-Black actions of people who could not help themselves, who against their conscious will simply *had* to act that way. The Delaware psychologists had discovered a behavioral expression of that which I am convinced is *civilization-level racism*. Though 85 percent of whites polled routinely deny prejudice and are ashamed of and even hate themselves for doing anything discriminatory, the racist reflex is too strong to be controlled. While earnest libertarians reject the overt hostility of the Ku Kluxers and cannot be counted among the hypocrites who lie about their feelings, the aversion to people of color even in small matters is so overpowering that, without thinking, they shy away from sitting next to a Black person on a bus, or hang up the telephone upon hearing an identifiably Black voice. Aversive racism is a pathetic compound of fear, discomfort, uneasiness, and disgust in the presence of Black people. The University of Delaware study confirmed that it is very common in the United States. Behind this is the belief that as a race Black people are incapable of being rational and civilized. This ultimately lumps libertarianism with the conservative brands of racism discussed above. It also leads to the conclusion that Black people require the "help" of white people because we lack the capacity to manage on our own. Which brings us to *racist relativism*.

*

Relativism is one of the most damaging and widespread racist conceptions. Relativistic racists profess the doctrine that "too much" civilization, science, culture, and learning can spoil "good-natured," easy-going, simple-minded Africans and other Black "children-of-the-sun." This is pointed, most obviously, at Africans, West Indians and Black Latins from South America, but in modified forms it is also used to ridicule the Black citizens of the United States and Canada. Racist relativism is premised on the belief that what comes naturally is good and beneficial, and therefore primitive peoples— i.e., non-whites—are best left alone to do what comes naturally. In a pinch, they should be required to express their "primitive" nature. We have all heard the comment about how we are "spoiled by too much education," how we become uppity and up-tight and forget our proper place. Why, with "too much" "Westernization" and "consumerism" (read: modern industrialization and high living standards), "exotic" places like Nigeria and Jamaica will "lose their authenticity." Particularly dangerous for us, according to the relativists, are advanced technology, military science, and the study of radical political doctrines—the latter in particular is said to make us surly. "Fun-loving," "genial" Blacks are turned into ludicrous imitations of white folks. Better leave serious economic, political, and technological concerns to their natural and habitual masters, i.e., to white men (and, reflecting current reality—to the Japanese as well). Africa's children do much better competing in athletic events ("after all, what would the Olympic Games be without them!"), singing, dancing, and staging Caribanas in Toronto and Carnivals in Trinidad and Brazil.

We need also take note of the scholarly ruse by which racism is stripped of its content. Here its historical record as oppression, genocide, and exploitation of peoples of color is diluted, or suppressed altogether. The aim is obvious - to whitewash the history of European civilization and explain away the misdoings of people derived from Europe. The concept of racism is ballooned up to the point where it means nothing more specific than to despise someone because he belongs to a particular group—any particular group. In this rendition, the person or group despised may be anything from a language to a religious, a national, an ethnic, or even a *political* collective. The *white* is whitewashed right out of racism. Canadians drone on about the alleged "racial" conflict between English Canadians and French Canadians, for instance. I have even seen gender discrimination slipped in under the general heading of race relations! Discussions of color-neutral class friction dominate sociological meetings advertised as devoted to the Black-white animosity.

This fraud pretends that racism is color-blind or "color*less*." The aim is to convince the general public that there are just as many Black and Brown "racists" as there are white racists. For a Black person may despise someone who belongs to a "particular group" just as easily as a white person may. This way the "nigger-loathing" white supremacist causes no more harm than the heterosexual who dislikes homosexuals, or the woman who despises rapists. The racists are taken under the warming blanket of general *"humanity."*

In a nutshell, stripping racism of its virulence is merely a refurbishment of the old "man's-inhumanity-to-man" chestnut, long employed to minimize the crimes of the Atlantic slave trade which occurred from the fifteenth through the nineteenth century. The "our-society-is-racist-and-everyone-is-guilty-Blacks-as-well-as-whites" theme is very like the "man's-inhumanity-to-man" theme, and, like it, it excuses inhumanity by making it too universal to overcome. By making racism everyone's disease, you make it incurable, something like bad weather, that one does not like but must put up with. We may bitch about racism, it may even be fashionable to be distressed about it, but nevertheless we must live with it. Of course, this universalization of blame implies that people of color must suffer discrimination without hope of escape.

The whitewashing of racism is often coupled with the view that Black people are subject to "social sicknesses," that we are the prey of "psychopathologies" variously called "welfare sub-culture," "poverty syndrome," "pimping on poverty," "underclass desperation," and such like. The academic psychological establishment insists that the terrible conditions endured in urban Black America are *not* due to racial discrimination, but rather to neutral causes like "damaging childhood experiences", "familial disarray" and "disfunctions built into the sub-culture and self-perpetuating," in the final analysis, always due to the nature of the "Negro's racial soul." The "Negro has himself to blame for his social predicament, but really he should not be blamed because it is in his unalterable nature to be inferior"—the circle is closed.

*

Since the latter part of the nineteenth century there has not been a day in which *"scientific" racism* has not been with us. Among its more fashionable offshoots at the present moment is a trend called "neo-racism." It is stylish in academic circles, launched for serious discussion about a generation ago with the publication of R. Gayle's *Mankind Quarterly* in 1960. Mainly, it has been its psychological disguise which has put neo-racism in high vogue. Racial attributes cause "psychic" properties which, in turn, determine the way we behave. Animalistic sexuality is seen as the distinctive feature of people of African descent. When not ridiculed as mentally deficient, Blacks and other non-whites are dismissed as "culturally abnormal." We are said to be addicted to "deviant" behavior, the compass for normalcy naturally being the white middle class. Bogus studies claim that certain brain abnormalities are linked to violent behavior. Proposed are government-funded genetic screening programs to ferret out inner-city youngsters at risk of becoming deviant, and then dope them up with pacifying drugs.

The only "normal" person is the garden-variety male Anglo-Saxon, the suburban white voter, complete with his conventional likes and dislikes and dream of "making it". Neo-racists see this "paragon of virtue" as admittedly aggressive, pugnacious if pushed, but decent. This sterling white man is even tolerant to a degree toward Blacks and other "racial inferiors", when they are "good", "clean," "hardworking," know their place, and "are a credit to their race." Of course, be it understood that this "average Joe" cannot stomach "weird stuff" like affirmative action, school busing for integration purposes, "welfare-cheating," miscegenation, and above all, racial "tipping" in his neighborhood, lowering the value of his residence.

The *sociobiology school* is another specification of "scientific" racism. Like other varieties of racist ideology, it fosters public policies harmful to people of African origin. Sociobiologists have compiled an elaborate enumeration of so-called racial psycho-social "differences" between Negroes and Caucasians. The differences range from ones of minor social consequence, like "Negro athletic prowess," to ones of major power significance, like Caucasian intelligence "superiority." Charles Murray's *Bell Curve* slanders are merely the hottest recent example.

Since about 1960, sociobiologists, along with their think-alikes in politics, have been emphasizing the "scandalous" Black crime rate. Human morality is reduced to the "morality of genes." Decency is innate in most white people, Black folks in contrast suffer an inborn tendency toward criminal activity. The guru of "racial conformity," professor Edward Wilson of Harvard University, set the trend, since continued by the notorious Phillipe Rushton, a Canadian. Wilsonian sociobiologists want the existing socio-economic inequalities to remain as they are, arguing that they accord with nature. They argue slickly that separately accumulated gene pools enabled racial superiority or inferiority to build up over time. Since Blacks and whites evolved racially over the last 12,000 to 50,000 years in separate continents, in Africa and Europe, their disparities and differing rapidity of development are merely matters of "scientific" fact, it is alleged. Borrowing the theory of polygenesis first announced in 1837, Edward Wilson yelled that *homo sapiens* is *not* a single human family of modern people, but a group of varying species or near-species, fundamentally different from one another. He claimed that social relations are rooted in the genes, implying that humanity is arranged hierarchically according to *races*, with Caucasians ranking at the top (Wilson 1975).

Rushton's professed willingness to concede the top spot to the

Asian Mongol race leaves Africans in the same position—down-trodden at the very bottom of the human ladder. Rushton pretends to reject the polygenesis credo that the modern races of humanity derived originally from separate, dissimilar species. Instead, the Rushtonians claim that "Negroids" are the *oldest* human stock and thus the most primitive. Since we are supposed to be ape-like, Black people are the most backward in the U.S. and Canada, driven by unevolved throwback urges. This is a racist caricature of racial differentiation, the classical anti-racist conception of which appeared in the works of the brilliant African scholar, Cheik Anta Diop.

In the 1960s, racist scholars felt hemmed in and discredited by the Civil Rights movement, and especially by the demands of Afro-Americans for Black Studies and equal education. They rebutted in 1969 in the person of Arthur Jensen whose lengthy article in the prominent *Harvard Educational Review* defended the theory of race-based intelligence. At the time Jensen was an educational psychologist at the University of California at Berkeley. William Schockley, a Nobel laureate from nearby Stanford University, seconded his effort. In sum, they contended that lower average Black scores on intelligence tests (IQ) indicated genetic inferiority. They ignored evidence showing that when white children were tested on the scientific Black Intelligence Test of Cultural Homogeneity, developed by a Black psychologist, they scored much lower than Black children. Jensen's and Schockley's malign theory went a long way towards trivializing racism, thereby making it easier for tender-conscienced white scholars to shrug off its impact on minorities. They implied that Blacks are discriminated against racially because we score lower in what are admittedly "unfair" examinations, geared against us. The chain of causes is thus sneakily reversed, and the damage of racism reduced to a trifle. In plain language, Blacks are by nature stupid and fit only for continued degradation. Neglect—whether benign or malign—must be our lot, for no reform can increase our potential, according to Richard Herrnstein and Charles Murray, the current stars of the IQ frolic. Sociobiologists add that the many unwed Black teenage girls who give birth are further weakening Black genes, for their children are being fathered by droput, jobless, and "inferior" young Black males. Social remedies may improve the lot of poor whites, but can have no credibility in respect to Black social and economic inequality, since that is the working of genes. To this school of thought, government initiatives (e.g., "War on Poverty,"

Headstart, Job Corps, Food Stamps, etc.) to reduce poverty and unemployment in the inner cities are misfounded, the utopian schemes of "bleeding heart" liberals. Far from "blaming the victim," say these racist scholars, they actually have the best interests of elderly ghetto residents and other "innocent" Black bystanders at heart— the helpless victims of predatory Black gangs, drug dealers, and muggers. Forget nutrition and pre-natal care, forget day care and affordable housing, forget schools, health care, recreational facilities, and equity programs, scream these hypocrites, the best that can be done is to try to protect the law-abiding ghetto inhabitants, and of course the broader society, from the Black criminal hordes by building more prisons, toughening the police, and stiffening mandatory sentencing.

•

There is a queer logic to racist ideology. The pitiless treatment meted out to people with African blood in their veins is cruelty which paradoxically is not cruelty at all, for Nature cannot be immoral, and it is by her law of selection of the fittest that the superior feeds upon the inferior, that the cat eats the mouse. What could possibly be wrong with a white man "disciplining" a recalcitrant Black, the white supremacist wants to know. The Black man plays the mouse to the white man's cat! The racist mind-set is so elemental in white supremacy culture that over the past three or four hundred years its imprint has been clear even in such an apparently remote science as *botany*. Why else would botanists commonly call the *Eriophorum vaginatur* grass "niggerheads" or the *Opuntia clavarioides* cactus "nigger's hand" and "nigger finger"?

Chapter 8

THE RACISM OF POWER: SEX AND SOCIAL VALUES

Social values are sticky and resistant to change. Among the many myths conditioning white antipathy to miscegenation and mulattoes is an old one going back to slavery. Miscegenation is marriage and/or interbreeding between a man and a woman of different races. The antipathy appears to have been strongest among Anglo-Saxon Protestants. Essentially it was an expectation that a mixed-blooded or mulattto population would be less willing to accept domination, degradation and exploitation. For example, prejudice assumed that, for having been sired by a white man, Frederick Douglass would be more likely to struggle for freedom and racial equality, more likely to be susceptible to currents of revolt and subversion and to revolutionary doctrines. This misconception remained rock-solid among racist pundits despite heavy evidence to the con-

trary. They ignored the Caribbean where captives recently imported from Africa were renowned for greater resistance to slavery than
Creole slaves (see Munford 1991, vol. III). They erected a wall of
silence around Haiti, where the entire slavery system was overthrown by Blacks while the mulattoes dithered. They spurned the
obvious example of such non-mulatto Black resisters to U.S. slavery as Nat Turner and Harriet Tubman.

These contrary proofs were ignored in favor of the myth that
"white blood" is by nature unwilling to submit to oppression and
domination, unlike "Black blood" which, being "inferior," is
admirably suited to servitude. To allow the intermixture of white
blood in a subject population of color is to breed future rebellion
against white rule. Of course, these doctrinal considerations were
spurned in daily practice as Southern white males slaked their lust
on helpless Black women. By the time slavery was done, four-fifths
of U.S. Blacks numbered whites among their ancestors.

The white man's disdain for his own mulatto offspring went
hand-in-hand with his sexual fear of Black males. During the ago-
nizing years of enslavement, Black men were forced to watch, torn
with rage, as white men, exercizing the prerogative of slavery, raped
Black women. Some were compelled to share their mate sexually
with the master. And until very recently, white women were off-limits for Black men. White dislike for miscegenation, particularly for
intermarriage, has long outlived slavery. Some 60 percent of white
Americans in the 1980s ranked their opposition to intermarriage
ahead of even their much crowed-about dislike for residential integration, while somewhat fewer still seemed to have anything against
contact with Black people in school or on the job.

As reaction to the circumstances surrounding the O.J. Simpson
murder case indicates, white attitudes have not changed much in
respect to miscegenation from what they were some forty years
before—only, then, they were backed by the force of law. At least
thirty states banned interracial marriage. The prohibitors included
not merely the obvious former Confederate states, but far northwestern Colorado, Idaho, Oregon, and Utah, along with chic, movie-
land California. Maryland boasted legal barriers to intermarriage
that went back to early colonial times and prohibited unions between
whites and "persons of Negro descent" to the third generation.
Georgia's legislators spurned "African, West Indian, Asiatic Indian,
and Mongolian blood" as equally tainted. Texas imprisoned Black-

white spouses the moment they entered the state, including marriages legally contracted in other states. Recognizing the danger to white supremacy in the possibility of different oppressed peoples joining forces, North Carolina, Louisiana, and Oklahoma banned marriage between Blacks and Native Americans. Nine states enacted statutes bastardizing the children of Black-white unions. White opposition to miscegenation ruled mid-Pacific Hawaii even during the war against Japan.

In the early 1980s 60 percent of whites remained stubbornly opposed to intermarriage as compared with 78 percent of Blacks who gave positive assent to intermarriage (Jaynes and Williams 1989:122). The only things whites seemed to dislike more in interracial affairs was government aid to minorities, i.e., spending money on Blacks and busing.

Simply put, in America miscegenation has always been viewed as a negation of white supremacy. In this way U.S. racists differ from Brazilian racists who have been willing to use white male miscegenation with Black women to "whiten" the population. The object of particular horror here is the Black man's seed germinating in the womb of a white mother. It is taken as flaunting Black male defiance in the face of white men. Fear that nearness will increase intermarriage is a main reason almost 60 percent of white people today feel uncomfortable about living in a neighborhood with as much as one-third Black residents. This is merely one of the many faces of homebrew, small-change racism, revealed further in the plainsong response in 1991 to Spike Lee's "Jungle Fever," a film which, while treating interracial mating, included additional main themes. "Cultural exchange interaction" has yet to cut inroads in white America's superstitious dread of Black sexuality. There was the same old lack of an image of Man common to both Blacks and whites. There was the same old white superstition about the Black "superstud," coupled with the reality of white-imposed evil-smelling, rat-infested slums for Black people. Lee's film elicited age-old white rage and denial frenzy.

*

These are tell-tale symptoms of the profound racism of the white popular masses. Young whites are hardly better than their elders, with 65 percent of those aged 15 to 24 opposed to affirmative action initiatives on behalf of people of color. Adult racists of the liberal stripe discount the need for retributive justice. Racists of the closet variety announce the "decline" of racism among the white public, while assuring, in the next breath, that most whites will never accept the legitimacy of entitlements based on race. And we are not supposed to notice the contradiction!

Derrick Bell, pioneering Black Harvard law scholar, has devoted years to deciphering current racism. Long term control exercized by the agencies of white supremacy is constantly being updated. Whites applaud African American entertainers and vicariously enjoy the triumphs of our athletes. White juveniles idolize the likes of Michael Jordan. This may appear contradictory and silly, but Bell knows it is not. He warns that this adulation too is a control device, and the very whites who clap for our actors and cheer our athletes are reluctant to work alongside Blacks.

The slave South regarded music as neutral and non-threatening. Slaveholders tolerated Black music-making, fostered the talented, often encouraging slave musicians to entertain the master's family and guests. Chants, hollers, songs, and ditties enlivened cotton field labor. It was less menacing for slaves to hum spirituals than to conspire at rebellion. Our musical genius was exploited as a source of profit and as a safety-valve. The tradition continues today. Mainstream America still tolerates Black music, using it to open profit avenues for white promoters who control the music industry. Today, just as a half-century ago, even whites who number individual Blacks among their closest friends are unwilling to allow Blacks whom they do not know buy or rent homes or apartments in their neighborhood, observes Bell (Bell 1992). He muses caustically that even the snooty, pricey restaurants which are most deferential to Black patrons are not about to hire a Black man as head waiter. Throughout the business world, "equal opportunity employer" all too often still means hire one or two Blacks and no more (Cose 1993; and Feagin and Sikes 1994).

At the outset of the 1990s, the Urban Institute weighed persisting job discrimination practices, "reverse discrimination," and "color blindness" in the private sector and compiled a report entitled "Opportunities Denied, Opportunities Diminished: Discrimination in Hiring." Empirical evidence was drawn from Chicago and Washington, D.C. Pairs of male applicants with exactly matching qualifications, one Black and one white, sought advertised jobs. In many cases there was overt discrimination against the

Black applicant. Whites were offered employment that Blacks were refused *solely* due to race.

The same pattern emerges in housing. A recent study by Massey and Denton brilliantly exposes residential segregation and the culpability of most whites in that obnoxious arrangement (Massey and Denton 1993). Andrew Hacker's *Two Nations* observes that there is a neighborhood "tipping point" which makes residential integration impossible in the U.S. When incoming Blacks reach eight percent, whites begin to flee the area. Nothing can keep them, not even proof that the newcomers are as affluent as themselves and share the same social standards. They simply refuse to live near that many Black people. They will not tolerate a quota even half the size of the 15 to 16 percent Black national population percentage. The Federal Reserve Board has admitted that banks will not grant mortgage loans to Black homeseekers. It makes no difference that the creditor could not lose his money, inasmuch as mortgage loans carry a federal government guarantee; Black applicants are still regularly rejected. In the course of 1990, some 9281 lending institutions turned down only 12.1 percent of white applicants—as patently bad credit risks—but cold-shouldered fully more than a third (34 percent) of Black candidates nationwide—many of them with excellent credit records. The action was clearly in violation of the federal Community Reinvestment Act which bans "redlining," but the guilty banks and other lending institutions had no fear of reprisals (*Black Enterprise*, February 1992).

New York, Los Angeles, Chicago, Houston, Philadelphia, and Detroit are the largest metropolitan areas in the United States, and all feature heavy residential segregation. In 1990, Cleveland—once hyped as the "best location in the nation" for Blacks—and Chicago led the pack in segregated housings for metropolitan areas with the largest Afro-American populations. To keep Blacks out, the white suburban Hammond, Indiana, built its own version of a "Berlin Wall" between itself and predominantly Black Gary, Indiana. A massive Federal Reserve Board study, released in 1991, documented the preference that American institutions continue to express for white skin. It showed that low income Blacks are denied the funds to obtain decent housing twice as often as poor whites. The study confirmed at once the skewed racial incidence of poverty and oppression, and the abiding capacity of American racism to shelter lower class whites.

The nation's schools remain, in Jonathan Kozol's phrase, the scene of "savage inequalities." Since the outset of the 1970s, white opposition to school busing for racial balance has been the norm. And while the greatest vituperation has always come from those aged 40 and over, at no time since such surveys began in 1972 have the majority of young whites 18 to 27 accepted the busing of Black and white school children from one district to another (Jaynes and Williams 1989:128). There is no appreciable difference in attitude between southern and northern whites. School funding rigmaroles steal subsidies for white middle class kids from poverty-stricken parents. Black pupils are left undereducated. The 1954 Supreme Court order to America to integrate its schools is a dead letter. The Bush Administration's fraudulent "Back to Basics" ploy was designed to deepen racial discrimination in the nation's schools, Kozol reported (Kozol 1991). "Freedom of choice" vouchers strip Black inner city public schools of funds and talented pupils. School privatization rides herd on Black teachers while lining white entrepreneurs' pockets. Schemes are being cooked to redefine inner-city crime as a special "biomedical" education problem. A federal government eugenics scheme to turn unruly Black youths into zombies has surfaced. Some 100,000 Black and Latino "dysfunctional" children, some as young as five years old, have been targeted for psychiatric behavior modification. Set to kick in in 1994, this "violence initiative" reeducation program was the brainchild of the National Institute of Mental Health. It presumes that Black and Latino pupils are "unruly," "ill-disciplined, and "unable to learn" due to genetic defects. "Defective" Black youngsters should be weeded out and injected with Ritalin, Prozac, and other psychiatric drugs before they become "violent" adolescents.

Direct democracy has been harnessed to serve racism in education, as exemplified in the state of California's 1994 Proposition 187. The proposal to expel Mexican "illegal immigrant" children from school—and refuse them health care—won a majority of white votes.

*

New York City is still home to the nation's largest Black community. There many of the Eastern European rejects whom the Immigration and Naturalization Service keeps parachuting in have been hired as taxi cab drivers. These foreign-born racists, favored because they are white, barely manage broken English, yet refuse to deliver native-born African American fares to "Uptown" Harlem addresses. As quickly as they learn to call Blacks and Latinos "niggers" and "spics," they learn that a white cabbie may disregard "no-go" Black neighborhoods. The car-rental giant Hertz Corporation was caught redlining the boroughs of Brooklyn and the Bronx where large numbers of Blacks and Afro-Latinos live. Though the action is of dubious legality, Hertz lays a hefty surcharge on car rentals in both boroughs, a "Black tax," as it were. Ritzy New York stores, particularly jewellers, become very "antsy" at the approach of Black shoppers, and some try to exclude them entirely. It is not alone Korean-American greengrocers and shopkeepers who insult and are brusque with Black and Latino customers. White salespersonnel snub them in large department stores. Blacks seated in certain New York restaurants are ignored for long spells as if they were invisible, get rude, glacial service when they are noticed, and at the end of the meal have difficulty making payment with credit cards (even American Express) without humiliating cross-examination.

The rise of environmental racism is a sign of the times, just as much as the disregard for Black concerns expressed by the activists of the lily-white environmentalist movement. The Commission for Racial Justice investigated the connection between white racism and lethal pollution. It discovered a sinister determination to locate toxic waste sites in or near minority communities. Robert Bullard observes that neither high income, nor high real estate values nor substantial homeownership have protected Black residential areas from poisonous dumping (Bullard 1992:190). And U.S. corporations have been shifting dirty, ecologically-damaging smokestack industries to the Third World for years. Africa is Common Market Europe's favorite garbage dump. In fact, pollution is now a dimension of racist political economy. Waste disposal, chemical and other toxic pollution generating firms prefer to locate in and around low-income Black and Latino communities. They regard these communities as politically defenseless. Their inhabitants provide the dirt-cheap labor required to operate the lethal facilities. Three of the five largest hazardous-waste dumps are located in Black and Hispanic communities, and the percentage of Blacks living in jeopardized areas in the five worst-polluting states ranges from nearly 75 percent to nearly 90 percent. In five others, the percentage of Black people residing in waste site areas is from 60 to 70 percent. At one time or another local governments, state Health Departments, and the federal

Environmental Protection Agency have all endorsed the policy, despite its violation of the fourteenth Amendment, the Civil Rights Act of 1866, and Title VIII of the 1968 fair housing law (Bullard 1993).

Yet the environmentalist movement which crusades against pollution, allegedly on behalf of everyone, remains pristinely white in outlook and personnel. The eight major national environmental private organizations were hide-bound racist, revealed the *New York Times* in January 1990. They avoided hiring and promoting minorities. The movement is estranged and isolated from Black and other poor minority communities—the very ones which suffer disproportionate dumping. As now constructed, environmentalism is for affluent, educated, white middle-class enthusiasts. Its prized issues—ozone depletion, tropical rain forests, and endangered animal species—are far removed from Black concerns and smack of dilettantism. Thousands of Green Peace types waged a near armed struggle to save the redwoods of Northern California. Yet few saw the urgency of combatting white racism. They stubbornly ignored the awful brutalization of millions of Black human beings right under their noses in their home state *off* California. Environmentalists rattle on about ecological damage without once mentioning the terrible war of attrition being waged against people of color. Lily-white environmentalism is silent about police brutality and economic marginalization, blind to criminalization and decapitation of Black resistance movements.

Despite the exalted rank of Colin Powell, despite the come-on of the "Be-all-that-you-can-be" ads, the situation in Uncle Sam's armed forces is not all that different from that in civilian walks. Anti-Black racism in the armed forces has not faded away. As reported in August 1991, racism is rampant at U.S. military installations in Germany. At six bases there was widespread discrimination in the hiring and promotion of both enlisted personnel and civilian employees, yet Black service people were so frightened by the threat of reprisals they did not dare file complaints. Defense Department schools connected with the bases Jim-Crowed the children of African American personnel. The youngsters were "streamed" into dead-end courses, denied access to extracurricular activities, and subjected to jail-like discipline.

In its effort to steal the thunder from the racial issue, the media has done more than hawk the line that the Black community is addicted to welfare, bent on narcotic self-destruction, and hopelessly divided politically. It deliberately diverts public attention from Black issues to military extravaganzas like the "Desert Storm" in the Persian Gulf. News commentaries are often far more concerned with what happens to white people half way round the world in Russia and Yugoslavia than with the fate of Black people right here in the United States and Canada. The historic centrality of Black civil rights is demoted in favor of discourse about the arms embargo in Bosnia.

The Canadian brand of racism talks about "visible minorities" in a "Canadian mosaic," flavored with "status Indians." "Dim-witted bigotry" has long been popular in parochial, remote farming and rural-related communities, and among the country's native-born Anglo-Saxon workers, European "ethnic" immigrants, and depressed Maritime marginals and "Newfies." Although Canadian racism holds the reputation for being less bloodthirsty than the U.S. version—in keeping with the country's sedate character—Prairie rednecks have a history of violence against the First Nations ("The only good Indian is a dead one" is also an old saying in the Canadian West). The Ku Klux Klan was strong in English-speaking Canada during the late nineteenth and early twentieth centuries, and the broad-based, near-fascist regime of Maurice Duplessis excelled in anti-Semitism and xenophobia. These quaint folk customs of the Canadian "True North" continue today in low-keyed, but relentless, racial discrimination against the patchwork category of "visible minorities," encompassing, among others, hundreds of thousands of immigrants from the Indian subcontinent, Latin Americans, Chinese, and Vietnamese. The economic and political heart of the country lies in the central provinces of Ontario and Quebec. It is there that anti-Black hatred is strongest, in metropolitan Toronto targeting Jamaican youth with the most ferocity. Haitians are harassed in Montreal. But other Blacks too (long-term Canadian Blacks, Afro-Americans from the U.S., West Indians, and immigrant Africans) are brutalized by the police, systematically ignored, discriminated against, and insulted by Canada's news media. Toronto's leading tabloid has built a wide readership among whites by running scare campaigns against "Black crime in the streets." At one time, the "public," tax-supported CBC radio network promoted the sale of South African Krugerrand in Canada (1984). World-wide sales of the coin financed the apartheid military establishment to the tune of almost 41.5 billion dollars a year, more than half the racist regime's entire 1983–84 military budget.

145

The lack of a national identity is much bemoaned by conventional Canadian political commentators. Yet if there is a national motto valid for most white Canadians, according to Canadian woman author Marlene Phillips, it is "keep Canada white!" Segregation and racism are widespread in the country, she noted, and the Homelands policy adopted by apartheid South Africa was modelled on the Indian Reserves in which Native people were corralled. The repressive cultural climate prevented the growth of any Black literary tradition, stunting Black liberation movements. Canadian jails are jammed disproportionately with Black and Aboriginal inmates. The slow-stream, "inferior-learners'" classes in Metro Toronto schools are lopsided with Black children of West Indian derivation. Scorning toothless Human Rights legislation and milk-toast enforcement, Canadian private employers and landlords routinely discriminate against Black job seekers and renters.

In 1992, Ontario's systemic racism was finally admitted publicly in a report on race relations commissioned by the Ontario Provincial Government: "First, what we are dealing with, at root, and fundamentally, is anti-black racism... Just as the soothing balm of 'multiculturalism' cannot mask racism, so racism cannot mask its primary target." In fact, the manner in which the whole constitutional debate and negotiations over Quebec's potential separation has always been conducted—i.e., between two white "founding solitudes," English and French—is a less than subtle message that Black Canadians are invisible and politically negligible.

Integration has not yet been banished completely to North America's trash can of history, however. It remains the goal of at least two distinct social groups. One—the lesser light—are large segments of the striving Black "middle class," along with neo-conservative "Buppies," the latter being the "affirmative action babies" torn with anxiety that white folks will not give them full credit for the "content of their character" and will not endorse their scramble up the ladder of the "meritocracy." The other—the locus of serious political pressure—is the top end of the upper-upper middle class of securely-buffered, compromise-oriented whites. These are well-heeled professionals, administrators, media directors, corporate agents, and foremost clergy, i.e., mild-mannered and "civilized" moulders of public opinion whose genteel existence unfolds far removed from the gritty reality of Black life. These are the ones who are tranquilled by the knowledge that there are plenty of domesticated Black "screens" to defuse the inner city. For these power brokers, token integration will yet vindicate the "American Dream." For them, "Black Power"—an uncomfortable but tolerable concept—means the election of Black mayors, sheriffs and Congressional representatives who can be trusted to play by the rules. These white integrationists campaign for, fund, and patronize the Douglas Wilders and the Colin Powells.

Genteel integrationism has been badly upstaged, however. During the 1980s, conservative Democrats joined hands with mainstream Republicans to strip the Black "underclass" of government entitlements. In their place were put only two options: either the charity of big-hearted wealthy whites, administered by churches and foundations; or hard-nosed police repression and jails. There are "no free lunches," they keep telling us, backing it up with the message that the white people who are alive today bear no responsibility for Black ills, even if their forbears may have.

*

In truth, global white supremacy is an institutionalized reality that often appears as remote from the daily doings of ordinary white folks as, say, the late summer formation of hurricane clouds off the South Florida coast. Millions of run-of-the-mill whites, who bear no particular animus against Black people, simply refuse any personal sacrifice to end racism and compensate its victims. As many as 77 percent of American whites oppose government spending to improve race relations, while 83 percent are against the use of tax revenues for welfare purposes because they think minorities are the main beneficiaries (Jaynes and Wiliams 1989:213). Public opinion polls in late 1994 were showing solid support among whites for anti-Black Republican Party proposals. Job security is honored over the affirmative hiring of Blacks. The U.N. Security Council, IMF, and the World Bank check the advance of national liberation the world around and block reforms designed to foster the well-being of peoples of color. In 1989 the U.S. Supreme Court's *Croson Decision* struck down a Richmond, Virginia, minority set-aside law which guaranteed minority-owned companies 30 percent of municipal building contracts.

Gerrymandering continues. Still very much alive is the classical practice of dividing states, counties and wards into electoral districts so as to assure white voters a majority in as many districts as possible, while concentrating Black ballot strength into as few as possible. Whites fear Black voter participation. They also dread Black predominance on Grand Juries and trial juries, in places of heavy minority population. State legislatures generate schemes to dilute the ballot effects of Black and Latino residential concentration. White politicians up for (re-)election pitch campaign appeals against "crime-prone" Blacks. Some 40 percent of Mississippi's residents are African-Americans. The state Senate took a look at the size of this Black population and decided to try to nullify the potential vote. The reapportionment plan proposed in 1991 was contrived to reduce the number of winnable majority Black districts. In 1993 the Supreme Court's right-wing majority vindicated white majority domination nationwide, repudiating electoral districts drawn to increase minority representation. The 5–4 decision (in which Clarence Thomas cast the deciding vote against his own people) says it may be unconstitutional for states to carve out new district lines with the purpose of creating districts where a majority of voters are people of color. More than two dozen "majority-minority" congressional districts and 13 Black members of Congress were put in jeopardy.

Since the U.S. Supreme Court has nodded approval of the disempowerment of Black voters, there now exists little recourse through the courts for redress of the politics of exclusion. The 1990s Supreme Court majority is hell-bent on upholding dilution of the Black bloc vote. Gerrymanderers are pretty much free to do as they please. Particularly in the South, where Black voter concentrations should be able to elect growing numbers of state legislators, Congressional representatives and even Senators, Black electoral hopes are still at the mercy of at-large voting schemes, runoff primary systems, open primaries and other devilish gerrymanders.

The determination to prevent African Americans from using the existing political system to our own advantage can be measured in the white political reaction to the Jesse Jackson phenomenon. Between November 1980 and November 1984, three million new Black voters were registered. The increase was mainly the outcome of Jackson's grassroots campaign to achieve a Black agenda and swell the number of Black elected officials. The movement culminated in his Rainbow Coalition campaign for the Democratic Party Presidential nomination, eventually harvesting seven million votes in 1988. Ironically, the very success of the Black voter registration program triggered the prejudice of white electors. An unprecedented white voter backlash galvanized. Whites feared that the new Black political activism would translate into more Black legislators pushing for reforms. So millions of whites who had never before bothered to vote poured out to register and to cast ballots for the likes of Ronald Reagan and George Bush. Not only did they check the Black offensive, but due to their greater numbers the beneficial impact of three million new Black voters—virtually all of whom opposed Reagan and Bush—was nullified. The phenomenon has been most intense in the South where hordes of first-time racist voters flooded the polls, particularly in North Carolina in 1990 in support of arch-racist Jesse Helms against Harvey Gantt, and in 1994 throughout the region, giving right-wing Republicans control of Congress.

Behind this is a demographic voter shift that is potentially lethal for Afro-American causes, given the limitations of two-party electoral politics. Its effect was felt in the 1992 decision of the Clinton campaign to ignore Black issues while wooing Reagan Democrats and white middle class suburbanites. The renewed "respectability" of a codified political racism manifested itself in strong white male blue collar worker support in 1980 for Ronald Reagan, repeated in 1984 and once again in 1994. This "meanness mentality" vocally blames "America's decline" on African American strivings for equality, and views Black people as an incubus in North American society, as a set of overly-demanding "whiners" dragging it down. The concluding decades of the twentieth century have witnessed a heavy growth of population in sections of the country where these opinions are particularly strong.

The spectre of racist populism stalks the Sun Belt. In the 1988 Presidential election, Klansman David Duke sharpened the vision of a white people's American *Reich* and collected 46,910 votes for his "Populist Party". The Democratic-Republican establishment nervously tried to explain Duke away as a tinsel Hitler, shampooed to look mainstream, heading a ragtail handful of Klansmen and neo-Nazis. However, the Duke message resounded in a receptive audience and his political shadow refused to go away. The 46,000 ballot total was merely the tip of an iceberg of popular support among both the working class and middle class suburban whites. In the 1990 Louisiana senatorial election, Duke skied to 605,000 ballots—an absolute majority of the white vote. He starred in the enclaves of white professionals, but also played well in the blue collar voter base. On 16 November 1991, David Duke was torpedoed only by a heavy turnout of Black voters, as he tried to win the office of governor of the state of Louisiana. Nevertheless, the former Grand Wizard of the KKK again polled a majority of the white vote. He ran as a "Southern Strategy" Republican. At the time, Duke was only 39 years of age and would most likely be around a long time. Parallels between his surge in popularity and the trajectory of Adolf Hitler during the first phase of his career do not appear far-fetched. Duke's allure is a measure of the mood of the white popular masses in the 1990s, of their true, if unspoken, feelings towards Black people. His 700,000 Louisiana backers—56 percent of the 1991 white vote—liked Duke's pledge to sweep away the present constitutional safeguards for minorities in favor of a more blatant white supremacist regime, one empowered to resegregate African Americans. He went to South Africa in April 1994 on the eve of the first real election in that country's history. Duke promised a Pretoria gathering of pro-apartheid whites that thousands of right-wing white Americans would be happy to join the fight for a white separate homeland in the new South Africa. He encouraged his listeners to secede in order to preserve an apartheid heaven. His pitch varies in timbre and shrillness according to audience and circumstance, but his all-white constituency clearly understands his intent, even though many do not yet consider the crisis acute enough to endorse it fully.

There is still a kind of hanging back from full-blown fascism, but for how long? Conservative Republican intent is clear and there is less and less difference between it and "boll weevill" Democrats. The ex-liberal Democrats have decided to counter the long-successful Republican Party "Southern Strategy" with a white middle-class strategy of their own, committing the party to sink or swim with the votes of white Reagan Democrats, white Baby Boom suburbanites, white Gays and Lesbians, white Pro-Choicers and white Environmentalists. The old liberal Democratic strategy had depended heavily on the Black vote. But now the party leaders ignore the Black "special interest," on the assumption that African American voters have nowhere else to go—either vote Democratic or refrain from voting at all. As the Democratic Party "whitened" its image, the Black vote would become progressively irrelevant, they figure.

Chapter 9

EUROPE TODAY
AND THE WINDS OF RACIST CHANGE

The latest battle in the epochal struggle between radical revolution and social conservatism has ended in victory for the latter. From one end of the world to the other, as we approach the twenty-first century, class-revolutionary movements lie in ashes, consumed by the fires of conservative capitalism and white supremacy. In just a few short years at the end of the 1980s, white socialist regimes tumbled like dominos across Eastern Europe, the Soviet Union disintegrated, and previously mighty Communist Parties evaporated in the counter-revolutionary conflagration, many pathetically relinquishing power with barely a whimper. Gone in one fell swoop were the gains of the 1917 October Revolution. Marx was calumniated, Lenin repudiated in his homeland. Right-wing forces had finally neutralized the impulse of class conflict within European civilization—at least for the time being.

This was not the first time in the age-old struggle between the status quo and rebellion that counter-revolution had won a long and exhausting battle in a war that appears unending. Two hundred years ago the great Black slave revolution in Haiti—the only slave rebellion in the annals of history to destroy an entire slavery system—was still-born, as white world supremacy quickly mobilized to keep its influence from spreading and liberating Africa and other Blacks of the Diaspora. From 1791 to 1804 the Haitian Black revolution convulsed Western civilization, throwing the system of Black chattel enslavement into severe crisis. The world appeared to be on the eve of Black liberation. The earth-shaking cleansing in Haiti began roughly coincidental with a bourgeois revolution in France—a conflict within that white society which pitted bourgeois and plebeians against feudal aristocrats and the monarchy. It was France which held Haiti in colonial thralldom and squeezed untold riches from the labor of Black slaves. The Haitians waged a long and bitter guerrilla war and took exacting revenge on their white oppressors. Eventually the Black freedom fighters were left to themselves without an international ally, as revolutionary France succumbed to Napoleonic despotism. Terrified, the forces of white supremacy rallied together internationally, ringing the revolutionary infestation in the Caribbean with a grim embargo. Having suppressed its own domestic class-revolutionaries, France led the way. Britain, accumulating seed-capital for its industrialization from the enslavement of Blacks and bent on consolidating the empire upon which "the sun never set," cooperated. Newly-independent America, the young United States of slaveholder Presidents Jefferson, Madison, and Monroe, anxious to protect Southern plantations, jumped in with obscene enthusiasm. These white powers ganged up to choke Haitian liberation in the bud. The revolutionary spark was doused before it could ignite the Black slaves of the West Indies, USA, and the Spanish and Portuguese colonies. Haiti was isolated diplomatically and prevented from setting off further conflagrations, as the white "Great Powers" of the time slapped a ban on the infant Black state as pitiless as the one the United States maintains against revolutionary Cuba today. Haiti became a pariah, and by the early nineteenth century had been driven into dire poverty. A series of corrupt puppet regimes were foisted on the people, culminating in the Ton-Ton Macoute, the Duvaliers, and military junta terror. Such was revolutionary Haiti's punishment for having dared to challenge white supremacy.

Much the same kind of counter-revolutionary triumph has taken place in our time, only on a larger scale and chiefly at the expense of white Communists and socialists. The twentieth century struggle was bitter and costly, the issue in doubt for decades, as the revolutionary contagion spread to Third World China, Vietnam, and Cuba, and even touched down tentatively in Africa (Guinea-Bissau, Angola, Mozambique, Ethiopia, and Algeria). But by the end of the 1970s Western imperialism had finally drawn tight its *cordon sanitaire*. Revolutionary Marxism had been quarantined, sealed off in Eastern Europe and the Soviet Union. Spearheaded by the United States, NATO capitalism bankrupted Communist Europe economically. It was dominated culturally. It was subverted ideologically. And finally, with the advent of the Gorbachev-Yeltsinites, it succumbed to political destabilization. Western capitalism was able to accomplish this master stroke by reaching out to the white racism widespread and deeply-rooted in the middle, urban working and peasant masses of Eastern Europe and Russia.

The richer West was bound to win in the long run for it shared a common foundation with the poorer socialist East. Western and Eastern Europeans all belong to *white civilization*—from which overriding impulses flow, urges which are racist in nature. Due to their membership in white civilization, it was only a matter of time until ordinary Eastern Europeans and Russians adhered to the message of white world supremacy coming from the West, finding it much more "natural" than a socialist ideology that preaches the equality of all mankind.

I myself sensed the onset of conservative revolution in Eastern Europe as far back as the late 1960s, having resided for a while in the eastern part of Germany. The social mood and street-level opinion suggested that neither socialist transformation of production relations nor the Communist remoulding of the political and ideological superstructure would redeem the racist common folk. Before his death, the great revolutionary Lenin himself came to realize that the image of the "noble and unprejudiced white proletarian" was a hollow myth. Much of the pathos of his final years sprang from his attempt to contend politically with white workers whose racial instincts were as base as any white capitalist's.

Why should this matter to us? It matters because global right-wing revolution has weakened the Black liberation struggle, particularly in Africa. Our position everywhere—in the Diaspora as well as in Africa—has worsened gravely as a result of the events at the end of the 1980s which altered the international balance of forces in favor of white supremacy. The collapse of Europe's white socialist camp has set people of color back everywhere. Why? The reason is simple. James Baldwin wrote that the small concessions won by the Civil Rights campaign, i.e. the removal of legal segregation in the statutes of 1964, 1965 (and 1968) would not have been possible without the pressure of the Cold War. Martin Luther King, SCLC and SNCC would have been ignored, or failing that, slaughtered wholesale, had it not been for the fact that the USA found itself embroiled at the time in desperate struggle with the Soviet Union for global dominance (Baldwin 1963). Feeling the heat, U.S. imperialism grudgingly placated Civil Rights militants, cleaning up the face that racist America presented to the outside world. Grinning and bearing it, white America tried to make it appear that discrimination against Blacks was at long last on its way out. This was window dressing designed to help the State Department win the favor of the newly independent African and other Third World countries in warding off the "Communist threat." Moreover, as Ishmael Reed observes, the CIA felt "a need to aid anti-Communist allies by using the inner cities as fund-raising drug bazaars for groups like the Contras" (Reed 1993:92). And no matter how small the actual concession, at least it was something. Abroad, the Cold War empowered African nations. They played off one white predator against the other. The FLN, MPLA, FRELIMO, PAIGC, ANC, and other anticolonialist movements got arms and diplomatic support from the USSR and its Warsaw Pact allies. The fact that one half of white civilization was at the other's throat gave African statesmen room to manoeuver. Kwame Nkrumah and Sekou Touré played the game adeptly; where Washington was not forthcoming, Moscow was sure to be. What better situation for oppressed people seeking power for themselves? "Friendship with my enemy's enemy" became axiomatic for Third World leaders bent on liberation. Faced with a self-liberating Africa, it was smart tactics for NATO to pretend fidelity to racial equality at home while it bellowed abroad about "freedom from Communist tyranny."

Now all that has changed. The rivalry has ended and the Kremlin and the U.S. State Department are "comfy" on the "same page."

Russia and America waltz cheek to cheek, planning cozy joint-voyages to Mars and beyond. The North stands united against the South. The white folks, including the majority in Central and Eastern Europe, have closed ranks, rallying around the very real, if undisplayed, banner of white domination. Japan plays along in the role of "honorary Aryan" imperialists. The world's people of color have lost leverage. We can no longer pressure the power elite for concessions on the claim that such conferments will strengthen State Department diplomacy.

What happened to the once mighty Soviet Communist Party? How are we to account for the loss of revolutionary calling by the party founded by Lenin and the Bolsheviks? The answer involves at once the quality of the civilization and a general rule of politics. There is, I believe, a political precept which sets a *time limit* within which any organized *revolutionary* political party must achieve power and complete and consolidate the intended social transformations. Thereafter, degeneration is inevitable, with or without achievement of the goal. The critical time span seems to be about one human generation, a leeway of some 20 to30 years for vital activity as a *principled* organization. Should a revolutionary political party not achieve power within that span of time from the date of its foundation, either through revolutionary seizure or through co-optation or through constitutional means like election, then it is doomed to shed its initial revolutionary integrity and dash. If it does not achieve power within a single generation, then impetuous ardor gives way to opportunism and careerism. Once that occurs, there is no likelihood that it will ever come to power, certainly not as a *revolutionary* force. In most cases, would-be revolutionary parties which have not gotten control of the state within twenty to thirty years have degenerated into warring factions and insignificant sects, or have been coopted as some sort of annex of the constitutional Establishment (i.e., one more electioneering party in a multi-party parliamentary set-up). Then its alternatives narrow to either being a marginalized fringe or a domesticated resident of the regular political corral.

However, even if a revolutionary party does seize power and implement its program, it nevertheless is bound to fail in the end if it lacks the proper *civilization* base to work with. This is what sank the Russian Red October Revolution. From its 1917 beginnings, Lenin and the Bolsheviks were overmatched in their endeavor to shake the world by the poor human material with which they had to work. Their raw material were white Europeans whose conservative traditions leaned more naturally to white supremacy than to socialist revolution and brotherhood with peoples of color. Lenin and his comrades were doomed before they started. With the Cold War now history, the present neo-imperialist arrangement between the USA and Russia condemns all subject peoples to continued servitude. Mikhail Gorbachev's legacy to the Third World in particular is "shut up and suffer."

In 1969 Dr. Han Suyin, a Eurasian commentator, expressed grave unease about the then still emerging European Common Market. She wondered how people of color should regard that "Great White League." We now know the answer. United Europe stands as a white super-colossus, glowering at the Third World. It is the latest manifestation of the expansionism inherent in the modernized white racist global economy. The European Economic Community (EEC), established in 1992 by the Maastricht Treaty, is a gigantic white free trade area, potentially the world's largest, protected by tariff walls and streamlined to step up exploitation of Africa and other "developing" parts of the world. It is likely to grow even larger as the Slavic-dominated Commonwealth of Independent States (CIS)—patched together by the Yeltsinites from the subverted USSR—and such Eastern European slum-nations like Poland and Hungary lobby for membership in the western European economic community as well as in NATO, the white league's supreme military coalition.

Already Europe is the scene of racist lynchings which have forced the Blacks residing there into organized resistance. In a move that calls to mind W.E.B. DuBois' 1905 Niagara Movement, a Standing Conference on Racism in Europe was founded in summer 1990 to defend the human rights of Black people in the new united Europe. Those rights are sorely contested and stand on very flimsy ground. Nazism is on the rise everywhere in Europe. Racist skinheads rampage throughout the EEC, committing race-bias crimes.

During 1990 in Britain alone racist assaults rose to 6,359 from 4,383 in 1988. At least a dozen racial murders were recorded in 1993. The British Home Office—the government ministry of the interior—has admitted that racist assaults occur at a rate of 130,000 to 140,000 a year. In a prison cell British jailers murdered Omasase Lumumba, 32-year-old nephew of Patrice Lumumba, the legendary founder of the Zairean state, assassinated on U.S. orders in 1960 (Omasase Lumumba had come to Britain seeking political asylum). British immigration agents seized a Nigerian woman, bound and gagged her and dragged her on to a plane. And in their execution of a deportation writ, the London Metropolitan police also killed a Jamaican woman in front of her 5-year old son. The victim's mouth, legs, and feet were taped. The officers then proceeded to pulverize her stomach, kidneys, liver, and brain.

A chronicle of contemporary German events reads much like the trail of events during the early 1930s, leading to the rise of Hitler. A branch of the American Ku Klux Klan has set up shop in Berlin and several smaller German cities. In the western parts of Germany there were 270 assaults on Third World refugees during the year 1990. The number soared to 990 the following year. Eastern German neo-Nazis staged 493 such outrages in 1991 and escalated the violence until attacks on people of color were occurring almost daily. Dresden in the east and Hamburg in the west were particular focal points. Racists mounted a serious assault on a house in Hamburg in the middle of 1990. They burned two Ghanaians to death. A half year later, in February 1991, another Ghanaian fell victim to the Black-haters, yanked from a bicycle and drowned in a pool. Over the next months, neo-Nazis continued to target Black Africans, as the scene shifted to Dresden. In April 1991 a white mob in that city set upon and lynched an Angolan. Two months later they hurled a Mozambican to his death from a train window. In September, skinheads torched an African refugee shelter in Saarlouis, burning alive one Yeboah, a citizen of Ghana. Two Nigerians were hospitalized with critical burns. On the last day of the month a mob attacked and incinerated a hostel filled with Africans and Pakistanis. The outrage took place in Hamburg, Germany's port city. Slobbering neo-Nazi skinheads were shown on TV besieging Black people before milling crowds of onlookers. The spectators yelled in jubilation and encouragement. This demonstrates the popularity of racism among average Germans, as did police inaction.

In the former East German Democratic Republic, police stood idly by and watched the attacks, exactly the way U.S. southern police used to observe and applaud KKK lynchings of Afro-Americans. Weak economically and militarily, and lacking the leverage of the Cold War, the OAU and individual African governments were unable to intervene on behalf of their citizens. They did not have the clout to pressure Germany to end the racist outrage. In fact, as if to flaunt the real significance of the fall of the Berlin Wall, white lynch mobs grew larger in the eastern section of unified Germany. In Wittenberg a gang of young white males savaged two large dormitories housing African workers who had been invited into the country by the former GDR government, now defunct. Two Namibians were hurled from the height of the balconies. In 1994 three young white Erfurt males kicked a pregnant 23-year old Nigerian woman in the stomach at a railway station. As racial incidents multiplied, Africans in the country feared to go anywhere near eastern regions. Observed one shaken young man from Ghana: "The violence is bad, but the other parts... the way people here look at you and talk to you. They hate Africans" (*The Globe and Mail*, Toronto, 7 September 1992). In November 1992 German neo-Nazis burned three Third World women to death. The uprising of 1989-1990 not only brought down the Berlin Wall, it also blew away the lid that had been holding down a volcano of racist hatred against Black people, suppressed in Germany since the Second World War. Today the lava of bigotry flows unchecked, a manifestation of the fundamentally racist character of white civilization.

Apparently unaware of the racist nature of Western civilization, Pan-Africanist historian Edward Scobie ascribed the new breed of extreme right-wing racism in EEC countries merely to unemployment. Yet recognizing the immediate peril to people of color, he warned that countries like Germany, France, Belgium and Switzerland are "building a big White summit house and we have no rooms in it." Non-white immigrants are being locked out (*New York Amsterdam News*, 4 January 1992).

Meanwhile the violence continued unabated, spreading to new countries. In January 1992 neo-Nazis murdered three Black Africans in Sweden, a land hitherto known for its tolerance. German pogroms swelled to the rate of seven a day, as a Togolese man was thrown in the path of a truck, a Sudanese refugee was pelted with stones, and a frail Vietnamese woman beaten within an inch of her life by a gang of white youths. It is the youth that shows the greatest support in Europe for neo-Nazism and other racist extremists. Within six months more than a thousand xenophobic attacks and threats were recorded officially by German authorities, but the majority of hate crimes went unreported. Italy chimed in with lynchings of African street vendors in Florence and immolations of East Africans in

Rome. The southern Italian *Mezzogiorno* confines thousands of African semi-slave farm laborers in concentration camp hostels. In Spanish Madrid, racist diatribes resound through the electronic media, spurning homeless Africans who "spoil the scenery" by sleeping in railway stations and public parks. From Prague in the Czech Republic, a white American woman professor on a Fulbright exchange program brought a tale of outrage. She was eyewitness to armies of racist Czech skinheads scouring the streets for Africans and Asians. They were on a hunt to kill, and a number of Nigerians were trapped and assaulted. The professor resided in a Czech apartment building. Her chief neighbors ostracized her upon learning that she had invited Black guests to her dwelling. In Moscow, white racist police brutality took the life of a Zimbabwean student in August 1992. Encouraged by the right wing Yeltsinites now in control, Moscow police gunned the African down.Two hundred and more special interior ministry riot troops were brought in to maul Third World students attending Patrice Lumumba People's Friendship University. As the helmeted troops pummeled the students, pinning many against walls, Russian bystanders cheered and made obscene gestures at the victims.

These obscene festivals of anti-Black hatred underway in Eastern and Central Europe are performed by working-class youth. Their actions prove the thesis that far from being revolutionary, white workers, if left to their own designs, tend to be racist "throwbacks." They are like this everywhere, from the working class suburbs ringing Paris to Brooklyn, New York. Many are filled with hatred for the three-quarters of mankind who are people of color.

On 2 April 1992, the media announced that the imperialist Group of Seven (G-7) which rules the earth, had clubbed together to bail out the former Soviet Union. The erstwhile bitter enemy of the West would be rescued with handouts totalling 24 billion dollars. The former Reds had returned home to the great white family, now forgiven, as all contrite prodigal sons are forgiven. $24 billion for the strapped white brethren in Russia, not a penny in the way of reparations for Africa and Diaspora Blacks and Native Americans, to whom the real debt is owed. This was a manifestation of global white racial financial solidarity. This was not only a bail-out program for the new right wing Russia, it was yet another reaffirmation of white world supremacy. The same can be said of the U.S.-backed "Polish American Enterprise Fund." This is a financial device to pump

American money into white Poland. Anxious to grace Eastern Europeans with interest-free handouts, the White House and State Department favor long-term loans for these beggars at the derisively low interest of three-quarters of one percent stretched over forty years. Another case of white folks taking good care of one another, the proposal allows loan recipients to wait a full ten years before having to ante up the first repayment instalment.

*

The United States of America is still the strongest military power in the imperialist club. It is the center of international repression, the dire enemy of global Black liberation, the "smart-bomb" destroyer of Iraqi civilians. It protects and props up countless puppet regimes, from El Salvador to Persian Gulf Emirates. It nourishes strawmen like Mobutu and Bhutelezi. It patronizes political ghouls like Boris Yeltsin. Worldwide it has assembled running dogs, lick-spittles, clients, lackeys, and Uncle Toms. It is as if the men on Capitol Hill have christened the earth "Dodge City," and then appointed the Pentagon as world sheriff. Jumping to orders, early in 1992 the Pentagon brass cobbled together a secret planning document to guide U.S. policy in post–Cold War diplomacy. The U.S. assigned itself the status of sole military superpower ready at a minute's notice to move unilaterally anywhere in the world, with the aim of eternalizing white North supremacy over the Third World South. Dubbed the *Defense Planning Guidance, 1994–1999,* the 46-page document lauded a unipolar "new world order," while implying greater impoverishment at home for Blacks and other non-white minorities. The Pentagon hopes to confine Japan, Germany, and Russia to mere regional military clout and convince them that their best intersts lie in cooperating to reduce the United Nations and its agencies to mere white men's playthings. With a firm grip on Persian Gulf oil reserves, the Pentagon sees itself positioned to counter the danger of Asia, still "home to the world's greatest concentration of traditional Communist states." Back-up would come from a CIA retooled to eviscerate Third World liberation movements.

It took the assassinations of Malcolm X and Martin Luther King to make some Black people in this country realize they should fear the CIA and FBI as white secret police. Third World people have long dreaded the Central Intelligence Agency. While the FBI stages frameups and assassinations and infiltrates militant movements at home, the CIA designs plans for international mass slaughter and super-exploitation of Third World people—racist division of labor. Recently, in the aftermath of the surrender of European Communism, the CIA has shifted its focus to the "darker brethren." No longer having to fear the Soviet Union, it has stepped up the recruitment campaign for career agents among Afro-Americans. The spy agency has now begun to imitate the decades-old U.S. armed forces policy of staffing Black and Afro-Latino "volunteers." The recruits will be put to work spying on and subverting movements of a nationalist color throughout the Third World.

How are we Black people to regard the changes in Europe? Why should it cut any ice with us? There can be no doubt that capitalism slaughtered and enslaved us for centuries. The capitalist system lynched, terrorized, segregated, brainwashed, and discriminated against us racially. Frankly, however, in the aftermath of the events of 1985-1990, the rap has crystallized against Marxism. The socialist system collapsed in eastern Europe. Save for only one instance, the ruling European Communists surrendered cravenly, without a fight. Astonishingly, they handed over state power without so much as a civil war, even though the Communist parties had controlled massive military and economic means for more than forty years; in the case of the USSR for more than seventy years! The "Reds" caved in even though armed defense of revolutionary gains is a fundamental dictum of Marxist-Leninist theory.

Now, we as Black people, as the throwaway appendages of white supremacy, as marginals confined to prison, unemployment and ghettoes, and as the military cannon fodder of imperialism, we cannot afford—by any stretch of the imagination—to be tied to any such historical 'loser' as Communism now appears to be. Dehumanized in the western hemisphere, recolonized in Africa to the point where we are prey to famine and AIDS, Black people should seek to bind themselves to none but winners in the global power struggle. It will cost us too much to back that which for the time being appears to be a lost cause. In the historic sense, Socialism/Communism interested us only to the extent to which it could deliver material benefits and concrete support. It was of benefit to the victims of racism only as long as it checked white imperialist aggression, only as long as it used imperialism's racist outrages to embarrass its Western opponents diplomatically, thus strengthening liberation struggles in Africa, Asia, and the Americas. In the aftermath of the events of

1989-1992, it would appear that the only lesson of value left to learn from the version of socialism that held sway in Eastern Europe and the USSR is that reaction and racism are immensely popular among the white masses everywhere. The fall of European Communism showed the egoism of white workers. It indicated stubborn refusal to espouse racial equality and friendship with non-whites. This is nothing to cheer about. For Marxian socialism claimed that it had the potential to become the only non-racist political economy ever created by whites in the annals of mankind. Sadly, however, the vast majority of white folk in Western civilization—including the common folk, white working classes—never endorsed that philosophy. Throughout the years of Communist rule, the common folk remained unregenerate white racists. The victory of counter-revolution in Eastern Europe and the former Soviet Union testifies to the repudiation of socialism by white working classes throughout the world in favor of the doctrine and practice of white supremacy. We of the Third World, all people of color, none more so than the Africans of Africa and the Africans of the Diaspora, must draw the proper conclusions—our very survival is at stake.

Chapter 10

LABOR, ETHNICITY, IMMIGRATION, AND RACISM

Let us turn to the political role of organized white labor. Created by successive streams of European immigration of various ethnic origins—Jews, Irish, Germans, Italians, Slavics, and others—the North American white trade union movement has never been known for a revolutionary class consciousness. Samuel Gompers, George Meany and Lane Kirkland are typical spokesmen. A distinguishing feature has been steadfast devotion to the capitalist system, qualified only by a mild affection for the Welfare State. "Blue collar ethnics" believe in white racial solidarity with "management" against Blacks. This white supremacist mind-set nullified or stunted concord between white and Black employees. Instead of uniting with their Black counterparts in a joint onslaught on the system, white workers have devoted much of their energies to escaping economic instability and unemployment. They concentrated on monop-olizing choice positions and on excluding Black workers from the competition for jobs. White workers cherished the bonus that came their way due to racial discrimination. They opposed the fear of their own impoverishment to the demand for justice and equality for Black people. Many have cursed minority "quotas" and affirmative action. The heavy burden of misery borne by Blacks spared white wage earners from proportionate effects of poverty and exploita-tion. Why, for instance, did so many white male industrial workers in Ohio and Pennsylvania—the heart of the "Rust Bowl"—vote for Ronald Reagan in 1980, and again in 1984? Why did Monongahela Valley Roman Catholic Italians flock to George Bush in 1988? Why do so many white male workers cheer for Newt Gingrich and Jesse Helms? How to account for Howard Beach–type lynchings in which very youthful white ethnic males transform instantaneously into mindless vigilantes who maim and murder Black people? Actually there are millions more of these types of unorganized white racists than of the organized sects of far-rightwing thugs.

We can no longer be satisfied to fob this behavior off as merely the spewing of turf-guarding frustrations. Nor should we duck the issue of its working class origins by merely attributing the phe-nomenon to the doings of skinhead crazies unlike so-called "pro-gressive" white workers.

The question is—how do these mainstream white workers and working class youths become virulent racists who support the Rudolph Giulianis, Daryll Gateses, and other right-wing conserva-tives? The answer seems to lie at least partially in a *special recruitability of white workers* under social crisis conditions such as those prevalent today in America and Europe. This seems to be a rule in societies based on white supremacy. The educational system and the mass media are influential. They help churn out predigest-ed, programmed, white worker families, as it were, conditioned in advance to respond to social pressure with anti-Black reactions.

Harmful it undoubtedly is, but by no means irrational, for it rep-resents the solid material interest the white working class owns in white supremacy (see above). The social environment, role models and ideas prevalent in white civilization predispose white workers to espouse and identify with jingoistic, militaristic, chauvinistic, right-conservative, and above all racist utterances. They see them-selves mirrored in "nigger"-hating, nuke-the-Third-World government policies. They are quick to want to sic the Marines on the Saddam Husseins and Muammar Khadaffis. Rambo is the model. Despite periodical wage-level disputes with management, admiration for the boss, based on shared skin-color, outweighs antagonism.

These are loyal, "patriotic" workers. The lives that these types live may often, in fact, be stunted, empty, deprived, frustrated and, of course, exploited. For the cancer lies in the innards of the white working class as it actually exists in North America and the rest of the West. The evil is inherent in the class. This is a phenomenon of historic proportions.

One of the more suggestive recent explanations for this phenomenon is the "segmentation theory" of racial discrimination, formulated from the mid-1970s through the 1980s. It recognizes that white workers have an objective material interest in *"crowding"* minority workers in low-paying, ghettoized job classifications. That the share of the social wealth available for allocation among Black and white workers is strictly limited, is a basic premise for segmentation theory. Other factors remaining equal, then, low wages paid to Black workers allow higher wages for white workers. The entire system presupposes white workers' political clout. Vested interest, according to this account, prompts whites to shield themselves from unemployment through the seniority system. Foremost lies opposition to affirmative action to achieve racial balance. Today ordinary white workers are much more against affirmative action than the corporate giants of the national economy (Bonacich 1976; Cottingham 1982; R.S. Franklin 1991; Glenn 1985:86–108; R. Williams 1987:1–15).

*

The South has hung on to its credentials as the citadel of economic racism. The South holds on to its status even though the Midwest, dotted with abandoned smokestack industries, housed the most economically depressed Blacks in the nation by the late 1980s. For one thing, despite the smokescreen of ambiguous figures implying that the wage gap between white and Black workers has been steadily lessening nationally, the traditional Black-white wage differential which dictates that a Black man must receive lower payment than his white counterpart for the same work, has held firm in the South. For another, for decades, at least until the Rust Bowl devastation of recent date, a regional differential has paid southern workers less than northern ones. Compare, for example, Alabama with Michigan. In 1982, the average wage for hourly workers, Black and white, in Alabama was $7.01. In Michigan it was $10.53, a gap of $3.52 per hour to the detriment of Alabamans. Deep South propaganda makes much ado of putting the "cracker"-, "redneck"- KKK-past behind it, tooting the horn of "racial tolerance." Yet its new-found liberalism does not translate as economic equality for its Black inhabitants. The level of unionization is still lower in the South than in the North, more states have anti-labor "Right-to-Work" laws, Black worker militancy is more dampened, and progressive Black political organizations and personalities are still subject to repression and harassment. The off-again/on-again persecutions of former judge Alcee Hastings and mayor Richard Arrington of Birmingham are just two instances among many.

The lastingly inferior economic status of African Americans is, in large part, caused by Dixieland's still very widespread loathing for Blacks, to which most Southern white workers are party. Prejudice insists on lower wage scales and inferior working conditions in the South than, say, in the Western or Northeastern part of the country, despite the fact that this runs counter to the betterment of the earnings also of *white* Southerners. Nationwide, the 1982 wage differential between Black and white workers totalled an average annual "circumstantial" extra-profit of $31.2 billion, without factoring in the extra sums derived from the regional differential.

We must factor in, however, the connection between white worker racism and plant relocation policy. By the early 1980s in deciding to relocate plants and enterprises, big business made it a rule of thumb to avoid choosing any region where Blacks constitute more than thirty percent of the work force. Now, before deindustrialization, Blacks counted for as many as one-fifth of all U.S. smokestack laborers. Relocating industries are in flight from trade-union-conscious, militant Black workers. Such businesses seek refuge instead among backward Southern whites who are politically conservative, hale from rural communities, are infested with prejudices and twice as likely to refuse unions as Black workers are. In short, enterprises relocating within the country rather than abroad like to seek out areas inhabited by laborers of the type who grooved to the music of David Duke.

It is nonsense to go on arguing that millions upon millions of white workers are just suffering from a dose of "false consciousness," and are about to recover their senses at any moment, wake up and fulfil their "historic destiny." White workers will go on being "duped" because they are not duped at all. They possess the hard-nosed common sense that one expects of members of a privileged group. They stick with their "false consciousness" because it is not in their interest to "overcome" it. "Hard-hat" racism and super-patriotism are slated to remain the white workers' special "bag" because they are means to defend surplus wages and the political and consumer privileges which surplus wages make possible. Many fighters for Black liberation, along with other progressives, have relied futilely on white labor militancy. White radical forces have long sought to rally us around a slogan of Black and white workers "unite and fight" for civil rights. For the entire twentieth century they have operated under the presumption that white wage earners are deserving of compassion, patience, and solidarity.

Now, although many millions of white industrial and commercial employees in the United States and Canada are deprived of ownership or control of the means of production and must sell labor power in order to live, that act of sale is privileged in comparison to minority participation in the labor market. Though they rank low in the hierarchy of privilege, they are a privileged class. For those who own the consign of privilege—white skin color—integration into the economy as an employed unit is comparatively easy, given the relatively wide job opportunities open to whites. Though squeezed periodically by recession and economic stagnation, the white employee never has to feel the sting of racial discrimination. He comes to take his surplus wage bonus and last-fired status for granted, considering them the norm.

A few figures will illustrate the fact. Black real wages peaked in 1978. Over the next 13 years the real earnings of Black workers declined 14 percentage points; Latinos, 19 percent. In comparison, the real wages of white full-time male workers fell only 10 percent. In the recession of 1990–1991, five percent of fully employed Black male workers lost their jobs, as against only three percent of white males. By the end of 1991, 53 percent of white males enjoyed full-time, year-round employment, while only 41 percent of Blacks held similar jobs. Hence the hollow ring to appeals like those raised in 1992 by Black Democratic Party politicians calling for backing of Bill Clinton's "racially neutral" agenda, contending that programs that rescue white suburbia, the white middle class, and white organized labor, will somehow trickle down to Black "welfare moms." Of course, the message played very well in the suburbs and with Reagan Democrats, 54% of whom returned to the Democratic fold in 1992, making Clinton the first Democrat since Lyndon Johnson to win a plurality of white votes.

The problem is that owing to the racist social economy, exactly these elements appropriate a slice—a thin one indeed—of the wealth created by the people of color here and around the earth. Spike Lee's depiction of New York Italian working-class types as hateful, sexually repressed, "every-man-for-himself" free enterprisers, enslaved to "good-hard-work" ideology, is not far wrong. It is no construction of fiction that the white characters in *Do the Right Thing* and *Jungle Fever* cannot imagine a life without racist putdown of Black and Brown people, or without a Puritanical ideal of "clean-cut" super-Americanism.

The Democratic Party is seen by many as minority-friendly. In fact, its office-seekers concede the white suburban babyboomers and the white blue collars a veto over social spending and other liberal measures. Clinton-era Democrats run scared that male Reagan Democrats will once again desert the fold in favor of the Republicans, so they are allowed to gridlock affirmative action. There is a "new breed" of Black politicians given to the same mouthings as American whites about crime, education, and jobs. Hardly had he arrived on Capitol Hill than J.C. Watts began talking this way, for instance.

In 1919 W.E.B. DuBois analyzed white labor's role in the exploitation of Third World people. Anti-imperialism motivated him. While the problem of the twentieth century was the problem of the color line, he insisted, the key to the economic malaise troubling the world at the close of World War I was the maladjustment in the distribution of wealth. The distribution of world income between the dominant and the oppressed peoples was unjust. White civilization had robbed the soil of its raw materials, raped people of color, and suppressed non-Western cultures. DuBois said white labor was a hand-in-glove accomplice with corporate management. "Unconsciously and consciously, carelessly, and deliberately the vast power of the white labor role in modern democracies," DuBois wrote in the Manifesto of the London Pan-African Congress, "has been cajoled and flattered into imperialistic schemes to enslave and debauch black, brown and yellow labor."

Depending on how one views the history of the twentieth century, this situation either exactly recurred during the 1980s, or had continued without a break through the New Deal era of affirmative action for white workers (1930s). White workers, many of them "ethnics," benefited preferentially from the Social Security Act, National Labor Relations Act and FHA housing subsidies. In much the same way, today's affirmative action has fostered white women's employment mainly, rather than benefiting Black men. As the civil rights movement surged in the 1960s, timid moves were made to redress some of the racist practices of government institutions. Yet hardly had they begun when the reactionary "New Right" sprang into motion. White backlash came of age. A crowd of white working class "ethnics," interpreted affirmative action as "reverse discrimination." Evidence proving the reverse discrimination concept to be groundless was swept aside.

White "ethnics" are cultural groups—mainly working class—created by *voluntary* migrations from Europe. Our position has been worsened by the nationwide tendency to weigh the Black experience on the same scales as white ethnics, thereby blaming Black victims of discrimination themselves for their inferior status in comparison with, say, Italian-, Jewish- and Polish-Americans.

Take the color bar against Black workers in New York state's skilled crafts as it stood a half century ago and more. Knowing that white craft unions and individual master craftsmen refused to permit any kind of apprenticeship for Afro-Americans, the first Black woman assistant principal in a New York public school, attended by 95 percent Black pupils, felt she had no alternative but to recommend that her charges prepare themselves instead only for the professions. This was the only road ahead, she was convinced, since stubborn white handicraft prejudice shut the door to the skilled crafts. Apparently unaware that the professions were just as closed to all but a tiny elite of Black youth, she exclaimed: "The same [school] standards must be maintained [as those for white pupils]. There must be Negroes in the professions. The trades do not welcome them, so we cannot concentrate on trade specialization" (*Claude Barnett Papers*, 1 October 1992).

During the 1930s the Congress of Industrial Organizations (CIO) trumpeted integration. But in the late 1940s and in the 1950s, CIO locals in Dixie grew more and more segregated. Around 1947 the CIO teamed up in Birmingham with the United Steelworkers chapter—a local run by Klansmen and other racists—to oust Black union leaders from the Mine, Mill and Smelter Workers local. They were replaced with lily-white bosses. By this time Birmingham steel mills had been invaded by Italian immigrants. Action like this smoothed the 1955 merger of the CIO with the jingoistic, conservative AFL, run by George Meany. To cite another example, a 32-year old fair-skinned Cleveland waitress lost her job when it was discovered that she was not white. Mistaking her for a Caucasian, a Tastyburger chain personnel manager had hired her. The chain operated thirteen lunch stands. When it came out that she was Black, she was cursed, abused, and fired. The point is that the woman was abused not alone by her supervisors, but even more virulently by her fellow waitresses, all of whom were "genuinely" white. One drop of "Negro blood," despite physical appearance, sufficed to trigger the racist reflex among ordinary white workers, female ones included.

George Wallace read the message as early as 1964. He realized that many Northern white workers hated and feared Black people. Four years later he cut deep inroads in the Democratic Party blue-collar constituency, setting a pattern. Later, Frank Rizzo, Richard Nixon, and Ronald Reagan were able to tap the well of anti-Black sentiments among white male workers in key industrial states from New Jersey through the Midwest. George Bush won the White House by fanning those same prejudices. And far from indicating any suspension of hostility towards Afro-Americans, the return of many white ethnics to the Democrats in Clinton Year 1992 was grounded explicitly on the political expectation that the White House incumbent from 1993 to 1997 would pay no special attention to Black "special interests." When Clinton seemed not to be living up to the promise, many of them punished the Administration by voting Republican in the 1994 Congressional elections. In the uncertain economic climate of transition from the twentieth to the twenty-first century, white workers cling to their marginally higher wages in comparison to non-whites, to substantially lower unemployment rates, seniority preferences, relative job security, and preferential hirings. They know the value of keeping apprenticeships for their own sons and nephews.

*

The complexity of the white working class' psychological stake in racism and the doctrine of white supremacy is often not appreciated.

We should not let white psychologists fool us into believing that whites have let drop their racial superiority complex and are merely sick and tired of hearing and talking about Black people and their problems.

The wealthy, elite white male, armed with the power and prestige of corporate ownership and command of government, enjoys the full array of economic, social, political, and cultural advantages which protects and isolates him physically from the competition of Blacks and other minorities. He can afford the self-satisfaction of being liberal and patronizing toward "deserving colored people," gazing down from exalted heights. The ruling class white male—take Senator Edward Kennedy of Massachusetts as a model—often seems above the marginal psychological perks of white supremacy, apparently taking no notice of white skin privilege, even denouncing it as morally reprehensible. In contrast, lower class whites are positioned much lower materially. Although much better off than Black people, they find themselves within our range of contention. There are many metropolitan centers in which secondary school districts straddle predominantly white and Black residential areas. Lower class white youth attend high schools with Blacks and dark-skinned Latinos. They compete with them athletically. Youth gangs "defend turf" against racial outsiders. They—and their fathers —feel constantly challenged by the minorities. Deprived of the real staples of white supremacy, they are more "irritable," as it were. Paradoxically, they are likely to even feel inferior to Blacks, especially in athletic competitions and other manhood-assertive activities, not to mention the teenage rivalry for girls that occasionally flashes into violence in gritty urban neighborhoods. The eclipse after the 1950s of Italian professional boxing champions by Black and Brown fighters was taken badly by the Italian-American community, for instance. Friction between African-Americans and Italians is long-standing and heated. The lynching of Blacks in, say, Bensonhurst is merely an echo of racist Italian onslaughts precipitated in 1935 by Mussolini's genocidal assault on Ethiopia. African Americans protested Italy's dastardly attack and condemned fascism. Italian-Americans supported Mussolini. Riots erupted repeatedly in New York City where Italian and Black districts adjoined. There was chronic warfare during the 1950s between Blacks and Italians all along the Murray Hill borderline in the Cleveland area. Current friction echoes the ill-will of the Italian-American mobs of Cicero, Illinois at the time of Martin Luther King's marches for residential integration. In metropolitan

Toronto's Scarborough area certain Italian restaurants are known to refuse to serve Black diners.

North and South, then, it is lower class whites who are most irritable about challenges to white skin privilege. In the words of a white construction worker nearly a generation ago (1970), we hear echoed the anti-minority populism which animates white male backlash today:

> "Look around....Look in the papers. Look on TV. What the hell does [liberal Republican mayor of New York City, John] Lindsay care about me? ...None of the politicians gives a good goddam. All they worry about is the niggers. And everything is for the niggers... And they get it all without workin'. I'm an ironworker, a connector....But the niggers they don't worry about it. They take the welfare and sit out on the street. They never gotta walk outta the house. They take the money outta my pay check and they just turn it over to some lazy son of a bitch who won't work. I gotta carry him on my back...." (Howe 1970:12)

This is the authentic voice of the David Duke "groupies" of today. The ballot box endows these types with considerable clout in American electoral democracy, and they are die-hard opponents of affirmative action and reparations. Before the Civil War, many lower class whites aspired to the ownership of Black slaves. In late twentieth century, related fantasies still swirl in the minds of white workers, dreams of striking it rich and joining the class of employers who hire and fire and lord it over hirelings. A lot of these visions are peopled with pliant Black and Brown workers, clients and servants, at the beck and call of the "deserving" white worker whose ship has finally come in, and for whom the American Dream has finally been realized. The fear that minority set-asides and parity-making indemnifications would trigger a radical change in the distribution of goods and services along racial lines, fuels massive white working-class resistance. This explains why for twelve years (1981-1993) Republican Administrations were able to win the confidence of countless white blue-collars, although simultaneously imposing intensely anti-labor measures. Reagan and Bush lubricated white supremacist navels.

*

Let us take another look at the David Duke phenomenon. It provides a striking example of white working class support for overt racist populism, and a very current one. In a state gubernatorial runoff, Klansman and Hitler-admirer David Duke won 30 of 64 parishes, thereby qualifying for Louisiana's November 1991 election for governor. His opponent, Edwin Edwards, was a standard white veteran Democrat. Duke carried the vote in white working-class suburbs as well as in rural districts. Certain tallies put his total at 700,000 votes. Here hundreds of thousands of American voters, the absolute majority at 55 percent of Louisiana's white electorate, rallied in support of a known advocate of the Nazi philosophy their country had fought in World War II. They did so because Americanized Hitlerism appeared sensitive to their predicament—the need to defend white supremacy against Blacks contesting social inferiority. Duke won between 56 and 63 percent of white voters with incomes *under* $50,000. He was equally strong among both blue collar and white collar employees of modest means. The Klan politician was the darling of the "poor white trash". These folksy categories voiced a 2 to 1 enthusiasm for white supremacy. To them Duke appeared to be someone they could depend on to beat Blacks back down into their "place." The chance to vote their hatred brought a huge turnout of Mobil, Shell, and other offshore and oil refinery workers in the white parishes of Chalmette and Arabi. Duke surged in Bernard parish, and in Metairie, an all-white suburb of New Orleans. He enjoyed strong support in northern and western Louisiana. His backers whined about being victimized by "reverse racism," boasted of membership in the American Association for the Advancement of White People, and sported Nazi insignia. To turn Duke back, it required an abnormally large mobilization of Black voters who make up 27 percent of Louisiana's electorate, and 80 percent of whom cast ballots against the Klansman. For the first time in the history of the state the Black turnout was proportionately bigger than the white vote. It had to be or Duke would have won. Nevertheless, the Black turnout still was only two percentage points higher than the white turnout, indicating racism's continuing ability to trigger massive white political responses.

North of the border, in Canada, during 1992 a similar outpouring of grassroots support favored white police outraged in metropolitan Toronto and other Ontario communities at a request to reduce their customary lethal violence against Black males.

As the 1990s dawned, white working class racism seemed to

swell rather than lessen. At work sites across the country remarks like "Black people don't need jobs when there are so many hard-working unemployed whites," were heard more and more often (*People's Weekly World*, 7 Dec. 1991). As the recession deepened, whites who still held jobs could be heard railling against "welfare queens," "Black pimps" and "dumb, lazy niggers." Black teachers, hospital workers, police officers, firefighters, and many others were ridiculed as "token niggers," deadwood holding down jobs that by right should have belonged to white men and women.

Trade union racism surfaced in Ontario. Local 721 of the International Association of Bridge, Structural and Ornamentation Workers was the culprit. Workers from this union built the world famous CN Tower and Skydome, as well as other landmarks of the Toronto skyline. Early in 1992 it was caught running a "request system" which discriminates against Black iron workers, knocking them to "the bottom of the barrel." Daily hiring at the union hall stretches from 6:30 AM to 10 AM. The white dispatcher routinely passed over unemployed Black iron workers, even though they were usually the first to arrive, and despite their status as paid-up union members. While some white members of the union were put in the way to rake in up to $100,000 yearly, the local's 250 Blacks were kept in the category of earning $20,000 yearly or less, doing jobs that last only a few weeks. According to Ontario law, these practices were clearly illegal. Nevertheless, on some construction jobs Blacks were the first laid off, even though they had been at the site longer than whites who remained working. The Coalition of Black Trade Unionists of Canada took to task the Canadian Union of Public Employees (CUPE)—the country's largest union. Despite sound and fury about addressing racism within its own ranks, CUPE is one of the worst footdraggers, in 1993 permitting only one Black person among its senior staff. Union leaders shut their eyes to racial discrimination in the workplace, defend flawed grievance procedures which hamper the fight against racism, and refuse to put specific anti-racist clauses in collective agreements. White union executives twist the arms of Black caucus members, dictating about how and for whom they should vote within Black meetings to select delegates.

In the big cities, the Irish have staffed the police forces. Even today they are heavily overrepresented among New York City's "Finest." Irish-American police officers nourish a reputation as Black- and Latino-hating killer cops.

Trouble with the Irish is mirrored by trouble with the Polish. Calumet Park is a suburb of Chicago. 75 percent of its residents are Black. But the Polish component dominates politically. Polish-Americans are notorious as perhaps the most rabidly anti-Black of all ethnic whites. Calumet's police force is kept lily-white, and in 1992 both the mayor and the police chief were Poles. Both the police and the Polish community regard all Black males as dangerous criminals. The cops are praised for showing no mercy, and the Polish-American officers excel at aggressive and sadistic brutality. Black prisoners in Calumet are known for the curious habit of "committing suicide" while in police custody.

*

In the course of the 1970s, *ethnicity* became a new code term for old racism. Appeals were heard to "common blood," "shared cultural heritage," "language-cultural community" and "neighborhood pride." Bobbing and weaving, ethnicity pundits ducked the direct connotation of racism (Ringer and Lawless 1989). Bare-knuckled racism had grown too crass for standard texts and its proponents were encountering too much flack from the victims of discrimination. To the rescue came the theme of ethnicity. It was discovered that the demands of Blacks and other people of color could be blunted and neutralized by arousing the counter-claims of white ethnics— usually Irish, Italian, Balkan, or Eastern European immigrants and their progeny. Whatever advances Blacks make, they believe, are made at their expense. They listen fervently to the message that civil rights for minorities, and civil rights spokesmen like Jesse Jackson, threaten their neighborhoods, jobs, schools, and churches (Block, Cloward, Ehenreich and Fox Piven 1987).

White ethnics are mostly skilled and semi-skilled blue collars with liberal sprinklings of small shopkeeper types and self-employed mechanics. The proverbial "construction company" boss makes a large figure in their communities. These are some of the most anti-Black communities in America (Reider 1985). Ethnicity theory flattered their "hardworking," "god-fearing" super-patriotism, and laughed at their "nigger"-hating antics. The ethnics suffer from split personality. On the one hand, they scream devotion to the traditional cultural values, extol "old-country" folkways, wail when second-generation offspring reject the old language for English, and swear undying loyalty to the church—usually the Roman Catholic

Church. On the other hand, few contract the social disease of "love-it-or-leave-it" Americanism faster than ethnic immigrants. Nowhere are "American Dream" illusions stronger. Among Italian-Americans this is sometimes linked to the capitalist-on-the-rise mentality of the Mafia. Rizzo in Philadelphia, and the Irish Catholic panic against school integration in Boston, were symptoms of the "ethnic age"—the decade of the Seventies. Twenty years later many racist scholars still prefer the term ethnic to race as less loaded with negative connotations. It is cherished for its capacity to inspire recent white immigrants—and some Asian newcomers—in support of overt racism and right conservative politics. Ethnicity now does for the northeastern and midwestern sections of the country, and for the west coast, what the old-fashioned doctrine of white supremacy did for Dixie, where the cry of "Negroism," for instance, rallied crackers in 1874–1875.

Hoaxers like Nathan Glazer assured us that Black and Latino slum dwellers are merely the latest (and the last?) of a series of "ethnic immigrants" who, like others before them, must pull themselves up the social ladder by their own bootstraps. Black neo-conservatives have rushed to endorse this bill of goods (Glazer 1975). Following the "underdeveloped" Jews, Irish, Italians, Poles and other Slavs, and Greeks, have come the "backward" Blacks and Latinos, last of the "newcomers." Glazer's friend, Daniel Moynihan, warned against the avalanche of social problems the "pathological" Black family was bound to unleash (Lemann 1991).

In a telling put-down of the "newcomers" thesis, Theodore Cross demonstrated that it is nonsensical to claim that underdevelopment is a natural stage through which Black America had to pass in the course of normal development. Its development had been perturbed by white oppression. The "retardation" or underdevelopment of Blacks and Afro-Latinos—"late" arrivals on the city scene—referred to, can only mean a relative weakness in saleable, high-tech work skills and business organization. This weakness is the result of an open racist *aggression* which robbed African Americans of independent development. The invaders from Europe seized America, eradicated the Indians, and established sovereign white political states. When they completed the operation with the enslavement of Africans, they extended their sovereignty over persons whom they still admit were *alien* to European culture. As a consequence, our heavily Black inner cities are nothing like the white ethnic ghettoes of the early twentieth century. They are the urban organization of an oppression of people of color imposed by white strangers.

And no matter how, or with what, the "banquet table" is laden, the Jewish experience in the U.S. is in no way comparable with the Black predicament, as ethnicity boasters pretend. Talk about the current emancipation and wealth of American Jewry is designed to convince the gullible that all the Black minority needs is patience; we need only wait another.... two, three, or four hundred years! In fact, throughout the history of North America, doors of public and private power that have been open to individual Jews (on a quota-basis) have been hermetically sealed to Blacks. For decades, Jews have been (over)-represented on the U.S. Supreme Court per population, for example, while there remains severe unease, even among liberals, at the mere suggestion that more than one of the nine justices be Black. Throughout their career, barriers were raised against men of such exceptional genius as Frederick Douglass and W.E.B. DuBois, while some quite ordinary Jews found preferment in the legal profession, academia, and politics. The widespread anti-Semitism of America may still not stomach the prospect of a Jewish President. However, the election of Jewish Senators does not raise an eyebrow, while the Black community has to burst a gasket just to break a single representative into the Senate. The main difference between Jews and Blacks is precisely the racial one. In North America color and race is the primary contradiction —not class, nor religion, nor anti-Semitic feelings. Jews have been *relatively* sheltered because they are white; African Americans are excluded precisely because they are Black.

*

Meaningful distinctions have been drawn between "old European immigrants" and "new European immigrants." The "old" category consists of English, Germans, Scots, Welsh, Irish, Swedes, Danes, Norwegians, Appalachian whites, and Finns. The "new" white immigrants to America's cities are Italian, Polish, Soviet Jewish, Hungarian, Slovak and Czech, Rumanian, Yugoslavian, Greek, and others. The blue collars among these "ethnics"—mostly Catholic and of central, southern, and eastern European origins—form the base for ethnic neo-conservatism in the metropolitan areas of the Northeast and North Central regions. Their impact began in the early 1970s, galvanized, in part, by fears that white job seniority privileges would fall before affirmative action to benefit minorities, and that unemployment would cause competition with Blacks for scarce jobs. Unwillingness to let Black teens attend school with white teens had much to do with it.

In 1990, Congress passed a new immigration statute designed to flood the U.S. with white European aliens and keep out Third World migrants. The Morrison Visa Act established a lottery mechanism through which a disproportionate number of visas are handed out to Europeans. Applicants are no longer required to complete an application form, no longer have to have an offer of employment in the United States, or even pay an initial filing fee. Of the thirty-six countries offered these alleviations, only one is African, Tunisia. Moreover, the majority of immigrants from Tunisia regard themselves as part of the Arab world and express no loyalty to the culture of sub-Saharan Africa. Estimates for the year 1992 pegged the proportion of Morrison Act immigrants coming from tiny Ireland alone at 40 percent. In contrast, not a single nation from Black Africa or the Caribbean was included. The intention is to make immigration from Europe as easy as possible, while preventing the influx of people of color, particularly Blacks. By offering 40,000 additional visas to newcomers on the basis of national origin (read: race) instead of the family relationships and employment prospects which by 1986 had encouraged inflow from the Third World, Congress gave notice that it intends henceforth to pick and chose in favor of white immigrants. The Immigration and Naturalization Service (INS) now lays out the welcome carpet to the relatives of Eastern Europeans, while shunning Africans and Latinos. Not only has it made clear it does not want any Haitian "economic refugees," the door has been slammed even on computer-literate English-speaking Black people. This "make-America-white-again" program qualifies Russians, East Germans, Hungarians, Poles, Croatians, and suchlike immigrants for entry. The cold welcome given Ethiopians and Somalis, in contrast, shows just how much the Black race is "dissed." Dark skin complexion proves beyond doubt in the eyes of the INS that these are either merely "migrants" seeking to take jobs from native-born U.S. citizens and unwilling to weather economic storms in their own country, or rejects from mindless Black-on-Black "tribal warfare" that is alleged to plague all Black nations. Either way, they are spurned as ineligible for entry here. Mexicans and Central Americans are also not welcome these days. How can anyone fail to catch the significance of California's Proposition 187? White

178

Canadians are no better. They too are swift to embrace displaced Croatians and Bosnians but turn their nose up at Somalis and Mozambicans.

All this is understandable, say ethnicity boosters, under the plea that ethnocentrism is a universal phenomenon, expressing nothing more harmful than group pride in cultural accomplishments. Favoring white immigrants is just a way of protecting Judeo-Christian values. All the world's "cultures" regard their own way of life as superior to all others, vow ethnicity racists. The racial status quo is the best defense of the "American way of life."

Poor whites fronted for the new bosses in the post-Bellum South and were the mainstay of Jim Crow until its partial dismantling during the 1960s. Today the role of the old Southern poor whites has been taken over, in large part, by a *racial hierarchy* of occupation based on "ethnicity." The media mask the conflict caused by this policy under the smokescreen of "clashing ethnicities." Of course, there is a hard material bottom line to ethnicity. Its political-economic substratum is a racial hierarchy of jobs, disguised as "ethnic," in which the hardest, most dangerous, least skilled, lowest paid, most dead-end, and least seniority-earning ones go to Blacks, Puerto Ricans, Native Americans, Mexican Americans and other despised racial categories. Middle level industrial, transport, communications, political, academic, and public service positions are occupied usually by "white ethnics," i.e., Jews, Italians, Poles, Greeks, Slovaks, etc. The majority of higher professional, middle management, and junior executive offices remain the privilege mainly of WASP males, seconded by Irish-, German-, Jewish-, and Dutch-descent crews. Despite publicity hoopla, the *Black Enterprise* corporate types rewarded with the key to executive suite toilets are few. The auto industry imported Arab workers and encouraged them to look down upon African Americans. The abilities and potential of workers from different backgrounds are alleged to be sufficiently different to require a distinct "ethno-racial" distribution of labor. Ethnicity theory insists that different races are culturally oriented to different kinds and styles of work.

Occupational and professional specialization bolsters the sense of ethnic exclusiveness. If all the foremen in a shop are, say, Italians or Poles, while most of the assembly workers are Black, consciousness of a white linguistic-ethnic heritage solidifies the occupational bond uniting the foremen. The sense of being white, and of being

Polish or Italian, is counterposed to the racial identity of the Black workmen. White solidarity certainly outweighs any feeling of "shared class interests" with the Black workers. Here membership in one and the same industrial union is of no avail. This has been found to be true of diemakers, electricians, and construction workers. A white collar version of the ethnic specialization syndrome appeared robustly in the American Federation of Teachers, when it was being run by Albert Shanker. A tight corps of Jewish teachers set themselves apart in enmity from Black pupils and their parents. Affirmative action to increase the number or upgrade minority teachers was viewed as a mortal threat. Shanker made "No to Quotas" his banner.

White immigrants who arrived in the 1970s and 1980s worsened conditions for Afro-Americans. Being white, they had no trouble getting citizenship quickly. As newly-hatched voters, they strengthened the conservative side of all issues from abortion to military spending to civil rights. They systematically opposed the rights of Black people. They applauded as the door slammed on Haitian refugees. They cast ballots for the Republican Contract with America and for the likes of Jesse Helms and David Duke. As jurors they exonerated police killers and KKK mass murderers. Eastern European refugees not only competed with African Americans for jobs, but being im America, they were now in a position to live out long-cherished right-wing fantasies. They refused to join unions, pushing instead for a "union-free" environment. They siphoned social service funds away from needy Blacks and Browns. They were coddled and lionized by federal and state governments in the late 1970s and throughout the twelve-year Reagan-Bush *Reich*. They assimilated quickly in the not-so-silent "Moral Majority." White "ethnic" immigrants have made America more right wing and racist than ever, and thus have helped make life that much more hellish for African Americans and other people of color.

In some residual liberal circles Canada still retains a reputation for racial tolerance. The rumor that the country to the north is tolerant comes from a historical comparison with the United States. At one time it was a haven for runaway American slaves. But that went down comparatively easy because until the 1960s there were few Blacks in the country, outside of the province of Nova Scotia. Lynching never became a pastime for white folks in Canada as in the United States. As recently as 1986 Black athletes from the States were astonished that they could date white girls in Toronto and not be looked at weirdly. Even now, after a generation of extensive Third World immigration, Canada's "visible minority" component—a composite of many different peoples of color—is smaller proportionally than the color component in its southern neighbor. Yet throughout the history of the country, Canada's dominant and warring "solitudes," Anglophones and Francophones, have cooperated in at least one form of action: a policy of genocide toward the once-large Native population. Native policy matured over the years, evolving from the crude mass exterminations of the past to the alcohol-drugs-penitentiary-suicide tragedy of the present. As we slide into the new century, treatment of the Aboriginals ranges from segregated reserves to urban unemployment, from neglect and homeless destitution to slick government buyouts of Indian, Innu, and Inuit chiefs, to referendum promises of self-government.

Much the same as Americans, Canadians overvalue white color and are addicted to its privileges. For a long time, Canada's immigration policy was racist exclusionism. And voices yelling "keep Canada white" can still be heard. Recently that policy has been purged, but merely of its most petty and irritating racist stipulations. The callous attitude toward Third World immigrants has made a comeback in recently revised legislation. The new law was applauded by the widely circulating Toronto Sun, a racist tabloid. A limited amnesty program for illegal immigrants, instituted in the 1980s, worked great hardship for many migrants from the Third World. The immigration department has been ordered to single out and deport Black Jamaican criminal code offenders. The crude and unpredictable behavior of immigration law enforcers causes underlying fear in Black, Brown, and Yellow communities. Prejudiced immigration officers operate at every level.

The criminal justice system is little better than the one in the U.S. Canadian police have been known to frame innocent Blacks. The notorious April 1984 case of a 17-year-old Black–Native Indian boy framed in Hamilton, Ontario, for second degree murder by two white officers and exonerated only at the cost to his father of $5,000 to hire a private detective, is merely one case of its kind.

Similar attitudes reign in the white regimes south of the Rio Grande. Brazil and Venezuela enforce immigration rules which check Africanization and strengthen white supremacy. Post–World War II migration from Europe to Venezuela has slowed the long-standing tendency in the country toward racial mixing. A gradual-

ly darkening population of Afro-Spanish and American Indian elements has been deliberately whitened with the injection of immigrants from Europe. Abdias do Nascimento has demonstrated that
the Brazilian government, faced with the western hemisphere's
largest Black population, has always sought to "de-Africanize" the
country. After 1945 the European influx into Brazil was thrown into
even higher gear (Nascimento 1979).

*

White feminism has fed off the techniques, struggles, and gains of the
civil rights movement in a manner similar to the way white "ethnic"
immigrants have fed on social service funds earmarked for Black people. Upwardly mobile white feminists have no intention of sharing
their good fortune with racial minorities—particularly not with Black
men. Middle class white feminists have had their way, both ways. They
hijacked the principle of gender equality, conveniently forsaking their
suffering Black and Latino "sisters." At the same time the feminists
manoeuvered to snare the 1964 Civil Rights Act, legislation extorted
from Congress at the cost of much suffering to Black men and women.
Title VII in the Act was framed in the hope of lessening racial discrimination in hiring and job promotion. It was preempted by white
feminists. Affirmative action programs and equal employment
enforcement entitlements were shifted off target to the benefit of middle class white women. Preferential settlements and compensations
went mainly to white females instead of Blacks. The Black community was hung out to dry as the employment prospects of Black males
deteriorated, while white females filled jobs that civil rights activists
thought would go to our people. The Black family was devastated as
a gender-equality interpretation of Title VII made white women the
principal beneficiaries. The fact that the median income of Black
women as a percentage of the income of Black men rose from 47 percent to 62 percent from 1969 to 1983, while the median income of
white women as a percentage of that of white men climbed only from
32 percent to 42 percent during the same period, is not a measure of
progress for Black women. Rather it is a gauge of the relative impoverishment of Black males in the U.S. economy (Jaynes and Williams
1989:536).

Feminism has done nothing to reduce the disparity in well-being
between Black and white women. Black women bear heavier child-
rearing, job, and family burdens, yet in 1989 had to get by on medi-

182

an annual earnings of $17,389 (full time, year-round employment), compared with $18,922 taken in by white women. African American women are much more likely to be restricted to low wage jobs than white women (P. King 1992:60).

White feminism has provided the excuse for both conventional politicians and radical activists to ignore and overlook the Black Liberation Movement, shoving it aside as "outdated," or as having "achieved its goals," or as representing only, say, a "15 percent minority," while women (white) constitute more than half the total population! White feminists have made low-down attacks on Black male fighters for liberation and equality under the pretense that militant Black men are sexist. An equally bewildering distraction has been the attempt to elevate the Gay-Lesbian movement to an urgency and legitimacy equal to the historic Black struggle. Suddenly more attention is given to narrow issues like the validity of same-sex marriage than to the persistence of racism.

These are the cynical doings of the racist media. In creating diversionary and demeaning smokescreens, these ideological institutions perform their social function. Calls for measures to protect "innocent" whites, or appeals against programs that "fight discrimination by discriminating," and against a so-called "racial spoils system," all in some way strike a responsive chord among white radical feminists, Gays, environmentalists, consumer advocates, libertarians, uncategorized leftists, housewives and retirees—all of whom feel alienated from and injured by conventional morality, or by the status quo and "big government." These groups worship "community control" and decentralization and cling to popular sovereignty (but so too did the slaveholding Jeffersonian democrats of the nineteenth century). For them, choice in the matter of abortion, sexual harassment, and the normalization of homosexuality overshadow all other issues. Since the real enemies, as they see it, are stone-hearted politicians, bigots, arms dealers, polluters, and militarists, "reform" for these elements means direct government, recall of legislators, democratized elections, abortion rights, popular courts, homosexual equality, and ERA amendment of the Constitution.

These slogans and diversionary trends are devices whereby whites, males and females, increase their "awareness" of their special material interests, interests supposedly threatened by the minority demands for redress. They serve to galvanize dissimilar groups of white people to defend one form or another of white skin privilege.

Chapter 11

THE PERSISTENCE OF RACIST TERRORISM

European civilization is violent, sanguinary, and cruel. Terrorism is one of its essential traits. American whites are among the worst of Europeans in this respect. The lynching of Blacks and other people of color stained the history of the Republic from its beginnings and, while now infrequent, has occurred recently in locales as distant from one another as New York, Chicago, Portland, and Los Angeles. We, sons and daughters of captive Africans, of brutalized slaves, should know that at any moment any one of us can still be hit by racially-motivated violence. White racist America is the product of one of the greatest crimes of violence in history, the genocide of an entire indigenous people, and is maintained by the most powerful machine of repression in the world today. There are white men in America who still want to terrorize the African in America.

Violent by the very nature of the act which constituted it, white collective mentality appreciates nothing so much as violence and terror. In North America the white man's proven instinctive response to any "problem" involving people of color is violence. Violence has served him well despite lip-service to "peaceful dialogue," "democratic process," and the "balancing of conflicting interests." The white man's preferred means of dialogue remains the billy club, the gun, the police dog, and tear gas. It is because he is a bully that he fears nothing so much as counter-violence, the threat of retaliation. This is the reason white neighborhoods ringing metropolitan areas periodically suffer spasms of hysteria. In fevered imaginings, Black counter-terrorism will one day open the same gaping wounds in the bodies of white people that have been inflicted on Black families for generations.

We have already demonstrated that institutionalized violence has an economic rationale as one of the social elements which preserves white wealth. Not only is the terrorism which has maintained its grip throughout the twentieth century instituionalized, it is sadistic. The *sado-racist* temperament was displayed—merely one example among thousands—by the gang of whites who lynched Mary Turner, a Black woman late in pregnancy, in Valdosta, Georgia in 1918. Noticing that she was heavy with child, the brutes ripped open her abdomen to pull out the unborn child. They stomped it to death. That same savagery can be found today. The LAPD patrolmen who assaulted Rodney King are spiritual descendants of the Valdosta ogres. During the month of April 1991, a dozen Los Angeles precinct stations received circulars from the KKK offering membership to white officers, presumably in celebration of the scourging of Rodney King. No one knows how many of the Department's white officers were secret members of the Klan during Daryl Gates' tenure as chief of police. We know that for years the Klan has maintained a very active Klavern in San Diego, including naval personnel along with police officers. It is also known that white prison guards have been recruited by the KKK throughout the length and breadth of the land.

Lynching, in one form or another, was once regarded almost as the divine right of the American white man. The lynching tradition is alive today in altered form—mainly as police violence against Blacks. But before we turn to its present police incarnation, we need be cognizant that the unalloyed form is still around.

There are many examples, past and present, from which to

choose. In 1982, two Klansmen invaded the Waco, Georgia, home of Peggy Jo French, a 44-year old white woman, mother of two teenagers. French's children were known to associate with Black youngsters on equal terms. For permitting this racial indiscretion, the mother was flogged with a leather strap. The very next year, in the same state, four Klansmen broke into the Tallapoosa home of Warren Cokley, a Black man, and his wife Peggy, a white woman. Enraged that a white woman would "pollute white blood," the hooded thugs terrorized and tried to murder the interracial couple. Cokley suffered a fractured skull. Fortunately, he was able to save himself and his wife, defending himself with a pocket knife. In 1984, the Greensboro, N.C. massacre revealed white Cuban immigrant support for the Ku Klux Klan. Nine Klan and Nazi confederates slaughtered a group of civil rights advocates in broad daylight, in full view of the public. Among the casualties shot through the head was Susan, the wife of Mark Smith, a noted Black activist. The assassins were brought to trial, charged with murder. The all-white jury was headed by a Cuban refugee foreman who used his authority to extort an acquittal. Unable to reverse the Cuban Revolution, the *Gusano* vented his hatred on U.S. Blacks, uttering the conviction that the Klan is a "patriotic" organization with the right to "defend" itself against "communists." The Greensboro massacre was a contemporary lynching, exonerated by the judicial system. The thugs faced a second sham trial, this time in federal court, charged with having "violated the civil rights" of those murdered. Once again an all-white jury was selected and once again the Klan-Nazi assassins got off scot free. As if to add insult to injury, the second acquittal came in April 1984, full steam in Jesse Jackson's first Democratic Party presidential nomination campaign. The ringleader jeered that he would celebrate his release with three beers and a weekend Klan meeting. He had made his point—as late as 1984 a Black person still had no rights which a Klansman need respect—not even the right to life itself.

And much the same held true in Spring 1991. In Long Island, New York, a group of white boys attended a youth gathering. As the party ended, they spied a Black lad chatting with a white girl, an old friend. The white boys objected, their racial jealousy aroused. In a wink, a lynch mob was thrown together to "get" the Black youth. He was set upon with baseball bats and sticks and beaten into a coma. Three white youths, including the girl to whom the victim had spoken, suffered injury when they came to his defense

(*Amsterdam News*, 8 June 1991). A similar outrage coccurred in the Pacific Northwest in 1992, this time involving Oregon skinheads. A vicious beating on a street in Portland's Black district left an African American man unconscious with skull fracture. The victim and a Black co-worker at the University Hospital had been the prey of a carefully laid ambush. As they walked the street, two white women called to them from across the road. When they approached the women, one of them assaulted the Black men and gave a signal to two white men hiding in bushes nearby. Shouting death threats and racial slurs, the assailants attacked their unprepared and unarmed victims with bats or sticks. The assailants, male and female, were known white supremacists, and the women held the injured man's arms during the beating. Police officers who arrived on the scene did nothing to assist the stricken Black man, neglecting to check his vital signs or cover him as he lay unconscious, and only one of the attackers was arrested. This outrage followed upon the Portland murder of an Ethiopian exchange student, clubbed to death by racist skinheads in 1988, and the Aryan Nations proclamation of the Pacific Northwest as a future all-white enclave, forbidden to people of color.

The Klan struck North Carolina during the summer of 1992. The Invisible Empire instigated a wave of racial terror set off in retaliation for Black men dating white women. In the worst atrocity a Black murder victim was found castrated with his penis stuffed in his mouth. Later, one Rickey Knight was found guilty of the castration and stabbing. Three other white men aided him in the assault. During a single year—1992—the number of white supremacist groups in the U.S. soared from 273 to 346. The Christian Identity Movement—a white supremacy group—stepped up its activity in 1993, as did the organization entitled National Socialist Skinheads of America. A terrorist campaign against the NAACP brought the bombing of two of the organization's West Coast branches—Sacramento, California, and Tacoma, Washington—within a single week.

*

The modern industrial way of life is a culture of cities, and urban clashes between Blacks and whites are a permanent fixture of the U.S. landscape. The span between 1913 and 1963 recorded 72 major "race riots." A few were Black insurrections for emancipation, local in character. The 1906 Brownsville and the 1917 Houston rebellions by Black soldiers were blows struck for liberty, and they were retaliatory. In contrast, those horrors during the first half of the twentieth century, termed "race riots" by the white media, were in reality indiscriminate slaughter of blameless Black people. There is little reason to believe that similar outbursts of murderous white paranoia may not yet recur.

Throughout the "Teens" and "Roaring Twenties", as policemen invaded the newly-sprung ghettoes to "police" the Black masses, they could count on the enthusiastic, if occasional, support of white civilian rioters, ready to spill Black blood indiscriminately. Any pretext served to set them off—housing disputes, use of lakefront beaches, the right to occupy a park bench.... Yet the gory white race riots of East St. Louis in 1917, Chicago in 1919, and Detroit in 1943 shared a significant economic dimension. They were staged to kill off Black workers who were competing too fiercely with white laborers for industrial jobs. Competition for scarce housing, leisure facilities, and health care and educational resources added fuel to white hatred.

The very same urges drive white vigilantes in metropolitan areas today. Italian Americans seem particularly prone to mob attacks on Blacks. Like New York City and Buffalo, the Chicago area is notorious for Italian hostility. As recently as summer 1990, when four African Americans had the bad fortune to seek service in an Italian-owned and -frequented bar in a Cook County Bridgeport suburb, they ran smack into a fury. Not only were they denied service, they were insulted and assaulted. Bar owner, employees and patrons all joined together in threatening their life. The victims were shot at, beaten, thrown into the street, and their car was trashed before they escaped.

The next summer it was a mob of Pennsylvania toughs. Some 500 white supremacists attacked 15 to 20 youngsters, most of whom were Black male youths under 25. The locale was Hanover, a town of 14,000 in southeastern Pennsylvania, near the Mason-Dixon Line. The Black youths used the town square for summer weekend evening meetings with their white girl friends—young women in their late teens and early twenties. Predominantly white, Hanover is located in an area which Black novelist David Bradley identified in *The Chaneysville Incident* as having always been a hotbed of Jim Crow. Hanover whites hate Blacks in general. But they were particularly incensed at the sight of miscegenation between Black men and white females. Long-standing fears of impending racial defeat were aroused. This triggered the old contention that any white woman romantically connected with a Black man is not merely a "traitor to her race," but loose in morals. Such a woman "ruins her reputation" and is "perverted" by sexual traffic with Blacks. She is "spoiled" forever for white men. The young people converged from neighboring towns which have Black dwellers. To force them out, Hanover residents recruited the aid of white motorcycle gangs. When the Black youths defended themselves, white policemen, until then passive onlookers, intervened to arrest and rough up the victims of the racist assault.

The baseball bat murder of a 22-year old Black man at the hands of five white youths prompted a grim *New York Amsterdam News* editorial which posed the question whether the majority of whites in this country harbored the secret desire to exterminate the Black citizens, concluding that "until that is answered....there will be no peace for us, so we might as well prepare for the fight that has always been here, but has been glossed over for all these years under the misconception that we shall overcome someday.... It must be a promise that there will be no peace without justice."

•

An old adage says that more Black people have been maimed and murdered by the haphazard acts of individual white folks than in all the race riots and lynchings combined. Much of the actual physical violence against Black people in the South from, say, 1945 to, say, 1965 was perpetrated by owners, managers, and employees of low-wage industries acting alone, and by the solitary initiative of small towners and rural planters. One such incident in Abbeville, Alabama, in 1944, had the humdrum aspect of everyday occurrence. Bored, and finding nothing more diverting, six young white men casually raped a 22 year old mother, wife to a Black GI. The crime was reported merely as confirmation of "white male supremacy, black female degradation" (*Claude A. Barnett Papers,* 10 December 1944). Such outrages were exceeded, as a matter of course, by the atrocities of thousands of redneck sheriffs and deputies, state troopers, and the other KKK police agents who stalked the region.

And individual spur-of-the-moment terrorism remains very much up to date. A case in point: Tampa Bay, Florida, 25 March 1983. Two young racists become incensed at the sight of two Black men, 24 and 26, in friendly conversation with two young white women in a Wag's restaurant. The women were close friends of the wife of one of the Black men. Storming into the restaurant, the more rabid of the two rednecks brandished a ten-inch hunting knife in full view of patrons and spewed slurs about interracial, mixed-sex groups, loudly promising his accomplice that he would kill the Black men —a clear case of premeditation. He insisted that interracial couples should be banned from the public, and certainly not permitted to enter restaurants together. The Black men parted company with the young women and drove away together. The "good old boys" stalked them in a white pick-up. Overtaken on the open highway, one of the Black youths was shot dead, the other wounded by a bullet fired from a 10-inch-barrelled 44 magnum. The justice meted out by Florida's juridical system? Sentenced to six months imprisonment in October 1983, the accomplice walked away a free man in April 1984. In a state noted for its stubborn upholding of capital punishment (33 inmates executed from 1976 to 1994), this killer stood convicted of nothing more serious than second degree murder, because the all-white jury could not be persuaded to blame one of their own for premeditation, and because presiding Judge Dennis Alvarez would not countenance the death penalty for a white man guilty merely of the removal of a Black man who "fooled around with white women."

If such individual-initiative violence against Blacks has appeared to tail off somewhat in the South since the mid-1960s, it is merely because whites with mayhem in mind fear that today's Black folks will retaliate with equal violence. Even so, individual attacks continue across the South. On 20 November 1989, the Southeastern Regional Director of the NAACP reported a rising tide of racist terrorism throughout the region, including physical assaults and cross burnings. He found a "very great and vehement resurgence of racial incidents in the South... We're still putting out fires," he lamented, "still fighting the old battles over and over again, not because we want to, but because there's no choice."

*

Police brutality is an even greater commonplace. Arguably, *police misconduct* —more inclusive term than brutality—has become the main, institutionalized aspect of racist terrorism. In many environs the main concern of local government is curtailment of African American residents, a mission for which white police forces have been militarized. The process began in the wake of the civil rights turmoil and accelerated through the 1970s and 1980s. By now it is difficult to distinguish city patrolmen in radio cars, county sheriffs, state troppers, even FBI agents, from the regular army. Least of all in armament. Already heavily armed, the police are constantly upgrading weaponry. They train in military-type crowd control, pre-plan anti-insurgency tactics, and are commanded, in many instances, by determined, sadistic, and unshakeably racist leaders. Daryl Gates was no mistake; nor was he as untypical of other white chiefs as made out to be. Tactically prepared and ever on the alert, many police officers are conscious enough of their own interests to be devoted to the preservation of white supremacy. Few white officers reside among the Black and African-Latino inner city inhabitants they police, and many now feel threatened by hiring procedures designed to increase minority representation on the force. Feeling their own longevity and promotion prospects jeopardized, and resentful that their sons, nephews, and cronies' offspring will no longer be allowed to monop-olize police employment, more than a few rank-and-file white offi-cers hate and distrust people of color. They become anti-crime fanatics. Hellbent on mastering the "mean streets," white officers assigned to cruiser patrol are the worst of all. "Weed and seed" pro-posals have legitimized police-state sweeps, and since the Los Angeles rebellion of 1992 special instruction in "riot control" has stepped up. So has Gestapo-like "preventive infiltration."

Even the briefest outline of the history of white police brutality in the twentieth century confirms the tendency. Police officers led the way in slaughtering Blacks during the Atlanta riot of 1906 (Shapiro 1988:96-103). In the *Crisis* in November 1911,W.E.B. DuBois denounced the rash of police killings of Blacks in the South. During the 1920s, police brutality grew so severe in New York City that Black women picketed police headquarters in Brooklyn on behalf of their tortured menfolk. In 1928, Florida cops went on a rampage that caused Black fatalities. The 1930s began with the Wickersham Commission's general condemnation of the whole sys-tem of police terror, and of the racism in the courts. The situation grew worse, typified by police atrocities against persons allegedly involved in the Harlem uprising in 1943. During World War II, white police vented their rage on Black GIs. Early in September 1942 cops set upon and beat a Black army nurse assigned to a Montgomery, Alabama, military unit hospital. She was singled out because she was a commissioned officer—a lieutenant—and because she was attached to the 99th Pursuit Squadron (later to become the famed 99th Fighter Squadron)—the renowned Black air corps pilots' training base stationed in Tuskegee. Four policemen beat her in a patrol car after she had been dragged from a bus. They aimed to teach her a "lesson." They did not want a "Negro" woman to think she could "get above herself" because she had achieved officer ranking. The police also stole one hundred dollars from her, and to top it off, charged the battered nurse with disorderly conduct. It was said that their action had been incited by racist utterances against Black servicemen by Alabama Governor Dixon (*Claude Barnett Papers*, 10 September 1942).

The Kerner Commission report, published in March 1968, exposed a national pattern of white police brutality and admitted to the world that the United States was, in truth, "two nations"—one white, policed benignly with respect for human rights; the other Black, a police state, the scene of extreme cruelties.

*

If anything, the police campaign against Black and other citizens of color is more intense now than ever. The nation's largest city—New York—houses the largest population of Blacks in all of North America. The chronicle of racist bestiality by police officers in the five boroughs is correspondingly long. It ranges from stun gunning in Queens to the pointblank shotgunning of Eleanor Bumpus—an elderly Black woman—in her own home to the beating and killing of Mary Mitchell by a white police officer called to calm a domestic dispute. New York's "finest" slew Richard Luke in Manhattan, put Stephen Kelly to death in Queens, sexually abused a Black woman elsewhere in the city, and beat Anthony Byrd to a pulp after he called for help when he was mugged. White cops on stakeout in Queens "mistook" an innocent Black woman for someone else, smashed a car window to get at her, dragged her out and pummelled her bloody. In Brooklyn, four policemen beat an unarmed Dominican in his own bedroom and then shot him to death. His crime? He was suffering mental illness.

Incidents in the rest of the country and in Canada reveal the same pattern. A Black female spectator watching a marathon race was slapped by a white officer, knocked down, and stomped. In two separate altercations in 1992, New Jersey police summarily executed three Black teenage boys suspected of weaponless auto theft. Since the mid-1980s the Twin City area of St. Paul and Minneapolis has witnessed a rash of brutal attacks on Blacks. In Los Angeles, a few years back, Don Jackson, a Black former LAPD officer, sought to obtain visual evidence of the mistreatment of Blacks and Chicanos. For his efforts white officers smashed his head through a plate glass window and then charged him with damaging property and resisting arrest. In 1984 a series of unprovoked police killings caused African American community organizations to demonstrate against the Indianapolis police department. In 1992 Las Vegas police borrowed armored personnel carriers from a U.S. Air Force base and used them to disrupt developing Black unity between local chapters of the Bloods and the Crips youth gangs. Police, armed with grenades and tear gas, broke up truce picnics and then proceeded to attack any gathering of three or more Black persons. Passersby in the Black-populated West Side were randomly stopped and harassed. These are merely a handful of hundreds of lethal incidents, the tip of the iceberg, as it were.

North of the border, metropolitan Toronto police welcomed the 1990s with a series of shootings of unarmed Blacks. Ontario's "white justice" courts then cleared the officers of all charges. In November 1990 a white constable was acquitted of manslaughter in the death of a Black man shot in his own home. In July 1991 the courts freed a policeman guilty of shooting and wounding a young Black woman. She was blameless of wrongdoing, sitting peacefully in a car pulled over for a routine check. In October 1991 a constable got off scot free despite firing three shots and killing an unarmed Black teenager whose car was involved in a traffic altercation. The April 1992 acquittal of two police officers in the shooting death of a 17-year-old Black youth triggered a storm of protest in Metro Toronto's Black Community.

There is, in fact, a long-standing tradition of racism in Canada which began several centuries ago with the genocide of the Native Peoples. It continues today in institutionalized practices of exclusion and the relegation of Canadian Indians to reservations, where they are demoralized and mistreated. In June 1991 a Montreal SWAT team slew a Black man, shooting him in the forehead. His family were Haitian immigrants. The victim was unarmed, without criminal record and completely innocent of any felony. He was assassinated under the age-old pretext that all Blacks look alike. The

Quebec cops claimed to be searching for two Black suspects who, it turned out, bore absolutely no physical resemblance to the slain man—except for the key one: they were Black. Though the victim was gunned down in cold blood, the Quebec Public Prosecutor's office ducked criminal charges against the SWAT team.

The savage assault on Rodney King, videotaped and rerun on screens world-wide, has been too publicized to require much commentary—except to emphasize that the beating was no "anomaly" or "aberration," as police apologists claim. It strayed from the norm only in that it sparked fight-back protests from organizations ranging from the NAACP, Urban League, and SCLC to the Mexican American Political Association, Justice for Janitors, and the American Civil Liberties Union; only in that it inspired a Los Angeles charter reform giving the mayor and city council more power over the chief of police; only in that it forced Police Chief Daryl Gates from office, and only in that it triggered the massive Los Angeles rebellion in the aftermath of the court exoneration of the guilty officers. The Rodney King incident deviated from the norm also only in that the police have "cottoned" on to the fact that community activists monitor and record their behavior in the streets. They do not like that any more than they could stand the surveillance of their activities mounted by the Black Panthers back in the 1960s. They have now taken to threatening persons who film their activities, pretending that monitoring citizens are criminals. They are on guard against any civilian armed with a camcorder. The cops destroy the cameras, claiming that they interfere with police procedure. New operational procedures have been adopted: while one set of policemen set upon some victim, their backup team scrutinizes the windows of surrounding buildings and nearby cars, in the hope of catching someone filming.

Early in November 1992 in Detroit two on-duty veteran white plainclothes officers—Larry Nevers and Walter Budzyn—with a reputation for being "tough guys" and known for disliking Blacks, decided to emulate the attack on Rodney King. Only they went further, they killed their victim. 35-year old Malice Wayne Green was pounded to death with a police flashlight as he sat in his car, beaten "down like a dog," according to a witness. Green had no criminal record, and his vehicle was stopped for no good reason, other than the usual custom of harassing Black male drivers. Five other police officers stood calmly by and watched the assault without intervening. Green died in the emergency room of multiple blunt traumas to the head. One of the guilty officers was a veteran of the STRESS police unit which terrorized Detroit Blacks during the 1970s, before Mayor Coleman Young called a halt. Affecting a macho "Starsky-and-Hutch" style, both men were notorious for their acts of police brutality over the years.

*

There is a clear ideological side to the misconduct of white policemen. On one occasion within recent memory, 10,000 drunken white cops—half the New York City police force—staged a white power rally, deliberately incited by the Police Benevolent Association and by the white politician, Rudy Giuliani, who had his eyes on the mayoral office. Streaming from the rally, the white officers rioted and stormed city hall. The action took place on 16 September 1992. They were enraged by efforts to establish an all-Civilian Complaint Review Board to curb police brutality against Blacks and Latinos. The infuriated cops screamed racist epitheths, attacking Mayor Dinkins as a "nigger" who had "shown his color." Their manner was crude, in accordance with the rough and inarticulate temperament of white policemen. But there was no mistaking their political statement.

A similar statement was made by white police officers of Queens, N.Y.'s 113th precinct, as they unleashed racial attacks on Black police officers. White cops hate Black and Afro-Latino officers, particularly those who organize in caucuses to protect their rights. In November 1992 Derwin Pannell, a Black New York undercover officer, was riddled with 21 shots by white police who excused themselves, claiming that Pannell looked like a holdup man or a mugger. Whites wondered what all the fuss was about, for what happened to Pannell was an occupational hazard. Undercover work is dangerous for Black officers, for it is the normal presumption of white cops that *all* Black and Latino males are criminals. The trigger-happy officers were sent off to undergo "sensitivity training." The prototypical white policeman simply does not believe that Black men should be allowed to join the force, and he loathes and resents those who have succeeded in becoming police officers. Even when a Black officer rises to high rank, jealous white cops still regard him as a "jumped-up nigger," and long for opportunities to be disrespectful. Something along these lines was brought home "in living color" in

1991 to a Black New York police chief, at that time Gotham's highest ranking uniformed police officer. In civilian clothing and on his way home, he was pulled over by two white officers in Queens. He was harassed in the fashion Black drivers are routinely harassed by white police, warned, and addressed disrespectfully as "Homey" by the pair who obviously did not recognize him. After all, since this Black man was at the wheel of a Jaguar, what else could he be but a drug dealer or some other kind of criminal?

The real deal is a serious lack of white police solidarity with Black and Brown officers. The Guardians Association—a fraternity of Afro-American police officers—came into being not just in protest against white police misconduct toward Black civilians, but more likely primarily because Black police themselves badly needed protection against their white peers. On the night of 2 May 1992, a Saturday, the Black and Latino rebellion was still going on in Los Angeles. The LAPD were whimpering about being "overwhelmed." White police constables in Metro Toronto chose that moment to voice their sympathy with their brother officers in Los Angeles. This solidarity was expressed in a predictable fashion—a Toronto cop shot a Black man dead. In time-honored fashion, the killing was passed off as justifiable defense against a felon who "lunged" with a knife. As a matter of fact, the 22-year old victim was unarmed. A few days previous to the killing, a large group of white Toronto police had gathered in a bar to cheer the Simi Valley jury's acquittal of Rodney King's assailants.

These provocations proved too much even for Toronto's long-suffering Black community. Young Blacks exploded on the night of 4 May 1992. To protest against the chain of police killings, and to show solidarity with the Los Angeles insurgents, they trashed establishments along Yonge Street (Toronto's main hub), blocked traffic at a main intersection, and attacked city hall. The night rang with the noise of running battles with the police riot force.

During the months that followed, a shaken social-democratic-leaning Ontario Provincial Government initiated a mild reform designed to curb police harassment and killing of Black people. Police officers were asked merely to submit a written report each time one drew a firearm against a member of the public. All across Ontario white policemen threw a fascistic tantrum. The new regulation was a slap on the wrist, a minor irritant—it takes only a couple of minutes to check blanks on a standardized form. Each report would be destroyed after thirty days, and the timid government promised not to bring charges against trigger-happy cops. The faint-heartedness of the reform did not deter the police. Commanded by a KKK-sounding police union boss, the white rank and file of the metropolitan Toronto force retaliated. They blackmailed the government, defiantly removing their badges to prevent identification. They refused to issue summonses for traffic violations, thereby depriving the Ontario government of millions in revenue. Unruly cops embarassed the Ontario Premier (head of government) at a Skydome stadium ceremony, shouting him down as a "nigger-lover" and hurling anti-Semitic barbs at him and his family. There was widespread support for this misconduct by other police forces elsewhere in the province.

In Canada as in the United States, when criticized, police spokesmen focus ire on high-profile leaders of the Black protest movement. Militant activists are singled out for persecution because, quite simply, the "men in blue" are convinced that Black people are too stupid to do anything without being masterminded from outside. That we are unable to act without the incitement of "agitators." They always believe that conspiracy and evil geniuses are behind any protest. The motto is: "Get the head nigger-in-charge and all the other coons will fall in line."

According to mainstream political science, there is a theoretical difference between the roles of the police and the armed forces. Theory says that the armed forces and the domestic police are designed to serve different ends. The duty of the various federal, state, county, and municipal forces is to hold down the ghettoes and barrios, i.e., to crush the "home folks" whenever the government deems it necessary. This is accomplished on a daily basis through routine police work. In contrast, the military establishment is supposed to carry out the corporate-military oligarchy's foreign adventures and defend its neo-colonial empire abroad. According to some minds, this basic division of labor is axiomatic. Nevertheless, as we have seen most recently in Los Angeles, the National Guard and regular troops are often called out to put down Black insurrections in the streets of America's cities.

This seeming clash between theory and practice has raised questions in the minds of some activists. Does this function signify that the armed services are closer to people of color and more sensitive to social movements than the police? Since its recruits over-represent the nation's minorities, does this mean that the armed forces' composition makes it more sympathetic to people of color than the police? On available evidence this does not seem to be the case.

*

These speculations need not distract us from the fact that anti-Black conservatism would reduce government—federal, state, county and municipal—to four essentials: *a)* military, *b)* police, *c)* courts, and *d)* penitentiaries. In the racist utopia, tax revenues would defray these expenditures. All other services—barring none—would be privatized and would benefit whites alone, along with a handful of affluent minorities able to pay for them. In this best-of-all-possible worlds for right-wing racists, people of color would face unmitigated terrorism. The official arsenal—armed services and police establishment—would be supplemented with an array of white voluntary legionnaire-type organizations and hard-hat super-patriotic squads—veterans and youth paramilitary associations, fascist survivalists, NRA gun clubs, ethnic neighborhood vigilante detachments, suburban defense leagues. The scope of the repression in the 1992 Los Angeles uprising is only a foretaste of what is to come, if hard-core racists have their way. Likewise, the paramilitary deployment to crush the Washington Heights uprising in July of the same year is a harbinger of a severe new form of "law and order" containment. Recurring urban rebellions would be met with concentration camps. The incarcerated would be subject to a forced labor regime reminiscent of the slave plantations.

Ultimate white terror would pass laws creating obstacles to Black ownership of real estate—buildings or land. Not that it has ever really disappeared, but the old educational segregation would be revived in absolute form, north and east as well as south and west. At the height of urban disturbances, Black and Latino children might be refused any instruction beyond primary school, under the pretext that the security problems involved in managing rebellious minority teenagers would overwhelm the high schools. Emergency restrictions such as those enforced during the Los Angeles uprising—requiring Blacks and Browns to show identity papers and imposing curfews— would likely be transformed into permanent legislation to limit minority freedom of movement. Command centers would be staged in Black and Latino districts. There would be rigid control over travel from place to place. The more nervous local authorities might lobby for rules requiring Black males in certain age groups to get special authorization to drive a motor vehicle. Ostensibly to protect public places from drug dealings and criminal activities, we might expect to see Black people refused entry into certain theatres, movie houses, libraries, and other cultural facilities. We could expect the stationing of Drug Enforcement Agency emergency squads. After all, Ross Perot suggested that the Black section of Dallas be cordoned off in search of guns and drugs and subjected to dragnets, house-to-house searches without special warrants, and wiretaps. Blacks might even be ousted from managerial positions and from opinion-forming posts in press and broadcast media and other jobs involving direction and responsibility. There could even be a move to make all African American residents register with the city police. The computer technology is available. At the age of puberty, residents of the inner city would be issued a special identity card. Not having it upon one's person when questioned by police would constitute a violation. The HUD Secretary's "war against drugs" in 1990 included a proposal to raise barbed-wire fences around minority housing projects.

One catches a whiff of apartheid South Africa's former Pass Laws. "Drug war" crackdowns are one phase of the psychological campaign to create a consciousness among white Americans that the Black community is a criminal community. A second phase is to create this feeling among Blacks ourselves—a new form of the traditional tactic of teaching us to despise ourselves. Before he left office, President Bush floated a "Weed and Seed" program, promising lavish funds to urban areas to weed out the "criminal element," supposedly as part of the fight against drugs, but really to root out rebellious minority youths before they develop political impact. The "no-knock-kick-the-door-down" policy is premised on police mobilization and concerted forays in "troubled neighborhoods" during which constitutional safeguards are ignored when Black residencies are the target. Militarized counter-insurgency programs have been crafted for the urban inner cities in the wake of the Los Angeles rebellion.

This is the background against which racist populists having taken to preaching white *jihad* in the 1990s. The events in South-Central L.A. prompted white supremacists based in faraway New York State and North Carolina to screech that "racial holy war" is upon us. They screamed for "total white unification." In anticipation of the "day of rage," each and every white family should arm itself. Conventional white professionals shed crocodile tears over the loss of any chance for "racial harmony," but basically blamed Black indiscipline and pushiness for the creation of a "great wall of silent rage within the white community." It is Black militancy, they lamented, which makes it impossible for whites to talk honestly with Black people. Whites have become adept, it seems, at "politically correct" mouthings in public, keeping their true feelings for whispers behind the backs of Blacks. When pressed, these sources admit that ordinary whites have no empathy, compassion, or sympathy for African Americans (*New York Amsterdam News*, 9 May 1992).

Black neo-conservatives close their mind to these warnings and certain veterans of the non-violent civil rights struggle will not allow themselves to believe, on ethical grounds, that white America has evil intent towards Black folk. Both groups have a difficult time facing up to the *indiscriminate* nature of white racist violence throughout history. They pray that white America will not make all Blacks collectively responsible for the misdeeds of an "underclass," branded as "criminals" by the media. These persons forget that when white slavers unloaded African "cattle" from dank, filthy slave ships, enslaved us on plantations for a quarter of a millenium, segregated, raped, castrated, tortured, and lynched us for a hundred more years, these actions were directed against the *whole* of our people, and not against a minority. Hence they cannot see that white repression is again descending on the whole community.

*

White racism has modernized the ancient *Fear Principle* upon which Western civilization has always based its dealings with Black people. The slavery economy was ruled by it. Raw physical coercion exacted slave labor, and individual Blacks were tortured and mutilated in full view, in order to intimidate and cow the entire community of slaves. Contemporary white world supremacy is footed on a *Terror Principle*, a transmuted form of the old plantation fear principle. In subtle and not-so-subtle ways, present-day Blacks are systematically terrorized, as are other people of color. We are conditioned to fear imprisonment, to fear being beaten to a pulp by white policemen, to fear sudden, unprovoked skinhead and redneck attacks, to fear loss of employment, to fear that our homes and other material possessions will be attacked and destroyed, or repossessed. We are conditioned to fear crime in our own streets, conditioned to turn our frustration and rage against others like ourselves, accustomed to being the victims of Black-on-Black violence. We fear getting sick without health-care protection, we fear loss of standing, we fear loss of reputation, and we fear ridicule. Ultimately, the white man holds the threat of death over Black people. His endmost trump is the police and military one. We know it, he knows it, and he wants us to know it. Should the need arise, he will try to impose his will by wiping Black America out.

The theory of the colonial origins of racism concluded that color prejudice was most rabid where white domination was most unstable and weak (see Jordan,1974). Be that as it may, white supremacy has great psychological reserves. The white man may no longer be able to rape Black women wholesale and lynch Black men at will, as he could then. He is still able to call on a kind of psychological rape, however, which compels some Black people to regard themselves as handmaidens of the "American Dream," or to shout that behaving in such a manner as to be a "credit to the race" will somehow lessen the sting of white whims and interests. We have all seen in the last little while how a band of Black "affirmative-action-baby" academics, claiming Booker T. Washington as their mentor, earn for themselves what Derrick Bell has aptly termed "enhanced racial standing." They embrace the idea that the chaos and pain endured by our people result from our own incapacity, indiscipline, and lack of morals—the bogus idea that we ourselves are our sole enemy. Constant exposure on the streets of North America to the arbitrary violence of white men in police uniform makes it difficult to overcome this syndrome.

*

Andrew Hacker, political science professor and author of *Two Nations: Black and White, Separate, Hostile, Unequal*, is one white man who knows his own folks. The whole apparatus of Black inferiority, he insists, is fuelled still by white male fear—fear of potentially rebellious Black males. In *Two Nations*, he explains that in their heart-of-hearts, white folks are convinced that very few Black men can be conned into playing by Western society's rules. While they suspect that Black women revere these values no more than their men, whites fear women less than men and are more willing to tolerate Black women than Black men. There is nothing new about this preference, and of course it fosters white interests. White middle class males have grown progressively effete, Hacker observes. This in turn breeds jealousy of Black men, envied for their physical virility. Hacker terms this the "Mike Tyson Notion," saying that white men fear that, given the chance, Black men are powerful enough to rip them limb from limb. Jealous frustration turns into murderous aggression—played out most times by white police officers.

The white man has a long memory and he suspects that the Black man has one too. White men remember what they have done to Black women, and they walk in terror of retribution, notes Hacker, dreading miscegenation, dreading the day when Black men will plant seeds in white women, mongrelizing Caucasian "purity." Willie Horton was far more than a political foil. He betokened Black insurrection, in the same way as, for many whites, the rappers betoken "guerrilla action." The reaction would be less severe, according to Hacker, were a white man able to look at a white woman with a Black man without feeling betrayed, without feeling rejected in favor of a better sexual performer. This enrages white men; it enraged them in the past and still enrages them on the eve of the twenty-first century. This rage fuelled all the efforts to "de-man" Black men, insists Hacker. In the old America, the most graphic efforts to de-man were lynching and castration. In today's America, the same quest takes the form of joblessness and imprisonment. North America is at war with Black males, says Hacker. A similar comment comes from the pen of yet another white analyst, author of a recent study of Black migration. In *The Promised Land*, Nicholas Lemann too concluded that "the heart of the matter was sex." I disagree. This is too near-sighted. To my mind the *"matter"* is the *entire* system of Black exploitation and oppression.

Very little indeed has changed in the racist structure of the white psyche in the century from the year 1900 to the year 2000.

PART TWO
THE STATE OF THE BLACK WORLD

Chapter 12

A WALK THROUGH HISTORY: STROLLING ON THE BLACK SIDE

We have endured a long march in the wilderness of white racism. In order to penetrate western civilization's heart, to this point we have had to invade the mind of white folks. The preceeding chapters drenched us in their cultural pathologies. Unfortunately, this is a task that no Black person has been able to escape, from the day of our first arrival in this land. To survive, Black people have always had to know white folks better than white folks know themselves, while whites understand little or nothing about us. Throughout the ages we have accomplished this task with more or less skill.

Now is the moment to return to home turf. This chapter examines, briefly, Black history's significance to Black people. We need to ask what the Black historical experience means. We need to gauge those inimitable features of the Black past which make our historic ordeal at once unique unto itself, and that which makes the entire western hemisphere what it is today.

There can be no greater tragedy in the modern era than that which descended upon Africans, beginning in the fifteenth century. The central premise of African American history is the cruel trick of minority status under white domination. All sorts of tragedies befall individuals, luck of the draw. A random selection of all races and colors inherits painful fatal disease. Who can ward off the devastation of hurricanes, typhoons, earthquakes and other natural catastrophes? Many accidents appear as "acts of God," bolts from the blue. It is the cruel destiny of some individuals to be born blind, to lose one's hearing, to suffer paralysis, to live the life of a paraplegic. The list is long and epitomizes the human condition. These are the workings of what the Hindus call "Karma," the inevitable injustice of nature; this is the destiny that Muslims believe "is written."

But there are also man-made disasters, *historic* ones. These are the greater misfortunes since they are social. Such was the heartless sentence of history against the children of Africa when it cast us into the cauldron of white supremacy. The pathos of Black history outstrips all others in modern annals. No other historical phenomenon should evoke greater compassion than the predicament of Diaspora Blacks born as a *minority* among white people, and even where not a minority, nonetheless subject to white domination.

This plight, however, is unlike the random cruelties of impartial Mother Nature. Our sad condition is the working of history—the outcome of white racism over the centuries. There is nothing chanceful about it—nor is it the result of the blind workings of nature. Black oppression is the crime of white civilization. And the inevitable consequence of that crime is the resistance of the oppressed. The struggle between the two—between white supremacy and Black liberation—constitutes the epic drama of U.S. history.

The existentialist way of thinking has influenced some of Black America's greatest literary luminaries, from the Langston Hugheses, Richard Wrights, and James Baldwins of the past, to the David Bradleys of the present. According to this philosophy, fear, desperation and hopelessness are inherent in human society. Each and every individual is free to create his own character from scratch, as it were, and no human being can escape responsibility for the whole of humanity. We are responsible for every one else. History is the attempt to do the best we can with the resources and knowledge of the moment. The fate of Black people is comprehensible, in this view, as a chain of events caught up in a continuous spiral of development. Each Black person "invents" him/herself, figuratively, according to this view. On one side, inherited genes and universal physical nature; on the other, culture transmitted by society—the synthesis is the individual personality. Afrocentrists observe, for example, that despite the existence of between seven hundred and fifteen hundred distinct African languages there is vivid cultural similarity throughout Black Africa. A clear impression of similarity, a common atmosphere, grabs every keen observer, be he in the western, eastern, central or southern part of the continent.

This affects the way Black history should be understood, and the way it should be taught. For our project, history is necessarily selective and utilitarian. We study African and Middle Passage history in order to contend with white supremacy today. This explains the emphasis Afrocentrists place on the glories of ancient Black Egypt, and on the achievements of the great African hegemonies and kingdoms of the pre-colonial era. Kemetic, Ethiopian, and Aja-Yoruba civilizations are highlighted to instil pride in the Black race. Investigation of the original Ghana and Mali, and of Songhay and Kanem-Bornu, reveal the legitimate features of African culture and its singularity. Benin is admired not only for its unmatched artistic genius, but as much for its famed resistance to British invaders during the nineteenth century imperialist "scramble." The overwhelming majority of Blacks in the Americas hail from western Africa. The reality of the anti-racist struggle requires this concentration on that region, for there lay the embarkation point for the Middle Passage. Exposing the damages of four centuries of slave delivery, we instill a sense of righteousness. Teaching our youngsters about the unspeakable atrocities white slave ship crews committed against their ancestors, helps to outfit them with the prudent distrust they will need to cope with whites in the course of their own lifetime. Slavery refused Black marriage legal recognition, and the post-bellum hardships of poverty and migration put great pressure on family life. Knowing this enables us to reject the lie which sees present Black family relations as "dysfunctional" and "pathological" for what it is—evil racist propaganda. Full description of the conscious attempt to strip Black people of their African cultural inheritance, combined with stress on the failure of that attempt, instills pride of self and can foster unity among Afro-Americans, while nourishing feelings of Pan-African solidarity between ourselves and our African cousins. The cultural habit of not accumulating material resources for investment purposes and technological development, and the resulting military inferiority *vis-à-vis* whites, is what made Africa weaker than Europe, not any racial inferiority. The only way to grasp that truth, however, is through careful study of the past. History has its utilitarian uses. The value of *Black Studies* is that it is mainly didactic, and not an idle ivory-tower pursuit.

Certain white philosophers have seized upon the fact that Africans were torn from their homes for permanent exile in the Americas, and the fact that Africa itself was conquered and carved up, as proof of an element of futility in the history of Black people. Since, it is claimed, the Black man allowed himself to be determined by an outsider, by an alien culture, he is suitable only for 250 years of slavery and "underclass" welfare handouts. Since Hegel, racists of this stripe have been dismissing Black people as the "infants of history," capable perhaps of "thoughts," but not of "Thought," famished refugees needing to be fed by the white nations of the world, unable to perceive "God and the Law" which make for "civilized" living. We must be aware, therefore, that history also has its utilitarian *misuses*. Racists seize upon the decisive and distinguishing feature of Black Diaspora history—white abuse and exploitation—as evidence of the lack of historical capacity on the part of Africans. The propaganda says that Black people can never be "history-makers" as such, or failing that, that our history is nothing to be proud of.

Yet history-makers we are, and the history that we *have* made is the history that makes the Americas what they are today. Since the sixteenth century, Black people have been the decisive element in Brazil, the entire Caribbean, and the continental USA. We are a people abducted from our homeland and carried into foreign bondage. That in itself puts us in a class by ourselves. The basic reason for the complexity of our continuing struggle against white racism—the reason for the *permanence* of that struggle, according to some—is the uniqueness of the history of the formation of Black America.

Afro-American psyche and culture exhibit features which are deeply rooted in our special past. Contemporary Black scholars of, say, the school of Molefi Asante, do not see eye to eye in all things with those of, say, the persuasion of Sterling Stuckey (Asante 1980 and 1990). Yet they concur that Africa survived in the perceptions, interpretations, psychological particularities, symbolisms, and reflexes of Black folk in the western hemisphere. White sociology, in tandem with the snarky media, has belittled these traits as "sub-culture." Mother Africa lived on in farming techniques, labor skills, oral traditions, dance rhythms, song, ritual, artisanry, and folklore. She conditioned temperament, folk sensibility, religion and psychic expression. Plunged, however, in a racist political economy which sought to strip the primary producer of his humanity, the African cultural heritage was bent out of shape. It gave birth to secondary traits alien to the original African social constitution, as it had been before the Atlantic slave trade. The crippling effect of racism has spawned the self-hatred and Black-on-Black violence which rip apart our inner-city communities. Cultural reflexes derived from deportation and fixed in Black sensibility by chattel slavery, sharecropping, convict lease labor, bottom-rung industrial hire, and permanent unemployment, by white violence, segregation and aversion, have been grafted onto our African cultural heritage. Diaspora Blacks are endowed with a creative culture that is distinct from the imitative porridge that passes for the culture of white America. However, our culture is also distinct from contemporary Black African civilization.

Though sharing a common, underlying, Kemetic-derived civilization, the Africans deported to the Americas spoke different tongues, worshipped different gods and, in most instances, had experienced dissimilar political and social organization. The common language we were compelled to learn on the plantations was the language of the white man—English in the USA. The exact same plantations saw the formation of a common mentality, compounded of an inherited cultural unity and a shared life experience, first as chattel slaves, and later as "second class citizens." The mother African mentality became bent, deflected, even deformed, but never eradicated, not even when mass migration during the twentieth century pulled our people from countryside to cityscape, from South to North. Nor did it ever become the custom-tailored "slave mentality" the planters tried to impose.

Trans-Atlantic cultural bonding between Black America and Africa is still happening. Even now, long separated, Blacks of the Diaspora and Blacks of Africa both remain masters of *extemporization*. The same cultural mentality still determines in an inimitable way most of the Black man's perceptions, the manner in which he sorts out his life experiences in a white racist environment. It still influences our elaborations and social reactions. It is what makes us *different souls* from white folks, and that which makes us different is not the cluster of personality disorders the Moynihans and Lemanns have chronicled —and which the white media make believe goes with us wherever we go. White racism makes our minds what they are, because all Black people experience it, even though we may

211

not all be conscious of racism to the same degree. Two sets of psychological experience make a person a part of Black America: the pain of racial discrimination, and sharing the Black community's history, aspirations and repulsions, social fears and enthusiasms.

For African Americans there is no freedom that is not freedom *from* white supremacy. White concepts of the Law, Truth, Beauty, and Good are—each and all—open to question. Black dignity, says liberation philosophy, requires a grasp of history as a conflict between two models of humanity—one Eurocentric, the other Afrocentric. A conflict which is the product of the long history of oppression, and which shows that the sole *original* collective contribution to the authentic culture of America has been the offering of America's unwilling (Black) "immigrants." Since leaving Europe, the dominant white immigrants have actually been relatively barren in the fine arts, resting on European laurels, endlessly recycled. Building on African foundations, American Blacks have, in a number of fields of cultural expression, from music to art to popular folkways, injected the original element. Ours has been the vigorous and vibrant element in the American social formation. Our rapacious "masters," in contrast, have spun their wheels culturally, whether by importing such ready-made traditions of Europe as classical music, or by smugly imitating and trying to grab as their own the products of the cultural genius of Black men (the Rap music pilferer Vanilla Ice—the latest in a long line of Elvis-like impersonators of our musical tradition—is no accident).

Basically this has been the "bottom line" since 1619. Even white authors have difficulty denying this. Surveying *de facto* segregation in force in the pre–Civil War northern "free" states, Leon Litwack, for example, admits the existence of two nations, one white, the other Black, developing side by side in antagonistic tension in the "same political environment," without ever integrating on an equal basis (Litwack 1961). At intervals, outbursts of mass white violence punctuated the tension.

*

The social makeup affects a nation's ideas and tendencies. National traditions are real phenomena. Even where, as in the United States, we are dealing with two nations—one Black and one white—within one greater social formation, each "nation" still reflects the economic development of society as a whole, as well as that mega-society's psychological and emotional temperament(s) and the balance of power and social equilibrium between races at a given time. Just as real are the special and unique characteristics derived from the history of Afro-Americans.

Many of these characteristics spring from a societal experience certainly unlike that experienced by any other people in North America. Contemporary Black America is the child of the history of a *unique series* of socio-formations, encompassing the traditional way of life back in Africa, two hundred and fifty years of chattel slavery, three-quarters of a century of Jim Crow terrorism, factory labor, and the present social isolation of inner-city Blacks, peaking in the ghetto "underclass." To the extent that a form of agriculture remained the primary productive activity of those Africans who arrived on these shores alive, little had changed in the labor of Black peoples from one side of the Atlantic to the other. What had changed was our status and living conditions. We were now white men's slaves, persons without juridical weight. To the extent that whites still find ways to make profitable use of many (if not all) Black folks, our status, in effect, is unchanged.

It was precisely our history as slaves which conditioned the formation of the African-American *race*, and this race identity was reinforced by post-slavery discrimination, segregation and second-class citizenship. These are social relations. Social relations, mediated in history, outweighed biological reproduction in creating North America's Black "minority race." Despite a rather common heritage of material culture, our slave ancestors came, as noted, from many different ethnic groups and spoke many different tongues. The boundaries of the plantations ignored these ethnic divisions. When the time came for procreation, the will of the slaveholder and the limits of the plantation regulated intercourse. Plantation endogamy smashed any surviving ethnic unity and integrity. Most marriages were within the same plantation or neighboring ones. Meanwhile the sexual rampages of owners and overseers injected a Caucasian strain in all but a fifth of African Americans. For a long time slaveholders were not concerned to balance the gender ratio among slaves. Not until the 1840s were there as many Black men in the United States as there were Black women. The only real "melting pot" of different peoples the U.S. has ever really had, in the true sense of that banal term, was stirred of transplanted Africans, a unique new people smelted in the crucible of slavery.

The factors that have made us a people are varied. We were forced to adopt a foreign, Western language—English. Nevertheless, it was a major force in drawing us together, as was a foreign religion—Western Christianity—that is, once our slave ancestors had worked it into a form suitable to the Black experience. The institutions of Euro-America, even the domination of the white United States government, imposed against the will of our embattled ancestors, were catalysts in pulling us together as one people—a new African American nation born of historical catastrophe. The presssures and distortions of white racism strengthened centripal forces within the community; to ward off the hatred we had to hunker down, pull together, rally in support of one another—at least most of us did, most of the time. For a minority of our people, unfortunately, racism's heat triggered the opposite reaction. It bred corruption and surrender; it separated the cream from the curds, as it were. This trend too is an element of the history that made us. Wilting before the implacable and powerful white enemy, craven figures emerged to do the master's will from within the community. Black America gave birth to numerous collaborators. By 1830, there were some 3,777 *Black slaveowners* in the United States. Louisiana and Old Dominion Virginia housed most of them. These abettors of their own people's disgrace grounded a tradition still sadly with us in the form of Black neo-conservatives securely niched today in posts everywhere from the Supreme Court to the armed services to the nation's universities and boardrooms

*

For some time now I have favored comparing the history of Black North America with the history of Brazil's Black people. These are the two largest components of the western hemisphere Diaspora—the Brazilian African population three times as numerous as the Blacks of North America; the U.S. Black community decades ahead of Brazilian Black folk in race consciousness and organization.

The two contingents shared a common historical womb—Afro-Americans and Afro-Brazilians, like all Africans in the western hemisphere, including the teeming Black citizenry of the Caribbean and Spanish-speaking America, are the spawn of the Mother African civilization born eons ago in the valley of the Nile. The modern era dawned in the same way for both Brazilian and United States Blacks. We both endured nightmarish centuries of chattel slavery. As yet there has been no adequate study by competent and trustworthy Black scholars, but a comparison of the forms and specific flavors of the slavery under which United States and Brazilian Afro-Americans coalesced as distinct national communities would surely benefit the struggle against white supremacy in the two countries. The ultimate nature and aims of white racism are the same everywhere. Nevertheless, the dissimilarities between Luso-racism and the Anglo-Saxon variety are instructive. For instance, there was a longer and more numerous influx of Africans into Brazil after 1807 than into the United States. This made for a stronger, or at least newer, fresher, more directly African influence in Brazil than in the United States and Canada. (Cuba fits closer to the Brazilian model in this regard.) Brazilian rulers made greater (or at least more conscious) use of the "whitening"-miscegenation path to white supremacy than did the Anglo-Saxon Negrophobes of North America. Unfortunately, we are taught nothing about Brazilian history, and the Africans of Brazil know very little about us. This whiteout is an aspect of deliberate racist educational strategy in both countries. It has never been in the interest of white supremacy for different African peoples to know much about each other. We need to compare our national experiences with slavery, and we require careful cooperative study of the nineteenth century which saw slavery hang on in Brazil until 1888, as well as the hopes and betrayals of Reconstruction in the United States.

Afro-Brazilians appear to have experienced nothing comparable to the accelerations of U.S. Black Reconstruction (1863–1877), the Great Migration (1915–1918), and the years in U.S. history spanning the Great Depression and World War II (1929–1945). These were hothouses of "forced historical development," times of rapid maturation which gave the Black community in the U.S. a leg up in the struggle for equality, and made it the role model for all other Black communities in the Americas as far as the struggle against racism and white supremacy is concerned. These episodes were unique to the history of the United States. They accelerated the growth of national/racial consciousness and group awareness, enabling the Black community to become a vibrant force by the time of the Civil Rights surge in the turbulent 1960s. These circumstances are at least part of the reason Black folk in the USA, the smaller of the two communities, appear more militant, self-possessed, and better equipped with the weapons of social struggle than the gigantic, "backward," and relatively passive Afro-Brazil.

There are other aspects of the Black experience in the U.S. for which there *seem* to have been no *exact* replicas in Brazil and the rest of the Americas; for example, the convict lease labor system and its precursor. The groundbreaker for the system of agriculture that replaced slavery appeared in the arrangements made by Union administrators during and right after the Civil War. Federal officials enforced contracts between Freedmen as farm laborers, and white landowners and leasers as employers. Payment for work was withheld until the harvest. Farm laborers were charged interest on purchases made to feed their families. This heralded the sharecropping and convict lease labor system, to which Brazilian Blacks do not appear to have had any directly comparable experience, surely not during the crucial years from 1862 to World War I, chattel slavery lasting formally until 1888 in Brazil. It would be interesting to determine, furthermore, whether Brazilian artisans suffered the same racist destruction of their craft skills as their U.S. counterparts, once slavery ended. On the morrow of emancipation, many Black men possessed master craftsman skills, inherited from Africa and sometimes nurtured through slavery. In the United States, the racist backlash against emancipation destroyed an entire Black masonry industry. Black stone masonry was ruined by the deliberate refusal of whites after the Civil War to grant building contracts in New Orleans and Charleston to Black craftsmen.

After having waited eight to nine generations for the Civil War and abolition, Black hopes in this country were dashed by the betrayal of 1876. When Reconstruction was brought crashing down, yet another of the unique features of its history was drawn on the face of Black America. All hope of social equality vanished as Jim Crow was imposed by superior might. Segregation affected all of life's social intimacies. For nearly four decades, Black Americans were banned from metropolitan white America. The white South set out to paralyze the Black man with the threat of murder and the reality of murder. Overcoming the ordeal of lynching tempered Afro-Americans to a degree unknown to Afro-Brazilians of the same time frame. From the Atlantic to the Pacific, Black men were castrated and burned at the stake on account of their color. From 1882 to 1968, there were lynchings in 43 states. Mississippi and Georgia led the way with 581 and 531 racial lynchings respectively, but white mobs hunted people of color down even in such seemingly unlikely states as California, Minnesota, Ohio and Utah, according to records compiled at Tuskegee University and the Southern Poverty Law Center. It remains to be seen whether Brazilian freedmen had anything like their U.S. brethren's history of organized resistance to post-slavery white oppression, and whether they needed anything like it. It would prove very inspirational for latent Pan-Africanist instincts should we learn that twentieth century Brazil has Black champions of its own comparable to New Orleans' Robert Charles, the Black paladin who faced down a mob 20,000 strong, and sold his life at the cost of death and wounds to some twenty lynchers. Earlier, during Reconstruction, Black men had armed themselves to resist white aggression. The domestic aftermath of World War I was bloody, and the burgeoning ghettoes moved to establish armed self-defense against white race rioters. Were similar scenes being played out in Brazil? If not, what made for the different conditions?

Another area of comparison is the rate of natural growth in the two communities. There are many more children of Africa in today's Brazil than in the USA. Have Afro-Brazilians enjoyed a faster rate of natural growth—surplus of births over deaths—than our community? From 1865 to the First World War, the great majority of Afro-Americans lived in belts and pockets across the rural south. Black America stabilized during those years and grew in numbers. The population doubled in size between 1860 and 1900, without immigration of Blacks from abroad, and grew even more rapidly from 1900 to 1960. Unlike the demographic increase of American whites, the swelling number of Blacks was due almost entirely to the surplus of births over deaths. Once slavery ended, the federal government banned the entry of any additional Africans. For more than a century since 1850, the rate of child delivery of Black women in the United States surpassed that of white women. Not until the modest influx of Afro-Caribbeans during and after the First World War were there any Blacks in the U.S. who were not native born. How does this compare with Brazil? Importation of African slaves became illegal in that country in 1850, but the ban was merely formal and some slave ships continued to land large numbers of newcomers from Africa for yet another whole generation.

Meanwhile, Black America was pushed along its own distinct path. For Blacks in the post-Reconstruction South there was no meaningful distinction between work and family existence. The praiseworthy attempt by freedmen during Reconstruction to free Black women from

217

field drudgery, keep their wives home, and enable them to tend their family, failed. The sharecropper regime eliminated any real division of labor in Black farming, all members of the family participating in all aspects of rural labor. Youths worked alongside adults, and women in particular were burdened with cotton "chopping." Farming tasks were indistinguishable from domestic tasks.

A saving feature was the blend of the family with rural activities, economic and social, religious and secular. On the farms and in the hamlets, villages and small towns of the Deep South's "Black Belt," everyone who belonged to the Black community knew everyone else—at least everyone who was not a transient. The Black community's proverbial informal and intimate "life style" jelled in this setting. Permanent and close contact made it very difficult for persons to escape the scrutiny of family and community. Families were defined as extended organs, not in the nuclear sense. White society's propensity to "segment" was rarely found. The positive attitude toward community, along with supportive institutions like the church, fostered a collective mentality. Terror too fostered social unity and solidarity. Sharecroppers lived in dread of white men. Ku Kluxers castrated men, raped women, and lynched both. They slaughtered Black children and babes. As hard pressed Black farm hands commiserated with one another over exorbitant land rents, wholesale fraud and cutthroat sharecrop "agreements," the bonds that formed a people were being woven. As Black communities wrestled with agricultural calamities, poor crops, and bad weather, as cattle and crop diseases took their cruel toll, our Black nation was being reaffirmed, consolidated well in advance of American white nationhood.

Soon to be born was a distinct Black industrial working class—a vital new component of the nation. From the end of the Civil War to 1914, Northern industries were at the stage in their development where they needed unskilled, underpaid labor. European immigrants supplied it until the outbreak of World War I. The mass exodus from the rural south to the urban ghettoes began in earnest around 1915–1916. The "Great Migration" coincided with the effects of the First World War. A new Black proletariat came into being. It encountered the immediate hostility of poor whites, the aversive contempt of middle class whites, and the manipulative patronage of wealthy whites. Competition ignited a brushfire of white race "riots" which flared through the nation's cities, cresting in the blood-red months of 1919.

Through lapses, and even rollbacks during economic down times, the migration continued even though the number of industrial jobs available to Black was always smaller than the number of migrants. The conditions they met in the industrial regions were invariably deplorable, but seemed better than life in the hellish Southland. The chief destinations were mining, steel and manufacturing towns in the Northeast and Midwest. But fewer went to Pittsburgh—the steel capital—than might be expected, kept away by white labor unions and the visceral racism of recent white "ethnic" immigrants. Blacks went to work in the steel and auto industries, in mcat packing and on the railways. The inrush slackened noticeably in the depressed 1930s. The situation in the nation's capital in the spring of 1939, for instance, was pretty much the same as in other cities. "There is no industrial work [in Washington, D.C.]...unless a man is fortunate enough to get in as a messenger or laborer for one of the governmental departments, few openings are available for Negroes. Some manage to get private jobs as chauffeurs and mechanics, others do regular laboring work for construction companies, but there is little opportunity for other than domestic and laboring work for men" (*Claude Barnett Papers*, 29 March 1939).

The migration resurged at the outbreak of the Second World War. The northern cities continued to absorb much cheap Black labor. Now, however, there was an alternative direction for the travelers—the West Coast. Benefiting from industrial decentralization of the national economy, the region became a new center of attraction. Black communities mushroomed in Seattle, Portland and Los Angeles. Jobs in naval construction and in the unloading of merchant vessels triggered a rapid influx of Black people to the Bay Area in Northern California. In the decade ending in 1960 a million and a half left the South for the West, Northeastern Coast, and Midwest.

The social compositions of Black America changed radically in the first half of the twentieth century. Black America took on a new profile. The most prominent new stratum was a vast urban industrial working class. Black folk became predominantly city folk. Nevertheless, the Black community remained an organism subservient to a bigger white nation. The meatpacker as much as the mill hand, the numbers runner as much as the jazz musician, each one of the now ghettoized Black community, slotted somehow or other in the bigger picture, in a way compatible with the white man's interests. Black folks found themselves assigned to more or less specialized functions necessary to white America, and/or to the Black community as a segregated entity—in which latter instance one ultimately still served white interests. Few escaped this functional role, not even the permanently unemployed. Put another way, having been made over anew by waves of migration and metropolitan overcrowding, Black America was handed a role to play that was really the same old role in new costume. There was little that was ambiguous about its function in the "social division of labor," even if often merely as an elastic pool of reserve labor, segments of which were destined for eternal joblessness.

The ghettoes were born of the great shift in population, while that legendary figure of early Afro-American history—the Black farmer—began a disappearing act. After peaking in 1920, with 900,000 Black-operated farms across the country, the decline has been precipitous. Projections say there will be no more Black farmers in America by the year 2000. As of summer 1991, there were only 23,000 left, concentrated in the Southeast. Small Black farmers are caught in the squeeze of scarce capital, markets, credit and technical assistance, and President Clinton's appointment of a Black Secretary of Agriculture—Mike Espy—in no way altered their status as endangered species on the way to extinction.

Naturally, non-economic motivations numbered among the "push-pulls" which fuelled the migrations. Revolutionary idealism inspired more than a few, not just fear and economic pressure. Blacks lamented the need to quit their birth place. We were driven out by white tyranny and exploitation. We sought the realization of impossible dreams. Like most oppressed people of color, we loved our native land with passion. We hated racist white *folks,* not the southern clime, nor Dixie's flora and fauna. Blacks were loath to emigrate. But the need to get away from Southern whites was more pressing, the need to follow the vision of freedom. Pursuit of noble ideals and utopian romanticism burned in the hearts of thousands of the men and women who pulled up roots and sallied forth to an uncertain future.

Arrived in our new homes we ran, unfortunately, smack into a Northern and urban version of the same old "race relations" we had known to our sorrow in the South. We were not permitted to enjoy the privilege—normal in human history—of continuing the organic development of our own social relations—a maturation begun in Africa before the appearance of Europeans, and which if it had been

left to leaven itself, would have differentiated our population socially, in our own way. What would have been the outcome is a matter of
speculation. Instead, all our travail and struggle were compressed into
the "race relations" with whites, so favored by white sociology. Before
the intrusion of white slave traders, the African way of life centered
on farming and crafts, on communalism and extended families, on
age-sets and *orishas*. For that we were forced to trade the servile labor
of America, unpaid labor which created much of the wealth of the
world capitalist economy. With the passing of chattel slavery came
sharecropping, poverty-stricken small farms, and segregationist lynch
law. How different this history is from the history of American whites.
The advent of the twentieth century and the migrations transformed
most of us into hyper-urbanized sometime wage-earners, assigned to
the more degrading tasks of industrial toil. Deindustrialization—the
latest scourge—relegates our young males to underclass status. This
is what the capsule view of Black history reveals.

The present disastrous condition of African American family relations, the self-hatred that tears the inner cities, the Black-on-Black
violence, the drug culture and the AIDS plague, are direct causal
effects of enslavement. The lack of positive self-identification as well
as family disarray spring from slavery. We are a captive people, a people in bondage to white supremacy—spiritually, culturally and ideologically. This is the flavor of North America's unique "race relations."

There is no substitute for the Black experience in American history. Black America has always been this country's agent of radical
change. It still is. The chief historical role for which the Black man
is singled out in the drama of the coming century is the same role
he has played in past centuries—the traditional role of progressive
change and founder of new social orders. His part in the drama will
keep him the most crucial figure in American history throughout
the twenty-first century. Everything ignoble among Black people can
be traced back to white supremacy.

*

Black experience in the territory that became the United States is
more than 350 years old, dating back to 1619. We do not know what
proportion of the ancestors of today's African-American citizens
were relative "latecomers" from Africa, i.e. were added to the slave
population only in the course of the nineteenth century. Some have
argued that constant infusion of new African blood nurtured con-

221

tinuing attachment to the African ideal, to things African. We do know that recent arrivals—*bossals*—from Africa triggered the Haitian slave revolution in 1791, and that they were less reconciled to slavery than Creole slaves were. The best known example of an Africanism in U.S. history is the title of the AME Church, the second largest denomination in the Black community for many decades. Some see this tradition as a validation of Afrocentricity, as a viable alternative to white supremacy in culture, historiography, ideology, and political economy.

Family building is seen as another validation of Afrocentricity. In slaveowning Virginia, hundreds of Black families—most of them freedmen-based—managed to establish a "house of the father", defined as one in which permanent mating was the chief characteristic. The practice was most prevalent among house servants and skilled craftsmen, a small elite stratum within the whole Black community. Legal marriage was common within the group, enabled usually by a freedman managing to purchase liberty for his wife and other relatives. Farm land was bought and handed down to descendants by last will and testament. This accomplishment was not limited to mulattoes or persons of light skin. Fully one-half of the Virginia families who extricated themselves from slavery were very dark or brown skinned. Family building continued throughout the life of slavery, right up to 1860. Yet, in affirming Afrocentric family building under slavery, we must be careful not to minimize slavery's disruptive impact on Black family strivings, thereby glossing over the evils of the "peculiar institution." The extreme pendulum-swing by some recent historians away from the E.F. Frazier–Moynihan family disruption thesis, carries that danger. We must bear in mind the informality and temporary nature of sexual couplings which plagued sharecropper families well into the twentieth century, and which troubles many of our inner-city families today—an enduring legacy of slavery.

The rope between the history of Black music in this country and the history of Black resistance and militancy is tightly drawn. It is a story that is justly famed (see, e.g., Jones 1963; Southern 1971). Black music is the cultural root from which springs Afro-American literature, poetry and art. Music played an inspirational and functional part in three hundred years of slave revolts. Our people's aggressive attitudes were displayed through music. Through song and instrumentation, Black folk showed our fighting spirit as a "defiant, spirited people." First came the spirituals and the genuine blues to sustain the slaves and the freedmen. Then came jazz to sweep the Eurocentric cobwebs from America's musical landscape. When in the early 1920s jazz was appropriated by slumming whites seeking a thrill, rhythm and blues sounded in to fill the gap, voicing the aspirations and "soul stirrings" of the alienated. Soul music followed to inspire the whole Civil Rights generation. And we are beginning to feel the impact of authentic hip-hop culture and the message of the Rap artists, trumpeting the soul stirrings of the wildly alienated Black youth of today.

Of course, all was not resistance. Those who would go-along-to-get-along have always been among us. Their presence and their activities have given rise to a school of thought that interprets Black history itself as a "dialectic" between accommodationism and rebellion, as a controversy between conformers and defiers. It views the Black experience in the U.S. as allowing only two concrete possibilities—revolt or accommodation. Lerone Bennett, for instance, defined the traditional protests of "Negro leaders" of the past as "an attitude of nonacceptance based on sustained contention via political and legal action within the system"—in other words, a willingness to limit oneself to more or less agile manoeuverings according to rules laid down by white overlords. The "middle ground" between collaboration and forthright revolt, an activist "program of direct action based on revolt on the edges" of the system, was historically unstable, according to this school.

The career of Rosa Gragg exemplifies the unspectacular accommodationism that has been an everyday occurrence throughout this century. In April 1949, the Detroit mayor appointed her the "first Negro to win [a] key city post," as described by the white press. Mrs. Gragg expressed her philosophy as follows: "I believe, as did Booker T. Washington, that as a race we shall prosper in proportion as we learn to glorify and dignify labor and to put brains and skill into the common occupations of life." Like others of such mind, her compliance made her attractive to Detroit's rulers, endeavoring to select Black leaders for Black people. She had been favored previously by a governor of the state, and by President F.D. Roosevelt. Born in Georgia, Gragg had graduated from Tuskegee Institute, the accommodationist bailiwick. By the early 1960s, Rosa Gragg had become President of the National Association of Colored Women's Clubs Inc., based in the nation's capital. She was a very different woman from, say, her namesake and contemporary, Rosa Parks. Gragg's is the tradition that is roundly claimed today by the Black neo-conservatives.

Counterpunching against white violence and against discrimination is one of our most cherished traditions. During Black Reconstruction, wanton brutality, lynching, and live immolation were met with the organized fight-back of Black communities, spearheaded by armed Union Leagues. Immediately following World War I, crazed northern white mobs rampaged. In Chicago, Washington, D.C. and elsewhere they were checked by a widespread movement to establish armed self-defense against white attacks. Many Black veterans, home from the western front, took armed reprisals against the racists (Shapiro 1988). Meanwhile, the NAACP riposted on the legal front. In 1912 it began a campaign of federal and state litigation. The main target was school segregation—well over a third of all cases fought—however, its battle in the courts also hit other aspects of white supremacy. Thurgood Marshall's epochal victory in *Brown v. Board of Education of Topeka, 347 U.S. 483 (1954)*— stripping public school systems of the racist privilege of segregating Black and white pupils—is justly renowned as the NAACP's crowning moment. By the mid-1980s the NAACP Legal Defense Fund had pestered judges to vindicate Black rights in every realm of social life from employment discrimination to police brutality, from housing and real estate to jury procedures, from public accommodations to voting rights. The court flurry peaked in the year 1970. Between 1944 and 1971, the Supreme Court was prodded to rule all-white primaries unconstitutional, along with some forms of racial gerrymandering, poll taxes, laws prohibiting interracial marriage, and racial discrimination in the sale or lease of real estate. The Court even ruled that the President may enforce affirmative minority hiring (Cross 1984).

The Montgomery bus boycott (1955–1956) brought militant civil disobedience to the forefront. It kicked off the modern Civil Rights Movement, devoted to integration. It enlisted the courageous action of the less compromise-minded members of the traditional Black clergy—pastors whose concern for the earthly tribulations of their congregations outweighed devotion to a distant and uncertain salvation. Martin Luther King Jr., and SCLC brewed a storm which brought legalized Jim Crow tumbling down. To the surprise of many, their action also spawned SNCC, "Black Power," and revolutionary nationalism. Parallel to integrationism, the Nation of Islam nurtured a separatist movement within which Malcolm X honed his formidable talents, and from which he parted to emerge as the paramount spokesman of a secular revolutionary nationalist and unitarian Pan-Africanism. The ghetto rebellions (1964–1968) resonated more to Malcolm's call to Self-Defense than to Martin Luther King, even though the greatest wave of urban uprisings was triggered by the assassination of the apostle of Non-Violence.

The late 1960s and early 1970s saw Black capitalism on the one hand resurrected as a Nixon Administration ploy. On the other hand, it was the legitimate revival of a strategy employed by Black businessmen during the days of segregation to maintain the service monopolies that had been afforded by Jim Crow. The Black capitalists hoped to improve their financial fortunes by expelling small white businesses from Black communities through race boycott.

In 1955, the Interstate Commerce Commission banned segregation of passengers on trains and buses used in interstate travel, and seven years later presidential *Executive Order 11062* struck down racism in federally assisted housing. In 1965, federal contractors were required to give priority to affirmative action. And in 1969, the mandate was broadened to include goals and timetables to counter discrimination. The pressure of mass Black "street heat" must be credited with the three main legislative concessions to Black citizens since the Civil War era. In 1964, the Civil Rights Act opened public accommodations and jobs to Blacks. The next year theVoting Rights Act suspended literacy tests and opened the ballot box to millions of disenfranchised southern Blacks. The 1968 fair housing law professed to prohibit discrimination in the sale or rental of housing.

Since then there has been reflux. Proprietary attitudes towards Civil Rights expressed by certain veterans of the movement injected a weakness. Afrocentric culture suffered. Certain veterans of the Civil Rights campaign began to feel their great personal sacrifices had earned them special privileges. This weakness became more prominent after the assassination of Martin Luther King. The late Ralph Abernathy's autobiography, for example, revealed a morbid obsession with personal slights. Infights over the mantle of Martin Luther King divided the leadership. Aid or deference refused was quickly denounced as betrayal. Criticism or advice from newcomers met with paranoia. The upshot was that by the 1980s, notables of the SCLC-genre had been outflanked and rendered obsolete by the course of political events, by the change in the mood of the country.

To make matters worse, along came placemen like Clarence Thomas. Early in 1992, with Thomas prominent among the anti-Black majority of justices, the Supreme Court struck a blow against the 1965 Voting Rights Act. The court sharply curtailed the law by upholding two Alabama counties that had stripped newly-elected African American county commissioners of their powers. The all white incumbent Board of Commissioners had changed the budget laws depriving the incoming Black Commissioners of traditional control of funds. The six to three ruling, penned by Justice Kennedy, dismissed their appeal. In advance of this judgement, Congress made a show of repairing this and other damages with the 1991 Civil Rights Act, requiring employers to show that measures excluding minorities are demanded by "business necessity," and insisting that no aspect of an employment decision can show bias. Yet on the whole, the statute was weak, allowing for the reopening of bias cases only under special circumstances, and shifting attention from race to gender. The damage done to the political right of Blacks to influence policy and make decisions was not addressed.

Chapter 13

BLACK NATIONALISM AND BLACK CAPITALISM: A CLOSER LOOK

BLACK NATIONALISM

Defiance resonates in Black history, and nationalist ideology has always ridden the flood of self-defense.

The most intense periods of the development of nationalist political theory and ideology coincide with the most feverish eras of exploitation and racist frenzy. Black nationalist political philosophy was born in North America roughly in the years from 1790 to 1820, when the white "founding fathers" showed their true color with the sanction of slavery in the Constitution of 1787, and with the first Congressional fugitive slave law of 1792, and in their glee over the new economic prospects opened for slavery by the invention of the cotton gin in that same year. Nationalist sentiment peaked again in the 1840s and 1850s, during the bitter struggle for abolition and the simultaneous debate over the future of Africans in a society that was virulently white racist. Black national-political theory spurted forward once more in the half century from 1880 to 1930, encouraged by the bitter experiences with segregationist lynch law, the Great Migration, ghettoization and white race riots in the north. Even though there is now a move to regard it as a West Indian import foreign to U.S. Blacks (Walker 1991), the Garvey movement was the high point in the history of nationalist agitation prior to the Second World War.

We have succeeded in expressing our national aspirations in ground-breaking political analysis, as shown in the large, complex literature of protest and justification of the right of insurrection, in voluminous writings on separation and national liberation, on full citizenship and integration. Our predecessors have been very adept at giving philosophic expression to our reflections on white racism (Bracey, Meier and Rudwick 1970; and Meier, Rudwick and Broderick 1971).

Take Henry Highland Garnet for example. He gave theoretical punch to our power to disrupt white America. While rejecting wholesale repatriation to Africa as impractical, Garnet reminded his tortured Black compatriots that it was ever in their power so to torment their white torturers that they would be glad to let Black men go free. The prescription was made in 1843, and has lost none of its validity. In its most general sense, the Garnet doctrine meant that social truth in America can have no other definition than the fulfilment of the aspirations of the oppressed Black minority. While slavery lasted, it meant as well that no Black man could be justly accused of stealing anything from a white man, because whites had stolen all that the African possessed, including the very person of the African himself.

There were others who leaned the same way. Though a champion of integration, Frederick Douglass—as early as 1853—termed Afro-America "a nation within a nation," laying the germ of a doctrine which, in the twentieth century, has come to see Black America as a domestic colony. Martin Delaney was a pioneer advocate of Black Power. He was born in northern Virginia in 1812. Until the moment of his death in 1885 he wrestled tirelessly against Black humiliation. Delaney knew that no people can be free who themselves do not constitute an essential part of the *ruling* element of the country in which they live. He was painfully aware that Black folk had no control at the policy-making level of U.S. society. "The liberty of no man is secure, who controls not his own political destiny." The white commonality consents to racism and racist ideals. In the mind of ordinary whites, dark skin color and African features alone are sufficient to preserve the Black man's social badge of inferiority, independent of costume, education, accent, emotivity, or any other distinguishing marks which "exceptional," assimilated Blacks might display. Martin Delaney was convinced that deep-seated prejudices had been engendered in white minds by centuries of crimes against African people, dating back to the fifteenth century. Incalculable ages might yet roll by, he suspected, before improved circumstances would elevate to equality the Black man in the United States. Delaney noted that as early as the 1850s the states of New York and Ohio had deliberately instituted distinctions among its Black residents in order to create "a privileged class by birth" in the Black community, a class dedicated to singing the glories of the United States and to faithfully serving the community of white masters.

From 1870 through the 1920s, Black nationalist sentiment enjoyed peak development. Actually there were *two* Black nationalisms. Both foreign emigration and territorial separation within the confines of the continental United States garnered popularity at the grass roots. These two sets of theories, sentiments, and schemes emanated from different social strata in the community. One was the creation of rural dwellers in the time from Black Reconstruction through the 1890s. The other was the expression of slum-dwelling urbanites at the time of Garvey. The two nationalisms were different in content and complexity.

The sixty years from 1870 to 1930 were an era of collective emigration—African, Kansan, Oklahoman, and Midwestern emigration. It was the time of all-Black Mound Bayou in Mississippi (1887), the time when Bishop Henry M. Turner prophesied that "manhood future" was not in the cards for American Black men (1896). Twenty-five African-American towns, including Langston and Boley, were the legacy of a brave effort to turn the Oklahoma Territory into an all-Black state in the Union. World War I and the migrations of the "Teens" and "Twenties" gave birth to our "inner city" landscape. This was the heroic age of migration in Black America's history. It provided the raw material for the theories of a whole generation of nationalist thinkers. It strongly influenced Duse Mohamed Ali, the

Sudanese-Egyptian nationalist and editor of the London *African Times and Orient Review*. Ali, in turn, influenced Arthur Anderson who conceived a plan in 1913 for the creation of a Black nation within the geographical confines of the U.S. He regarded his people as "a nation apart," whose relations with white America should properly come under the heading of international law. He wanted our historic goal to be a separate, suitable territory—suitable in clime and resources, and suitable to the Black temperament. Only there, he was certain, would Black folk be able to enjoy a life free from the insanities of whites, those "polite savages." Later on, Marcus Garvey too would feel the influence of Duse Mohamed Ali.

Feeling similar currents, W.E.B. DuBois defined a race as "a vast family of human beings, generally of common blood and language, always of common history, traditions and impulses, who are both voluntarily and involuntarily striving together for the accomplishment of certain more or less vividly conceived ideas of life." Though couched in the language of race, it can be argued that he was describing a nation more than anything else. For DuBois, the American Black community constituted a *racial nation* or a *race-nation*, one of whose *non-essential* peculiarities happens to be certain physical characteristics (skin pigmentation, hair type, lip formation, nose shape) inherited from African forebears, in the same way that most members of the Chinese nation inherit a characteristic eye-lid form, or many Germans a propensity towards large bones. He flirted throughout his long life, on and off, with integrationism. Nevertheless, in 1897 DuBois wrote an article on the "Strivings of the Negro People," wherein he lauded the African-American's refusal "to bleach his Negro blood in a flood of white Americanism." While he knew that many Blacks embraced assimilation, DuBois was plagued with the question of security for American Black folk, given the intimidation of the smaller nation by the larger, more powerful one, especially seeing that the larger nation was racist-minded.

Many are familiar with the role-modelling career of Marcus Garvey, and with his message. Garvey was the apostle of Pan-Negroism. Ultimately, his "Back-to-Africa" ideology did not play in the United States and Canada. Garvey did not know that the word *"Negro"* appears in no indigenous African tongue—it was foisted on Black people by Portuguese slavers. He used the term, just as did his rival DuBois. His knowledge of African history was sketchy and his grasp of the politics of the Africa of his day was tenuous. He championed the liberation of the mother continent from its colonial masters, but knew little of the real impact that imperialist colonialism was having on Africans and African society. But his heart beat with an unparalleled Black patriotism and his clarion voice trumpeted the study of, and respect for, African history. In this respect he can be seen perhaps as the popular, plebeian counterpart to Carter G. Woodson, founder of the famed *Journal of Negro History*. While opposing integration with all his being, there was nevertheless that in the "Get-Aheadism" of Garvey's strivings which dovetailed with the "Join-America-be-all-that-you-can-be-and-Ride-to-the-Top" ideology.

The same spirit shines forth in George Wells Parker's precocious Hamitic League program of Black nationalism, race consciousness, Black studies, and resistance to media racism. Parker was a Garvey contemporary, but appears to have reached his conclusions independently. To quicken racial self-consciousness he worked to spread knowledge of the part played by Black Africans in the development of the human civilization. In order to arouse a powerful race pride, Parker called for the revision of all textbooks that falsified and deleted the truth concerning Black folk. And like W.E.B. DuBois, he fought for the capitalization of all terms used as an ethnic designation of the Black race. He foreshadowed our current fascination with the Egyptian part of ancient Ethiopia as the land of the pyramids, and mother of civilization for the Mediterranean and the entire Western world. Parker insisted that Africa was the birthplace of humanity. His pamphlet eloquently proclaimed the Black character of pharaonic Egypt—a fact later proved by the master historian Cheikh Anta Diop and publicized by the *Journal of African Civilizations* and the Afrocentric school led by Molefi Asante. George Wells Parker, the nationalist, lived in Omaha, Nebraska.

Once the much-discussed Harlem Renaissance had passed, swallowed by the Great Depression, Aimé Césaire, speaking from Paris, seized the baton and created the *Négritude* movement in the mid-1930s along with Leon Damas. He defined it simply as the awareness of being Black—an intuition rare among the brainwashed Black intellectuals of the day. Césaire insisted that acceptance of one's Blackness was no simple feat. For it meant taking charge of one's fate. It implied a revolutionary determination to fix the destiny, future history and culture of the Black man. Césaire knew this simple proposition had to be repeated time and again, since Blacks worldwide were still running ashamed of their race. For instance, the war in the Pacific brought an influx of Afro-Americans to Hawaii. By the end of the 1940s, some of the more self-despising Black residents were touting the islands as an opportunity for "the American Negro to lose his racial identity" (*Claude Barnett Papers*, 23 September 1949). They strutted about, pretending to be Puerto Ricans or part-Hawaiians, although white migrants from the deep South were not falling for the trick, and were forcing Blacks to the bottom of the Hawaiian social fabric, one rung lower than the Filipinos who had above them the Japanese and the Chinese, going up. It was to counter this kind of self-humiliation that Aimé Césaire (A. Césaire, *Tropiques*, 3 October 1941; and *Cahier d'un retour au pays natal*) was joined by Leopold Sedar Senghor and Léon Damas in celebrating epic "black deeds." Their connection, if any, with the English-speaking Pan-Africanists George Padmore and C.L.R. James has yet to be explored by Black scholars.

Out of the nebulous realms of Négritude emerged Black cultural nationalism in all its manifestations—from soul music to soul food, from Afro-garb to natural hair styles, from "Black folk's vernacular" to neo-African harvest festivals. Where it was not misused, where it was not permitted to degenerate into "pork chop" complacency, and where it did not become an excuse for a cop-out, cultural nationalism was a powerful ideological weapon. It prepared Black activists emotionally and intellectually for greater struggles.

However, the rhetoric of certain cultural nationalists turned out to be not so very different from traditional Baptist religious mythology, which lived in an Old Testament past. To more than a few cultural nationalists the Black nation had no real substance. It was more like a mystical projection of mighty kings and valiant warriors than the Black socio-economic reality embedded in twentieth-century white America. It was a matter of telling tales of omniscient African sorcerers and virtuous amazons, of the Black pyramid-builders of the long-lost African past. Some latter-day cultural nationalists seemed to seek an extraterritorial cultural-national autonomy that was very hard to pin down. They seemed to say that they would be satisfied were all individuals of Black nationality in North America allowed to form a group endowed with autonomy in cultural affairs. They lacked any plan for political power. Economic analysis rarely got beyond buy-Black programs, appeals to keep consumer dollars within the community, and applause for boycotts of white retail outlets.

*

By the time the 1950s rolled in, major political tendencies contended for favor in our community. The mainstream favored integration, particularly in the South. It featured the fight to end legal segregation and win voting rights, with the aim of giving priority to electoral politics. Very prominent were business and church leaders whose agenda called to mind Booker T. Washington's National Negro Business League, and whose plans for social advancement were being thwarted by white racist prejudice. Segregation had both enabled and limited this group's financial, educational and professional prospects. They rubbed shoulders, ideologically, with the volatile big-city folks, pressed together in northern and West Coast ghettoes, for whom Malcolm X now emerged as paramount spokesman. The "underclass" shared the landscape with the families of a Black working class, many of whom were still organized in unions and still employed in manufacturing. There were urban dwellers of recent rural origin—migrants who had left Jim Crow only within the preceding half-century. There were students, poets, preachers, and writers. All these tendencies were poised in a kind of suspension, awaiting the triggering news of *Brown versus Topeka, Kansas* and the Montgomery bus boycott.

One trend in particular recognized the existence of two distinct nations in the USA—a Black domestic colony and a racist white imperialism—and proceeded from there. This trend defined the Black struggle as a national liberation movement of the same sort as that which was then freeing Cuba from U.S. tutelage, and Algeria from French rule. It ranked our struggle with the Indochinese peoples' efforts to ward off French and U.S. aggression, and applauded the Chinese Revolution. It insisted that the key to social transformation in America is the Black national liberation movement, while admitting that American imperialism was the strongest link in the chain of white supremacy. Nonetheless the United States was vulnerable, they claimed simultaneously, because of the presence on the home front of a dangerous Black "fifth column." U.S. imperialism is menaced from the "rear," they contended.

Meanwhile, the then-flourishing Nation of Islam took a different tack. Elijah Muhammad condemned white "blue-eyed devils" on religious grounds, proposing a nationalist option that offered voluntary territorial separation as the remedy to the evil of white domination.

233

The highwater mark of Black separation, as articulated in the demand for the establishment of an independent Black republic on U.S. territory, came in 1967. That year a Chicago conference for a "New Politics" brought some two hundred left-wing organizations, mostly white, together at Palmer's House Grand Ballroom. Black representatives dominated the gathering. Caucusing separately, the Blacks imposed a 13-point platform endorsing the right to partition the United States into two separate nations, one white and one Black. Other militant demands included the right to form a Black militia, and the right of Black people to rebel whenever we deem it necessary.

About the same time, one segment of the Black liberation movement tied the fate of American Blacks to the creation of a revolutionary base in a completely liberated and unified Africa. Not until power had been seized by revolutionaries throughout the Black continent, and a base established in which all Africans would speak a single language and respond to the command of a single Black government, did these latter-day Pan-Africanists consider it possible to extend emancipation to the embattled African people of the Americas. To American Black folk they assigned the role of supporters, to be sacrificed, if necesary, for the freedom of the mother continent. This thesis was criticized as a fallacious interpretation and a misapplication of the doctrine of the revolutionary base area developed by Vietnamese general Vo Nguyen Giap and China's Mao Tse-tung. Its advocates tried to make the Chinese leader's teachings on national struggle relevant to the strategy and tactics of Black liberation (Mao Tse-tung 1965, Vol. II, Peking:213-214). They regarded the overthrow of imperialist rule in Africa as the point of departure for Black struggles everywhere, particularly those in North America. The struggle of American Blacks was demoted to a mere *form* of the struggle to emancipate the Black continent, or alternatively, efforts were made to demonstrate identity between the two, i.e., to prove that one was the same as the other. Divergent political and economic demands from the western side of the Atlantic would merely upset the apple cart.

This attitude marked the philosophy and program of the All-African People's Revolutionary Party (AAPRP), a spinoff of this country's 1960's Black Power Movement.

Despite U.S. origins, the AAPRP leadership felt it had to base its headquarters in Africa, not in America, were the party to ever become a truly independent, permanent, and revolutionary Pan-Africanist organ. The mother continent is revered as the focus of a Pan-African and world socialist revolution: "All people of African descent, whether they live in North or South America, the Caribbean, or in any other part of the world, are Africans and belong to the African nation." AAPRP admitted that Euro-Christian and Islamic intrusions had changed the traditional African way of life forever. The Black homeland has been ripped to its seams by competing and conflicting slave, "feudal" and capitalist modes of production, and for a time during the 1960s and 1970s, by would-be socialism. Nonetheless, insists AAPRP, Black people, scattered in over 113 countries, are one people, sharing a single identity, history, culture, and destiny. Though we suffer from disunity, disorganization and ideological confusion, we have one common enemy—white supremacy. AAPRP made total liberation of Africa and its unification under an all-African socialist government the party's primary objective. The policy has made recruitment and organization extremely difficult on this side of the Atlantic.

The Nation of Islam bungled its way through the assassination by its own "zealots" of the movement's greatest product—Malcolm X—and through splits, schisms, fratricidal conflicts and doctrinal disputes. Its popular influence dwindled. Of late it has rebounded, its program, philosophy and interpretation of history is projected in *The Final Call*, a news journal. The Nation of Islam continues to call for a separate territory for Blacks in North America or elsewhere and to demand that intermarriage be abolished. It calls for the release of all believers in Islam now in U.S. prisons. Some scepticism greets its vision of separate-but-equal Black schools, given our painful experience with the historical reality of separate-but-unequal education enshrined in *Plessy vs. Ferguson*. *The Final Call* pleads for equal justice and employment until a separate territory is created. Minister Louis Farrakhan, successor to Elijah Muhammad as head of the Nation of Islam, suspects there is a plot to inject Black people with AIDS. He has pushed for a three-year financial savings program as a model for Black economic empowerment. Funds contributed by Blacks themselves would go to establish a banking system and buy farmland. The purchase-of-farmland idea calls to mind the remedies of Booker T. Washington and Thomas T. Fortune. Put forward as an updated strategy capable of dealing with twenty-first century stress, *The Final Call's* economic proposals resonate with self-help. In October 1995, Farrakhan mobilized adult Black males for a Million Man March in the nation's capital. The themes of the march were atonement, rededication, and recommitment.

By way of contrast, in the year before his murder, Malcolm X had become very subtle and discriminating in his condemnation of the white man. He ceased to talk of Elijah Muhammad's "blue-eyed devils." Instead he substituted the "collective white man's cruelty." By the collective white man, he meant the *system* of white society and civilization, white cultural traits, and the racist political economy developed through history. He realized that targeting any one specific white individual, or group, was not enough. According to the mature Malcolm, the fundamental political-economic racial contradiction pitted all the world's Black and other people of color against the collective white man, that is, against the *global* system of white supremacy.

*

Nationalism has shown like a bright pearl in the history of Black political philosophy. It has given us a yardstick by which to measure our options—and an attitude which gives form to the choices made. Nationalist ideology had to serve preservation. It offered survival strategies to a people jeopardized by the evolution of the U.S. economy from one in which we were restricted to low caste manual and domestic labor, to one which is well on its way to dispensing altogether with the labor of many of our Black males. Moreover, there was the malevolent social rituals of racist white America with which to contend.

Nationalist thinkers defined the community, figuratively, as an organic unit endowed with its own existence. They perceived Black America as a collection of Africans brought in chains to these shores. Those Africans—remaining Africans despite the long exile—are now bound together by a common historical destiny, and a collective psychology which constitute a unique American Black national character. Nationalists grasped the Black man's character as the condensation of the whole unique history of the nation, the history of his African ancestors, the history of one nation sprung from many different African ethnic groups, yet all united in a common Black culture or civilization (see C.A. Diop and Chancellor Williams). They knew that until late in the nineteenth century Black slave labor was the fuel that drove the expanding capitalist world machine. This gave them reasons for a sense of group pride. Nationalists lauded the Black cultural heritage, and our accomplishments in mass culture, athletics, and elite entertainment. But nothing mattered more to nationalist ideology than the record of Black socioeconomic and scholastic achievements, of identity and racial solidarity—the nationalists were unwavering "race men." Unfortunately, throughout the history of nationalism there also runs a thread of fanatical hatred for mulattoes. The disease ravaged writers from E.W. Blyden to Marcus Garvey to Chancellor Williams. Mulatto phobia has tarnished Black nationalism, diminishing its political credibility.

Nevertheless, despite many disagreements, nationalists have—since the nineteenth century—shared a collective mode of perceiving, a way of feeling, which colors all cultural elements assimilated from other peoples. This, they say, endows our folk with the renowned personal touch one still encounters when entering Black communities, even in the dangerous inner-city. This, paired with the long fight to preserve the Black national character from racist obliteration, solidified the "underdog" community. It built a distinct racial consciousness. The fact that racist white America handled an imprisoned Black America as a domestic colony, say some of the nationalists, conditioned at once the community's ability to feel and express itself, and the social cohesion of its constituent elements. In short, the racial question has kept Black folk "down" with each other, despite life-style, religious, and proto-class differences. Insightful nationalists acknowledge that white-imposed cultural devaluation has resulted in self-contempt and a massive inferiority complex that defame the purer forms of Black culture. According to certain *cultural* nationalists, the only ones isolated and alienated enough from white values to identify fully with unadulterated Black culture are the "grass-roots brothers and sisters." The latter are said to be less bashful about embracing the "gutsiness" of Black culture. The least social and psychological ambivalence is to be found at the "grass-roots" (Kelley 1994).

Black Capitalism

Whatever happened to Black capitalism? Well, it has been a little like the proverbial "Perils of Pauline"—a story filled with sound and fury, fates worse than death, exaggerated reports of demise, pulse-thundering rescues, and last-minute resurrections, phoenix-like, from the ashes. It has been a procession of gurus from Booker T.

Washington with his exhortations, to Reginald Lewis with his leveraged buy-outs. Of late, if one thumbs the pages of *Black Enterprise*
magazine, it comes across as not merely alive and well, but downright flourishing. Reality is much less encouraging.

Actually, too much and too little has been expected of Black capitalism. If minority economic enterprise could have duplicated, say,
American Jewish capitalism, then Black capitalism would have
served Black America magnificently. One in five of the super-rich in
this country is Jewish, in a Jewish population that is barely more
than two percent of total inhabitants. When was the last time one
encountered a Jewish garbage collector, a Jewish janitor, or Jews in
similarly humble occupations? Where is the Jewish ghetto "underclass"? Jews are underrepresented among the homeless and vastly
overrepresented in wealthy retirement settlements. If our experience
had been similar, capitalism would have made Afro-Americans 30
percent and more of the super-rich. For generations Black governors and senators would have been common in a dozen and more
states. Not just one, but always three or four Supreme Court justices would be Black, and Black people would dominate (monopolize in some cases) such solid middle class professions as secondary
school teachers and principals, university professors and administrators, doctors, lawyers, stockbrokers, and psychiatrists, as well as
the movie and print industries. We would be almost non-existent in
heavy, dirty blue-collar jobs and low-paying service industries. That
is what any really significant Black business enterprise would look
like. In truth, our real situation is ludicrously different.

Yet our attitude towards capitalism remains stubbornly positive.
Some 65 percent of American Blacks believe the economy can run
only if businessmen make large profits (Jaynes and Williams:211).
And surprisingly, 29 percent of our people even thought that business profits are distributed *fairly* in the United States, according to
a 1984 survey.

However, Census Bureau data compiled at the beginning of the
1990s show that Black capitalism continues to be weak. Black businesses constitute only three percent of the United States' companies, and a mere one percent of gross receipts. White resistance to
minority set-asides is stronger than ever, and the Black proportion
in corporate management remains anemic, with little prospect for
swift improvement. At 5.9 percent of all managers in the United
States, we are grossly underrepresented. Blacks make up three per-

cent of *corporate* management. Many of our most talented business minds are still locked out of the choicest executive positions. In 1990 the federal Equal Employment Opportunity Commission (EEOC) revealed that African Americans represent only about eight percent of the executive corps even in what were described as the "25 Best Places for Blacks to Work."

It is a sad fact of life that Black capitalism is miles from self-reliance. It depends heavily on government for credit, custom, and contracts. At the end of the 1960s, one-half of Black firms were located in the South, numbering some 163,000—a mere 2.2 percent of all American firms. As a legacy of segregation, most were concentrated in personal services and retail trade, and pocketed less than one percent of all national business receipts. In 1987, the share of Black sales revenue was about one-third of one percent of the total U.S. sales receipts. As the 1990s began, Black entrepreneurs owned and operated somewhere between a low estimate of 300,000 businesses and a high estimate of 400,000 (Henderson 1990: 55; and Billingsley 1992). In either case, more than 90 percent of them were supplying or servicing government agencies. In contrast, less than 50 percent of all enterprises run by whites or other non-Blacks were chained to the government chariot.

Racism causes this dependency, and racism shackles the Black entrepreneur, for most white private sector businesses refuse to do business with Black businessmen and find a myriad of excuses for the thumbs down attitude. Only because it is somewhat sensitive to political prodding does the government itself comply. With only two percent of the nation's population, Jews dominate whole sectors of the economy. Black capitalism, representing at least 15 percent of America's inhabitants, amounts to one third of one percent of the nation's sales receipts. David Swinton, former Jackson State University economist, observed that Black capitalism generated receipts only about 1.2 percent of what would have been expected if our people had business ownership parity (Swinton 1990:42). Moreover, Black enterprise is not merely small business, it is a micro-small affair. A 1987 survey reported African American enterprises as averaging only $47,000 each in annual receipts, as compared to $146,000 for all other (i.e., mostly white-owned) small and mid-sized firms (Census Bureau, *1987 Survey of Minority Owned Business Enterprises—Black*). And it is notorious that even among the star companies in Black America's economic firmament, less than 20 percent have anything to do with key industries like computers, construction, energy, and metal works. The best performers are still concentrated in such tertiary sectors as entertainment, food and beverage, and hair care and beauty aids—areas that do not command the macro-economy. Combined revenue for the 100 largest Black-owned companies finally reached the $10 billion ceiling in 1993. Those 100 top firms employed a total of merely 38,649 persons. Not enough to make a dent in the job-needy Black work force.

Where considerable wealth is amassed, it is not clear that it is always used in a manner conducive to the Black general interest. Deceased in 1993, Reginald Lewis was reputed to be the richest Black man in America. At his death at age 50, he was chairman and largest shareholder in TLC Beatrice International Holdings, a multinational food company, valued at close to a billion dollars. TLC Beatrice's chief operations were in France. In 1992 Lewis' personal net fortune was pegged in excess of $400 million. Shortly before his death, Lewis saw fit to endow Harvard Law School—his alma mater—with $3 million, the largest grant from an individual in the history of the law facility. Shortly before the gift, Harvard Law School officials dismissed its senior-ranking Black professor—Derrick Bell—for protesting the faculty's refusal to appoint a woman of color to a tenured position. Lewis donated in full knowledge of the Bell case.

These are the real-life dimensions of Black capitalism. Most corporate doors remain closed to Blacks—or have barely cracked. As the 1970s ended, persons of color were nearly invisible in the nation's managerial class—a mere 3.6 percent and only three African-Americans among senior executives. Along came the Reagan-Bush era to further slow, or bring to a standstill, what little progress was being made.

Mouth-froth from such apologists as Thomas Sowell and Walter Williams fails to disguise the facts that as soon as the recession of the 1990s hit, the corporate establishment raced to lay off its Black MBA's, that three to four percent remains the glass ceiling for Black students enrolled in MBA programs, and that African-Americans are less than one percent of all mid-to-upper level corporate executives. Publicity-stunt appointments of high-level Blacks in a handful of corporations merely lend media gloss to disparity.

It is difficult to avoid the conclusion, therefore, that Black capitalism has weight only with a numerically insignificant segment of the whole Black population. Nowhere in North America has it ever been able to provide jobs, income and career opportunities for substantial numbers of the community. Economically it is essentially different from the real capitalist class—the imperialist white corporate elite. This is not due to any fault of Black entrepreneurs, for they too are the victims of racism. Black capitalism owns none of the crucial means of production. Exclusion from ownership and control of the latter, in turn, signifies that our businessmen control little capital and will never be allowed to accumulate significant blocks as long as white supremacy holds. Black capitalism finds the ascent to real economic and social power blocked on all sides, in the South as well as in the North and West. The business activity of Black capitalists is marginal. *Black Enterprise* magazine's hopes are unrealizable without stunning change in American political economy. Black entrepreneurship vegetates in tiny, arbitrarily restricted, separate niches in the economy—woven in intervening spaces. We are still limited mostly to retail trade, car-dealerships, fast food and beverage franchises, restaurants and service enterprise (where morticians still star), entertainment and the manufacture of cosmetics. The Black consumers' market is starved by under- and unemployment, overpricing and multiple hoodwinking commercial practices. North America's largest Black community still lives in New York City. The list of Black-owned businesses in Gotham in 1991 included barber and beauty shops, Nation of Islam enterprises, shoe repair, real estate brokers, dressmakers, bookstores, newsstands, accountants, restaurants, public relations firms, grocery stores, advertising agencies, bars, magazines, clubs, newspapers, banks, radio stations, and insurance companies. A fair range, but all these enterprises were small. And the banking, savings and loan associations, and insurance companies are famished by the poverty of their Black clientele.

Hoping to remedy the situation, some strategists bank on minority set-asides and seek to get around the *Croson v. City of Richmond* Supreme Court decision which declared race-based, set-aside programs as unconstitutional, unless overt discrimination were documented. They have been helped a little by the Civil Rights Restoration Act of 1991, weak though it is. Atlanta Mayor Maynard Jackson tried a race-neutral gambit of bonding, financial, and technical assistance for small businesses. His Equal Business Opportunity (EBO) legislation attempted to facilitate minority participation in city contracts. It mitigates the effects of discrimination against minority-owned enterprises. A five-year program, EBO set annual contracting goals of 30 percent for Black-owned businesses. Set-asides were earmarked for Native Americans also. EBO is applauded as a model for other Black-administered municipalities seeking to reverse affirmative-action losses. Operating from exalted heights, Xerox, a multi-billion dollar document-processing and financial services corporation which employs nearly 9,000 Blacks (13.5 percent of its work force), offers a piece-of-the-pie strategy. Blacks hold 10 percent of Xerox management positions, and the corporation boasts that its 26 Black vice presidents make it the top equal opportunity employer in private industry. A Black executive, Richard S. Barton, was appointed president of Xerox Canada, Inc., and Yvonne M. Wilson, a Black woman, was installed as vice president of the New York-area field operations in the corporations' U.S. Marketing Group.

The strategy that champions electoral politics as the road to Black business empowerment touted Lawrence Douglas Wilder as its darling. Wilder, a Democrat, was elected governor of Virginia in 1989. He had fashioned a coalition which included trade unions, community activists, pro-choice white women, peace activists, environmentalists, and business leaders. His basic constituents were African-Americans, roughly 20 percent of the state's voters. Wilder's fiscal conservatism and refusal to raise taxes on corporations and the wealthy were somehow supposed to create a "trickle-down" effect that would encourage the Black small business community. However, this strategy melted in the political heat of 1992, as support for Wilder wilted in the Black community at large. He faded further in 1994.

The problem facing Black-owned business and Black entrepreneurs today is essentially the same old one—the inability to provide gainful employment to a *substantial* segment of the Black work force. This casts shadow and doubt on Black business enterprise. Ultimately, Black capitalism's standing in the Black community must depend on job-creation. This task far outweighs the aura of personal wealth. The radiance and hero-ranking of Black tycoons are little in comparison. After all, we have long ogled a handful of super-rich entertainment and sports superstars, little to the benefit of our poor. The visibility has been there, as has the role modelling. This is not to imply that Black business people as a group are not devoted to their community's welfare, and are not to be trusted. Many are trustworthy. Black entrepreneurs must start small, and there is nothing wrong, intrinsically, with starting small. But the point is that white supremacy and institutionalized racial discrimination against Black entrepreneurship condemns Black business to second-fiddle or bankruptcy. Black firms are still uniformly redlined by banks. Black capitalism cannot function as a provider and nourisher.

*

These circumstances force Black capitalism's historical limitations to the front and center. Over generations its greatest success has not come from manufacturing, commerce or finance. Not even from service, publishing or entertainment enterprises. The master strokes of the Johnson Publishing company and Motown were merely exceptions that proved the rule. If Black capitalism is taken to mean independent wealth (income) generation for American Blacks; stable and secure livelihoods; prestigious occupations; and sums of money free from white control; then the Black *clergy* has been the champion creation of Black capitalism. Though it may seem paradoxical and ironic, its main accomplishments have come through the efforts and professional status of the Black ministry. Preachers were the largest body of Black middle income professionals (ca. 18,000 as early as the 1940 census) whose regular paychecks did not come from white people. Black congregations ranged from large, "respectable" Baptist and AME ones to small storefront flocks. They paid the bill for the Black minister—for the imposing Baptist patriarch as well as for the "jackleg." These church folk endowed their ministers with a wonderful independence. The clergy alone were not directly beholden to whites for their daily bread. The near-monopoly of leadership assumed in the community for so long by the reverends was rooted in this financial autonomy. The only other seemingly independent group—small farm owners in the South's Black Belt—were, in fact, usually mortgaged to white merchant bankers. Any attempt to act independently could cause foreclosure. Only in the last twenty-five years or so have accountants, lawyers, and physicians outpaced the clergy in numbers. The bulk of today's Black white-collar "middle class" consists of engineers, computer programmers, registered nurses, college professors and other teachers, journalists and managers and administrators—all *salary earners*, i.e. not the kind of people who hold significant profit-yielding capital assets. (According to 1992 Bureau of Labor statistics, Black public relations specialists were 8.3 percent, physicians 3.2

243

percent, journalists 4.6 percent, and college professors 4.8 percent, respectively, of the national totals of these professionals.) The government—once again—is the backbone of the current Black "bourgeoisie." Municipal, state, and federal jobs are the economic mainstay for Black middle-incomers. The old maxim—"preach, teach or farm"—gave way to the dictum, teach, preach (less and less), entertain, or work for the government, and, since the 1970s, civil (and military) service substitutes for the absence of private capital.

Black capitalism has remained a secondary phenomenon, and without a startling change in circumstances will remain so; one lonely pimple on a vast epidermis, figuratively speaking. Black-owned business provides a negligible number of jobs for Black people. A disappearingly small percentage of our folks are employed by Black entrepreneurs. Black capitalism is not unrighteous; it is not morally bankrupt; it is merely irrelevant to the life-shuffle of the majority of the Black community. And, saddest fact of all, since the formal abolition of Jim Crow in the 1960s, it has become less and less of an economic life-saver.

*

THE SCHOOL HOUSE AND THE SCHOOL YARD

White supremacy could not have flourished without a nourishing *collective mentality* ordaining the miseducation of both white and Black children. This particular collective mentality can be defined as an edifice of bogus logic, all the component ideas and beliefs of which support one another, and are bound together by content relations, principle, and consequence. All the parts of this collective mentality provide mutual proofs, as for example where the crime of the inner-city, coupled with poor minority pupil performance, are taken as the sign of inherent racial inferiority of Blacks, and where, turnabout, alleged Black racial inferiority is cited as the cause for the degradation of the inner-city, and for slow-learning minority pupils. By a kind of osmosis, young whites have confirmed for them during their years of schooling a prejudice which is as prevalent in the social environment as oxygen is in the air we breathe. They grow accustomed to the idea they are superior to Black human beings and come to act as if they were. Black youngsters are made to believe they are innately inferior and are trained to behave accordingly.

The false consciousness dictated by this collective mentality has withstood two entire generations of changing patterns in Black school enrollment, per-pupil expenditure, and years of formal schooling, as well as changes in Black adult education.

For a lot has changed since 1930. Without ever fully catching up, Black lads born in, say, 1965 had a much higher enrollment rate in comparison with whites, than their fathers born in, say, the year 1925. While "savage inequalities" persist, it is no longer likely that even Mississippi could still get away with spending more than 600 percent more on the education of a white child than on the schooling of a Black child, as it did in the 1939–1940 school year. In 1940 nearly 70 percent of adult Black women had had eight or fewer years of schooling, while more than 75 percent of adult Black males were similarly unschooled. By 1980, in both instances that ratio had fallen to less than ten percent. Meanwhile, by the end of the 1970s, more than ten percent of adult Black women and men were earning college degrees. Completed high school diplomas had become common. Black kindergarten enrollment in the 3 to 5 age range rose from ten percent in 1968 to over 90 percent in 1985. In fact, Black kids made very good progress over those seventeen years. Data from the National Assessment of Education Progress and reports from the Educational Testing Service registered real academic achievement in mathematics and science, the disciplines in which Black youngsters traditionally lagged most. More Black students were taking algebra and geometry, and more were mastering those subjects. By 1982, 16.5 percent of Black male high school seniors, and 15.5 percent of female seniors were earning at least three credits in advanced mathematics, within hailing distance of white male and female seniors at 21.9 and 22.9 percent, respectively (Jaynes and Williams 1989:350–351). Literacy tests for adults aged 21 to 25 showed that Blacks still experienced much greater difficulty writing standard English prose than whites, and that Black teacher competency test scores in deep South states fell below white teacher scores, but the failing merely reflects the inadequate training of Black teachers and the racist bias of the tests. Census Bureau statistics show that African-Americans are completing high school at an increasing rate. In 1970 nearly 28 percent of Blacks dropped out of school. By 1989 the non-graduation rate had declined to just under 14 percent, i.e., had been cut in half. Reading at the "adept" level rose for Black students from eight percent in 1974–1975 to 26 percent in 1987–1988.

Yet, despite these efforts, Black males in the northeastern and southern regions of the country who attended college continued to suffer higher rates of unemployment than white residents in those same regions who did not even complete high school. What was amiss? The same old shaft—the harder we strive, the less we seem to get. College enrollment slackened among Afro-Americans during the Reagan years, although women made some gains. The earnings of Black high school graduates slumped noticeably, as the white-run economy learned more and more to dispense with Black labor. In 1973 the percentage of our high school graduates earning less than $12,000 stood at 16 percent. By 1987, some 38 percent were taking home less than $12,000.

A generation ago, Black students pressed hard on college campuses everywhere in North America to have Black Studies recognized as a legitimate academic discipline. They won concessions. In March 1969, Harvard University itself announced plans to establish a degree program in Black Studies in response to the demands of Black students. The nation's premier institution of higher learning acknowledged that "[we] are dealing with 25 million of our own people with a special history, culture and range of problems." And it added that "[it] can hardly be doubted that the study of black men in America is a legitimate and urgent academic endeavour."

But since then much has grown worse as racism has increasingly devalued education for Black people. Correspondingly, a slander campaign spread reports that the Black males have become a gender of drones of little help to their women. By 1989 Black females owning high school diplomas had increased their earnings to 71 percent of the earnings of Black male high school graduates. Higher education, in particular, was beginning to pay off for Black women. In 1989 those with four or more years of college were pocketing 3.27 times the income of Black females who had dropped out of high school, according to data presented by David Swinton (*Black Enterprise*, vol. 22, no. 6, January 1992). Yet as a measure of the downgrading to which white supremacy subjects the Black male, the advantage for comparably educated males over school dropouts is only 2.4-fold. Frances Cress-Welsing has commented that while white males do not fear Black women and expect to manipulate them, many white adults hate and fear grown-up Black men. The more education African-American men get, the wider the income gap, as compared with a white index. In 1991 the disparity for Black men with eight years or less of schooling was 13 percent; 25 percent for high school graduates, and a whopping 32 percent for Black men with four years of college. This severely reduces the monetary value of higher education for Black men.

Black male university graduates of all age groups still earn less than the average of white males who only complete high school. That fact alone refutes the argument that all we need do is improve our educational level and related skills. Post–Cold War cuts in the armed forces have proliferated. It is doubtful whether the Blacks discharged from the armed forces with enhanced specialist skills in everything from radar to electronics will fare any better than the average white high school graduate. Surely they will not do as well as whites discharged with similar enhanced skills. The opportunity to improve educational and specialized occupational skills has been a major inducement for Black and Brown youths to join the "volunteer" U.S. armed forces. Minority recruits hoped to catch up with whites in similar social categories and command higher earnings later in civilian pursuits. Anyway, a Black person with a completed college education is still two and a half times more likely to be unemployed than a white person with a college education.

The likelihood that a Black youngster, fresh out of high school, would matriculate in a college or university, hit its zenith in 1977, whether causally or coincidentally connected with the Carter Administration. Ominously, the odds against college entry have been greater since then for Black high school graduates. The decline in minority presence on the nation's campuses directly parallels the cutting of minority scholarships. At one juncture, the Bush Administration even tried to prohibit "race-exclusive scholarships." It meant scholarships set aside for Blacks and other minorities. Even now, Republicans hope to further lower minority enrollment and retention. Even without the attempted sabotage, all minority scholarships make up only a paltry three percent of financial aid, far below the population percentile of Blacks alone. Already waiving the $4,000-a-year tuition fee for out-of-state Black students, the University of Florida announced in 1993, for example, that Blacks were a mere 5.7 percent of the institution's student body.

It bodes ill that the youth crisis in formal education also has a gender dimension. Comparing 18- to 24-year-olds reveals that during the 1980s, fewer Black males graduated from high school than females. The ratio of Black male high school graduates aged 18 to 24 attending college is now noticeably lower than that of Black females. The spillover this has on Black male earning power is bad.

It predicts a diminishing share for male income in the household budget, and that spells trouble for an already battered Black family structure. The median earnings of Black males age 25 and older with only a high school education was $20,280 in 1989. In contrast, the median for Black females with a college education was $26,730.

As the 1990s began, there were some 1.2 million Black undergraduates and graduate students. The overwhelming majority pursued studies in predominately white institutions. Still it was the gender breakdown that was most unpromising—with 747,000 studying in colleges and universities, females outnumbered males almost two to one. There were only 476,000 Black men on the nation's campuses.

＊

Of course, unfairness is found not only at the top of the educational hierarchy. It reaches deep in the American public school system, down to the primary level. Recently Jonathan Kozol exposed the unfair practices and racist inequalities inherent in the primary and secondary education. He surveyed 30 schools in six cities. His findings show that white supremacy is alive and strong in the "Little Red School House." Education in the suburbs is computerized, clean, healthy, and backed up with fine libraries; and suburban schools are typically white, which explains why money is thrown at them—$15,000 per annum per student in suburban New York. Television audiences were treated to the comforting fairy tale of the Huxtable kids being nurtured through adolescence in safe schools by intellectually stimulating teachers. Reality in inner city schools is somewhat different, where, as Kozol reports, less than half as much is spent on each child than on the education of rich white suburban pupils. Children are packed in like sardines. Minorities are rigidly segregated according to race and color, warehoused in filthy, broken-down constructions, lacking even in toilet paper. Frightened, harassed, underpaid, and under-trained teachers contend with drugs and guns. Teenage pregnancy and dropping-out are commonplace (Kozol 1992).

The focus of educational segregation has shifted to the northward inner cities. Public schools in South Carolina, Alabama, and Georgia are now less segregated than those in the state of New Jersey, where school *apartheid* has raged unchecked since 1968. And New Jersey is not the only state to run a dual school system, an adequate one for whites, and another, grossly inferior one for Blacks and

Latinos. The nightmare is compounded by "missing" Black teachers. As Floretta Dukes McKenzie observed: "Projections are that by the year 2000, only five percent of the teachers in public schools will be black; how ironic is such a decline in minority teachers at a time when minority student enrolment will be continuing to increase..." (McKenzie 1991:104-105). North Carolina, for instance, was short some 15,000 minority teachers in 1995.

The twenty-first century will open with all too few Black teachers in charge of America's blackboards. It is already too late to alter that prospect. Yet already in many localities, the majority of children in the public school system are non-white. This trend will accelerate through the twenty-first century's early decades. Current misery will worsen and magnify. Nor has Canada escaped the problem of "missing" Black teachers. A similar lack in the Greater Toronto Area triggered modest affirmative action in the 1990s, designed to boost the "visible minority" contingent in Ontario's Teacher Training Colleges. Black-on-Black violence has compounded the school crisis. 56 incidents involving firearms were recorded in New York City schools in the 1991-1992 year alone. Five teachers were shot—one fatally; six children were fatalities; a parent was wounded; overcrowding, coupled with the removal of 2,500 teachers from the staff, fueled the "open season."

Though the problems are different, the prospect is equally bleak for Black college and university teachers, especially for males. There are precious few Black Ph.D.s in North America, and their ratio is not growing. In truth, between 1978 and 1988, there was a 22- to 27-percent drop in the number of Blacks who were awarded the Ph.D. degree. There was a small increase in the first half of the 1990s, but not enough to make a difference. At the time of this writing, less than 4.5 percent of professors are Black. This scarcity alone makes it hard to better the plight of Black professors, still concentrated in education and the social sciences, after a whole generation of campus struggles to validate Black Studies. The quandary facing Black faculty has many facets. It ranges from underrepresentation at predominately white universities to low retention rates, from a quota ceiling to lack of seniority, from the hostility of conservative white colleagues to workloads which in practice far exceed the job description. Posing as the champions of "merit" and "excellence," the majority of white male faculty in North America are bitterly opposed to affirmative action in their own "backyard." They cast slurs on aggressive hiring and promotion of racial minorities. They make life miserable for Black professors. Once an initial appointment or two have been made, other minority candidates are shut out by the "one-or-two-is-enough" syndrome (Jaynes and Williams, 1989, pp. 375-377). Career development, evaluation, and promotion procedures cause high turnover among those Black faculty who do manage to get appointed. Caught in a revolving door, as it were, Blacks on short-term contracts are swept in and out. Tenure-track appointments—leading to permanent appointment lasting an entire career—are still relatively rare for Afro-Americans and dark-skinned Latinos. The professorial staff at the nation's elite universities are still mostly lily-white. The rate of faculty and staff hiring of minorities has stagnated nationally. There is continuing reluctance to recognize the scholarly value of Black research. Afrocentric studies on social problems, history, and race relations are subject to concerted "putdown." The white scholarly establishment puts its stamp of approval only on those Black faculty who toe the line and avoid the slightest whiff of controversy.

Black professors who do make it into the ranks of the tenure-track faculty face daunting disadvantages. Demands on their time far exceed the demands on white professors. For if they retain any sense of commitment to our people, they cannot escape the need to act as role models for the Black students on campus. This constitutes a heavy load of counselling and mentoring. This and other forms of stress unknown to white faculty are likely to diminish research productivity—particularly for young faculty struggling for tenure. It is not the fashion of academia to allow for the burden of white racism Black professors must bear.

The total enrollment in the nation's 41 Historically Black Colleges and Universities (HBCUs) has swelled recently. Still, these collegians are but a small percentage of all Black college students. Southern Black colleges are being undermined under the guise of *eliminating* racial segregation! The incongruity of desegregated higher institutions is illustrated, for example, in the recent attempt by Mississippi authorities to close Mississippi Valley State University— a historically Black institution.

The Black college would have been sacrificed to budgetary constraints while Delta State University, a predominately white institution, would remain open.

My own experience as a university professor for 35 years has convinced me that some African-American students are impaired psychologically when their higher education is confined to "integrated"—i.e., historically white—institutions. Particularly in facilities where whites are 80-90 percent of the student body, and where almost the entire faculty and administration are white (Black personnel five percent or less). The "chilly environment" instills self-doubt. It cannot fail to engender paranoia. Being where one is not wanted is humiliating. More so than in the classroom, it is in extracurricular events and in campus social life that inter-racial stress and strain are most evident. Feeling merely tolerated as a token damages personal esteem.

The historical track record of Black national leadership seems to indicate that alumni of the HBCUs are more self-confident and demanding. Certainly, the HBCUs have provided the community with leaders, generation after generation. This holds true even if skewed by the fact that since slavery most of our leaders have come from the clergy, and the natural place to train Black ministers were the Black colleges. For long there were really only three professional career options—teach, preach or farm. Noteworthy, moreover, has been the prominence in U.S. Black political affairs of West Indians, offspring of Black-majority societies. It seems that there is something about being with one's own race during one's college days, which instills self-confidence and self-respect, qualities which persons swamped in a white sea seem to have difficulty developing. Only time will tell how future graduates from predominately white institutions will fare.

The best Black athletes flock to white universities, drawn by scholarships and publicity conducive to post-university professional employment. However, the HBCUs continued to attract and educate the majority of Black undergraduates who actually manage to *complete* a degree program.

The struggle has no signs of letting up. In Spring 1993 Starksville, Mississippi, Afro-American residents were threatening to sue the state over equity funding for school systems. The NAACP voiced outrage at Mississippi's equity funding legislation. The law discriminated against low-income school districts. Black pupils are concentrated in poor districts. At that same moment, Black collegians attending the University of North Carolina at Chapel Hill were staging a 1960s-style sit-in, unable to get University officials to agree on a suitable site for a Black Cultural Center.

There is a substratum underpinning each basic civilization—Black, white, Chinese, Native American, and any others. This substratum (under/over) determines socio-economic relations. The substratum issues a kind of unconditional command which governs folkways and customs which, in turn, give each civilization—and each society within each civilization—its own flavor. However, we must distinguish between this ultimate determination and the ideological trap that contends that neither the Black African in his native setting, nor his descendant in any of the Americas can be improved, or that the circumstances in which Black people live cannot be radically altered because those circumstances are inherent in our nature. As we have seen, this malicious claim sets Black folk outside History and Time. Unfortunately, a version of this idea appears in some extreme Négritude philosophy, as well as in some varieties of cultural nationalism. Predictably, it is traded upon by white supremacists. Today's sophisticated racists increasingly discuss Black-white relations in terms of a moral dilemma, as an exercise in the achievement of the "American Dream." Discrimination against Black people is made out to be nothing more than a faltering of American ideals. Change becomes an illusion. Change and time are abolished, and one is left facing an impenetrable conservative wall. The happenstance that since the fifteenth century the white race has dominated people of color is construed as proof of inherent white racial superiority. It is used to validate a "white man's burden."

Nevertheless, the struggle will continue, but on different terms, in the twenty-first century. The race has not yet been run to its conclusion, the historical outcome is still in doubt, very much up for grabs. History is laying seeds of circumstances that should spell the end of white domination over people of color. There is reason to believe that the twenty-first century will also turn the tables on the whole educational project.

Chapter 14

THE STATE OF BLACK AMERICA-I

DEMOGRAPHY: RUNNING NUMBERS

Analysis of the current living and working conditions of a people must
entail demographic considerations. In fact, it would be downright
foolhardy not to run some numbers on you. The science of demography inquires into the composition, movement and development of the
population. Without it, we can neither predict social trends, nor arrive
at any reliable social and political perspectives for the future.
Demography is closely connected with political economy, sociology
and statistics. It enables us to gauge a people's quality of life. Through
population statistics we comprehend our people's makeup as well as
such vital processes as the evolution of the Black family, occupational and spatial mobility, the skill level of the Afro-American work force,
gender and age ratios, social stratification within the community, living standards, and the birth rate. Demographic investigation tells us
whether the African American population is growing rather than
shrinking and whether it is likely to continue in the same mode. In

the North American context, demography must also deal with the practice of census undercounting and with immigration policy—life-and-death issues for Black folk.

*

Right off the bat there is an intriguing outlook—the 1990 U.S. Census revealed that minorities of color will account for one-third of all entrants into the labor force by the year 2000. There is of course no likelihood that even a large minority of these new jobseekers will actually procure employment, or that they will face any less racial discrimination than encountered by their resemblants of the previous two decades, although their arrival is only a few years away. Minorities will bulk large in North America's future labor force.

A look at the *1962 Statistical Abstract of the United States, Table 30,* shows that even federal government undercounts could not hide the fact that Black America swelled by some five million between 1950 and 1960. The civil rights movement drew much of its vitality from this rapid growth. By 1960 there were upwards of two million more young Black adults than there had been in 1950. Federal government enumerators put the 1960 population total for Black America between 20 and 21 million (Malcolm X and other militant fighters for Black liberation talked of 22 million). Even discounting the undercounting of those actually enumerated, the figures were grossly inaccurate, for they omitted Blacks in prison, persons in transit from city to city, Blacks temporarily not living at home, and the permanently homeless, just for a starter. In the space of the nine years between 1 April 1960 and 1 July 1969, the Black community expanded by more than 20 percent as compared with an 11.8 percent growth in the number of whites. Between 1967 and 1992, the Black population in the United States grew by more than 50 percent. What is more, by the latter date any honest estimate had to reckon that, taken together, the various contingents of the people of color added up in the U.S. to considerably *more* than 70 million.

Conservative estimates peg the growth of the Black population during the 1990s at 12.8 percent, as compared with a mere 5.2 percent expansion of the white population (Tidwell 1991: 219).

In 1991 the total population of the United States was somewhere around 259 million. Most probably it was a lot more. For instance, the census net never catches the many undocumented illegal immigrants who live clandestinely—the vast majority of them people of color. Both in the U.S. and Canada many of these "illegals" are Black, especially in the eastern half of the continent. Countless thousands manage to live out their entire lives in the shadows, residing for long decades in our midst, beyond the purview of the authorities. Of the officially registered population, 69 million were racial minorities, more than half of whom were African Americans. This meant that the government was owning up to the fact—reluctantly—that more than a quarter (26.2 percent) of America's total inhabitants were racial minorities, but it knew that the percentage in truth was higher yet. And the twentieth century had yet another whole decade to go. Following Black folks, the largest minorities are Latinos, Asian Americans and Native Americans whose estimates vary greatly. But even given our large presence in North America, in comparison Black Brazil dwarfs Black America. Brazil's real population is now anywhere between 180 and 200 million, and people of African descent there represent the *majority* of the inhabitants, the largest concentration outside Africa. Moreover, the Brazilian Black population is youthful (i.e., under 18 years of age) and expanding more rapidly than Black America.

However, what matters to us here is that Black America is younger than white America. Demographic comparison shows that, although gradually aging, the Black population in the United States is marginally younger than the white population. For every 100 whites over 15 years of age, there were proportionately in 1987 only 91 Blacks over 15. The prospect is positive, therefore. For the immediate future we can count on a larger proportion of Black women able to bear children, and during a greater number of years, than the fertile proportion of white females. Other circumstances not intervening, we can expect our ratio in the general population to continue to rise for a considerable span of time, or at least to rise in proportion to the Caucasian population. Negatively, this means that a smaller portion of the Black population is of an age to earn income. Our families face an enhanced burden of nourishing more children than whites must bear. That there are about 15 percent fewer adult Black males than white males in comparison to the female population, is another problem. Many of these "missing" males have been killed off. Hopefully, this will balance out in the future, for among the very young there are now slightly more Black boys than girls.

In Canada, Blacks are bunched up in the greater metropolitan Toronto area. Other clusters may be found in Nova Scotia, Montreal, and in Hamilton and other southern Ontario locales. Although the Black presence in Canada is ancient, dating as far back as 1608, most Afro-Canadians are twentieth century immigrants. The Caribbean has contributed the largest group, but significant numbers hail from the United States, and since the 1970s, many immigrants from Black Africa have arrived. The Canadian government lumps all people of color together as "visible minorities," the fastest growing component in the country. Aboriginals—native Indians and Inuit (Eskimos)—Chinese-Canadians, South Asians (Hindus, Pakistanis, Sikhs) and Blacks lead the way in numbers. By the year 2001, Chinese-Canadians are expected to number 1.29 million people, or 23 percent of the "visible minorities," slightly ahead of South Asians who with 1.08 million should be 19 percent of the total. While the 1991 Black Canadian population was estimated at 527,000, Canadian demographers project a rapid rise to 750,000 in 1996, soaring further over the next five years to a figure of more than a million in 2001. Black Canada's social profile is similar to Black America's, with more than three-quarters of the population ranking as working class. Unemployment and wage differentials—rooted in white racism—cause familiar problems. Metropolitan Toronto has become the most racially diverse city in North America, far more heterogeneous than New York or Los Angeles. As of 1991, "visible minorities" accounted for one-third of its total population. Some demographic projections expect Metro Toronto's "visible minorities" to account for 45 percent by the year 2001. Better appraisals predict an outright majority for the people of color. Nationally, a low estimate puts Canada's "visible minorities" at 5.7 million by 2001, i.e., 17.7 percent of a total population of more than 32 million.

South of the border, in the United States, the regional distribution of African Americans has followed its own trend. From the beginning of the Second World War through the late 1970s, the "Black Belt" below the Mason-Dixon Line constantly lost population density. As late as the year 1940, more than three-quarters of all Afro-Americans still resided in the South. However, migration to the Northeast, Midwest, and West during the following generation reduced Dixie's proportion of America's Black citizenry to barely more than half. Recent Sun Belt industrialization, coupled with "Rust-Belting" in the Midwest, has reversed the trend. The South has once again become home for a palpable majority of Black folk.

By 1988, 56 percent (55.9 precisely) of Black people in the USA were residing in southern states, tangibly more than half of the total Black population. The region's share seems destined to grow further—at least through the turn of the century, according to demographic projections.

Yet considerably more significant than the regionalization of the Black community has been its hyper-urbanization. In 1915 there were 44,000 Black Chicagoans. In 1940 the group had swelled to around 300,000. In 1991 East St. Louis proper had a population that was 98 percent Black, earning it the label of "America's Soweto." Like most heavily Black "inner cities," it was thoroughly polluted, due to racist neglect. Its Black residents had to battle a sewage system in such disrepair that raw feces backed up repeatedly in homes. Between 1940 and 1980 the Black percentage of the population grew from 28 to 70 percent in Washington, D.C.; from 9 to 63 percent in Detroit; from 21 to 58 percent in Newark, N.J.; from 30 to 55 percent in New Orleans; from 10 to 44 percent in Cleveland, and from 8 to 40 percent in Chicago. Today, racial minorities collectively are more than two-thirds of the inhabitants in Gary, Ind., Newark, N.J., Detroit, Paterson, N.J., Washington, D.C., Oakland, Atlanta, and New Orleans. Birmingham, Memphis, Savannah, Ga., and Jackson, Miss.—all are now majority Black cities. In New York City, where Census Bureau authorities refused statistical adjustment to remedy a severe undercount, a 19 percent jump in Black inhabitants was recorded in the 1980s, confirming Gotham as the number-one population center in the nation for African Americans. The Borough of Brooklyn alone is home to more than a million Black people. The state of New York has the largest Black population of any state in the Union. The five New York City boroughs together house more than three million.

At the outset of the 1990s, racial minorities—Blacks (including Haitians), Latinos, and Asians—constituted between 53 and 60 percent of New York, the largest metropolitan area in the country. Upwards of 800,000 Haitians live in New York, Conecticut, and New Jersey. More than 10 percent of the island nation's population has joined continental Black America. Every one of the top ten metropolitan statistical areas have large Black concentrations, including the Los Angeles–Long Beach area, Houston, and Dallas. A half million Black inhabitants reside in the sprawling San Francisco Bay Area—made up of San Francisco, Oakland, Berkeley,

San Jose, and their suburbs—more than eight percent of all residents. The collective spending power of the Black American consumer market equals that of the ninth largest country on earth.

                        *

Yet nothing has lessened relentless census undercounting. The 1980 census failed to count many more than the 11.2 percent of the Black community which—seven years later (1987), after much arm-twisting—it finally owned up to having missed. In March 1983 timid critics suggested a rounded total of 50 million for the combined Black, Brown, Red and Yellow minorities, citing notorious and incorrigible undercounting by the Census Bureau. More forthright faultfinders rejected 50 million as a figure much too small for the real situation as it was at the outset of the 1980s. Even the most blatant apologists for the government knew that the 1990 census failed to enumerate many more than the four million Blacks and Latinos admitted to. Invisible to the authorities, these people received no Congressional representation. More immediately damaging to their life chances, they were also locked out of federal transfer payments allocated on a per capita basis. In 1993, federal spokesmen "confessed" to having omitted 4.8 percent of Blacks and 5.2 percent of "Hispanics" from the last enumeration, hoping that acknowledgement of a small error would silence criticism. The 1990 tally missed at least 45,000 tots locally, nearly all of them children of color, said the New York City Board of Health. It was as if minority neighborhoods had been proclaimed off-limits for enumerators, for children living in minority districts were almost eight times less likely to be counted than white children. Ignored also were most minority youngsters born out of wedlock. Where more than half the births were to unwed mothers, the census missed about 20 percent—the vast majority Black and Brown. Homeless children and poor children were nine times more likely to be left out than mainstream white ones.

Given these sloppy nose counts and deliberate slights, it should surprise no one that there is grave suspicion of the government's claim that African Americans are no more than 12 to15 percent of the national whole. For some time now, nationalists, inspired by Malcolm X, have been insisting that there are actually *upwards* of 40 million Blacks in the USA, not the underestimated 34 million suggested by the Census Bureau. There is no convincing evidence that the federal government demographers are right, and the nationalists wrong.

Frederick Douglass' last battle plan—formulated at his death in 1895—relied on the relatively high Black birth rate to change the balance of power in favor of our people. The demographic weapon— a higher birth rate than the white one—is even more of a factor today. The Black population is increasing faster than the white population. This "revenge of the cradle" remains one of the most potent long-term historical forces influencing the power equation to our advantage. Even given the losses caused our community by the "passing-for-white" sickness, our demographic vitality has held firm. 5,000 Blacks were crossing over annually by 1929 to "pass" for white. As of the year 1950, the defectors had soared to 12,000 per annum. By 1980 the yearly tally was 17,000. If that number held steady during the 1980s—conceivably it was greater—then during that decade alone, some 170,000 persons abandoned Black identity and the Black American community. Even a conservative estimate would place those who slipped away to pass for white in the sixty years from 1930 to 1990, at some 630,000.

Any time arch-racists like William Shockley and Charles Murray are frightened by the rapid rate at which Black folk are expanding, then we should know we are on the right track in multiplying our children. Human beings, not things, constitute the decisive factor in any long-term historical struggle. By the year 2000, Blacks and other people of color will make up at least one-third of the American citizenry. By 2020, among residents under 45 years of age, more than 25 percent will be persons of color. In the year 2050, people of color will be the majority in the United States, while European-descended whites will have become the minority. This is a shorter time than the six to nine generations it was once thought it would take for the racial minorities to overtake white folks. Serious-thinking racists know this and have become more earnest about recourse to genocide to ward off this population trend. They are haunted by the spectre of a planet swamped with people of color. In the words of Frances Cress-Welsing, "Few Blacks or other non-white people were aware that white scholars and experts are discussing the projection that by the year 2073, whites will represent fewer than 3 percent of the people on the planet ... these white experts are concluding that they will be left in a state of peril if these facts are ignored" (Cress-Welsing 1991:254). February 1993 brought a proposal to boost funding for the Norplant birth control device in Virginia state health clinics. The surgically implanted device would be marketed to Black, Native American, Afro-Latino and other minority teenage girls, rendering them infertile. Baltimore Blacks objected to the introduction of the Norplant device in local schools. Norplant was condemned as a means of shrinking the reproduction rate of the Black race. The whole proposal smacked of genocide.

*

NO "SLAVE" FOR THE CHILDREN OF SLAVES:
UNEMPLOYMENT AND THE JOB MARKET

Present living conditions are woeful. All the long-term processes of marginalization outlined above seem to be hitting the Black community with concentrated fire as the century ends. Robotization, electronically operated devices, fiber-optic, Internet and other constantly evolving communications networks, computerization and data-processing systems, genetic engineering, aerospatial breakthroughs, and technical efficiencies are radically transforming elements in U.S. economic life. Their effect is compounded by productivity schemes, deunionization, and the shift of production facilities to cheap labor locales "offshore" and to "sun belt" states within the confines of America. Given this country's white-supremacist political economy, these new elements are finally enabling American capitalism to dispense with much of its super-exploited but now redundant Black labor force in many phases of social production. Permanent unemployment, homelessness, and the hopeless misery associated with these conditions, impact a growing number of Black folk. Numbered among the victims of this washout are the discharged Black "veterans of foreign wars," crunched in post-Cold War military "downsizing" and base closures. The conventional view is that that which holds true for white male-female gender relations is duplicated in Black male-female relations, with Black women the objects of the worst economic exploitation. On the contrary, however, examination of the percentage of men and women (both races) employed during the whole generation beginning in 1950, shows that Black men—not Black women—are the ones singled out for the rawest oppression (especially police brutality), and the worst exclusion and joblessness. This is most true in regard to relative status in comparison with whites of the same gender. Black male status is much lower *vis-à-vis* white males, than Black females relative to white females.

In an effort to illuminate the current plight of Black folk, B.J. Tidwell, director of research for the National Urban League, has advanced the theory of a "bad fit" of the African American labor force to the economic and occupational demands of the 1990s and beyond (Tidwell 1993:35-57). He blames much of the desperation on the instability of a "secondary labor market," where the time-honored racist privilege of "last hired, first fired" continues to reign. Trapped in low-paying jobs—the kind of employment known as a "slave" in street vernacular—without benefit of tenure and seniority, or disproportionately concentrated in manufacturing and other goods-producing industries subject to closure or relocation, Blacks endure worsening racial inequality. The racial gap in wealth has widened as Afro-American family income remains stuck at a percentage of white income that is below pre-1980 levels. The predicament is systematic, says Tidwell, connected to the business cycle. It goes without saying that our people suffer disproportionately during depressions (now called "recessions"). However, the post–World War II record reveals that we lag very badly behind also during recovery phases of the periodic cycle, with the jobless rate among African Americans actually increasing during certain general economic recoveries. In its waning months, the Bush Administration confessed to an African-American unemployment rate of 12.2 percent, twice that of whites. That was a gross minimization, the National Urban League making it plain that in truth actual unemployment in the Black community stood at 25 percent as of January 1991.

Many Michigan Blacks were destitute, haunted at the outset of the 1990s by 20 percent unemployment. Republican governor John Engler cut welfare payments, leaving at least 82,000, mostly Black men, to freeze and starve. Most of them were homeless. Of those pushed off assistance rolls, 58 percent were Black, a wildly disproportionate rate in a state where the Black population totalled somewhere around 14 percent, although heavily concentrated in the Detroit area. This reflected the unevenness of poverty typical of the racist economy of the industrial Midwest. The corporate decision to shut down much of the auto industry had the effect of "whitening" parts of the Motor City. The loss of 80,000 jobs during the 1980s decimated the inner city, creating conditions under which droves were killed by drugs and violent crime. Large stretches of urban real estate lay abandoned. Former residences were torched. Halloween-eve arson became fashionable. Developers planned to replace unwanted Blacks with a new 740-acre super-luxury enclave. They envisioned a self-contained downtown reserve, exclusively for whites, consisting of its own school, recreation facilities, expensive housing, offices, shops and a special police department.

The *income differential* is the shortfall from what macro-income should be. Its cost to Black America in 1993 was some $122.7 billion. That is the additional sum Blacks would have received during that year were there no discrimination and had we been treated with parity to whites economically. A report released in January 1993 by the Fair Employment Council of Greater Washington made it known that African American job applicants are still experiencing discrimination 24 percent of the time while seeking a job.

Wage standards for Black males regressed badly as full-time, lower-paid women (Black and white) were hired to replace laid-off men, settling the annual real wages of Black women at only one-third the gap below those of full-time Black males, compared with the gap between the wages of white women and white men. Thus in one respect nothing has changed. White domination has always humiliated the Black man in the eyes of the Black woman. Under slavery he could not protect her; today he cannot support her. White women maintain their traditional advantage over Black women. "Even when women hold equal amounts of education, job training, and work experience, women are three times more likely to earn low wages than white men. African-American women are four times as likely to be low-wage workers. The average family income for Black women is less than that for white women" (P. King 1992:60). Recession combined with deindustrialization pushed unemployment rates for Black women in the early 1990s to 18.7 percent in Louisiana, 18.4 percent in Michigan, and 17.3 percent in Wisconsin. But the toll was even worse among Black men, where in Michigan it denied work to 22.1 percent, to 19.1 percent in Louisiana, and to 18.8 percent in Wisconsin, according to official sources.

The Washington, D.C.–based Urban Institute probed hiring bias against Black males in Chicago and the nation's capital, two key localities (Urban Institute 1991). Ten pairs of matched testers—Black and white—fanned out in summer 1990 to apply for randomly-chosen entry-level jobs. The white job seekers were allowed to advance further in the interviewing process than the Black testers in 20 percent of the cases. At the final hiring hurdle, Black job seekers were turned away 15 percent of the time when the job was actually offered to white counterparts with no better qualifications. The study confirmed that whites routinely equate African race with inferiority.

In Canada, 27 percent of "visible minority" women with a degree or diploma were employed as low-paid clerical workers compared to 11 percent of white women, and three percent of white men with the same qualifications. This was the situation in 1993, without real hope for betterment in the rest of the decade. "Visible minorities" of both genders with the same skills as whites earned between 74 and 85 cents for every dollar their white counterparts earned. For every job offered to a Black person in Metro Toronto, a white job seeker with equal qualifications got three job offers. All told, Blacks can expect widespread discrimination when applying for jobs. And even where there is decent work available, social isolation excludes the Black "underclass" from the job network system. Our misery is worsened by the ingrained practice of allowing Black people less income from welfare, social security, and pensions than whites.

*

INCOME DISPARITY

For more than a few, the guns of August 1914 ushered in the twentieth century. World War I opened an epoch of dizzying changes, transformations which have remade the features of human society—at least its scientific and technological hallmarks. One element, however, remained remarkably constant though—income disparity between America's Blacks and whites. In 1914 median lifetime earnings of Black men after age 25 amounted to about one-third of the white median. Nearly a half-century later, in 1959, Black median earnings were barely more than half of white median earnings, having peaked in 1944 at some 60 percent of the white total, spurred by Second World War job opportunities. Remarkable also has been the constancy in the gap in dire impoverishment suffered by Black and white males. From age 20 to normal retirement at 65, Black men deprived of all earnings averaged 22.4 percent of the whole Black male population, during the years from World War II to the mid-1980s. The comparable percentage among white males was 13.7. And, basically, young Black men (aged 20 to 24) were penniless during the 1980s at almost the same rate as at the end of the Great Depression decade! White supremacist political economy is premised on a more severe racist earning differential between white men and Black men than between white women and Black women.

From 1939 to 1984, for example, the per capita ratio of Black women's annual earnings to the earnings of white women averaged 80.5 percent, against a paltry male ratio of per capita Black-white earnings of 51.2 percent. "Even-handed" exploitation of cheap female labor (Black and white), and super-exploitation of Black males—both policies are vital to the racist social formation.

1967 was one of the years that civil rights legislation was enacted. Since then, median Black family income, according to the U.S. Census Bureau, has remained well behind that of white families. In 1967, the Black median was 61.5 percent of the white. By 1990, it had fallen to 56.6 percent of the white median family income. More reliable computation indicates that the spread between Black and white family incomes widened by about 10 percent, actual median purchasing power of Black families nesting about half that of white families. Of the millions of Americans the government admits are poverty-stricken, always about one third are African Americans. But even with the undercount distortion corrected, by no means do Black people alone constitute anything near a whole third of the entire American population. These poverty figures starkly confirm the racist character of the political economy of poverty in the U.S.— Blacks are heavily overrepresented among the poor and the hungry, and vastly underrepresented among the rich and the sated. This pattern of over/under-representation recurs in all areas of social living which are said to constitute the "way of life." There is, once the mask is torn from the face of Black poverty, a real sense in which this can be said to be the proverbial "American way of life." Negative overrepresentation recurs not the least in areas of social living where, according to popular myth, it should not appear. Affluence and higher education fail to lift apartheid-like ostracism from Afro-Americans. During the 1980s, nearly 80 percent of Black families enjoying income of $50,000 or more were, nevertheless, corralled in segregated residential districts, throughout the nation's 16 major metropolitan agglomerations, including New York, Chicago, Los Angeles, and Philadelphia. 71 percent of college-educated Blacks were likewise segregated in the same metropolitan areas.

In Canada and the U.S., the key form of wealth is ownership of the means of production, and financial, communications, and service businesses. Racial discrimination has assured that wealth distribution among Blacks is weakest precisely in those assets. This accounts largely for the fact that while Black women may now look forward to lifetime earnings not much behind the earnings of white women, Black men can rarely expect lifetime earnings more than half that of white male lifetime earnings, no matter how hard we endeavor. For the one aspect where the disparity between Black and white men is the greatest is the ownership of profit-yielding assets— white males own the sources of wealth; Black men do not. This extends to real estate holdings, family dwelling equity, and savings.

In the Black community, a "high"-income household may usefully be defined as one enjoying a stable annual income of at least $50,000. Even these solid income households, however, lag far behind similar income-bracket white households in the vital fraction of wealth held as retirement assets. And contrary to the suggestion that the disparity may be due merely to the difference in age (*Common Destiny*:293), it is *race* which dictates that high income Black households have less than 40 percent as much wealth in the form of stocks and mutual funds, business and professional proprietorship, and interest-bearing accounts, than their white counterparts. The identical pattern prevails at the opposite end of the social hierarchy too. In 1986 a Black female head of a family, with no spouse present, had to make do—because she was Black—with less than sixty cents for every dollar which went to a white female head of a family, living without a spouse. Across America, the median net worth of Black households in 1988 totalled $4,169, far below the $43,279 median net worth of white households; white households are *ten times* wealthier than Black ones. As the 1990s began, 70 percent of whites enjoyed median family incomes over $25,000. Comparative statistics showed that more than 56 percent of African Americans had median family incomes of *less* than $25,000. Half of our families earned less than $21,500 in 1993, and 70 percent of our households less than $35,000. In northern cities, a college degree was worth $4,000 less per year to a Black graduate than to a white graduate (Population Reference Bureau, Inc. 1991). Nearly half of all our children are officially classified as below the poverty line, many of whose parents strain to provide for them on less than $5,000.

Such is the real face of inequality—nothing like the pacifying myth of a successful, contented Black America, the television Huxtables fed to white suburbia, inadvertently confirming the prejudice that none but slackers come to grief (Jhally and Lewis 1992:95). "[A]lways one paycheck from being homeless," in the words of Walter Stafford, associate professor of urban planning at

New York University (*The New York Amsterdam News*, 23 November 1991), even the Black middle class is perched precariously. The incline is greasy, and many slipped in the late 1980s and early 1990s as *real* income declined from a high in 1973. In fact, without double and triple wage earners in the household, the whole Black so-called "middle class" would go up in smoke. One can only agree with David Swinton, that "[t]he absolute and relative economic status of African Americans is very low," as well as with his conclusion that there is no solution for the economic problems confronting African Americans as long as the current racist economic conditions stay in force (Swinton 1991).

●

SCHOOLING—THE ROAD TO THE TOP?

Rarely, not usually. The observation that college-trained Black folks earn less than white ones is so commonplace as to be trite. In fact, this particular injustice is a secondary rule of U.S. political economy which holds from the bottom right to the top.

Take Black and white male workers with less than eight years of formal education. The latter's wages are seven percent higher than the former's. This is a concrete measure of the surplus wages accruing to white men, solely as a token of white skin privilege. For high school diploma-holders, the wage gap for similar jobs was 25 percent in 1991. The Census Bureau reported that Black men holding four-year university degrees, aged 25 and over, are paid 33 percent less than white graduates in comparable occupations. The tally in 1989 was $31,380 against $41,090. It is a nasty piece of irony, therefore, that not only are Afro-Americans rewarded less for schooling themselves, but the higher they climb the ladder of scholarly achievement, the greater the gap between their earnings and the earnings of their white peers. In the course of a lifetime, the Black school-dropout is much more likely to achieve income parity with the white dropout than the Black college graduate is with his white counterpart. One economic dimension of white racism requires that university education should be worth less in dollars to Black males than to white males—a mere $798 for every $1,000 that goes to white men with those credentials. Those of us who persevere on through graduate studies fall even further behind—earning only $771 as compared with $1,000 received by our white counterparts. The message is clear. Black males are advised to persevere in education, but they must understand that doing so only moves them ahead of others of their own race; they are never permitted to catch up with their white peers.

These higher education earning-disparities sit on an elementary and secondary public school system which, self-serving rhetoric aside, has grown increasingly segregated and dilapidated since 1978, increasingly reminiscent of apartheid South Africa's Bantu schools. The Harvard Project on School Desegregation found the exact opposite of its mandate. It unearthed a national "drift" back to segregation so severe that the racial separation of Black youngsters from white pupils is now higher than it has been since the assassination of Martin Luther King. School segregation is most intense in the Northeast—overwhelming in Illinois, Michigan and New York—but reviving swiftly in the southern states of Tennessee, Alabama and Maryland. School segregation in the 1990s is not confined to the inner city any more than it is confined by region or state: 58 percent of Black kids in suburbs go to mostly minority schools. Even "golden" California has pressed four-fifths of her Afro-American pupils into schools where minorities make up more than half of the student body. New York City, home of the largest number of Black and Latino pupils anywhere in North America, runs a public school system in which more than 85 percent of minority children attend *de facto* segregated institutions, up from 18 percent over the last two decades. Chicago's public schools teach thousands of Black youngsters to be marginal illiterates. The miseducation is facilitated by assuring that most of the Windy City's Black children attend schools in which more than 90 percent of pupils are of their own race. America's schools do not even come close to meeting the needs of minority youngsters, Black male teens least of all. Jonathan Kozol—a white critic—has done the best job recently of exposing the savagery with which our children are treated in the system of "education" in America.

The system's resistance to cure has sparked cries for all-Black male high schools. Not alone in New York, but in Wisconsin, Minnesota and other locales as well, the demand is being heard. It represents a search for effective Black adult male role models for Black lads inadequately prepared to fend off the onslaught of racist North America. Greatest urgency for all-Black male high schools is felt by those convinced that far too many Black lads, growing up in a fatherless environment, have been damaged by the absence of relevant adult male role models. The vacuum is hurtful, given the special oppression meted out to Black males. While female-headed households are competently led by very strong Black mothers, these women, though indomitable, nevertheless, as females—say the advocates of male schools—are unable to arm their sons with the social weapons required by a Black male in this society. This concern is coupled with the desire to escape the downgrading of Black culture and history institutionalized in the educational establishment. Canadian Blacks with the same worries have proposed "Black-focused" Middle or Junior High Schools in each of the Metropolitan Toronto boroughs with the most Blacks. They hope a "Focused School Model" would provide Black youths with a sense of identity and a sense of belonging. The existing system is rejected as a sad caricature of real primary and secondary education.

Those who want to build high schools exclusively for Black youths also want to get away from white teachers, from whom Black boys, more so than girls, feel alienated and estranged. They are not deterred by the charge that their proposal represents a step back from the victory over school segregation enshrined in the 1954 Supreme Court decision. The schools are in fact still segregated, they retort, nowhere more so than in the big cities, the place where most Black people reside anyway, and will continue to reside. Many white teachers are hostile to Black pupils and parents, and are met with hostility in return. White educators seem indifferent and irrelevant to the fate of their charges, concerned instead mainly with pay scales, benefits, retirement pensions, and tenure job security. Proponents of all-Black schools further cite the physical trepidations of white teachers. In the eyes of many white educators, Black male teenagers, as they grow in size and assert the male characteristics triggered by testosterone, loom as a physical danger and sexual threat that Black women and teenage girls do not.

*

SEGREGATED HOUSING

The twentieth century watched as waves of Black migrants poured forth from the South. Generation after generation of Mexicans have sieved through the porous border, joined in recent decades by thousands upon thousands of immigrants from the Caribbean, and from Central and South America. Asians too have come in an unending trickle. Like magnets, the metropolitan areas have drawn these "minority" groups. There is a crucial difference in their residential pattern, however. Asian-Americans, and those called "Hispanics," are much less limited in the spots they may reside than Black folk—native-born or foreign-born.

The residential pattern, perhaps more than any other contemporary social design, reaffirms the overwhelming primacy of the Black-white contradiction; for in the American context during the foreseeable future, the *ghetto* will remain a thickly populated slum section packed mainly with African-Americans. To escape the ghetto is much easier for Hispanics and Asian-Americans. The Jewish ghetto has long since disappeared. Urban renewal and gentrification continue to take the form of "Negro removal." In 1989, about one-third of all poor Blacks lived in substandard housing—that is about two-and-a-half times the proportion of poor whites living in such circumstances. As poor Blacks and Afro-Latinos are forced from their homes, they increasingly double-up, crowding in on relatives and friends, straining nuclear, extended and augmented family structures to the limit (Billingsley 1992:27-64). Those who cannot find domicile hit the streets and public shelters, becoming the homeless. Denial of mortgage loans on properties in Black neighborhoods is as much a nation-wide practice as ever. Not only do whites hog 83 percent of conventional home mortgages, but even smaller "minorities," including Asians and Hispanics, receive more private housing loans than us. We trail the field with just three percent of mortgages. It is true that over the last twenty years or so, large numbers of Black folk have moved to the suburbs. Many inner city cores—rotting—have been abandoned to growing concentrations of Black and Latino paupers, "underclass," and homeless. But even this suburbanization is compelled to fit the national mold of Black-white residential apartheid. Black suburbanization proceeds on the basis of Black *resegregation*. Chunks of the inner city ghetto are dispersed as all-Black pockets around the wider urban area. The ghetto does not disappear, it multiplies with smaller offshoots hiving off. Residential segregation is alive and well, and now also living in the suburbs.

America's residential pattern requires wealthy Blacks to live near poor ones, running roughshod over class differences—or more to the point, effectively treating all Afro-Americans as one single race-class. Prompted by factuality, sociologists are now challenging the popular notion that there has been a mass flight of Black middle incomers to the suburbs over the past generation. Housing discrimination holds most upper-income Black families in or near the inner-city core. "As a result," observes the Urban League, "both high- and low-income Blacks tend to live in proximity to the nation's major cities" (Urban League, Inc., *The State of Black America, 1991*: 266-267). Even the relatively very affluent Black "bourgeoisie" of the District of Columbia find it twice as hard to get mortgages than do comparable whites. Analysis of 130,000 deeds of homes sold there in 1985 and 1991 showed that race, not income, was the key factor. White folks will live next to just about anybody but African Americans. Eighty percent of Blacks live in neighborhoods where they are in the majority. In a study undertaken for the Urban League, R.D. Bullard found that a Latino resident would have to earn ten times less than an African-American before he would have to live in segregated housing (Bullard 1992:185). Asians or Hispanics with a third grade education are more likely to live in an integrated environment than a Black with a Ph.D. While middle class status does seem to work for white Hispanics and Asian-Americans, as far as neo-residential segregation is concerned, membership in the "middle class" brings no comparable relief to Blacks. No more than do education and occupational status.

Home insurance redlining is a cornerstone device. Black and Brown residents must pay significantly higher rates for homeowners' insurance than whites with similar incomes. In some regions Black home buyers in 1994 were being charged interest rates higher than 30 percent. The Association for Community Organizations for Reform blows the whistle on this mean double-dealing. Take the cases of the Federal National Mortgage Association ("Fannie Mae") and the Federal Home Loan Mortgage Corporation ("Freddie Mac"), two government-private mortgage purchasing agencies which reinforce the discrimination practiced by private banks. By refusing to buy more than a token number of mortgages on homes in minority districts, Fannie Mae and Freddie Mac discourage private mortgages for Blacks, since bankers like to turn around and sell to these agencies at a profit. Real estate firms insist on steering Black would-be home-buyers to ghettoized areas and then the banks refuse to grant mortgage loans. One analysis revealed that African Americans were turned away 2.35 times more often than whites. Black applicants with annual incomes between $75,000 and $100,000 were turned down more than twice as frequently as whites in the same category. Even persons with incomes of more than $100,000 were rejected. Chicago was the worst location in the nation for this treachery, although Milwaukee, Detroit, Cleveland, and Newark also rank as hypersegregated.

One result is sky-high homelessness among Afro-Americans. The army of the homeless in New York City, for instance, is over 90 percent Black or Latino (especially Puerto Rican). Though over 20 percent of homeless people have jobs, they cannot afford the high rents for apartments, and mortgage discrimination puts home ownership out of the question. Security problems have grown so immense in public shelters, where drug addicts are housed along with everyone else, that the more fearful homeless rather sleep on the streets than go into the shelters.

*

DOING BUSINESS IN THE GHETTO

Be it shopping, farming or the entrepreneurial scuffle, the private sector in Black America continues to resemble a disaster zone. The causal connections between race, economic chance, and poverty are pretty well established by now. Black folks suffer in the most routine details of everyday life.

Think of what happens when we go to the store. Retail establishments rip off ghettoites regularly, siphoning extra profits from customers held captive by residential segregation. In fact, social services spending in general, unemployment compensation, and welfare payments to racial minorities function, at least in part, as a means of redistributing a portion of the national income to profiteering whites at the expense of middle income taxpayers. The poor who receive transfer payments are merely the conduits by means of which these funds are passed on to rent-gouging landlords and chain food stores situated in Black neighborhoods which sell inferior produce at inflated prices to people who cannot move. Shopping in Black neighborhoods is a dilemma of high prices, limited selection, disappearing bank branches and dreary conditions—along streets where shoppers run a gauntlet of purse-snatchers and muggers. In the nation's largest city, Black New Yorkers pay 8.8 percent more for groceries than middle class and wealthy whites (who can afford to pay more)—and the stores they must patronize are dirty and cramped. One and the same supermarket chain charges Harlemites 13 percent more for the exact same basket of groceries than its white customers in Queens. At the outset of the 1990s, such surcharges

271

cost a poor Black family of four an extra $350 a year for food. Higher prices and dirty stores are born of less competition in the inner city, compounded and licensed by supermarket management wedded to racist stereotypes. The situation resembles shopping in many dirt-poor Third World countries. But then, what are the ghettoes but "Third World" enclaves within America?

From the Reagan era to the Clinton administration, business spokesmen—Black voices are heard here alongside the dominant soundings—keep hawking *enterprise zones* as a panacea for inner city economic woes. Lauded as a "take-off" stage in industrial development for the country's ghettoes and barrios, enterprise zones have been likened to "off-shore enclaves on-shore." The notion jumped back into prominence as the Bush administration—in its death throes—splashed around in search of a solution to the urban crisis highlighted by the 1992 Los Angeles rebellion. The scheme has made Jack Kemp a Republican Party luminary. Like the off-shore operations of many multinational corporations, "free enterprise" zones in U.S. cities would do without effective workplace safety regulations and would function with (grossly reduced) wages and hours—statutes designed to protect workers. But since the workforce is to be drawn from desperate, jobless Blacks with no alternative, the lack of these protections is regarded as not merely alright, but as a downright blessing. The inner-city "beneficiaries" would be expected to be grateful and not complain. And forget pollution controls! Environmental racism would run rampant. Any job is better than no job, say enterprise zone boosters. Since the hostile reaction of Blacks and dark-skinned Latinos to complete unemployment threatens social stability, the "underclass" is to be appeased with a take-it-or-leave-it offer of slave-wage jobs and slave working conditions. The Clinton administration endorsed its own version of the plan. Softened and renamed "Empowerment Zones," the design remained essentially the same.

In agriculture, appeasement took the political form of the appointment of a Black Mississippian—Mike Espy—as Secretary of Agriculture. As a remedy to the rural crisis, the move had even less substance than the enterprise zones. For Black farmers are a vanishing breed. In 1980 there were 242,000 African Americans living on farms in the United States. By 1990 that number had dropped to a mere 69,000, according to the Census Bureau. Accepting, for the moment, the government's underestimation of the number of Black citizens, that amounted to less than 0.19714 percent of the total Afro-American population! The economic trend is well on its way to leaving Black America without any agriculturists of our own by the turn of the century. And agriculture is the basis of collective living.

The disorder and turbulence plaguing Black-owned business nationally show no sign of letting up. Black companies continue to be starved of revenue nationally, and they rank below other minority firms, many of whose owners are only recent immigrants. Black businesses earn less than Hispanic businesses, and rank far behind Asian American (mainly Japanese and Chinese) companies. Although Black America outnumbers the Asian American community more than four times over, our businesses yield less than 60 percent of the gross receipts of Asian-owned companies (U.S. Department of Commerce, Bureau of the Census, *Survey of Minority-Owned Business Enterprises, 1987,* Washington, D.C.). Most hurtful for future prospects, Black performance in the pilot industries in a modern economy—technology, communications, manufacturing, construction and engineering—remains feeble. The "hard" industries provided only 18.2 percent of the sales of leading Black enterprises, as of year's end 1992. Black entrepreneurs in media, food and beverages, health and beauty aids, and auto dealership still hold the lion's share in sales. The weakness of Black capitalism is mirrored in (and in part causes) stagnating incomes for African Americans nationally. Blacks owned only 424,000—mostly very tiny—of a total of 17.5 million businesses.

Knowing that the control of capital is the key to ultimate power in our society, David Swinton has concluded that "it is unlikely that economic parity can ever be obtained in our capitalistic economic system without significant attenuation of the racial gaps of ownership" (Swinton, January 1993:136). No such diminution is in sight, so long as the federal government remains committed to its welfare system for rich white folks. Since the outset of World War II, the federal government has coughed up highway subsidies to make white suburbs accessible to and from downtown areas. It has paid subsidies in the form of tax deductions for mortgage payments, in the full knowledge that white borrowers were usually the only ones able to get mortgage loans. As indicated by the response to flooding along the upper Mississippi in 1993, federal assistance is most effective and swiftest in the aftermath of natural disasters in regions inhabited mainly by whites. Wealthy whites benefit from subsidies in the form of deductions from real estate taxes. Federal loans and grants for higher education have accrued primarily to white students. The record shows that since the moment it saw the light of day, the Federal Housing Administration has benefited whites disproportionately. Even Medicare has favored white patients more than Black patients. Economic circumstances are rigged in such a way that it is the white middle class which is best positioned to take advantage of both Social Security and the Small Business Administration. White armed forces veterans have been the disproportionate beneficiaries of the G.I. Bill and Social Security, while Black veterans number disproportionately among the homeless.

This has been the way, historically, in which "American Self-Help" works. The white government helps its own kind—white people. The welfare system for whites—White Self-Help—works through the government, which is the reason why many activists in the Black liberation movement insist that influence over the policies of the state must become the first-line priority.

●

Black Folk are Poor Folk

The governing authorities in this country are very slippery when it comes to defining poverty. Admission of too much poverty, of an absolute standard of impoverishment, is politically damaging. So there are constant efforts to minimize the phenomenon, define away the poor, overlook them, deny their existence, and—most important—deny any necessary connection between race and poverty.

Nevertheless, for a half-century and more, not to mention the awful years from Reconstruction to the Second World War, every Black person in America with any sense has known that he or she faces much greater odds of being poor than any white person. At no time since 1960 has the rate of poverty for Black children been less than four times the rate endured by white youngsters. Folk wisdom of sorts assures us that a husband-and-wife nuclear family with both spouses employed and earning, has better prospects of beating poverty than any other familial living arrangements. Just the same, the yearly prominence of Blacks (and Hispanics) among recipients of the Earned Income Credit—established by Congress in 1975 to offset the effect of regressive payroll taxes on low-income working families—shows how difficult it is for minority parents, living with and supporting children, to escape poverty, even when both spouses are employed. In 1990

Earned Income Credit eligibility kicked in for working families at $20,264—and the large number of our people eligible is a measure of the widespread poverty throughout the Black community. The Clinton budget passed in 1993 qualified many Black families for earned income tax credits to be distributed over the five-year span from 1993 to 1997. For some time now, the most poverty-stricken metropolitan areas for Black folks have been New Orleans, Philadelphia, New York, Chicago and Newark—home grounds for a large proportion of African Americans. By the end of 1983, nearly half (46.7 percent) of U.S. Afro-American families were living in poverty, according to the U.S. Census Bureau. The poverty line—as decreed by the federal government—then stood at $10,178 in annual cash income for a family of four. Close to half of all Black families had less than that in income. In 1986, 42.8 percent of the Black poor resided in inner-city areas, with only a quarter in non-metropolitan areas, a situation strikingly different from the residential pattern among the white poor, more than 60 percent of whom live in suburbs and non-metropolitan areas. In 1989, 30.7 percent of the African-American population were living in poverty. Actually, there were a lot more, heeding the undercount. Most were women and children. The 1989 poverty line was drawn at $12,675 for a family of four. Two years later, the number of Black people officially counted as poverty-stricken had risen above 10 million for the first time since the Census Bureau started collecting separate figures for Afro-Americans. Racist politicians beat their breast over Black "welfare mothers" and such like. Nevertheless, white folks are the ones who gobble up the welfare budget, and they—not Blacks—are the majority of those who draw upon Social Security. They receive almost twice as much per capita, for an aggregate advantage to the white race of $10 billion a year.

Throughout its existence, the welfare system has worked primarily to the advantage of white people, despite Black people's greater needs.

*

MEAT AND POTATOES

The growing wealth gap between Blacks and whites is, of course, essentially a power gap. The Urban League's *Racial Parity Index* (RPI) scale pegs parity between the two races at 100 (Miller 1991: 111). In 1967 the index stood at 51.2. By the end of 1989 it had

275

fallen to 47. At the current rate of change, we will *never* reach parity with whites in blue collar employment. Furthermore, current projections require 54 to 58 years for the achievement of parity in executive and managerial jobs, and 73 to 77 years to close the racial gap in earnings. It will take at least 170 years for Blacks merely to have a *poverty* rate no higher than whites. That will put us in the second half of the twenty-second century! In fact, over the next twenty years, we will suffer a *widening* gap of inequality. The ebb from the high tide of Civil Rights and the 1960s economic boom connected with the Vietnam War, is daunting. Little can be more infuriating than the cost of racial discrimination, when it is measured in actual dollars. For example, African-Americans jointly lost $179 billion in this country in 1988 alone due to racism. The 1984 value of benefits accruing to white folks from occupation, education, employment and wage discriminations against Black people in the United States from 1929 to 1969 amounted to roughly $638 billion. From 1980 to 1989 the total income loss to our people due to racial inequality was $1.4 trillion.

For more than a decade the RPI has read like an *in*equality file. Black America entered the 1980s in a critical state. More than 41 percentage points separated the rate of Black infants born out of wedlock from the rate of white babies born in those circumstances. Female-headed families were already nearly four times as frequent among Blacks as was child poverty. Black teens were jobless at a rate five times that of whites. On average, whites could expect to live somewhat more than five years longer than Black persons, and the homicide rate was already nearly seven times greater in Black communities. Any comparison of 1990 Black social indicators with the national average confirmed either stagnation or further slippage. Rather than narrowing, in twenty years (1970–1990) the gap in median family income had widened further by upwards of $1,800. The *national* infant mortality was 10 per 1,000 live births; the *Black* infant mortality, 17.6 per 1,000 live births—worse than in some Third World countries. Out of every 1,000 Black inhabitants 17 were imprisoned, as compared with merely 3.9 inmates per 1,000 inhabitants for the nation. As a whole, Black homicide was still nearly 6.6 times the national rate. Food cost the average Black household about 20 percent more than it did the average white household.

Canadian statistics present a similar picture of America's northern neighbor. In the Toronto metropolitan area, according to data drawn from the 1986 Census, the earning power of "visible minorities" is much lower than that of their white counterparts. This in an area where one of every three people is an immigrant. Statistics Canada—the Canadian equivalent of the U.S. Census Bureau—identifies Blacks, Chinese, and Indo-Pakistanis as Toronto's three largest visible minoriities. But Blacks are clearly the most despised, disadvantaged and discriminated against, even though other people of color also face racism. Only six percent of Black men are allowed in white collar professions, as compared with about 20 percent of Chinese men and 14 percent of Indo-Pakistanis, despite the fact that virtually all Toronto-area Blacks can speak English or French, while 17 percent of Chinese and five percent of Indo-Pakistanis cannot speak either official language. Forty-seven percent of Blacks are confined to manual labor, and the community as a whole suffers a higher unemployment rate than the general population. Civil rights for Black Ontarians is a sham. The Ontario Human Rights Commission —the very government agency charged with protecting minorities from racist abuse—is itself plagued with racism and discrimination. Inasmuch as racism is not an enforced criminal offence in the province, Ontario activists insist that dogs, cats and pigeons have better protection in Ontario than members of an oppressed and exploited race. About half of the 70,000 dwellings on Ontario's Indian reservations are unfit for human habitation. The 1986 overcrowding rate in Indian dwellings was 16 times the non-aboriginal rate. The reservations lack water and sewage, almost one-third of native Indian households are completely without running water or piped sewage, or septic fields. Indian reservations are ravaged periodically by hepatitis, tuberculosis and other diseases related to poor sanitation and water contamination, and Indian deaths from house fires in Ontario are three and a half times the Canadian national level.

*

The problems confronting African-American men are not limited to the ones at the bottom of the ladder. A couple of rungs upward, employed Black male university graduates are earning less than their white counterparts, as noted above, and the gap is widening. In 1975, Black males with four or more years of college earned 90 cents for every dollar pocketed by whites owning similar credentials. By 1987 this had dropped to 79 cents. Well into the 1990s, some 52 percent of white female college graduates—versus only 28 percent of Black female college graduates—have husbands who earn as much as $700 per week (i.e., $36,000 per annum).

Stress and strain are compounded by the inequities of the racist criminal justice system. Once arrested, Black males are more likely to be convicted, sentenced and jailed than white males. In illustration, Black males comprised 23.2 percent nationally of the arrested for all crimes in 1985. Three years later the percentage had spiked to 29.6 percent—a steep jump reflecting stepped-up police surveillance, harassment, and repression, and a militaristic racism, symbolized by slogans like "war on drugs" and "operation hammer," etc. Blacks also were slapped with longer sentences than whites for the same crime—the disparity in punishment between the use of crack cocaine as opposed to cocaine powder is so outrageous it has become the butt of sick humor. By the year 1990, Black men made up 45 to 48 percent of all inmates in federal, state and local prisons and jails. This was double the current number of Black males enrolled full-time in college. Blacks are a third of the patients admitted to New York City municipal hospital psychiatric units, and more than a third of those treated in the state's mental health programs. Afro-Americans are 68 percent of New York's single homeless mentally ill population. For years at least half of Black youth between the ages of 16 and 21 in the nation's largest city have been jobless. During the frigid first quarter of 1992, the portion of Blacks laid off, discouraged out of the work force, or forced to accept part-time jobs, was about 30 percent—reviving conditions of the Great Depression of the 1930s. Deprived of adequate health care and services, Black seniors at that moment were four to five times more vulnerable to influenza and other illnesses than the white elderly. In Black communities AIDS runs ahead of the national incidence. Epidemics of cancer, tuberculosis, hypertension, diabetes, heart disease, measles, and other maladies ravage the compressed, run-down inner cities.

This is the national pattern. Black people are underrepresented in all the good qualities of life, and overrepresented in all the bad ones.

The Population Reference Bureau (PRB), a private non-profit educational organization, commissioned a demographic study of the 1990s. Entitled *African-Americans in the 1990s*, the report was released in Washington, D.C. in summer 1991. Its authors—William O'Hare, Kelvin Pollard, Taynia Mann, and Mary Kent—admonished Black folks to rely heavily on one another, for racism is bound to continue its rampage throughout the 1990s. Institutional racism, they pointed out, remains the single greatest cause of Black misery. Although African-Americans claim a larger share of the U.S. population today than at any time in the twentieth century, and maintain higher birth rates than whites, we remain the most residentially isolated U.S. minority group. Integration is an exceptional thing for the majority of our people, and to the extent that economic restructuring dispenses with our labor, we face growing social isolation. The PRB report revealed that median Black total assets less liabilities is only one-tenth that of whites. Poor Blacks continue to be much poorer than poor whites—an inevitable long-term political-economic consequence of white supremacy. To repeat, Black-owned farm land in the South is disappearing at a rate of 9,000 acres a week, five times that of white farms. In all probability, there will be no African-American farmers left by the year 2000. By then the land will have been lost to the tax office, or to real estate speculators and sharp white lawyers. The culprit is discrimination from farm suppliers, private banks and public lending institutions. In 1982, for example, Afro-Americans were extended only one percent of all farm ownership loans, 2.5 percent of all farm operating loans, and just one percent of soil and water conservation loans. The Congressional Black Caucus estimated in 1992 that merely as an emergency stopgap to meet the big-city crisis nearly $31 billion in federal funds were needed right away for community and housing development, job training, and education.

*

Uncle Sam's Soweto

Some suggestions put forward of late arouse distrust, particularly those intended to better chronic unemployment, particularly among Black youth. One suspects that in truth what is envisaged is a migratory labor system, Yankee-style. For most of the twentieth century Blacks in South Africa were herded to backcountry "homelands," or locked in all-Black suburban encampments, viz. the Bantustans and Soweto. Pouring forth from these locations, each day the people travelled often long distances to jobs in homes and firms in whites-only cities, towns, and farms. At night there was an exodus— flowing in the opposite direction. Like beasts of burden, the African multitudes traipsed back and forth from their apartheid settlements. Now in the U.S. we hear proposals—sometimes well-meant—for transportation subsidies for mass transit to enable inner-city residents to reach jobs located in white suburbs. These schemes conjure up the nightmare of a massive twenty-first century migratory labor system for African-Americans. Hundreds of thousands tramping to and from white realms—daytime toil in Caucasian suburbia and exurbia, eveningtime ride in public transportation back to the inner city for night-time slumber. Ghettos ringed with police perimeters drawn for "containment." Hired hands during daylight hours, safely warehoused where we can do no harm to white folks and their property at night—pundits increasingly tout this as the prospect for Black people in "post-industrial America."

Many inner cities are already "*Sowetoized*." Crowds of inner city youths rub shoulders in the streets, "hang out," shoot hoops, rap and "style out," and, unfortunately, all too often maim or slay one another. Like the so-called "Black-on-Black" violence in a South Africa ripped by Inkatha-thug assaults on ANC followers on the eve of free elections, rarely do these young Blacks harm any white persons. Whites keep well away from the inner city murder scene. Our youths act out their frustrations—rooted in racist oppression—mainly against one another, while white America looks on with detachment and tut-tutting bemusement. Only when the prospect arises that the violence might spill over into white neighborhoods, or that a truce between warring gangs of Blacks might divert the anger (e.g., truce between Crips and Bloods in 1992-93), does the white community grow nervous. In many ways the violence unleashed by racist cops, skinheads, and neo-Nazis against Afro-American males is full acknowledgement of the system's refusal to provide them with jobs, education and a decent life.

This process of Sowetoization or inner city Bantustanization is a compound of the effects of structural changes now taking place in the economy, of the reversal of civil rights gained, and of general physical deterioration of urban centers, particularly in the smokestack industrial quadrangle. It reflects Reagan-Bush era decisions to neglect the social needs of Black urbanites, while controlling them by means of police repression. "No-go" districts for public transport blossomed in the 1980s. They indicate a political resolve to ignore ghetto residents, as well as the near-bankruptcy of city governments. Philadelphia and other cities took the lead in designating certain minority districts as off-limits for buses and other forms of public transportation. Bus lines were drawn to skirt "no-go" districts, leaving their residents without transportation service. In other words, it is one thing to truck cheap Black laborers out to places where white employers may require them, it is another thing entirely to provide minority residents with the public transportation they need to move about the municipality like normal citizens.

The advent of American Sowetos is sometimes excused as a fear reflex aroused by the high-crime reputation of "no-go" districts. The root causes—namely, runaway unemployment, squalid housing, grinding poverty, and the escapism of drug addictions elicited by these afflictions—are unmentionables. A prominent feature of the bantustanization is the refusal of police forces to protect innocent residents of the inner city from criminal violence and plunder. Police routinely neglect to answer calls from poor neighborhoods in urgent need of police assistance, or arrive hours late. White police refuse to live in the minority precincts they patrol, behave like an army of occupation, and balk at foot patrol duty. When required to investigate crimes of violence within the ghetto against ghetto dwellers, they are slipshod, bored and disinterested, merely going through the motions. They only become eager and dutiful when it comes to making sure that no unsuspecting white person gets lost, goes astray, and wanders into a Black district. White folk wisdom teaches that the ghetto is "no man's land," especially after dark. It is too much to ask of "overstrained" police resources that it not be surrendered nightly to the tyranny of anti-social elements, organized criminals, and strung-out addicts. There is an accepted division of labor in racist America in which depraved thugs are allowed to pimp on criminality to the sorrow of their innocent Black brothers and sisters, while white police agencies steadily beef up their manpower and firepower. Efforts are made to patrol the circumference of the area in order to reduce the number venturing out at night into business and white residential districts. This assignment gets priority even if it means violating the constitutional rights of Black and Latino men to freedom of movement. The police violence which occurs in South Central Los Angeles and in every other Black district daily, is meant to forestall mass popular uprisings and to indicate to us, should they occur, the white Establishment's resolve to crush them with overwhelming weaponry.

Galloping physical dilapidation of Black residential areas is a trademark of bantustanization. Walls and roofs crumble from disrepair and rat and roach infestation spreads. Garbage litters the streets, laying about uncollected. Houses stand abandoned, locks gone, windows smashed, doors askew. Lawns are pressed into service as parking lots, mostly to reduce the likelihood that one's car will be stolen. Car owners load ignition and steering wheel with heavy chain locks. Vacant lots become dumping grounds for worn-out vehicles. In New York's South Bronx and Cleveland's East Side, abandoned, boarded-up buildings march rank upon eery rank. Homes are barred and dead-bolted three, four, and five times over, doors bolstered from the inside with massive metal shafts anchored to the floor. Formerly bustling industrial Black communities like the East Side of Cleveland have declined woefully, undermined by shrinking population. Bank branches have long since closed down and moved away from Black neighborhoods. Folks have gone off in bewildered search for livelihoods to replace jobs lost to plant shut-downs and plant runaways. "De-industrialization" depopulation was worsened by the Reaganite shift of Job Corps offices from northern centers to the non-unionized Carolinas and elsewhere in the low-wage Sun Belt. As well-paying industrial jobs dry up, it's back to teaching Blacks cotton-chopping "skills" in what is now termed "training for *real* job opportunities"! As if price-gouging were not enough, supermarkets located in the inner cities refuse to renew grocery stocks until a few days immediately prior to the arrival of the monthly welfare and social security checks and food stamps. The excuse—fear of being robbed by the famished. On the day the checks and stamps arrive, long lineups form outside supermarkets and shops, long before opening hour, as early as four and five in the morning. People know they must arrive early if they hope to find provisions on the shelves. The merchandise is shoddy, and priced sky-high. All the good stuff is reserved for stores with predominately white customers. The shopping blitz soon depletes stocks, leaving those at the rear of the line out of luck. Scuffles break out, fights are common. Incidents occur which the white media term "looting."

Parallel to the Sowetoization of Black America proceeds the construction of fortress white America. Just as Blacks and Afro-Latinos barricade themselves in their houses, apartments, and fire-trap tenements, compelled to lock themselves away from the carnage in the streets by the lack of police protection, so a fortress mentality has taken hold of white middle class suburbia. Fear of Black urban guerrillas seeking retribution for racism, fear of the have-nots, fear of non-white intruders, has given birth to fortified dwellings in white neighborhoods. The richest white people are already barricaded in bunkered luxury high-rises with electronically-controlled access, closed-circuit TV monitored corridors, instantaneous alarm connections with police headquarters, and a growing army of hired security guards, packing murderous firepower, accompanied by guard dogs, and instructed to keep out "the wrong people" by any and all means. Between the first and second Rodney King beating trials, white middle class householders went on a gun-buying binge in the Los Angeles region.

The economic wealth and military might of the United States of America have depended on the sweat and courage of African-Americans since the very birth of the republic. Our reward has been small-potatoes. Black America stands low when compared with other peoples around the globe. Early in the decade of the 1990s, a United Nations team studied living conditions in some 173 countries. The quality of life for U.S. Blacks—major contributors to the riches of the most powerful country on earth—and for many dark-skinned Latinos and Native Americans, ranks, the team reported, on a level with impoverished Third World nations. As a nation within a nation, Black America graded *thirty-first* internationally. The report confirmed what many in this country have long known. The minorities of color are, in fact, poor Third World nations within the confines of the United States—one reason for the lasting attraction of the domestic colony thesis in Black nationalist circles. American whites, in contrast, ranked just about first in the quality of life on earth—they and the white folks in apartheid South Africa.

Chapter 15

THE STATE OF BLACK AMERICA–II

BEING BLACK–A HEALTH HAZARD

Earlier in the century, white demographers claimed to have
unearthed a causal connection between the growth of the Black population and the incidence of disease. They suggested that the fall in
the Black birth rate registered between Reconstruction and World
War II was caused by widespread tuberculosis and venereal disease—mainly syphillis and gonorrhea. There was indeed a steep drop
in the *rate* of Black population growth during that span, the Black
proportion of the U.S. population falling to around 9 percent—an
all-time low. Although the number of Afro-Americans did increase
absolutely, this was more than offset by massive white European
immigration during the period. In other words, it was not the drop
in the birth rate, it was the European hordes flooding the country.
The point is, rather, that there has been a healthy rebound since
1940, despite continuing racist deprivation of pre-natal and post-
natal care which has kept infant mortality relatively high among

African-Americans. Death rates for Black youngsters remain from 30 to 50 percent higher than for whites, mostly caused by injury. While death from infections and other natural causes have fallen radically since 1950, fatalities from injuries have risen. These injuries can be catalogued under the heading of racial oppression, since they derive from the painful living conditions imposed on black parents. Smoke inhalation and burns enact a grim toll in firetrap housing. Unlike the quiet streets of white suburbia, traffic is congested in Black neighborhoods, and children are often run down, or suffer injury while riding in vehicles. Many tots fall victim to unsafe stairwells. Uncollected garbage not only breeds rats, roaches, and lice, but dangerous cuts, wounds, and injuries plague children who must play on grounds strewn with litter and trash.

In the mid-1980s, the United Nations compiled a list of infant mortality rates in various countries. White infant mortality in America ranked in twelfth place, behind seven white European countries, two predominately white non-European countries (Canada and Australia) and two Asian nations (Japan and Singapore). The infant death rate for African-Americans was far worse, ranking in twenty-sixth place internationally, trailing Cuba significantly. In 1988 the infant mortality for whites was 8.5 deaths per 1,000 live births. For Blacks it was 17.6. Lack of primary care is the main culprit. Since they are deprived of pre-natal care, Black mothers suffer adverse births, including many low birth-weight infants. It is common knowledge that the United States is lax in its child immunization program. All American children are jeopardized by this lapse, just one more manifestation of right-wing conservative determination to dismantle social services. But here too the familiar racial disparity sticks out. National Health Center statistics covering the span from 1976 to 1985 show that far fewer Black children than white, aged 1 to 4, were immunized against measles, diphtheria, mumps, and polio. It remains to be seen what long-term effect Clinton Administration immunization legislation will have in closing this racial gap. Black children have nearly two and a half times as many decayed teeth as white youngsters. Trips to the dentist are too expensive for many Black parents to afford. Adequate health care in this country has long been synonymous with the health care enjoyed by white people. Cost factors, coupled with the relative scarcity of Black physicians, have given whites much superior doctor's care per capita annually. All medical records kept since the Second World War tell this story.

Average life expectancy of Afro-Americans in 1991 lagged behind whites by more than six years. White males then enjoyed an average life span of 73 years. Life expectancy for Black males stood at 64.9. Black men were shortchanged by nearly a decade. In the course of our life, we frequent hospital emergency rooms two to three times more often than whites. This is because we cannot afford expensive insurance, and because regular medical checkups are much too costly. By the time one needs to visit a hospital emergency room, it is often too late to salvage one's health. According to data from the National Center for Health Statistics, there has been no time during the twentieth century when very many more white elderly than Black did not enjoy personal care and nursing in reputable old folks homes. In 1991 there were at least six and a half million Black citizens completely without any medical insurance. During the three years from 1989 through 1991, the percentage of the uninsured among African-Americans averaged 19.8, as compared with only 12.7 among whites.

Premature death is defined as fatality from causes that are not fatal when treated. For instance, Blacks are more than three times as likely to succumb to diabetes than whites. The racial health gap shows up here in glaring fashion, since Black folks account for 80 percent of premature deaths, countrywide. The lethal duo of racial discrimination and poverty are at fault for this atrocious statistic. According to *The New York Times*, whites suffering serious ailments are routinely granted benefits under Social Security disability programs by government administrators. In contrast, a Congressional investigative agency unearthed evidence that Black people with similar ailments are turned down.

Death puts paid to all our accounts, closing down all our possibilities, shutting off all alternatives, once and for all. This notion illuminates the causal connection between white racism and hypertension among African-Americans, since, given the social cirumstances, for a Black woman or man to be completely calm and utterly self-assured, is to be dead, I suppose. Anxiety may be the normal state of humanity, but among Black folks in America this becomes hypertension—a pathological elevation of systolic or diastolic blood pressure—because of the unresolvable conflict between socially-instilled American values and aspirations, and racist-imposed prohibitions. Every Black man and woman in North America must live with excessive tension. No wonder many of our people suffer from high blood pressure. Apologists for the system claim that the high incidence of the disease is caused by diet and sedentary ways, as if food habits and lack of exercise are not instilled by social customs and pressures. It is no wonder that desperate people seek desperate escape in drug addiction, a kind of half-hearted suicide. Too many Black human beings are forced to live under circumstances they know to be demeaning to human beings. From 1960 to 1980, hypertension was nearly twice as prevalent among Black adults as among whites, as measured by the U.S. Department of Health and Human Services. A study published in the *Journal of the American Medical Association* noted that the prevalence of high blood pressure in U.S. Blacks results more from the stress of living in a racially divided society than from genetics. The disease is tied more to racism-induced poverty than to any inherited traits. The investigation upon which the study was based, and whose results were released in February 1991, tested 457 Afro-Americans living in Maryland, Colorado and Georgia, widely separated parts of the country. From the American Heart Association comes evidence that millions of Black children suffer from untreated high blood cholesterol levels, leading in adulthood to initial heart attack at an age about five years younger than white victims of heart disease.

It is as if the entire book of diseases has been scoured, and every illness imaginable dumped on Black America. Cancer continues to rage through the Black community, many malignancies caused by the carcinogens of environmental racism. The chemical pollution of East St. Louis—an all-Black city—is merely one item in a very long ledger. Nationwide, we have come to expect tumors to kill four or more Blacks, proportionately, to every three whites. There is no genetic reason why this should be so. Homosexual men aside, AIDS in this country has become a much greater risk to the racial minorities than to whites. Recent studies say that 11 percent of AIDS cases among Blacks were contracted from heterosexual contact, as compared with a figure of only one percent for whites. AIDS among whites is the outcome of mainly gay doings, sparing the non-homosexual majority. There is still greater social stigma against homosexuality in Black America than in the white community, where it is more tolerated, and increasingly defended in some influential circles, despite redneck gay-bashing. Homosexuality and bisexuality appear to be only about half as frequent among Black males as among white males. Nevertheless, the AIDS epidemic is a much greater danger among our people, spreading chiefly by means of intravenous drug users. Heterosexuals plying dirty needles contaminate their heterosexual partners. Through the HIV vector, infants are born with the contagion, infected in the womb.

This takes us back to the way racism has structured death rates by race. Being Black in North America increases the likelihood that one will die before one's time. For every age group under 70, death by misadventure is more frequent among Blacks than whites, be it from pedestrian mishaps, drownings, residential fires, or from homicides—above all from homicide. After having fallen off from a peak around 1970, the homicide rate for young Black males, aged 15 to 24, has since 1985 created a serious concern that Black males are becoming "an endangered species." There is a perception that the killing has soared to an all-time high. According to Census Bureau projections, even as far ahead as the year 2020, barely more than half as many Black senior citizens will survive as white elderly, proportionately, and among those who do survive to old age, Blacks will continue to be sicker than whites, suffering more restricted activity, more bed disabilities, and more chronic ailments. During his tenure as Health and Human Services Secretary, Dr. Louis Sullivan, a Black "moderate" not given to statements calculated to disturb the white powers-that-be, said that average African-Americans must expect to live a life six and a half years shorter than European-Americans. Black people accounted for 80 percent of the nation's premature fatalities. Panelists at the National Medical Association 1989 Convention agreed that the widening health gap between white folk and Black people is due, at least in part, to the trauma of racial discrimination. And they singled out as chief afflictions cancer, hypertension, and drug and alcohol abuse—maladies either aggravated or caused outright by the stresses related to racism.

*

It is easy to lose one's way in the shower of official data regarding conditions in our community. In the summer of 1993, civil rights organizations came together to stage a mass demonstration on Capitol Hill, 30 years after the historic 1963 March on Washington. The 1993 gathering occasioned stocktaking, comparable to the critical appraisals that rang through Black America in 1913, 50 years after the Emancipation Proclamation. As then, the degree of progress was measured in terms of Black accomplishments, current conditions, and ultimate goals, nationally. And like those of our forefathers who mourned 1913 as the "nadir" of our hopes—the lowest point—the 1993 marchers agreed that we are once again living through a "worst of times."

Many moons have waned since we were Southern rural folk. As the twenty-first century dawns, Black folk are the most citified people in America, 85 percent of us trapped in ghettos. In most inner cities, one out of two of us is jobless. Educational apartheid has flipflopped regionally, Northern public schools now more segregated racially than even Mississippi during its bad old 1960s days. J. Kozol's definitive analysis exposes the systemic nature of the miseducation dealt our children. One of every two African-American children is poverty-stricken, the government confesses. Many more Black males are locked up than attend college—200,000 more. Our people toil long and hard each day, yet four in ten of us are paid so little for our efforts that we cannot break the grip of poverty. From California to Michigan to Québec, the Rodney Kings, Malice Greens and Anthony Griffins are legion, as white police continue their open season on African-Americans. White international drug trafficers wax wealthy, flooding our communities with addictive narcotics, while alleged suppression of the scourge sanctions police maiming and murder of young Black men, and violent police invasion of Black homes. The Florida immolation of Black tourist Christopher Wilson—signature happening in the rising tide of random, populistic racist outrages—signals a new era of insecurity for Black citizens as we move around in our own country. Not only are out neighborhoods notorious for awful housing and landscape, not only must we make do without basic municipal services (how often is the garbage collected?), not only must we endure inferior health care, but some 30 years after Martin Luther King's "Dream" oration, four of every ten Black men in their twenties were in prison, or otherwise entangled in criminal "justice." And as enlistment opportunities in the scaled-down armed services dry up, who could say how many more would be added.

*

The "Crisis" of the Black Family

We are tired of hearing about the alleged "crisis" of the Black family. The white-run media din constantly that the Black fmaily is seriously diseased as an institution, and that, lacking immediate cure, the outcome will be fatal. We, of course, do not recognize this as describing the family relations in which we have grown up, and in which we continue to live as adults, least of all are we willing to buy the slander that claims that Black people "lack family values."

What we are actually contending with is the negative impact of the evolution of the industrial economy on family structure, compounded by the racism inherent in North American society.

Emancipation enabled African-Americans to adopt three types of family arrangements—nuclear, extended, and augmented. All three were viable and strengthened the bonds of the wider community. From 1865 to about the 1950s, the dominant household structure in Black America was that of the extended family, centered around a husband and a wife. Most children were born in wedlock and were raised in the home by their parents. Until about 1960, uneducated Black men were still able to find adequate-paying blue collar jobs in industry. They had the earning clout to head and support a family. In 1960, according to Andrew Billingsley's *Climbing Jacob's Ladder*, fully 78 percent of all Black families with children were headed by married couples—the father was firmly in the household, at the head of the family. As restructuring, computerization, "downsizing" and deindustrialization eradicated union-wage-scale industrial jobs for Black males, single-family headed households began to proliferate. The phenomenon became noticeable during the decade of the 1960s. So what white critics call "disappearing family values" in the Black community are really disappearing jobs for Black fathers. By 1985, said Billingsley, the number of married couples had dwindled to 40 percent, and the trend has grown since. In 1992, only 36 percent of our children lived with both parents.

The hammer blows of a racist economy, casting off Black men, have pulverized the family arrangements which had served us in good stead over an entire century since 1865. The overall birth rate of Black women in the U.S. has remained higher than that of white women. However, since the Second World War Black birth rates have traced the same temporal pattern as those of white women, spiking and declining in the same rhythm. Indeed, the fertility rates of Black and white women aged 25 and over are just about the same. The noticeable difference is among younger women, Black teenagers giving birth twice as frequently as whites (Jaynes and Williams 1989:514-517). The productivity of very young Black women accounts for the relatively elevated Black birth rate remarked upon by Malcolm X, among others, for lifetime fertility rates are now roughly similar for Black and white women, and have fallen off for both. Black teenage motherhood provides the surplus, of course making it difficult for many young mothers to finish high school. By 1985 there was almost no difference, on average, in the number of children born to married women aged 20 to 45, Black or white.

"Illegitimacy" is a purely artificial convention. However, it still occasions hypocritical furor in white conservative circles. After having held more or less stable through the 1940s and 1950s, the incidence of births to unmarried women of color rose steeply from 1960 to 1980. In the course of the 25 years from 1966 to 1991, the number of Black infants born out of wedlock more than doubled. In 1990 such births outnumbered so-called "legitimate" births by a rate factor of two to one. Today about 15 percent of white births occur outside of marriage, nationally, as compared to nearly 64 percent of Black births. Nowadays almost two-thirds of Black babies are born to single women. This is a multiple of more than four times that of whites.

Of course, this has much to do with the marital prospects of Black men. We are single more, have shorter first marriages, and are separated or divorced more than white men. White males remarry more often, and are widowed more often. Unable to escape the unending economic depression imposed upon us, many Black men find it impossible to act the roles of husband, father, and provider. Reviewing data from the period from 1940 to 1985, *Common Destiny* concluded that "Black women face a somewhat tighter marriage market than white women." (Jaynes and Williams 1989:538). This does not mean that there are actually not enough Black men to mate with Black women. The shortage is a *perceived* one, not entirely free of class and prestige prejudice—one of "suitability." There has never been a real *demographic* shortage of unmarried Black men aged 20 to 26 to wed with unmarried Black women aged 18 to 24. Social attitudes rank not only convicts but also the poor and the uneducated as unsuitable spouses for Black women seeking husbands. It is a question of "eligibility"—a social rather than a biological lack. The quandary is that the proportion of Black men with jobs has declined more rapidly than the proportion of white men with jobs. If Black men enjoyed the same income as white men, 20 percent fewer would be separated, widowed or divorced, and the number who had married, rather than remaining single, would swell by more than a third. Perhaps the most socially-approved matches are those between college undergraduates. Yet by the mid-1980s, there were roughly only some 880 Black men on the nation's campuses for every 1,000 Black female undergraduates. *White* girls, by way of contrast, had a small *surplus* to chose from, there being roughly around 1,060 white male undergraduates for every 1,000 females. In 1960, 24 percent of Black families with children were headed by a woman. Over the next 25 years that family status more than doubled in frequency to 50 percent. Among the generation of Black women who came of age in the 1960s, hardly more than one in four was living with a husband as the 1990s began. By then, only 30 percent of Black men aged 25 to 44 were married. The pressure on the family structure can be measured in the fact that there are now virtually no U.S. Black males 25 years of age or younger who are married; or so few as to be statistically insignificant.

The uneven development inherent in the racist system has, for an entire generation, been sharpening income stratification within the Black community. Poverty is worst among female-headed Black families. Andrew Billingsley's *Climbing Jacob's Ladder* is one recent work that contrasts a middle stratum of two-parent families to a poverty-wracked stratum composed largely of female-headed households. The ejection of Black males from the workforce is, thus, the economic foundation for the much-touted "decline" of the Black family. Afro-American household arrangements wither as industrial employment with decent wages phases down and comes to a complete halt in many locales. The flight of jobs southward to Mexico and other low-cost spots kills not only upward mobility hopes, it destroys family life as such. In 1960 the Black family was still father-centered, focused on child rearing. 78 percent of Black families were husband and wife teams, residing in a family home. By 1985, this traditional family—one that dated from Emancipation—had come apart at the seams, as Black fathers were no longer permitted to support a family. Only 40 percent of Black families remained under the leadership of a gainfully employed male in 1985. In the nation's capital—a Black-majority city—80 percent of the city households are headed by females who make less than $20,000 a year. Meanwhile, more than 80 percent of white children, nationally, are being reared by both parents in households headed by the father. A 1991 U.S. Census Bureau report measured the widening national social gap between a white America, more than half of whose entire population comprises married-couple families, and a Black America, merely one-fifth of whose population is made up of married-couple families. The 1991 median income for Black families remained stuck at 57 percent of the median for white families. Low income led to poverty and shattered or prevented union between man and wife, not the consequent fact of single families headed by women. For, as ever, Black families headed by gainfully employed men are better off financially, and hence more stable.

It would appear, then, that we are midstream in a major restructuring of the Black family in America, traditional father-headed two-parent families declining from 78 percent in 1960 to 37 percent in 1990, according to the U.S. Bureau of the Census. Failing reversal in racist oppression, a century-old tradition in the living arrangements of Black persons closely related by blood seems doomed. Census Bureau data indicates that 1969 was the best year in American history for the typical Black family, relative to white Americans. That was the year our median family income reached some 61.3 percent of median white family income. The gap was at its narrowest. Since then it has widened to about 56-57 percent, perhaps even more. Was there a causal connection between the gains and the remedial measures effected during the first years of the Johnson Administration under the slogans "War on Poverty" and "Great Society"? Some think so. More likely it simply reflected the long economic boom connected with the Vietnam War.

Claims are heard that racial discrimination is declining, that society has grown "color blind," and that conditions are "improving" for Black people. These claims are ludicrous. Such claims fly in the face of the fact that even were our median family income to gain on white median family income at the same rate as from, say, 1964 to 1981, then Black median family income would not attain parity with white median family income until 2334—another three hundred years and more! (Cross 1984:194). But we have not even maintained that pace; instead, there has been regression. The modest economic gains of the late 1960s were undoubtedly linked to the upsurge in the Black liberation movement, imposed by civil disturbances, freedom marches, sit-ins, and serious ghetto rebellions in eighty or more urban centers. Militant action raised the heat on the Establishment, winning small concessions. Since then, material well-being has stagnated and declined. Homelessness and destitution torment the inner cities. For the "underclass," real earnings are lower than they were a quarter of a century ago. Family assistance benefits are the only lifeline for innumerable single parent households. Even the postponement of marriage, now so general among our young people—for whites, on average, now wed at much younger ages than Blacks, on average—has not helped much. Nor has the willingness to work hard, for there is clear evidence that African-Americans are more work-oriented than comparable whites, that our people are more likely to try to earn a living through heavy, hazardous toil than leisure-hogging whites, and that whenever given the opportunity, the Black family is likely to derive *more* of its income from wages and salaries than a comparable white family. The alleged "cultural pathologies" are merely the manifestations of severe racist victimization.

There is little wrong with the Black family that a dose of racial equality, economic parity, and political empowerment would not cure.

The oft-cited "fluidity" of Black familial relations, the so-called "irresponsibility" of Black fathers whose desertions leave decapitated families is—like so much else in American social life—a legacy of the enslavement of the African. But that is not all that it is. The alleged "promiscuity" and "familial irresponsibility" are more than just another terrible heritage of the past. The "crisis" is the sign of ongoing racist oppression; precisely the result of present-day exclusions of Black men from gainful employment.

*

TRANSPOSITION, PROJECTION AND CONFUSION:
ANTI-MISCEGENATION AMONG BLACK WOMEN

The stresses now perturbing family affairs in Black America have their spinoffs. In particular, these macro-problems have caused anxiety in a micro-group whose public profile has grown of late. The severe constrictions racism has placed on Black men, injuring the male role in marriage and the family, have been construed in a narrowly self-interested way by an articulate, upper stratum of Black women. Having devoted time and effort to higher education and upward mobility—to good results—some of these professionals and businesswomen are very worried about growing miscegenation in North America. Weeding out the vast majority of Black bachelors as beneath them, leaving as "socially acceptable" potential spouses only those of our men who are professionals, businessmen, and the very wealthy, they see marriage or cohabitation between Black men and white women as destroying their own mating hopes. This perception has nourished alienation and frustration in the group. It is felt as a blow to just expectations. In justice, the issue is contentious only for a very small number. Yet the reactions of this anti-miscegenation 'club' breed serious political confusion. From such bewilderment can come the kind of mischief that will damage the ultimate Afro-American interest, which is full empowerment of the community and real liberation of every Black person—man, woman and child.

With quickening sassiness, some of these college-trained, upper-income Black women have taken it upon themselves to chastize Black men who associate with white women intimately. The aggrieved are very vociferous. Everything from mere dating to sexual intercourse, to courting and marriage, is censured bitterly. In a way, for these zealots the crusade against miscegenation has become as much of a single-issue obsession as the "right-to-life" campaign is for anti-abortion leaguers, or as much as "outing" is for certain Gay rights activists. Jealousy, rejection sensibilities, and mating insecurity—all serious hurts for the persons experiencing them—have been transposed into aims of the Black liberation movement. Slighted feelings have taken voice and pen. Black female students at predominately white universities count among the most vocal. Rage is nursed against the white women allegedly "taking our men away." Any Black male considered to be a "good catch" who is caught courting a white woman is branded as a "traitor" to the African race.

Unfortunately these passions are stoked up by certain male figures in the Black community and manipulated in the interest of a certain political agenda. Perhaps to curry favor, if not for cynical political calculations, certain men, known for their nationalist credentials, have taken it upon themselves to applaud these counterproductive outbursts. Ignoring the disunity caused among an already sorely disunited Black community, male individuals egg these women on with demagogic exhortations, like the following:

> "Lastly, I have stated before that under no condition will I marry a white woman... It has to do with the distinction of my race... I'm going to struggle for my survival... I will look like an ass walking in here with a white wife, talking about 'Black is beautiful'... Can I lay in bed tonight with a white woman, then plan her father's murder and tell her: 'I'm going to kill your father tomorrow?'" (Y. ben-Jochannan 1991:38-39).

Now, besides the fact that no one had suggested that the speaker marry a white woman, besides the fact that this exactly mimics the way white arch-racists talk about "racial purity," as they scorn Black people, and beside the fact that the statement conjures up *race war*— the fondest dream of Nazi skinheads—it is the height of irresponsibility to reduce Black resistance against racism to the level of bedding with a white woman and murdering her father. Prattle about Black men's alleged "flight-to-white-love" disorder is frivolous. It insults and ridicules our historic liberation struggle. The affront continues in the burlesque dream of archetypal encounters between super-lovely, brilliant and strong Black women, and successful, ultra-sensitive, Black businessmen or professionals. The women must be very dark complexioned with prominent African racial features, and hair in corn-rows. The men must never have even heard the terms "ho," "bitch" or "pussy," as applied to womanhood, and would never utter such slurs had they heard them. In this lampoon, the male idol has nobly rejected the abject love (*read:* servile subjugation) of the most ravishing white Nordic-type female on earth. Why? Because he is repulsed by her non-African features! He finds beauty exclusively in the "pure" African somatic-type. These paragons wed and live happily thereafter, raising youngsters suspiciously like the Huxtable kids, if not for their Afrocentric attire instead of Buppy Gucchi styles.

Surely there is more socio-historical significance to our toil and tribulation than female pulchritude! There is much about this male support for the anti-miscegenation club that is self-serving. One wonders whether the effort to appear as "race-pure" warriors is made in hope of winning personal "favors" from "grateful" single-issue women. Over-blown war-survival rhetoric raises nothing but a smokescreen of mystification. Only in the bogus world of pretenders and poseurs can a pronouncement of personal marriage preference pass for a political manifesto. A poseur is one who tries to bluff others by pretending a virtue that is hollow or unreal.

Personal marriage preference just does not make it as a racial political agenda. The danger inherent in making one's choice of a spouse the content of one's politics is lampooned in the stage drama *Tragic Mulatto*, a biting satire from the pen of talented young Black playwright Lisa Jones. She is the daughter of Amiri Baraka (Leroy Jones) by his first wife, a white woman. The drama hit the New York stage in December 1991. The "mulatto" heroine seeks to embrace her Black heritage. Therein lies the tragedy, for her Black father rejects her. Resplendent in Afrocentric dashikis, the latter trumpets his ultra-militancy. He primps Black consciousness like a garment of ebony and gold. The ultimate "race man," he preens himself on his preeminence at the cutting edge of Blackness. For all that he has nothing for his own daughter. He abandons his child to the care of her mother. He leaves to her—his white ex-wife—the job of instilling African-American values and pride in his Black daughter.

This whole anti-race mixing mess is weak. For one thing, this prejudice against miscegenation flies in the face of history, and ignores the political economy which prompted white supremacists to outlaw interracial marriage until very recently. For another, nearly all voluntary Black-white unions have been decided upon romantic reasons, almost never as an exercise in racial amalgamation. Then as now, such weddings are the coupling of two spouses, not the union of two races. Moreover, it is a rare Black person who will renounce love for a person of another color in the name of Black "racial purity." In demanding such abstention, the anti-miscegenation lobbyists in our community show that they have lost touch with how folks actually behave in Black America. This blunder accords neither with the letter nor the spirit of our historical struggle to lift the ban against interracial marriage. And let there be no mistake about it—veterans of the civil rights movement pioneered in the fight to obliterate anti-miscegenation statutes along with other racist laws. Having won the battle, they certainly did not intend for us to reimpose the ban ourselves. Our people remember only too well how blood-lusting mobs of white men, desperate to preserve white domination from the "ultimate threat," mutilated and lynched Black men for having "looked at a white woman," decorating Southern trees with the "strange fruit" of Black bodies. The memory of Emmett Till is still fresh. Nor have we forgotten that belief in a "pure Black race" helped sink Marcus Garvey, blundering him into roundtable discussions with the KKK. It is a queer loyalty to Black womanhood that boils down to abstention from miscegenation. To be sure, such promises are cheap and easy to make, and just as easy to break. And even if kept, contribute nothing substantial to Black America's quest for power and self-determination. Interpreting Afrocentricity as a crusade against "the curse of many colors within the Negro race," as a war against "bastardy in the race" is a travesty (Garvey 1969:37). It is a ludicrous distortion, and at the very least a gross misunderstanding. The women seeking protection against miscegenation lack a sense of situation (Hutchinson 1994).

White civilization was the entity which imposed the rule against "race-mixing" in order to keep the Afro-American population separate, entailed, isolated, and easily-identified. It was *their* rule, *not ours*. They wanted us as pariahs, set apart from the majority of the people for special mistreatment. Nothing was more vital to white supremacy's cultural and political integrity, said racism's spokesmen, than preventing intimacy between Black men and white women. All sorts of legal hurdles against interracial unions were in force until about 1965; since then extra-legal barriers of a social and economic character have functioned nearly as effectively.

*

What is droll about the anti-miscegenation hullabaloo is that there is no substance to the panic. Sober analysis shows that the alleged spate of race-mixing is a pure figment of the imagination. "Eligible" Black bachelors are not disappearing into white women's bedrooms. Attitudinal surveys reveal that a strong majority of Black people know this, and are not panicked. In a national survey of African-Americans, 69 percent either thought there was nothing wrong with Black men dating white women, or deemed it the private affair of the persons involved (Jaynes and Williams 1989: 199). Here the nationalists are clearly swimming upstream against the current of Black attitudes—if it is at all true that the nationalists insist on racial exclusivity. Although Black-white births more than doubled in the United States in the span from 1978 to 1989, the birth of children with one Black and one white parent remains rare—only 45,000 in this nation of more than one quarter of a billion people, according to National Center for Health Statistics. So-called "mulatto" children make up only about one percent of all annual births in the country—hardly enough, one would imagine, to scare even the most skittish defender of "pure African posterity." (The fact that four of every five living African-Americans have mixed racial heritage does not seem to faze these purists.)

The most high-profile Black-white unions are those between Black men and white women. Those are the ones which elicit the most hostility and jealousy among the opponents of miscegenation. However, statistics show a nearly equal number of marriages in America between Black women and white men as between Black men and white women.

Marriages between white men and Black women tend to be less visible to the African-American community. When Black men wed white women in this country, this usually occurs in a big city. It is an urban phenomenon, noticeable to the media, often involving celebrities. The couple is unlikely to reside anywhere but in a predominately Black neighborhood, or in an integrated suburb "in transition." In contrast, mixed marriage uniting Black women and white males typically occurs in small communities, in suburban, rural and farm areas where it passes unnoticed, as far as the Black general public is concerned. The Black wives of white men disappear from our view.

Be that as it may, single-issue zealots have a substantial pedigree. One that reaches back at least to 1971, when Black female anti-miscegenationists first banded together on campuses to "Save Our Men." Today increasing numbers of Black women are earning higher education degrees and commanding higher incomes. Many are better educated and earn more than their male counterparts. Black males currently get only about 67 bachelor degree diplomas for every 100 B.A.'s awarded to Black women. If anything, this trend has accelerated since 1985. More than any other factor, this appears to be the rock-bottom cause rallying Black professional women around this single issue. Considering potential mates worthy of themselves to be in short supply, they object vociferously to Black "eligible" bachelors romancing and wedding white women. It is a battle over scarce resources. Ordinary Black men are rejected as "inappropriate spouses."

A Los Angeles group is ticked off at the alleged enhancement and enrichment by upper-status Black men of the lives of the daughters of white men—the enemies of Black people. It has organized formally under the title *"Black Women's Alliance Association."* It wars against miscegenation as hurtful to the entire Black race, since it "hurts and neglects" Black women. Most Black men in this country between the ages of 25 and 44 are unmarried and partnerless—a situation indicating anything but a scarcity of Black adult males as potential spouses and lovers. Nevertheless, the Alliance Association's sight seems to be limited to famous entertainers, rich athletes, prestigious academics, successful entrepreneurs, leading lawyers and physicians, prominent clergymen, and top-rung military brass. Is there a degree of snobbishness about this rigid selection in favor of "comparable partners"? Is there not a suggestion that this obsession with high status Black men conceals a contempt for the millions of *ordinary* Black males, desperately in need of the support of loyal Black women? Does this mean that these women despise the "grassroots brothers," as the latter go about coping with the racism which thwarts their assertion of manhood and threatens their very existence? Would there be such stubborn resistance to interracial nuptials were white males with the social clout to "enrich a woman's life" willing to marry Black women? Would devotion to the "purity" of the Black race then crumble? Is there not something about this that reminds one of those in Booker T. Washington's circle who were interested in maintaining the segregated Jim Crow economy of the Old South, because their profits depended upon it?

The Alliance Association has taken dead aim at Spike Lee. It did not like his film *Jungle Fever*. It did not like Wesley Snipes making love to a white secretary. Borrowing a page from career-hungry white middle class feminists, the Alliance Association thumbed its nose at *Jungle Fever*, for having "missed the opportunity to uplift Black actresses, Black women and the Black race." "You blew it," they scolded Spike Lee. Such peevishness creates the impression that Black women sit around fuming about a marginal, irrelevant sexual issue. Black females outnumber Black males, somewhat. Black womanhood mothers the African-American nation. It is not helpful to act as if one half of our sorely oppressed people wastes time on a paranoic aversion. Not while we face *real* political, economic, and cultural problems.

Fortunately, the women enrolled in this single-issue sect are a tiny minority of Black womanhood. Nearly all come from a relatively elevated social stratum. The chief spokeswomen are above-average educated professionals, representative of what is usually termed the "Buppy" phalanx. Not the uplift of Black people as a whole is their concern, but narrowly the acquisition of "appropriate mates"—a "special interest" if there ever were one. Racial pride is not the concern, but rather *class* prejudice. Ignored are the poor and the undereducated, a large proportion of Black males. Deemed unworthy are the inner-city jobless. Instead of receiving sympathy and support, those Black males who are harassed by the police and herded into prison by the hundreds of thousands, are dismissed as "ineligible." Worshipful attention focuses on a small group of "preferred" males. Drawing an analogy across the racial line, it is as if white women were to resist marriage with any white males, except rich ones. This is *class* behavior, *not* action in defense of the race. Egocentrism of this sort is not very unlike the selfishness of white middle-class feminists. The single-issue agenda shares little in common with the needs, worries, and aspirations of American Black working class women. Nor do "underclass" single mothers, coping with the stresses of inner-city life, waste time imagining Black men chasing after white skirts. This worry cuts no ice with people facing real predicaments.

*

There is, of course, a more analytical view of sexual competition between Black and white women. White feminists have sought recognition for white womanhood as more than mere "decorative sex objects." Black women, on the contrary, have never been in flight from their femininity. Historically, they have actively sought it. For slavery ran rough-shod over the womanliness of the African female, or denied it outright. To the slaveholder, Black womanhood may have meant docility and submissiveness (*read:* vulnerability to rape), it always meant a beast of burden, but never any feminine delicacy he had to respect. Throughout America's long history Black women have equalled their men in misery, even outpacing them in the severity of their oppression. Slave women complained, therefore, not about their inequality with the "brothers," but about an unenviable equality they did not care for. After slavery they functioned—and were saluted by Black men—as co-workers subject to the rigors of the factory and the farm, and to the indignities of domestic labor in white homes, a tradition harkening back to slavery. Some Black women envied middle class white girls, women privileged to luxuriate in "femininity." Some came to suspect that Black men longed for such soft and decorative sexual objects. Black women lacked these qualities, it was alleged. Under slavery, the Black woman's body was viewed as a machine of labor, as well as a reproductive organ at the disposal of the slaveholder. As manipulated by the present welfare system, many Black women are doled a "social wage" (welfare payment), miserly compensation for participating in social life at the very bottom of the social well. According to every statistical indicator—educational, economic, health care, job income, employment, and welfare benefits—white women are significantly better off than Black women. Life satisfaction measurements tell the same tale. Spread across the color line, the "sisterhood" vaunted by feminism becomes a very thin veneer indeed. It is about as thick as the flimsy "brotherhood" which binds white male workers and Black male workers.

Black mainstream women's issues diverge accordingly from the fixations of the feminists. For years the latter have been warring chiefly against sexual harassment. Black women's concerns have been elsewhere. They worry about pre-natal and post-natal care, about affordable, high-quality health care for themselves and their family. They require timely information about family planning options. For them, abortion is one of a broad array of reproductive choices. Patricia King, Black law professor at Georgetown University, says, "Black women interpret (the right of reproduction) as the right to choose to have a baby, as well as the right to choose not to" (P. King 1992:61). This is as far a cry from single-issue anti-miscegenationism as it is from white feminism. Unfortunately some Black women do not even have time to worry about Pap smears, let alone reproductive health, since they find that warding off violence is their prime priority. "In Georgia, for instance," Black health care activist and founder of the U.S. National Black Women's Health Project, Byllye Avery, told the Black Community Committee of United Way of Toronto, "the No. 1 killer of young black men and women is homicide" (*Globe and Mail*, 4 October 1991). The reality check for many Black women is not a stampede of Black men to white women, but how to feed the family, bail a son from jail, or rehabilitate a relative on drugs.

We are the most racially-mixed people on earth. In the western hemisphere, Blacks come in all shades and complexions and hues. The small amount of Black-white interbreeding that occurs on the margins of society hurts nothing, and has no impact on the basic social makeup of the Black race in this country. It changes nothing of social significance. To see it as an attack on Black America's integrity is ridiculous. On the contrary, those who campaign against miscegenation, diverting attention to an acrimonious side-issue, open themselves to the charge of deliberately sowing disunity within the ranks. Malcolm X said that unity is the essence of racial self-love. By pulling people away from the prime socio-economic and political issues of our empowerment, are the snipers not creating a diversion? Is not as much *blackening of the U.S. population* as possible a good counter-strategy to the mean doctrine that would "keep America a white man's country"?

It is an established principle in the history of "race relations" in the United States and Canada, that any child born of African ancestry is to be regarded simply as Black, under the age-old "one drop" rule. Yet, pathetically, there are now advocates of "biraciality" who object to being considered "monoracially" Black and who define racism, bizarrely and narrowly, as "thinking about people in terms of categories of race." One such grouplet has surfaced in Chicago's Biracial Family Network, centered around Ramona Douglass, another in San Francisco's Association of Multi Ethnic Americans, chaired by Carlos Fernandez, another in the Atlanta-based Project Race (Reclassify All Children Equally). This is sad. For these people lobby against enfolding children of mixed Black-white ancestry in the bosom of the Black community. They fly in the face of our history which proudly acknowledges the leadership of Frederick Douglass, W.E.B. DuBois, Walter White and many others, figures who by this strange definition become "biracial" and no longer Black. Doubt is cast on the entire meaning of these giants' life-long fight against white supremacy. At the heart of "biracial identity" lies the wishful thinking of "wannabes" who are ashamed of the African strain and who in the grand old American passing-for-white fashion want to be seen as anything but Black. They want "in" on white skin privilege, if only at the tail end. While seeming to be 180 degrees opposite to the anti-miscegenation purists, the bi-racialists inflict similar damage on the struggle for Black emancipation. In this part of the world, white racism has never allowed a mulatto buffer-caste, as a third force, unlike racist practice in the Caribbean and Latin America. In North America each white woman who gives birth to and nurtures a Black child is a white woman who bears and nurtures one *less* white child. Misconceived activities like these of the biracialists help the tricksters. It aids the federal government's traditional undercounting. This is a way to deduct up to two million children from the census count of Afro-Americans.

*

ARE WE ONE SOCIAL CLASS, OR SEVERAL?

Black America's class composition, its social stratification, and its slot in the system of white supremacy can best be understood under the notion of *race-class*. It is the one concept which most aptly describes the racial quarantine imposed on Black people in the white civilization's North American slice.

The whole issue of social class is Janus-faced in Black America. Janus was the ancient Roman god of doorways, usually depicted as one head with two faces, back to back, gazing in opposite directions, seeing contrasting aspects. Class structure in the Black community can be said to have this dichotomy.

It does help comprehension to break Black America into as many as five or more *analysis categories*, as suggested by Black family expert Andrew Bilingsley: 1) upper class; 2) middle class; 3) working non-poor (i.e., job income above minimum wage); 4) working poor (i.e., families whose earned income falls below minimum wage levels); 5) jobless paupers—the "underclass." His is merely one notion of class division. Other schemes are equally valuable. For example, according to the old, classical leftist thesis, the Black community was headed, toward the end of the 1940s, by a "capitalist class" of landowners and businessmen, kept economically weak through racist confinement exclusively to the segregated African-American market for its profits. The rest of the social hierarchy consisted, in descending order, of a professional class, a middle class, a "petty bourgeoisie," and a strong proletariat. Each one of these classes drew recruits from a remaining peasantry (sharecroppers, tenant farmers, smallholders) strung across the South. This thesis spotlighted the years 1877–1915 between Reconstruction and the massive migration from country to town. It pointed to twentieth century Black America's class roots in the soil of the Southern "Black Belt" region, with its debt-enslavement, KKK terrorism, and lynch law. Not until the First World War demand for cheap factory labor did the Black community acquire a status and function more in accord with the normal class structure of capitalist society—and then only briefly. For a half century and more thereafter, classical leftist class analysis acclaimed the proletariat—concentrated in urban ghettoes and assigned the cruder tasks of industrial toil—as the "decisive" class among the Black masses. Despite the deindustrialization and plant relocations of the 1980s which marginalized much of Black America, relegating young African-American males to a "superfluous" underclass, left-wing class analysis is reluctant to admit that the Black industrial working class may have relinquished its "leading" role.

The criteria for nearly all such class breakdowns are income, education, occupational status, and/or political prestige. Such analyses are useful and reliable inasmuch as they reflect real diversity within the Black community.

Nonetheless, I maintain that all Black people living in North America fit *also* within a single class category—all are comprised in a single *race-class*, despite membership of one or the other social strata internal to the community. Race-class is as "American as apple pie"; in its peculiar form and function it is certainly particular to America. Race-class is the creation of white world supremacy. It embodies the concrete discrimination endured to some degree by each and every Black person in North America due to ingrained systemic racism. Race-class is the factual manifestation of the global status of persons of African blood at the very bottom of the international pecking order. In simpler words, it is the line-by-line, word-for-word display of the way white society inflicts misery on our people. Every place in North America where Blacks reside as compact and identifiable communities, they continue to be the victims of choice for super-exploitation, oppression, marginalization, preventable disease, social ostracism, and dosed genocide.

Collective social awareness is a concept sociologists deal with. Among us, as a people, that awareness is still essentially a racial-national one. The rage uttered in "gangsta" rap lyrics, the heavy Black votes for Jesse Jackson cast nationally in the 1984 and 1988 Democratic presidential primaries, and the renowned "cool pose" Black men assume to cope with the dilemma of life in a racist society, are very dissimilar phenomena. Yet each seems to reveal an awareness of race—a shared experience of belonging to a disadvantaged caste. Race consciousness is much stronger among Black folk in North America than any class consciousness, and by all indication is likely to remain stronger for a long while indeed. Though perhaps not held as consistently and militantly through all the different strata of the population, anti-racist sentiment and resentment against discrimination are, notwithstanding, common to all African-Americans, regardless of class.

Frances Cress-Welsing agrees that U.S. Blacks make up *one* single class, or, alternatively, that there are no significant class differences among us, reasoning that people who are oppressed and powerless under white supremacy can have no *class* identity. For her the essence of class status is power (Cress-Welsing 1991:156-157). South Africa's Bernard Magubane too sees us as a single class, a marginal one. He acknowledges that many societies are set up primarily along class lines. But the color-bar nullifies class struggle in the United States, Magubane thinks. History has voided class solidarity between skin-privileged white workers and oppressed Black people (Magubane 1987: 8-9).

There is no question that we as a people are fragmented and fractionalized today—wrought so by racism's hammer blows. Yet and still, we constitute one single race-class in respect of the dominant racist social relations. White America has *one* predominant social reaction to Black America—a paranoic one. It used to be the fashion to say that the whole white working class was exploited by the whole class of capitalists. This did characterize class conflict in Europe and European-dominated societies. Current wisdom deems this portrayal an error, or an overstatement, or true only in part, or dependant on one's personal perspective. When it comes to Black folk, however, no such hedgings are warranted. We maintain flat out that the entire African-American minority in North America is super-exploited and discriminated against as one *entity* by the *entire* racist white establishment. In subtle ways often unnoticed by the general white public, white supremacy accords with the interests of nearly all white persons in America, including white wage workers. This is evidenced in the proprietary attitude of the white public toward "our" "American" Black athletes when it comes time for them to win medals for the United States in Olympic Games. In a hallowed ritual every autumn, white football coaches pit *"their"* "nigras" against opposing white coaches' "nigras." The white men who stage the NCAA's annual basketball "March Classic" manipulate the "hoop dreams" of Black youths in a national extravaganza. Television and the film industry encourage the belief that it is not merely alright for Black entertainers to entertain white people, but moreover that Blacks possess "instinctual talents" which enable them to accomplish the task better than anyone else, especially the job of making white folks laugh. Black sitcoms have become an essential ingredient of the recreational pastimes served up to white people.

As confirmed by a four-month investigation by *Money* magazine, not even comparatively wealthy Blacks escape the disgrace of the race-class stigma imposed on Black people as a whole. The probe revealed that not only does racial discrimination prevent upper-class Black families from earning as much money as their white counterparts, it actually lessens much of the enjoyment of their wealth. Their homes do not increase in value at the same rate as white homes. It is more difficult for them to get mortgages. Financial services are doled out to Black-owned firms very reluctantly and sparingly. Black entrepreneurs have a tough time getting business loans (Walter L.

Updegrave, "Race and Money," in *Money*, December 1989:152).
Though it may ruffle the feathers of the more prideful among us,
the wealthiest among us belong to the same *race*-class as the destitute homeless. Metropolitan agglomerations the length and breadth
of the land resemble one another in one key fashion. Poor Blacks
and rich Blacks alike endure much the same residential segregation.
The 1990 census confirmed this racial affliction as applicable to all
strata in the community. Residential apartheid grows more intense
with each passing year. It devalues the possessions of the wealthy,
because sooner or later Black neighborhoods always equal out to
inferior housing, higher rents and mortgage rates, second fiddle
municipal services, dirt, dereliction, and crime.

*

I maintain therefore that Afro-Americans constitute one single class,
one single social category as far as systemic racism is concerned,
even though the behavior of individual racists may be nuanced
toward the different strata of the community. In fact, the essence of
tolerance for white America merely means easing up a bit on Blacks
in certain, approved walks of life, while coming down hard on the
remainder of "the lazy lot." In order to function, institutionalized
racism must work its wiles on the group as a whole. Racism as a
socio-historical phenomenon runs a "game" on all of us—period!
Yet institutionalized white racism does impact, say, a Black senior
citizen in one particular way, for instance, often as sickness-aggra-
vating poor health care. It impacts on, say, an underclass crack-head
another way. Not infrequently the latter feels the assault crudely as
a thudding police club. It impacts Black intellectuals and professionals in subtle, sophisticated fashion, with the polished hypocrisy
that sets some of our celebrities and "eminent" academics lapping
from the master's hand. Black workers confront racism's economic
dimension daily in respect to unemployment, underemployment and
speeded-up assembly lines. The single mother sees it in the eyes of
her undernourished child, and hears it in the growls of the rent collector. The homeless experience police brutality and harassment
minute by minute, swelter the summer through and freeze in the
winter, tyrannized by the elements and the unshielding "shelters"
alike. Racism's bolts strike certain Black supreme court justices and
heads of Harvard University's Afro-American Studies Department
so obliquely, they seem not to know racism exists at all.

Not so long ago a white think-tank, the Population Reference Bureau, put the blame for the shrinkage of the Black "middle class" squarely on the Reagan-Bush episode. The Reagan administration went out of its way to fan bigotry and erase civil rights gains. But today there is a new wrinkle to the game of blaming the victims. It is now the fashion to pit the upwardly mobile opportunists among us against the inner-city poor and homeless. These unfortunates are badmouthed as walking embodiments of pathologies—crime, broken families, addiction to the public dole, and lifelong joblessness. At the behest of their white patrons, a small, conservative Black clientele scrambles desperately to cut all ties with the high-poverty, low-income districts which continue to spread in the Black central cities. Neither social strata polarization among us, nor distant residence alters the situation fundamentally, however. Try as one may, racism proves over and over again that its reach is long enough to snare any and every Black person anywhere in North America, whenever and as ever it wishes.

*

Moreover, our cultural traits help to bind us together—even the unwilling ones among us. Black culture has unified African-Americans as a people distinct from any other race or nationality group in America. It certainly has made us different from the white folks in this country. More than our skin color sets us apart from them. But this has not come easily. To assert a cultural identity, one with vigorous African roots, we have had to wage a never ending, bitter struggle. At times the battle has been silent, at times, clamorous. Ian Haney-Lopez, Latino activist and legal scholar, reasons that the history of the white supremacist United States has resulted in the formation of a distinct white *American* culture different from the original, seminal, national cultures of Europe (Haney-Lopez 1991:50). Whether he is right or not, what saved *us* was our *own* culture. In surviving, the Afro-American identity warded off the dehumanization that would have issued from complete immersion in the behavior and ideology of the white European civilization transplanted to these shores. Slave ships docked on our shores directly from Africa, and indirectly via the West Indies. Admittedly, they did not deposit here the purely African concept of the family as including the living and the dead, as did the vessels which arrived in, say, Brazil or Cuba. Nor did an unadulterated African pantheon of deities survive the Middle Passage. Yet the ease with which *Santeria* has been transplanted to Florida, and the current vitality of *Shango* worship in New York, indicate just how much U.S. Blacks revert to their African roots, if free from interference. And everyone knows just how many Black *Christian* women in North America believe in a pure immaterial force which is imperceptible to human beings except when it takes possession of a person. Well, the true name of this force is *Orisha*, fundamental principle of the Yoruba religion—a principle fiercely condemned in May 1990 by Eurocentric Pope John Paul II. The views of Black women are decisive in respect of religious faith, for while the Black Church is still headed predominately by Black males, the congregations are overwhelmingly female. Black men are as missing from the churches today as they are from some Black households. More than half of all Black church-goers belong to churches attended solely by members of their own race. And even if merely symbolic, the two most ancient major Black religious denominations in America—AME and AME Zion—still flourish the proud prefix, *African*. Together, these two denominations are home to some 20 percent of Afro-American Christian church-goers. The captive Africans arrived in America with a cultural leaning towards listening and looking. With the exception of literate slaves from book-oriented, Islamized Sudanic cultures, west and central African ways of life had inclined ordinary folk to oral rather than to script literature. They now found themselves on strange shores, compelled to speak a white man's alien tongue. The slaveholder's prohibition against teaching slaves to read and write accentuated this leaning. Thus today, unlike, say, Jews, many Blacks are not known as "book people." Less enamoured with reading and assimilating printed works, "grass roots brothers and sisters" choose audio and visual devices as much better mediums of education. As Geneva Smitherman in *Talkin and Testifyin: The Language of Black America*, and R.Majors and J. Mancini in *Cool Pose: The Dilemmas of Black Manhood in America*, make clear, this comes through in the street lingo and other elements of popular culture. Music is the most renowned of Black cultural expressions. It was the abstract vehicle for the aggressive philosophical and emotional attributes of folkways prevented from producing artifacts. Music was the strong, thick, tangled root from which springs contemporary Black art, prose, and poetry. And our music is unique unto us.

Black social stratification remains stuck at the sub-class or interclass level. North American whites are in truth divided along class lines. There are true cleavages between the white ruling, middle and working classes, and such distinctions are even more salient in European societies. Our situation is different, however. The differences in life-styles and life-chances that we ourselves commonly describe as "underclass," "middle class," and "upper class" are, in fact, *subdivisions* within one and the same large social class. This is because in the racist socioeconomic edifice, Afro-Americans (and Afro-Latinos) constitute one single great *race-class* whose cellar-ranking in the overall social structure is enforced most rigidly by labor-market discrimination/high unemployment, and by a residential segregation that has proven impervious to change since 1900.

*

TYING KNOTS IN FOOLS' PARADISE: BLACK CONSERVATIVES OR TINPOT GENERALS IN SEARCH OF PRIVATES

What goes around comes around. The spanking brand-newness of Black neo-conservatism is merely old accommodationism teflon-packaged. In 1884 Booker T. Washington remarked: ."..the best course with regard to the civil rights bill of the South is to let it alone, left alone it will settle itself." Conventional wisdom now regards this as a condensed representation of the entire capitulationist strategy. It bequeathed us the political legacy of men like Hiram R. Revels, Black post–Civil War politician. Resurgent Southern racists drove Reconstruction governments from office with the brand and the sword. Revels timidly supported the outrage as a need to conciliate white folks. Hindsight teaches us that this attitude contributed to a century of disaster for our people. Many commentators, from W.E.B. Du Bois' *The Souls of Black Folk*, to Louis Harlan's biography, *Booker T. Washington, The Wizard of Tuskegee, 1901-1915*, to V.P. Franklin's *Black Self-Determination: A Cultural History of African-American Resistance*, have weighed in on this theme. The 1980s and 1990s have generated a raunchy update of the accommodationist program. There are some strange beasts out there. Today the neo-conservative express is crewed by a motley gang, ranging from Armstrong Williams and Alan Keyes to Clarence Thomas and Anita Hill, Judge Thomas' estranged alter ego. Like Booker T., they intone the refrain that "brains, property and character for the Negro will settle civil rights," if only we will finally get off the white man's back and shoulder the blame for our own faults. Cut the white man some slack, they urge. To most of us this sounds suspiciously like condoning the servility and degradation we have suffered for so long. It calls to mind Bishop Henry M. Turner's rejoinder to B.T. Washington: any Black man who justifies the oppression of his people at the hands of the white man is "either an ignoramus or an advocate of perpetual degradation of his race." Yet this is what Black neo-conservatism is about.

Fronting for the racist political economy, Black neo-conservatives exalt free enterprise as a divine precept. Competitive capitalism has never injured Black people, they claim, and will never injure us. On the contrary, Blacks would benefit were free enterprise to function unfettered and under ideal circumstances. A more or less unregulated market would put us in the winner's circle and reward merit. Free enterprise is not the culprit, they claim. The guilty party is a bias that is somehow not connected with the economy. By mandating closed enterprise, race prejudice has excluded Blacks from market competition and destroyed true capitalism. In its place it installed color selection and racial etiquette.

The right-wing Blacks preaching this sermon shut their eyes to reality. Whether as free enterprise, or as a racially-closed shop, the economic system, historically, has not worked for Black people, and there is no prospect that, as presently constituted, it will ever work for us. What it has done is tear us from our African homes, slap a 250-year sentence of hellish slavery on us, and most recently has marginalized us with hopeless economic prospects. What the economic system has done is to institutionalize centuries-long affirmative action for white males, helping them to everything from business to home ownership.

Yet Black neo-conservatives on university campuses seem unable to understand this. Stephen Carter, Yale University law professor, for one, whimpers about the alleged inconveniences, insults and injuries he endured as an "affirmative action baby." His pride is shaky. He is prey to anxieties and self-doubt-maladies he somehow imagines to have broad social significance, something about which the rest of us should concern ourselves. He appears hurt that no one has given his private woes much thought. The neo-conservatives have redefined autobiography as the art of bookish tantrums. Pouting, Carter demands affirmative action be banned from the Academy, as well as from other professions. He, the "affirmative action baby," would deprive other Afro-Americans of the benefits of affirmative action, because he failed to appreciate them, and felt

slighted by his white colleagues whom he appears to worship mainly because they are white. His solipsistic egoism could be dismissed
as infantile, were he and his ilk not lionized by the media. Solipsism,
by the way, is the doctrine that nothing but the self exists. Like
Walter Williams and Dinesh D'Souza, Carter seems to suffer from
an acute color inferiority complex. The most that can be done for
him is to excuse him for heeding his master's voice.

The same goes for such run-of-the-mill Black conservatives as
Thomas Sowell, Glen Loury, David E. McClean, Shelby Steele, and
Stanley Crouch. They are annoyed at the self-confidence and artic-
ulateness of those they term "Civil Rights Establishment" spokesmen, and irked at the creative originality of the Afrocentrists. Unsure
of their ability to compete with them for attention, Black neo-conservatives have turned opportunistically to the bosses of racist
America. They have become bagmen for white patrons. Not that
their services are not well paid. Dubbed super-star "dissidents," they
are paid, published, and promoted. They are put on the fast track
to tenure and, for them, white academia never seems to run out of
speaking invitations. Harvard University, in particular, seems well
on its way to becoming a hang-out slum for Black neo-conservatives.
Pretty good for boys who might have a tough time making it, if they
had to win a following among their own—Black—people, and were
it not for the approval and pamper of their white overlords.

A lot of us have grown weary of hearing the *nightmare* that
began in 1441—or 1492, or 1776, or whenever—called a *dream*,
"American" or otherwise. Yet this is the theme of Shelby Steele's
The Content of Our Character: A New Vision of Race in America
and of Stanley Crouch's, *Notes of a Hanging Judge*. Both croon a
self-obsession melody. These callow middle class "success" stories
strike a contrapuntal note with the biographies of "successful" Black
dealers of crack cocaine. Both drug dealers and neo-conservatives
are about "making it" in an every-man-for-himself environment. The
devil take the hindmost. Shilling for the white status quo, the conservatives spoon us such bromides as "we should just stop whining
and feeling victimized." (Too bad if the majority of Black folks can't
make it, but such are the "neutral" workings of the free market, and
each individual must accept the responsibility for his own failures.)
This much can be said for the drug dealers: unlike the Negro neo-
conservatives, they do not publish tomes of canting self-justifica-
tion. They do not scamper about begging Black people to like them

despite their misdeeds. That indignity is left to our conservative intellectuals. The cocaine kings just go about their work of destruction. Period. Just who is morally superior to whom—our latter-day accommodationists or our drug dealers? The neo-conservatives see unlimited "opportunity" for Black people on all sides. Shelby Steele *boasts* of having made a bargain with himself in the early 1970s to fake Black racial identity, in order to get on with his life. Pleading the need for self-advancement, he pretended to support the cause of liberation, so as to make a way for himself.

But doesn't the drug dealer do something similar as he enriches himself at the cost of destroying young Black lives? Isn't this similar to what an eighteenth or nineteenth century slave-selling African chief did, as he went about bartering his fellow Africans to white slave-buyers? How is Steele's "embracing opportunity" morally different? This is individualism run amok, is what it is. No wonder he concludes that Black people may, in fact, *be inferior* to whites. Neither the fact that his mother is a white woman, nor that his wife is white, makes Shelby Steele the arch-trumpeter he is of Brazilian-style "racial whitening." Rather it is his deliberately chosen stand against Black interests.

It has been suggested that in seeking the root causes of the accommodationist disease, sexual orientation should not be discounted in some cases. The journals *Transition* and *Reconstruction*, high-gloss intellectual periodicals slanted to the Black world, have made a point of depicting Black gay males as ostracized and isolated from mainstream Black America. In some cases this causes resentment leading to extreme individualism. It can breed a desire to strike back, to take revenge on an unfeeling community that views gays as pariahs. Blacks, as we know, are good at "dissing," and equally quick to feel the sting of disrespect. Feelings of rejection may inspire a Black homosexual to embrace neo-conservatism out of spite. He may adopt a nihilistic disregard for our people's collective needs. He may succumb to an absolute denial of the standards of morality and justice elaborated by Black people in their struggle over the centuries of the Diaspora. The gay intellectual may see accommodationism as means of personal vindication and gratification. Not that this eventuality is, by any stretch of the imagination, the inevitable outcome of homosexuality. The great James Baldwin, for example, never allowed his sexual orientation to distance himself from his people and their sufferings.

*

Black neo-conservatives have even mounted a populism of their own. Home-grown conservative populism combines outdated utopianism and economic romanticism with militant rhetoric about the alleged "evils" of federal government-"foisted" welfare dependency. Its chief propounder nowadays is Robert Woodson, president of the National Center for Neighborhood Enterprise, and a familiar of the Reagan-Bush administrations. Operating out of the nation's capital, he insists that the civil rights movement says "racism is still hurtful" only in order to squeeze money grants and welfare programs from a nervous and guilt-ridden federal government. So the table has been turned, and it is now Blacks who do the intimidating! Around every corner, Woodson spies civil rights lobbyists lurking to stop us from "doing for self." The benefits of affirmative action, according to this fiery moralist, have all been purloined by upper-income Blacks. Woodson terms this alleged practice a racial "bait and switch game." The civil rights veterans pimp on poverty, implies Woodson. His populism is as bogus as the other forms of Black conservatism.

Exposure of the sham is never more riveting than when the neo-accommodationists are seen in practice:

Alan Keyes, dean of Black neo-conservatives, fronted for right-wing racists at the 1992 Republican Party Convention in Houston and then ran for U.S. senator on the Republican ticket that same year. Since he had no chance of winning support among Black voters, sarcastic observers wondered whether his role was one of self-aggrandizement or that of "coon." But he does not give up easily, for he was back again in 1995, this time running for President. As if to prove that an easy fool is a knave's fool, Roy Innis, sinecured national chairman of CORE, has long since doffed his 1960s militant garb for a right-wing conservative coat of many colors. Burly Glenn Loury hung on to his status as favored political commentator on election newscasts run by white media, despite accusations of sexual violence against women. The Boston University economics professor distinguished himself in 1992 as a foremost apologist for Clarence Thomas. Michael Williams could think of nothing more appropriate as Assistant Secretary of Education than to try to further curtail Black youth's chances for higher education. He goose-stepped out to announce on behalf of the Bush Administration that federal scholarships for colleges should no longer be given to minority students. Armstrong Williams, vocal member of the gang, drones his what's-wrong-with-Black-people sermon over more than 40 radio stations. Wealthy white conservatives pick up the tab.

Colin Powell is a special case. He was appointed Chairman of the Joint Chiefs of Staff. Nevertheless, his function was really a limited one—that of a lethal instrument, triggered by white men and aimed at the Third World. General Powell was authorized to kill people of color, but not to war on white people in Europe, or white people in South Africa. Upon his retirement in 1993, conservative Republicans speculated that Powell might make a fine figurehead presidential candidate, particularly now that American foreign policy is devoted to stepping up the oppression and exploitation of Third World people. He might serve as an exemplary symbol under which to induce Black Americans to join with white Americans in screwing the rest of the non-white world. These conjectures caused some members of the Nation of Islam to wonder whether Powell might also be groomed to command bloody repression of his own community here at home.

Similar career enhancement has rewarded judge Clarence Thomas' willingness to oppose everything of benefit to his own people. His is the worst instance of Black neo-conservatism, and the most damaging of all to the Black community. George Bush, with the aid of bipartisan Senatorial acolytes, plopped Thomas down in the United States Supreme Court, for the rest of his life, ironically to fill the chair vacated by the great Thurgood Marshall. Thomas got the most choice legal plum in the land. Booker T. Washington served white supremacy by persuading his people to eschew political empowerment. As remuneration he had to be satisfied with chump change payouts and the empty nickname of "black President of the United States and advisor to Presidents." The cost of Thomas' betrayal is much higher. It is bitter irony that the higher cost is due primarily to the sacrifices made by the freedom fighters of the 1960s. Today the reward for Clarence Thomas' toadyism is the Supreme court, where he is expected to serve his masters faithfully for at least a generation. Trademarking his own brand of "Black Face Politics," Judge Thomas smugly faults Black people for their white-imposed failings.

His biographical file reads like something scripted by the producer of the film *Birth of a Nation*. He is himself an "affirmative action baby," yet condemns affirmative action for other Afro-Americans and other minorities. Perhaps he feels that too much of a good thing, spread around, spoils it. He once hung a Confederate flag in his office, perhaps feeling that the wrong side won the Civil War. His Supreme Court nomination drew the endorsement of David Duke, Ku Klux Klansman, signifying that the "right" people knew the "right" man when they saw him. The ultra-right Washington, D.C., Heritage Foundation certainly backed him to the hilt, a pat on the back for his close ideological bonding with that think-tank. The Heritage boys see to it that his speeches circulate widely. In his time as bagman for the Reaganites before joining the High Court, Thomas associated avidly with a lobby firm registered as an agent of the then-apartheid government of South Africa.

Once ordained as an Associate Justice, it did not take him long to demonstrate treachery toward Blacks, the other side of the coin of fierce loyalty to white supremacy. In February 1992 he struck down a Federal Communications Commission program giving preference to minorities in granting licenses to operate radio and television stations. Next he nixed Black-majority congressional voter districts. Following the cue of plantation mistress Justice Sandra Day O'Connor, Thomas ruled "unconstitutional" a redistricting plan designed to give Blacks more political clout in various states. He voiced outrage at the "racial gerrymandering." He really meant that he is disgusted at any gerrymandering likely to give African-Americans a bigger slice of the electoral pie. Never mind that the measure was intended to undo the injustice perpetrated over the years, as white legislators deliberately drew district lines in a way that diluted the Black vote and obliterated Black transfer payment entitlements. The prospect for Black empowerment within the existing system was shot down under the pretense that race no longer matters. That Thomas is the blackface symbol and representative of white interests on the high court bench, is underscored by his adulation of white men like Paul Weyerich, a New Right pilot and a fighter to reserve tax breaks for racially segregated schools during the Reagan Administration.

After two years on the Supreme Court, an emboldened Thomas emerged from his sinkhole to assure his puppeteers that they need not worry about him "evolving" in a direction favorable to Black interests. He promised to remain staunch in his attacks on all civil rights organizations and causes that enhance African-Americans. What made him think they had any doubts about his loyalty is not clear. To reassure any doubters, however, he hosted Rush

317

Limbaugh's wedding party for the "Big Man's" third marriage.

The grim prospect of a very dark-complexioned judge using the highest court in the land to strike dagger blows at Black America has prompted more highly educated and more affluent Blacks to disapprove of Thomas at rates higher than the ill-educated and poor. This is mainly because the upper strata (so-called "talented tenth") are better informed. The less fortunate knew little of Thomas' record, and they did not understand the dire implications of his conservative philosophy. They saw only his Black skin. Thus when Thomas pulled his "high-tech lynching" trick at his controversial Senate confirmation hearings, many fell for it. His was one of the most cynical manipulations of Black solidarity, by a schemer who shares no such sentiment of racial solidarity.

Thomas is not the only anti-Black African-American activist; he is merely the most powerful. Others are equally zealous. Take Gary Franks, for example, a Republican Congressman representing Connecticut's 5th district. The district is 90 percent white. On behalf of his white constituents, Franks boastfully opposes Black empowerment political initiatives. He has labored to block implementation of the section of the 1965 Voting Rights Act that enables "majority-minority" Congressional districts. He lauded the Supreme Court ruling on *Shaw v. Reno*, which savaged new majority-minority districts. Adding insult to injury, Franks even tried to give further muscle to *Shaw v. Reno*, proposing federal legislation to bar "intentional creation" of new electoral districts based on race, and designed to create Black majority districts boosting Black membership of the House of Representatives. Yet all the while this fellow insists that he is a member in good standing of the Congressional Black Caucus. Shelby Steele and Stanley Crouch helped Bruce Perry, a white racist author, collect material for a scurrilous biography of Malcolm X (*Malcolm: The Life of a Man Who Changed Black America*). Perry used the "dirt" they unearthed to defame the great revolutionary nationalist martyr. The book tries to "out" Malcolm as a closet homosexual! Juan Williams, author of the companion volume to the PBS television series, *Eyes on the Prize*, has made dubious remarks on New York talk shows (*Juan Williams*,1988). Basketball superstar Charles Barkley is so neo-conservative, his name is mentioned as running mate for Rush Limbaugh in a future Republican campaign for the presidency. This Jester's Court also has its distaff wing. Prominent in the uncrowded ladies' parlor are two Black women.

One, sociologist Anne Wortham, is known for teaching junkets at Harvard, Boston University, and the University of Missouri. The other, Harvard-trained psychologist Eileen Gardner, has nestled in a comfortable cage at the far-right Heritage Foundation.

From Roy Wilkins (who refused to take a stand against U.S. foreign wars against people of color) to Clarence Thomas, the same sinister threat runs through our twentieth century history. Film-maker Spike Lee calls Black conservatives sell-outs who can be trusted only to be untrustworthy. By definition, business in America is conservative in its ways. Yet even Earl Graves, publisher of *Black Enterprise* and leading cheerleader for entrepreneurs, has lambasted white media efforts to create a national audience for Black conservatism. Its activists are, he scoffed, a fringe group who are "the new phantom army" (*Black Enterprise*, October 1991). They hold way-out views on everything from South Africa to affirmative action, from education to access to health care. They have eccentric views on housing and minority business development. A shadowy band, gnawing at the edges of the Black community, the neo-conservatives most resemble moth-eaten self-proclaimed generals in search of foot soldiers—and not finding any. Under normal circumstances, noted Graves, they would be dismissed as deviants far removed from central thinking. Yet white opinion-makers insist on magnifying their influence.

If there is a logic to the neo-conservative philosophy, it is the claim that Black people are divided along class lines, combined with the belief that class divisions far outweigh racism. Racism is seen as residual and diminishing, in North America anyway. According to neo-conservative dogma, antagonistic contradictions wall off the interests of the Black "underclass" from the special interests of the elite. The inner-city is spurned as the denizen of "underachievers," the unmotivated, and the criminally inclined. Conservatism best shields the interest of the elite, runs the conclusion.

The argument is patently false. Racism curtails the life chances of *all* American Blacks, regardless of social stratum, and regardless of difference in form, incidence and weight. It is merely more or less subtle, more or less frequent, more or less unrefined. If Ellis Cose's *The Rage of a Privileged Class* and J.R. Feagin's and M.P. Sikes' *Living with Racism: The Black Middle Class Experience* prove anything at all, they demonstrate that even the most advantaged African-Americans fume at the racial discrimination from which they are unable to escape. Suppressed rage pushes many a one to the edge of psychosis. If Black, even the "privileged" are numbered in the *class* of U.S. citizens subject to racial oppression. For the time being, Black neo-conservatives are being rebutted intellectually. When the time comes, they are very likely to be called to account physically by a new generation of militants, and a Black Liberation Movement with its second wind. Meanwhile, no *ethical* confrontation with Black neo-conservatism is called for, inasmuch as the entire movement has been morally bankrupt since its birth.

Chapter 16

BLACK FOLKS AS BUGBEAR: HANDCRAFTING THE CRIMINAL RACE

In Lieu of Introduction: Racism's "Gorillas in the Mist" Syndrome

Sometimes racism isn't everything; it's the only thing. Hopefully, people of color the world over will come to realize this one day. North American Black folk had better know this, for right now in fact, racism is hell bent on criminalizing our entire community, every last one of us. Let us be clear what we are talking about. A criminal is someone guilty of an act harmful to morality and the public welfare. He injures the interests of society as a whole, as defined by the state. A particularly aggravated example of a criminal would be that of one who deliberately poisons a community's water supply, or one who slaughters an entire kindergarten in cold blood. To the religious-minded, a criminal is one who offends against divine law, one who is evil and sinful. To the legal-minded, he is a felon, one who acts illegally, an outlaw. Common lay people call him thug, hoodlum, gangster.

North American white supremacy has moved to criminalize Black America. This is not a matter of speculation, it is not a matter of maybe, nor is it simply a matter of the hateful behavior of bigoted cops. The criminalization we are facing is a series of grave social measures, progressive and interdependent, by which white society comes to view African Americans as dangerous felons and treat them as such. Though the entire Black community is targeted, the main victims are young Black inner-city males ("boys from the 'hood"), with Canadian criminalizers zeroing in on aboriginals (Canadian Indians) equally along with young Black males from the Toronto and Montreal areas and Nova Scotia.

For all the hype about little old white ladies' and small convenience storekeepers' "fear" of Black delinquents, there is nothing spontaneous and unprogrammed about this process of criminalization. For it has a bottom line—political and monetary profits. This criminalization has its own custom-tailored political economy. It has its own special vocabulary, voiced by elite academics as high-falutin "concern" about Black "cultural pathologies," "criminal subcultures," and "genetic inferiority," and mouthed by low-down white cops as slurs about "gorillas in the mist" and "jungle bunnies." It has its own ideology which defines Black males as the number one peril to society. It has its own peculiar white paranoia which sees a mugger in every nocturnal Black pedestrian, a holdup thug in every Black jewellery store customer, a shoplifter in every Black department store shopper, potential rioters and looters in every gathering of Black teenagers. It has its own *Gulag* syndrome, entailing frenzied prison construction, courtroom railroadings and frameups, and mass imprisonments. Those who are in the business of criminalizing our people have made it their religious rule that the Black male is by nature prone to violence, that he lacks self-control and must thus be narrowly regulated. That the best places for him are boot camps and stockades on decommissioned and functioning military bases. Such a one is less than human. Upon this assumption, white society feels justified to handle him as one would handle a mad dog.

To the optimists among us, prospects appear sunny; for hard-headed realists the outlook for the future is bleak. These are very dangerous political-economic times for Black men. Our young men are being held in suspension, in a holding pattern as it were. They are hung up between several bleak alternatives. Some pin their hopes on staffing the armed forces whose downsizing is now, inopportunely, mustering out rather than enlisting personnel. Others endure police brutality in the inner-city "hole in the doughnut." Others search neverendingly for jobs that have disappeared, jobs that are not there, or jobs for which they "lack the skills." Still others do time in the nation's prisons. Nearly a third of our young males are caught up in the criminal system at any given moment. A Washington D.C. Center for Social Studies survey predicted that, at the current pace, fully 70 percent of all young African-American men will be left out of the work force by the year 2000. Many of those left out will be locked in jail or addicted to drugs. However, this situation cannot last much beyond the turn of the century. The holding pattern is unstable, for the logic of contemporary American political economy dictates an imminent solution, of one kind or another. It can be a solution that will result in our salvation as a people. It can be a solution that could be fatal for the Black community. Either alternative appears equally possible. In the hope of eliciting the protest of those who should protest, judge Bruce Wright mused, "[t]hat Black men have stood mute when their rage should have compelled them to scream, to rant, to rave, and to be insane has never ceased to amaze me" (Wright 1990:162-163). He, like others, reflects on white supremacy's new personification as the "thin blue line" and the "super-prison."

THE POLITICAL ECONOMY OF INCARCERATION

The economic dimension of the criminalization of Black America mushrooms by the moment. The United States has put more than a million men and women behind bars, and the pace of incarceration just keeps on growing. It jails a higher percentage of its citizenry than any other nation on earth. The Bush Administration tried to up the percentage even further. The Clinton Administration takes much the same view, proposing to "attack crime" with 50,000 additional cops. "Law-and-order" legislation has imposed longer minimum jail terms for certain offenses. Conservative sentiment favors police use of illegally obtained evidence. The number of federal crimes punishable with death has been upped by more than 50. The "just-say-no" constituency insists that serious drug offenses warrant

capital punishment. Black and Latino drug peddlers are the targets—
the small fry in the rat race for personal wealth. Minority hustler-
entrepreneurs are being heavily hammered. The real sharks, the big
international drug traffickers, are white. They will continue to escape
retribution. Lawmakers have imposed a "three-strikes-and-you're-
in-for-good" policy that puts three-time convicted felons behind bars
without parole.

The consequences of these policies are felt on two levels. The
count of Black, Afro-Latino, Mexican, Central American, and Native
American inmates continues to soar nationally. There are more and
more prisoners to be fed, clothed, housed, and controlled daily—at
soaring cost. This has become yet one more way of redistributing
national income to the benefit of poor and lower middle class conservative white persons. It enables the appropriation of tax revenues
to provide them with employment—jobs maintaining, guarding, and
servicing prisons filled with racial minorities. For instance, in New
York state there is almost an exact match colorwise between the
watchers and the watched-over—82 percent of correctional officers
are white, while more than 80 percent of inmates are Black and
Latino. Deliberate incarceration of minorities is a major federal and
state job-creation program for whites in needy locales. It is a whole
sub-economy.

On the other hand, the cost of locking up so many people without a labor-value return is, of course, economically unpalatable. It
is very likely, therefore, that municipal, state, and federal levels of
government will act to transform the jails into a forced, convict-
labor production system. That is, where they have not already done
so. I envisage a prison-factory system, "employing," so-to-speak,
convict labor on a mass scale to turn out low-capital, high-labor
intensive commodities. More and more enterprises, like the Fort Dix
federal prison factory whose convict textile workers manufacture
camouflage clothing. Envisioned are the kind of commodities where
most of the value component is added by unskilled or semi-skilled
manual labor. Imprisoned workers are susceptible to all sorts of pressures, manipulation, and intimidation. This will be forced, unfree
labor. One menacing model is the Nazi *Strength-through-Joy* labor
camps. Expect a kind of Black *Gulag Archipelago*. A second phase
will bring privatization of the American prison network itself. Much
like hospitals now, the time is near when jails too will be sold to the
highest bidder, and run as private profit-making enterprises. The

political-economic forecast must make room for a twenty-first century update of the convict-lease labor system of the old Jim Crow
South, a rerun of the scheme that guaranteed dirt-cheap Black labor
to Southern businesses a century ago.

This twenty-first century-style convict lease labor is already well
underway, according to a CNN Television News report datelined
from the California penal system. By summer 1992, some 54 San
Quentin prisoners had been enrolled in a cooperative job program
with private industries outside. The enrollees remained in jail but
were taught skills to enable them to work on private firm projects
while inside, like computer assignments. They earned rock bottom,
Third World-level wages. Pay is scaled according to Mexican, South
American and Thailand benchlines. Both government and private
capital find satisfaction. The state of California makes money from
the project. The private firm cashes in, employing docile (because
imprisoned) jail-disciplined, non-unionized cheap labor. Here the
nineteenth century Southern convict-lease labor scheme is transformed to fit the age of computers. 1992 also witnessed the beginning of a move nationally to use inmates from privatized prisons in
labor disputes as strike-breakers. As of 1991, the prison system in
the U.S. was a $37 billion industry and growing. It was beginning
to appear recession-proof. The country was already spending $16
billion a year to incarcerate the world's largest prison population.
The prison building boom stood at $32.9 billion in mid-1994.

Diana Gordon detailed the cost of keeping Blacks in jail in *The
Justice Juggernaut: Fighting Street Crime, Controlling Citizens*. Black
imprisonment eats up half the total expenditure on incarceration,
as Afro-Americans are nearly half the nation's prisoners—an obscene
overrepresentation, attributable alone to racism. The annual cost of
maintaining half a million Black inmates in U.S. jails is 15 to 20 billion dollars, and climbing. When the court and police components
are reckoned in, the total outlay on the criminal "justice" system
nationally amounted to some $70 billion annually as the decade of
the Nineties began. Clearly there is more involved than merely sup-
pressing criminal behavior and "controlling citizens." The whole
business is too lucrative not to involve financial profit aims. Equally,
the whole affair is too sensitive civically not to entail partisan political machinations. A growing economy of criminalization demands
an ever-swelling army of Black, Afro-Latino, and Native American
prisoners, in order for public revenues to be diverted to those pri-

vate interests in the business of investing in the penal system, and, to pay the herds of lawyers, police and jailers, whose business is to round up, process, and watch over the captives. Battle cries like the "rights of victims," "mandatory sentencing," "war against crime," and the "death penalty" rally the racist white majority round the banner of continued white supremacy. There are economic and political grounds for the gigantic machine of repression.

Both Democrats and Republicans bellyache about how strapped-for-cash government is nowadays, and about how impossible it is to squeeze another dime in revenue from rebellious middle class taxpayers. Yet the U.S. Senate thinks nothing of throwing additional tax billions at police and prisons, while the Clinton Administration floats brash schemes for boot camps, new jails and thousands more police officers. The feeding-frenzy of political paranoia about crime just goes on and on. It began way back during the Nixon Administration. It came to a head in the Crime Bill of the 1990s. Mega-billions are being shifted from the federal government bureaucracy to be spent solely for more cops and more jails. The two fastest growing white employment sectors in America are security personnel and prison jailers. The ancient feudal principle of fortresses for the wealthy, shielded by private cops, has resurfaced, while poor and weak people of color are abandoned. There are two and a half times more private cops than public law enforcement officers, as criminalization has come more and more to also mean privatization. Private security firms are projected to be spending $104 billion annually by the year 2000, and to have 1.8 million persons in their employ by that date, including locksmiths, security guards, and alarm installers.

The penal organization is a new plantation system in the making. New prisons are constructed in white towns and run by white personnel. They are job-creation agencies. Like the slave plantations of the old South run by hired poor white overseers, the new lockups are stuffed with Blacks and dark-skinned Latinos watched over by mainly white personnel. The penal system combines career opportunities and earning for white folks with social control of Black people. Prison construction took off in the 1980s, as an episode of Reaganism. Since then it shows no sign of abating. During the ten years following 1982, the number of prisons in New York State rose from 34 to 69. In boondocks like Attica, Dannemore, Greenhaven, and Clinton, the number of inmates soared from 24,798 to 62,209, of whom 85 percent were Black and Latino, nearly all drawn from just seven neighborhoods in New York City. Governor Mario Cuomo used his 1994 State of the State address to announce the erection of a new superprison. A multi-million dollar high-tech detention center glowers over East Baltimore, kingpin in a ten-year drive by Maryland to construct a vast new criminal complex. Prison investment is lucrative. The profits line the pockets of white unionized building trades workers, white-owned construction companies, and white bankers. Contractors rake in profits supplying handcuffs, fire sprinklers, body armor, medical care, chewing tobacco, razor wire, dandruff shampoo, and infirmary beds. Advertisers and private consulting agencies that specialize in inmate services make small fortunes. In upstate New York, as in downstate Illinois, as in the rural hinterlands of every other state from Florida to Colorado with a sizeable Black population, whole communities have come to depend totally on the income and revenue of the prison system. Its benefit to whites is so obvious that Mujahid Farid can aptly call the prison system an affirmative action employment program for rural white males, without fear of rational contradiction.

A whole new geo-politics of prison location has sprung up to coordinate the subsidization of small white towns. The material dimension of racist criminalization and mass incarceration of Afro-Americans is the key dimension, although often overlooked. In the first half of 1991 the federal government announced a step-up in the "war on crime" in Black communities using high-tech measures similar to those employed in its Persian Gulf War against Iraq—expensive measures, the supply of which would be very profitable for certain private interests. The project was designed to redistribute fractions of the national income to the advantage of politically-sensitive segments of white America. It is also a means of compensating special fractions of the military-industrial complex for post-Cold War defense budget cutbacks. If over the next ten years the near half-million Black males already incarcerated were to, say, double, a bonanza would result. Many more right-wing rural and exurban whites would find steady jobs in the penal system; and not only white males. For the mass jailing of minorities creates employment opportunities also for white females. The penal system's jailor, janitor, administrative, medical, psychological, counselling, food and laundry service personnel does not exclude womenfolk. The small-town, conservative, white working class as a whole—male and female—

are acquiring a vested material interest in measures which generate convicts from the inner-city. They batten on the penal system. Construction companies compete, tendering for contracts to build penal facilities funded from tax revenues. This has become a subsidy for the building industry. Since prisoners get "room and board" after a fashion, laundry, cleaning, maintenance, and food—catering contracts are awarded.

Thus the political economy of incarceration is justly political *and* economic, serving both distinctly political and distinctly economic aims. Politically, it captures the loyalty of a section of the white working class, guaranteeing reliably conservative downstate-upstate voter majorities. Economically, it is a pork barrel of subsidies for certain manufacturing, construction, and service industries. Moreover, the incarceration economy has a mirror image in the militarization of police work. Federal, state, and local contracts for para-military equipment for the suppression of urban crime are bound to increase. "Smart" weaponry and other high-tech police procedures are fantastically expensive. Private firms supply this "state of the art" technology, and these firms charge high prices.

We are witnessing a domestic militarization designed to police America's racial minorities that parallels the anti-Third World Rapid Deployment strategy of today's U.S. Armed Forces. War abroad in places like Panama, Libya, and Iraq cascades profits on defense industries. War-like police policies at home intimidate the racial minorities, purchase the loyalty of rural whites, and promise safety for the white middle class. Thus the rise in street crime caused by economy-wide restructuring, a shrinking industrial base, and the disappearance of good jobs for young Black males, have, under racism, become yet one more way of raining benefits on white people at the expense of Black people.

BLACK INCARCERATION: THE HOUSE THAT ECONOMIC RESTRUCTURING BUILT

Permanent joblessness, high-crime-rate ghettoes, and the underclass are now all but synonymous. Inner-city underclass lads are dismissed contemptuously as "unemployable" and as school "dropouts." Congress is constantly crafting schemes to reform welfare and cast these "freeloaders" afloat. Self-important sociologists debate rehabilitation strategies. In truth, many denizens of the inner city are permanently without mainstream jobs, and most are youthful. The

328

category includes transients and the homeless. Economic racism and the ostensibly global "technological revolution" combine to deprive them of jobs, as well as of any prospect of satisfactory legal earnings. The underclass does not work in the legal economy because deindustrialization and the shift to high-tech enterprise have reduced the number of jobs considered lowly enough for inner-city Blacks to be eligible. They must choose between the burger-flipping wages of the service industries, and the high-risk street economy. Add the fact that during recessions or any other tight economic situation, the "privilege" of employment is restricted primarily to white males. As always, white entry-level applicants get first pick at choice high-tech training. Permanent unemployment is one of the specific modes of degradation imposed on Black people—especially on young Black men. The "do-nothingness," "aimlessness" and disproportionate criminal behavior for which they are blamed are merely manifestations of enforced Black redundancy, merely a way built-in racial discrimination shows up. The inner-cities are the proving grounds of *marginalization*, the process by which an entire population is isolated and turned into a human surplus. The government is free to deal with these Black "redundants" mainly in terms of how to police them, and how to incarcerate the unruly. It becomes a matter of how to fine-tune the penal system. In fact, there is evidence that many Black males are given long prison terms in order to artificially lower the unemployment rate among African Americans.

Further pressure on those Tony Monteiro terms the "chronically socially disabled" (Monteiro, 1991, pp. 9-10) comes from the growing presence of Third World immigrants—legal and undocumented. There are large influxes of Haitians, West Indians, and Spanish-speaking Dominicans and Mexicans and Central Americans. These, along with poor immigrants from the Philippines, China, and Indochina, compete with Blacks for low-paying jobs in manufacturing and service industries. And even though few African-Americans are in the running for hire in agriculture, the large pool of dirt-cheap Hispanic and Caribbean farm workers exerts downward pressure on wages generally, helping to keep pay low in the non-unionized services and sweatbox manufacturing still open to Blacks.

The process by which "street people" are forced into the underground economy and criminalized is instructive. Through no fault of their own many are estranged from the concrete experience, responsibility, and work habit discipline that spring from going to a job day in and day out. Refused employment, left without funds to fend for themselves in a voracious, heartless economy, the street brothers are forced to live by their wits. Survival becomes a hand-to-mouth hustle. Some see no other option but to prey on their own people. The homeless are vulnerable to criminalization. Poverty and street life are incentives for criminal behavior. "[W]hen captured from such an environment," observed Bruce Wright, "defendants who are poor find little difference between the jails and their homes." (Wright 1990:202). Indeed, for the homeless jail may represent a step upward—warm bed, toilet, and three square meals.

*

SATAN'S CHOICE: DESTITUTION OR THE UNDERGROUND ECONOMY

Everyone knows that Black plumbers and electricians are about as common as hen's teeth. Everyone also knows that those occupations, along with top construction jobs, have long commanded decent wages. Skin-color discrimination, which excluded Blacks from apprenticeship, all but closed such occupations to our people. In any case, the financial incentives for young Black males to engage in such para-economic enterprises as pushing drugs, snatching purses, and other street crimes, appear to outstrip the remuneration from even the most high-paying "lawful" blue collar trades. This is not something new. It only seems new because white demagogues and the media hype the issue with unprecedented fury. The disparity in financial prospects have been with us since at least the 1950s. It has plagued the big city scene for even longer than that, as far back as the Second World War, and in locales like Philadelphia, Chicago, and New York, as far back as the Teens and Twenties. Extra-legal work in a parallel economy has long paid better wages to a lucky few than legal employment. Far more important, illegal enterprise is the only one open to many Black males. Many do not make any once-and-for-all decision for one form of enterprise rather than the other. Some move in and out of legal work, and hustle on and off. The vast majority of Black and Latino common law delinquents would not place themselves in jeopardy outside the law if they could secure productive employment at decent wages. Thousands who abandon the legal labor force for criminal activity do so only intermittently, with the full intention of returning to the labor market at the first opportunity.

The fast food industry is touted as one of the fastest growing sectors of the service industry. It offers fertile comparison with the crack cocaine economy in respect to job opportunities for Blacks. In Baltimore, for instance, more Blacks had work hustling and dealing crack cocaine than the total number of Blacks hired by the local Burger King, McDonald's, Roy Rogers, and Kentucky Fried Chicken franchises put together. This was the situation in 1990, and there is little evidence of real change since then. Furthermore, Baltimore fast food concessions employed African-Americans at the minimum wage scale of $3.65 to $4.50 per hour—semi-slave earnings in view of the consumer price index. Obviously much more could be "earned" as a *minimum* in the parallel drug economy. Far-northern Milwaukee recovered from its "rust-bowl" depression in such fashion as to greatly benefit Caucasians, two-thirds of the city's inhabitants, reducing white unemployment city-wide to well below the national average. But Black Milwaukeeans are saddled with one of the highest jobless ratios in the entire Untied States. At one time or another more than half of all African-American residents have been on some form of public assistance. In this desert of poverty and despair some young Black males turned to the lucrative drug traffic. Where one in five was jobless, and where drugs became the means to wealth, it is no surprise that Milwaukee's Black homicide rate doubled in just three years from 1988 through 1990. White Milwaukeeans did not seem to care.

The Black underground economy is stoked by large-scale white-run drug trafficking which floods Black America with narcotics. Fabulously profitable, the network churns out wealth for white entrepreneurs engaged in extra-legal business enterprise. Its reach is international, in fact global. Its profits are laundered and reinvested in "legitimate" businesses, juicing the corporate establishment. Government agencies from local police forces to the federal CIA have been implicated. The import, processing and distribution of drugs mark a new "postmodern" phase in the history of entrepreneurial capitalism. Black and Latino neighborhoods rank at the top of the list for delivery and distribution. A modest estimate makes this a $160-billion-a-year industry for the white men who control the international pipelines. During one span in the 1980s the amount of cocaine pumped into Black America increased 19-fold.

While at the top end of the drug traffic gold showers white high-rollers, at the bottom the repressive machine herds small-time Black drug offenders into jail, securing jobs for city policemen and poor, small-town white Americans. In the penitentiaries themselves, white prison staff is being progressively Ku Klux Klanized, while prison authorities tolerate racist and Nazi organizing campaigns among white inmates.

These are the dire consequences of redundancy. Truly this is a dangerous time for Afro-Americans. For white folks are confused and have not made up their minds. For the first time since they hauled us to these shores in the slave ships, they do not know what to do with us. Growing numbers of whites believe they now can get along without us. The belligerent insist they have no further use for us. During 500 years, whites in the western hemisphere have felt one overriding need for Black folks—the need to *profit* from our labor. That is why the first Black slave was brought to the Americas and why the last one was delivered. Now it increasingly looks like the final decision regarding us will be made for white America neither by its political leaders nor its clergy, nor by conservative Foundation thinktankers. It seems that white America's collective mind will be made up by the evolution of the political economy. The market is not infallible and all-foreseeing, as some claim. It works blindly and blunderingly. The racist economy is in a quandary as to how to dispose of Black folk whose labor has been rendered superfluous and redundant, and from whose presence large profits can no longer be squeezed. What to do in the long run with restless Black inhabitants? What else to do with us now but "contain" and "welfare" us in inner city ghettoes, whites wonder. With near unanimity, the white suburbs see this as a costly proposition entailing an unacceptable redistribution of the national income to their disadvantage. If Blacks are no longer needed, why keep them around? The danger of genocide grows hourly. Right now white society is in a funk, torn by indecision. But it will not remain undecided for long. The ultimate danger is that the racist economy may at some point mandate our elimination.

*

The Criminal Injustice System

The criminal system of racist injustice squats firmly on four pillars: a) anti-insurgent overpolicing of Black urban core communities; b) a much higher rate of arrests of Blacks than whites; c) differential sentencing according to race; and d) an elevated rate of Black incarceration. During the Great Depression not only were white arrest rates low, but so were the rates for Blacks, perhaps reflecting the general doldrums of a society in the grip of poverty, as well as stagnating urbanization as big cities momentarily lost their pull on rural Blacks. Nevertheless, Blacks were arrested twice as often as whites. But compared to what has followed, Black arrest percentages were relatively low throughout the Second World War and the immediate post-war years. The turning point seems to have coincided with the end of the Korean War, the number of Blacks (mainly males) hauled in by the police spiking suddenly around 1953, and despite easing off in some years, soaring to atrocious heights since then. By the mid-1980s, the national Black arrest rate was three times the white rate. This for a Black population that is much smaller than the total white population. As the 1980s began, Blacks were being jailed on homicide charges at a rate seven times the rate for whites (Jaynes and Williams 1989: 458-459).

California has a reputation for being the nation's pacemaker—flaky and otherwise. It has lived up to its reputation in respect to racist police repression. By 1992 two-thirds of all Black and Chicano Californian male youths had been arrested at one time or another. California locked up 9.7 million men, women, and children in 1989, most of them people of color in a state whose entire population stood then around 30 million. The slave-plantation-like beating of Rodney King by Daryl Gates' LAPD was certainly no fluke. Mark Fuhrman's dreams of burning Black people are shared by many of his former brother officers.

The pattern is duplicated on the Atlantic coast, however with a more specifically anti-Black bias because more African-Americans live in the east. In New York State, the system expresses itself in numerology that is curiously coincidental. The personnel of the courts, including its judges, is 81 percent white. The state's convict population consists of 82 percent non-white minorities—on the one hand white supremacy, on the other modernized racial bondage. The state of New York houses the largest Black population in North America. It jails Afro-Americans at a rate 15 times higher than the rate at which it incarcerates white New Yorkers. Young Black males are 23 times as likely as white males to end up in jail. In the New York City metropolitan area Blacks and Afro-Latinos are one-third of the inhabitants. Yet the four boroughs of Manhattan, Brooklyn, the Bronx, and Queens—the sites of heavily Black and Latino districts—have been ransacked to furnish eight of every ten inmates in the state.

The Northwest seems to specialize in the criminalization of Black children. African Americans—adults and children—make up only about seven percent of Seattle residents. Nonetheless, 42 percent of those in juvenile detention are Black youngsters. State-wide, Black youth amount to a tiny four percent of total youth, but police arrest them 150 percent more frequently. No wonder the Aryan Nations believe their dream of the Pacific Northwest as a "pure white enclave," to be a realistic one. Black youth are regularly rounded up for trivial offenses which are overlooked when committed by white youth. The norm for them is pre-trial detention, followed by lengthy jail sentences.

Dixie is still Dixie as far as law enforcement and Black men are concerned. On drug charges, Montgomery, Alabama, locks up Blacks at a rate six times as high as whites; Little Rock, thirteen times; Miami, five times; Richmond, Virginia, eight times; and Raleigh, North Carolina, eleven times!

In cities of more than 100,000 population in eight Midwestern states, Black persons are arrested on drug charges at a rate eleven times as high as whites. Yet no one has been able to demonstrate that drug abuse is more common among Blacks than among whites (*USA Today*, 23 July 1993).

In 1990 Marc Maurer published two statistics, often quoted since: in 1986 there were 436,000 Black male college students in the United States; as of 1990, some 609,690 young Black males were subject to the supervision of the criminal justice system. In short, almost one and a half times as many in trouble with the law as there are collegians. Maurer worked for The Sentencing Project, a Washington, D.C., non-profit research association. Research revealed the ouster from the national work force by the beginning of the 1990s of half of all Black male youths aged 15 to 19. Black America contains no more than 12 percent of the nation's drug users, yet 44 percent of those arrested for drug possession are Black. Law enforcement arrests far fewer white abusers as a matter of policy. Some 80 percent of the cocaine users in this country are Caucasians. Cocaine is available in two forms—powder and crack. Powder is expensive and the narcotic of choice for whites. Crack is retailed in cheaper units and is consumed by minority addicts primarily. For this reason, law enforcement is selective in respect to the two forms.

Relatively few are arrested for use of cocaine powder and the penalty is light, because the offenders are white. Droves are rounded up and jailed for years for possession of crack cocaine, because they are Black or Afro-Latino. Search the length and breadth of the land and on any given day one will find fully one-quarter of Afro-American men between the ages of 20 and 29, either on probation or on parole or in jail or in prison. Fully 75 percent of those convicted under the federal drug kingpin act have been white, but 90 percent of those sentenced to death under the same statute are Blacks and other racial minorities.

Figures like these, and the cost of warehousing these men, confirm that the entire criminal justice system is a gigantic business designed to generate jobs and income for those administering "justice." It has certainly bred conservative political loyalties. And the situation worsens as the rate of incarceration increases. By May 1992, 42 percent of District of Columbia Black men between 18 and 35 were under some type of correctional supervision. A Black man in Texas must expect to serve 13 years longer in prison for attempted murder than a white man convicted of the same charge, an expression of differential sentencing racially. What matters most in the lone star state is the color of the victim. The average sentence for the killing of a white person is 30 years, compared with 20 for the murder of a Black person. The rape of a white woman costs a median sentence of 10 years, but one can get off with just 2 years for the rape of a Black woman. Only one white person was executed in the 18 years from 1976 to 1994 in the entire United States for killing a Black person. Funds dispensed nationally on courts, police, jails, prison maintenance, and other aspects of criminal justice have quadrupled.

As the gold showered on the criminal justice system by Congress and state legislatures has increased, so has denial hardened that there is anything racist about the system. Apologists scream that juries and judges assess higher sentences on Blacks, Latinos, and Native Americans solely because of the severity of the offense, or because the convict is a repeated offender, or—major concession—because of the weight of poverty and class—but never *race*! The Supreme Court itself has okayed more severe penalties—including the death penalty—for criminals whose victims are white. It coupled its decision with a baldfaced denial that this has anything to do with racial injustice, even though a comprehensive analysis of 28 geographically diverse areas revealed glaring racial disparities in the imposition of the death penalty. A ton of evidence shows that Black people are arrested and jailed for minor misdemeanors much more often than white persons. In fact, it is a rule of legal thumb in racist America that as the seriousness of the transgression diminishes, racial disparity increases. Nevertheless, the system's defenders assure us that the great discretion given law enforcement and prosecution is not used in racially discriminatory fashion. Tell that to the white cop in a Black neighborhood about to make an arrest for a minor drug offense! We are also supposed to believe that race has no influence on parole decisions for Black inmates.

*

Political economy is about who gets what, about who cashes in and who goes home empty-handed. Nowhere is this more obvious than in the bitter controversy over mandatory sentencing, for the antagonists are at each other's throat over alternatives. Loud-mouthings about "incapacitating criminals to protect society" cover greed for tax-derived income transfers. They drown the noise of tussles between segments of the electorate over income redistribution. Take the mandatory prison sentence program in New York state, for example. In 1973 Nelson Rockefeller was governor. He pushed through a law which sentenced repeat felons to jail automatically. Rockefeller's law blazed a trail for today's three-strikes-and-we-throw-away-the-key legislation that is now cropping up all over the place. New York judges were stripped of the right to fix alternative forms of punishment. The alternative would have allowed judges discretion to prescribe different penalties for non-violent, mostly drug-related and otherwise "victimless" offenders. This was an option favored by Black and Afro-Latino community activists with an eye toward rehabilitation. The alternative envisioned probation for Black and Latino convicts that would have let them remain within the confines of their own community and be intensely supervised by members of their own community. This pro-Black alternative to mandatory sentencing offered a substantial political-economic pay-off. The program would have created a windfall of supervisory jobs in Black and Latino communities. For the offenders it raised the prospect of day-reporting, community service and jobs. Job-training and mandatory participation in community-based job programs would have figured in the package. And rehabilitation would have a leg up, for it does not take the proverbial rocket scientist to know that the convict's own community understands his needs and failings better than any remote white prison staff.

But such was not to be, even though the vast majority jailed in the state of New York and elsewhere are non-violent, petty-property and minor drug offenders. They are not a danger to the public, yet the hammer of mandatory sentencing has lowered.

Prison personnel are drawn from just about anywhere but from the inmates' own environment. With negligible exceptions, the white police officers who patrol the inner cities maintain family homes tucked away in white suburbs at a safe distance. Every time a young Black or Latino man is locked up, a job is created for someone to guard him—and that someone is usually white. In contrast, alternative sentencing programs would generate employment for Blacks and Latinos skilled in rehabilitating members of their own community. For instance, funding could be provided to reimburse the Nation of Islam for some of the rehabilitative work it does voluntarily. Furthermore, an offender held within his own community can more easily be induced, or compelled, to reimburse his victim. Indemnification for stolen property may be possible. Such procedures would make restitution more than just a pipe-dream for the victims who themselves are nearly always Black and members of the same community as the offenders. Restitution is never forthcoming when prisoners are incarcerated far away in a white area.

Another glaring example of the racial discrimination inherent in differential and mandatory sentencing comes from Florida. In certain jurisdictions in the state two persons charged and convicted of one and the same offense may have entirely different treatment, if one is Black and the other white. Both may be classified as "career criminals," but never get the same punishment. Here sentencing guidelines mean nothing. One and the same court will give the Black offender 30 years, while the white man convicted of the same crime gets away with a five-year sentence. And this is passed off as simply the result of the white criminal having the "better" lawyer. Regularly Black convicts are hit with ten-year minimum mandatory sentencing; whites no minimum mandatory. It has been calculated that it would take five to ten times as many white inmates to make up the discrepancy in length of sentences meted out to Black convicts. "White convicts themselves say they don't know how they get off with such easy breaks, when Blacks triple their sentencing." According to federal court research, sentencing of Blacks for firearm and drug violations now averages 49 percent longer than for whites.

*

It is not new for Black people to be complaining about the refusal of American courts to apply the same measure of punishment to Black as to white offenders. It is also nothing new for us to be lamenting the injustice built into the jury system. This century began with the Niagara Movement decrying the miscarriage of justice entailed in the exclusion of Black citizens from juries (1905). The Committee of Forty on Permanent Organization which prepared the way for the founding of the NAACP joined suit in 1909 in condemning the practice subjecting Black defendants to all-white juries; as did Marcus Garvey's UNIA at its first convention in August 1920. Since then little has changed, though the lipstick and eyeshadow of white supremacy have been freshened several times over. The composition and the decision of the Simi Valley Rodney King trial should have surprised no one. The outlook of all-white juries in the 1990s is not essentially different from that of the white "Anglo-Saxon" jury in Mississippi which exonerated Emmett Till's lynchers in 1955, or that of the two all-white juries which returned not-guilty verdicts to Byron de la Beckwith in the first two Medgar Evers cases. The Simi Valley jury consisted of ten whites, one Asian and one Hispanic— but no Afro-American. Although in the second (federal) Rodney King trial, the system did not succeed in stacking the jury completely, and two of the officers were found gulty of a little bit of something or other, nevertheless juror names were drawn from a pool which included a white ex-Marine, a sexagenarian Danish army veteran who admired the Simi Valley jury, a white man who moved in police circles, a youthful white man who saw no injustice in the Simi Valley decision and a middle-aged white businessman whose idea of virtue is obedience to the police. Their opinions indicate the wide disparity between the two races in attitude toward the criminal justice system. Nearly three-quarters of all Black people in the United States say that they are treated more harshly than whites in the criminal system. But only 35 percent of whites agree with them. Two-thirds of the white population insist that African-Americans are getting a fair shake or that they should be treated even more harshly.

The exact same jury-room racism dominates civil cases where Black plaintiffs receive only three-quarters as much money as whites for the same type of claim, injuries, or lost income. For instance, when a Black couple in Florida sued an insurance company in 1992, after they had been hurt in a car accident, the all-white jury compared them to chimpanzees with drug dealers for children. The plaintiffs were awarded less than five percent of what was due them.

In Canada, north of the border, the jail system is much the same in harsh treatment of Blacks. Leaked reports were so embarrassing that even the government had to appear to favor remedy. A Commission on Systemic Racism in the Ontario Criminal Justice System surveyed the province's 85 correctional facilities and made some uncomfortable admissions. It is common practice in Ontario's jails for Black inmates—called "spooks," "savages," "camel jockeys" and "cotton pickers" by the white guards—to be denied combs and other grooming equipment and personal care products. At one detention center, African womanhood is so spurned that Black women inmates are refused sanitary napkins during menstruation. Pregnant Black inmates are burdened with physically taxing assignments while white female prisoners get lighter work. A rigid form of apartheid is practiced. Black inmates are separated from white ones and segregated in all-Black holding pens known as "Jungles," "Madhouses," "Animal Houses," "Bumboclot Ranges," or "Monkey Ranges." Segregation is justified on the grounds that racial hostility between Black and white inmates would endanger prison security. We are describing a situation not, say, from the pre-1950s U.S. jails, but as it existed in Ontario's correctional institutions in 1994. Rehabilitation for Black prisoners is a laughing stock, as classification officers routinely impose race-based discrepancies in educational programs.

＊

WHO GOES TO PRISON?

According to inner-city street lore, the distinction between life within prison walls and life on the outside has become a blur, and it is unclear to some that things are better on the outside than within. Which is the prolongation of the other—the civilian life of the penitentiary, or the penitentiary of civilian life? Haki Madhubuti has some very trenchant insights in this vein (Madhubuti 1990: 45). The confusion arises because it has become the norm for many young African American males to be imprisoned, rather than to walk around free for any length of time. Incarceration is a rite of passage for many young Black males in America, a ritual marking the change from puberty to adulthood. Ever since the early 1980s, Black youths in their twenties have been 16 and more times likely to taste prison than white boys of similar age. As of 1994, the incarceration rate among Afro-Americans of all ages was more than seven times the rate among whites.

Who goes to prison? Mostly young, poor, urban Black males, men unable to find jobs in the legal economy, many of them school dropouts. The United States which locks up Black males more than four times as often as apartheid South Africa at its worst, outstrips all other countries in the rate at which it incarcerates its citizens, ranking well above such lands as South Africa, the former Soviet Union, Britain, and France. North America is a prison of *Black* nations!

Latinos are twice as likely as white males to be "busted" by the NYPD, Black men three times as likely. New York City is the foremost jailer of Black folk. For instance, in the month of November 1991, New York City jails were jammed with 18,000 Black prisoners. There were only 2,500 whites in its cells in a metropolis where whites outnumber Blacks. Derrick Bell's brilliant allegory (Bell 1992: 190) marshals testimony of the National Center on Institutions and Alternatives to show that the same disproportionality prevails in the District of Columbia, the nation's capital. In the far northwestern corner of the country Black residents are about four percent of the State of Washington's population. Typical of the countrywide pattern of racial harassment, though, 23 percent of the young in prison in that state are Afro-Americans. Scanning the entire country, we find that there are two African-Americans in lockups, state and federal, for every one (18 to 24 years old) enrolled in post-secondary education. Nearly two thirds of Black men in the lock-up experience difficulty reading even the most simple text with comprehension. Nine of ten are unable to solve elementary math problems. The army who "graduate" from jails is twice the size of the Black male college student body.

Frederick Douglass warned, "find out what people will submit to and you have found out the exact amount of injustice and wrong which will be imposed on them." White power has weighed us down with an "imprisoned generation" of young captives for whom prison is the only place to learn to be fit for life in companionship with others, or, more realistically, to learn lifelong aversion to caring social behavior. These are the prisoners of the "growing American gulag" that white racism hopes to make the hallmark of the coming century, a plantation system risen from the ashes, run by the new master class of criminal justice personnel (Jhally and Lewis 1992:63).

*

As we all (should) know, capital punishment has a racist face. What seems to matter most in determining who will be executed is the color of the convict's victim. Between 1930 and 1979, 2,066 Blacks were executed by the criminal justice system in America. During that same span only 1,754 whites were put to death by the state, though one could not convince even an alien from outer space that there were not far more white folks in America than Black people. Of African-Americans sentenced to death and actually executed, 1,659 were in the Old South—heartland of racism and white supremacy.

After being suspended for a brief period as unconstitutional, the death penalty was reinstated in 1976. In the interval since then, judges have been sentencing people to death with growing alacrity. The Reagan rehabilitation of racism politically fed the judiciary's lust for blood. Once again more than 40 percent of inmates sitting on death row are Black. The NAACP Legal Defense and Education Fund has clocked this grisly performance, but has had little luck in persuading the right wing majority on the Supreme Court to condemn the racist character of capital punishment as practiced in the U.S. South Carolina, for instance, has a history of murdering and lynching Blacks. Over the years it executed droves of our people for alleged crimes against white folks. But it was not until Octobr 1991 that South Carolina finally got around to executing a white man for murdering an African American—the first and only time in its long history. Yet conservative Supreme Court justices refuse to admit that the death penalty is a terrorist weapon of intimidation against Blacks—a racially selective weapon. It has been deaf to Urban League proposals that would allow defendants to challenge death sentences that may be influenced by racial bias. Nationally, approximately 90 percent of those (white as well as Black) put to death since 1976 have been convicted of killing *white* persons. Kill a white person and you are likely to die in judicial revenge. Kill a Black person, or a Native American, and your chances of avoiding death row are very good indeed, regardless of your own color.

Death penalty freaks know full well that execution is not—and has never been—an effective crime deterrent. It has never reduced crime, never stopped a murderer, and the hardliners know this, despite lies to the contrary. But they are driven by psychotic urges for raw revenge and primitive retribution. Some of them imagine that we may some day pour out of the inner cities to hunt them down in their suburban havens, and they cling to the hope that the threat of execution might deter our anger. Deep-down, the advocates of capital punishment are motivated by white racial protectionism, coupled with a passion to inflict genocidal punishments on non-white offenders. Maybe there is something to the Cress-Welsing theory of fear-induced obsession in white supremacy culture after all.

Again, crossing the northern border does not bring much relief. 40 percent of prisoners in some Toronto-area jails are Black,while it is doubtful that even ten percent of the people in the metropolitan area are African-Canadian. The percentage rises further for the province as a whole, with Blacks comprising more than six in ten inmates in Ontario lockups. Canadian courts perform more and more like American courts, the appearance of a large Black population in southern Ontario since the 1960s and 1970s having triggered a racist coordination of the two judicial systems. For example, on the same day (31 October 1991), verdicts in two separate Toronto courts exonerated perpetrators of violence against Black victims because the aggressors were white. In one courtrom, an all-white jury acquitted a white cop of attempted murder of a 16-year old Black lad, even though the policeman admitted that he shot the unarmed youth in the back twice. In the other courtroom, a white female judge freed three white hoodlums who had attacked and stabbed a Black pedestrian in full daylight in downtown Toronto. She ignored eyewitness identifications of the assailants, as well as an admission by one of the defendants that he had indeed injured the Black man. White racial solidarity overrode any gender friction that might pit white females against white males. For the judge it was more important to make sure that white men did not have to go to jail for knifing a "visible minority," as people of color are termed in Canada. North and south of the border, the jury system is consistent. It is very reluctant to convict whites for aggression against Black people. White racial preference always kicks in.

When the Metro Toronto Police Force got wind of Black community efforts to establish an independent civilian police review board, stamp out racism within the police and enact mandatory affirmative action, it moved as swiftly to obliterate Black dissent as any American police force. Starting in the spring of 1989, it compiled a

Confidential Intelligence Report on activists within the Black community. Inside informers were recruited. Black police officers infiltrated Black groups. Entrapments framed outspoken critics. And, as in American jails, white Canadian prison guards beat Black inmates to death—an outrageous incident occurring at Kingston (Ontario) Penitentiary in October 1993.

The criminalization of U.S. racial minorities was rejuvenated legally in a series of laws beginning during the Reagan era. The Comprehensive Crime Control Act of 1984 inflated the powers of law enforcement. The Helms Amendment of 1988 encouraged police-state blanket surveillance. The Omnibus Anti-Drug Act of 1988 enshrined presumption of guilt rather than innocence, and cut into the heart of *habeas corpus*, the provision that is supposed to protect us from illegal imprisonment. Following in his predecessor's footsteps, George Bush pressured Congress for even more repressive legislation, this time broad enough to criminalize Black women as well. Lisa Maher, a specialist in the affairs of poor women, observes that under the guise of shielding the unborn from so-called "crack pregnancies," pregnancy itself is viewed as a criminal act, if the pregnant woman happens to be poor, jobless, and Black. The real aims are to push sterilization and control the number of African American citizens (Maher 1990:113-135). The 300 percent increase since 1980 in the rate of incarceration of Black women is topped only by the 500 percent increase in the incarceration rate of Black men. Municipal "anti-gang" laws enable any policeman who observes two or more young persons "loitering" in a public place, to order them to disperse or arrest them as "gang members." One is reminded of the vagrancy laws of the Jim Crow South under which thousands of Black men were rounded up for "loitering." Federal "anti-gang" measures provide for federal preventive detention to block release or bail pending trial; more wiretapping and entrapment; and federal investigative grand juries with dictatorial authority. The 1994 Crime Bill broadened mandatory minimum sentences, boosted appropriation for an already over-funded criminal justice system, and added new offenses to the list of crimes eligible for the death penalty. Seizing control of both houses of Congress in 1995, the Republicans provided further muscle through their "Contract with America."

Chapter 17

CONTAINMENT AND THE POLICE STATE

The *prisonization* of Black America is scaled on an escalator of sorts. At the upper end there is maximum security incarceration in the nation's new, high-tech, "super-prisons." In the middle there is the network of conventional jails, reformatories, penitentiaries (and now boot camps). At the lower end, whole inner-city districts and public housing projects have been turned into minimum security concentration camps or reserves, ringed and patrolled by racist white cops with a licence to harass, brutalize and kill recalcitrants at will. White cops are aided in this task by certain Black (and Hispanic) police officers who have internalized white myths about Afro-Americans as jungle folk. They have the same leeway to inflict injury, as long as they refrain from savaging white citizens. The "war against drugs" has spawned plans for barb-wired housing projects, elaborate ID-pass systems, and other restrictions on the free movement of inner-city residents. On Capitol Hill there is bipartisan effort to popularize the notion that violent Black crime is the number one crisis facing the nation. With the Cold War now history, "gun-toting" domestic Blacks have replaced foreign "Commie Reds" as the demon image.

One hundred and seventy metropolitan areas are "threatened" by youth gangs, say news journals. In reality, there is evidence that many of the drive-by killings in Black communities, ascribed to Black-on-Black gang violence, are actually staged by off-duty policemen in plain clothes and unmarked vehicles. These missions seem modelled on the actions of Central American and Brazilian police death squads. Police drive-bys were triggered in particular by four major gang summits in 1993, pledging peace and truce among Black youths. Cops were "scrambling around trying to figure out what to do about all those unified Black folks." Disinformation is leaked to hoodwink a neighborhood into thinking that its "turf" has been hit by a rival gang. Fragile peacemaking is sabotaged, truces undermined, street gang warfare revived and prolonged, costing more fatalities. The media campaign to convince the world that Black "gangsta" youth are lethal, a danger to themselves and everyone else, is given more fuel, and police repression more excuse. Police drive-bys masquerading as street gang shootings confirm the nervous white middle class in its yell for repression against Black residential areas. The lid must be slammed down on them before they explode and export "*their*" violence into white neighborhoods. The countrywide hysteria unleashed by the white media in the aftermath of the Long Island Railroad attack on 8 December 1993 was an object lesson in the manipulation of such incidents.

The effort to foment disunity in our neighborhoods, to provoke renewed bloodshed, is also part of a law enforcement fiscal planning scheme. By creating the impression of a need for stern measures against street gangs, police strategists seek tax appropriations for more jails, stiffer sentences, larger police forces, high-tech equipment with greater firepower, and higher salaries for white cops. The image of carnage in Black neighborhoods drums up support for increased spending. It is like the old Cold-War Pentagon ruse of inventing foreign "threats to the national security," in order to justify spiralling defense budgets.

The criminalization of the Black citizenry proceeds under the cover of an elaborate vocabulary designed not to call the thing by its real name, a vocabulary redolent with terms like "gang members," "irresponsible parents," "delinquent youth," "gansta rappers," "street hustlers," "public safety," "safe streets," "thugs and hoodlums," "repeat felons," and so forth. Self-incrimination, preventive detention, and arbitrary search and seizure, are becoming common measures of law enforcement. The fact that these tactics violate the Constitution of the United States is shunted aside. The plea runs that just as the invasion of U.S. territory by foreign troops would justify the suspension of basic civilian rights pro tem, the "present emergency" of violent crime makes it alright to deprive "suspects" of their constitutional rights, or to place whole minority neighborhoods under federal control. The Chicago Housing Authority has ordered "lockdowns" which require special identification papers and sign-ins. This is the philosophy behind "street-sweeping" and *Weed and Seed* round-ups of inner-city youth—catching many innocents in the same net indiscriminately with the few guilty. In the early 1990s, Omaha, Trenton, New Jersey, Kansas City, Missouri, Philadelphia, Seattle and Denver, all tried pilot Weed and Seed programs.

Every night the police make false arrests, beat those who protest, and then charge the pummelled with resisting arrest and assaulting police officers. Preemptive arrest has moved from the planning stage to the operational stage. Suspects are grabbed and held without bail in the mere expectation that they *might* commit a crime. The anticipation of crime is strongly connected with pigmentation—young Black inner-city males are suspect on sight. Some public housing occupants live under police-state regulations which deprive them of the right even to entertain visitors. Police sweep apartments, supposedly in search of illegal drugs. The uprising in Los Angeles, sparked by the first Rodney King trial verdict, provided a pretext to step up blanket repression. Ever since then, at the slightest hint of protest against police brutality in the streets or the death of a Black man in police custody, city officials immediately ban alcohol and weapons sales, and close off whole districts. Police go into the riot control mode at a moment's notice. The adoption of racial profiles in law enforcement has further institutionalized police harassment and presumption of guilt for Black people. State police in New Jersey, Pennsylvania, and elsewhere regularly use racial profiles to stop motorists for drug searches. Denver compiled a police list of gang-member suspects, 93 percent of whom were either Black or Hispanic, making likely the persecution of two of every three Black youths in the city age 12 to 24. Blacks and Hispanics accounted for 90 percent of felony arrests by special "gang-crackdown" units.

*

Crime is indeed a vexing problem in America. The dizzying array of "white collar" crimes, everything from embezzlement to insider-dealing, occurs so universally in "mainstream" America as to liter-ally make it difficult to find many white adults with clean hands. Corrupt police officers are the cancer of the United States. For example, recently (1994) the Mollen Commission exposed the mis-deeds of well-organized gangs of NYPD cops who prey on Black and Afro-Latino districts. Police crews coordinated operations, using radio networks and code names to deal drugs to supplement their income by some $8,000 a week. Rogue cops practiced "collars for dollars" record falsification. A "blue wall of silence" in the depart-ment buried evidence of forcible entry and looted drug trafficking locations in mysteriously lost or destroyed "tickler files." The Patrolmen's Benevolent Association—the police union—backed the conspiracy.

The quandary for Black and Latino communities is coping with the blight of self-destroying street violence. Of course, there is an obvious and sole remedy for the curse: Employ Black parents at steady, secure and decent wages which would enable them to estab-lish and maintain stable families; provide Black people with attrac-tive, affordable, single-family housing; ensure decent clothing and healthy nourishment; furnish adequate leisure and entertainment facilities; assure every youngster quality schooling; make remuner-ative, meaningful jobs available for each and every minority youth as she/he enters the workforce—in other words, establish human living conditions, and the crime rate among Blacks would melt down like a snowman on a hot day in the Arizona desert.

But such a solution is incompatible with white supremacy. Any such resolution cannot exist together in harmony with the existing racist political economy. Instead, we get a two-pronged containment strategy, one prong aimed at Black people, the main target, the other prong pointed at whites as a support resource. In the dozen or more biggest urban agglomerations, high unemployment (two to two-and-a-half times the white rate), underemployment (part-time jobs with-out benefits), and low-wage service jobs (with cut-rate benefits) are accepted as fundamental parts of the national culture. These "free market effects" keep the Black community in its traditional "place" as a cheap labor reserve and reundancy pool. As a system—reformed or unreformed—with its childcare traps, welfare functions socially as a means of controlling Black women. The inner-cities are flooded with narcotics, the ultimate origins of which are far outside the boundaries of the United States and totally under the control of white men. AIDS has appeared as the "political disease" programmed, it seems, to decimate African Americans and reduce the Black population worldwide, cutting its grimmest swathe across the African continent. Black-on-Black violence has surfaced as the surrogate for lynching: the internalized self-hatred that leads Black youths to execute one another without whites having to lift a hand. We face a lethal manifestation at the young adult level of the same self-denigration revealed in our small children by Kenneth Clark's dolls experiment in 1952.

Naturally, racism's containment strategy must ignore evidence that many of the offenses committed by Black males express a desire for revenge against white society. Many act from an utter lack of respect for the white man's ownership rules grounded in the historical reality that the white man has ever approached the Black community as a thief in the night, even to the point of stealing Black people themselves. Furthermore, the criminalization process incorporates an occupied zone syndrome. Police patrol patterns are put together in such a way as to contain and isolate Black (and Latino) sections from white neighborhoods. Notice how Black motorists are shadowed suspiciously in certain exclusive and wealthy white residential areas after dark. And woe to any Black man on foot in the area at night. He better have a good explanation ready when he is halted and called to account by some white cop or security guard. Afro-American individuals hard to deal with are brutalized in order to overawe and intimidate the mass of Afro-Americans. Riot control methods have been honed and para-militarized with surveillance helicopters, armored vehicles, and special weapons training.

Law and order freaks raise a ruckus about stamping out crime. But they really mean only the kind of activity which jeopardizes the racist status quo. They have no intention of stamping out anything that is profitable and system-affirming. No establishment figure in his right mind would do anything to injure the profits of the "prison-industrial complex," or those of the private sector security industry. High-roller white collar crime is sacrosanct. The policy of containment tolerates the parallel, shadow, underground, illegal, and paralegal economy. In fact, it does more than just tolerate it. The illegal economy is regarded as a generator of jobs of sorts. It handles, retails, and consumes stolen goods. There are two sides to drug-dealing (the kingpin of the underground economy). First, narcotics are supplied to minority communities by white major traffickers. Second, ghetto peddlers are convenient targets for right-wing demagogues who specialize in arousing anti-Black prejudice. One is a source of white wealth, the other a political boon. The shadow economy functions as the carrot in the carrot-and-stick aspect of containment strategy. It is an "equality of opportunity employer" of sorts, much like the armed forces used to be during the heyday of Black troop recruitment. It is a safety valve allowing for '*hood* entrepreneurs who, if frustrated, might otherwise turn their talents to dangerous political dissent. After all, the average hourly pay from crime ranges from twice to four times the average hourly minimum wage in the legal economy.

But the ground strategy to perpetuate white supremacy through the criminalization of Black folk is broader yet, and more supple. It provides for systematic harassment of Black elected officials, for instance. It mounts elaborate entrapments, such as the spectacular sting which brought down Mayor Marion Barry in Washington, D.C. African American officials are tied up in grotesque court cases and Capitol Hill investigations, required to defend themselves against never-ending rounds of alleged corruptions, IRS tax evasions and even more bizarre charges. They never have time to govern or administrate. Reform is paralyzed. Pro-minority initiatives die on the drawing board. Black Trojan Horses gallop in from all directions. A tiny minority of modern-day equivalents of the Black slave drivers of old are well rewarded and much publicized—men like Clarence Thomas. Lionized are Negro scholars, journalists, and public personalities who rush to condemn any of their fellow Blacks who boldly criticize white supremacy. These are the Quislings who embrace policies hurtful to their own people under cover of conservatism. Undermining our community from within, these characters voice outrage at quotas and affirmative action beneficial to the racial minorities, while lauding "color-blind" "merit-only" alternatives. The Black Trojan Horse is a key pawn in the containment power play.

So too is psychological warfare which, in the 1990s, increasingly relies on racist coding. The anti-Black psychological campaign now speaks in a language urging "war on crime," "war on drugs," "take back the streets," "reverse discrimination," and suchlike. It talks about rejecting quotas in favor of a "color-blind America." It dotes on negative political campaigning. The "Willy Hortonization" of political life has been discussed too often to need elaboration. We are swamped psychologically by a discourse crafted to nurture middle class paranoia. An image is fostered in white minds of lazy, good-for-nothing, irresponsible, violence-prone, welfare-loafing Black folk who really do not know what they want, who constantly make demands and who want to be coddled. Such people should be ostracized. Sermons like this assure that white majorities will continue to vote for right-wing conservatives, politicians who can be depended upon to oppose minority set-asides and civil rights legislation as measures allegedly harmful to white job security. Furthermore, the psychological war is tailored to win curtailments of the government services and transfer funds which go to people of color.

Curtailment of transfer funds owing to Blacks, Native Americans, and Latinos of African origins, and cutbacks in municipal, education and health subsidies, allow redistribution of national income in favor of poor whites and medium-scaled white owned businesses. As noted above, prison construction is one of the fastest growing sectors in the white-dominated construction industry, and the deliberate location of penal facilities great distances from the inner cities extorts funds from Black women who must spend time and fares chartering buses and paying for transportation to far away prisons to visit their male relatives. But this is understandable, for the overrepresentation of poor whites as police, jailors and prison guards, administrators and caterers must be funded from somewhere. And the vast white middle class—already chaffing from perceived overtaxation—does not want to subsidize criminal justice system affirmative action for poor whites.

In the face of containment strategy, can Black police officers be anything but modern slave drivers? Does the current system leave room for them to act as true "guardians" of our people? Where does Black community policing fit in a police state? In the last little while, African American police professionals have been posted to high office as commissioners and police chiefs, usually appointed by Black mayors. Some have climbed arduously up through the ranks. There are even a few spectacular namings of Black men as "Czars" for the prevention of some crime or other. In 1994 a Black woman, Beverly Harvard, became the first female police chief of Atlanta.

Do they make a difference? Can they make a difference? Despite misconceptions created by movies and TV shows, Black officers are still very rare in the topmost ranks of America's police forces—less than 2 percent of captains and above. It is at the top where the vital decisions are made. These are the officers who can either rein in or unleash the racist cops on the beat. At the present rate of promotions—or even at an accelerated affirmative action pace—how long would it take for African American top-ranking police officers to approach, say, 12 percent nationally? The picture is no better even in cities with many Black inhabitants, like New York, Chicago, Detroit and Philadelphia. The ordinary cops are mostly white men and nearly all the top cops are white men. Blacks are heavily underrepresented at the rank of captain and above, with five percent seeming to be about the ceiling. Washington, D.C., Newark, N.J. and Detroit are renowned for their Black majorities, yet the number of Black policemen never exceeds a quarter of the total number of officers—even these police forces are dominated by white cops, a racially-hostile occupation force in Black and Afro-Latino districts. The same is true in Atlanta, Baltimore, Memphis, New Orleans and St. Louis, all cities with sizeable African American contingents. And in the forty years from 1954 to 1994, 20 Black police officers have been shot down by the "friendly fire" of white cops—an average of one every two years. Even in terms of personnel, self-policement is as far from reality today as it was in the days of Marcus Garvey.

Occasionally Afro-American police associations are capable of bold racial solidarity in defense of embattled civilians in their community. They have been known to defy white reprisals. Such militancy and potential for good deserves support. Despite the disabilities inherent in the chain of command we must continue to strive for more and more Black law enforcement officers.

*

The whole criminal justice situation yeasts paranoia in suburban Lalaland. The hype against Black "criminality" has now even replaced fear of "race-mixing" as the chief means of conditioning the white public to sanction tyranny against people of color. Under the cover of crime control, white racism seeks to grab the moral high ground and turn the table against the testimony of history. As if slavery were not the arch-crime, the victims themselves of white civilization's crime against humanity—Black males in particular—are now branded as crime-prone. In utter disregard of the primeval transgression against black people which gave rise to "delinquen-

cies" and retaliation by the victims, the philosophy of criminalization makes the victims out to be the villains.

The "war on Black crime" is a self-fulfilling prophecy. Even
though the incidence of violence among Blacks shows no factual
increase, the overall rates of Black male arrests continue to spiral
skyward, the result of ideology-inspired strict and heavy anti-drug
enforcement efforts. Sweep up drug users and petty dealers and use
the catch to vindicate further dragnets. Black-crime ideology hard-
ens the white public's perception of Black male criminality and fuels
the "war on drugs." The war on drugs, in turn, confirms white middle class paranoia that Black males pose a threat to personal safety.
This view is further substantiated by the endless shots on evening
news broadcasts of handcuffed Blacks under arrest for something
or other.

It is the task of this ideology to blind white society to distinctions in the personal behavior of young Black men; all must be seen
as the same, all must fit the stereotype—the "all-Blacks-look-alike"
doctrine, 1990s style. As conditioned, white public perception blots
non-violent, law-abiding, educated young Black males out of the picture entirely. More and more, the response is a visceral one of dread.
White women clutch at their purse as Black men pass. Timid white
businessmen hurry to the opposite sidewalk to avoid Black
teenagers. Ritzy stores refuse to admit Blacks without ludicrous riga-
marole. Department store security agents dog the footsteps of Black
shoppers up and down the aisles like faithful mutts. White cops cannot bear not to stop and search an expensive motor vehicle if there
is a Black male at the wheel.

President Clinton's law-and-order sermon on 13 November 1993
in Memphis aided in the conditioning of the white public. Throwing
the blame on the African American community, he preached a "crisis of the spirit" as the root cause of crime. He proposed more police
hardware, more prisons, and the death penalty. He ignored the social
causes of crime in the Black community. Like Congress, the President
was blind to the hopelessness and despair. Clinton delivered a fol-
low-up speech, hardening the tone even more, immediately after the
Long Island incident involving Colin Ferguson.

The conditioning campaign has had its effect. In 1993 a Jewish
agency poll revealed that two out of every three whites in America
think that "cops are tops," express full confidence in them and
admire the way they hold back the tide of Black and Afro-Latino

lawbreakers. They dimiss minority complaints against racial bias in the national criminal justice system as a figment of minority imagination. Nearly half of the white population (46 percent) had been fully convinced that big city police treat Blacks as fairly and as courteously as they treat whites. Almost three-quarters love the "fairness" of white judges and believe the courts to be absolutely impartial in racial matters. Most ominous for the future, the survey revealed that young whites today hate Black people more than their elders do. Whites aged 18 to 30 during the 1990s were more anti-Black than their "Baby Boomer" parents, aged 30 to 49.

We have fallen into the habit of saying that it is the *system* which is racist. Often our implication is that ordinary white folks are decent and not really racist. We insist that racism is inextricably institutionalized, and of course it is. But what, say, about the members of the jury in the first Rodney King trial, what message does their acquittal of the guilty cops convey? These were ordinary, "decent" white folks. The Simi Valley jury was all-white (or as nearly so as to make no difference; certainly it contained no Blacks). Did its action not provide fresh evidence that racism is widely popular, deeply rooted in the white public? The members of that jury were human beings, white individuals, not some faceless, impersonal "*System.*" They were a fair cross-section of ordinary white middle class suburbanites. And their attitudes and opinions were a fair reflection of what millions of others like themselves think and feel. These jurors expressed hatred and contempt for Black people, in rendering their verdict. They confirmed that Blacks can get little justice in this country's criminal "justice" system. They bore witness that the run-of-the-mill white citizen is still steeped in racial prejudice, regardless of the wishful op-ed pleadings of certain much-praised Black academics, the darlings of the white establishment. Ordinary whites are still convinced that a Black person has no rights a white (police) person need respect. Perhaps his social betters and his "polite" political leaders are now careful to deny they share any such opinion, but white "*Joe Citizen*" thinks that Supreme Court Justice Roger Taney got it right way back in 1857, when he rendered the Dred Scott decision. The jury system is a pillar of white supremacy. It will function as such in every locale with a heavy white majority. Most white jurors can be relied upon to identify with white policemen and prosecutors, despite the constitutional rights owing to minority defendants and despite overwhelming evidence, such as the videotape of Rodney King being beaten to a pulp. White Nobel Prize-winning author William Faulkner once personally acknowledged the justice of the Black cause, but admitted that if push came to shove, he would fight to see that the white man kept the upper hand. Like Faulkner, ordinary white jurors are hardnosed—they can be relied upon to decide verdicts that reaffirm white supremacy whenever they perceive that principle to be at issue.

Frame-ups are an essential feature of the criminal justice system. They have been occurring with increasing regularity since the Civil Rights-strained 1960s. There has been much common law skullduggery, such as the outrageous 1973 framing of Clarence Chance and Benny Powell for the murder of a police officer. The main focus, however, has been on railroading an entire generation of Black political dissidents from H. Rap Brown to Dhoruba Bin Wahad to Assata Shakur. In Canada too, smashing Black critics of white racism sits at the top of the agenda. Ontario's Dudley Laws, leader of the Black Action Defense Committee, has felt the crackdown. He was entrapped, jailed, tried, and in February 1994 convicted.

Out on the streets the chronicle of police brutality has been equally unbroken and just as much to the point. The length and breadth of the land, there is a deluge of formal minority citizen complaints against police misconduct. In 1991 there were some 15,000 cases of police brutality pending with the federal Justice Department. Sometimes the brutality is costly for the establishment, as plaintiffs win injury damages against police and municipalities are compelled to fork out. By the end of the 1980s Los Angeles, for instance, was coughing up at least $4 million a year to settle cases of police brutality and misconduct. Many such judgements originate in the police recreational sport of harassing innocent Black citizens. Edward Lawson, for one, a Californian, was arrested 15 times for merely walking in affluent white neighborhoods. Yet these are the unavoidable costs of police repression. The authorities recognize them as such and are clearly of a mind to pay the price. The expenditure is simply charged to the public purse, a small cost to pay for putting the boot to African Americans and dark-skinned Latinos; a small cost to pay for white middle class peace of mind.

The willingness to ante up for unlawful arrests and police brutality is yet further indication of the authorities' determination to impose a police-prison state. There is a political will to control the movements of Black people. The costs entailed in reproducing the system of white supremacy and security are calculated and accepted. For there is a strategy behind police brutality. Unrelenting police violence is designed to inhibit any organized Black resistance by "decapitating" the community of those most likely to show rage. Or at least nip in the bud any fight-back. It is more than a coincidence that the Rodney King beating occurred precisely at the moment when Los Angeles power brokers were starting to feel pressured by organized Black and Mexican-American local political initiatives. Paired with the inoculation of the ghetto with drugs, the policy is calculated to weaken community response and paralyze the Black political will.

*

BLACK-ON-BLACK VIOLENCE: ITS PATHOLOGY

The destruction of Black persons by Black persons is the sickest phenomenon in a sick society. African Americans are the prime victims of crime in this country—not the scared white folks who are always bleating about crime. Black people are six to seven times more likely to be murdered as whites (Jaynes and Williams 1989:12). Our people are the ones who are robbed, our people are the ones who endure devastating physical and economic injury. Nearly half of all homicide victims are Black (49.6 percent in 1994 as against 47.2 percent white). The mortality rate for Black males ages 15 to 25 is 3.25 times that for Black women.

Tragic indeed, most of the robbing and killing suffered by our people are at the hands of our own people. Homicide is the leading cause of death among young Black males, the main cause being guns fired by members of our own race. This Black-on-Black violence exhibits a pathology that has a clear socio-economic pattern. The majority of the predators are have-nots, the "strung-out," the poverty-stricken and alienated, those from the very "bottom of the well." The majority of their victims are solid, hard-working, grass-roots Blacks, seniors, middle-incomers and the not-so-poor backbone of the community. Most Black professionals and business types, and nearly all white folks, never become the victims of a crime. Desperately afraid for their life, growing numbers of these middle strata Black victims are being stampeded into the law-and-order camp. Unwittingly, they are joining cynical white politicians— diehard enemies of the entire Black community—in calling for more cops, more police surveillance and tougher sentences. This is one of the most hurtful ironies of the African American calamity.

This situation breeds escapism, accommodationism, and self-destructive violence. Ceaseless confrontation with the norms and institutions of white society mars the personality of many youthful Black males. It engenders defense mechanisms and compensatory behavior. Who does not number among one's acquaintances someone who seeks to shield himself from racist hatred by pretending it does not exist? Who does not know some poor "blood" who stumbles about bleating that racism is "lessening with time," or who seeks to rob it of its sting by proving to "massa" that at least one of us is "responsible," trustworthy and loyal? Can anyone of us honestly claim to have never met some brother or sister who is trying to compensate for being Black by outstripping whites in sports, entertainment, or other white-sanctioned "fields of endeavor"? Such types have always been among us.

Well, times have changed. For as many of these old familiar types we may encounter, today there are many more who vent their frustration in acts of aggression and crime against fellow Blacks. The criminal activity which poisons the air in Black and Afro-Latino districts and selects innocent people as its victims, rarely if ever touches the real enemies—racist whites. We face an uncontrolled explosion of aggressiveness accumulated under long and intolerable pressure and badly misdirected. There are murders, muggings, shootings, drive-by's and drug-turf wars in our streets.

Dr. Amos Wilson, Black psychology professor, offers the seminal concept of Blacks transformed into "surrogate ventures of themselves," a brilliant if rather complex way of describing Black-on-Black violence. What he means is that we tear each other apart, ultimately, in the service of white domination, although those committing the crimes seldom realize that, being individualistically motivated. Instead of reaching out and destroying the oppressor, we seek to annihilate that which has been humiliated—Black humanity itself. One enduring theme of Afro-American history has been survival against overwhelming odds. Straining in the opposite direction, unfortunately, is a suicidal tendency to destroy ourselves in self-inflicted violence, a tendency which seems to make many desperate individuals not want to survive. A curious and bitter logic, indeed. Not only are young Black males murdering one another, the frequency of suicide is also on the rise.

We lament this phenomenon not only in North America, but also among our brothers in Africa. We saw it in the strife in the Republic of South Africa. By unleashing Inkatha against ANC, the forces of apartheid figured to block the long march to freedom. We saw it in the clan warfare-induced famine in Somalia. We saw it in the genocide in Rwanda. We saw it in the endless civil war in Angola. Injury done by Blacks to one another anywhere stymies and fractures Black liberation everywhere.

Black-on-Black violence expresses the self-hatred of alienated individuals. It is a politically negative blockbuster, whereby entire Black communities and nations themselves assist in perpetuating white world domination. It is an aspect of the criminalization of our entire race. It makes it impossible for those of our people who have managed to clamber up several rungs of the social ladder to rejoice or relax. As Black America's historian emeritus, John Hope Franklin, put it: "The most tragic thing is, they are being dehumanized and alienated and destroyed; if they're not being destroyed, then we put guns and dope in their hands and say, 'Destroy yourself'."

The utter disregard shown in the grim inner-city by some Black males for the life and property of fellow Afro-Americans is what can be expected of the powerless and the rudderless. These are the enraged and the frustrated, seeking blindly for a way out of their predicament. These are desperados whose options apppear to have shrunk to only one means of survival, or to only one path of social "success." As one Black evildoer expostulated: "Man, fuck some Black people!"

The drug traffic accounts for many of the fatalities not related to domestic disputes. And, according to a study of youth behavior, most of drug-related violence is triggered by revenge, territoriality, reputation, honor, and loss of "face" in the Oriental sense of suffering disgrace (Williams and Kornblum 1991:204). Drug dealing sits at the cutting edge of entrepreneurial activity in the parallel economy. Increasingly it is paired with gun-running and the sale of prohibited weaponry. Just about any boy in the 'hood can get his hands on an automatic weapon, if he has a mind to. Small children have been known to pack handguns. Many critics have detailed the connections between addictive drugs and high-powered firearms on one side, and the international drugs and arms cartels, the CIA, FBI and local police, on the other. Black America is fed a lethal diet of guns and crack. African American mortality is profitable, both in the monetary and the political sense.

*

Let us look at the ideology of the alienated who prey on other Blacks. According to some, an "outlaw culture" has emerged among low-income youth forced into the underground economy by straitened economic circumstances. Their mind-set brings back to life the dog-eat-dog business ethic embraced by the white Robber Barons of the 1890s who clawed, cheated, and slaughtered their way to the top of America's corporate heap. Traditional community-caring is out, predatory individualism is in. The capitalist marketplace writes the laws; only, as with Mafia doings, it is the *underground illegal* aspect of the capitalist marketplace which here legislates. "Business is business, gentlemen," and the breathless competition leaves no place for racial solidarity. With the iciest calm and complete detachment, one Black drug entrepreneur will execute another (Naison 1992:128-129). The life snuffed out counts only as competition removed. Weighing the disaster from the perspective of the political economy as a whole, Ron Daniels talks of "an internal implosion of self-destruction" (*The New York Amsterdam News*, 1 June 1991). So frightened and desperate are some Black residents in crime-ridden districts, they are even willing to trade constitutional safeguards for real police protection. They are too shaken to realize that surrender of precious civil liberties is a giant step back to enslavement, playing right into the hands of our worst enemies—the diehard white supremacists.

White men have ruled over us for so long, to some it seems like one of the physical laws of nature. Propaganda has led some of us to believe that cowardly Clark Kent really is Superman. If indeed he is, then it is futile to strike at him, so we turn our rage in among ourselves. Violence—administered by white folks—was a major constitutive element of the original Afro-American community. Now, much of the violence has become self-administered, as we have taken over the job of brutalizing and murdering ourselves.

*

Care must be taken when it comes to scrutinizing the Black prison population from the angle of class, and in respect to social stratification. All too frequently Black inmates are damned as the worst of "underclasses." Here the notion of underclass is taken to mean a tangle of all kinds of dire "pathologies." Before jail, while in jail, and upon release back into the community, inmates are blamed not merely for crime, but as ultimately the cause of unwed motherhood, permanent unemployment, female dependency on welfare, extreme poverty, child neglect, single parenthood, unmarried and involuntarily celibate Black women, juvenile delinquency, role-model-less male children, and a host of other counterproductive behavior (Edari 1991:31-56).

Tony Monteiro says that our prisons are contemporary North America's answer to Charles Dickens' nineteenth-century British poor-houses (Monteiro 1991:4). While on the outside, most ex-convicts remain jobless, penniless, unless for the proceeds of crime, and uneducated. More than half of Black inmates are single, having never married. There are slightly more divorced Black convicts than married ones. Most are adult, nearly seven in ten between the ages of 25 and 44. The great majority have dropped out of school before high school graduation. No more than 15 percent had ever earned as much as $25,000 a year legally before prison. And they are drawn disproportionately from certain geographic regions. For example, 75 percent of New York State's inmates come from just seven neighborhoods in New York City—districts where Blacks and Afro-Latinos are thick on the ground. Black inmates have the shortest life expectancy of any group in the country.

The answer to the question who goes to jail, then, is clearly *poor* Black men.

*

Black people, not whites, are the primary victims of crime—and at high cost to the Black community. There is a national norm that says that Blacks and Native Americans and dark-hued Latinos are *not* entitled to full protection under the law. Our claim to full and equal legal recourse is denied. We do not qualify for basic services. Police "protection" for Blacks in America's big cities now more likely means running from someone trying to rob you, being seen fleeing for your life by white cops who immediately conclude that *you* are the felon, and being beaten to a jelly for "resisting arrest" when you try to explain that you are the victim, not the criminal. Should a white officer, in a good mood that day, deign to offer protection to a Black person, it is done as a favor, as one stoops to help an inferior. Aid is extended patronizingly, not as a duty that must be performed for a first class citizen, not as an obligation for which one is officially responsible to tax-paying civilians who pay one's salary and who are one's employers. *Since criminals*—Black ones as well as Latino,

Asian and white criminals—*are not fools, they pick mainly on Black people and on African-Latinos, for they know that the police are not going to protect Black and African-Latino citizens.* They take full advantage of the situation to prey on defenseless victims. The detective squad will come down on them with the full force of forensic science should they murder a prominent white figure—and God help you should you kill a white cop. But even children know that a Black fatality merits only the most slipshod, bored, perfunctory attention. Have an emergency as a Black person in any non-white district, call the police for assistance, and see how long it takes for them to respond; and when they do arrive they are more likely to be hostile, careless, insulting and, even injurious to the victim rather than helpful.

Black residential areas are *overpoliced* when it comes to harassing law abiding Black males, and *underpoliced* when it comes to protecting Black citizens in jeopardy. Blacks are robbed three times more than whites, are assaulted more often, have their homes burgled nearly twice as often and suffer almost 20 percent more household larceny. More than three-quarters of the victims of crime in neighborhoods with a substantial minority population are Black. The police's lax attitude encourages Black felons to prey on their own people.

We are the real victims of crime, the greatest cost being human losses tallied in the slaughter of our young people. Kill-counts show that Black homicide victims 15 to 24 years of age outnumber the white body count four to one. Even though we have always had to endure less and inferior health care, since World War II we have been shelling out about $30 in medical expenses caused by violent crime for every $26 disbursed by whites for the same reason. The same goes for time and wages lost from work spent recovering from being the victim of crime. Household crime has cost us some $29 for every $20 it has cost whites.

Like the hound chasing the fox, lethal violence tracks our youth. Young Black males aged 15 to 34 are ten times more likely than comparable whites to be firearms homicide victims. In the 15 to 19 age group, 105.3 Black males are killed by firearms per 100,000, as compared with 9.7 white males per 100,000. No wonder people consider our male youth an "endangered species" and talk of genocide. We should be equally vocal about the elaborate pains taken to spare the lives of white boys. Ours are dying while theirs survive to manhood, an exact measure of white skin privilege today. The feminine gun fatality rate registers 10.4 Black females for every two white females. Homicide is the leading cause of death among young Black men at a time when the country is *not* at war abroad. And on top of this, Black people are facing racist hate crimes at an alarming rate. In a recent work devoted to the predicament of the Black talented elite, Ellis Cose observes that not merely do far more whites attack Blacks for racial motives than Blacks attack whites, but Blacks are *thirteen times* more likely to be assaulted for reasons of race bias than white persons (Cose 1993:108-109).

*

TESTOSTERONE AND TOPSY-TURVY GENDER DISCRIMINATION

The triple oppression which falls on Black women has been exactly chronicled, feminist critiqued, philosophized on, and lamented. It is roundly condemned and struggled against by right-thinking Black males. Ironically, however, without bringing any improvement in the status of Black women, the last thirty years or so have altered the two genders' relative positions on the misery barometer. Young Black males are now worse off than Black women. Today there are more jobs for Black females than for young Black men. Since 1960 the Afro-American masculine jobless rate has consistently averaged two times—double—the unemployment rates for Black females.

This malignant gender twist to racial discrimination is a powerful propellant of criminal behavior among our menfolk. The very last persons on earth that white employers want to hire for any job of work are Black male youths, 15 to 24 years of age. In the lurid white mainstream imagination, they are the most feared images around. Dread of Black testosterone has turned gender discrimination upside down. Perhaps not, someone may object with eyes on the past: haven't there always been jobs for Black women cooking and cleaning up after whites, while Black men were forced to stand aside with hands in pockets?

In any case, this sadistic twist has definitely flavored the morality and ideology of Black "crime in the streets." It has helped make that which the white media terms "looting" an accepted way for many minority youths to get even, to take back those things of which one has been unjustly deprived. Decoded, "looting" becomes a procedure by which a few persons among us recover in the form of goods some of the alienated labor and capital stolen from us over the centuries of slavery, segregation, and racial differential.

Of course, this relieves none of the social consequences of locking up Black men. The incarceration side of the criminalization of Black America has created the *"missing male"* syndrome. As the 1980s ended, there were 93.5 white males in the active working-age population for every 100 white females. But among our people there were only 83.1 males to every 100 females in this same category. There is a staggering total of well over a million "missing" Black working-age males. Where have they gone? Half of them are locked behind bars. Others are dead, strung out on drugs, or dying of AIDS. Growing numbers commit suicide. Some have been reduced to the level of utterly disfunctional, sociopathic zombies who neither know who they are or where they are.

People shake their head bewildered at the apparently suicidal fearlessness exhibited in the "mean streets" by many Afro-American urban youths today. But really this social trait is the product of white racist violence. In the view of many of these adolescents and youths, why in the world should they be afraid of the white man's doing them any further harm? What more violence can be done to one who is spat upon, rejected as unteachable by one's teachers, and scarred emotionally in his own native land day in day out? Be it actual or merely threatened, the violent behavior of Black youth is the creation of white racist violence. Suicidal fearlessness is a reflection of "crime consciousness" and of an attitude towards white man's law. As one Black police officer—a veteran of the District of Columbia scene—put it, disappointment and frustration have destroyed belief in the system among young African American men, leaving a "by any means necessary" code of survival. The criminalization of the "underclass" is rooted in despair. Progress and optimism are dependent upon self-awareness. For a people to be hopeful, to believe in "doing for self," it must believe that headway can be made. The U.S. is predicated on the oppression and degradation of Black people. Folks in the inner city feel that their condition is hopeless, that they are doomed no matter what they do. This is more than just a counter-productive defeatism. This view also represents reality—the odds really are stacked overwhelmingly against.

The ultimate socio-political significance of Black crime thus begins to come into view. In most instances it is a manifestation of *individual* struggle against an unjust society. Lone-wolf combat against the system is doomed to failure, however. When one takes on social injustice by oneself alone, the result is nearly always ineffective and chaotic. The same goes for small group, gang, and ultimately even for "organized" crime. Individual struggle almost always ends in disaster—for the person(s) involved—usually imprisonment and/or death. Family and friends are left shattered. This is not to imply that drug-dealing, thievery, robbery and such like doings are anything but solid social outflows. They are. They generate jobs. Illegal activities give income and employment to quite a number of otherwise unemployed and unemployable Blacks. It is a mistake to underestimate the economic clout of the para-legal economy. Contemporary North America incorporates an underground parallel system of managing and distributing goods and services. Where the constitution of society is based on racist refusal to respect the rights of persons of color, person after person rebels and dashes himself individually against the system. In the words of judge Bruce Wright: "Success in crime becomes the criminal's private *coup d'état,* his momentary victory" (Wright 1987:213).

*

Suicidal fearlessness and individual struggle against injustice go hand-in-hand. For the ideologically rudderless, criminal activity is seen as the only viable alternative. It is a choice dictated by the survival impulse.

White racism drives Black people literally insane. But there are degrees of the mental and emotional disorder. They extend from sheer self-destructive madness to a state approaching political rationality and significant historical impact. In this sense the most insane are those who commit suicide or succumb to drug addiction, abuse and kill members of their own family, murder their "home boys," maim women and children, and other such self-hating misdeeds. The next stage—a half step toward social rationality, though still far short of the real thing—are the criminal entrepreneurs, everyone from muggers and robbers to the organized crack cocaine hawkers. These are would-be capitalists. In the haste to "get paid," they slaughter rivals in turf wars, slay innocent bystanders in gang fights, get dragged off to jail. Some end up on death row. Some die in the street at the hands of racist white cops. At the next level, though still misdirected and counter-productive, we find those who direct their destructive anger away from their own people, who seek out victims in, say, affluent white exurban reaches. Ever so often the news flashes a tale of *Black Rage*—the story of a Black person lashing out indiscriminately, inflict-

364

ing injury and death on any white person within reach, in retaliation for suffering inflicted by institutionalized racism. Hating white supremacy and finding no effective political alternative available, they rampage, creating carnage.

The incident which occurred on a Long Island commuter train on 8 December 1993, as it pulled into a suburban Garden City station near Mineola, New York, is often cited as one such example. Are such incidents isolated oddities or do they presage many more such outbursts in the near future? Or will a revived Black liberation movement emerge to channel righteous aggression in a politically and historically meaningful direction?

*

Folks thrash about trying to remedy the awful consequences of having so many of our menfolk locked in prison. We search for constructive alternatives to recompense the community. One agenda suggests compulsory community rehabilitation service for offenders. Another looks to community policing.

By community policing, at a very minimum, activists mean Black and Afro-Latino law enforcement personnel. During the 1980s, Atlanta and Detroit led the field by a wide margin in bumping up the percentage of Black officers in the municipal police department, leaving key metropolitcan jurisdictions like New York and Miami lagging badly. However, no jurisdiction brought Black representation on the police force up to equal the percentage of Blacks in the local labor force.

Community service as an alternative to serving time focuses on constructive punishment. The program would tie probation to public tasks designed to improve the quality of life in Black districts. Offenders would be required to renovate living quarters for senior citizens, tend parks and playgrounds, provide services to the homeless, keep vacant lots clear of refuse and subways and bus stops free of graffiti. Care for persons with AIDS is one of the most worthwhile ways of paying the debt owed the community. The program aims to instill positive job experience, work ethic, as well as routine, and non-violent conflict-resolution skills.

The downside is that funded by the federal government, the program is being taken over by the establishment and manipulated to suit the purposes of criminalization. Police mini-stations open in Black neighborhoods. These stations are manned by officers assigned to walk the beat. They collect information on the local residents. Efforts are being made to improve the network of police informers in the 'hood. The streets are blanketed with "finks." Neighborhood groups recruited to monitor the drug trade are duped into becoming an arm of repression. Civilian watch groups are bought and paid for by police and state, federal, and municipal government. They help create a pretext to arrest and imprison yet more young Black males.

There are two contending principles. On one side we have a nontraditonal approach which is restorative, empowering the powerless while confronting the irresponsibility of crime in one's own community. On the other there is a notion of "justice" which says be tough on crime, lock up these Black thugs and throw away the key, and, whenever possible, stifle any further discussion with the finality of capital punishment. Racism assures victory to the second principle, the principle of brutal retribution and behavior modification. There is nothing restorative about the "justice" meted out to Black offenders. Vindictive white legislators have run amok enacting "three strikes" mandatory sentencing laws, condemning thrice-convicted small time crack cocaine addicts and dealers to interminable and lifetime sentences. Black inmates have no civil or human rights white prison authorities must respect. They can be overcrowded, beaten, and "locked down." They can be lobotomized, injected with behavior-altering drugs, and subjected to sensory perception deprivation—subjected to the whole arsenal of Nazi-like techniques crafted to control "subhumans." The state of Louisiana has enforced its own version of a three-strike law mandating life sentences for three-time violent offenders. It locks up more of its residents per capita than any other state in the union. Yet Louisiana still has the second highest murder rate in America. Clearly the tough-on-crime hype has nothing to do with making our cities safer. It has much to do with more nice cop jobs and more jobs and profits for those in the prison construction industry—at taxpayer expense.

*

Ever since the advent of COINTELPRO, the penal system has played a major role in controlling and repressing *political* dissent. Imprisonment is used to snuff militant Black rebellion. America's jails teem with Black, Afro-Latino, and Native American political prisoners. Those of our spokesmen who are not being assassinated

366

are thrown in dungeons. Incarceration of dissidents of color is now a prominent aspect of social control. U.S. prisons have been aptly termed "twentieth century slave ships" whose prime captives are Blacks and Browns. And if in the case of the U.S's northern neighbor, "Brown" is taken to mean Native people, then the description is an apt one also for Canadian penitentiaries.

Penal measures to root out militant commitment among Black and Afro-Latino political prisoners are an offshoot of the COINTELPRO program begun in the 1960s by the FBI. It programmed prisons as socio-political control agencies. More than that, it factored the penal system in a monetary political economy. Suppression of political dissidents was made a key mission of the *incarceration-control political economy*. J. Edgar Hoover penned the COINTELPRO memorandum on 25 August 1967. In the months following, the Black Panther Party was drowned in blood. Key leaders were assassinated by the police, a thousand members of the party were arrested, hundreds disappeared into cells. George Jackson was murdered, bestial white National Guardsmen brutalized and butchered the unarmed Attica prison political rebels (1971), and a few months later, in order to tighten the reins on Black political prisoners, the federal penitentiary at Marion in southern Illinois was established—the country's first "supermax facility."

Marion set the model for super-maximum security prisons. With time it too became outdated. The old COINTELPRO has been modernized in the guise of today's "Prisac," a prison activist program. The 1990s have witnessed construction of the Federal Correctional Facility—Florence (Colorado). It is a state-of-the-art super-maximum house of detention designed to hold political prisoners from the Black, Afro-Latino and Native American communities. It is only one of ten such maxi-penitentiaries planned for construction by the Federal Bureau of Prisons leading up to the year 2000 (Mauer, 1991). Within six years of the Attica uprising, $13.4 billion annually were being spent on police and prisons. The country now spends more than $20 billion a year on penal facilities alone. It is easy to see that this translates into a lot of jobs and business procurement profits for a lot of white folks. To keep a Black political prisoner in jail costs about as much as it would to educate him for a year at Harvard, which shows that a *conscious decision* had been made to jail Black men rather than educate and train them for decent jobs, regardless of the cost of imprisonment. "The most reasonable explanation," Marc Mauer concludes, "is that prison is [indeed] a control mechanism for people of color, some form of counter-insurgency which has as its purpose the goal of preventing rebellion by people of color within the borders of the U.S."

Looking back, this is how we must gauge the bloody suppression of Attica and subsequent prison uprisings, the persecution of the captured prisoners of the Black Liberation Army, the witchhunt against members of the Black Panther Party and the Republic of New Africa, the disrespect for the womanhood of Angela Davis, Assata Shakur, and other female political prisoners—i.e., as jobs for whites, policing and guarding Blacks.

The prisons *are* the twentieth century slave ships. They are the warehouses in a social control equation. There are no other barred windows and blank walls in the world behind which people yearn so constantly, so intensely, with such passionate longing and with such rage, every hour, every minute, every second of every day. Voices among us can be heard intoning that these men have gone wrong and have gone to waste. That since they chose to engage the system in a losing individual criminal struggle instead of effective organized political action against white supremacy, they have chosen a dead-end route and are a lost cause.

This is a mistaken view. Many thousands of today's Black convicts become militant while serving time. There is an amazing prison phenomenon of *political* rehabilitation underway behind bars. Most inmates are neither docile, apathetic nor passive. Although often misdirected, "pre-political," and occasionally hopeless, Black inmates have one of the highest rebel-dissident rates in the entire world. The prisons are a crucible of potential revolutionaries. Tanaquil Jones, a community activist, is the wife of Dhoruba Bin Wahad. Dhoruba, a former N.Y. Black Panther Party field secretary, was framed in 1971 and buried in prison for 19 years, one of many prominent Black political prisoners. Commenting on her husband's case (*New York Amsterdam News*, 4 January 1992), Jones tried to make the community aware that "our movements are always criminalized... political dissent in this nation is always represseed, especially militant dissent... and Dhoruba clearly proves there are political prisoners inside the U.S" Moreover, it proves that Black political prisoners often strengthen their resolve behind bars. Men like Dhoruba Bin Wahad emerge from the pen more militant than ever. And while some may dismiss this rebelliousness as "pre-polit-ical," at the street level there is even a growing *pre-prison* aware-ness of white racism, as a five-day National Gang Peace Summit held in Chicago in October 1993 indicated. The gathering of gang members—prime candidates for arrest and mandatory sentences—denounced whites for fostering poverty and crime in Black neigh-borhoods.

The world sat riveted in late April and early May 1992 as rage clawed at Los Angeles. During these hours for sure, and it seems also during the tense smoke-filled weeks that followed, the frequency with which young Blacks had been killing one another dropped off radically. For a time the guns of drive-by shootings, like those depict-ed in the film *Boyz 'n the Hood,* were stilled. The "bloods" now had something better to do—out they popped as rebels. They jetted for-ward on the slogan—*"No Justice, No Peace!"* The senseless Black-on-Black killings were put on hold. Long-overdue outrage at LAPD racist brutality put private trivialities in deep freeze. While the rebel-lion went on, a lot of street corner crack deals did not get done in South Central. The potential healing power of collective direct action against white supremacy stood bared for all with eyes to see. Young Black men "trashing the power" have no time to destroy one anoth-er. Lust for your brother's blood wanes, for here come the white cops and the white national guardsmen. The adrenalin rush that comes from destroying the symbols and sinews of oppression is so strong that, for a time, one no longer needs to seek solace in the realm of drugs. For a while the rebellion gave young Black men an alternative occupation to defending drug-dealing turf. Freedom fighters may fall in combat, but they do not destroy themselves or their comrades, or trip into narcotic stupor.

Unfortunately, like any emotional flight, the high is merely tem-porary and will crash to the "same-old, same-old," if not sustained by lasting and organized mass political struggle. Yet in all, the Los Angeles events were a striking confirmation of Frantz Fanon's maxim—an embattled people fighting against white oppression heals itself psychologically and morally in the course of the struggle, and the more so as it engages in physical combat.

Meanwhile the long list of repressive new laws and measures orchestrated to kick in the twenty-first century indicates that white America is deadly determined to react rather than remedy. Main Street, appalled at taxation for social services like welfare and public education, is willing to foot the bill for 500 and more new prisons throughout the United States. It does not skimp funds for its favorite "uniformed service"—the police force. Estimates which put the federal prison population at over 100,000 by 1995—70 percent of them petty drug offenders—bring a cheer. The vast majority of U.S. prisoners—more than a million—are in state and local jails. Savage new sentencing guidelines and mandatory minimum sentences roll off the legislative assembly line at breath-robbing pace. Minimum sentences are mandated in drug cases in which a firearm is found—upping the incentive for police to plant evidence on suspects of color. The economic aspect of the criminalization escalates. Pekin, Illinois, offset layoffs at Caterpillar by erecting a penitentiary, "as jobs leave town, more prisons are moving in." What would the economic future of a place like Tamms, Illinois, look like were it not for the $60 million super-maximum security prison rising there?

*

It may still be a little too early to inscribe young Black males on the rolls of the "endangered species." But it is certainly past time to recognize that they are becoming an *imprisoned* species.

Chapter 18

AFRICA, THE DIASPORA, AND THE "NEW WORLD ORDER": TWENTY-FIRST CENTURY PAN-AFRICANISM

Five and a half centuries ago, our Mother Africa lay under velvet skies pondering the mysteries of existence and the secrets of the centuries. Suddenly she started and gazed perplexed, as a gang of white raiders crept up on her western shores. Exhaling the foul breath of savagery, they fell upon her children in the still of the night. Thus began the rape of Africa. Not for a moment since has Africa's Black humanity known respite. Twist it as one may, Africa's fate since that night in 1441 has been defeat and humiliation. Hard on the heels of the slave trade came colonialism and white settlers, came dispossession and apartheid. Even the euphoria that rode the triumphant wave of independence at mid-twentieth century has since drowned in neo-colonial dependency.

Today the continent lies prostrate, her people starving, sick with diseases designed in foreign laboratories, weltering in bloody retribalism. Scarred landscapes bake drought-stricken, as alien corporations rip the mineral wealth from the bowels of the earth—and run.

Harried Africans are now wracking their brains, seeking the reasons for the continent's historic defeats and humiliations. Equally anxious to draw the lessons from the Black race's debacle is the African Diaspora—those people of African descent uprooted, transplanted and dispersed over hundreds of years. Those whose forced labor and cultural and technological genius created the wealth and material civilization whites enjoy in the western hemisphere.

In the scramble for answers, fatalists suggest that perhaps the legendary goddess Fortune decided somewhere along the way to abandon Africa and her children. Others, attuned to the heroic traditions of the Old Testament, say the God of Battles is a Caucasian god, and that the God of Battles smote the Gods of Africa and slew the Gods of the Native Americans. Yet others, absorbed with the wrap of ethics with race relations, say the answer lies in white lust for African labor and white hatred and contempt for Blacks.

Reality does not belie these figurative depictions. Infant mortality gnaws away, holding down an expanding population. Short life expectancy cancels female fecundity. Current population guesstimates of 600 to 700 millions may or may not be too low. Africa's population growth of three percent annually is nonetheless the highest on earth. But each year nearly half of all deaths on the continent are children. Ten times as many African infants die as western European and North American babies. In many parts of Africa 25 percent of youngsters are lost in the first five years of life. African life expectancy is the shortest on earth, upwards of 30 years less than that enjoyed on the average by Northern Europeans and Japanese. African women, on average, give birth to six or more children, but the death rate for mothers ranges from 110 to 1,000 or more women per 100,000 live births. Northern Europe has the world's lowest rate of maternal death—a mere 1/10,000. In Africa it is one in 21—the worst on earth. The highest risk is in sub-Saharan Africa, where a pregnant woman is 75 times more likely to die than a white western European pregnant female.

In an Africa whose foreign debt millstone had topped $270 billion by 1993 and was still growing, and where more than $190 billion of this was owed by sub-Saharan countries, the condition of children is deteriorating badly, according to U.N. findings. Somewhat more than 12 percent of the world's young children are African. 60 percent do not have safe drinking water. About 35 million suffer from malnutrition. Of African tots under five years of age, one quarter are underweight for their age. It is no wonder that nearly 13,500 African children under five die every day, and the death toll is rising.

Not surprisingly, this scourging of the infants is rooted in economic collapse. Hunger stalks adults as well as children, as per capita income has declined by 25 percent in most sub-Saharan countries. The per capita decline is not just in income; however, it is even more damaging in food production, causing thousands of deaths daily from starvation. Two-thirds of African women are illiterate and primary school enrolment for both boys and girls dropped roughly seven percent in the 1980s.

Health care—or its absence—is an unmitigated disaster. In sub-Saharan Africa there is an average of merely one doctor for every 24,500 people, so 40 percent of the people lack access to even the most rudimentary health care. This is compounded by that which many Africans believe is a white-made genocide, tailored to smother the Black population explosion—the AIDS epidemic. Black Africa is being ravaged by AIDS worse than any other region in the world, and if unchecked the disease could reverse the population growth trend. Striking down young adults in their most productive years, it will wipe out hard-won economic gains. The World Health Organization (WHO), itself suspected of having unwittingly introduced AIDS infection in Africa through a smallpox vaccination program in the mid-1970s, estimated that 10 million Africans would be infected by 1995.

There even appears to be a strain of the HIV virus that causes AIDS especially for Africans. HIV-2, a strain of the virus, rides on normal sexual intercourse. It is most common in West Africa. It is almost as if someone, concluding that the homosexual-focused HIV-1 virus would make limited inroads in the general African population, cooked up the heterosexual HIV-2 strain. The latter does not show up in routine tests and is resistant to drugs and vaccines. In 1994 western scientists were saying HIV-2 is less virulent than HIV-1. It seems to develop at a slower rate and seems to have less secondary-disease-causing potential.

Afro-American investigators have pointed the finger at a Fort Detrick, Maryland, laboratory as the locale where the original AIDS virus is likely to have been manufactured. The WHO indicates that some 100 million Africans are at risk. The figure reminds one of losses inflicted by the Atlantic Slave Trade!

With the Cold War over, there are signs that the West is determined to dump Africa for good. Suck as many resources out as possible, dump polluted garbage, and forget the place. South Africa with its investment opportunities is the single exception. The terms of trade worsen steadily for an exchange in which Africa ships 83 percent of its exports to the Caucasian West in return for 84 percent of its imports. Today African exports buy 25 percent less than a decade ago. Meanwhile Europe is shifting to other sources of supply. But the African continent remains as deeply dependent on European markets as in colonial times. Sub-Saharan economies shrank throughout the 1980s, laying 15 percent on average lower in 1991 than ten years earlier. Debt servicing in a number of countries eats up 75 percent of export earnings. In 1994 Africa's foreign debt equalled 93 percent of the continent's gross domestic product. Service payments alone devoured 32 percent of all annual export earnings.

The population projection for Africa in the year 2100 is 2.9 to 3 billion. If achieved, this would give Africa nearly three times as many people as the white industrialized nations, projected at only 1.2 billion in the year 2100. Pressure would inevitably rise for changes to the advantage of Africans in the balance of power and consumption of world resources. White supremacy knows this and worries about it. The projected African population growth cannot be achieved, however, unless AIDS is checked. Can we avoid the suspicion that AIDS is a man-made scourge designed to curtail the Black population worldwide?

This leaves us with dire and frightening prospects. Check out the current situation in the mother continent. There you have famine, civil war, drought, and AIDS epidemic. Here we have sneering white media which constantly rub our noses in the mess. Who can escape the endless pictures of emaciated, belly-bloated Black babies begging for a scrap? How ego-building for the "Aryan citizens" of the world! How humiliating for self-respecting African Americans! CNN regales us with shots of huddled piles of African bodies, the bloody anonymous dead from the unexplained civil strife of Kigali, Liberia, southern Sudan, and other locales otherwise never mentioned. For years we have seen photographs of Angolan amputees, mutilated Liberians, Ethiopian and Somali refugees.... We are sick to death of this propaganda. For any Diasporan Africans who had contrived to escape the psychological damage of centuries of white domination, these symbols were crafted to renew feelings of inferiority. Such views of our ancestral home are intended to make us feel worthless, to make us feel we cannot govern ourselves even in our native abode. These media images are calculated to make us crave the rescuing hands of the rich, "benevolent" white North.

Africans are shown to us as the most destitute, beggared people in the world—the truly pauperized "wretched of the earth." Yet we know that there are no poor countries in Africa, only the people are poor. We know that Africa has immense resources, a nearly inexhaustible store of wealth upon which to base future development. The sorry plight is the outgrowth of upside down priorities, priorities that suit World Bank and IMF agendas, but churn Africa's people as in a meat grinder. The international capitalist market integration—the global economic dimension of white world supremacy—misuses Africa's people and its resources. Africa is not *poor*; it certainly is not unendowed, and it has been the crucible of great civilizations. The Africans we see on TV are degraded, exploited, and brutalized because, a whole generation after "independence," they in fact are still subject to white rule.

Africa's wellsprings are not only material, they are also cultural. Though composed of many different tribes, ethnic and language groups, and nations, throughout its long history since its pre-pharaonic Nile Valley origins, Black Africa has maintained a primal *unity* of cultural and material conditions. This explains why the uprooted Africans brought in slavery to the Americas were nevertheless able to retain their essential Africanness. All keen observers have noted the basic unity behind the apparent diversity of Black Africa. Not the least of those observers was Cheikh Anta Diop. He saw that this unity consisted of similar productive forces, means of production, and modes of production. It entailed a common farming technique and a common instrument—the hoe produced by refined iron technology. A common social framework consisted of lineage groups expressing kinship, uttered spiritually in ancestor-reverencing ritual.

*

A nation's weight and importance are not measured in square miles. Mere area is not the crucial factor. Much of it may be barren desert or frozen tundra, unfit for human settlement. Past events may have gathered huge territories under a single flag, but few people. Look at Siberia and Canada. If sheer expanse were the pivotal factor, then Canada with its immense territory but tiny population would be the world's largest and greatest state (with 30 million inhabitants Canada is actually "smaller" than California). Magnitude and ranking in the family of nations depend on the size of a country's *population*—the number of human beings living within its borders. It's about human beings even more than it's about GNP statistics, untapped natural resources, or "size of the economy." Make no mistake; that is why China and India rank as numbers one and two in the world. People make history. More folks, living their lives make more history than fewer folks. Of course, white philosophers and historians will tell you otherwise. They will try to convince you that the lives of, say, one hundred white men have greater social meaning than the lives of a million Africans. This is simply a lie. In the final analysis, a nation's historical significance is tied to the size of its population—the more human beings housed within its confines, the greater its importance. The neglect (or refusal) of some white historian to chronicle the life of one or the other group (usually people of color) does not nullify that group's real impact.

Nigeria covers a smaller area than, say, the Sudan or Zaire. Nevertheless Nigeria is the largest country in Africa. It has more Black Africans than any other country, anywhere. By the same token, the second largest African country on earth is not located in Africa. It is part of the Americas. More Black folk live in Brazil than any other land, save Nigeria. This is a fact of immense historical and political significance. Neither continental African statesmen, nor the Black activists of North America and the Caribbean can afford to ignore or be ignorant of the condition and the struggles of Pan-Africa's Brazilian branch. Nor should the language barrier which sets English off from Portuguese be allowed to serve as an excuse any longer. For there can be no definitive emancipation for Africans worldwide without the liberation of African Brazilians.

Hawking the bogus myth of "racial democracy," Brazil's white-dominated government publishes official statistics which underestimate the number of Afro-Brazilians at half the total population.

Moreover, Eurocentric Brazilian demographers fiddle the country's African racial composition, splitting it arbitrarily into "Blacks" versus "Browns," indoctrinating the "Browns" (or "mulattoes") to believe they are "nearer" to whites and superior to their Black cousins. To hike Caucasian population figures, census authorities encourage "Browns" to classify themselves as whites. Great efforts are made to falsify a racist hierarchy which elevates Caucasian race and European culture to the very heights, and pushes African race and culture to the very bottom. The leader of Brazil's Black consciousness movement, Abdias do Nascimento, makes this clear. Millions of Brazilians are hoodwinked into believing they live in a land freed of racism by a "historic process of amalgamation" in which one single mixed-race is alleged to have emerged, bolstered by a miraculous "mulatto escape hatch," which by conferring upward mobility on "Browns" has pulled the teeth of Black protest (Nascimento 1989:vii-ix).

In the first half of the nineteenth century Black people—slave and free, racially "pure" and mixed—were the large majority of Brazil's inhabitants. But when slavery finally ended in May 1888 the government, determined to gain the day against the "Black peril," packed the country with hordes of white immigrants. Millions descended from the ships, mostly Portuguese, Italians, and other Latins, but as time passed increasingly Germans and other Nordic types. Almost to a man, these European expatriates quickly embraced racist doctrine, rescuing endangered white supremacy. Wallowing in white skin privilege, they scorned and ridiculed the ex-slaves and their descendants. Government labor policy eased the newcomers into the skilled jobs and crafts, while slamming the door on African Brazilian participation in the preferred job market. Both the school system and the Catholic Church lauded the "values" of a phoney Luso-culture (modern Portugal is located on the territory of the ancient Roman province of Lusitania). In the mines and on the ranches and plantations much the same conditions prevailed for Black people as during slavery. The Northeast became one gigantic Black plantation homeland, the scene of hunger, disease, illiteracy, oppression, and "surplus" people. Religious practices derived from Africa were spit on and stomped as being devilish and heathen. Country-to-town migration swarmed Afro-Brazilians into a half dozen or so large cities, where they squat today in some of the world's worst slums, rigidly segregated from posh white residential districts. Whether as peasants, sharecroppers, or migrant workers, whether as *favelados* (slum-dwellers) or as odd-jobbing "service employees," whether scratching the soil for a tyrannical landowner, shining shoes, washing cars and delivering packages, or hustling a living on the streets, the great majority of African descendants are subjected to police-state authoritarianism. Police brutality and arbitrary arrest for the adults; murder for the street urchins by off-duty police and security guards moonlighting at the hire of white shopkeepers and merchants—such is the fate of Africans in today's Brazil.

In many ways Brazil is a real model of Black social oppression. The litmus test of a racially egalitarian society would be an economic and educational affluence for Blacks at least equal to that of the white middle class, paired with massive and conflict-free dealings between Blacks and whites. Paid propagandists pretend this to be reality. Nothing could be further from reality. A white superiority complex and a white criterion of humanity rule the roost in Brazil, greased on a policy of miscegenation misused to dilute the unwanted "Black lump" and preserve "white civilization."

Under slavery, and particularly it seems from 1819 to 1910, there was massive racial blending in Brazil of people of African descent with whites (mostly Portuguese and other southern Europeans), compounded with a native Indian admixture. White slave masters and post-slavery landowners had their way with Black women. During those years the proportion of "Browns" (mulattoes) increased from 20 to 60 percent of the total population. A 1983 study calculated that African-descended mixed-bloods account for about 75 percent of Brazil. The power and wealth, however, are concentrated in the white Eurocentric one-quarter. The Brazilian ruling class is recruited overwhelmingly from the "pure" white minority. Thus racial blending cuts no real ice. Or rather, it is a device manipulated deliberately in such a way as to eliminate the African element over time.

Brazil now ranks in the bottom half of the dozen largest industrial powers in the world. It has become a major manufacturer. Annual per capita income averaged $2,540 as the decade of the 1990s began. There are well over 100 million Brazilians of African descent. Three-quarters of the national income is hogged by the whites. Corporate boardrooms, the upper ranks of the military, and the diplomatic corps are still pristinely Caucasian. It is the custom for the U.S. government and mass media to slander Cuba. The island nation is cursed as a "backward Communist dictatorship." Well, the Cuban infant mortality rate is 16 to 17 per 1,000. Infant mortality runs 105 per 1,000 for Blacks in Brazil, deemed kosher by the U.S. State Department because its economy is capitalist.

Here racism wears a face that is distinctively Brazilian, unlike any other variety. Some observers aptly term it a *sub-categorizing racism.* Abdias do Nascimento lays emphasis on its genocidal intent. For while what occurs is not genocide in the sense of large scale violent physical extermination, a systematic government policy of *"whitening"* Brazil has long been in place. The goal is accomplished by marginalizing Blacks economically. Massive white European immigration was encouraged and is still going on. Latinized Aryan cultural domination has generated the heat to "melt the Black lump." Ideological brainwashing has conditioned Black people to accept their fate. Brazilian miscegenation establishes cascades of contempt. A subtle, sliding scale of prejudice distinguishes between shades of color, odium falling on the darkest skin tones. Light-skinned mulattoes are tolerated most, the ones who most closely approximate white physical body types and racial features. But white racism is white racism, despite subtleties and refinements.

Sub-categorizing racism has worked to stabilize the country's status quo. Its most powerful effect has been to block the emergence of racial solidarity among people of color. Many mulattoes enjoy opportunities for social mobility not open to Blacks. They look down upon their black-skinned relatives. They scorn them as underprivileged pariahs, persons with whom any association might jeopardize one's own status. These "Browns" refuse to identify with Black interests. Black consciousness in Brazil thus is undergoing a more difficult and long drawn-out birth than in the United States, where the dichotomy is more simple. Under U.S. racism, a person is either white or a person is not. Anyone who is not white is simply "nonwhite," the most despised edition being Black. Brazil's mulattoes have comparatively fragmented loyalties and drag their feet in supporting the cause of Black liberation. There has never been a massive civil rights movement in Brazil comparable to the one in the United States. In that country the racist establishment would have upended mountains to coopt leaders like Frederick Douglass and W.E.B. DuBois. It would have sought to ween them from their own people and integrate them in the power structure. It would have keened in their ears the refrain that as "mulattoes" they were more "acceptable" than "full-blooded" Africans.

Regardless of the difficulty of its birth, it should be obvious that the Black liberation movement in Brazil is an infant without whom the family of the African Diaspora can never flourish in the western hemisphere.

A brief glance at the country's politics reveals the predicament. Early in the decade of the 1990s, there were less than a half-dozen Black representatives in the Brazilian Congress, all deputies in the 564-member lower house of the bicameral legislature. This in a nation three-quarters African.

One such deputy was Benedita Souza da Silva, a remarkable female activist and vice-president of the Workers Party, an influential national party. As in North America, Black women are perceived as less threatening than Black men, less likely to rebel, less likely to sport a "chip on their shoulder." She is a rare bird in her country, for there are no Blacks in positions of authority. Her people are in jail, however. Blacks are 80 percent of Brazil's inmates, but only 2 percent of the university student body. In autumn 1992 Da Silva ran for mayor of Rio de Janeiro, half of whose residents are of African descent. She lost her bid although capturing 1,326,000 votes. She fought to overcome the political retardation and apathy of Rio's crowded Black hillside slums and working class neighborhoods. There were only four Black members of the 42-member city council, a body notorious for its racist slurs and jokes. There is no real Afro religious-cultural autonomy in the city. The widely-followed Yoruba *orisha* religion called *candomblé* has been forced to tailor its calendar of celebrations of each *orisha* according to the calendar set by the Catholic Church. And the Pope has condemned this whole form of worship which is an integral part in the daily life of Black Brazilian womanhood.

Recently African Brazilians have had to contend with a creeping tide of racist violence. Neo-Nazi and skinhead gangs have gone on the rampage. A string of violent assaults have occurred in Rio de Janeiro against Black and Brown migrants from the northern region. Ridiculing Afro-Brazilians as "sub-human," neo-Nazis want to kill Black Northeasterners. Surging white supremacy draws its main support from white middle class right-wingers, impassioned believers in "White Power" and "Aryan racial purity." In 1994 they were killing an average of eight Black street kids a day in Rio de Janeiro. The hands-off stance of the police authorities to the campaign of extermination prompts the national Black organization, *Articulacao Nacional de Negros*, and the Black nationalist *Quilombismo* movement (which identifies itself with Pan-Africanism) to adopt active self-defense.

Does the rise of genocidal atrocities mean that Brazilian racism now recognizes the failure of the traditional policy of maintaining Caucasian domination through "whitening" the Black population, and is going over to mass physical extermination?

*

PAN-AFRICANISM: THEN, NOW, AND IN THE TWENTY-FIRST CENTURY

Like other profound political movements, the Pan-African phenomenon has had its varieties, problems, and contending strategies, as it has moved through history. The literature on Pan-Africanism is extensive and accessible and there is no need to review it here in detail (see UNESCO, *General History of Africa*, Vol. VII; and articles in *Freedomways, Journal of African History* and *Présence Africaine*). *Neo*-Pan-Africanism—as it is termed by those who wish to emphasize newness and recentness—is vitally important also to North American Black people in the 1990s, and will be even more so early in the coming century. We cannot dispense with the insights and lessons it offers.

Pan-Africanism is no Johnny-come-lately, however. Its precursors and founders can be discovered among various branches of the Black world—African and Diasporan. Should we focus our attention merely on this country, for instance, we hear Martin Delaney (1812–1885) calling, long before the Civil War and Emancipation, for strong alliance among people of color—the majority of humanity. Today this is known as "Third World solidarity." Away back then, Delaney—physician, traveller, and Union Army officer—was explaining that such a union would overwhelm the numerically inferior but potent racist white international of colonizers and slavers. The white man's territorial domain, he taught, had been created solely by usurpation and encroachment on the rights and native soil of the peoples of color. The worst villains were North America's own, Delaney said. Anglo-Americans stand pre-eminent for deeds of injustice and acts of oppression, "unparalleled perhaps in the annals of modern history." He knew that white men will only respect those who resist their usurpation, acknowledging as equals only those who will not submit to their rule. Where racial domination and colonial conquest come in, class struggle is modified, noted Delaney, restructured, even nullified, by the conflict that pits oppressed Blacks against oppressing whites, regardless of the latter's class status. Delaney's proto-Pan-Africanism saw white commoners joining with rich whites against enslaved Black people. It was axiomatic in a racist society where every white person, by virtue of Caucasian race, was held to be superior to every Black person, that no permanent alliance between Black and white common people against the "higher classes" would ever be possible.

An acknowledged father of Pan-Africanism, Edward Wilmot Blyden was born in the West Indies in 1832. A brilliant scholar, he died in 1912, having spent the most productive years of his life in the mother continent of Africa. While his interest was piqued by the white Fabian socialism of such Europeans as H.G. Wells, Blyden's novel idea of "African socialism" was entirely his own. He worked to expel Eurocentric education from Africa and replace it with Afrocentric education. Early in this century (1908) Blyden realized that ancient Pharaonic Egyptian civilization, with all its monumental glories, had indeed been Black. Footed on this knowledge, Blyden invented the concept of the "African personality," a notion he held firm to despite a church allegiance to western Christianity, and despite the adoption of such ideas as the "social character of production," "capital" and "labor" as tools of analysis. He learned to admire Islam, mainly because it espoused polygyny, a form of marriage allowing a man to have more than one wife at a time and thus not disruptive of traditional African culture. Valuing the universal Black African custom that made land the collective property of a kinship group, Blyden came to the conclusion that when free of white or Arab interference, Africa was a place where there were neither rich nor poor. From this he concluded that the African social structure was the original "communalist or cooperative one." Class formation and class struggle were foreign to Africa, in his opinion. African society had been "everlastingly socialist," and if left alone would never descend into capitalism with its sharp class divisions.

Blyden preached a reformist Pan-Africanism, regionalist in character. West Africa (Liberia in particular) was his arena of action. The balance of power then existing, and perceived "differences" between rival white colonial powers, led him to believe that one had to *choose* between British and French imperialism. He chose in favor of Britain. Blyden's concrete political ambitions for West Africa may thus seem timid to us today. He hoped at most for Dominion status within the British Empire, like that held by Canada from 1867 onwards.

*

The year 1900 is conventionally taken as marking the coming of age of Pan-Africanism. Its formal organization began with the initiatives of Sylvester Williams, Henry Walters, and W.E.B. DuBois, the "Renaissance" genius of the Afro-American Diaspora. The South African ANC came into being in 1912, beginning one of the most remarkable walks to power in the history of the Pan-Black world. In 1916 Marcus Garvey brought his Universal Negro Improvement Association to the United States. Undaunted by the shadow of British imperialism, Joseph Casely-Hayford (1866-1930) triggered an activist nationalism based on the knowledge that Africans were an ancient civilized people who once had had proud institutions and ideas peculiar to themselves alone. And would again once free of the yoke of imperialism. Casely-Hayford fathered modern West African literature, penning the first African novel in English, *Africa Unbound* (1911). His name is connected with the "principle of hospitality," a key doctrine in many varieties of Pan-Africanism.

Between 1919 and 1945, W.E.B. DuBois organized and led five Pan-African Congresses. These gatherings had to meet in France, Belgium, and Britain, for white domination forbade African soil to Black activists.

And the imperialists knew what they were doing, for the logic of Pan-Africanism led inevitably to political self-determination. It encouraged the formation of African nation-states, independent ones. It fostered continental unity—continentalism. And it looked beyond to a great confederation of Black peoples on both the western and eastern shores of the Atlantic Ocean, to an "Atlantic community" of African peoples.

Black men born in the West Indies continued to play a major role in Pan-Africanism after World War II, none more so than Frantz Fanon. Dubbed the "Patron Saint" of the national liberation movement by some, he steered Pan-Africanism towards revolutionary action and away from conference debates, theoretical speculation, and doctrinal wrangling. Fanon taught the importance of proving

383

one's manly qualities in combat, on the frontline against white supremacy. We emancipate ourselves, he explained, through a process of cleansing—discharging pent-up emotions, fears, and self-hatred by going head up against the oppressor. Concentrate on the real enemy—white domination—and forget ethnic and religious disputes among ourselves. Fanon's advice is particularly appropriate in the 1990s, given the threat to Pan-Africanism now posed by creeping Pan-Islamism and by such ethnic strife as that in Rwanda. Another West Indian, George Padmore, influenced Kwame Nkrumah, the first statesman to lead a Black African state to independence.

For an entire generation, beginning in 1945, Pan-Africanism enabled Blacks to view their struggle against white oppression from two angles: a) as a struggle against colonization in all its forms, in Africa and elsewhere; and b) as the affirmation of the right to a common civilization, Black in tone and African in culture.

A useful distinction can be drawn between *"Global Pan-Africanism"* and *"Diasporic Pan-Africanism."* Global Pan-Africanists advocated back-to-Africa movements of one sort or another. Martin Delaney and Marcus Garvey were Global Pan-Africanists. In contrast, Diasporic Pan-Africanists demanded justice for Africans brought to the western hemisphere against their will. The debt owed them should at long last be paid in citizenship rights and financial reparations. These claims spring from the decisive contribution Black forced (and semi-free) labor has made to capital accumulation. This trend was epitomized in the magnificent career of W.E.B. DuBois. Both trends were united in admiration for Africa's place in the history of human civilization. Both wished to reconstruct Africa's true history. Both Global Pan-Africanists and Diasporic Pan-Africanists dreamed of an Africa of independent nation-states, although the Globalists were more sensitive to the need for continental unity, for without it, they were convinced, Africa would never equal the white Great Powers.

The Nkrumahist tendency projected the clearest image of continentalism. This group contends that the fate of Diasporan Blacks is dependent upon the creation of a revolutionary base in a completely liberated and *unified* Africa. Key to the equation is the industrial might of Black-controlled, post-apartheid South Africa. Only after power has been attained by Pan-African revolutionaries throughout the Black continent, according to the Nkrumahists, and a base established in which *all* Africans answer to a single government and military command, will true emancipation be extended to the embattled African peoples of the Americas. A unified Africa would henceforth depend totally on itself alone, both materially and ideologically.

The Organization of African Unity (OAU) came into being in 1963 as a loose organization of nation-states geared to cooperation by means of the unwieldy mechanism of diplomatic negotiation. It was inspired vaguely by Pan-African philosophy. In the years since its founding, OAU Pan-Africanism has shifted the focus of its activities to a restructuring of the United Nations organization. Restructuring's advocates can be found in the United States as well as in Africa. They lobby to have Africa's largest nation, Nigeria, appointed as a permanent member of the U.N. Security Council with veto power. It is likely that OAU Pan-Africanists had a hand in boosting Boutros Boutros-Ghali of Egypt into the position of Secretary General of the United Nations. While it is obvious that Boutros-Ghali speaks on behalf of some Arab circles, there is little evidence he represents Black African interests. And therein is traced the limits of the OAU brand of Pan-Africanism, prisoner as it is of stuffy international diplomacy.

The Pan-Africanism that is connected with *négritude* has a completely different flavor. Not that it is very practical in present circumstances, nonetheless it is anything but stuffy and dull. Négritude Pan-Africanism is usually associated with Leopold Sedar Senghor and Alioune Diop (1910–1980). Senghor, renowned poet and pro-French statesman, was the first president of independent Senegal. He championed the philosophy of *négritude* as the key to the cultural liberation of French sub-Saharan Africa. Although *négritude* was originally the brainchild of Aimé Césaire and his fellow West Indian, Léon Damas, the tool of cultural rebellion against white supremacy, Senghor—and Diop—gave it a continental African dimension. Each people and each culture was an inalienable yet singular part of world civilization, believed Senghor. The "African personality" was peerless and inimitable. According to Senghor, this personality had more to give to the world in the way of emotion, traditionalism, and harmony with nature and instinct than in the way of science, logic and technology. With Senghor, Pan-Africanism took on a mystical hue.

Wrestling to throw off European imperialism and contending on a day-to-day basis with Parisian racists, Alioune Diop was less wont to trip off into mystical intuition. He founded the renowned journal *Présence Africaine* shortly after World War II and stayed with it in Paris working untiringly as publisher and chief editor until his death. Like Senghor he believed in the reality of a unique African world view, one which honored vital forces, venerated ancestors and gave pride of place to tradition. But he had real-life political concerns. He puzzled over the part authoritarianism would play in modern African statescraft. Africans, he said, were down-to-earth folk. They valued earthy pleasures and shared little liking for the mean-spirited, tight-assed individual "freedoms" Europeans worshipped. Alioune Diop wanted to take the white man's weapons and his industrial know-how and use them to throw off his domination.

✳

The U.S. State Department has tried to horn in on Pan-Africanism. Dusting off the time-honored principle of "he-who-pays-the-piper-calls-the-tune," it bankrolled a gala three-day "summit" in Abidjan (Cote d'Ivoire) in 1991. Dubbed the "first African-African American conference," it gave the world a peek at a "New World Order" version of Pan-Africanism, scripted at the State Department. The lure of dual citizenship was waved before a concourse of Afro-Diaspora luminaries. To harmonize "moderate" African American Pan-Africanists with U.S. foreign policy in Africa is the aim. While no concrete provisions were forthcoming for actual citizenship of western hemisphere Diasporans in the more than 50 separate, sovereign African nation-states, the more than 300 summit delegates acted as if it were a "done deal," agreeing "in principle" to establish African citizenship for Black Americans. Seeking to revive a personal prominence that had slipped since the "Sullivan Rules" era, Rev. Leon Sullivan spearheaded this move to create a triangle connecting African statesmen, U.S. policy aims, and American Black middle class spokesmen. Leering over Sullivan's shoulder stood a white man, Herman Cohen, then U.S. Assistant Secretary of State for Africa. Pulling on the purse strings, Cohen was there to see that if anything lasting came out of the gathering, it would be plans for even more African integration in the international division of labor on terms fixed by the U.S. Manipulating the facilities of the U.S. Embassy in Abidjan and its personnel, Cohen steered conference deliberations toward the mobilization of capital for the kinds of economic development and investment opportunities that are profitable to U.S. businesses. Linking land, labor, and capital for the purpose primarily of uplifting wretched African masses did not top his agenda.

Neither the Bush nor the Clinton administration—the latter endorsed the second African-African American summit—seemed to know where they were really heading with this policy. Yet its long-range implications are profound. It is a grand design to manipulate Black American citizens—their skill, devotion, and passion—as surrogates through whom to secure United States control of Africa and its resources for the entire twenty-first century. At stake is a "post-modern" ultra-recolonization by the USA that would make Africa the prize American imperialist reserve, closed to the United States' European and Japanese rivals. American diplomacy and corporate capital would put a lock on the Black continent.

With six African heads of state in attendance in Abidjan—the presidents of Cote d'Ivoire, Botswana, Gambia, Burkina Faso, Uganda, and Guinea-Bissau—the summiteers concentrated on dual citizenship for U.S. Blacks wishing to live and work in Africa, but remained silent about comparable privileges for the millions of Black people throughout the rest of the western hemisphere.

"New World Order" Pan-Africanism is thus tailored to more efficient exploitation of Africa's labor and resources. While there was talk of cancelling the government-to-government component of Africa's foreign debt, the burdensome debts owed to private Western creditors would remain intact. Plans for a new bank for the reconstruction of Africa omitted any demand for reparations. Funding for the proposed bank would depend on the success in the U.S. of an Africa lobby, yet to be established.

A second summit was scheduled for two years later in Gabon and did come off, with energy directed toward formation of a permanent secretariat. Congressional Black Caucus participation lent the project legitimacy and delegates vaingloriously pledged to pay taxes in two nations—in America and in an African host country. There was no mention of hard fiscal reality. Such as the fact that in the early 1990s the United States doled out in aid to sub-Saharan Africa an annual average of less than $19 million per country. There are more than 600 million people in these countries. As a measure of the insult and contempt for Black Africans concealed in these paltry sums, note that America spent more than $1 billion every day during the Persian Gulf war against Iraq.

*

"New World Order"-style Pan-Africanism contrasts sharply with the militant stance taken by some of today's individual Pan-Africanists. Tribute is often paid, for instance, to John Henrik Clarke, an elder statesman among contemporary Pan-Africanists.Clarke has never spelled out whether Diasporan folk are to spearhead the socioeconomic and political development of the mother continent, or the other way round. Nevertheless he has provided Pan-African leadership for many years. A prolific author, he urges Diaspora Blacks to work together. The former Hunter College professor and founder of the African Research Institute insists on a "Pan-African perspective," advising his fellow African Americans to "look to yourselves" for liberation. The destructive cultural influence that Western civilization exerts on Black people has been one of his chief worries. Thus he fosters African and Caribbean research, while championing *independent* Black struggle. "Our mission," he intones, "is not only to claim our African-ness, but to make Africa the jewel of the world." Regardless of how the chips of international relations may fall in coming decades, there is no way either Africans outside of Africa or Africans on the continent can protect themselves, Clarke believes, without a powerful *African World Union*.

Gerald Horne has concentrated on restructuring the U.N. Security Council to reflect the real world order, one which is no longer stifled by a Washington-versus-Moscow, white "bipolarity." To his mind, permanent vetoes for Nigeria, Brazil, and India would be a first step toward recognition of planet Earth's vast majority of people of color. A long term shift in the international balance of economic power is underway. It is accompanied by a potential revolution in the distribution of military clout. Reducing Europe's overrepresentation in the Security Council is a sensible way, thinks Horne, to pay tribute to the change. He would collapse the separate British and French vetoes into one common European Community veto. Japan's economic preeminence would be rewarded with permanent non-veto membership on the Security Council.

Throughout its history, international Pan-Africanism has been a secular movement. The great Pan-Africanists of the past were concerned primarily with non-religious subjects, preferring a discourse about how to overcome African social disintegration and world fragmentation. Pan-Africanism pertained to worldly things and, recognizing that African people follow many different faiths, it wisely

388

decided to leave religious, spiritual matters alone. Now, however, there has come a break with this tradition. Recently two stalwarts of the Pan-African Movement, Nigerian professor Naiwu Osahon and Canadian Charles Roach, a lawyer, have suggested a novel and surprising approach. They are convinced that the spirituality imbedded in African culture will block the advancement of Pan-Africanism should the movement fail to adopt a religious world view. To avoid the danger, Osahon and Roach want to set up a Pan-African Spiritual Priesthood. An ecumenical body, as envisaged by the pair, its mandate would include the teaching of Afrocentric philosophy, anti-depression therapy, and the promotion of Pan-African unity throughout the world. The role, if any, of such priests in the management of the Pan-African Fund and Pan-African Foundation (proposed at the same time) is not explained.

Debate swirls concerning the appropriateness of the initiative. Some doubt whether Pan-Africanism, an essentially secular movement, has the capacity to absorb a religion, or whether it even should. Is there any real need for a formal body of priests, or is this just a way to saddle the movement with another bureaucracy? Does this represent the birth of yet another hierarchy, yet another elite? Or is this an attempt to ward off an aggressive fundamentalist Pan-Islamism which threatens to swamp secular Pan-Africanism? If indeed so, the proposal can be seen as a clever move on the political chessboard. From another angle, whether the call for a "Priesthood" is religious obscurantism (i.e., opposition to the spread of practical knowledge) remains an open question.

Whether Pan-Africanism survives as a secular movement or not, it is clear that it is cut up into all sorts of factions, organizations, sects, and doctrines, ranging from groups advocating wholesale return to Africa to organizations proposing to negotiate with the white governments for land and reparations right here in the United States and Canada. Some suggest buying enough real estate in the western hemisphere until Blacks own coherent territories. Reparation payments could fund the purchases. Some restrict their vision to community control. Others seek moral regeneration through cultural rehabilitation. Others place their hopes in Afrocentric education. Yet other tendencies reject politics completely in favor of an "extraterritorial cultural-national autonomy" that would allow an individual to "be Black" without resolving the contradiction between true Black cultural development and continued white political manipulation of the bodies and souls of Black people. There is everything from Afrocentric history and curriculum reform to otherworldliness and belief in apocalyptic divine intervention. Some dream of *Ujamma* and African communalism, while others would have the Diasporan man wait for salvation to come from Mother Africa. There are even those who advocate shipping our ex-convicts to Africa for rehabilitation where, it is believed, they would contribute positively to modernizing the economy, to raising living standards, and to rejuvenating civilization.

*

The Seventh Pan-African Congress met in Kampala, Uganda, 3–8 April 1994. It gathered to confront a looming "recolonization crisis." Only this time the threat was not white territorial imperialism, or European settlers seizing African farms and pasture. This time the recolonizers were "impartial," supra-national agencies established by "post-modern" imperialism to police the Third World. The World Bank and IMF had imposed Structural Adjustment Plans (SAPs) in one African country after another. "SAP-ed" economies effectively nullified African governmental sovereignty. Delegates at the Seventh Congress tried to figure ways to reverse the loss of authority. They also addressed the devastation of the continent by civil wars that never end. And for the first time in Pan-African conference history there was a serious look at the predicament of Brazilian Blacks. But the major agenda theme was unity—unity *of* the continent and unity *between* the continent and the Diaspora.

The most riveting suggestion proposed the year 1999 as the date for the formation of a United States of Africa. The crux would be an all-African continental parliament. According to the design, this assembly would be made up of elected representatives of the peoples of the continent, as distinct from the OAU, which functions as a kind of trade union of heads of state. This version of continentalism would endow the All-African parliament's decisions with the authority to command individual African nation-states.

Perhaps the most visionary edition of contemporary Pan-Africanism is one born on the United States' east coast. Though secular in purpose, it nonetheless exudes an almost millenarian quality in conjuring up a time of general righteousness and fulfilment in the indefinite future. It looks to the day when an Atlantic Ocean–spanning International African State will emerge as one of the world's truly great powers. It will bind together under a single sovereignty all the disparate parts of the African world—(1) a unified African continent, (2) a totally decolonized Caribbean, (3) Black communities in Spanish-speaking America, (4) a "blackened" Brazil, and (5) U.S. "city-states" (i.e., Black inner-city districts in the twelve largest metropolitan areas). The inspired political leadership of a World African Party would steer this magnificent neo-African superstate.

Chapter 19

AFROCENTRICITY
AND PAN-AFRICANISM

Today there is a fit between Pan-Africanism and Afrocentricity. Firm mooring in the spirit of Pan-Africanism enables Afrocentrists to shine the spotlight on Africa as the birthplace of humanity and honor African civilization as the mother of world civilization. To Egypt is restored its rightful place as the glory of antiquity and the original mentor of Western civilization. The Hegelian construct that Africa was "historyless" is rebuked.

Afrocentricity has also knocked the pins from under the cultural pathology thesis, while exposing the falsification of the African past. Thus it vindicates Pan-Africanism. The Afrocentrists uncover the nakedness of cultural pathology, showing that it avoids scrutiny of the *structure* of Black oppression and exploitation in order to divert attention from racism and white world supremacy. To mes-

merize the public with tales of alleged failures, frailties, incapabili-
ties, and criminal proclivities of the victims is part of racism's grand
design. Afrocentrism does not permit this blaming-the-victim syndrome. It has turned up the heat on the denigrators of the Black
man's contribution to world history. It proves that anyone who
claims that Africa had no part in the conception of men as human
beings is a liar. This is why Afrocentric scholars get such a bad press
in white mainstream media. They are performing their task too well.

The same can be said of those educators who advocate a curriculum of inclusion and who are under heavy attack for doing so.
The white man never admits that the African is capable of any superiority, no matter what the sphere. For centuries he had disallowed
any excellence in his victim, since such fessing up might make his
victim realize his own potential for resistance. Everything that Black
folk have done in the past is said to have been somehow or other
either "borrowed" from other civilizations, "diffused" from centers
foreign to Africa, or invented independently and simultaneously in
several areas, most of those places outside the Black continent. No
priority for Africa is admissible. The same goes for contemporary
life. Despite the testimony of our senses and the weight of popular
folk wisdom, any trace of excellence, be it physical dexterity, emotional perception, intelligence, or volition, is dismissed as "myth."
The "big guns" of white academia are brought to bear to "prove"
that the priority or equality in question is merely "apparent."

New York and Ontario are a couple of the places where vigorous
moves have been made to incorporate the history and contributions
of Africa and the African Diaspora in the school curriculum. There
is a drive to make public education somehow relevant to Black youngsters. As Professor Dona Richards of Hunter College's Black and
Puerto Rican Studies Department stresses, relevance is not merely a
curriculum of inclusion. Nor is a relevant African-centered curriculum merely one of inclusion, nor is it one that is pablumy "multicultural." The same insistent spirit infused the 1994 discussions of Black
professors in Ontario about the formation of a Black Faculty
Association, devoted to the defense of Black needs in higher education. They stressed the need for an organization independent of the
established Ontario Council of University Faculty Association
(OCUFA), a body dominated by white professors and insensitive to
Black interests. In fact, their action revived an initiative a generation
old in that part of Canada. A 1970 international Black conference

held in Ontario resolved that "it must be the sacred task of every teacher of Black History to emphasize that our people were removed from their native soil and enslaved in a foreign land, facilitating their subordination and spiritual mystification and estrangement."

Not only should Black studies be taught in this forthright and uncompromising manner, the Afrocentrists are also insisting on the need for North American Black scholars to learn Portuguese. Tangible links with the single largest contingent of the Diaspora are now vitally important, yet are sadly lacking. At the very least, activists require reading command of Portuguese in order to begin the essential "networking." Concerned Afrocentrists say that priority be given to the task, even if it means diverting attention temporarily from the study of other foreign languages, such as French and Spanish, and even if at the expense of lessons in African tongues, in, say, the ever popular Swahili. The outreach to Black Brazil cannot wait. Black Brazilians are beginning to be invited to North American international confabs devoted to the development of people of African descent.

Abdias do Nascimento, Brazilian legislator, chief of a national agency devoted to the defense of Afro-Brazilians and main champion of the Black power awakening in that country, links the Afro-Brazilian struggle to that of all Africans in the Diaspora, as an indispensable condition for nation building. The fact that Africans were the victims of the greatest holocaust ever to occur should appear, he said, as the number one item in textbooks. A real curriculum of inclusion would not merely be purged of negative stereotypes of Africa and Africans, it would reflect the true dimensions of the cultures and civilizations built by African people. Only such an Afrocentric education would provide the training required for Afro-Brazilians to rein in racist police killers, house their homeless, and provide legal assistance for victims of racial discrimination. Nascimento's Afrocentrism is about toppling the white ruling elite; it is about Afro-Brazilians seizing hold of their own destiny. It stands squarely in the tradition of Pan-Africanism.

*

In many ways the attention of contemporary Pan-Africanists, the continental ones, has narrowed to the current crisis. They seek swift answers to today's headaches—to problems of debt, deteriorating terms of trade, political instability and heart-rending civil wars, demoralizing structural adjustment programs, collapsing commodity prices, health-care emergencies and famine. These seem much more pressing than dreams of continental unity or the predicament of Diaspora cousins an ocean away. The great white league—the European Community—has dumped Africa for white Eastern Europe. Under the terms of the renewed trade pact signed in 1990 between the European Community and its former colonies in Africa, the Caribbean, and the Pacific, the bank teller's counter has been slammed shut against any further special capital loans. The new Lomé Convention provides grants only and concedes no debt cancellation. Africans can no longer count on agricultural export income stabilization reimbursements. There had been a time when the European Community compensated its Lomé "partners" for lost earnings on more than 40 primary export commodities when world market prices dropped.

In the face of this unprecedented economic and social dislocation, some neo-Pan-Africanists now argue the need primarily for African *economic* unity. Lacking real prospects of continental unity, regional economic integration has become a theme. Others warn of the dangers of tying Africa to Europe's economic coat tails. Zimbabwean financial expert, Bernard Chidzero—at one time a serious candidate for the U.N. Secretary-Generalship—praised the concept of a monetary union of African states. An Africanist kind of "New World Order," Pan-Africanism has surfaced. It concedes domination of the post-Cold War world to the West, hoping for a favorable integration of regional African economies. Beginning at the sub-regional level, it is hoped that the move can be made to full-scale regionalism and that the New World Order will allow full African continentalism some day. Critics reject this as a pipe dream, noting that African economies are already integrated in the world capitalist system on terms that are so favorable to the West that white financial moguls are very unlikely to want to change. Moreover, the present African state apparatus—the vehicle of corrupt native ruling class enrichment and the mechanism which keeps Africa locked in the world market—is irrelevant for the needs of the African masses, argue the critics.

Debate swirls over retribalization, and the question of African identity in the Diaspora. Some are for a "we-are-an-African-people" ideology, others are against it. The latter maintain that the idea is nullified by the fact that in the real world of African inter-state relations there is no such thing as an *African nationality* in the sense of specific citizenship. No one walks around with an *African* passport.

There are only Nigerian, South African, Malian, and other passports. One can indeed be an Angolan, Tanzanian or Cameroonian citizen. But as yet there is no African citizenship as such. Nevertheless, retort those who claim Pan-African identity, all Nigerians, Ghanaians, Namibians, Kenyans, etc., share the African past, share ancient Nile Valley origins, and a kind of lowest-common-denominator culture. They are alike much in the same way the English, French, Italians and Germans (now straining toward a common citizenship) are all Europeans. African too are the Blacks of the Diaspora, insist the "we-are-an-African-people" forces. Some of them are enthusiastic about the term *"African American"* as a description, rather than *Black*. Does the term imply a kind of dual citizenship? Or is it merely a semantic way of paying tribute to a new and historically distinct entity, a new nationality which is African-American? Debaters who are most consistent in their belief that the total liberation of peoples of African descent everywhere can only be achieved through the overthrow of white world supremacy, prefer the designation *"Black."* For it emphasizes the basic contradiction of global society which is the antagonism between Black liberation and white supremacy. It is a more adequate reflection of the real task.

However, these critics do not reject Pan-Africanism. They endorse it as the valid underpinning for a distinct American Black national identity—with all the unique features peculiar to it. A powerful identification—emotional and political—with Africa *as a whole* is indispensable. No healthy Diasporan identity is possible without immersion in African-derived culture. Diasporan Blacks also sorely need to support politically those African nations which have the potential to rise to Great Power status within the near future, states like post-apartheid South Africa and Nigeria. Our dignity requires us to reaffirm Pan-African ties. Pan-Africanism can also help remedy the western hemisphere strain of retribalization, the "island tribalism" that plagues Caribbean Blacks. Both the United States and Canada have experienced the parochialism of West Indian migrants who, long after arrival, still identify themselves according to insular loyalties rather than face up to a North American racism which lumps all Black people together, regardless of birthplace. Island tribalists remain hostile towards those from neighboring islands. Hence many are unable to cope with a racism which does not differentiate between Jamaican and Trinidadian, between Barbadian and

397

Dominican, between Afro-American and Afro-Canadian, but instead sees only "Negroes." Submerged in the waters of a levelling white racism based on "Negro blood," for these unfortunates the awareness of self as Black—if ever arrived at—is forced upon them by the wider society, as it imposes an inferior social status.

*

Multiparty democracy and parliamentarianism—both being Western imports—cause many Pan-Africanists unease. Are they suited to Africa? Is there any match between them and an authentic African political tradition like consensus-through-palaver? Can a marriage between Western-style representation based on formal elections on one side and ancient instincts born of egalitarian communalism on the other ever be harmonious?

Critical-thinking Pan-Africanists reckon that Black people should take a neutral attitude toward "democratic" as well as toward opposing forms of government. Mulling over prospects for the twenty-first century, they conclude that neither the continent nor the Diaspora can afford the false luxury of espousing any one form of government to the exclusion of any alternative. As a rule of political life, being doctrinaire and dogmatic about any one form of government is a prescription for disaster. As borrowed from the West, democracy is a political system which enshrines majority rule through some arrangement of election. Why should Black people fall blindly in love with this, ask canny Pan-Africanist philosophers? The British and the French—the two main colonizers of Africa—were certainly well served by the system, but is that any recommendation for Africans who have had to sacrifice so much to throw off the colonial yoke? From 1619 to 1865 African Americans endured chattel slavery administered by a system of majoritarian democracy and were kept down for another whole century by segregationist white voters and duly-elected racist legislators. Why should they dance with joy at the continuing prospect of being outvoted by the white majority year after year?

Of course, it is no wiser, these thinkers note, to become an enthralled devotee of dictatorship, defined as one political group's or individual's control of social power and coercion.

Recent multiparty electoral experiments have failed spectacularly in Africa. Military dictatorships have turned into fiascos. In the

United States, race remains the single most decisive determinant of voting behavior, limiting the election hopes of African American candidates to districts where Black votes predominate. These facts create a growing sense among Pan-Africanists that it is too costly for our people, and too restrictive, to hitch our cart to any one form of government. It is wiser to espouse whichever system at the moment does the best job of delivering the goods. The form of government does not matter as long as it delivers quality education, high nutrition, and health standards. Black people, Africans *and* Diasporans, need cultural freedom, intellectual excellence, and advanced consumer services, *not* specific forms of government. In places like, say, Rio de Janeiro, where Black street urchins are exposed to racist police and to merchants bent on genocide, even a dictatorship would be acceptable, provided it were dedicated to the protection of *Black* rights. There are circumstances under which one-man rule, or the dictatorship of a minority political party or class, could do a much better job of protecting the interests of a Black minority than a populist democracy where the majority of voters are prejudiced whites. Government coercion may be blunt and unrestricted. But if it defends Black human rights it is justified. Black interests must always head the agenda. Black needs set the criteria for preferring one political system over another. It is a question of performance. If dictatorship delivers the goods, so be it. Benevolent despotism is not a contradiction in terms where the despot serves the interests of our people.

The following refrain is heard with increasing frequency in Pan-African circles: find a Black alternative to white democracy. In the words of Edward Scobie, advising the Caribbean region to turn its face away from European-style democracy, "we must stop paying tribute to Europe. Stop creating institutions, states and societies that get their inspiration from Europe."

*

Equality for Black folks worldwide can come only through the emergence of some Black nations as Great Powers. In order to survive economically and politically, Pan-Africanism must set itself a new agenda for the twenty-first century. Global equality is accessible only through raw, naked *power*—power that is economic, yes, but power that is also *military*. All other avenues have been tried and found wanting.

The military component is perhaps the key component in relation to membership in the circle of great powers. Now, the military need not be omnipotent, it need only be a protective shield. For this is where the concept of *finite deterrence* comes in. Required merely is the military ability to scare off a would-be aggressor. An African state need not be as strong as its adversaries in numbers or material resources and firepower to avoid annihilation. It need only be capable of retaliation—and to make its resolve to use that capability credible *to white imperialism*, to let the white world know we mean business. It is unlikely that any military threat to Africa will come from non-Arab Asia any time during the twenty-first century.

Military power is needed to overcome the fear that has paralyzed Black people for so long and that has made Africa a cipher in the diplomatic power equation. There is no ducking the need, therefore, to acquire weapons of mass destruction. Any Black nation which truly aspires to Great Power status must have them. The news of full-power weaponry at Black disposal would mean that our people could no longer be ignored during international emergencies. It would inspire confidence in Black folk wherever they live. We would know that our interests would be taken seriously. Black diplomatic input would not only be sought, it would finally have some clout. Just knowing that the hand of a Black statesman is poised somewhere over an Armageddon button, like the hands of white statesmen have been for decades, would neutralize the fearful inferiority some of us feel. It would also inspire some respect in the white man, causing him to fear us for a change. None of this is possible without a Black-controlled state-of-the-art defense industry, capable of manufacturing the sinews of war. It is indeed difficult to function as a great power, if one has to purchase one's weapons from one's adversary. Presently, with perhaps the sole exception of Mandela's South Africa, no Black nation anywhere has a modern armaments industry.

Increasingly this need is acknowledged by leading Pan-Africanists, among others by Naiwu Osahon, who rejects the argument that African countries should avoid expensive technologies because they lack the funds and skilled manpower. "The sciences leading to the production of the bomb or the landing of man on the moon," he says, "are indispensable to mankind's combined advancement and control of his environment, and the Black man cannot afford to lag behind the rest of the world in these or other areas."

More than anything, this has to do with morale. Glorification of the African past, say, can be a morale booster. It can help one feel

400

impervious to racist insult. It builds self-confidence, gives one a sense of worthiness in the day-to-day struggle for Black liberation. The same is true of certain religious beliefs. Moral certainty that God is on our side inspired Martin Luther King. It also imparted tremendous courage and enthusiasm to hundreds of thousands of Black Southerners fighting for civil rights. Malcolm X's belief in Allah was deep and genuine. In the past the Voodoo tradition, which is still alive in Haiti, armored Jacques Dessalines and his warriors in their guerrilla victory over the troops of Napoleon Bonaparte, come to reimpose slavery.

But morale too has its limits. Feelings of invulnerability alone do not get the job done. They do not make one impervious to the white man's bullets. Suicidal bravado is counterproductive. It is merely suicidal. Conviction by itself is no substitute for concrete military strength. Faith by itself can divert one from the effort to acquire and master superior weaponry. The key to liberation is to restrict our own losses to the minimum while inflicting the greatest damage on the forces of racism.

Here as in other contentious issues, militant Pan-Africanism has a tack of its own. It is incumbent upon Third World statesmen, particularly African ones, to overcome the inferiority psychosis that makes us presume that Black nations are condemned to military weakness henceforth and forever more. Diasporan leaders must shake free of the servile illusion that Black communities are, by some dictate of God or Nature, forever restricted to *non-violent* political means. Whether we like it or not, violence, particularly military violence, has been a major agent of historical change. It is not some divine right restricted alone to white countries.

The only real equality is equality based on equal material strength, i.e., economic and military power. The United States has never practiced a non-violent foreign policy. Notice how seriously Washington, D.C., took Stalin and the Soviets when the USSR got the means to deliver nuclear warheads to targets in North America. America continued to take the USSR seriously until the day the Gorbachev-Yeltsin "government" buckled and submitted to U.S. global domination.

Postwar Japan earns respect of a different order even though it still seems to suffer from a psychosis caused by being the only country to suffer nuclear destruction. Throughout the 1980s it performed as the economic powerpack of the world, stirring much resentment in white power circles. Should the Japanese decide in the near future, under different leadership, to translate their economic strength into military might, they would figure ominously in the Great Power complex.

China is the world's fastest growing mass economy today. However, it is its possession of nuclear weapons and a missile delivery system that forms the basis of its clout in the U.N. Security Council and respect in international affairs. China has become a real factor in the international power equation because it has nuclear capability.

One assumes that fairly soon India too will occupy its rightful position as a Great Power. It already has the ability to manufacture and deploy weapons of mass destruction. Eventually its rivalry with Pakistan will likely compel both nations to upgrade their armed forces to include the latest weaponry. While still under white rule, South Africa brandished the nuclear sword over Black Africa for years. In 1991 it was revealed that Israel had developed a panoply of nuclear weapons. It even implemented its "Sampson Option," the biblical implication being that if Israel went down it would take its enemies down with it. Arab population centers were targeted. On at least three occasions the Israeli government proclaimed nuclear alerts, placing its nuclear launch forces at trigger-readiness. Thought of nuclear weapons production in Iraq and Iran causes nervousness in Tel Aviv. Similarly, there is much handwringing in the Pentagon at the prospect that North Korea has the technology to deploy nuclear weapons.

Given these models, Black people would be foolish indeed were we to remain the only race on earth without the final deterrent. Blacks too must seek to acquire the "Great Equalizer," i.e. the means to checkmate imperialism by rendering an attack on Africans too costly for white society (or any other enemy that may materialize in the future) to contemplate. At that moment Africans and people of African descent will walk to the table of international diplomacy as equal players. We will have arrived as winners in the power game of bargaining and negotiation. The road to the promised land of full human rights for the Black people of this earth passes through the savannah of military might.

Admittedly, non-violence can be a supple weapon, suited to the ploys of the weak in the face of the strong. It is the means for Aesop's wily fox to dismay the lion. But the lion can be put off guard only temporarily. If he is to prevail, at some point the fox must get the firepower to take the lion down. Nonviolence is often a good strategem for the weak. It can never be the ultimate shield.

The stage is set for sweeping confrontations between North and South in the coming century. Major contradictions plague imperialism in the world at large. The prospect for armed conflict exists throughout the Third World. In all probability a rash of wars will blanket the Third World over the next several decades, very likely including much of Latin America. In March 1992 it was rumored that China would actively recruit former Soviet scientists, including those with nuclear expertise. They were to be offered employment in Chinese defense-related industries. The grapevine buzzed with the news that China was exporting nuclear know-how to Pakistan and Algeria. 1994 resounded with reports that high-grade plutonium was being smuggled abroad from the former Soviet Union. Access to nuclear weapons proliferates worldwide. Africa can ill afford to be left out of this high-tech windfall. Black countries should seek to get in on the valuable "brain drain" from the former USSR, even at the cost of inflated expatriate salaries and fringe benefit inducements. This expertise could help the continent close the military-technological gap.

Imperialist conquest taught Africa a bitter lesson during the age of Scramble and Partition. Africans were not morally or ethically inferior to the white invaders. African warriors were no less courageous than European soldiers. In many instances they were braver, for European fortitude often depended entirely on superior weapons. The Black warrior looked the white man in the eye. Even so, he sadly came out on the short end. Africa's fighting forces proved inferior in the very thing that in the last analysis determines who dominates whom. African warriors were defeated in combat everywhere between, say, 1880 and 1914, and very many times in history it has been combat that has decided who bosses whom. Spears were no match for maxim guns.

The lesson is stark. There is no substitute in the international arena for state-of-the-art weaponry, nor for the political discipline and will to use it. On the eve of the twenty-first century up-to-the-minute armament means stealth bombers and nuclear warheads, it means rocketry and sophisticated satellite warning and surveillance systems. It implies independent defense industries. It entails control of air and sea spaces, and territory secure from foreign encroachment.

It will be incumbent upon a full-fledged African military power to implement a Monroe Doctrine-like policy for the African continent, excluding non-African intervention from Africa, in the way the United States keeps the western hemisphere closed to extra-continental powers.

•

On 10 December 1965, Dr. Martin Luther King, Jr. gave the world a warning. He said that the Western passion for white supremacy would condemn humanity ultimately to race war. After all, the vast majority of the human race is anything but Caucasian. That majority is wallowing in misery and poverty. They will not put up with those conditions much longer. The coming century may see the price of white supremacy soar to international racial warfare. The contradiction between the North and the South is the main contradiction in today's world. Elimination of white "Northern" supremacy must top twenty-first century Pan-Africanism's docket, and head the historical agenda for the whole world.

This course of events gives new meaning to the time-honored Pan-African concept of Black unity. And new urgency, for time is running out. Continental and Diasporan Africans can ill afford any diversion from the relentless pursuit of *real* power, i.e., decision-making authority in economics and politics combined with the armed might to back it. Each group of Black people must pursue this, according to its own local circumstances and limitations. But the ultimate goals for all branches of the African family must be the same—international clout, domestic control, and universal respect for those of African race. Without these minimum requirements Pan-Africanism will be a joke.

Furthermore, as Diasporan Africans search for the best for ourselves in the Americas, we must be aware of ancient ties between ourselves and the native American peoples. We must try to revive the tradition of alliance with the descendants of peoples who were here long before Columbus. The Diasporan phase of the Pan-African struggle cannot be separated from the mutual liberation of the indigenous Americans. They "are also the victims of the racism and wanton destructiveness introduced and enforced by the European colonists and their heirs," observes Abdias do Nascimento, founder of Brazilian *Quilombismo* Pan-Africanism (Nascimento 1985:180).

Pan-Africanists tend more and more to distinguish between long range plans of action designed to achieve ultimate aims and a short term agenda for the remaining years between now and the first years of the next century. Understandably, most attention is focused on the latter. Stripped to the bare bones, the immediate agenda seems to consist of the following: (1) consolidation of the Black political rule established in the Republic of South Africa in 1994 and its extension to the commanding heights of the economy; (2) a permanent U.N. Security Council seat with veto for a stable Nigeria; (3) reestablishment of South Africa as a significant voice in the United Nations and in international diplomacy; (4) debt cancellation as a first step toward economic independence; (5) loosening the reins of structural adjustment programs, IMF, and the World Bank, to enable modernization and diversification of African national economies. Success in these early stages would create the breathing spell for long-term work on: (1) modern military power including nuclear weapons and chemical and biological arsenals; (2) breaking out of the existing economic integration in the world imperialist system in favor of an African economic integration rising from sub-regional to regional to continental unity; (3) the kind of prestige and influence in international relations that would enable continental Africans to exert protective sway over the status of Diasporan Africans; and (4) extracting full reparations from historically liable white Western powers payable to both the continent and the Diaspora.

None of this is likely to be achieved painlessly. In fact, there is the sobering possibility of a series of wars extending over several generations. Comparable historical changes have seldom occurred without strife and conquest. The emergence of European nation states and the rise to preeminence of England, France, Spain, Germany, and Russia involved bitter repercussions which Europeans could not duck. The emergence of one or several African states as Great Powers on the way to continental unity is unlikely to be much less painful. History does not work that way. Achievement of an African continentalism that concentrates strength, morale, resources, and military clout for optimum effect will probably require strife among regional powers, an era of defensive and offensive alliances, shifts in the balance of power, *realpolitik* diplomacy (i.e., policy based on advantage rather than on ideals), and trials of combat renewed over generations, as was the case with Europe. Large chunks—and in the end maybe even all—of the continent may be conquered by one great warring African state. Who knows, one African state may emerge to unify all of Africa under its sway, the way Prussia came to dominate

405

and unify all of Germany. Such power assemblage has recurred throughout history. We have seen it, briefly, in Ghenghis Khan's empire spanning Asia and Europe. It occurred in the Mediterranean under Rome. The gathering of the territories which went to make up the United States of America coincided with the awful genocide of the Native Americans. The Great Mogul's empire in India was a forceful assemblage of lands and peoples. There is no guarantee that something similar may not happen in tomorrow's Africa. Such historical processes often entail blood and suffering, sometimes hecatombs. History is cruel. This may prove the path along which Africa is modernized militarily, raised to Great Power status, and ultimately united under a single sovereignty. Whether or not this comes to pass, only history will tell. One prospect is clear, however. Without unity and modernization, regardless of how arrived at, the alternative is continued disease epidemics, famines, degradation, and the hecatombs of retribalized warfare. We would experience many Rwandas. The alternative, in short, is the continued yoke of white world supremacy. That is why many Pan-Africanists are willing to look upheaval and revolutionary conquest coolly in the eye. Upheaval is preferable to slow, whimpering death.

Major input in Africa's immediate future development is envisaged for a "big four"—Nigeria, USA, Brazil, and South Africa. Nigeria and South Africa, along with the Black communities in the United States and Brazil, are envisioned as the *motor* for the entire Black world. Each has a special gift to offer, a unique contribution to make. *Nigeria* is the *most populous* Black country and has the potential to eventually mount large armed forces. The *United States* houses the world's *wealthiest* Black community, the one that is the most sophisticated, and the one with the greatest organizational experience. (And as British white supremacist J.A. Froude observed in 1881, "organization creates superiority of force" [Froude, *The English in Ireland*, vol. I:2].) *Brazil* is the *largest* Black nation in the western hemisphere. *South Africa* is the most *industrialized* state in the continent and has nuclear capability.

The color line DuBois saw drawn in the sands of twentieth century Western civilization has thickened into the titanic North-South bifurcation set to dominate the coming twenty-first century. Pan-Africa stands in the front line of the struggle. Manning Marable is right on in observing that the close of the Cold War has revalidated the racial question as the key to international affairs.

*

Pan-Africanism is on the rebound. It lives on after many reported demises. One of its main tasks in coming decades will be to win and retain support from anti-imperialist, non-Black elements throughout the Third World. Albeit that Black interests will not always dovetail with the interests of other people of color, and occasionally may even diverge sharply, the empowerment of African peoples worldwide requires support from as many non-Black peoples of color as possible, on as many issues as possible. Specific measures, attitudes and policies can be tailored to merit fraternal support. Focusing world attention on the misdeeds of white supremacy and on its brutal repercussions is a most helpful measure. Calculated use of the international media to spotlight discrimination against and repression of Black peoples can sway Third World opinion—a concentrated drumfire that never lets up, exposing racist atrocities. And the Pan-African community must reciprocate. Third World support would evaporate without a mutuality on our part, indicating an exchange of sympathy and obligation. The Diaspora, African Americans in particular, must increase their sensitivity and sympathy for the struggles not merely of continental Africans, but of the rest of the Third World as well. Even when certain Asian or Latin American issues appear irrelevant to Black interests, Pan-Africa can ill afford politically to tune them out. There is no excuse for insensitivity, certainly not where issues vital to ordinary people in, say, Bangla Desh, Viet Nam or Mexico, in no way countervail Black interests. Cuba, for instance, is a glaring example of a Third World nation in precarious peril of U.S. invasion and badly in need of the solidarity of all people of color.

Yet in all, this does not mean that Pan-Africanism should not seek the *Black Interest* in all issues of concern to mankind. We need learn from our enemies, emulate their relentless style of pursuing power. Wise flexibiltiy dictates neutrality on our part toward parliamentary democracy, authoritarianism, populism, and benevolent dictatorship, depending on circumstances. Diasporans sure have had a bellyful of the jury system, for example, governed as it is by one of white folks' is-now-and-ever-shall-be precepts—the rule says that white jurors will never meet a Black-killing white cop they cannot acquit. The wisest tradition of Pan-Africanism is eclectic, borrowing whatever works. By not following any one system, but selecting the best and most workable elements of all systems, Black people—Diasporans and continentals—best control their own destiny.

There is a dichotomy in Pan-Africa. People of African blood are divided into two great halves. The bifurcation clearly has grave consequences for strategy and action. The tasks and issues of continental Blacks are peculiar to Africa, its inter-state relations, its domestic affairs, its ethnic and religious frictions. These tasks and issues are not the same as the ones which grip Diasporan Blacks. Both sides need to recognize this. Both Africans of the mother continent and Africans of the Diaspora must accept that in order to be achieved, local aims must be distinct and evolve according to local conditions. For a long time the *macro*-goal will remain identical for both wings—destruction of white global supremacy. However, circumstances differ radically on the two shores of the Atlantic, necessitating local strategies and tactics that diverge sharply.

*

The moment has come for a remodeled Pan-Africanism, tailored to the twenty-first century. Required now is a revolutionary new Black *supra*-nationalism, tall enough to look beyond tribal frictions, island snobbishness, and Disapora myopia. We need an African continentalism which confronts the "flag independence" of a myriad of African nation-states. A remodeled Pan-Africanism must refocus its vision to encompass sub-regional initiatives, rising to regional economic integration, as steps along the way to full continental unity. It must decide what to do with the Arabized North. Military might is the key to Great Power status. Military modernization is a need that will not go away. Diasporan Africans living in the western hemisphere will always lack prestige and protection as long as there is no great African military force. The new Pan-Africanism will seek the realignment of the balance of world power first through transformation of the U.N. Security Council. It will insist upon Black state participation in the G-7 power bloc which now rules the world. But it will not stop there.

With growing volume, the drum must sound in coming decades for *reparations*. There can be no lasting peace internationally until the West pays adequate compensation in money, material, and technology to Africans for colonization and to Diasporans for slavery and racism.

Diasporans must end their solitudes. We must overcome our self-imposed ghettoes which divide and hinder unity among native Afro-Americans and Afro-Canadians, West Indians from the Caribbean, Afro-Latinos and recent immigrants from the mother continent. A restyled Pan-Africanism must teach us to overcome ancient parochialism because North American white racism proclaims that all persons of "Negro blood" fall into a uniformly and distinctly *Black* social category. It is folly to pretend otherwise.

Neo-Panafrican coalition policy will entail widening concentric circles of alliances having a common center—*the Black Interest*. The tightest circle will consist of fraternal alliances with the Non-Black oppressed, e.g. Native Americans, Pacific Asians, non-Black Latinos (where possible), etc. The more remote alliances will involve provisional, tactical coalitions. This type will be temporary and opportunistic. Here the "partners" envisaged are mainly white liberal and "progressive" movements, say, organized labor, women, church groups, etc. Based on compromise and negotiated agreement, these coalitions will be entered cautiously, wary of the ever-present racism waiting to surface among the white "partners."

Pan-Africanists need to check out the credentials of China and of India too. Those are poor and very populous Third World countries whose economic growth has been remarkable in the last few years, particularly China's. They also cover large land masses, especially China. They may serve as *relevant* role models for Africa, offering lessons on how to feed the people, spur economic development, and increase the nation's weight in international affairs. The Chinese example shows how a large, relatively weak, once brutally semi-colonized Third World country can muster the economic and military power to assert real independence. It now figures seriously in the international power equation. And the most inspiring lesson in this for the children of Africa is that the misson can be accomplished within a *single* generation.

White folk around the globe have repudiated socialism. In Russia they threw the Soviet baby out with the bathwater of communism. Yet socialism was the only *potentially* non-racist political economy white civilization ever produced. These events strengthen Pan-African suspicion of white men bearing ideological "gifts." Expect Neo-Panafricanists to be increasingly wary of Caucasian political philosophers. We must resist the lures of Western civilization. Most white-derived ideas about political economy are poisonous to Black folk, or crafted to create wealth for white folk at our expense, or both. Like the illusions of European religions, white-formulated philosophies are devious come-ons. Third Worlders must seek economic and military power, and not get run off track trying to salvage something good for themselves from white political doctrines and values. Africans must liberate ourselves, for if we do not, no one will do it for us.

Twenty-first century Pan-Africanism can be expected to work to block the influence of white consumer culture. It will lobby against all efforts of white demographers to persuade Black people to reduce their numbers. "The more of us the better," is likely to become a leitmotif of the more forthright strains of Pan-Africanism.

If the ultimate emancipation of people of African heritage can be nothing else than the attainment of *real* power, for Diasporans that power must be absolutely equal on a parity basis to the power held by the whites with whom we share the same society. If it is to mean anything substantial to continental Africans, that power must be equivalent to that wielded by the collective white man in Europe, the Americas, and on the world scale. True power has two pillars. One is substantially economic, the other military, the latter enabled by and confirming the former.

Pan-Africanism *is* Black internationalism, now and for the future.

PART THREE

WHAT IS TO BE DONE

Chapter 20

REPARATIONS

Today, with increasing insistence, historically-conscious Black folks are toting up social bills, wondering if we will ever collect the much-in-arrears debt owed us as a people, whether we can ever even so much as find out what and how much we are owed. Restitution-minded nationalists are not alone in this any longer. Even convention-bound HBCU educators now want to know exactly what we should be demanding from white Western civilization at this stage of our struggle.

The answer proposed here is blunt and plain-spoken: *Demand it all!* Insist on collecting everything owing to us as a people historically, down to the last penny, and not one whit less. Make indemnification item number one on the Black political signboard. We need to calculate the gigantic debt owed the African creators of the wealth luxuriated in by the white industrialized North and once that is done, get right down to negotiating the forms, accrued interests and period of amortization. As Manning Marable observes, public policy toward Afro-Americans has been up in the air ever since desegregation was legally won 30 years ago and more (Marable 1984:83). *Reparations*—and its Siamese twin, Black empowerment—are imperative if the end of formal segregation is ever to amount to anything but a sham leading absolutely nowhere.

Despite all our sacrifice we have been handed law-book freedom without make-right compensation. That is why, for the life of me, I cannot find it in my heart to condemn as a *crime* any act against white-owned property committed by a Black person—be it robbery, larceny, fraud, defacement, vandalism, or such—which white legal codes themselves classify merely as *"transgression."* Many perpetrators are not themselves conscious of the fact, yet the Black "felons" in America who infringe white property are merely recovering values stolen from us as an oppressed and enslaved people. In an individualistic and usually unsuccessful manner, they are merely *recovering* surplus value created by the unpaid forced labor of their enslaved ancestors, capital assets, technologies and services for which we have never been reimbursed. Some felons are not even engaged in reappropriation, deliberate or otherwise. A few strike, damage, and destroy entirely to deprive the heirs of those who robbed our ancestors of the enjoyment of the fruits of ill-gotten gains.

Let us test the furor over reparations. For legalistic minds, we can justify indemnity by defining the concept and looking at its various global economic rationales.

Actually there is little that is radical or even at all beyond the usual about the practice. The best known example the world over are the payments Germany continues to make to the victims of the Jewish holocaust since 1945. On the argument that responsibility survives even the defeat and eradication of the offending government (the Nazi regime in this instance), Israel and individual white Jews (and their heirs) have been buoyed financially for nigh onto half a century. Germany and Austria have paid more than a billion dollars to Jewish individuals and many billions more to the state of Israel. A further $630 million are earmarked for Eastern European Jews by the year 2000. Both the United States and Canadian governments have shelled out to Japanese-Americans (Nisei) and Japanese-Canadians as restitution for wrongful internment after Pearl Harbor. The U.S. paid the Nisei $1.25 billion, amounting to $20,000 per person. In 1992 the U.S. Office of Reparations agreed to increase the amounts to the Nisei or their descendants.

Although American Indians continue to be shortchanged in all emoluments that make human existence tolerable, the federal government has at least sporadically recognized the principle of reparations in respect to aboriginals, distributing one billion dollars and 44 million acres of land to the Native Americans of Alaska, $23 million to the Oattawas of Michigan, $81 million to the Klamaths of Oregon, $31 million to the Chippewas of Wisconsin, $12.3 million to the Florida descendants of the Seminole holocaust, and $105 million to the Sioux of South Dakota. Canada has anted up $200 million and 250,000 square miles so far to aboriginals and Japanese individuals.

The Florida legislature passed an enactment in 1994 responding to an outrage committed early in this century. The state lawmakers thus admitted that the passage of time does not erase the obligation to make amends. Money was set aside to compensate the heirs of Black victims of white mob violence in one locality. Moreover, nowadays even law and order freaks are acknowledging that government must shoulder the responsibility to compensate the victims of ordinary, everyday common-law crime. These compensations in money, material and transferred technology embody the obligation to make right damages and losses suffered as a result of the actions of individuals and sovereign states. These examples are grist for our mill. In 1994 the World Jewish Restitution Society persuaded Hungary and Slovakia to agree to restore land and other property to the heirs of Jews dispossessed during the fascist period. Here is yet another model and justification for our demands for reparations. For who can think of a greater dispossession and genocide than that of white civilization against the children of Africa, beginning in the fifteenth century and continuing today?

Now if the white world can compensate white Jewry, it should compensate Blacks for our much greater losses over a much longer span of time.

Furthermore, there is an intriguing global economic rationale that goes with Black reparations. Macro-economists admit that the basic ailment behind the fits and starts, the recessions and fitful recoveries that have plagued the world economy throughout the 1980s and 1990s, happens to be the enormous *excess* productive capacity in every highly industrialized country. As long as this is the case profits will be low or uncertain or will stagnate. The private sectors will hesitate to increase their purchase of new plant and equipment significantly. The results, as we know, are little high-wage job creation, runaway industries, relocation of production facilities offshore, and stagnant real wages and salaries. There is little likelihood domestically of any rapid rise in family incomes in the foreseeable future.

Here is where reparations could be a remedy. A massive reparations program in Africa and the western hemisphere could help turn the corner. Excess capacity could be worked down in programs designed to provide goods and services to needy Diasporan Blacks and Native Americans, and in indemnity deliveries to Africa. As assets are worn out and depreciated producing these goods and services, room would be made for new plant and equipment. The ensuing economic boom would be something like that triggered by the long drawn-out reconstruction of war damage and worn-out plant which covered the years from 1945 to 1969. Post–World War II reconstruction of Germany and Japan, together with the Marshall Plan—that stupendous bill of reparations for white Europeans footed by U.S. taxpayers—spurred the global economy for a quarter of a century. Reparations could function as the post–Cold War spark plug, helping to keep the world economy from spinning its wheels. Reparations for Black people can jump-start the global economy, if only there is the political will. If we, Black people, are ever to be restored to good condition, they are an absolute necessity.

Widespread renewal of fixed capital, with the inevitable higher organic composition of capital, would also stimulate and accelerate technological innovation, i.e., hasten the scientific and technological revolution worldwide, not least in Africa and America.

The only long-term macro-economic alternative which appears to be available to the white North economic system is a monstrous third world war, this time against the South (Third World). Already some white supremacists are viewing that option as a means of reviving flagging defense industries and generating a boom in military production. The North would hope to defeat the world's people of color once and for all, rejuvenating white *colonial* domination over the entire earth. Conflict on this scale would be an unprecedented holocaust of human and material destruction. Super-war strategists expect, however, that enough of the earth would remain intact, useable and inhabitable with exploitable natural resources. The treasure-trove of Africa's mineral and other resources would be wide open to Caucasian takeover. They see the decades immediately following such a war as spent repairing the damage and replacing worn-out, obsolete production facilities, in the expectation of pumping out "prosperity" for a victorious white world, postponing the day of reckoning for perhaps the whole twenty-first century.

*

Sankofa is an Akan word meaning to return to the past in order to move triumphantly into the future. (Why do you think white movie-goers stayed away from Haile Gerima's film *Sankofa* in such droves?) Perhaps it is from that perspective that the bill for reparations proposed in Massachusetts by state legislators Bill Owens and Shirley Owens-Hicks suggests the thirteenth (1865) and fourteenth (1866) amendments of the Constitution as the basis for compensation of Afro-American citizens. The wording of the thirteenth amendment in particular sanctions procedures to correct the economic disparity and discrimination between whites and Blacks as a result of enslavement. *Section 2* of the thirteenth amendment abolishing slavery stipulated that "Congress shall have power to enforce this article by appropriate legislation." The fourteenth amendment conferred citizenship on African Americans as persons native born in the United States. In *Section 5* it too specified that "Congress shall have power to enforce by appropriate legislation, the provisions of this article."

The actual term "*affirmative action*" as relating to remedial measures does not seem to have emerged until the twentieth century. White lawmakers first employed it in the Wagner Act of 1935, spelling out the duties of the new National Labor Relations Board with respect to the right to form unions and bargain collectively. John F. Kennedy first mentioned the affirmative action form of reparations in 1961 in his Executive Order 109255 covering the hiring of Blacks in firms with federal government contracts and banning discrimination by those contractors (Smith 1991:96). In 1965 Lyndon B. Johnson twice evoked a policy of racial reparations. And speaking at Howard University, he even paid homage to the concept of *equality of results*. He said, "we seek not just equality as a right and theory, but equality as a fact and equality as a result." His Executive Order 11246, issued that same year, reiterated Kennedy's ban on racial discrimination by firms doing business with the federal government. To qualify for or retain government deals, contractors were required to take "affirmative action" to remedy discrimination and its effects. The federal government thereby revived and endorsed the principle entrenched in the thirteenth amendment. Of course, these concessions were the result of pressure brought to bear jointly by the civil rights movement and the ghetto rebellions. Predictably, the Johnson orders aroused widespread white resistance and Blacks continued to suffer job exclusion and disproportionate unemployment.

While these vacillations were troubling the halls of white power, reparations were being embraced widely in the Black community. The Republic of New Africa was founded in Detroit in March 1968 by Gaidi Obadele (Milton Henry) and Imari Obadele (Richard Henry), two prominent nationalists. One of their first calls was for $400 billion in reparations from the United States Congress to finance the establishment of an independent Black republic, covering the territory of the states of South Carolina, Georgia, Alabama, Mississippi and Louisiana. Martin Luther King Jr.'s valedictory political campaign—the Poor People's March (April 1968)—was designed to win for all American citizens a federally guaranteed minimum income policy. Lamenting the fact that African Americans were still tortured by the effects of slavery and subjugation, militant SNCC activists voiced similar demands the next year. Speaking to a Detroit audience, James Forman launched the *Black Manifesto*, insisting that the time had come for whites, the beneficiaries of racial exploitation, to pay up. He reserved his most concentrated fire for white Christian churches and Jewish synagogues, hypocrites knee-deep in racism, but limited the reparations demand to a modest $5 billion. White liberals shamefacedly admitted that Forman might have a point (Berry and Blassingame 1982:406). On 12 May 1969, a group of Blacks, including a daughter of the great writer Richard Wright, interrupted a service at the American Church in faraway Paris, France. They marched in to demand reparations for the enslavement and super-exploitation of Afro-Americans.

I share this opinion personally, and I have made public my conviction in writings since 1969–1970. I am convinced that ample reparations are a necessity that cannot be avoided and are eminently just, for there is no white man living or dead in the Americas who does not owe the people of the Black communities so huge a debt that it could ever be repaid in a single lifetime.

In fact, our claim to reparations in one form or another is no longer really controversial among most Black people. And we, Black people, are the decisive ones for whom it matters whether the demand is contentious or not. We know that the large majority of white folks are against it at the present time. However, most major Black spokesmen now agree that some form of compensation is owing to us. Reparations activities are gaining momentum throughout America and Canada.

For example, when the International Tribunal on Reparations for African People in the U.S. met in Philadelphia in November 1991, it was the tenth such session to be staged by the organization. Via the Oakland-headquartered Yeshitelist African Peoples Revolutionary Party, the Tribunal is an offshoot of the original Black Panther Party.

A briefing to American minorities on the subject of minority rights was held in New York at the United Nations on 8 November 1991. The Afro-American delegates raised the issue of reparations. They briefed the chairwoman of the New York office of the U.N. Center for Human Rights. Those who spoke out were following the advice of Malcolm X who, on 3 April 1964, advised his fellow American Blacks to internationalize our cause by laying our plight before the United Nations and the World Court in The Hague. The Los Angeles-based Cosmopolitan Brotherhood Association, headed by Robert Brock, entreats Uncle Sam to indemnify descendants of enslaved captive Africans for the loss of their culture and the insult to their humanity. After all, on paper the U.S. is a party to the United Nations' covenant outlawing crimes against humanity. Brock says, "the government owes us money on a number of different fronts; for time, for labor... It's like an inheritance. We have inherited the ills of slavery" (*New York Amsterdam News,* 1 February 1992). Reparations are long overdue for a people whose foreparents were forcibly locked into disadvantage.

When Ron Daniels took to the stump in 1992 as an independent candidate, replacing Jesse Jackson, who decided not to run, he made reparations a keynote of his bid for the presidency. He advocated material redress for African Americans and Native Americans as retribution for centuries of oppression. Daniels also supported the Urban League idea of a domestic "Marshall Plan" to reconstruct the cities. His "Campaign for a New Tomorrow" envisaged a progressive convention of Black strategy-mappers, and a Black-led progressive cabinet, as the key elements in "a human rights crusade to create a new domestic order." Another Third Party independent, Black Studies professor Gerald Horne also called for reparations during his California Peace and Freedom Party run for U.S. Senator in 1992. Horne and other African American academics echoed the demand for reparations raised in May 1991 by John Hope Franklin, the dean of U.S. Black historians. For years Dr. David Swinton, economist and Black college president, has made reparations the centerpiece of his analysis.

Though the initiative has been snubbed by his white colleagues, Democratic as well as Republican, U.S. Rep. John Conyers from Michigan has drafted a reparations bill for the House of Representatives. The bill calls on the U.S. government to at long last formally acknowledge its liability for the crimes of chattel slavery and of legal and de facto segregation. The Congressman's proposal would provide "appropriate remedies" for racial and economic discrimination against Black Americans. Rev. Alfred Sharpton's *Black Agenda* demands $6.6 billion in reparations over ten years. On 5 June 1993 Jesse Jackson too weighed in on the side of reparations, as did such African-Canadian defenders of reparations as "A Medium Against the Debt" (AMAD) from north of the border. The National Coalition of Black Reparations Associations (N'COBRA) sharpened its initiatives and strategies in November 1994. A leading spokesman for the Coalition is Ronald Walters, chairman of the Political Science Department at Howard University.

By 1994 more than 20,000 Afro-American citizens had rallied to the cause of reparations and filed tax rebate claims to the IRS. They cited the hidden "Black tax" of racial discrimination as the basis for their claim, to which they put a dollar value. No surprise, the racists at IRS treated the claims as "frivolous."

There is much similar agitation outside North America. In 1987 a formal demand for reparations was submitted by African Brazilians to their country's Constituent Assembly. A world Conference on Reparations to Africans and Africans in the Diaspora met in Lagos, Nigeria, in December 1990. Two of Nigeria's leading statesmen— General Ibrahim Babangida and Moshood Abiola—bitter political enemies on nearly every other issue—made public statements in 1991 and 1992 indicating agreement on the right of Africans to reparations. In January 1992 OAU Secretary General Salim A. Salim endorsed the idea at OAU headquarters in Addis Ababa. Twelve months later, the First Pan-African Congress on Reparations brought together in Nigeria Black members of the British parliament and representatives from OAU, NAACP, SCLC, the Reparations Movement of Brazil, the Reparations Committee of Jamaica, and the U.S. Congressional Black Caucus. As indicated in the preceding chapter, Pan-Africans of all stripes and from all countries are enthusiastic about the reparations campaign. A confab in Abuja, Nigeria, on 27-28 April 1993, insisted that monetary reparations are not the only form of restitution required. Psychological and cultural amends must also be made.

*

The fundamental validation of the claim to reparations of African-Americans and every other Black person in the western hemisphere, lies in the Atlantic slave trade and chattel slavery. The enslavement imposed on our ancestors by white civilization entitles us to compensation. We are aware that the alleged slave "trade" was not a trade. It was anything but. It was the biggest and most successful robbery, human abduction and genocide in history. Africa got nothing worthwhile or healthy for its lost children whose labor was indispensable for the plantations and mines which were for such a long time the unique source of extracting the great wealth of vast regions of the Americas. This history of grossly unequal "exchange" has left Black Africa and Diasporan Blacks the chief *creditors* of the white world. It would denude the United States of most of its ill-gotten wealth were it ever to repay Africa even a fraction of the debt, let alone the settlement due to this country's African-descended citizens. "An integrated cup of coffee is not sufficient pay for 400 years of slave labor," Malcolm X observed caustically. Today's fighters for Black emancipation will not be fobbed off with the establishment of modern Haitis. We should no longer permit outselves to be cheated with calming-down schemes which inevitably end where they began—in poverty and degradation. We are not the hoodwinked Haitians of 1804. We know better than to be satisfied with mere legal emancipation, even when accompanied with the sham "independence" of statehood. We reject any new form of recolonizing the Third World, disguised as "international cooperation without recrimination" (*read:* without reparations). Equally we reject any "neo-modernization" approach that is Eurocentric.

*

Ours are ancient demands, as old as the river of Black protest. David Walker's *Appeal* did more than just hint at our right to reparations. That was as far back as 1829. The demand for compensation for wages unpaid to slaves is as old as Black America itself. Insistence that deficits caused by post-slavery discrimination be made up began the day chattel slavery ended. Today AMAD wants African Canadians to write letters to individuals and institutions in North America and overseas, asking them to turn the screw on Europe and the United States to pay reparations for slavery, slave labor, and colonialism. As part of the atonement, Third World debts and IMF and World Bank-imposed Structural Adjustment Programs should be cancelled.

Thanks in part to the support of the Congressional Black Caucus, Congress passed a law to provide some reparations to thousands of Japanese-Americans, interned illegally and unconstitutionally during World War II, many of whom lived in California. African American spokesmen as well as the OAU say that reparations from the major European powers and the United States must be paid to continental as well as Diasporan Africans because of the slave trade and slavery. Descendants of African slaves who helped make this country what it is today deserve reparations, particularly since the U.S. has become the world's preeminent industrial power. Compensation is owed also to the African continent whose underdevelopment in no small part can be laid to the ravages of the slave trade.

A few years ago the OAU Secretary General held talks on the issue with a high level Nigerian delegation. The two sides emphasized the need to encourage scientific research to support the claims advanced. A group of eminent Africans and people of African ancestry is being organized to establish the extent of Africa's exploitation through slavery and colonialism and to fix the legal liability of the perpetrators. Suing the U.S. government in 1994 for $2 million in slavery reparations, one Black plaintiff cited the kidnapping of his ancestors from Africa, their enslavement and forced labor, the breakup of their families and other wrongs. He demanded a formal apology and "compensation for forced, ancestral indoctrination into a foreign society."

We are making headway in calculating the dollar costs of discrimination. As of 1987 wage inequality, according to the Urban League, along with discriminatory transfer policies (i.e. unemployment insurance, medicare, medicaid, welfare payments, etc.) and other racist differentials was costing each Black man, woman and child in the U.S. an average $5,566.78, or a total of $151.9 billion in the aggregate in that year. David Swinton calculated the total 1987 cost to the Black community of *wage* inequality alone to be

$87.7 billion, a mind-boggling $1.5 trillion for the whole 1980s (Swinton, 1990: 40). These totals measure the dimensions of merely present-day, ongoing racial discrimination, without including amounts owing from past enslavement and discrimination going back three centuries, not to mention their accrued interests.

"Downsizing," leading to plant shutdowns, job speedups, job export, recession, and redundancy—"New World Order" maladies—have made certain white (and Japanese) corporations think they can now finally manage permanently without Black labor. And as ever, "last hired, first fired" remains the rule in the United States and Canada.

Given these circumstances, not only are reparations doubly necessary, they are, in Swinton's judgement, the sole viable option to bring an end once and for all to racial inequality. Otherwise, as long as the current economic system is in place, racist discrimination will continue costing minorities annually more than the entire huge 1990 military budget (i.e., before post–Cold War defense reductions cut in). By the early 1990s, losses sustained by African Americans due to racial discrimination were running in excess of $216 billion each year. The total was much higher if one included the losses in transfer payments caused by census undercounting, the higher prices our people are forced to pay for goods and services, and the costs of racist oppression to Native Americans.

*

WELFARE FOR WHITE FOLK

There is no denying that some whites are incensed at the idea of reparations for Black people and there are timid African Americans who fear that indemnification for our sufferings would only further poison the atmosphere between Blacks and whites. Consideration needs to be given to the thousands of Black social workers who fear the kind of reparations program that would dismantle the welfare system as we know it. Would their jobs vanish were reparations in the form of a federally guaranteed income for African Americans put in place? The Nation of Islam would postpone the demand for reparations until such time as when the economy has healed, thus it does not like the Conyers reparations bill, claiming it fails to foster independent nationhood for U.S. Blacks. Confused members of the Black community see a contradiction between affirmative action and reparations and think we must be satisfied with either one or the other, preferably affirma-

tive action. Black conservatives oppose both reparations and affirmative action. This gang rejects reparations as a one-shot opportunity lost forever when we did not get forty acres and a mule at the close
of the Civil War. They slander affirmative action as humiliating to
Buppies.

Black conservative barkings are a toothless irritation; white resistance to reparations is a serious matter. Grassroots racist emotionalism says that Afro-Americans should not receive reparations
because one's ancestry should not give one rights ... because Black
slavery and World War II which provided the context for Jewish and
Japanese-American reparations were somehow "two different situations"... because Jews qualify as whites and there is less white
antipathy against Asians than against Blacks... because the law compensating the Nisei has already been enacted and it is okay to compensate Jews since the money is paid by Germans far away over in
Europe... because reparations for Blacks would be much more
expensive... because slavery happened "long ago" and the Jewish
holocaust and Japanese internment more recently... and finally
because, as contended by the likes of Charles Murray, a white Jew,
Blacks being a genetically inferior lower order of humanity condemned by Nature never to improve, any remedial action is a waste
of money and effort. Less emotional hypocrites maintain that financial reparations are not the right way to make up for past wrongs
because the effort "to treat each other equally and as human beings"
will only be soured by recriminations and payments to some but not
all members of society; hence, they recommend, "let bygones by
bygones." For instance, Jewish delegates at a Black-Jewish workshop
meeting in New York in the aftermath of the 1991 disturbances in
Crown Heights insisted that Jews will never support Blacks on the
issues of affirmative action and reparations.

*

An objective reading of history would reveal a long-term white commitment to the preservation of racial inequality in economic life, for
it underpins the whole system of political, cultural and psycho-social
white supremacy. Economic inequality glues white society together
and holds many benefits for many white individuals. Consequently
white resistance to reparations for Blacks goes hand in hand with
enthusaism for the ancient system of welfare for whites.

In fact, throughout most of history the proper generic name for "welfare" in America should have been *transfer payments to whites*, many of the recipients being anything but poor. In the propaganda war over reparations it furthers our claims to recall the free grants the federal government has made to whites throughout the nineteenth and twentieth centuries. Largesse from resources stolen from American Indian tribes or from tax revenues, including taxes and values appropriated from the toil of African Americans. In this context Black reparations would merely be a long-delayed effort to reach a norm long since established by government practice on behalf of whites. From the Homestead Act (1862) during the Civil War on into the first years of the twentieth century, the federal government made handsome concessions of licenses, grants, and franchises to whites—native-born citizens as well as those just off the boat! Whites in America were the first to freeload off the government. The original "handouts" and their value consequences are worth hundreds of billions of dollars today and are still owned by the descendants of the original grantees. Some of the descendants are direct blood offspring, others are financial offshoots. The predecessors of today's wealthiest elite received huge government grants and privileges allocated free of charge under strict racist handouts-for-whites-only policies. Much of this government largesse for white persons came during the fifty years following Reconstruction. While they were pocketing handouts, our ancestors were locked mostly in the Jim Crow South, occupied cleaning up after white folks, sharecropping, and doing time as convict lease laborers—farm, mine and domestic labor. The early "Robber Barons"—the Carnegies, Mellons, Rockefellers, Fords, etc.—fed from the pork barrel of government dole, getting real estate, utility, and railroad franchises, mineral rights and broadcast licenses.

The government did much for ordinary whites too. Particularly after the Second World War poor whites benefited from a public housing program and national mortgate system which encouraged home ownership among ordinary white families. Tax incentives, exemptions, and preferences boosted white middle class consumption. Meanwhile, the very same lending institutions were redlining Black neighborhoods, denying mortgage money. The public housing program which spurred single-family home ownership in white suburbs built the bleak projects casting in concrete the residential segregation we find today.

In comparison to the charity showered on white Americans, our demand for reparations seems modest, a diffident request for a second wave of government bounty to repair the injustice which created the yawning gap between Blacks and whites. The disparity in wealth is the result of deliberate government intervention inspired by racial prejudice. It did not come about as the result of some "color blind" *laissez-faire*, functioning automatically in a free market. African Americans are demanding support and subsidies from a national government which a century ago laid the foundation for the present mega-billionaires, all of whom are white.

The briefest survey of federal transfer payments from the 1930s through the 1980s refutes the racist propaganda which casts Black folk as the "welfare loafers." New Deal administrators discriminated racially throughout the 1930s in the allocation of relief and WPA jobs and payments. INRA-NRA sectional wage differentials favored whites. The decline in the relative level of minimum wages that has ruled since 1968 has hit Blacks hardest. By the time the Reagan administration took office, for every one dollar that whites received in transfer payments on a per capita basis, Blacks were granted only 81 cents. Yet more than one-third of all Afro-Americans are poor, as against only 12 percent of all whites. Throughout the 1980s poor white people continued to get more "welfare" in America than poor Black people, and "welfare for the rich" continued to pour on affluent whites in the form of massive subsidies and contracts which exceeded the total of all transfer payments to needy persons. A glance at unemployment insurance right now reveals an unemployed Black worker typically getting half as much compensation as an unemployed white worker. Poor Blacks in the 1990s are getting only one-half to two-thirds as much as poor whites in welfare payments. The bailout of the corrupt Savings and Loan industry (S&L) amounts to a giveaway of $190 billion in public revenues. S&L compensation goes overhelmingly to affluent whites.

There is one issue on which both Black liberals and conservatives agree. Both pray that when a "fortunate tenth" of the Black community manages by hook or by crook to become rich as Midas or Rockefeller, white prejudice against people of African blood will fade. The expectation that wealth in the hands of a select group of Black personages—our Bill Cosbys and Oprah Winfreys—will eradicate white bigotry is an illusion. It is an illusion nourished in part by the by-now familiar spectacle of white corporate bosses bowing and scraping to Japanese moguls. For Japanese financiers now top the international money hierarchy.

Unfortunately there is no evidence that even were the present handful of rich Black celebrities to become a significant number, that would influence whites as a group to abandon their opinion of Black people as being economic failures and poverty-stricken dregs; and not merely because whites would continue to be served the media images of Africa as a famine-ridden backwater. Prejudice would survive for the simple reason that despite the proliferation of wealthy Black celebrities, the vast majority of our people would remain poor, for Black poverty is inherent in the selection principle which governs the racist political economy that is the American way of life. That is why reparations is the only viable alternative, the only reformist project likely to break the ice. We do not have at our disposal an independent economy like the Japanese have, and we have no gigantic high-tech-generated trade surpluses to rub in Uncle Sam's face. White racial hostility is unlikely to yield to the argument that the success of wealthy Black celebrities, or business tycoons (like the deceased Reginald Lewis), or top military brass, or influential polititicians refutes the stereotype of Black *racial* inferiority. Racism among the white public is a lot stickier than that and the American market economy itself has inherent limits on the distribution of wealth among minorities. The number of Blacks at the top is strictly limited, financially as well as politically. The historical evolution of racist capitalism allows only a select few Blacks to pass the turnstiles of financial dominion in any one slice of time. Nothing has yet subverted the common racist belief that Black people are born to labor, while whites are born to employ Blacks and enjoy the fruits of our labor.

At most, the common notion has modified to the belief that while the vast majority of African Americans are destined to work for whites, Nature, in her wisdom, also provides a social pressure reliever in the guise of a small number of lucky or talented Blacks who are rewarded with wealth. The group is useful to the system, for it makes the status quo appear fair, "color-blind," and respectful of merit. The rest of us are to remain trapped, as Charles Murray and Richard Herrnstein see it, in a low-IQ ghetto of irresponsibility and poverty.

An extrapolation of the rate of development which has prevailed over the last one hundred years shows that not until about the year 2480 would American Blacks catch up with whites in percentage wealth holdings in personal property, bank accounts, and homeownership. Actually this projection makes the situation seem less terrible than it really is, since it does not factor in the key element of possession of production assets. It focuses solely on "overall" wealth holdings, highlighting private homes, automobiles, and savings accounts where present disparities are less than the gap in capital ownership. For us merely to approximate white equity holdings would take about 500 years at the current rate of progression. And that does not address the crucial issues of Black holdings of dividends and interest income, of stocks, mutual funds, government bonds, and deposit certificates. Nor does it deal with the prospect of African American ownership of major means of production—the real delights of capitalism! So instead of the year 2480 as catch-up date, without reparations we will have to wait through several thousand years of "normal" "organic" economic development to finally arrive at parity with the white folks with whom we share this country.

Obviously we must find another way as a people to obtain the resources to acquire equivalent ownership of capital and power. "The possibility of obtaining the required surpluses through internal community sacrifice is nil in the absence of compelling political power," observes David Swinton (Swinton 1991:75).

*

In one estimation, by no means overblown, between 1619 and 1865, slaves just in the United States were forced to perform 222,505,049 man-hours of unpaid wages. The claim for reimbursement for those wages (arrears with interest) devolves on us their descendants, to whom the debt is now owing. Larry Neal, Illinois professor of economics, reckoned that the 1983 value of the slave labor expropriated between 1620 and 1865 from Black Americans ranged from $96.3 billion to $9.7 trillion, depending on whether a 3 percent or a 6 percent rate of interest is applied. Neal is the author of a book on *The Rise of Financial Capitalism* (1990). James Marchetti of Rutgers University came up with a lower figure. He figured the 1983 value of slave labor performed from 1790 to 1860 at between $2.1 trillion and $4.7 trillion. Updating the ripoff to the 20th century, Richard America and other scholars in a recent anthology entitled *The Wealth of Races: The Present Value of Benefits from Past Injustices* (1990) set the white benefits from labor market discrimination against Blacks from 1929 to 1969 (a short 40 years) at $689 billion in 1972 prices, compounded at an interest rate of 6 percent per annum. Adjusted for inflation, the 1983 total came to $16.3 trillion. In view of these and similar calculations, David Swinton concludes that it would take more than the entire wealth of the whole United States to compensate Black folk fully. In order merely to attain an equality that would give us parity per capita, it will be necessary to shift major capital stock to Blacks. Ownership of major means of production would be the only way to do justice to the magnitude of reparations owing to African Americans (Farley and Allen 1987).

Yet and all, to this point in time the claims being submitted are strikingly modest. One suggestion calls for the small sum of $25 billion. That is like targeting for the enrichment of our sorely tried people no more than what it takes to develop a single stealth bomber—a tiny fraction of the equivalent of the wealth our foreparents were forced to create for the white people of this country. A similar underestimation burdens Professor Everett Green's proposal that payment of the debt to African Americans for four centuries of slavery and oppression would run into hundreds of thousands of dollars per capita. However, there is much to recommend his suggestion, made while speaking in Peekskill, New York, that all qualified Black youth be funded for the cost of tuition, room, and board and other family responsibilities to enable them to complete a college education. That would be a start. Al Sharpton"s *Black Agenda* includes a fiscally-restrained request for $6.6 billion in reparations from the federal government every year over ten years. Jesse Jackson has voiced the need for "some" reparations to compensate for over 350 years of rape, slavery, and exploitation, saying that "if the U.S. could dole out billions to European countries and Japan, it could pay reparations to its Black citizens."

In contrast to such modest claims, the African National Reparations Organization, for one example, is bolder and closer to the mark. It has figured a *minimum* of $4.1 trillion for unpaid labor alone owing just to Black people born within the borders of the United States. This does not account for sums owing to Blacks in the Caribbean and Latin America, most of them in Brazil. Nor does it account for Africa and its claims for damages from colonialism.

*

FORMS OF REPARATIONS AND REAL EMPOWERMENT

The debate which sets affirmative action off against reparations has marred real understanding of the issue. I oppose the "narrow construction" of reparations as a mutually exclusive *alternative* to affirmative action. Narrow constructionists view affirmative action as programs based on equal opportunity, along with regulations to moderate and govern the behavior of the corporate elite who own disproportionate shares of the economy. The narrow constructionists fear that if Black people are to have meaningful affirmative action we must do without reparations. Why? One does not exclude the other. On the contrary, I envisage large scale reparations programs transferring the capital to fuel Black corporate ownership, combined with comprehensive affirmative action, parity, minority set-asides, as well as race-conscious quotas. There is no contradiction; one is not the negation of the other. All come under the single umbrella of rectification of past and present racial wrongs.

Black reparations may even eventually come to appeal to Rightwingers, because they would expect a Black corporate-owning class to become faithful center-right Republican voters and financial contributors to Republican Party election campaigns. Support from a full-blown class of Black capitalists would also remove much of the blatant racist taint which besmirches right-wing Republican discourse nowadays. A reparations solution will grow more attractive to conservatives, furthermore, once the now-dampened challenge to the capitalist system as such revives internationally. It is only a matter of time before the challenge is renewed globally, making the defenders of capitalism once again sensitive to criticism and willing to clean up their racial face.

Reparations should appeal to old-line Leftists as well, because compensation would finally remove that ancient bugbear of the Left, i.e. the economic disparity that leftists are convinced has always "split" the poor and the workers along color lines, weakening the liberal-left appeal nationally. John Hope Franklin said, "If we can spend a billion dollars a day on what has been rather theatrically described as Operation Desert Storm, we can spend a billion dollars a month to rebuild our inner cities, to repair our dilapidated infrastructure, that would provide employment for many thousands, and spend whatever is necessary to save a generation of Black males....from the scourge of drugs, disease, despair and crime."

Properly understood, reparations for Blacks should be broadly construed as encompassing affirmative action, employment equity, race-conscious quotas, parity, minority set-asides, equality of results, free, state-of-the-art health care and, above all, legislated and government-administered remittances of assets and monies. A reparations program might also include a family income plan (FIP). Given political reality, however, this benefit would have to extend to the entire citizenry. It would be politically inexpedient to confine it to African Americans. A national FIP would state that when a family income fell below a certain dollar value, the federal government would immediately step in and provide payments from public revenues to make up the shortfall, bringing the family income up to a prescribed national, regional or state minimum. Since a much larger proportion of Black families fall below the poverty line, a disproportionate benefit from this program would accrue to Black people. Moreover, since racism condemns Black families to annual incomes barely half that of white families, Afro-Americans should be granted mortgage loans at half the going interest rate. The shortfall would be subsidized from the federal budget.

In order to achieve all this we require as a minimum a mass political campaign in favor of reparations encompassing all the main components of the Black community. In order to make reimbursement for the past five hundred years of plunder and spoil a recognized principle of international diplomacy—enshrined in United Nations policy—we need mobilize the support not just of Canadian Blacks, but as well of Black people in the Caribbean, in Brazil, and throughout Spanish-speaking South and Central America. Together, the Africans of the Americas must march arm-in-arm with Africans in the continent, fighting for indemnification. There is no other way in the United States to avoid the social abyss, neither for Blacks nor whites. Booker T. Washington's constantly recycled doctrines of hard work and accommodation simply have not fulfilled dreams of autonomous community development. Self-improvement through education and talent raises the odd individual, but leaves the mass in the mire. White-sponsored Black conservatives carve lucrative careers for themselves, but merely replay the age-old role of house nigger–Uncle Tom sellout. Civil Right–vehicled integration is a task never accomplished, having to be redone each new day. Legions of white "experts" blaming the victims have not reduced the number of Black victims by even one, and have not succeeded in concealing white responsibility for the oppression.

Social betterment aims that would be fostered by reparations include union-protected employment with equal pay, working conditions and fringe entitlements, as well as real social equality that is not merely formal-public but informal-private too. Reparations would promote decent, factually non-segregated residential patterns and Black ownership of profitable businesses. Respect, recognition, and funding for core Black culture would finally become real. At long last we would possess the independent financial means to back our demand for government-enforced freedom from racist violence, abuse, and insult.

A strategy to counter the "downsizing" which has led to plant shutdowns and job speedups requiring fewer workers to be more productive, would have a crucial place in comprehensive reparations. "Last hired, first fired" could be knocked down by giving priority to Afro-Americans in retraining programs, by putting us at the top of the list for company recalls and new hirings and by raising Black wages to the level of white employees. Many other measures are also conceivable. For example, a lump sum payment to Black America as a whole to spark economic "takeoff" has been suggested. Another option would channel all funds to housing, education, and job skills, giving priority to the young as the best bet for the future. Investment of the reparations payments in profit-yielding assets, perhaps with the dividends allocated annually on a per capita or per household basis, is usually lauded as being superior to and likely to yield better results than a per capita cash payment to each individual African American.

Where is the money to come from? Fiscal conservatives are forever crying the blues about how cash-strapped and deficit-ridden government budgets are. Reparations activists are not taken in, however. There are definite ideas about the sources of funds to pay for reparations. For instance, rather than continue to pour the so-called "peace dividend" down the maw of budgetary deficit reduction, at least $200 billion could be transferred from military spending to finance the initial stages of the reparations program. After all, the U.S. deficit ballooned after Ronald Reagan launched the biggest military-spending binge in peacetime American history. Another $300 billion can be derived from postponing interest payments on the "national" debt. Servicing bonds held by rich whites is a massive liability drain on public revenues. The government increases already large deficits just to pay the interest charges on the debt. It would further help were Congress to increase the rate of income tax on banking profits as well as on private incomes over, say, $250,000. By now everyone should know that less taxation of persons at the upper end of the income scale does *not* yield more government revenue through expanded economic activity. Closure of notorious loopholes such as tax abatement gifts to real estate speculators would yield considerable revenue. Similar reductions and transfers in Canada would free up funds in that country to indemnify Aboriginal Canadians and extend equity to African Canadians and other people of color. The sums saved would go to achieve the primary goal of the initial stages of reparations— the elimination of the shameful poverty which scourges the lives of between one-third and one-half of all African Americans. As far as overcoming the racial gap in ownership of profit-yielding assets, massive capital infusions and transfers will be required, for, in a racist political economy, market forces, as David Swinton was quoted, "would tend to perpetuate and even exacerbate racial gaps in ownership once they have been established" (*New York Amsterdam News*, 28 March 1992) as the legacy of slavery and discrimination.

*

Personally I foresee an epochal recasting of American social life extending over decades. Without involving any immediately apparent system-threatening changes in the basic market economy, federal government-sponsored indemnification would be tailored to close the racial gap of ownership in means of production and other key resource assets. A major land reform is required to establish our people's rights to abodes and landlord privileges. These would come in the form of government-awarded franchises. I am talking about a kind of twenty-first century homestead law for Blacks (plus Native Americans and Chicanos) comparable to the nineteenth century Homestead Act for white settlers. But since American Blacks are townsfolk nowadays, primarily big city inhabitants, land reform must not focus on farm land, but instead on real estate containing mineral deposits and precious metals, and on choice acreage in the suburbs and exurbs. And we most assuredly will not be content with desolate stretches in the inner city, the ownership of which many whites would be only too happy to see us satisfied with. Included must be ownership of large office buildings in choice downtown locations. It is essential that federal, state, county, and municipal tax authorities stimulate wealth formation among Black citizens under the headings of tax deduction, incentives, subsidies and abatements, including enactment of Rep. Albert Wynn's *Small Business Lending*

Disclosure Act (H.R. 918), designed to shield minority-owned businesses from discrimination by bankers. Federal agencies must finance purchase by Black persons of major segments of the nation's primary means of production, from metallurgy to chemicals, from service industries to high-tech electronics, from aircraft to computers. Black people would thereby finally take a slice of the surplus value pie of North American capitalism. That is the only kind of "economic base" which will permit us to influence the State apparatus (the supreme socio-economic tool in human affairs). As David Swinton puts it: "Only when Blacks own enough to be equal participants in the nation's economy will they be able to ensure their own prosperity and equality. If Clinton-Gore do not choose to call such policies reparations, that is fine..." (Swinton 1993:199).

How would we measure the progress of reform? The key standards of success of capital-transfer to create racial parity in ownership would be the capacity of Black-owned business in, say, two generations (i.e., 50 to 60 years) to provide employment to around 15 to 20 percent of the total North American Black labor force. And to maintain that level year-in, year-out. The remaining 80 percent of gainfully employed Blacks would seek and hold jobs in white-owned enterprises. Besides creating a viable Black capitalism, the main result would be to provide an *employment alternative* sheltered from the indignities of racism for a significant minority of Black workers. The opportunity for life-long employment for several million African Americans in major enterprises owned and managed by fellow Blacks would severely reduce corporate capital's ability to continue the present racist practice of marginalizing inner-city Black males. As double-digit unemployment would shrink in our community, it would prove more difficult for white corporate decision makers to assign Blacks disproportionately to labor's reserve army of unemployed. Lastly, we might finally even begin to see emerge concrete preconditions for the much-talked-about but never-achieved *"integration"* of Blacks and whites, at least in economic affairs. The opportunity for 20 percent of the Black labor force to find jobs in Black enterprises would be a mighty bargaining weapon for the remaining 80 percent employed by white owners. Deracialization of the economy would sound the deathknell for white supremacy which has always relied on its monopoly of economic control to maintain its sway over our conquered and captive people. Nullification of white skin privilege in job placement would, in turn, open the door for society to move on to the next stage—the prospect of completely different socio-economic arrangements designed to meet the human needs of everyone.

We must have a care, however, that our demand for reparations not be seized upon and mistranslated by subtle, sophisticated racists intent on updating the white man's alleged *noblesse oblige* obligation. We must guard against allowing our just claims to become a twenty-first century edition of the old "white man's burden" doctrine. I can just imagine liberals, missionaries and Rudyard Kipling-minded anthropologists ganging up with "conscience-stricken" racial theorists to give our demand for restitution exactly that coloration. Therefore it is crucial that control over any future indemnifications must rest completely and unconditionally with the Black community itself. Reparations payments must be free of white tutelage in countries where Blacks are a minority. In the case of the African states, administration of payments must rest with the local governments and not with any white international "aid" agency. "Shared control" schemes, or "power-sharing" compromises with so-called "socially responsive" white corporate pundits, "sympathetic" governments or liberal politicos would only be a rerun of the McGeorge Bundys of the 1960s and the Daniel Moynihans of the 1970s and 1980s. We have had enough of that.

There is a tight bond between independent third-party politics and reparations. The latter is very unlikely to ever occur without the former. We will require an independent Black political party to set the general line, to act as claimant on our behalf, as negotiator and administrator of reparations. What other force would have the capacity and clout to supervise the transfer of high-tech information and wealth to our people, the most urbanized people in North America? Independent politics is already the coming thing in Black America. Sentiment in its favor is surging in Black communities all across the country, fueled if by nothing else than by disillusionment with the Democrats and hostility towards the Republicans as a white folks' lobby. Such a party would have to be all-inclusive. It would have to be home to reformers and revolutionaries, home to separatists and integrationists, nationalists and cultural assimilationists, home equally to Muslims and Christians, Afrocentrists and adherents of "mainstream" education. The only common denominators among supporters would need be African American identity and devotion to the principles of parity, empowerment and anti-racism.

435

Through little fault of its own, Black capitalism has not performed well for us, historically. African American entrepreneurs are often compared unfavorably with Jewish entrepreneurs. Yet it was racial discrimination that stopped Black businessmen from accumulating capital like the mountains heaped up by their Jewish counterparts. From 1969 to 1977 America witnessed a public relations campaign lauding Black capitalism. The campaign was a fraud and the economic outcome was bleak. Tokenism in executive positions, government employment and educational establishments was never anything more than a manoeuver or stratagem designed to lull discontent. Given this history, we must insist on decision-making power over any future compensation program, as well as over all derivative political, educational, or cultural projects which spin off the deployment of reparation funds and initiatives. The danger will always be present that white helpmeets would do as they have done in the past and channel efforts to non-Black purposes. The only form of white "positive intervention" acceptable will be the payment of reparations owed as partial reimbursement for centuries of forced capital-creation by Black labor for the benefit of white exploiters.

Reparations are a demand for the long haul, to be retained and repeated tirelessly in the confidence that long range historical tendencies will eventually swing the political pendulum our way. It is by far both the most rational and the most hopeful of the options available to us. Frances Cress-Welsing's theory of color confrontation claims, for example, that it is futile to beg white folks to cease racism and instead embrace affirmative action to foster the uplift of their Black fellow citizens. However, if we cannot extract reparations through militant struggle (not begging), then it is "game over" anyway. She is right that a white racist war is being waged against Black folk. But should we fail to win reparations, we will have lost the war forever, there will be nothing left for North American Blacks but gradual extinction in the course of the next century or two. Cress-Welsing suggests as a survival strategy a program of separate development, i.e., self-help, self-respect, and rigid voluntary birth control (Black families limited to two children only). Due to the lack of any political economy in her theory of color confrontation, she fails to realize, in my opinion, that there is at least as much chance for a mass sustained struggle for reparations to succeed, as there is for separate development, and the reparations payoff promises to be much richer.

436

•

We African Americans are not the only ones after reparations. In Lagos, Nigeria, a World Conference on Reparations to Africans and Africans in the Diaspora met in December 1990. Low-income Africa's foreign debts are equivalent to 100 percent of its annual gross product and 500 percent of its exports. Some dozen and more African countries are poorer today in per capita terms than they were when they won independence during the 1960s and 1970s. For the continent, the program of reparations that seems to offer the most promise focuses on debt cancellation and on diplomatically-negotiated indemnity payments to individual African governments from the former slave trading Western governments. The details, as well as the strategy for investment of the funds received, will best be left to an overall African organization like a thoroughly reformed OAU. Somehow and some way the separate African states must some day band together to "form a more perfect union." The enigma of South Africa's economic leadership role in a future reparations Africa haunts Black thinkers' minds, even as that country enters its post-apartheid dawn. The development strategies implemented by South Africans over the next few decades will be very instructive for all the other Black states of Africa.

A group of leading Africans have planned a campaign to make Western nations live up to their historical responsibilities for centuries of slavery and colonial exploitation. The lead has been taken by the Group of Eminent Persons, an independent commission on reparations established in 1990. Stressing that the forced impoverishment of their continent is an issue too bulky to stay covered under the rug of disregard, the 1990 Lagos gathering saw the demand for cancellation of Africa's huge foreign debt merely as a first step. Prominent Africans have taken to calling upon Western governments to reorganize their foreign priorities. They are enraged that NATO investors are hell bent on forgetting Africa in favor of Eastern Europe, now that Africans are no longer needed to support Western Cold War efforts.

The demand for indemnification from the Western countries is gaining momentum in international forums. Africans hold meetings to work out the ways and means to implement compensation from the industrialized countries in Europe and the Americas for the damages and losses incurred by their actions. The issue keeps coming up at each general session of the United Nations. Diplomacy is being used to direct the world's attention at compensating the Black continent for the forced loss of opportunities which barred it from economic development. Political independence did not dissolve the financial yoke of neocolonialism or the slavery legacy. Africa insists that it be helped over the hump by means of programs similar to the Marshall Plan which rebuilt Europe following the Second World War. Otherwise the development gap with the West will widen inevitably, threatening humanity with war and disasters on unprecedented scales. African statesmen demand that the West pay the slaves' wages for work spanning five centuries. As the white Western world celebrated 1992 as the fifth centennial of the alleged "discovery" of America, international organizations condemned the event as the beginning of the worst possible kind of slavery. And African demands rely heavily on recent historical precedents in which Germany was compelled to pay war reparations following both world wars and in which Jews were deemed entitled to compensation for damages and casualties inflicted by the Nazis.

Bringing to bear its weight as one of the most advanced countries—and the most densely populated country—in Africa, Nigeria as been in the forefront of the indemnification movement. Nigerians base their claim on the massive forced "export" of slaves along their "Slave Coast" littoral which for centuries fueled Western development. Chief Moshood Kashimawo Abiola, media tycoon and contestant for Nigeria's presidency, wants white people in Europe, America, and the Arab Middle East to pay the African continent for the damage done to it during that slave trade. In 1992 Nigerians upped the urgency, putting reparations near the top of the agenda at the annual meeting of the Organization of African Unity. Prodded by the Nigerian efforts, OAU leaders vowed to pursue the matter at the United Nations. The reparations issue has been a hot potato in Nigeria since at least 1977. Nigerians flayed the hypocrisy of the UN resolution which backed the payment of reparations by Iraq to Kuwait but said nothing about the bill owing for the rape of Black Africa. A full Pan-African Congress on Reparations took place (1992). At a five-day summit in Gabon in 1993, more than 1,000 African American delegates joined 3,500 African participants in asking for debt relief for African nations, groaning under a foreign debt of upwards of $255 billion. Stringent economic austerity measures imposed by the World Bank and IMF have worsened the situation. The summiters agreed that the descendants of the millions of

Africans sold into bondage in North and South America, the Caribbean, and Europe, have a right to reparations. In 1994 a United Nations Special Rapporteur was given a mandate to document continuing anti-Black racism across the United States. The UN General Assembly promised to review the compiled testimony.

Among the demands now being voiced by Brazilian Blacks is one calling for a constitution-rooted principle of equality that would sanction restitution for past wrongs. They want a law enshrining compensatory measures designed to give preference to Black citizens in order to guarantee their equal participation in and access to employment, education, health care, and other social rights. To protect against backsliding, the teaching of Brazilian history would have to be reformulated at all educational levels.

*

The cry for reparations on both sides of the Atlantic represents two sides of a single coin, as it were. One side of the coin is white aggression, 550 years of Caucasian assault on the peoples and the continent of Africa. The other side of the coin is history's greatest Diaspora, the scattering of Blacks to live lives of exile outside Mother Africa in communities born of suffering. The assault which began on Africa's west coast and continued through the Middle Passage has culminated in a western hemisphere wracked from Edmonton to Buenos Aires with Black-white racial discord. Both the Diaspora and the continent have irrefutable claims to reparations. However, the forms of indemnification, its extent and context differ noticeably as between the Diaspora and the continent. To some extent these divergent concerns are reflected in the different tone and tack taken by today's Global Pan-Africanists as compared with Diasporic Pan-Africanists.

Chapter 21

OUR LEADERS AND OUR ALLIES

et us pose a question: How should we as a people meet the challenge we face? We would be fools were we to believe that the answer is in any way a simple one—or that there can be any *single* response. Anything this complex and this threatening requires compound solutions.

*

First off, we cannot duck the issue of leadership. Just who are our preeminent leaders? Who have been the ones who have spoken for us, with or without our authorization?

For better or worse, our pacemakers have been drawn substantially from one and the same social source since Abolitionism: from the clergy and sundry other intellectuals. This is merely a fact of Afro-American life. DuBois' "talented tenth" is alive and well and still performing its long-standing function. I mean the collection of reverends, teachers, professors, journalists, doctors, dentists and lawyers, entrepreneurs and other workers-by-brain-more-than-by-hand. These personalities, along with their families, relatives, friends, and acquaintances, continue to serve up our elected officials, influential government appointees, senior police and military personnel, and political lobbyists. They have been doing so for generations. Weighed on the historical scale, they have served our public interests, in the full meaning of the term. Ever enlarging and flexible, the circle has never been closed. New blood is constantly rejuvenating our "talented tenth." Nevertheless, the leadership core is stable enough for its members to be identified and tagged.

The archetypal figure can be described as a technician of practical knowledge, one whose work entails garnering, comprehending, and generalizing concepts. Black folk have seen their leaders as prophets who transmit practical knowledge—knowledge of how to achieve well-being and freedom from racist oppression. They are the producers of our ideologies, i.e., the ideas and symbols of our liberation movement. The wisest have been creators of theory, a labor which compels the thinker to "get his head together," collect his thoughts, and translate vague urges and aspirations into concrete political programs.

But all has not been sweetness and light with our elite. For it is in the nature of things that the creation of theory and ideology be mainly individual, and it is more difficult for an individual than a collective to withstand the lures of domineering white civilization. Throughout the nation's history, most of our thinkers have lacked the independent finances that would have enabled them to avoid earning a living in white racist society. So when push came to shove, certain Black intellectuals did not serve their own people. Many of us can cite figures in the history of the "talented tenth" who catered mainly to white needs, at times even misusing their knowledge and talents to intimidate their racial brothers and sisters. We have observed accommodationists at the beck and call of Presidents, private foundations, and college trustees. Such persons' skills help the white Establishment, not the people in the inner-city. In this case, the Black intellectuals' conceptual knowledge and expert skills are turned in upon themselves.

Therein rests the dilemma. Not all who belong to the leadership corps do as they should. The political attitude of the Black elite towards the people as a whole has often been ambiguous and given to vacillation. Then and now, the irresolute desert the liberation movement, go into hibernation and become politically quiescent. Some seek refuge in artistic endeavor—art for art's sake—or immerse themselves in the chase for research grants and academic perks. We have seen "movement defectors" who, after much self-congratulation for "super-Blackness" and much talk of "revolutionary war" against Caucasians, sell out completely and hire on as shills for the established order.

On the eve of the Second World War, clergy, teachers, and managerial government employees were 9.6 percent, 36 percent and 0.7 percent, respectively, of the African American white-collar work force. A half-century later, the category of Blacks in managerial positions in government had ballooned to 11.6 percent, while the proportion of teachers had slipped to a little over a quarter of our white-collar workers. Until the demise of legal segregation, Afro-American professionals and business owners were restricted to their own people for customers and clients. Although now probably less than one percent of Black America's top socio-economic category, the clergy still today retains an extremely high profile in Black political life. Along with lawyers and judges (an equally small group), reverend ministers head our most prestigious Civil Rights organizations and sit in Congress. And the National Baptist Convention, USA, remains the single largest African American organization in the country, numbering eight million members and 36,000 churches in the early 1990s.

Unlike certain of their white counterparts, Black superstar entertainers have yet to parlay media notoriety into high political office. Although our high-profile athletes are beginning to milk commercial endorsement in a big way and push into the business arena once their playing days are over, only a handful seek elected political office. Top-rank athletes and entertainers fill the Black community's desire for symbolic display and vicarious gratification in a way roughly comparable to the role of royalty with the British public. They are a tiny group. The Michael Jordans and Michael Jacksons are our "kings," and their family tragedies and personal tribulations have as much bite among the Black public as the vagaries of the Queen and the royal family among the English. They are Black folks' version of pomp and pageantry.

*

LEADERSHIP STYLE

The predominant style of political leadership was set very early in Black America—defiant prophecy and messianic militancy, as distinct from the conciliatory strain later associated with B.T. Washington and the "Tuskegee Machine." David Walker was already evoking multi-faceted struggle in 1829. His concept of fighting on all political fronts, using any and all means in the interest of the people, extolled armed struggle as well as opinion-mobilizing united fronts composed of different social and racial elements. In 1843, Henry Highland Garnett, pioneering nationalist and intrepid fighter against slavery, exhorted Black people to "let our motto be Resistance! Resistance! Resistance!" A dozen years later Frederick Douglass, in an assessment that can also apply to twentieth century relations between Blacks and white liberals, wrote that no people that has solely depended on foreign aid or upon the "benevolent" efforts of those in any way identified with their oppressors, "ever stood forth in the attitude of freedom."

Douglass maintained this tone of leadership to the edge of oblivion, crying out on his death bed in 1895 to his people to "Agitate, Agitate, Agitate," and never renounce the quest for empowerment. Whatever the cost, an oppressed people must itself always take the leading part in the contest, he admonished, if it is to assert its humanity. He discoursed on white racist patronization of the Abolition movement. Douglass issued stern warning against relying on white initiative and leadership in Black causes.

The same note resounded down to the twentieth century. James Baldwin—prophet of like timber—eventually renounced dialogue with white Americans. "[T]hat hope is gone... There is no one to talk to; no one is listening" to the anguish and appeals of African Americans (*Globe and Mail*, 28 April 1983). His 1955 *Notes of a Native Son* had analyzed the psychological and social circumstances involved in a "Black man's love for whites." In fiery letters, *The Fire Next Time* gave white America just one last chance—it would either be rescued from its own self-destructive racist "insensitivity" or be engulfed. Years later, and that much wiser, it was clear to Baldwin that most whites had simply turned a deaf ear to "those petitions and marches and those kids during the Civil Rights movement." The bomb in the Sunday School in Birmingham had not meant a damn to them. Shoring up and disguising the status quo are what whites

444

do best. Baldwin's own career summed up the stressful odyssey of leading Afro-American intellectuals through the Civil Rights upheavals and their aftermath. Towards the end of his life he expressed the hope that his people would finally learn to "refuse to believe anything white Americans say." To Baldwin the prophet, those whom the gods would destroy, they first make racist.

Nevertheless, confrontation as the style of militant advocacy has always been paired with a tradition of very pragmatic proposals. Take for example the proposal for a "Marshall Plan" of assistance for urban (predominately Black) areas, first put forward in 1963 by the National Urban League. Whitney Young pleaded for Congressional enactment of a domestic program of economic and infrastructural recovery honed for the central cities. At the time there was little prospect for its adoption. In one form or another, the appeal is still with us today. Though its present prospect appears more bleak now than in 1963, the Congressional Black Caucus and Black mayors renew the call for a domestic Marshall Plan at each new legislative session. At its 1991 convention, the Urban League called for $50 billion of annual domestic funding. The measures would cover ten years, totalling $500 billion.

To make the proposal politically palatable to white lawmakers, John Jacob, then Urban League chief, claimed that a domestic investment plan would be racially-neutral, not a "social program" designed especially for Blacks and Native Americans. That same year the Urban League temporized concerning the Supreme Court nomination of Clarence Thomas, the meanest of Black conservatives. Failure to oppose the nomination seemed to indicate disarray and abdication of duties on the part of some of the old-line Civil Rights leadership.

Pragmatism has not been any kinder to the Rainbow Coalition. Since 1984 it has spun its political wheels. The failure of its *Stop the Violence* campaign to catch fire is an indication of the rut it is in. For years Ron Daniels was the most effective Rainbow organizer, and a chief lieutenant of Jesse Jackson. He now heads the Center for Constitutional Rights and chairs the Campaign for a New Tomorrow. His style of leadership combines progressive with conservative features. Cut the military budget in half, he urged in 1992, and divert the funds to a domestic Marshall Plan, to housing, education, and infrastructure construction—a progressive initiative. His call for a ban on all nuclear power stations in the country reflected "Green"-

445

style environmentalism, however, an issue that really does not speak to problems of environmental racism, the scourge of many Black communities. And to top it all, Daniels touted Gorbachev, of all people, as one of the "greatest men of the century."

Smarter Rainbow pragmatism is evident in Jesse Jackson's manoeuver for statehood for the District of Columbia that would not require a constitutional amendment. The Black majority in the nation's capital could become residents of a new state called "New Columbia," achieved through legislation with a simple majority in both houses of Congress and presidential backing. The Afro-American voter majority would guarantee for the foreseeable future a minimum of two Black senators in the Senate. The move would give the residents of the District of Columbia the budgetary autonomy and representation in Congress they are now denied and would be a real political boon for Black America as a whole. But what chance for enactment can such legislation have in a Congress dominated as now by right-wing Republicans and boll-weevil Democrats?

*

Pragmatic integrationists have always rubbed shoulders in the leadership corps with nationalists whose aims may be different, but whose style has been even more defiantly messianic.

Let us take several examples, beginning with the territorial separatism of the Republic of New Africa (RNA) and the Nation of Islam. The RNA demanded the establishment of an independent Black republic engrossing the territory of five specific southern states. Elijah Muhammad's Nation of Islam was vague, envisioning a separate entity somewhere in America, in some locale of concentrated Black population, with more or less entailed facilities.

Nowadays critics consider both options obsolete. The main reasons are lessons learned from the example of apartheid South Africa. There Africans were herded into Bantustans in order to enshrine a migratory labor system. Under Bantustan separation, African migrant workers were tolerated in "white areas"—cities, farms, mines, and factories—only as "temporary sojourners." They were allowed in white areas only on permission. Entry was restricted strictly to the number required as dirt cheap laborers. Paid paupers' wages, Africans were denied permanent residence, without special dispensation. Yet economic necessity forced millions to trek from the Bantustans to seek jobs in the so-called "white economy," and there is no reason, say critics of the separatist option, circumstances would not be similar in any scheme which would separate Afro-Americans from whites spatially and concentrate them in one or several regions. Skeptics doubt whether any Black economy in continental North America could ever be functionally detached from the white-controlled advanced capitalist economy. When South African workers ceased to be functional, or wore out, or were disabled physically, or became superannuated, or merely displeased whites for one reason or another, they were unceremoniously booted back to the Bantustans. Similarly, when downturns in the periodic economic cycle occurred, they were sent to the reserves to wait out the depression in utter destitution.

This, we the Africans of North America will not tolerate. Many thus believe the separatist card no longer playable. And they have similar doubts about current versions of Marcus Garvey's Back-to-Africa movement. There is too great a danger of degeneration into deportation fantasy. Nor are "we-are-an-African-people" options which focus attention on struggles in Africa any better, for they may lead to neglect of "right-here-right-now" struggles.

Louis Farrakhan issued a new policy guide for the latter-day Nation of Islam in 1993. *A Torchlight for America* is a kind of manifesto. Among other suggestions, the Black Muslim leader urged that imprisoned Black men be freed and given a new start. He wanted to remove them from alcohol and drugs and "corrupting home environments." However, Farrakhan's proposal chimes in higher register. He wants Black men released from America's jails to move to the continent of Africa, a voluntary emigration and repatriation. The idea is one that finds favor among white far-right-wingers who jump at any chance to get rid of Black folk. Safeguards that would prevent this from deteriorating in effect into a contemporary *deportation* of Black inmates are not suggested. Given the malevolence of American racism, nothing can be taken for granted. It is also not clear why this is not merely a recycling of Marcus Garvey's star-crossed Back-to-Africa enterprise. Even more telling, the authors of this and other neo-deportation schemes demonstrate little or no real knowledge of present-day African conditions. What makes one think that Africa can be made to absorb significant numbers of the U.S. Black convict population, regardless of the injustice of their imprisonment? Africa already suffers from a wicked refugee problem involving millions of displaced persons with no place to go. The Congressional Black

Caucus assistance Farrakhan solicits in meeting statesmen of African countries who might favor his rehabilitation scheme would not make the mother continent a refuge for our convict population. The limitations of any religio-political movement comes to the fore whenever it is forced to grapple with secular political problems. Curiously, Minister Farrakhan and the Nation of Islam have suggested that the demand for reparations be postponed.

On the other hand, it is the nationalists who have shown the greatest stamina in voicing the call for Black *empowerment*. Yet the demand is new only to those suffering from historical amnesia. It punctuates the whole history of Black America since Emancipation. Charles Sharrod of SNCC revived the theme in 1964, insisting that were empowerment not to come through reconciliation, it would have to come through rebellion. Malcolm X's *"Ballots or Bullets"* was all about Black empowerment. Equally pointed were the political plans for his Organization of Afro-American Unity (OAAU). Malcolm's call for liberation schools, rifle clubs to defend against racist civilian and police aggression, and election of Black candidates free of Democratic or Republican party strings, were empowerment prescriptions which strongly influenced the Black Panther Party after his assassination.

Unfortunately SNCC's most renowned alumnus, unwavering revolutionary Pan-Africanist Stokely Carmichael (Kwame Ture), has been shoved to the periphery of political life in the post-civil rights era. Unintentionally Ture has fostered his own marginalization by inadvertently mirroring the career of Marcus Garvey in geographical reverse. Garvey sought to galvanize Africa from a base in America. British and French colonialism combined with the U.S. federal government to assure that he galvanized neither one nor the other. For more than two decades now Kwame Ture has been straining to mobilize and organize the Diaspora Americas from a base in Africa. He has yet to make significant headway.

In order to ignite the people as a revolutionary force, they first had to be mobilized, the Black Panther Party dared say, energized, and engaged in political activity. And the people had to be *organized*. The Panthers were right, of course. They deployed a dizzying array of community survival programs. Their initiatives ranged from voter registration and liberation schools to breakfast for children, from free plumbing repairs and free groceries to sickle cell anemia screening, from free bus transportation to visit inmates to community counselling to free shoes, from health and free clothing to legal assistance and the Black Panther newspaper. They dabbled in Mom-and-Pop stores, at one time even trying a hand at manufacturing golf bags.

In performing all these services, the Panthers probably did too much. The group fell prey to hyperactivism. Too much was attempted for an organization of its size and resources. The Panthers dispersed rather than concentrated their organizational energies. While it is wise to be bold and energetic, the range and scope of programs need be reasonably focused. Focus by all means on the realizable, on delivering the goods to the community, but keep the end political goal in mind. First succeed in one, or a few, enterprises and only then move on to bigger, more politically provocative undertakings.

On the other hand, the Panther legacy should not be misconstrued to mean that liberation forces should go underground and hide from ordinary grassroots folks. The hidden is the unknown. Secrecy is a road to isolation, infiltration by police agents, and ultimate ineffectiveness.

In the same vein, the fate of the young urban rebels of the "Sixties generation" can teach us a lot. During the second half of the 1960s many boys 12 to 15 years old took part in the ghetto rebellions sweeping the country. In the course of Cleveland's Hough district "riot" in 1966, for one example, lads of 14 and 15 bravely appropriated clothes and shoes for themselves and seized electrical apparatuses. Described by shocked white reporters as "utterly brazen," youngsters hurled fire bombs at heavily armed police. These teenagers were rebelling because they needed food and clothing. They felt their situation so desperate they were willing to risk life and limb.

But what has happened to those young rebels since? What are they doing now 30 years later, now that they are men in their mid-forties? We really do not know. How many are dead? Have the survivors been "domesticated," de-fanged? Have some simply "dropped out"? Did the armed forces gather some of them up? Are many of the young urban guerillas of the 1960s the prison seniors of the 1990s? What is their rate of unemployment? In most instances we cannot say. We have not tracked the street fighters. We know much more of what has become of members of groups active in the former Southern Civil Rights movement, particularly SNCC and CORE. Careful track has been kept as some have moved up to political preeminence, while others have fallen by the wayside. A few have deserted to the enemy, enrolling as charter members in the neo-conservative band that fronts for their white patrons. But we have lost track of the anonymous young urban ghetto warriors over time. Nowadays it seems that the attitude that motivated the Hough kids and others during the "long hot summers" of the Sixties—that is, the belief that life is so miserable one might as well take chances, for life and death are one and the same—has shifted away from collective rebellion. All too many of the present crop of fifteen-year olds struggle nihilistically against racist society, resorting to criminal behavior and the self-hatred of Black-on-Black violence. Some 30 years after the great ghetto rebellions the attitude that life is not worth living still pulsates through the inner cities; however, it is not expressing itself in the same way.

*

Liberal integrationists have a very different leadership style. Take the strategy of Lani Guinier, for instance, who aims to nix white supremacy by nixing the white voting majority's winner-take-all trick. She has been vilified as an "undemocratic" "Quota Queen" because she dared demand for her Afro-American minority in this country special protections which the overwhelming majority of U.S. white folks insist are required to shield the interests of the white minority in a post-apartheid South Africa ruled by the ANC. As one remedy for the "tyranny of the majority," Guinier advocates a procedure called cumulative voting. Paradoxically, she has drawn support for her ideas in the writings of "Founding Father" James Madison, himself a Virginian slaveholder, as well as in the practices of the Reagan and Bush administrations. Cumulative voting gives each voter multiple ballots which may be distributed among candidates to express intensity of preference and ensure the election of Black candidates in jurisdictions where solid white racial bloc voting shuts Blacks from public office.

In contrast, communalist integrationists believe in "plowing profits back into the community" as the means to "giving people the right to participate in the social and economic decisions that affect their lives." Here the dream is to humanize U.S. society through direct democracy. The more freethinking communalists have advanced schemes designed to ensure the security of African Americans, Puerto Ricans, Chicanos and Native Americans.

450

Proportional representation of these "nationalities" in such popular institutions as workers' caucuses, local and regional assemblies and autonomous interregional assemblies would do the job, they think. Where such institutions do not already exist, their creation is seen as the indispensable condition for a just and genuinely multicultural America. The nationally-syndicated Black political scientist, Manning Marable, has made suggestions along these lines, as elements of a social democratic solution to racial conflict.

Voices that emanate from the Martin Luther King Jr. Center for Social Change and from SCLC have been insisting for some time that the dreams and aspirations of the vast majority of American Blacks are categorically integrationist and not nationalist. They reject separation in whatever shape. The baffler, however, is the *quality* of the integration. The champions of strict integration are constantly looking over their shoulder, spooked by the shadow of assimilationism. They feel a need to reassure everyone that their dream of integration is not a desire to disappear and melt away in white America. It must not be an ideal that requires Afro-Americans to transform themselves into incognito beings, indistinguishably whitened culturally. Integrationists of the Atlanta trend are anxious to distance themselves from a marginal fringe of Buppies that spent the entire 1980s pursuing precisely that vain fancy. These types insist that the integration they seek is one that aims chiefly to appropriate for ourselves the high material standard of living enjoyed by white mainstream millions. Black people want for themselves the same good schools, well-paying jobs, fine homes, safe neighborhoods, beautiful surroundings, and quality leisure. That has been the main thrust of Black integration historically. But beyond that, the integrationist ambitions of grassroots Blacks are less incompatible with separatism than doctrinaire integrationists imagine. Granted, there has never been mass support for Back-to-Africa emigration, or for the formation of a separate Black territory within American confines. Nevertheless, as shown by the tandem pressures exerted by Martin Luther King and Malcolm X during the Civil Rights era, throughout African American history integrationism and separatism have always united to further the interests of the Black community.

Of all secular political organizations in the United States, the NAACP, until the melt-down of 1994, rated highest among Black people as the most effective leadership organ defending our interests. Under the brief stewardship of Ben Chavis its total membership shot up from 500,000 to 680,000. It outranked the Nation of Islam, SCLC, and the Urban League in popular support. Its name recognition surpasses all other groups. Chavis' initiatives included a high-profile three-day summit of scores of Black leaders in Baltimore during the month of June 1994. Summoned under an "interdisciplinary" hammer designed to reconcile warring views, the gathering was a first in seeking a common political agenda for the coming century. It targeted economic development, community empowerment, and spiritual renewal. Debate was lively and frank, as participants ranged across the ideological spectrum from Louis Farrakhan to Kweisi Mfume of the Congressional Black Caucus to Jesse Jackson. Coretta Scott King and SCLC's Joseph Lowery did not attend (probably in protest against Farrakhan's presence) while Jewish demonstrators marched in protest outside. Lacking the consensus, the conferees were unwilling to draft a final document with a list of recommendations. But they did agree to continue the quest for a united Black political agenda.

*

The debate on strategy and tactics in the late 1960s and early 1970s was the liveliest in a century, or at least since the days of W.E.B. DuBois and B.T. Washington. Community regroupment and control of our own economic destiny confronted scenarios for breaking into white society. Militants gathered around Martin Luther King plotted a society of reward according to personal merit and content of character. Social judgement would lose its racial vision and become "color blind." We know that this kind of integration never came close and King's legacy has become ambiguous, even coopted.

The alternative strategy has fared no better. Through the mid-1970s nationalists talked a quasi-separatism that would have us first cocoon in our own communities and then come out powerful. The hindsight exposes this too as a failure.

Black mayors began taking over big-city municipal government in the mid-1960s. They ran into insoluble dilemmas. Dark-skinned mayors have been elected in Cleveland and Gary, Newark, Berkeley, and East St. Louis; in the nation's capital; in Detroit, Atlanta, New Orleans, Baltimore, Philadelphia, Memphis, Seattle, St. Louis, Denver, Chicago, Los Angeles, and even in New York, the "Big Apple" itself. These electoral victories teach Black people a very bitter lesson at the cost of long and useless compromise. Conciliation, accommodation, and "coalition-building" have proved vain. The experience of some 30 years confirms that the mayor's office can be just one more devalued trophy, tainted by the all-pervasive racist system.

The well-being of the Irish and other white "ethnics" soars when the Daleys—Irish "godfathers"—sit in Chicago's mayoral office. A Fiorello LaGuardia or a Rudy Giuliani in New York's Gracie Mansion means that Italian-Americans will be catered to royally. Things do not work that way for Black folk, however. Suddenly control of municipal government, long a pork-barrel for white residents, becomes a nearly empty cupboard, stripped of goodies, the moment Black voters prevail and elect one of our own. Black mayors spend their years in office either with hands tied by budgetary deficits or scrambling to hang on to white "crossover" voters, or caving in to every "special interest," except to the Black special interest, or in court fighting indictments. Community activists have discovered that hard-won "independent" Black educational and health institutions depend on funds controlled by racist white city councils and state legislatures. Black mayors find they must protect white corporate property and enforce white-defined "law and order", or the system will smack them down. They find they must placate white neighborhoods at all cost to prevent the remaining whites from quitting the city, further reducing the tax base. "Community control" has turned out to be a poisoned gift, if anything, of benefit only to the wealthy donor. It has proved a device to reduce the cost of local administration by letting the "niggers" and the "spiks" police their own filth-ridden, crime-plagued ghettos. Control of the mayor's office has proved a big disappointment to our people. Usually a Black mayor means more Black policemen. Unfortunately, all too often on city streets that can mean merely more Black police than white police. Both groups of officers beat, gas, and stomp Black youths, enforcing curfews to preserve the "American way of life."

Despite 30 years and more of Black-dominated big-city government, housing segregation sits firmly entrenched in metropolitan neighborhoods. The upper hand at the municipal ballot box has yet to make the slightest dent in the discriminatory housing patterns which keep African Americans piled up on one another in racially isolated, urban ghettos, aptly described as "American apartheid" by Massey and Denton. Chicago, Cleveland, and Detroit lead the nation in residential segregation, with some of the "meanest streets" and worst housing anywhere. All three cities have been governed by Black mayors at one time or another. Washington, D.C., where no one other than a Black candidate has the faintest chance of winning a mayoral election, is notorious for its residential hypersegregation.

Criticizing traditional civil rights agitation, Black South African political scientist Bernard Magubane has written:

> Hankering after middle-class goals limited the programs of the civil rights movements to futile and spiritually deadening aims... The Afro-American is black and because of his color, he stands out and cannot melt into a crowd— which is what I understand as integration. Socially he occupies the lowest rung and although he may be equal (which, of course, he is), his equality would not affect his socio-policial status (Magubane 1987:236)

*

THE QUESTION OF ALLIANCES

He who is an ally at one juncture of history can be transformed into an enemy at the next. Historical moments are very brief nowadays, sometimes lasting no more than several months, a few weeks, even just days. Any effective political alliance between progressive forces in society must operate on the basis of carefully established priorities. We are Black people and we must be more concerned about ourselves rather than about others. Nothing should take priority over our own interests, neither alleged "national" interests nor any general human interests. It is a simple matter of fact in this post–Cold War world that no nation has the military strength to threaten the security of the United States. We are not dealing with some science fiction in which a silicon-based intelligence invades from outer space to destroy all carbon-based bipedal life forms. Only then might there exist general human interest that would temporarily override our Black concerns. Historical development itself has placed Black liberation at the very top of the political agenda in the United States and Canada. Some of us drew this conclusion 25 or 30 years ago. Nothing has occurred since to lessen that conviction. Instead, the condition the world has fallen into in the meantime would suggest that the very fate of mankind, the progress of humanity, depends on the rise to power of Diasporan Blacks, continental

Africans, and people of color everywhere.

A by-any-means-necessary Black agenda is imperative. We must hammer out the shifting and time-limited political alliances required by our condition as a minority in a hostile society. That our oppressors outnumber and outgun us must never be forgotten. Malcolm's renowned "by any means necessary" is nearly always interpreted as merely urging retaliatory, self-protective violence against racist attacks. Malcolm's dictum is regarded primarily as a payback. It should not be. "By any means necessary" covers a much broader range of options. It includes the crafting of coalitions. Within its scope lies every action from, say, coolly-calculated political trade-offs to, say, self-interested power brokering in electoral district reapportionment designed to maximize African American representation in state and federal legislatures, or to, say, lobbying in the Canadian constitutional debate for "distinct society" status for First Nations (the aboriginal Indian population) and "visible minorities" (as people of color are termed in Canada). Malcolm meant for us to learn that Machiavellian politics may serve more than just the interests of white civilization. It can also be an effective tool in our struggle to achieve our historic goals.

Actually, the need for flexibility and experience in forming friendships and seeking confederates has never been a mystery among Black leaders. For instance, Ron Daniels, former executive director of the National Rainbow Coalition favors alliance primarily with other people of color. To his mind, unity among the nation's racially oppressed keys the struggle. "Principled coalitions" with other people of color must be based, he says, on mutual respect and "common" interests and concerns. But Daniels does not restrict his pattern alone to the racially oppressed. He would bolster the phalanx with poor whites and the trade union movement. He appears to underestimate the problematic nature of bonding with rank-and-file white workers. The dynamics fuelling alliance between peoples of color is one thing; the circumstances surrounding blocs between ourselves and ordinary white folks is something else again. While certainly not impossible, it is a different kettle of fish entirely and very problematic. According to a 1985 Michigan state Democratic Party survey, working-class whites "express a profound distaste for Blacks, a sentiment that pervades almost everything they think about government and politics" (Massey and Denton 1993:94). This is a rock-hard prejudice that has not eroded over time.

Don Rojas, one-time participant in the Grenadan revolution, is more exact in analyzing the potential for broad coalitions of people of color with working class and liberal whites. In locales like New York City, where people of color (Blacks, Afro-Latins, South American immigrants, Asians, etc.) are now the majority and comprise, in his opinion, one of the most sophisticated populations in America, it is possible to negotiate from positions of strength with the interlocking power brokers and "invisible government" which control political affairs. Caution is required to win the coalition battle, however. Setbacks can be enervating, Rojas has warned, for the mechanisms of public policy are beyond the effective control of the electorate, particularly beyond the control of Black voters. Coalition policy should be defined, therefore, as an exercise in *maximizing* Black political power.

Inevitably, the reverse side of the coin of Black-led coalitions of people of color are tactics aimed at fragmenting the white mainstream along its natural fault lines. We must strive to undermine the bipartisan *"Democran"* consensus that has ruled the country at least since the Korean War and the McCarthy era. We must try to intensify discord between white women, affluent-educated white males, poor white "Bubbas," Catholics, Protestants, Jews, religious fundamentalists and liberals, anti- and pro-abortionists, feminists, senior citizens, gays and lesbians, and others. It is vital to worsen the ill feelings between those factions. If their differences are not exploited, Black political power will never be achieved. Contradictions inherent in their relations with one another must be incited with the aim of pulling one or the other group temporarily into progressive political blocs. A major target for disruption should be the Congressional bipartisanship that engineers Democratic and Republican party domination of the federal government. A comparable model might be construed in the current fragmentation of ABC, NBC, CBS and FOX network domination over the TV audience nationally in favor of proliferating and divergent sets of viewers, facilitated through cable and satellite and special-interest channels.

*

As far as *fraternal* alliances in North America between African Americans and the other people of color go, the American Indian Movement (AIM) seems a good place to start. There are vibrant Native American resistance movements and equally vigorous ones in Canada. AIM was formed by students in Minnesota in July 1968. The organization is dedicated to Indian land claims, political sovereignty/autonomy and the cultural rebirth of Native American peoples. It straddles the border with chapters in both the United States and Canada. The will of indigenous Americans remains strong even though the genocide they have been suffering for the last 500 years has few equals in history. From an original population of some 25 million around 1492, there remain only somewhat more than 905,000 Native Americans combined in the five states with the most Indians. The state of Oklahoma houses the largest Indian population, yet even there they number only a few more than a quarter of a million. Canada too has few survivors, somewhere between ca. 500,000 and a little more than 1,000,000, thinly scattered across the immense expanse from Labrador to British Columbia, according to the 1991 Canadian national census. Yet the spirit of Wounded Knee and Oka is unbowed. Furthermore, no two peoples are more intertwined by intermarriage and blood than Native Americans and African Americans are with each other. As far back as the Seminole Wars in the 19th century the prominence of "Black Indians" has testified to the symbiosis of the two peoples, to mutually beneficial living together. Native Americans are our most natural allies.

*

While it would be utopian to imagine that mutually constructive dialogue and cooperation between the Black Liberation Movement and the Disability Community is automatic or an easy matter, close fraternal alliance between African Americans and the disabled is not only natural, it is also morally worthy and politically worthwhile. Shunned as political equals by the white upper-middle-class' "beautiful people," the Disability Community is "under the gun" of eugenics. On the rebound today after flourishing in the 1920s, eugenics is a false doctrine concerning the improvement of the human race, based on the idea that social inequality is due to genetic, psychological, and physiological disparities among human beings. The eugenicists bray that human progress ceased with the disappearance of natural selection. Fearing the potential political clout of disability as the one and only "minority" status that cuts across all racial lines, hard-core eugenics racists would "improve" America at the very least by introducing artificial selection through the sterilization of disabled persons, and through prohibiting marriage between people with disabilities. This is the kind of oppression and contempt that has been aimed at Black people for ages.

Nevertheless, inasmuch as the Disability Movement's current priority rightly is de-institutionalization and "community placement" for all the disabled wrongly incarcerated in state-run "development centers"—a move that makes the predominantly Black "disability-care" staff in these state-run institutions fear for their jobs— the achievement of any marching-together accommodation between the Black Liberation Movement and the Disability Rights Movement will take a lot of hard work and much patience. Be that as it may, it is a crucial job that must be done.

*

Hispanics present a special problem. Mostly because few know precisely to whom they are referring when they use the term. For the word *Hispanic* merely means Spanish or Latin American, in fact connoting more about language than national or regional origin. Hispanics are those whose mother tongue is Spanish. That is all. The designation Hispanic alone says nothing about racial identity, and *race* is the key social identity in North America. Hispanics may be of any race. Millions are white, millions are Black, and millions are of mixed Black-white-Native American race. Similar confusion surrounds the term *Latino* which, although taken by most people to mean an American citizen or resident of Latin American or Spanish-speaking descent, really designates a culture. Just as many Latinos are of predominately African descent as others are mainly European in blood. The matter is further complicated by the fact that the U.S. Census Bureau plays tricks on us. They lump Black and white Hispanics/Latinos together as a separate group, or simply add *all* Hispanics, regardless of race, to the *white* category in order to inflate the white population artificially and cheat Black people of transfer payments and other federal entitlements allocated according to size of population.

Hispanics or Latinos—applying the terms synonymously—in the continental U.S. now number around 23,000,000. During the ten-year span between the censuses of 1980 and 1990 they increased more than 50 percent. At least those were as many as census agents managed to count. There may be a lot more—legal residents as well as the undocumented. The U.S. houses the fifth largest Latino population in the world. Hispanics are already the majority of entry-

458

level workers in many Southwestern metropolitan districts and soon will be the majority of entry-level workers in such large markets as San Antonio and Los Angeles. More than a quarter of the inhabitants in both California and Texas are Hispanic. Large Latino communities are found also in New York, Florida, Illinois, New Jersey, Arizona, Colorado and New Mexico. As of 1991 there were 4,004 Hispanic elected officials in the country, a 27.2 percent increase over 1985. One quarter of all U.S. Latinos are bunched up in just eight metropolitan centers: Los Angeles, Chicago, San Antonio, Houston, El Paso, San Diego, Miami, and New York City (whose 1.7 million [officially] makes it one of the largest Hispanic centers in the world). Three fourths of all Latinos reside in California, New York, Texas, Florida, Illinois, and New Jersey, key states with the biggest Congressional delegations and the most presidential electoral votes. Like Blacks, Latinos in the U.S. are heavily citified.

Mexican-Americans, with high birth and immigration (legal and illegal) rates, far outnumber Puerto Ricans as the largest group among Hispanics. Nearly all Mexican-Americans are confined to the Southwest and the Chicago area. Next in order of magnitude come the Puerto Ricans who outnumber Cubans living in this country by three to one (ca. 3,000,000 Puerto Ricans to ca. 1,000,000 Cubans). White Cubans are the most intractable of all Hispanic groups, the large majority embracing anti-Black racism and supporting right-wing policies. Cuban hordes have overrun Miami and southern Florida, yet make up less than five percent of U.S. Hispanics.

Latinos are intensely regionalized in this country. They are not evenly spread throughout its territory. In a few distinct regions they seem to be everywhere and one hears Spanish in every nook and cranny. Then one can travel over huge distances—mainly through the center of the country—and find nary a one. The Puerto Ricans are concentrated in the Northeast. Less than a third of the Cubans have made it out of Florida. With the exception of Chicago, all the Mexican-Americans are west of the Mississippi. And, like Blacks, poverty is rife among them. The federal government reckoned that every fourth Hispanic family lived in poverty in 1988, as the number of poor Hispanic families swelled by 30 percent in the Reagan era. As the 1990s began, one quarter of Hispanic youths who finished high school left without acquiring any marketable job skills. Forty percent dropped out of school before graduation (Aspen Institute Conferences 1989, 1990).

But these generalizations hide great disparities between ethnic contingents, for the Latinos living in this country are most definitely *not* all in the same boat.

Hispanics come color-coded in white, Brown, and Black racial hues. They are also divided sharply along *class* lines. A comparison of the three main groups—Mexican-Americans, Puerto Ricans, and Cubans—shows great disparity, with some faring much worse than others.

Mexican-Americans are poor. Less than half are home owners. One in five families among them is headed by a woman and 15 percent of adults lack fifth-grade schooling. The federal government admits that almost 30 percent of Mexican-Americans live in poverty. Two-thirds of Mexican-American males are either farm laborers, low-skilled blue collar workers or low-paid service employees. In the West the maid-drudgery, cleaning up, and keeping house for wealthy white women is usually performed by Mexican-American women. Only around eight percent of Mexican-Americans are hired for what the Census Bureau terms technical, sales, managerial, and professional jobs.

Puerto Ricans are pestered with one of the highest poverty rates of any group in the nation. Of course, the majority of Puerto Ricans are Black which goes far toward explaining the 40 percent poverty ratio. Half of Puerto Rican males are in low wage blue collar and agricultural labor, as are 15 percent of Puerto Rican females. For thousands, men and women, cheap service industry jobs are the only ones to be found—flipping burgers and such like. Unemployment is high, usually double-digit and usually twice as high as the jobless rate for non-Hispanic whites. Puerto Rican households earn the lowest median income among Hispanics. Only around one in four owns his own home. Sixty percent of Puerto Rican children are poverty-stricken.

Cuban-Americans are the richest Latinos, reward perhaps for being racist and reactionary. They certainly fare well in socioeconomic status, with one in five Cuban males and one in four Cuban females holding managerial and professional jobs. In contrast only 11 percent of Cuban men have to put up with low-paying service employment.

Rapidly expanding in size, Dominican and Haitian communities face fierce discrimination. Stalked by AIDS, jobless, plagued with crime, poverty stricken, hounded by immigration agents, these latest Latino newcomers are pitiful. In 1990, Latinos in New York

City—most prominently Puerto Ricans, Dominicans, Haitians—numbered around 1,800,000, or ca. 24 percent of the officially recorded population. About half were Puerto Ricans. However, the Puerto Rican contingent fell proportionately in the course of the 1980s, as Dominicans, Columbians, and Haitians flooded Gotham.

The U.S. Census Bureau, by the way, has yet to figure out how to categorize Haitians. The designation "Hispanic" as used by its demographers includes Spanish-speakers only. The Haitians speak French and Creole, yet fit unmistakeably under the Latino cultural umbrella. Furthermore, where to put Brazilian immigrants? Their tongue is Portuguese. I use the terms "Latino" and "Hispanic" as meaning the same thing in the United States context, and include both Haitians and Black Brazilian immigrants in the Hispanic-Latino category.

In any case, it is vitally important to enlist Latino support and cooperation in some form or another whenever possible, if Black aims are ever to be accomplished. The common ground is there. There are enough "walking together motivations" for coalitions of our people with Puerto Ricans, Mexican-Americans, Dominicans, and refugees from Central America. There is, however, no objective basis for knuckling under to the reactionary coterie of Cuban *Gusanos* who run Miami. Their politics is right-wing reactionary; their prejudices white racist. The social consciousness of Miami Cubans, shared with the Cuban communities in New Jersey, is passionately anti-Black. Having fled the Castro government's race-mixing policies enshrining Black equality in their native Cuba, they reject affirmative action. They spurn the African American claim for reparations and parity-making indemnifications as compensation for the scars of slavery and racial discrimination. White Cubans living in the USA are loud in support of the principle that whites have the right to keep Black people out of white residential neighborhoods and vehemently oppose any concrete measures to break up the hypersegregation that disfigures the urban landscape of the Northeast and Midwest. There is no objective basis for amity with such people. They are our adversaries.

Race is decisive in America. Far from declining in consequence, its significance is growing as the new century dawns. Race is the fundamental social criterion, the great divide. It retains its validity also in respect to Latinos. Once foot is set on U.S. soil, the latter are not exempt from the rule. Hispanics are not one race. They are

461

not a monolithic social category. They do not rank as a single racial class, as do Afro-Americans and native-born whites. Thus it is misleading—i.e., in accord with the habits of Census officials—to say that the Hispanics are the fastest growing "minority" and will surpass Blacks in that status. Not so. For there are white Hispanics, persons who assimilate as *white* folks, exempt from racial discrimination and eligible themselves to join in the racist aversion to the African citizenry. For there are brown Hispanics and Black Hispanics. The Latinos in this country make up two, if not three, distinct racial groups, each with divergent interests. They are united only by a language, Spanish; and not even by that when it comes to French-speaking Haitians and Portuguese-speaking Brazilians.

Hispanics do not even share a uniform culture. Mexican-Americans, for instance, bear a strong Amerindian stamp which puts them worlds apart culturally from white Cubans. Hispanics cannot even be said to be set apart by religion, by adherence to Catholicism. For there are Italian Catholics, German Catholics, Irish, Polish, Dutch Catholics, English ones too, etc., and surely these other Catholics are not Hispanics. By common agreement, one's religion is not what makes one Hispanic. The one trait that Hispanics seem to have in common is where they or their ancestors started out. The only feature all share is derivation from a vast *region*, Latin America. But Latin America is not merely vast; it is also very diverse. How can, say, Puerto Ricans, Mexicans, Cubans, Central Americans, and Columbians be reasonably viewed as hailing from one and the same location? Central Americans in the U.S. alone now number in excess of 860,000. There are many *different* Spanish-speaking immigrants from the hemisphere to the south—as dissimilar from one another as English-speaking Pakistanis are from English-speaking Hindus, though both native to the Indian sub-continent. Furthermore, we should not forget that the Spanish tongue is not peculiar to migrants from Latin America and the Caribbean, for immigrants from Spain speak Spanish too! And the Spanish are certainly Latin in culture. Yet few insist on including these Europeans in the category of people that Americans mean when they say "Hispanics." Many of the more than 900,000 Filipinos who live in the U.S. speak Spanish, yet we understand that they are Asians, not Hispanics.

Thus in tailoring its alliance policy toward Latinos, the Black liberation movement must apply the inescapable Gringo equation of *race* as the sorting principle. We need separate the Black Hispanics from the white ones and recognize a (brown) Amerindian contingent (e.g. Mexican-Americans and Central Americans), and proceed accordingly on the bases of fraternity, cooperation, neutrality, and—where appropriate—enmity.

When it comes to trying to work with Hispanics, therefore, we need to adopt a *color-conscious strategy* and *race-coded tactics*.

A steady effort must be made to woo and win over Black (darker complexioned) Latinos, particularly Haitians, and African and mixed-blooded Puerto Ricans and Dominicans. These groups face prejudice in schooling, social services, political patronage and in the job market—prejudice motivated by aversion to their African heritage. Black Puerto Ricans, in particular, are spatially segregated in the fashion in which they are housed. They and other Afro-Latinos are prime candidates for broad coalitions with Afro-Americans along racial lines, fraternal alliances cemented by shared membership in the oppressed race, transcending the cultural and language differences which set our communities apart. Faced with unrelenting anti-Black discrimination, self-interest motivates immigrants of African descent towards coalition-building with native-born Black folk. The patronage and other perks derived from the enhanced political clout that will come from cooperating with the native Black community will provide the glue to hold such political coalitions together. We can depend upon the practices and prejudices of white America to help split Afro-Latinos away from allegiance to non-Black Hispanics. As racist whites treat them as Black folk first and only secondly as Hispanics, self-interest will weaken their identification with white Hispanics. It is increasingly obvious to Haitian immigrants that they are spurned while white Cuban refugees are pampered. To build lasting coalitions with Afro-Latinos we simply need respect their culture, religion and language. Cooperation is worth substantial concessions, including promoting talented Afro-Latinos to leadership roles in the established Black organizations. A real effort should be made to understand the needs specific to Afro-Latinos, concentrating on their agenda and integrating them without bias fully in the life of the Black community at large. The expectation that the integration of Afro-Latinos will prove more difficult than assimilation of some 600,000 and more English-speaking West Indians (Jamaican and other English-speaking Black West Indians are often not fully integrated with native African-Americans, the fault being mutual) should not be allowed to dampen the effort.

While conceding less fundamental concessions, the Black liberation movement needs to form coalitions in descending order of priority with the remaining Hispanics according to the degree of their color; i.e., a *complexion criterion* will lend greater urgency to cooperation with the Browns (i.e., Mexican, Salvadoran, Guatemalan and Nicaraguan immigrants of mainly Indian descent) than with, say, Chicanos and Latin Americans with less American-Indian heritage. Along with sensitivity and flexibility in applying this policy goes the realization that self-interest will prevent *most* light-skinned Hispanics from being as fully supportive as Black-skinned Hispanics or even from seeing eye-to-eye with their Black Hispanic brethren. Yet in all, the hands-across-the-table approach is appropriate in dealing with Hispanics of color, regardless of hue.

Our attitude toward white Hispanics should be hands-off and neutral. Here the wait-and-see stance is best. The Linda Chavezes are no accident. We must maintain a wary and correct distance. Temporary coalitions around issues of momentarily coincidental interest are possible. We must be prepared for frequent clashes with white Hispanics and hostility on racial issues, for such is inevitable given social circumstances in this country. Black people will continue to experience open confrontation with right-wing Cubans and other conservative white Hispanics, and not just in and around Miami.

*

With Asian-Americans a differentiated policy of sometimes-alliance, sometimes-opposition is necessary.

Asians are said to be the fastest growing minority in the United States, now totalling around seven million. On the average they are extremely conservative. Alliance with them is thus questionable most of the time, complicated in all instances. This most likely reflects either personal political history in their homeland or social status and financial resources. Many recent immigrants from Vietnam, Cambodia, Laos, Korea, mainland China, Taiwan, and Hong Kong were handmaidens of Western colonialism and fled retribution when anti-imperialist forces took over in their native countries. The South Asians who came to North America from India, Pakistan, and Bangla Desh are usually highly educated, well-off professionals—doctors, mathematicians, computer specialists, scientists, and technical experts—classic brain drain. Immigrants from Samoa and other parts of Oceania and from the Philippines are exceptions to these rules. They are poor. Many are progressive, seeking an end to color discrimination and open to political cooperation with African Americans. Asians born in the United States and who have been here for several generations, particularly the Chinese, are not nearly so right wing and anti-Black as the newcomers. Unfortunately these moderates now seem to be in the minority in the Asian community, at least on the west coast. Fifty-six percent of Asian voters backed George Bush in 1992. That was a higher proportion of conservative votes than that cast even by traditionally conservative Southerners (42 percent) and nationally by affluent voters with incomes above $75,000.

Moreover, beyond the much-publicized frictions with Korean retailers in Black neighborhoods, anti-Black racism has long been rife among the Nisei (i.e., Japanese-Americans born and educated in the U.S.). During the 1950s, a correspondent of Dr. Harry Richardson, then President of Atlanta's Gorman Theological Seminary, observed:

> When the Japanese were driven out of California and put in concentration camps, the only people who succored them, or the principal people who did, were colored folk. They visited the camps, took them food and did errands for them.
>
> When the ban was lifted no one could have been more cooly indifferent to colored people than those same Japanese when they were permitted to return to Little Tokyo in Los Angeles and other areas and reclaim their possessions.

(Claude A. Barnett Papers, 10 August 1954).

Chapter 22

POLITICAL BEHAVIOR AND THE WHITE PROBLEM

How about the white folks? Do they figure in our strategy of political blocs? We do not have to worry about our bond with the 12 percent of American whites who are staunchly anti-racist. This component is sound, has been re-stocked generation after generation since before Abolitionism. It is time-tested and every day it reinvents its loyalty to our cause, not in mere words, but in response to the query, "What have you done for me lately?" It proves its fidelity daily. These white people are much more trustworthy than today's Black "crossover" politicians, not to mention the Black neo-conservatives. Anti-racism is mother's milk to these people and the ruminations that follow concerning the trouble we experience in trying to work politically with the rest of white America does not apply to white anti-racists.

Black people have tried time and again to trust political cooperation with whites. A long history of trial and betrayal stretches
back at least as far as Reconstruction. We have been left in the lurch
over and over again. Massey and Denton argue persuasively that residential segregation immunizes today's white politicians against any
urge to form mutual interest coalitions with Black politicians. Many
of us doubt the wisdom of political dealings with white folks. Despite
our long-term servility to the Democratic Party, even the bare suggestion that we can get anything good from coalitions with whites
is now greeted with understandable suspicion in some quarters. Any
matter this vital merits careful scrutiny.

Nowadays the credentials of even the far-left leaning white liberals and self-proclaimed radicals appear tainted. During the 1950s
and 1960s young white "revolutionaries," "peaceniks," "flower children" and "anti-imperialists" screamed "counter-culture" and undying hatred for the "System." They vowed to reduce U.S. imperialism
to ashes. But time passed, the Civil Rights movement waned, Nixon
changed the "color of the corpses" on the battlefields of Indochina
and the Vietnam War finally ended. The withdrawal of U.S. troops
from Vietnam removed the fear of the draft from the mind of many
white youths. As the Sixties generation matured, it shuffled off its
radicalism, graduated from college, married, sought employment,
settled down and acquired a stake in society. Many former liberals
succumbed to anti-Black Yuppyism. One band of left-liberals turned
right-wing conservatives, excused their defection claiming hurt feelings that Blacks were not adequately "grateful" for the "sacrifices"
white progressives had made in the fight against Jim Crow segregation. Others shifting allegiance to Zionism pointed to our lack of
affection for Israeli interests as the reason for deserting the cause
of Black liberation. Still smarting thirty years afterwards from the
loss of control of SNCC, CORE, NAACP and other activist agencies, and spooked by the rhetoric of the Nation of Islam and other
nationalists, many white former radicals still cannot bring themselves to admit the political independence and hegemony of the
Black liberation movement at home in the United States. Some insist
instead that the initiative for progressive change must come from
the outside, either from the Third World or from alienated white
youths or "exploited" white workers, or from environmentalists, animal rights protectors, white Women's Libbers and gays and lesbians—from anyone but Afro-Americans. A few are stuck in the

time warp of "Black-and-white-unite-and-fight" under (white) work-ing class leadership.

Today no class of the white population of the United States and Canada is objectively revolutionary.

*

Racistization of white ethnic immigrants and blue collar workers is a fact of North American life, an unbroken process as old as the U.S. republic itself, incriminating white popular culture, official pol-icy, and private institutions. Left-liberals would like to see blanket Black resistance to generalized white supremacy dropped in favor of a united front of Blacks, whites, Natives, Latinos and others, against a so-called "common enemy", i.e., against a power-hungry white "elite" which hogs wealth, media and political influence. The rub is that ordinary whites do not regard the elite class as their enemy. Most identify racially with the small minority of their "bet-ters" who rule society. Instead when it comes to seeking enemies, they are more likely to regard African Americans as the common foes of both themselves and "white elite supremacy." Racial blood runs thicker than the water of mutual political aims.

And it has always been this way. Those who cherished fond mem-ories of, say, frequent intermarriage between Blacks and Irish immi-grants in nineteenth century Boston conveniently forgot New York's Draft Riot in 1863 during which Irish mobs hunted Blacks like par-tridges, including women and children. Throughout the 1930s Italian immigrants fought bitter street battles against Afro-Americans over Mussolini's attack on Ethiopia. In Chicago and Buffalo, Polish-Black antagonism is legendary. Advocates of alliance between separate and equal Black and white entities have to some-how work around the hard fact that millions of white workers, immi-grants and middle class have been lobotomized by racism, as it were.

About 12 percent of America's white citizenry stay the course in the battle for Black equality, through thick and thin. Unfortunately this percentage is smaller, probably, than the percentage of hard-core racists who would go as far as genocide to keep Black people down. The white racist obstacle to Black empowerment persists intact, despite enactment of such recent federal remedial legislation as the Civil Rights Restoration Act and the 1988 amendment strengthening the Fair Housing Act.

Even if by some improbable mutation of history the Black community would succeed in transforming the existing ghettos into real citadels of autonomous Black culture expressed through institutions controlled by the people and with a viable economy organized in the "enterprise zone" manner advocated by some Black leaders, or with Black workers integrated through proportional representation with other minorities of color in a broad, interracial U.S. economy under "workers' control" and direct democracy for the entire population, as advocated by the Democratic Socialists—grave danger would still loom. Why? Because the superstructure of notions and attitudes, ideology and prejudice has a reciprocal and at times "over-determining" influence on the socioeconomic infrastructure. And, as argued in the first chapter, an ultimate, last-word, "under-determination" spills upward from the civilization level; such urges are historically racist in European-derived civilization. Hence even were the institutional and policy foundations for racial discrimination destroyed in the USA, white racist behavior would survive for a long time. In fact, the existence of prosperous, seemingly-privileged Black islands in a white sea would provide a focus for constant surges of white envy and jealousy, for racist currents. There is much raw material for a social-fascist backlash. Envy of renovated inner-cities might ignite even more intensive racial hatred, like the Aryan Nazi tide which engulfed Germany in the 1930s. Black well-being could lend plausibility to a new social-fascism riding on dissatisfaction among those whites considering themselves "reverse-discriminated" against. The capacity for self-pity in such circles is immense. The spectacle of Afro-Americans enjoying culturally confident and economically successful careers in Black "wards," integrated in an "America of nations," might open the door for personally or socially frustrated whites—social incompetents who themselves lack the talent to compete on equal terms—to flog the myth of a "foreign, privileged incubus" in the body politic, to create a legend that Blacks were "strangers" without real connection or loyalty to the country. This is the danger of self-contained neighborhood fastnesses, of Black islands in a vast white sea, of flourishing Black urban centers in white suburban doughnuts. Would they be allowed to exist inviolate as a kind of fetus curbed in the womb of white America, or would they be under constant attack?

Yet if we disperse outside of the ghetto we lose the safety in numbers and set ourselves up to be picked off one after another. Hence the lasting ambivalence: compacted communities facilitate the election of Black officials—yet because of their isolation—are vulnerable to white racist hate campaigns that claim that autonomous Black communities are alien enclaves foreign to America's body politic and should be cut out. White elected officials, answerable only to white constituents, find it easy to ignore or oppose Black interests. On the other hand, scattered integration threatens to dissolve the Black community as a bloc, reducing the Black presence to isolated, politically weak, and voiceless families residing in districts surrounded by whites, far from friends and relatives—invisible people with diluted voting strength. Of course, nobody dares talk about proportional political representation on the basis of race, a reform that would ensure Black political clout *without* African Americans having to be compacted in unbroken residential clumps with all the problems that entails. "Power sharing" between the races is simply not looked at in the USA.

According to some statistical projections, "minorities" (i.e., Blacks, Latinos, Amerindians) will be the official majority in the United States some time early in the century, if counted all together. To what limits might fearful white folks go to nullify this "threat"? Old-style independent Black revolutionaries (Boggs 1969) envisioned the Black community as the vanguard of a socialist revolution to make the United States a single socialist republic uniting Black and white citizens. They envisaged a great upheaval in which the Black "domestic colony," functioning as a revolutionary class, would seize power at the head of an *alliance of classes* comprising large segments of a radicalized white majority. Today the vision appears something of a pipe dream. American Blacks and whites share the same country, but events since 1968 have hammered home the reality of two different racial groups, two separate communities. Each is marked by highly visible skin color and other racial features. Those who would overlook the racial barrier in favor of a class analysis, underestimate the depths of racism in North America. White racism is objective reality in the American scene. It is the cause of the dehumanization and cultural alienation taking place in our inner cities. Over and over again racism has choked Black-white mass solidarity before it has broken ground.

Any Black-white alliance under Black leadership, in which the white commitment to change would be real, now seems far-fetched. That is why we hear more and more voices in the community insisting that "dialogue" between Blacks and whites is merely a manifestation of our emotional dependency. Many see it as an inferiority complex, requiring the approval and indulgence of white superiors. These critics have trouble understanding that like all other relations between the Black community and white society, dialogue too should be treated in terms of political expediency, requiring a specific talent. There is no confidence in our ability to manipulate "interracial dialogue" to our own benefit. I am referring to the "melanists" among us, otherwise brilliant and original thinkers. They are fearful of "dialogue" with the enemy, and refuse to see that it behooves the Black activist to listen carefully when "Whitey" speaks, especially when he bellows his rage and frustration at Black aggressiveness. Viewing social behavior as a function of genetic inheritance, the melanists leave themselves open to many blind-side shots. For instance, how are we to evaluate the social character and the political alliance record of people of color like the Native Americans, the Chinese, and others who possess less melanin than Blacks? Does it make any sense to regard them as some sort of "semi-melanists" and assume that the sometimes unreliable and half-hearted support we get from them is caused by a genetic "semi-albinoism"? Evoking theories of energy absorption through melanin neurochemical agencies, while scientific-sounding, is no substitute for a credible political economy and a reasoned strategy of alliances.

The Republican Party has evolved into a white united front spanning the middle and upper classes. It is a particularly tough nut when it comes to devising strategy. Former Ku Klux Klansman David Duke, a Scots-American, came within a whisker of winning Louisiana's U.S. Senate race on the Republican ticket in 1990. He strengthened his draw among the state's Republican voters in the gubernatorial contest. He was expected to make another run for the Senate in 1996, once more as a Republican. Republican candidates ran white supremacy campaigns in 1994 and did very well indeed in contests for both houses of Congress.

Straining in the opposite direction, the party contains a "Compassionate Republican" faction whose chief spokesmen include Jack Kemp and Ron Stein. Shortly before his death, Richard M. Nixon is alleged to have been converted to "compassionate Republicanism." This faction wants to dump Reaganism, deeming George Bush's "thousand points of light" rhetoric a joke. It is leery of Newt Gingrich's Contract on America. They favor a revised agenda that would restore social service cuts, accept affirmative action, and be "productive" in remedying the plight of the homeless. If the government can afford to pump billions of dollars into Gulf War adventures, contends Ron Stein, it can surely afford to wage war on poverty. For years men like PBS' Tony Brown have drummed for Black voter support for Republican candidates. One assumes that it is this faction Brown has in mind. Whether at this late date Black America can make any beneficial deal with a party more in the process of being captured by far-right Fundamentalists than by its "compassionate" faction remains to be seen.

Other devotees of two-party politics among us see valuable lessons for coalition-building in Harold Washington's 1983 victory in the Chicago mayoral election. The leverage to frustrate the Windy City's deeply-rooted white racist populism came from an alliance of Blacks with Hispanic voters. While 82 percent of the white electorate took an unambiguously racist position, 79 percent of Latino voters opted for Washington. Firm Afro-American unity around his candidacy energized a successful campaign to register Black electors. A massive turnout on ballot day coupled with a 99 percent tally of Black votes in his favor put Washington in office. Also 18 percent of white electors voted for the Black candidate in 1983. Speculations about the liberal-leanings of well-heeled white lakefront Chicagoans aside, we still are in the dark about the special appeal that won them over in 1983. We are equally in the dark about the general psycho-social and political influences that can mould such whites into temporary coalitions with us.

White electors are sharp enough to know the difference between tame "crossover" politicians unlikely to cut into white privilege, and progressive Black candidates with the gumption to defend our interests. In the eyes of whites the latter are "strident militants." White voter support for progressive Blacks, if any, will always be a shaky and sometime thing. In 1984 Jesse Jackson got a grudging five percent of white ballots. Four years later, after a cascade of media recognition, he garnered 17 percent. That figures to be about the upper limit nationally for white voter tolerance for forthright Black candidates and causes. Anomalies in which Black female candidates up this threshold with larger shares of the white female vote, riding the crest of debate of such issues as abortion rights and sexual harrassment, are temporary deviations which do not suspend the common rule. By remaining silent about race and ignoring Black concerns, "crossover" candidates like Douglas Wilder have demonstrated an

ability to woo condescending, affluent white voters anxious to foster the American myth of racial tolerance and equality, as long as it
costs nothing. Why not cast one's ballot for a "nice," non-threatening Black gentleman when one is assured his election will have no
more impact than viewing the Huxtable family on television. But
what good is this to Black people?

Affluent white middle class voters gave Jesse Jackson a measure
of support, but white workers were emphatically opposed. Gomes
and Williams observed that "[i]n both contests, Jackson did better
among whites 30 to 49 years old, midwestern and western whites,
college-educated whites, whites in white-collar occupations, and
whites with household incomes of $25,000 or greater." (Gomes and
Williams 1992:148). The flood of Rainbow Coalition propaganda
left poor whites unmoved. There was no way they were going to let
go of their hereditary prejudice and join a coalition with Afro-
Americans. With them, race—as always—outweighed class.
Upwardly mobile white suburbanites and liberal college campus
types might afford the luxury of flirting with the Jackson candidacy, but blue-collar whites were certainly not going to budge for a lot
of talk about lower income persons of all colors getting together
politically. Like their forbears a hundred years before, poor whites
of the 1980s knew what mattered most: they were not going to jeopardize their hopes of enjoying white skin privilege for any class-
based appeal that would put themselves in the same category as
Black people.

The Gantt versus Helms U.S. Senatorial campaign in 1990 measured political racism's refraction through North Carolina's contemporary class structure. This campaign has been cited as a special
case because the poorest whites with incomes under $15,000 broke
their usual racial pattern. Harvey Gantt, a polished Black moderate, took on arch-racist and social dinosaur, Jesse Helms. Gantt
scored a high 35 percent of the white vote, attracting wealthy, well-
educated white voters, yet doing surprisingly well among poor
whites. White females and the youthful, affluent liberal university
elite were the ones most willing to put aside racial prejudice.
Nevertheless theirs was a vote mainly against Helms' repugnant
social conservatism (homophobic anti-intellectualism) than an
endorsement of Black interests. Ordinary white males, churchgo-
ers, middle incomers, and married couples gave solid support to
Helms who won the election. They voted not so much from love of

Jesse Helms, as from a rock-solid determination to *prevent* the election of an African American, of any African American (McCorkel 1991:23-24).

David Dinkins' adventure as mayor of New York City illustrates the dilemma that haunts every Black elected official, "crossover" politicians more than any. They must cater to white liberal voters. Many white liberals will vote for the Black candidate his first time out, as a conscience-salving "feel-good" trip. Once that is done, they feel they have paid their "tolerance dues," lose interest, swing over to a newly-fashionable cause, be it "clean air," animal rights, or abortion on demand. Or perceiving the incumbent administration they helped put in office as "too minority-oriented," they swing their ballots to white candidates in subsequent elections. Afro-Americans chosen by slim majorities forged by "liberal coalitions" ride a razor's edge. Such coalitions depend on a significant minority of white ballots. From inauguration day the winner spends inordinate time worrying about the prospect of *reelection*. Mesmerized about the next campaign, typically the Black office-holder forgets his Black voter support base. Our vote is taken for granted on the grounds that it has nowhere else to go, no alternative. Surprise and disappointment is registered on reelection day when many Blacks just stay home and refuse to vote. Campaign promises are designed to placate the white sections of the liberal coalition. Much energy is wasted trying to win over hostile whites whose votes had gone to the opponent in the preceding campaign. David Dinkins hastened to placate Jewish tempers in Crown Heights. He even chased after Italian-American voters, the overwhelming majority of whom spurned him in 1989 and rejected him again in 1993. His supplications were useless.

Sharon Sayles Belton's experience is not unlike David Dinkins'. She became the first African American mayor of Minneapolis, a city only 13 percent Black. She quickly found that she had better favor powerful constituencies like gays, lesbians and white women, and that she had better not emphasize the needs of her own community. In this country public opinion polls are regarded as scientific when correct within 3 to 4 percentage points, positive or negative, 19 times out of 20. Surveying Black and white youth in the 15 to 24 years -of- age group, a 1992 Peter D. Hart Research Associates scientific poll found growing hostility between young Blacks and whites, not only in Dinkins' New York City, but nation-wide. Children of the very liberals who applauded Martin Luther King Jr.

and the Civil Rights movement are now often the ones who are most disdainful of Black people. Sixty-five percent of young whites born between 1968 and 1977 oppose affirmative action, and a plurality of young whites espouse the myth of "reverse discrimination."

•

Given these obstacles and intense resistance, are political alliances with white folks possible? Yes, some alliances are possible. (They'd better be!)

However, if such coalitions are ever to mean anything positive for the economic improvement and political enablement of the rank and file in our community, they must be on our *terms*, and under our *leadership*. They make sense only if they serve the general Black Interest. We have no permanent friends, only permanent interests. Likewise, we have no eternal foes. One loyal, capable white ally, ready and willing to obey Black commands to a tee, committed to infiltrating the white establishment on our behalf, an unyielding foe of white racism, owning a long and proven record of devotion to African-American interests outweighs, in my estimation, a whole gang of ultra-nationalist brothers, draped in black, red, and green, blowing *cheeba* on the street corner while boasting to all within earshot about how many white women they refuse to sleep with! There are reliable whites in the United States and Canada. The depressing fact is that they are such a small minority.

It is wrong and dangerous therefore to maintain that we should not form political blocs and coalitions with whites from time to time. My point is that there are no natural or permanent allies (or enemies) for Black people among the components of the white population—be they Hispanics, Jews, liberals, radicals, revolutionaries, or whoever else. Those few whites who are able to break through the bonds of their racial identity, cast off the fetters of American ideology, renounce white skin privilege, and strike effective blows against racism are eligible for temporary political alliances with the Black liberation movement. Those who reject all contacts with anyone having a white face, male or female, regardless of his/her political action, do us a disservice. There is no place for pouting emotionalism in such serious matters. Sex-oriented Black conservative "militants" who waste time censoring bedroom activities in order to prevent sexual relations between Blacks and whites are just excess baggage. But—and the exception is large—the coalitions must be on African American terms. The question is how to assure that they remain on our terms.

The answer is that whites, no matter how consistently revolutionary and adept at theorizing, must be kept *out* of the leadership of African American organizations. The same goes for the leadership of Puerto Rican and other Afro-Latino, Chicano, Asian, and Native American organizations. Black associations must be headed by Blacks—in fact, not just symbolically. Whites may be allowed in the rank-and-file membership, used as auxiliaries, united with and sought for supporting actions, but they cannot be permitted to determine policy. Over the years the NAACP and the Urban League, the two most established civil rights agencies in the nation, have sweated to juggle the conservatism of influential, wealthy white backers with the stout-hearted demands of rank-and-file Afro-Americans. The NAACP must still peer nervously over its shoulder before opening dialogue with Black nationalists, for fear of alienating Jewish donors.

These pressures showed up in the disarray which swamped these two oldest civil rights agencies in the mid-1990s. The Urban League took a sharp swerve to the right as its new director's inaugural address exonerated white racism, instead joining the blame-the-victim chorus. The NAACP went the same route, ousting Ben Chavis. He fell victim in 1994 to a concerted conspiracy of the board's closet neo-conservatives and Jewish backers nervous about Black political independence.

If the forces of Black liberation are to mature and learn to focus exclusively on our own interests, we must grow more adept at exploiting white inter-tribal disputes. Not just in the U.S. and Canada, but in all countries where whites rub up against each other in anger. It is in the interest of Pan-Africanism worldwide to take advantage of such white inter-tribal brawls as the IRA struggle against British rule, the civil war in Yugoslavia, Russian-Chechen strife, or Hungarian-Rumanian frictions, etc. We should milk them for all they're worth. After all, whites have been doing just that to us since at least the fifteenth century. Turn about is the fairest of play.

*

The Jewish question causes much tearing of hair and wringing of hands among Black activists.

As of 1994 there were some six million Jews in the United States, 2.4 percent of the national population, as officially estimated. For more than two millenia world Jewry has centered around Judaism, a monotheistic Middle Eastern religion, precepted ethically, ceremonially, and legally in the Old Testament and chiefly in the rabbinical teachings of the Talmud. However, millions of Jews are not religious, many being atheists. Therefore, to encompass both the religious and the non-religious, Jewish identity actually has a secular, biological character, founded on being born of a Jewish mother. Given the ambiguity of being regarded by some as a biologically constituted race, by others strictly as a religious group, Jewish thinkers define their folk as a *"people,"* sharing a common sense of history and a commitment to a set of values and beliefs grounded within Judaism. In North America, *white* Jews are the vast majority of the group, descendants of the Ashkenazim, i.e. Jews from central and eastern Europe, as distinct from the Sephardim Jews hailing from Spain and Portugal, and as distinct from the Falashas of Ethiopia. Black Jews are only a handful, oddities in North America, although Sephardim (so-called "brown" Jews) and Falashas are numerous in other places. For more than 2,000 years the Falashas, or Black Jews, lived in Ethiopia's Mountains of Semien before decamping for Israel recently. In Israel both the Sephardim and the Falashas endure racist discrimination from the dominant, mainly Polish-derived Ashkenazim.

While fewer than three Americans in a hundred are Jews, the most significant datum about them is the fact that fully one-third of U.S. billionaires are Jewish. Per capita, Jews have more economic clout than any other people. By the mid-1990s there were about a million more Jews in the United States than Muslims, but the latter are projected to outnumber Jews early in the twenty-first century. Blacks and other people of color are growing as a percentage of the nation, while Jews are declining. The drop seems to be caused by a combination of secularization of Jewish communities, a low birth rate and growing intermarriage between Jews and white Christians— clear measure of mainstream white America's acceptance of Jews as valid members of the Caucasian race.

It is this integration which enables U.S. and Canadian Jews to share in white skin privilege. White America is obsessed with the racial contrast between Caucasians and Africans. Most now have little patience with virulent anti-Semitism, seeing it as an irksome diversion from the true fight to keep Blacks down. There is no more striking evidence of white tolerance towards Jews than the growing number of marriages between Jews and Italian-Americans. In this, most North American whites are different from Europeans, among whom anti-Semitism earns more time-honored attention. This willingness to allow Jews under the blanket of white skin privilege is the reason Jews esteem North America so much, as contrasted with, say, Germany, where many still spurn Jews as "polluters" of Aryan racial purity.

Jewish racial status, Jewish wealth and the social stratification of the Jewish community all have bearing on unprejudiced assessment of the likelihood for political alliance between Afro-Americans and American Jewry. In 1993 there were 73 billionaires in the United States. Twenty-four of them, i.e., 32.8 percent, were Jewish. The overrepresentation is classic, for Jews are only a tiny portion of the population. It is estimated that some 20 to 25 percent of North America's "super-rich" are Jews. Thus Jewish wealth is magnified even more disproportionately, for it is clustered at the very top of the monied pyramid. At least a hundred of Forbes magazine's 400 richest Americans are Jews. Given the conservative proclivities of the wealthy everywhere on earth, more and more analysts are questioning the very possibility of a Black-liberal Jewish coalition. On average, Jews are the richest ethnic or religious grouping in the U.S., with incomes exceeding WASPs. The few remaining Jewish poor are retired workers. But the children of even these poor tend to be well-off professionals. 20 percent of U.S. doctors and lawyers are Jewish, some very high profile. 10 percent of American professors are Jews. American investment banking has been heavily Jewish since the 1850s. And more than half of the 110 richest Jews are realtors. In Canada about 1.1 percent of the population is Jewish. Around 140,000 to 150,000 Jews reside in Toronto, roughly the same number in Montreal, and a mere 7,000 in Vancouver, Canada's three largest metropolitan areas. Yet a whopping 41 percent of Canadian university faculty are Jews. Thirty percent of Ivy League professors are Jewish. Wealthy Jews influence the U.S. Republican Party (more and more the tool of anti-Black conservatives) by contributing a quarter of the party's funds. Jews exert even greater influence on Democrats by forking out the lion's share of Democratic Party money. And wealthy Jews—Democratic and Republican—identify with Israel and bankroll it. With the exception of Florida, relatively few Jews reside in the deep South. Yet in the mid-1980s half of all middle class Jewish women employed a Black cleaning lady. The African American domestic service sector is disproportionately dependent on Jewish patronage.

More than any other factor it is their heavy overrepresentation in the arts and well-paying professions that has created Jewish hostility to affirmative action for Black people (masked as opposition to "quotas") and it was challenging Jewish control of Hollywood movies and other media that got Len Jeffries in hot water. In New York, Diane Ravitch, a Jewess from Texas, led the fight against a school curriculum of inclusion. Unwilling to relinquish cushy teaching jobs to Black and Latino teachers better qualified to train minority pupils, for many years Albert Shanker, union boss of the Jewish-dominated American Federation of Teachers, lobbied against the interests of Black parents. Even in the "liberal" Northeast, two-thirds of the Jewish vote since 1966 has been running solidly against Afro-American needs and demands. Even the one-third still willing to vote for Black Democrats has grown shaky, susceptible to demagogery about so-called "Black anti-Semitism."

Workers—ordinary folk who had to work for a living and who did not possess the wealth to hire others to work for them—constituted a majority of North American Jewry up until the 1940s. Since then working class Jews have become a disappearing species. This decline strongly reduces the likelihood of mutually-beneficial coalitions between Blacks and Jews. Progressive Jewish critic Lenni Brenner concludes that American Jews are well on the way to becoming the first ethnic group in all history without a working class of any size (Brenner 1984:107-123). Eighty-five of every 100 American Jewish youth enter university, the highest rate for any people on earth. Today the Jewish social structure extends only down to the lower middle class. There is really no mass rank-and-file bottom layer below that. Jewish social stratification is top-heavy, ours is bottom-heavy; there are few common life-experiences left between the two communities. Rarely do the prince and the pauper look at the world the same way.

Despite its small numbers, American Jewry today is one of the strongest and most influential forces supporting the system. It is enthusiastic in its support for the status quo. Most Jews feel they have much to lose and nothing to gain by change. This is why there is no automatic trust or real alliance now between people of African descent on one side and conformist Jews on the other. African American academics who traipse the lecture tour attacking "Black anti-Semitism" and trying to "revive" Black-Jewish cooperation, do a lot of whistling past the graveyard, tiptoeing around in the dark trying to unearth something that has past. Rather than as allies, nowadays Blacks are as likely to appear as mercenaries serving Jewish interests. Israelis and American Jews had a powerful stake in the Gulf War against Iraq in 1991; African Americans no stake whatsoever. Yet more than 30 percent of the 500,000 plus U.S. troops sent to the battle zone were Blacks and Latinos. Only 1,500 were Jews. Black and Brown soldiers were at risk in a dispute where international Jewish interests predominated. Between 1992 and 1994 fully ten percent of U.S. Senators were Jews, i.e., ten Jewish senators for a people who are less than three percent of America's inhabitants. In Canada a Jewish politician was elected Premier of Ontario, the wealthiest and most populous province. The lesson: while a majority of white "gentiles" gladly cast ballots for Jews, acknowledging the latter as Caucasians, racial aversion denies Black candidates the votes of more than 70 percent of whites (Christians and Jews) regardless of the political affiliation.

There is a virulent anti-Black current running among North American Jewry. So how should we deal politically with Jewish racism? It reared its political head recently in the defeat of New York mayor David Dinkins in 1993. It has been suggested that in retaliation we lend increasing voter support to such white populists as Ohio Congressman James Traficant. He and like-minded politicians vote in favor of civil rights bills while refraining from criticizing Black people. They do not blame us for the social woes tearing at our communities, but they certainly lambast Jews. Temporary, selective support for the Traficants who are neutral or pro-Black might be one way of sending a message, of neutralizing Jewish anti-Black racism, of making clear to Jews that there is a political price to pay for prejudice, at least in electoral politics. Jews must learn that "Schwarzer"-bashing is a no-no.

Nevertheless, as Lenni Brenner points out, there are thousands of young Jews on the nation's campuses who have nothing to do with the conformist Jewish establishment and who are eager to join the struggle to reorder American society from top to bottom.

*

According to the principle which elevates our own advantage upper-most, the Black agenda for this decade and for those that follow entails four different types of alliances and coalitions, keeping in mind that while African Americans have eternal concerns and stakes, we are unlikely always to have the same friends and allies—or ene-mies. The blocs are arranged in descending importance.

First, we must form lasting bonds with Native Americans (called "First Nations" in Canada), Afro-Latinos, Mexican-Americans and others from *La Raza*, Pacific Americans (i.e. Samoans and others), and the remaining progressive Hispanic immigrants. African Latinos and American Indians are our kinfolk and must form the preferred circle of fraternal allies. This union must also incorporate other will-ing Third World ethnic groups resident in the United States and Canada, targeting specifically Central Americans, Philippinos, and Arab-Americans as communities smarting from discriminatory slights. Efforts should also be made to work with South Asian and Chinese communities whenever possible, even with Korean-Americans and Nisei Japanese. Unity against the common enemy, comradeship-in-struggle and full equality combined with long and hard bargaining sessions to reconcile competing agendas, will cement the bloc. In mind is a union of people of color.

Second, coalitions can be formed with groups, movements and political parties which contain whites, *provided* the whites in ques-tion have a history of unrelenting struggle against the racist system, are actively engaged in programs committed to fundamental change, and provided they are constantly on guard to suppress within them-selves the racist reflexes from which few white persons are exempt.

Thirdly, it would be a smooth tactical move to conclude tempo-rary, contingent agreements with pacifists, civil libertarians, femi-nists, white student unions, senior citizens' groups, homeless organizations, teachers, artistic and cultural associations, health care professionals, philanthropists, radical professors, AIDS activists, tenants' associations, environmentalists, gays and lesbians (contin-gent, of course, upon white lesbians and gays purging themselves of their anti-Black racism), consumer advocates, disability-rights activists, and church groups. Tied to special issues and events, these coalitions will naturally be time-limited, kaleidoscopic, and ephemer-al. One should not expect to grow old in them, nor should too much be expected from them. Moreover, it must be made clear that each such alliance is feasible only on the basis of priority for the Black Interest and on the basis of Black leadership.

Lastly, we must look carefully at cooperation with the sectors of white organized labor which are willing to condemn and struggle actively against the many racists among white hard-hats and blue-collars and which oppose aggression against the Third World. Of course, these sectors of white organized labor must first be identified, and that is not easy for they are few. For this kind of bloc to work, these trade unionists must accept the primacy of affirmative action for Blacks and other people of color, aimed at achieving equality of results, up to and including altered seniority rankings, minority set asides, and full reparations for African Americans and Amerindians. Furthermore, for this cooperation to be effective, white labor leaders need demonstrate that they can, in fact, discipline and control the political behavior of their rank and file, finally putting an end to white labor's spasmodic lurches into racism. The Lane Kirklands cannot be allowed to continue to sit back complacently while their white union members quick-change into Reagan Democrats in every election where Black interests are at stake.

*

BLACK POLITICAL BEHAVIOR

Throughout the twentieth century, electoral behavior in America has had two phases (registration and voting) and one regulator—race. In the year 1988 more than 64 percent of eligible Afro-Americans were registered to vote—up from 25 percent in 1965, the year of the Voting Rights Act. But in Mississippi, for example, the state with the largest African American population percentage and the most Black elected officials, white registration as of 1988 continued to outpace Black voter registration 79 percent to 54 percent. In spring 1992, a presidential election year, it was calculated that a 25 percent increase in voter registration in 50 major cities would add some nine million electors to the rolls. Since most of the new registrants would be Black, analysts believe there is serious potential to expand the Black vote nationally. These estimates were made shortly before passage of the Motor Voter law.

Whites have always turned out to vote in greater percentages than Blacks, even in presidential election years. This is to be expected; after all the political system is theirs and there is little reason for middle class whites to be disaffected. The greatest white voter turnout proportionately was for the Kennedy-Nixon contest in 1960; the weakest came in 1976 as Carter edged Ford. In 1964 Lyndon Johnson pulled the heaviest ballot cast by Blacks in this century—nearly 60 percent of eligible voters. There was minimal Black participation in the 1952 election which brought Dwight Eisenhower to the White House. It is noteworthy that the pro-Johnson turnout occurred *before* enactment of the Voting Rights Act which opened the polls to millions of Southern Blacks for the first time. The nearest that Black participation in a national election has approached the 1964 peak took place in 1984, when 90 percent of Black ballots were cast for Walter Mondale in a losing cause. It is a tell-tale fact that since 1976 the president that had the least Black electoral support, Ronald Reagan, was also the one most widely beloved among white voters. Presidential candidates aside, registration practices seem to condition voter participation markedly, spurring hopes for more Black ballots in the wake of Motor Voter law alleviations. Black turnout tends to surge in the presence of a strong Black candidate—an obvious readout from the Jesse Jackson primaries of 1984 and 1988.

Southern Blacks were enfranchised in 1965, and Black voter participation in presidential elections soared to an all-time high in the region in 1968, topped slightly only in 1980. Nevertheless, Southern white voter participation continued to outstrip the Black vote, with the single exception of the year 1980 as Black voters in the region came out in record numbers in a vain attempt to keep Carter in the White House. Despite the surge in the Black vote enabled by the Voting Rights bill, Southern whites remain racially conscious of the need to keep their rate of voter participation above the Black rate, thereby maintaining tight hold of the region's political reins. The same is true of Northern whites, who have been beaten only once in voter turnout, and that once was in 1964 by a mere hair. Given the racial polarization of voting in this country, coupled with keen white political awareness, exercise of the ballot alone does not yield political power for Black people. Much more is required, and much that is qualitatively different. Of course, one realizes it is a fool's game to tamper with Black folks' present love affair with the ballot. Our people sacrificed long and bloody for the right to vote. The road to the polling booth is paved with the blood of countless martyrs. At this juncture in history, pointing out the limitations inherent in voting and running for office in a political economy like ours is futile.

Yet in all, a reverse trend in Black voter participation has set in as disillusionment has grown. The percentage of African Americans voting in presidential contests declined from nearly 60 percent in 1964 to 44 percent in 1976. In 1980 it lay at 50 percent, climbed to 56 percent in 1984, but slumped back to ca. 51 percent in 1988. Black voter participation in mid-term congressional elections waned from 44 percent nationally in 1970 to less than 30 percent in 1978, recovering only to 43 percent by 1986. In many local areas the percentages have been even lower. Many Black people do not vote because they feel there is no one to vote for, and even if there were, it would bring no improvement in their circumstances were he or she to be elected.

Moreover, white racist politicians continue to manipulate unsophisticated Black voters. For instance, it still has not been adequately explained why George Wallace—the most notorious racist of his time—was able to win overwhelming reelection as governor of Alabama in 1982, with the reported support of 79 percent of the state's Black voters! Black men described as "field hands" lined up to elect the leader of a white supremacist gang which earlier had fought to deprive them of the vote. This is the concrete political behavior of some of our people and it is dangerously utopian to ignore this reality. Alabama Blacks bore no malice against a man who had done his best to turn back the clock to terroristic neo-slavery. Is this blindness, short memory, foolhardiness, masochism, or what? Surely this carries the no-eternal-enemy rule a bit too far. One still comes today across Southern Blacks leery of "militants" "come from outside to stir up" the stagnant pool of local "race relations." An inculcated master-servant mentality is alive in many backwater counties. Unconvincing are arguments which explain away this behavior as merely a "pork-barrel effect" (i.e., that racist local politicians control the public purse strings, federal revenue, and many grants, doled out to local Blacks in return for support at the ballot box). Something more fundamental and subtle is at work.

On 12 April 1983 Harold Washington won in Chicago with 688,176 votes to 619,926 for Bernard Epton, a white Jew (51.5 percent to 47.99 percent). Washington carried 22 of the city's 50 wards, Epton 28. Although Epton won more wards, Washington carried the African American wards by huge majorities, well over 90 percent, and 87 percent of the Puerto Rican and Mexican precincts, while getting some good splits in the integrated wards. Certain analysts point to the 1983 election as a bellwether. Washington got only 18 to 20 percent of the white vote, but the so-called "lakefront liberals," mostly white middle-class professionals, had "come through" for the Black candidate.

But time passed. Once Washington died, the "lakefront liberals" grew tired of "Black domination," wandering off home to the traditional Irish machine headed by son Daley. Crueler cut, many Hispanics defected from the progressive coalition. Then, in 1991, many Black Chicagoans could not be bothered to make the effort to vote for a lack-lustre Black mayoral candidate. By way of comparison, and as an indication of the political regression nationally in the 1980s, at 700,000 votes in the Louisiana gubernatorial election of 1991, David Duke, avowed white supremacist, polled more *white* voters alone than Washington got from all races together in his 1983 victory.

Ronald Dellums is regularly elected to the House of Representatives from California's 8th Congressional District. His constituency is unique. It has been described as America's "radical" district. While this is an exaggeration, it certainly appears the most *liberal* area bar none. The 8th District encompasses Berkeley, site of the famous university, along with sections of neighboring, predominately Black Oakland. The original Panthers sprang from Dellum's power base and the Black Panther Party was headquartered within its precinct. The voting pattern in the 8th suggests that a race-class mixture composed of African Americans and a large white intellectual and artistic community, if stable residentially over a long period, can nurture a long-term progressive electoral coalition. The snag is that such congressional districts are few and far between in the United States—in fact, there are no others. Given current demographic trends, combined with the residential (hyper-)segregation which is institutionalized nationwide, future prospects for similar districts are slim indeed.

David Duke's Louisiana forays are a more likely harbinger of the future. Positively, the outcome of the gubernatorial election in 1991 shows that Black people, often cursed for political apathy, are capable of the most intense political activity, provided enough stimulus. African Americans had the highest turnout in the state's history. 80 percent of eligible Black voters went to the polls. Duke's opponent, Edwin Edwards, routine white Cajun Democrat, outpolled the erstwhile Klansman with a 61-percent electoral vote, supported by 96 percent of the Black vote. Blacks made up more than half of Edward's total vote. The anti-Duke turnout's coattails were long. Blacks elected 12 additional Black representatives to the state Legislature, bringing their number to 32, amounting to 21.5 percent of that body, a tally for the first time actually approaching the proportion of Afro-Americans in Louisiana.

Still and all, Edwards never got more than 30 percent of the white vote. Seven of every ten white Louisiana voters stood firm in support of white supremacy. Now, in the history of elections, 70 percent is considered a very large majority—only two-thirds are needed to override Presidential vetoes, impeach the President or change the Constitution itself (constitutional amendments must be ratified by two-thirds of the States). Here a large number of white adults were saying frankly that they have no use for Black folks. We would be foolish not to take such testimony for what it's worth. Failure to heed the warning could prove fatal.

Similar electoral behavior occurs in a nearby state. The first elected Black mayor in Memphis' history was sworn in on 1 January 1992. Willie Herenton ran a "crossover" campaign, urging racial harmony and a truce to ancient grievances. Fifty percent of Memphis' 610,000 residents are Black. More Afro-Americans registered to vote than whites, giving Herenton a razor-thin victory by 142 ballots. But here again the same malignant pattern recurred. The vote split heavily along racial lines. The vast majority of whites vote only for white candidates.

This mountain-high obstacle frustrates those seeking minority empowerment. Some think the only way around the barrier is to radically increase Black voter participation nationally. They take dead aim, therefore, at low minority turnout as the chief evil. Toney Anaya, Democratic governor of New Mexico from 1982 to 1986 and a member of the Executive Board of Jesse Jackson's National Rainbow Coalition, harps on the fact that 75 percent of eligible voters in the United States—white and minority—do not participate in the electoral process. Critique of this kind keys the registration programs that Jackson has been running for years. Black neutrality toward the whole electoral contest irked Dennis Walcott, president and chief executive of the New York Urban League branch: "[w]hat is so interesting and ironic about these times," he observed in autumn 1991, "is that while other nations appear to be embracing democracy, voter dissatisfaction and apathy is on the increase in New York and the rest of the country" (*New York Amsterdam News*, 5 October 1991). He lamented "the lack of faith in the process."

Though the recent-immigrant status of the large majority of the community creates different circumstances, non-activism and electoral apathy prevail also among Canadian Blacks. The largest Afro-Canadian community resides in metropolitan Toronto, where people generally vote for those from their own racial group. Where the contest is confined to whites, balloting divides strictly along ethnic lines—Italians choose Italians, WASPs, elect WASPs, etc. As a rule, when there is no one running from one's own racial or ethnic group, one does not vote. Toronto Blacks generally do not vote, rarely even when Black candidates appear on the local, provincial or federal ballots. Most Toronto Blacks hail from the West Indies. Since as much as 90 percent of West Indians at home in the Caribbean vote in their own local elections, i.e., in societies where they control the machinery of politics—some analysts conclude that the alienation and apathy apparent among African Canadians manifest the estrangement of Black immigrants new to the country, hence a very different dynamic than that conditioning African American non-participation. An immigrant mentality is at work in Canada, it is argued. Not everyone agrees. Some having noticed over the years that apartment dwellers in Toronto do not vote, as opposed to single family homeowners who do, say that Toronto Blacks fail to vote because they are overwhelmingly apartment renters. Others ascribe the "fault" to the refusal of Black people in Canada to read political campaign literature. Encouraged by vigorous rank and file protest in Toronto and Montreal against racist police killings of Black men, and against media stereotyping, certain activists reckon that African Canadians are simply too disillusioned with the racism institutionalized in old-time machine party politics to whip up any enthusiasm, even when Black candidates are involved. Moreover, crouched at the bottom of Canada's economic well, they are overwhelmed with the gritty details of daily survival. In any case, despite metropolitan Toronto's large Black population, very few Blacks are elected to public office in Canada, and not a single one enjoys political prominence comparable to that of African Americans.

*

Which brings us to Black folks' Clinton song and dance. Except perhaps for Ron Brown and the Arkansan's Black cronies from his home state, few Afro-Americans were enraptured with William Jefferson Clinton as a presidential candidate. It is unlikely that he would have been elected had Ross Perot not thrown his hat in the ring and siphoned away disgruntled Bushites. Yet Black support showed up for Clinton in November 1992. That poll provided classic proof—if proof is still required—of Black America's subservience in the two-party system, as the Democratic Party's taken-for-granted captive vote. Clinton was the star of the Democratic Leadership Council, the faction determined to win back the Reagan Democrats, racists included. During the campaign he went out of his way to thumb his nose at Jesse Jackson, belch flatulence at Sister Souljah, and jet back to Arkansas to oversee the execution of a mentally retarded Black convict. He grandstanded coast to coast for the white Bubbas, but yawned at the Black community.

Nevertheless, Clinton garnered 82 percent of the Black vote despite his aloof attitude. Puerto Ricans helped out in the cities of the Northeast. This is a gauge of the concrete performance of the Black voting public. Theoretical speculations and contrary pleadings aside, this is what we actually do. During the 1992 primaries Black voters had turned out in much smaller numbers than in 1984 or 1988, when Jesse Jackson was the draw. In the Georgia primary, for one example, Clinton polled 74 percent of the Black vote in the absemce of anyone more attractive. In the national election African Americans gave him the margin of victory he needed to defeat George Bush. The Black vote—only eight percent of the national total—had a magnified effect for being concentrated in key electoral college states. Jews (78 percent), gays and lesbians (75 percent) and Latinos (62 percent) gave Clinton substantial, but weaker, voter support than Afro-Americans. Once again Black folks came through for the Democratic Party with the highest level of support that its candidate received from any group. Even though many were voting *against* the Reagan-Bush regime rather than *for* Bill Clinton, it did the trick. Blacks swung the vote in Georgia, Illinois, Louisiana, Tennesse, Michigan, New Jersey, Maryland, and Ohio, putting Clinton in the White House. Sixty-one percent of white electors voted against him: 41 percent for Bush, 20 percent for Perot. Clinton did a little better among white males than Dukakis had done in 1988 (37 percent versus 36 percent), but being less popular than Dukakis among white women, Dukakis actually outpolled Clinton among all whites, 40 percent versus 39 percent.

The Southland was the heart of American slavery, and still today half of this country's Black citizens are concentrated in ten southern states. It was in this region that the voter registration campaign fostered by Jesse Jackson and the Congressional Black Caucus bore the ripest ballot fruit. The African American turnout was nearly twice that of 1988, extra votes crucial to Clinton.

Elsewhere the outcome was muddy. Black America went into the 1992 "Fall Classic" with only some 12 million registered to vote, less than half the total population of adult Blacks eligible to vote but unregistered. Of those registered, only two-thirds found the Clinton-Bush-Perot trio enticing enough to go and vote. In all, less than one in three eligible adult Afro-Americans cast a ballot in the 1992 presidential contest. The decisive factor seems to have been income. According to census calculations, the top 20 percent of Black families earned incomes averaging $61,000 in 1990. Of these 75 percent voted in the 1992 election. Families whose annual income was less than $10,000 sat at the bottom of the Black social hierarchy. Of these, only ca. 35 percent could find anything for which to vote. It has not been determined whether the 464,000-plus Black votes for Ross Perot (2.9 percent of his total) came entirely from the affluent Buppy contingent. Without Perot in the contest, how would his Black supporters have been divided between Clinton and Bush; would they have just stayed at home?

In Illinois Carol Moseley Braun's run for the U.S. Senate galvanized the Black community, swelling the Afro-American vote by 90 percent over 1988. Riding her coattail, Clinton squeezed through in the presidential contest in that strategic state.

Braun leaped into the U.S. Senate with a term from 1993-1999. Her success is both phenomenal and (perhaps) contingent. This single mother from Chicago's Southside garnered 92 percent of the African American vote, mostly within metropolitan Chicago. A lawyer by training, she is the first Black woman Senator in U.S. history. There has been wonderment about the remaining eight percent of Black electors who cast ballots against her. They call to mind the African kings and other corrupt elites of the Atlantic Slave Trade holocaust who made the deal to sell millions of their own people to white slave handlers. One is also reminded of the Black slave drivers, depraved creatures who wielded the whip on the plantations against their own kind for cast-off raiments, second-hand shoes, separate cabins, crumbs from the master's table and the sexual run of female slaves. One has visions of eight Clarence Thomases trudging to the ballot box for every 92 normal, sane Black voters. Moseley Braun picked up half of the white vote, provided mostly by white women, for right-wing Republicans made the mistake of pitting a rich white *male* against her at a moment when feminist sentiment was running high. She did particularly well in Chicago's predominately white Northwest and Southwest sides, topping the best totals ever received there by Harold Washington.

The *conditional* element was the Clarence Thomas-Anita Hill confrontation which inspired many white women voters to back Moseley Braun as a *female* rather than reject her as a Black person. One wonders how lasting this feeling will be. The test will come in the November 1998 election.

On the same flood tide, former Black Panther official Bobby Rush won a Congressional seat in the U.S. House of Representatives. He won his set in a Chicago district where, according to reports, some voted for him out of nostalgia for the Panthers and others because they were persuaded that Rush had repudiated the Panther legacy.

Out west, Ben Nighthorse Campbell of Colorado was the first Native American elected to the U.S. Senate. In California Blacks are not the only voters of color. There is a huge Hispanic component as well as many Asians in the northern part of the state. But while west coast Asians tend to be conservative and as a rule vote for right wing types, Blacks, along with most Hispanics, are vital elements of the progressive bloc. Clinton's victory in California was an easy one, a foregone conclusion months before election day. However, there too Black voters contributed solidly to his majority. Black third-party candidate Gerald Horne totalled 287,358 votes running for the Senate on a Peace-and-Freedom platform. One source reported that Horne had been cheated in the count and that the scholar-activist had in fact polled nearly 300,000 votes. Much of his support came from left-leaning white liberals. His campaign was assessed as one showing the positive potential for Black independent political action.

The situation in New York State was intriguing. Clinton enticed 86 percent of the Black vote. But Dukakis had taken 89 percent of Black ballots in 1988. Nydia Velasquez from New York City became the first Puerto Rican woman to go to Congress. But the endorsement of the *Amsterdam News*, the leading Black weekly, threw 20 percent of the Black vote in the state's U.S. senatorial contest to Republican Alphonse D'Amato, providing the margin to reelect him. As expected, D'Amato took virtually all the Italian and Irish votes.

The defeated Democrat, Robert Abrams, Jewish, was being punished by politically-savvy Black voters for his vicious attacks on Al Sharpton and lawyer Alton Maddox.

A cautious estimate placed the total national Black vote in 1992 at 8.32 million. That was up from 7.36 million in 1988. How much of an increase in the rate of participation this amounted to is in doubt, for the Black population had grown in the four years since 1988.

All told, African Americans in the House of Representatives increased from 25 to 38. Most of the 13 newcomers were from new districts in the South. They held seats created in the aftermath of the decennial reappointment mandated by the population shifts documented in the 1990 census. By 1994 however, some of these new seats were being threatened by the Supreme Court's anti-Black *Shaw vs. Reno* ruling against majority-minority "snake"-shaped districts. Ironically, a number of the districts under attack were the brainchild of a Republican plot to redistribute seats and redraw electoral boundaries, creating majority Black districts, leaving more all-white ones where conservative whites are the majority and can always outpoll liberal whites once Black minority votes are gone from the district. The transparent aim of the *Shaw vs. Reno* decision is to expel some of the Blacks from Congress.

Chapter 23

WHAT IS TO BE DONE: VOCABULARY, INTERESTS, AND TWO-PARTY POLITICS

L ike it or not, never once in this century has our formal "politicking" escaped the ritual parlor game controlled by the two "national" parties. More times than not the Republican Party has controlled the White House. Even more frequently, the Democratic Party has dominated Congress. From nil in the Woodrow Wilson era, Black influence within the Democratic Party inched turtle-wise ahead, cresting about 1988, only to be deflated shortly thereafter by the conservative Democratic Leadership Council takeover. Meanwhile, Black input in the GOP shrank from little to nothing. Afro-American influence, as measured in delegates at Republican national conventions, melted from six percent in 1912 to three percent in 1984. Pork-barrel patronage has remained wafer-thin for us under the system. Despite the election at various levels nationally since 1965 of thousands of Black officials, public sector jobs, promotions, and government contracts for us are still hard to come by.

The two-party system is a major obstacle to Black political self-determination. There is, for instance, a contradiction between Black seniority rights in Congress and the formation of an African American political party. The considerable seniority rights built up in Congress by members of the Congressional Black Caucus (CBC) hinder establishment of any independent national Black third party. CBC members are Democrats, with two negligible exceptions. It takes at least ten years of seniority to get within striking distance of chairmanship of key legislative committees. Before the Republicans took control of the House of Representatives in 1995, John Lewis was a House deputy chief whip, with authority to corral other Democratic members of the House. Ron Dellums chaired the House Armed Services Committee, while Charles Rangel, Cardiss Collins, and John Conyers were prominent on the Ways and Means, Energy and Commerce, and Judiciary panels, respectively. Kweisi Mfume hoped to take the chair of the Joint Economic Committee in a few years.

Furthermore, each individual in the Caucus has her/his own individual career objectives to see to and those aims may not always coincide with the general Black interest. There is also the galling fact that white racist legislators are incumbents in many districts where the Black population exceeds 15 percent but is not large enough to elect one of our own. The present CBC has a vested interest in the Democratic Party. Yet they are heavily outvoted by a united, bipartisan front of anti-Black Republicans and conservative white Democratic members of Congress. Thus it is extremely difficult to translate the CBC's presence into payoffs for the Black community as a whole. Perhaps the Republican sweep of both houses of Congress in 1994 will bring the lesson home at last. Before the debacle, senior members of the CBC had high expectations of controlling key congressional committees based on seniority. That was before white males went to the polls in November 1994 and cast their ballots strictly along the color line. Two-thirds of white men voters chose the Republican Party as the surest defender of white male interests. Instead of power and influence, the CBC found itself shoved in the corner. Instead of the Kweisi Mfumes and Ron

Dellums influencing public policy, lawmaking fell to old-fashioned "Negrophobes" like Jesse Helms and Strom Thurmond, and new-fangled ones like Newt Gingrich.

Perhaps now more of our people will turn to the concept of *proportional representation* as the means of securing Black interests in the politics of the American Republic. We require a constitutional amendment acknowledging once and for all the centrality of African Americans in U.S. history and society. Until the rights and interests of its Black citizens are entrenched forever, the entire country remains in jeopardy. Given the political settlement established in 1787 under which we continue to practice government, the best way to anchor our rights is a constitutional amendment guaranteeing Blacks proportional representation in the House of Representatives and the Senate. The statute must require the election of 50 to 60 African Americans to each and every House of Representatives, as long as the House consists of about the same number of delegates as it does now. Should it expand in number, its Black core would increase accordingly. The amendment would also have to guarantee a dozen to fifteen Black members of the U.S. Senate. One of the two Senators in states with a substantial Black population should always be elected from among Black candidates alone. Were the stipulation on the books today, one of the two Senators from each of the states of South Carolina, Georgia, Alabama, Mississippi, Louisiana, Florida, Texas, New York, Illinois, Michigan, Ohio, and Maryland would be Black. Whether the African American Senator in any given state would be chosen by a closed list of voters restricted to the Black residents, or by the state electorate at large, might vary according to local provisions. Statehood for the District of Columbia would enable the election normally of two Black Senators from the same circumscription.

*

Hefty debate rages over how well African American politicians perform for their people once in office. As some see it, Black elected officials do the best they can against insurmountable odds, every once in a while bringing home the bacon in the form of patronage and progressive legislation. In the opinion of others, elected officials would not be running scared of unity conferences and grass-roots militancy if they had a clear conscience concerning their doings in office. They spend too much time and effort on damage control,

495

say these critics. The corps of Black elected officials has grown dramatically across the country from the few hundred in 1965, when there were only four in Congress and 102 in state legislatures. Today they are most frequently seen in the South and the North Central regions.

From the standpoint of the entire American political system, however, Black representation is still quite small, less than 10,000. Black elected officials are overrepresented nationally only in a single aspect, a negative one—they are singled out for harassment by law enforcement agencies, "above and beyond the call of duty."

Afro-Americans have always been underrepresented on the bench. Even the self-styled "friendly" Clinton Administration was slow to fill federal court vacancies with Black judges. Even though a larger proportion of Black law school graduates than white ones end up in government and public interest practice. As with elected officials, the largest concentration of Black municipal and state judges continues to be in southern and north central regions.

So-called "Reagan Democrats" should really be called "anti-Black Democrats." They stampede to vote for white Republicans whenever a Black Democrat is perceived as even mildly interested in defending minority rights. His affiliation with their own traditional party cuts no ice with Reagan Democrats. That is how David Dinkins was booted out of the New York mayor's office in the election of November 1993. By ousting him in favor of a hard-line Republican, white Democrats were affirming their racial identity. Black Democrats regularly vote for white Democratic candidates, Jews as well as Christians. Whites rarely return the favor. And with Hispanic Democrats it is an on- and-off thing, a very fickle affair. Whether "crossover" politics and politicians pay out for Black folk is questionable. Once in the governor's office, Virginia's Douglas Wilder kept a cool distance from his Black constituents. He had no intention of "alienating" his white supporters. And it was primarily to his white supporters that he appealed in his campaign as an independent for the U.S. Senate in 1994. Denver mayor Wellington Webb has enforced a police list of gang-member suspects 12 to 24 years old, even though 93 percent of those catalogued are Black or Latino. Seattle's Norman Rice has okayed police-state measures aimed primarily at Black youth. Cleveland's Michael White has keyed the city's "revival" to white business interests. Much of David Dinkins' time in office was spent paralyzed, politically. He seemed to neglect those who had put him in the Gracie Mansion. Instead he courted Jewish and Italian voters, all to no avail. Disillusioned Black electors were so turned off that when the moment came for reelection, many did not care and stayed away from the polls, depressing his vote total. They had watched their Black mayor waste months shaking the hands of white voters and kissing white babies. Some felt that he had demeaned himself, crawling to placate irate Hasidic Jews. Dinkins bent over backward, only to find on election day that no matter how hard he tried, the white folks did not like him because of his blackness. They crossed party lines to vote over-whelmingly for his white Republican opponent. Almost to a man New York City Italians voted for one of their own. And the major-ity of Jewish voters preferred the Italian Republican to the Black Democrat. Whites joined forces to "take back" their city.

The refusal of Reagan Democrats to reform their racial ways prompts growing numbers of Black Democrats to rethink partisan political affiliation and reflect on the wisdom of building a new third party—an *independent* national Black political party. Again, though, a major obstacle remains the CBC and the seniority some of its mem-bers hold on key Congressional committees as Democrats. Nevertheless, many feel that something must be done about "dera-cialized" crossover politicians, increasingly regarded as "*postblack*" by critics.

But we must try not to be iconoclastic in our criticism of accu-mulated seniority. For in our haste to attack a traditional institution as based on error, we may end up in bed with the enemy, as Carol Swain has done. Without persuasive evidence, she claims that "elec-toral passivity" is a distinguishing feature of historically Black Congressional districts (Swain 1992). Swain condemns Afro-American voters for reelecting the same Black congresspersons over and over again, for ten years and more. She throws a tantrum over districts in which Congressional representatives do not have to worry about appeasing conflicting policy preferences among competing racial groups. She hates race-conscious districting as "less constrain-ing" of elected officials. Sounding like Supreme Court Justice Sandra Day O'Connor and other white racists, Swain is against drawing lines to enhance the electoral clout of Black voters. She calls taking race into account in order to overcome racism, "gerrymandering." Hers is the resounding refrain of today's Black neo-conservatives everywhere: appeals premised on the alleged "declining significance of race in society," precisely at the moment when the significance of race is soaring, not declining.

Maxine Waters (D.-Calif.), in contrast, is a forthright and reliable defender of Black interests. She has explained her support for Clinton as preferring to "fight with a friend" rather than continue to be frozen out completely by hostile Reagan-Bush style administrations. However, the only way for Black America to capture the "friend's" attention may be through "street heat," including Los Angeles-like explosions. For since the 1992 presidential ballot the new conventional political wisdom is that Democrats win the White House chiefly by ignoring Black issues, while playing footsie with white suburbia and Reagan Democrats. How many blasts of the "bombs ticking" in the inner cities would it take to get the Democratic Leadership Council to notice the plight of its Black "friends"? The toll of the 1992 Los Angeles uprising was 58 dead, 3,000 injured, 15,000 jailed, a billion dollars of property destroyed and another billion dollars lost in wages and salaries. Black South Central and Latino East L.A. were swept up in the firestorm. The rebellion stretched to Long Beach, Compton, Hollywood and Beverly Hills. Black districts in cities across the United States rumbled in sympathy—Atlanta, Madison, Wisconsin, San Francisco, Cleveland, Seattle, New York, Omaha, Pittsburgh, Las Vegas, Chicago, Minneapolis, Birmingham, and New Rochelle, NY. Even Black Canada stirred in the aftermath of the Los Angeles rebellion. An outburst by young Blacks fed up with police brutality was ignited on 4 May 1992, following a Black Action Defense Committee rally against the first Rodney King verdict and in protest against the Toronto police killing of an unarmed 22-year old Black youth.

Yet once the ripples from the Los Angeles explosion subsided, the establishment reverted to business as usual. Obsessed with issues like Whitewater, Bosnia, and the President's reelection chances, the Oval Office is not concerned with Black interests.

Of course, tricks on the Black community are played from both sides of the political aisle. Not to be left behind in the business of prodding (*read:* controlling) Black political behavior, the Clinton Administration dreamed up its own answer to Jack Kemp's Republican enterprise zones. President Clinton unveiled an $8.1 billion *"Empowerment Zones"* plan, targeting tax breaks and federal programs on depressed Black and Latino areas and Indian reservations. Here the Democrats were playing a game of one-upmanship with the GOP. Businesses operating in the targeted zones get up to a $5,000 tax credit for hiring, training, and educating someone from the 'hood or barrio. Clinton's empowerment zones give employers *outside* the zones—i.e., in affluent white suburbs—up to $2,400 in income-tax credit for hiring someone who lives *inside* a zone. Schemes like these, along with rhetoric about America's alleged "commitment to civil rights" are viewed in bipartisan circles as painless substitutes for *parity of results*. There is no reason to change them as long as mass Black political behavior continues in conventional grooves. The acquiescence and apathy that spring from being caught on the horns of a Democratic-versus-Republican Party dilemma is no threat to the status quo. Away back in 1827, the very first issue of *Freedom's Journal* pleaded with us not to let ourselves become the tools of any white political party. Now almost two hundred years later we still need to be admonished not to allow ourselves to be the fools of the Democratic or Republican Parties.

At the outset of the 1990s, 21.1 percent of Black workers in the U.S. were union members. In contrast, only 15.5 percent of white workers were union members. In absolute numbers, there were upwards of 2.4 million Black workers in the ranks of organized labor. We should not overlook the positive role militant Black union caucuses have played in creating an atmosphere favorable to the struggle for social gains for our community at large. Praise is due, for instance, to the Coalition of Black Trade Unionists (CBTU) for its herculean efforts to broaden the Black agenda and meet the challenge of new urban dynamics. At least since the Great Depression of the 1930s, Black trade unionists have confronted racist bosses, technicians, personnel directors, factory doctors, office workers and foremen. And they have taken on Black-hating union bosses and shop stewards within organized labor's own ranks. Frustration or rejection of their demands have led to wildcat strikes and demonstrations. Black union activism has proven most effective when it concentrates on racial discrimination.

*

PRESCRIPTIONS

The major problem Black trade unionists now face is the declining relative power of the Black industrial working class. The CBTU must own up to the prospect that its constituent base will occupy fewer and fewer of strategic heavy industry jobs from which to exercise direct economic pressure on national production. Gone are the days when steel, auto, meat packing and mining industries employed armies of unskilled and semi-skilled African Americans. Deindustrialization, "rustbowling," "downsizing," the lure of "offshore," and high-tech restructuring have all had fateful consequences. Under their heat, decent-wage employment for untrained Black men has all but dried up. Redundancy imperils an entire generation. Non-unionized service industry jobs at minimum wages are all that some can get. The potential power over the white economy of Blacks in primary industry—even negative power—is condemned to shrinkage during the first decades of the twenty-first century. The haunting expectation of a "Black general strike," raised, say, in the minds of the Dodge Revolutionary Union Movement (DRUM) and the League of Revolutionary Black Workers in the late 1960s, is likely to grow less and less terrifying to white capitalists with the passage of time.

This presents the Movement with the challenge of creating new alternatives. With the "industrial proletarian" option now much reduced, we are left with two major ways to organize the Afro-American masses for political action: *1) directly* through councils at the basic community level (e.g. schools, city blocks, the homeless, tenements, housing projects, city districts, churches) or at work where folks join as individuals or as elected representatives of, say, Black-employee intensive light industries, labor caucuses, military personnel, students, teachers, professionals, etc.; *2) indirectly* through local committees which represent various organizations and collective bodies (e.g., appointed delegates representing political parties, NAACP, Urban League, SCLC, Rainbow Coalition, PUSH and other civil rights agencies, Nation of Islam, nationalist organizations, Christian churches, etc.). In the first instance, solution of problems confronting the community will require massive ancient-African style debate-to-consensus based on individual contributions and the persuasion of competing ideologies. In the second, a general strategic political line and a set of tactics—the much-touted *Black agenda*—can arise only from confrontation between the partisan positions, theories, programs, platforms and strategies of the various organizations with real standing in the community. The fulminations of sects and self-proclaimed messiahs will impede progress, but are inevitable. Right now both methods seem prevalent in our community's general ideological ferment, with a bias toward the first tendency, although recent leadership summit initiatives (1994) look promising.

Because of the nature of twenty-first century racist oppression and economic exclusion, large numbers of Black workers can no longer be organized at the "point of production" as they could in the 1940s and 1950s. Many of our young people will never experience a manufacturing point of production, and more and more of them are excluded lifelong from gainful employment because corporate capital is determined to locate production facilities in predominantly white surroundings (among foreigners who invest in the U.S. the Japanese are the worst offenders) while encouraging runaway automation, "rationalization" and the export of jobs to cheap labor reserves in foreign lands. Even during the mid-1990s with the economy humming along, inflation held in check, and white unemployment down below five percent, joblessness among our people remained more than double the white rate, without counting our massive "hidden unemployment."

*

Any Black political movement seeking to mold opinions at the grassroots must never tire of repeating its arguments, even though the literal form of presentation may change. Repetition is the most effective teaching method of influencing the public. Incessant effort is needed to raise the political level of ever-widening strata of our people. Only in this way can personality be imparted to the amorphous "river of struggle," to borrow a phrase from Vincent Harding (Harding 1981). There can be no end to the search for leaders of a new type, trail blazers who arise directly from the masses and remain organically in contact with them.

What to print in the Black press that is politically relevant and what to broadcast over Black electronic media that contributes to the flow of our struggle, have always caused puzzlement. Early in the twentieth century there was a spontaneous rebirth of the African American press, made up of publications of all descriptions and sorts.

Our periodicals and newspapers must push the tradition of exposing the harmfulness of white supremacy on into the next century. How bad it is and how humiliating for Black people to be dominated by racists, must be repeated time and time again. No people with self-respect can allow itself to be muzzled with, say, the appointment of a Black-faced sellout to the Supreme Court. That we cannot sit back and be content merely because we now see many Blacks on TV may seem obvious to the few, but our opinion-setters are shirking their duty if they leave off reminding the many to whom it is not obvious. Sit-coms are not an adequate diet for a people in search of empowerment. While it is alright for Black celebrities to line their pockets doing TV commercials, sneaker advertisements are not the sign of liberation. Our media are doing their job when they explain that nearly all of the "progress" Afro-Americans are alleged to have benefited from since 1980 has been merely for show and that, in fact, the shafting of the "grassroots" brothers and sisters is what is really going down.

By the year 2000 our people will have increased and multiplied in these United States to around 40 million, from one million in the year 1800. Despite the genocide pursued by white supremacy against us over those two centuries, Africa's seed bears bountiful fruit on these cruel shores. Our journalists, commentators, and theatre people should reveal the shame of our being subject at this late date to the whims and spites of racists. Our media should hammer home the message that we dare not trust the federal government to throw us a "safety net." The history of all successful Third World struggles has shown such frank and repeated messages to be the heart of liberating publicity. For a long time our more militant publications have emphasized white America's determination to exploit and dupe Black people. More ink needs to flow on environmental racism, to expose it as a conspiracy to kill us off gradually in an underhanded manner; explaining that our water is being poisoned and the air we breathe befouled under the cover of "waste recyclement." The idea is to interpret current events and put a "spin" on contentious issues in such a way as to turn them against the powers-that-be. For instance, Disney flicks and Disney theme parks should be interpreted for what they really are—great circuses put on to excite our passions and starve our minds, while squandering stupendous resources that could be used to feed, house, and educate our children. We need to challenge such allegedly "Black-friendly" films as *The Lion King* for what they really are—ploys to get us to buy tickets and decoys to make us believe that we have been "accepted." Even though our situation seems bleak, white world supremacy faces oblivion in the long run, doomed at home and abroad because people of color everywhere are destined to fight it. This message builds confidence. Tell

Black people that white civilization is not invincible. Tell us that over and over again and it will embolden our attacks.

Perhaps it was to address these issues, among others, that the National Association of Black Journalists joined Asian, Latino, and American Indian journalists in a Unity 1994 conference. At the very least the almost 6,000 members of the four groups tried to bring down walls between them. They recognized that the fight against white racism had to be a joint one.

It is essential for Black political propaganda to have popular appeal. The picturesque is a big draw for the inner city man-in-the-street. The ecstasies and extreme emotions of many Black church services are proverbial. If we are to reach the masses, the message of cold social analysis and political strategy and tactics had better be joined with fervid rhetoric and lots of concrete illustration. Dry-as-dust presentation ignores the Black life style and is likely to leave us cold and unmoved. This added requirement complicates the task, but it is the elementary duty of the activist to learn and speak a language understood by the ordinary people of color.

The same goes for African Canadians. Like no other people in their country, Blacks in Canada are tied to the economic situation and political climate in the U.S., south of the border. The fate of each and every Black person in Canada is bound inextricably to the fortunes of the 35 to 40 million-strong community of African Americans in the United States. I have contended that all Diasporans—North Americans, Caribbeans, Spanish-speakers, and Brazilians—are linked. However, in the case of Afro-Canadians, the bond with the Black United States is more than a connection; it is a life line. This is because Blacks in Canada rank as an *ultra*-minority, merely one of several "visible minorities," in many localities numbering much less than South Asians, Chinese, and Native Canadians. This small community can forego economic, political, and cultural links with Black America only at great cost to itself. Canada may or may not maintain its national unity. That unity is constantly threatened by the separatist ferment in the province of Québec. Québec may or may not separate and form an independent, sovereign state. Whether French Canadian nationalism takes Québec out of Confederation really does not matter all that much to Black people. For whether racism speaks English in Toronto or French in Montreal, it is all one to the Black people. In both places African Canadians must deal with white supremacy. There is no evidence French-speak-

503

ing Black residents in, say, Montreal would face any less white racism in an independent Québec; it might even be worse.

Hence ties with Black America are immensely significant for Canadian Blacks. They enable them to overcome the inferiority complex that can come from contemplating their ultra-minority status in Canada. As time passes, Afro-Canadians must become more cognizant of the fact that they are part of an immense Black community centered in the United States—that they are, in fact, its northern tip. Their main loyalties should be with the African Americans, not with the lily-white Canadians. Surely it is far better for Afro-Canadians to rank as equal members of the African Diaspora family than as the second-rate stepchildren of a "great white North" dedicated to European cultural standards.

There is urgent need for Canadian Black organizations to establish lasting ties with American Black liberation associations. The border between the two countries means little to Black folks culturally. It is detrimental to the struggle of the smaller, poorer, and weaker Black Canadian contingent. Afro-Canadians can benefit from emulating the organized labor model, in which many Canadian unions are branches of so-called "international" unions with U.S. parent bodies. The payoff is greater clout in collective bargaining. For those who lack the stomach for anything stronger, at least there should be a Toronto branch of the NAACP. Organizations like Ontario's Black Action Defense Committee would be much aided in the fight against racial discrimination if they could call on the experience, resources, personnel, and legal moxie of American civil rights and Black nationalist agencies. These recommendations may upset a few African Canadian leaders intent on running their own local show. But "independence" hype aside, partnership in broader North American–wide associations need not stifle local initiative and it is high time for all Diasporans to suppress particularistic egoism on behalf of our people as a whole. The recent-immigrant character of Black Canada's West Indian majority is the chief psychological obstacle. Having arrived in the country only during the last 20 to 30 years, many are insecure, fear expulsion, and thirst for naturalization, praying that formal Canadian citizenship will somehow shelter them from white racism.

*

POLITICAL VOCABULARY

The "Movement" is an old shoe that Black activists kick around with familiarity, reviving or burying it verbally as need be. As a real phenomenon with a history and structure, it has always been rent by divergent interests and ideologies. In its best aspects the movement is the spontaneous organic creation of Black America's long resistance to racism and devaluation. It swims in that which Vincent Harding has aptly termed the mighty river of Black struggle. At times the term *"Movement"* is used to lump together all the different political factions representing different segments of the community. From the mid-1950s "revival" of struggle, this condition stamped the features of the civil rights crusade. In common usage, the term refers to that vast collection of liberation forces juxtaposing parties, organizations, institutions, and prominent personalities, each enlisting and directing its own followers.

As a whole, the activity of the movement has always been non-specialized, with fluctuating membership. Call to mind, as merely one illustration in many, the short-lived alliance between the Black Panthers and SNCC at the end of the 1960s. Historically, the component parts of the movement have split more easily than they fuse. This has been one of its weaknesses, a manifestation of that disunity which caused Malcolm X such agony. Spawned by ambition, bitter rivalries have often paralyzed effective political work.

The donneybrook over unity and self-definition is illustrated clearly in the continuing debate over self-denomination. At the beginning of the 1990s, when the Joint Center for Political and Economic Studies asked the community to name itself, it learned that 72 percent of Black people still wanted to be called "Black." The national survey found that only 15 percent were partial to "African-American"; the designation favored most by college graduates. Eight percent did not care one way or another, and there was still a hard core residue (two percent) that chose to be called "Negro," three percent preferred "Afro-American." Opinion ran the gamut. Since then the term "African American" has gained in popularity and usage.

Use of the term "African American" is sponsored most prominently by the Jesse Jackson forces. Many intellectuals and the young

505

like its resonance. The one qualm that can be raised about its adoption as the general designation is that it may be interpreted as homage to the ethnicity concept which denies Black people a more socially deserving plateau in American society than, say, Irish-Americans or Italian-Americans. Ethnicity is deployed as camouflage to divert the heat away from white racism. In contrast, the term "Black" has the strength of highlighting that which is most fundamental in America—the centrality of racism and the struggle of African Americans against it. As the primary designation, the term "Black" acknowledges Black folk as the *motive* force in the entire history of the nation. The basic contradiction in our society is still the Black-white one.

One and the same term may mean different things to different persons. In Chapter One I characterized the struggle between Black people and white world supremacy upcoming in the next century in near-Darwinistic terms. While my meaning is one of confrontation between two fundamentally antagonistic social collectives, that is not necessarily the way the concept "Darwinism" is used and understood by some other Black thinkers. Haki Madhubuti, for instance, observes that many of the brothers loitering on street corners in city after city are unfortunately hung-up on a survival-of-the-fittest code toward one another. Theirs is a brand of Darwinistic survival in which each person strikes to achieve his own ends regardless of others. The usual outcome is Black-against-Black destruction.

If liberation is ever to come, some way must be found to channel these self-destructive energies into fruitful political avenues; into reparation campaigns, for example.

At most, a political party or movement retains the capacity to effect real social transformation for about the length of one generation from the date of its birth. As a rule, if it has not overturned the status quo within that 30-odd years span, it never will. From its Free Soil foundation in 1854 to the end of the Grant Administration and the betrayal of Black Reconstruction, the Republican Party, for instance, fulfilled its historical destiny as an anti-slavery factor in 22 years. Since then it has been a malevolent, reactionary drag on the Republic. Any new, truly radical political movement which has not taken over control of the government within a generation never will. Should its trip to power take longer, it will no longer have any thing new or progressive to offer when it arrives. It lives on solely as a sorry rump of opportunists, of timid and conservative time-

506

servers, spurred mainly by personal career goals, lucrative and prestigious posts, and winning elections. Movements that escape domestication and remain true to original ideas, but have not made it
within the prescribed period, are usually marginalized, ostracized
to the sectarian fringe of the political arena.

In white society, even those movements which make it, those
which seize power, implement their program and institutionalize
their rule— nevertheless fail in the end, essentially because they seek
to install justice on a white civilization base organically opposed to
justice and equality for people of color—an impossible task.

The ultimate victory of the Black struggle depends on the ability of Black political formations to avoid these fates. To date not one
of our political creations has as yet succeeded. Not one of our political organizations has come close to real political power.

*

Since the day we first arrived as slaves on these shores nearly 400
years ago, three political options have been available to those among
us involved in the community's public affairs: accommodation,
reform, and rebellion.

At the outset of the present century the accommodationist trend
was best personified by B.T. Washington, most agree. At the tail end
of the twentieth century it is personified most starkly by Clarence
Thomas. Accommodationism is willing to view ordinary Black people as expendable. Countless sellouts at their expense have marred
its career.

There have been moments in the history of Black rebellion, when
rebels—fierce and proud—have avowed an inherent reformism, i.e.,
a readiness to make do with the small change of today in the hope
of a better, richer tomorrow. The anger and frustration which have
spurred our revolutionaries, from Nat Turner to the Black Panthers,
have cost much in blood and sacrifice. Any direct challenge by Blacks
pushes white supremacy's violence button. The jack-booted military
repressions in Miami's Liberty City and L.A.'s South Central are still
fresh in the mind.

Yet, indomitably, the advocates of independent politics keep trying. One recent example of this resilience came in Detroit. Perhaps
out of nostalgia for the heady, revolutionary-seeming days of the late
1960s, DRUM (Dodge Revolutionary Union Movement) joined with
the few League of Revolutionary Black Workers cadres still around

to call a conference at Wayne State University in 1993. The occasion was the 25th anniversary of those two revolutionary organizations. It could be that the real aim of the gathering was to commemorate a lost revolutionary spirit among Black blue-collar workers. Lamenting the slippage, conference oganizers pleaded with Detroit's depleted industrial ranks to carry forward the legacy of Malcolm X. The roster of organizations evoked in retrospect read like an honor roll of the revolutionary 1960s and 1970s: African Liberation Support Committees throughout the U.S. and Canada, the Black Panther Party, the CTA Black Caucus of Chicago, the Black Student United Front, the Congress of African Peoples, the Motor City Labor League, and the Republic of New Africa.

Knowing at first hand the economic havoc caused by the new technology of computers and robots which is throwing Black industrial workers out on the streets all over this country, General Baker, an early leader of DRUM and of the League, hoped the conference would revive revolutionary resolve. If not, Baker and his remaining comrades felt, Black America will strangle in poor health care, concentration-camp public housing, and an expanding police force and prison system.

Canada too sees efforts to prod Black workers to take action—defensive in this case. Racism in white organized labor has prompted formation of a Coalition of Black Trade Unionists of Canada. It held a forum in Toronto in the fall of 1993 to discuss white racism in the work place and to try to find a way to counter the discriminatory hiring practices of unions, particularly in the construction industry. The organizers recognized they would get nowhere without Black unity. Strategies designed to boost Black worker participation in union affairs were put forward, and plans were made to lobby for adequate Black worker representation among the leaders of the Canadian labor movement. Clearly, the Canadian CBTU is modeled after its American counterpart.

America's Muslim segment is growing by leaps and bounds. Surprising to many, the largest single group of Muslims in North America are Blacks, not Arabs. African-Americans make up 42 percent of the Muslim population, perhaps more. South Asians follow at about one in four. Arabs are only 12 or 13 percent.

Although the majority of Afro-American Muslims are orthodox in the Sunni or Shiah sense, for most people the Nation of Islam comes to mind when they speak of "Black Muslims." The movement founded by W.D. Fard, developed by Elijah Muhammad, the organization which nurtured Malcolm X, is unquestionably the most prominent Muslim institution in the United States, and its concrete political actions impact the Black community at large with great force.

Thus when Nation of Islam leader Louis Farrakhan seems to advocate that job-needy Blacks now offer themselves as a cheap, docile labor force, it is a serious matter (Louis Farrakhan, A *Torchlight for America*, FCN Publishing Co., Chicago 1993:81)— even if the white media do distort his remarks. A fair interpretation would see the proposal as the Nation of Islam's way of attracting white-owned manufacturing to Black urban districts. It is also fair, however, to view the proposal as refurbished Booker T. Washingtonism. The Nation of Islam's combination of radical-sounding rhetoric with an ultra-conservative economic program is in keeping with the legacy of Elijah Muhammad.

I, for one, am a firm believer in conspiracy as an influential social phenomenon, not in the narrow sense of a treacherous plan formulated in secret, but rather as the unplanned, but purposeful, behavior of key groups in society. A grand conspiracy to exploit and oppress Black people has been the heart pump of white supremacy for 500 years. There is room under its umbrella for all sorts of specific *enabling conspiracies*. As things happen, some of these enabling conspiracies may even contradict others—reflecting the often dissimilar or conflicting immediate interests of one or another faction among white power brokers.

Current today is an enabling conspiracy by means of which the white Establishment continues to pick and appoint Black leaders, only now the selection is sly as well as negative. Wickedly-wise upholders of white supremacy know that in the current atmosphere any public endorsement by white pundits of any top rank African American political personality will most likely immediately bring the Black community down on his head for being an Uncle Tom. The individual in question is likely to be spurned as the white man's puppet. But they know also that Black folk will rally round and acknowledge the "leadership" and virtue of those among our political leaders under attack by whites. Even left-leaning Black feminists began to think that Anita Hill, a conservative Republican, was alright the moment she was manhandled by white male Senators during the Clarence Thomas hearings. Nowadays when the white power structure wants to advance the fortunes of some Black political figure whose program actually confirms white supremacy, the best way to accomplish the task is to orchestrate a massive media, political, and academic *attack* on that personality, triggering reactive Black support and solidarity for the one assaulted. White media badmouthing combined with radical and militant-sounding rhetoric, confers respectability in the eyes of ordinary Black folk, and wins their trust.

In view of this process there are those among us who are uncomfortable about the Farrakhan phenomenon. They wonder whether there is a negative selection at work to elevate the public image of the Nation of Islam chief who has become a major celebrity in the Black community on the strength of sympathy for a brother dumped on by the white media, rather than for the reasoned appeal of his political message.

There is also movement at the other end of the political spectrum. Milwaukee is a retooling, restructuring, and developing service-oriented center, notorious for residential hyper segregation. Its Black residents kicked off the 1990s with Panther-like militancy and a coalition-building mood. Michael McGee, a former Panther organizer, won election as an alderman, buoyed by a hard-core constituency including 600 members of a local Black Panther militia. Structured along para-military lines, the militia staged unarmed patrols of the Black community with an eye on police brutality. Desperation could drive Milwaukee Blacks to urban guerrilla warfare, it was warned. The time may not be far away when oppressive institutions will be attacked physically. McGee, an advocate of militant struggle, favors the recruitment of determined cadres unafraid of white supremacy. He also favors anti-drug dealing, building restoration and aid for the elderly and the homeless. McGee, a Vietnam veteran, blames much of the frustration and alienation that characterize Black life today on the total vacuum in radical leadership since the demise of the Panthers. Unless Black men get back to the 1960s tradition of going head-up against white supremacy, they will continue to kill each other for less than nothing, McGee believes.

In a parallel political initiative in nearby Illinois, the Chicago Chapter of the National Conference of Black Lawyers founded the African American Defense Committee Against Police Violence in 1992. The next year the group held workshops on police brutality, trial advocacy, and Black political empowerment. In Indiana, during the spring of 1994, the leader of the Indianapolis Black Panther

Militia called for Black reprisal for lethal judicial sentencing. Reacting to a trumped-up charge of murder against his own son, the militant predicted retaliation should his son be executed. Even relatively placid Canada has begun to see omens of retaliation against racist police violence. Victims of racist cops in metropolitan Toronto have warned that if they continue to be denied justice, the oppressed would "find out where [the guilty cops] live and who their children are" (*Globe and Mail*, 1 April 1994). Black Torontonians were particularly enraged at police provocations like the deliberate entrapment of popular local activist Dudley Laws. Is payback the harbinger of the near future in urban North America?

The reactions illustrate what is likely to happen in the absence of an organized, militant Black mass political movement sworn to obliterate white supremacy. The void leaves those made desperate by racism, those who have identified well-off whites as the real enemy, feeling there is no other meaningful alternative but physical confrontation. The failure of Black elected officials and police officers, and the inability of established civil rights agencies to mount a credible challenge to white domination, goads the disillusioned warrior to act by himself; to isolated, individual strikes, planned and carried out alone, choosing white locales to spare Black bystanders from harm. In such an undertaking the casualties tend to be indiscriminant, hurting even anti-racist whites, even white persons who are members of Black families. Another fault of such a solitary operation is the death or imprisonment of the attacker. A freedom fighter is lost whose contribution to Black liberation under other circumstances might have the potential for greatness. Colin Ferguson, for instance, is alleged to have warred against the instituionalized racism of a university and of the New York state government. Though he disparaged some Asian-Americans as racists, he despised "Uncle Tom Negroes" more, convinced that collaborators and upwardly-mobile types are selling out the community.

*

INTERESTS—"NATIONAL," WHITE AND BLACK—NEVER IDENTICAL

The torrent of Black struggle is broad and deep, much too diverse to be captured in one bucket. After all, we are 40 million here in North America. Yet it is clear that our people *as a people* have a general binding *Interest*—an interest in freedom, *power*, self-determination, and development of our full human potential. And it should be equally clear that the key to that interest is that ever elusive Black unity.

From the brash streets of New York City has recently come a catchy slogan—*"Just Us Revolution."* Besides the obvious play on the word "justice," the slogan was coined to call together all of Black America's contemporary trends, movements and ideologies— reformists, nationalists, republicans, liberals, Christians, Muslims (orthodox and Nation of Islam), and all other religionists, Afrocentrics, communists, socialists and conservatives—the masses and the "classes." The Just-Us-Revolution concept dovetails with the circumstantially revolutionary demand for reparations. It envisages indemnification especially ("just") for Afro-Americans in long-overdue recognition of our unpaid labor contribution to the creation of the wealth and power of the western hemisphere. The call is revolutionary, for the establishment of Black unity arrived at through mass dialogue to consensus, and a mass campaign for reparations, could hardly fail to trigger a ferment that would alter the fundamental nature of the society in which we live. It is also the movement that is most appropriate (at the moment) to the post–Cold War global struggle against white supremacy.

The children of the Diaspora have multiplied and spread over the western hemisphere. In addition to the 40 million in North America, there are more than 100 million in Brazil, and millions more in the Caribbean and Spanish-speaking America. The garbage of oppression—"the shit that comes down," in street vernacular— is endured solely because Black people for a myriad of historical reasons put up with it. Were we to join forces as a unit tomorrow, or next year, or during the next decade, and say *No*! to the system of white supremacy, were we to free our minds from the fogs of Eurocentric brainwashing, the situation would alter radically. The movement might be a non-violent one of civil disobedience, one in which our people pour into the streets, clog the arteries of transport, clutter the country's factories and financial facilities, straining police and political resources to the limit. The movement might have to combine direct physical confrontations with the above mass measures. Either way, we could literally paralyze the country—close America down and force the white man to finally face the issue of Black liberation and the payment of his debt to us. Such a movement would put to rest the blame-the-victim ploy used to exempt white racism from moral, social, and economic responsibility for the plight of Black people. It would put "paid" to the hypocritical preachings of "racial autonomy" reconciled with continuing superiority for white values, white institutions, and Western [white] civilization. Resounding in the slogan "Just Us Revolution" is the realization that none of this is possible without massive and continual Black street-level action across the length and breadth of the continent.

As should be expected, the prospects of any such political self-reliance sets alarms ringing in the halls of white supremacy. Quick as lightening, "friendly" pundits jump to warn us against the "fatal" consequences of any attempts by Black people to go-it-alone. That we should place our trust in white "moderates" is an article of faith in Caucasian circles and among our own more timid brethren. Evidence that real independence is still a no-no in certain African American circles can be seen in the alacrity with which NAACP board "moderates" responded to white pressure in 1994. No sooner had they gotten wind of the displeasure of white moderates at executive director Ben Chavis' "extremist" overtures to militant forces in our own community, than they organized a coup against him. The lesson of white "moderation" is hammered home in white South Africa's desperate solace at Nelson Mandela's assurance following his victory in the 1994 election that reconciliation rather than retribution would guide his post-apartheid government. A self-pitying collective sigh of relief was heard round the earth, broadcast by globe-spanning Western media.

In essence, the *white "moderate"* is one who can live with discrimination against Blacks and other people of color, but when that injustice ceases to be possible, prays that whites escape payback. He/she is one who is lukewarm in defense of Black rights, but downright passionate in fearing that white folks might get their just deserts. Yet the influence of white moderates in prominent Black agencies still compels us to deal with repeated betrayals, repudiations, and petty backbiting by misguided elements among our own folk. Affection for white "moderates" remains the basic condition of existence for many simpering, spineless "Negroes" and "hankerchief heads." Anyone of us who dares insist that we should never allow our demands to become dependent on the assistance of white allies is dismissed as an "extremist" by our own "moderates."

Even so, white supremacy can buy, seduce, and suborn only so many of us. Its ability to train and grubstake house pets is finite. The system can afford politically only a tiny handful of Clarence

Thomases and still retain its integrity as a *system* of white supremacy. Conversely, the Black liberation movement can flourish only
where it succeeds in mobilizing the ordinary Black folk to whom the
system offers nothing but the "same old, same old" poverty and discrimination. That is why the Chavis-progressives' loss of the NAACP
springboard was a serious setback for the movement as a whole.
The best mass mobilizers of Black rank and file in recent historical
memory have been Martin Luther King and Nelson Mandela.

And mass mobilization depends, in turn, on the ability to capture and maintain the focus of national political attention. A pow-
erfully unified and goal-oriented Black liberation movement must
have an array of strategies and techniques. Above all, the movement
must generate a kind of *sensation-a-month* in order to electrify the
national media and keep everyone thinking and talking about our
issues. America and Europe are notorious for their short attention
span, a flaw cultivated by the mass media. Western civilization has
a thirty-second sound-bit brain. For example, the energizing impulse
that the Jesse Jackson campaign generated among Blacks and among
some whites in 1988 lasted only until the Democratic National
Convention in Atlanta which pegged Dukakis as its contender. After
that, Jackson was thrown into an anonymity limbo and his political
clout fizzled.

The Black liberation movement must be able to churn up one
political issue after another, month after month, one controversy
after the next, or at least be perceived as having that potential, year
in, year out. Only then will we keep Black demands and aspirations
at the top of the national political agenda. White America must be
allowed no respite. That means constant pressure—not just reacting with protest when some racist cop shoots down an unarmed
Black youth, thereupon falling back to sleep until the next outrage.
To date we have not done a very good job of this. The U.S. media
focuses abroad on every European spat from the Crimea to the Mafia
in Italy. It ignores positive news from Africa. On the home front
Black issues are upstaged by abortion pros and cons and stories
about penises snipped off by alienated wives. Worse, we have
allowed the media to trivialize Black problems. By minimizing white
racism, by promoting environmentalism, homosexual rights, animal
rights, and white feminism, the media have made the struggle for
Black liberation seem no great shakes in the public eye. If the centrality of Black folk in American history is denied, then we are

demoted to the rank of merely one issue among many of allegedly equal status.

Race turns the wheels of American society. We must never permit the powers-that-be to slumber the racial issue in neglect. If we reduce the pressure, the media are sure to divert national attention to white concerns, to the Chechnyas and Bosnias, to the Boris Yeltsins and Helmut Kohls of world politics, to U.S.-Japanese trade balances, to the personal tribulations of Hollywood celebrities, to sporting events, to natural disasters—to anything but those circumstances troublesome to Black folk.

*

It is hard to overestimate the galvanizing effect of correctly formulated, timely political slogans. The search for ever more active, ever more demanding, yet easily understood political slogans needs to continue day and night. Rallying cries and catchwords should be of the type which agitates the community and draws folks into demonstrations, resistance, and direct action. Kariamu Welsh Asante has devoted her career to examining the social and political symbolism of African dance, for example. They should not be the merely reactive calls to "free this or that political prisoner," or to "end the persecution of this or that Black organization," which we are all so used to. Yet it is vital that they be down-to-earth and the kind that ordinary people consider *attainable*—not some castle in the sky entreaty like, say, asking the western hemisphere's Black citizens to return to Africa, or appealing for us to renounce our Black birthright to ownership of America's "land" in favor of the "Red Man." For the broad masses, action is usually kindled only by matters of immediate concern, realizable goals. They are seldom swayed by abstract discussion or party dogma. The turn-off and tune-out are most evident in the apathy of unregistered and non-voting Blacks in the 18 to 25 age group. The leadership needs to propose steps to restore Black self-respect and dignity in the face of white supremacy. It must have an intermediate program of true humanism. Short of total liberation requiring the final eradication of white supremacy, there are moves that can be made to lessen the self-hatred and feelings of worthlessness expressed in Black-on-Black violence, despair, and inferiority complex in regard to whites. This is where the Nation of Islam has excelled, by the way. The strength of Louis Farrakhan's followers resides in the rehabilitation of addicts and common-law felons and in cleaning up neighborhoods and public housing projects.

One such strategy envisages radiating "circles of love," nucleated around self, spoking out to family, finally encompassing Black folk as a whole on the principle that one likes those most like oneself. A little far-fetched seeming, but intriguing as a notion. The end purpose of this sphere of affection is concerted action to destroy white domination. And it is only on condition of the overthrow of white world supremacy that it would become possible to include white people as an entire civilization in a love for humanity as a whole.

Just as empty, extremist rhetoric must be avoided, so must outlandish behavior and life-styles, if activists are to win popular support. Care should be taken to avoid the voluntarist styles, impatient over-enthusiasm, "way-out" homo-and heterosexual irrelevancies, and drug "trips" that have become as "American as apple pie" but turn off the decent, down-to-earth, hardworking Black and Afro-Latino majority. Instead what we need is a sober line of political demarcation. It is not wise to go running after every new political fad.

Consequently, plans to force through affirmative action and other partial gains are an essential part of the struggle. Plans for reform and amelioration should be massive and bold, not small and timid. They must aim to raise African Americans to parity, proportionately with whites, in all levels of the economy, cultural life, and education. We must not shy away from huge federal expenditures and policies in fear of white conservative tax revolt. White backlash is inevitable; however, the tension between it and Black demands creates destablizing ferment from which may arise historical transformation. White opposition must be confronted head-on. Indeed radical reform is bound to be unpopular with the racist white majority. No matter how weak-minded, all politicians can count electoral votes. No incumbent president chosen under the present two-party system would fight faithfully to enact and enforce such reforms. Never mind his promises. The white majority would never reelect him. Hence this stragegy should entail programs and reforms which can be completed within the four-year span of a single administration, measures least amenable to repeal under subsequent administrations.

We are talking about reforms that would *commit the system* and be very difficult to undo without jeopardizing the entire socio-political organism. That is why we must envision Afro-American *ownership* of major assets as the key element of palliative reform. *It is very hard to rescind private ownership under the capitalist system.*

While not invulnerable to right-wing take-backs, property legally vested in Black hands would cause a dilemma for the system. It would be very difficult to order uncompensated seizure of Black assets without infringing the bedrock principles of capitalism itself. Such action would reveal private property to be less than sacrosanct and encourage radicals of all stripes, colors, and races to attack it, including white leftists. Expropriation even of Black holdings would set an example very dangerous to capitalism. Subsidized, mortgaged, and guaranteed by federal funds, sanctioned with bought-and-paid-for valid deeds and contracts, property transfers to Black owners would create a thundering headache for anyone determined to strip new Black owners of reform-generated assets, given the philosophical and constitutional presumptions of the system of private property. It could be done, but the act might destabilize the entire political economy. It could ignite bitter political strife comparable to that which set one group of whites against the other during the 1850s leading up to the Civil War.

*

Many Afro-Americans now feel that no meaningful affirmative action is achievable without an independent Black national political party. The call for one reverberated through the National Black Political Convention in Gary, Indiana, in March 1972. The demand was resurrected in 1976 when Ron Dellums was encouraged to run for President as an independent candidate. It has surfaced again in the 1990s, as people yearn for political action free of Democratic Party strings. Support ranges from social scientists like Michael Dawson of the University of Chicago to DeWayne Wickham, *USA Today* columnist. The independent frame of mind of Black voters shone brightly in Marion Barry's reelection as DC's mayor in 1994. Black Washingtonians refused to let federal prosecutors lead them by the nose. Visionaries yearn for the day when the more than 8,000 Black elected officeholders break free politically. After all, nearly all of our officials are elected in Black majority districts and are not dependent on white voters. Almost all of them are Democrats. Since when has the Democratic Party not taken the Black vote for granted? Since when has it not ignored Black interests once elected? Clinton ran after the white Bubba swing vote with the ardor of a maiden in fear of becoming an old maid. He pandered to their prejudice, posturing as "tough" on any Blacks who step out of line.

517

Clinton lectured Sister Souljah, marginalized Jesse Jackson, and retracted Lani Guinier's nomination for assistant attorney general for civil rights. The other party is even worse. The GOP openly courts the racist backlash vote. The last time the Republicans even winked at Black folk was 1948.

Those who back the move to independent action envision an independent party as controlling a *swing vote* capable of throwing national elections one way or the other—either to the Democrats or to the Republicans, depending upon which group offers the best payoff. Michael Dawson sees good prospects for this kind of manoeuver. However, third-party advocates still have not come up with a way to deal with the vested interests of Black elected officials, especially those seated in Congress and in state legislatures. How to overcome the reluctance of long-term Black Democrats who have built up much seniority, which they would lose if they left the Democratic Party? Could they even retain their seats as independents? This puzzler has led to the suggestion that maybe the drive to form an independent Black third party should not kick off at the national level, thereby avoiding injury to the seniority rights accumulated in Congress by Black Democrats. Perhaps it should start at local levels, in municipal electoral politics. The initial effort could be made in locales like New York City, where the 1993 defeat of David Dinkins demonstrated once again that white Democrats refuse to support Black Democratic candidates when they are pitted against white Republicans. Or in states like North Carolina where white regular Democrats endorsed the likes of arch-Republican Jesse Helms—vintage Confederate-style white supremacist—given the ballot choice between himself and a Black Democrat.

But then who at this late date can credibly claim that anything is race-neutral in America, let alone political democracy? We are supposed to believe in the existence of a particularized free voter "marketplace," where totally unconnected individuals cast ballots on a purely private basis. This is a resounding myth. Our world is not constructed that way. At birth we inherit a social structure composed of conflicting large blocs of persons, united or at least joined together in racial, ethnic, national, religious, gender, class, age, and other groupings. The overriding antagonism in the society in which we find ourselves is racial—one that pits white supremacy against the Black struggle for first-class humanity. There is no, say, brown-eyed electorate competing against a blue-eyed one. The real antagonism leaves no room for alternative, imagined ones. The way history has panned out, we most definitely do have a white majority electorate at loggerheads with a minority Black bloc vote. We would laugh at the suggestion of a political party of heavyweights to contest against a party of people weighing less than, say, 150 lbs. But Catholic, Jewish, Fundamentalist, Hispanic, anti-abortionist, and gay-lesbian lobbies are indeed realities. We do not live in, say, a science fictional universe where all the land masses riding the earth's crust are joined in a gigantic "Pangia" supercontinent, eliminating the need for navies to protect national borders. Nor has Homo sapiens evolved wings. If people could fly think how easy it would have been for Rwandan refugees to escape the slaughter in their homeland for shelter in neighboring countries. Nor do we live in a world where people could swim like dolphins. If so, millions of our ancestors would have leaped from the slave ships and swum safely home to Africa, and the Haitian boat people of the 1990s could not have been so easily intercepted by U.S. naval vessels and herded back to their purgatory.

In the real world, the children of Africa in countries where they are a minority must view the institution of democracy for what it is— a device to perpetuate white supremacy by means of racist voter majorities. Apartheid-like residential segregation, white racial preference, and low rates of Black-white intermarriage indicate non-assimilation between the two great racial groups for a long time to come. Black conservatives are the only ones still talking about a "color-blind" society and the "declining significance of race"—characters estranged from reality. Our list of grievances is long, ranging from joblessness, poverty and poor schooling to substandard, segregated housing, police brutality and neglect, and an unjust legal system. Continued confrontation between the races is unavoidable. White majority rule is an instrument of our subjugation. There is nothing holy, nor anything carved in marble about counting ballots. Owning a voter majority does not give the white man a divine right to rule over Black people. We need not be hypnotized by two-party idiocy.

Even the system-affirming campaign of maverick billionaire Ross Perot in 1992 exposed a potential to explode the Republican-Democrat tandem. Proposals like Lani Guinier's cumulative voting scheme—which proved the kiss of death for her candidacy— deserve careful consideration in our effort to work out provisional strategies. She wants authentic representation in the political process for our people, something which winner-take-all and at-large elections rarely provide. Her political philosophy is anchored in a politics of "like minds" as opposed to one of "like bodies" (Guinier 1994). To accomplish this aim she would revive the more-than-a-century-old U.S. tradition of cumulative voting. Approval of the latter would make it impossible for white majorities to continue to shut out Black candidates, yet would still assure that a majority of the voters will elect a majority of the representatives. She looks, furthermore, to the U.S. Congressional supermajority rule which requires two-thirds, rather than a simple majority, to override presidential vetoes, impeach a president, and ratify treaties. Across-the-board adoption of legislative supermajority regulation would in effect give the Black minority a "veto," forcing white majority lawmakers to bargain and accept compromise solutions. Guinier's search for broad-based consensus is thought-provoking. At the same time it is one that confirms the adage that a technique effective in one situation is not automatically suited to a different situation. In South Africa the supermajority rule would hinder the drive to establish Black majority control.

Thus the Black world needs one set of plans for combatting white supremacy in the United States and another set for combatting the same in South Africa. And that is as it should be. Given the demographic situation in racist America, where Blacks are a decided minority, and given a political system in which white politicians court a white majority electorate that is either indifferent or hateful towards Black people, we are unlikely ever to receive redress from our electoral constitution which enshrines the "will of the majority." Again this calls into legitimate question our political loyalties to the democratic political setup. The primary skill of white politicians is to attract votes and win elections. To ask those selfsame politicians to remedy the vast structural woes plaguing African Americans is naive. Say all one wants to about "gridlock," it is like asking the highly trained professional football player, one who has spent long years honing *football* skills, to win a world chess competition, on the misapprehension that a world-class athlete should be able to perform effectively in any sporting contest.

Our people have never been polled as to *their* wishes about their destiny in the western hemisphere, never been asked how they regard their place in the U.S. and Canada, never even been allowed to say whether we are content to live alongside white folk. The Black

Panthers once called for a referendum on the national aspirations of Afro-Americans. It might make sense for the Black community to be presented over a number of years with a series of carefully prepared inquiries concerning the economy, cultural life, education, leisure, preferred locality, and even religious preference—a series of referendums, as it were, of plebiscites limited to Blacks. The procedure might even culminate in a plebiscite concerning national identity and allegiance—as sensitive as those queries might be. True referendums and plebiscites which consult every adult in the community would be ideal. Short of that, massive, scientifically-established polls which sample Black opinion on relevant issues could be effective tools in policy-planning. Even though it is understood that polls take *samples* and never really rest the will of the *whole* people.

For example, we know that Black families spend more per capita than whites for fresh fish, bacon and sausage, sugar and flour, baby food, orange pop, boys' clothing and infant accessories, while renting far more electronic gadgets than whites. However, despite tough-jawed blather about "economic multiculturalism," we have done nothing yet to boycott the white-owned companies which sell and rent us these commodities, but which have done little or nothing to promote African American hiring or joint ventures.

Chapter 24

A CONCLUSION: SAFETY, POWER, AND PARITY

White supremacist extremists intent on race war—groups such as the Aryan Nations, National Socialist Skinheads, and Church of the Creator—run military training survival camps for their recruits in which they give them weapons training. Black organizations, as a rule, do not. What measures are being taken to prepare Black folks to at the very least defend themselves against trained racists bent on violence? The racists have para-military camps. They collect money to purchase land in remote, non-urban and topographically favorable terrain for military training. Racist para-militarists take refuge in Montana. They stockpile up-to-date, high-tech weapons—all legally purchased. We watch this idly and take no counteraction. Black veterans of the armed forces could be recruited to instruct some of our youth in the art of self-defense.

Many veterans are jobless and need employment; harnessing their skills would give some of them jobs doing what they know well. Who knows when we will need our own explosives experts to defuse bombs planted by crazed racists? Can we trust white demolitions men to do it for us? Letter bombs have already arrived in the mail at Black agencies. Black intellectuals, political activists, and church leaders face the threat of right-wing bombings. It is irresponsible to sit back and watch KKK-types training and stockpiling for our destruction without taking similar measures legally for self-protection. How reliable are the police and armed forces when it comes to protecting us from race-motivated attacks? The Jewish Defense League and the Israeli armed forces testify that Jews, for one, certainly have learned the lesson of armed self-defense.

A whole generation of young inner-city Black males is being flushed down the drain, so to speak. They are lost, hopeless, deprived of meaningful human life prospects. Never employed, or always underemployed, they are prevented from expressing the primal urge of a male in this culture to affirm one's manhood by taking unto oneself a woman, remaining with her, fathering her children, and—most vital—supporting his wife and children with his own *sufficient* earnings. This is a function that most white males in this society take for granted, but which fewer and fewer young Black men are allowed to perform. A whole generation of Black males has been deprived of this prime instrument of self-respect. This is why many urban Black youths feel they have so little to lose, turning to gangs, drug-dealing, and violence. Their life could be salvaged by a relentless drive for real empowerment, one that would offer meaning and direction for an otherwise directionless, aimless existence marred by bravado and self-destructive behavior. This generation has nothing to lose, but a world to gain. They are the ones most susceptible to an updated version of Malcolm X's "Message to the Grassroots." They are the ones for whom the struggle for Black liberation is a life and death issue.

These are also the ones, the public housing project dwellers, for whom the issue of police harassment and brutality is not academic. Can we afford to be the only ones who are forgetful? Columnist Herb Boyd commented: "[o]ur approach in the future should be well-calculated, and if we strike back let it be selective... we need a complete arsenal of tactics to challenge the potent racism that engulfs us" (*The New York Amsterdam News*, 9 May 1992). When they see the long arm of true justice reach out and lay punishment on those who commit racially-motivated acts of injustice, white racists—be they police officers, judges, prosecutors, or private citizens—would for the first time in history begin to respect the slogan "Black Power." They would begin to realize that sooner or later, no matter how long it takes or how much tracking is required, retribution would come.

One could compile a "shopping list" of Black injunctions that would range from punitive political action on our part to the defeat of racist candidates, to a repudiation of the national debt and annual interest services charges owed to the top four percent of U.S. citizens whose annual income equals the combined annual income of the bottom 51 percent of all Americans. The list would pair favorite son bargaining in presidential primaries with Afro-American bloc voting. The slate would not be complete without the call for numerical parity for Blacks in judiciary and law enforcement agencies, without the travesty of appointees like Clarence Thomas. There would be no room any longer in the police force for Black quislings who sell our people down the river. For example, in 1994 Los Angeles police chief Willie Williams—himself an African American—demoted a Black deputy chief for favoring Black over white officers for promotion. Williams-style betrayal would merit immediate dismissal. National law would appropriate money for an independent minority development corporation mandated to encourage Black business ownership. Since the era of the Freedmen's Bureau we have been demanding the kind of vigorous federal government enforcement which provides assistance without control.

✳

THE BLACK INTEREST

Just as traces of aversion to Blacks occur in all white societies where people of African origin are present, so there is a general and overriding Black Interest that can be classified under the heading of a general category—i.e., a main concept formed in the process of historical development on the basis of social practice in North America. It should not be confused with specific Black interests which vary according to issue and happenstance. The general interest should be accorded a kind of determining veto, as it were, over all Black strategy and tactics.

Continuing white racism all around the globe is the basis for the existence of the general Black Interest. All continental Africans and Africans of the Diaspora have a stake in the uprooting of white world supremacy. As seen from these American shores, the general Black Interest also has a heavy international aspect to go along with our domestic worries, for, as Garvey, DuBois and Malcolm explained, neocolonialist imperialism has corralled "flag-independent" Africa in the world economy on the most degraded and super-exploitative terms. Furthermore, everywhere one looks in international diplomacy, everywhere from Africa to Haiti to Brazil, the scene is the same—Great Power statesmen regard Black folk as of little account in the international power equation. The general Black Interest is an all-class and above-class interest, because all of us, from the highest to the lowest, female as well as male, regardless of wealth and prominence, remain subject to racial putdown. The contingent interests of the different "classes" and social strata that make up the community often diverge and cause disunity, but never in such a fundamental way as to nullify the residual bond that continues to exist outside and independent of the willingness (or ability) of individuals to admit to reality—a bond forged by the pressure of racism.

The specific worries of Black homeless, single mothers, government employees, businessmen, workers, clergy, and professionals, for instance, are all *partial* concerns. They are not the same as the parallel concerns of their white counterparts. Institutionalized white racism affects *every* Black person in the U.S. and Canada—as a nerve-wracking likelihood if not as an occurrence felt daily. It is a reality in every land in the western hemisphere to one degree or another. Racism's influence conditions the life-chances of every Black individual from the cradle to the grave. The influence may be very remote and indirect as, say, in the case of backwoods central African villagers who have never seen a white person, but whose whole economic existence is nevertheless structured by mechanisms of an international division of labor controlled from Paris, London, Zurich, or New York.

The general Black Interest "downloads" on specific issues. Take the controversy surrounding capital punishment. Most Black leaders are firmly opposed to the death penalty. Why? Because of the way it is applied in the United States. Because white racism dictates that judicial execution will be inflicted disproportionately, perhaps even genocidally, to slaughter Black men. We recognize its potential as a means to assassinate militant Black political dissidents under the cover of legality. Nearly half of all convicts on death row today are men of color. However, in a place like, say, Nigeria, where white racism is not in *direct* control of the criminal justice system, there is less reason to oppose the death penalty on principle. Presumably it can be a weapon of stern but true justice for Nigerian transgressors guilty of heinous and callous offenses. This is not to claim that the death sentence is administered evenhandedly in Nigeria at the present moment, given that nation's ethnic strains and class disparities. But there is at least the *potential* for it to be just, whereas in racist America capital punishment throughout history has been just one more weapon of intimidation against Black people.

Consequently there are no truly "national goals" in America, nor for that matter are there any *"national* interests." There are only Black goals, white goals, Catholic and Protestant goals, white ethnic ones, feminist goals, environmental and gay ones, the goals of oil or tobacco industry lobbyists, white and Black organized labor goals, "Hispanic aims," and so forth. The great constant in North America are racial goals, meaning Black, white, Native American, Asian-American interests, etc. National interests reputedly uniting one and all are a fairy tale, however, unless something obvious and empty is meant, like measures to prevent everyone from being wiped out by some monster earthquake, tornado, or hurricane. Or the hope that the country will not be conquered and enslaved by non-humanoid aliens from outer space. Even seemingly universal aims like the common interest in a cure for cancer elicits disparate responses, for health care in America is administered unevenly in a racially discriminatory manner. A measure to uplift one group in our society is invariably viewed as hostile by another. One proof of divergent national political interests comes from the white response to Black voter registration in the South in the wake of the passage of the 1965 Voting Rights Act. In order to shield racist political domination of the region, white folks countered with their own massive new voter registration that all but offset the increased Black voter pool. Whites repeated the exercise during the 1984 presidential primary campaign, trying to destroy the effect of Jesse Jackson's Black voter registration campaign. That which forwards Black political empowerment injures white political dominance. Thus any real effective political alliance between interest groups must operate on the basis of carefully considered and established priorities, requiring a tug-of-war for predominant influence of one ally over others.

527

＊

EMPOWERMENT AND THE STATE

In the final analysis, should Black empowerment ever become more than a mere slogan, it must come to mean decisive influence for Black America over the principles and policies of the United States Government. That is the bottom line. Only by triumphing over the systematized racism which rules the U.S. and Canada can we achieve this, a victory which in turn is contingent upon uncompromising overthrow of white supremacy worldwide. We must seek this our macro-goal with unrelenting singlemindedness. For the prospect of our success represents humanity's last real hope for a just and humane society. It is our last chance to save mankind from the ultimate catastrophe of North-South nuclear conflict in the coming century.

Is this prospect difficult? Of course. Is it utopian and unrealizable? No indeed. For as the collapse of the Soviet Union—one of only two superpowers—and the defeat of South African apartheid's political aspect bear witness, in the politics of today it is the politically "impossible" which now seems bound to occur. We should insist therefore upon loyalty to Black empowerment as coming before all else. We need a relentless modernization and *secularization* of the entire Black liberation movement which would unite Black Catholics, Black Protestants, Black Muslims, Black capitalists, Black communists, Black socialists, Black nationalists, Black Democrats and Black Republicans, as well as others, while insisting that our aims are non-sectarian and non-partisan. We must maintain our equilibrium in the whirlwind of current events. We must uphold *the primacy of the Black agenda* in all dealings with so-called "reform" and "progressive" trends.

And among current problems we will find few more pressing than the political implications of our own demographic growth. The growing relative size of the Black population in North America conceals both positive and negative prospects. A larger community can muster greater political strength. However, pressured by ever more potent Black bloc-voting, more and more whites will want to abandon political democracy entirely, in favor of an American-baked apartheid eternalizing white rule far into the future, even beyond the moment when Caucasians will have become the minority in North America. We need further be vigilant against any cultural nationalist melanism in our own ranks that would blind us to the real racial composition of the Diaspora: 80 percent of African Americans have Caucasian admixture (the legacy of slavery and subsequent miscegenation) against 20 percent of whites with African ancestry. "Negro racial purity" doctrines are nonsensical, divisive, and counter-productive.

An equally urgent problem that we have made much of in this book is the structural economic redundancy, or "surplusization" which has altered the face of industrial America, i.e., the joblessness, failed education and irrelevant training that are expelling urban Black males from the work force permanently. We need emphasize that the fate of Black womanhood is tied to the destiny of this young male "endangered species," and finally put a stop to the disabling, anti-Black male discourse that mars the writing of all too many Black women today (Alice Walker, Terry McMillan, Ntozake Shange, E.R. Shipp, and Michele Wallace are oft-cited examples).

*

We are on a quest for state power. Now, one cannot effectively be on more than one quest at a time. That means we cannot simultaneously set out on quests for "democracy," "salvation," "socialism," "racial harmony," "freedom," "fundamentalism," "communism," "capitalism," "free enterprise," or any of the other "ism" pacifiers, surrogates, and soporifics with which we have traditionally been injected by white cultural, ideological, and religious domination.

The call to seek power at any cost confers a heavy responsibility because it is a frightening prospect. It is scary because we are not just talking about the formal so-called political "power" that comes from having a handful of Black-faced representatives elected to office in the two-party system (in Canada the three-, now, four-party system), or appointed to "high office" as figureheads. We are not talking about window dressing, but rather about the *real* power which implies at the very least major participation in and influence over the institutions that control the State, especially the economic sinews of society. The uncompromising policies apparently required will at first shock certain persons. However, I predict that, given time to sink in, these notions will seize hold of the minds of Black youth everywhere, not just in the United States and Canada. They will gradually penetrate, spread among, be embraced by, and enthuse coming generations of Black youth. Already some in the inner cities and on campuses across the nation are taking the first steps in this direction. These exhortations are addressed to them. They are espousing a *"realpolitik"* philosophy, one that is unswervingly power-oriented. Among college students this new attitude sometimes wears the garb of a "revised Pan-Africanism" free of illusion and wishful thinking; one that seeks fulfillment on this earth in the here and now, leaving the hereafter to take care of itself. They will pass this vision on as a legacy of seeking the kingdom of earthly power before all else. These youngsters aim to make the twenty-first century the century of the Black man.

This notion of real Black power requires that one embrace yet another concept which conventional, old-style activists may find shocking. It tells us to forget the "beloved community." It says "later: for that." Restrictions which hobble the pursuit of power should be cast aside—be they Semitic religious restrictions, philosophical qualms, or the prohibitions of such pacifist traditions as Buddhism and Bahai. It begs Black people to quit trying to be liked by white folks. We should forget about loving the collective white man and put a stopper on endless drivel about the "table of brotherhood." Quit trying to win professional approval from white occupational peers and stop aping white folks. There is growing admiration in Black *realpolitik* circles for astute expediency and political cunning. In the spirit of learning from one's opponents, let us study the calculations of white historical statesmen who let nothing stand in their way as they transformed their nations into Great Powers.

We are engaged as a people in a life-and-death struggle. We cannot afford diversions from the effort to defeat white racism. We dare not turn aside from the effort to reduce white world supremacy to ashes. Radical young activists are insisting that such be the content of any new, relevant, contemporary Pan-Africanism. Otherwise, despite its great traditions, Black protest will have become mere sentimental romanticism, hot air best suitable for excitable adolescents, but not appropriate for true political warriors.

A salient feature of European history has been its religious fervor. Actually, on close scrutiny, it is a religous fervor of a very practical and hard-headed sort. Despite pious disclaimers and elaborate hypocrisy, throughout history white civilization—Malcolm X's "collective white man"—has really adored only one god, and that god above all others—the god of supreme earthly power. A god whose favor enables white men to rule over the world's people of color; a deity who sanctions Caucasian sway and dominion over creation.

Judeo-Christian doublespeak notwithstanding, the white man's god has ever been a patriarch whose good graces are won by faithful application of the precepts of the lord of battles! White civilization's religious fervor is militaristic, and militarism has given the white man dominion over the earth. Since the fifteenth century the white man's most effective prayer has been mastery of science and technology. We are now saying that the god of power should also be our god; he should become the god of Black folk too. "It was good enough for Moses; it's good enough for me." We must learn to worship him as a race of people, and worship him even better than the collective white man has worshipped him for centuries. For—as our ancient Egyptian ancestors knew— if religious fervor instills a sense of righteousness and purpose, a worship that brings mastery of science and technology leads to military might and economic wealth. There is no question here of power merely for the sake of power, but of power to accomplish the well-being of Black people. "Had whites been treated in America as the Blacks have, I feel certain," says judge Bruce Wright, "that they long ago would have undertaken either guerrilla warfare or prolonged civil disobedience for their rights. The American revolution stands as precedent for how much white victims of oppression accept before they rebel" (Wright 1990:175). In the *Declaration of Independence*, Thomas Jefferson took it upon himself as spokesman for a band of disgruntled white men to proclaim that whenever government becomes destructive of "Life, Liberty and the pursuit of Happiness," "it is the Right of the People to alter or to abolish it..." Have slavery and segregation schooled out of us a similar healthy impatience?

Whatever one's view regarding our mild manner toward whites, the question of power remains imperative. The quest for the temporal power to raise people of African descent to a status and well-being equal to the status and well-being of persons of European descent, encourages us to run any risk, make any sacrifice, uphold any truth, make any compromise, and break any promise if need be, twist facts, betray the "trust" of white supremacists, commit any "transgression" against racism, in the pursuit of our goal. The quest for power requires steely determination. It is ours not to persevere and merely survive; it is ours to persevere and prevail.

Some of our leaders still believe there is an irreconcilable contradiction between the "moral high ground" occupied by the victims of racial discrimination and the adoption of "any-means- necessary" modes of struggle. If we adopt the latter, they claim, we will lose moral authority. This is a fallacy. The moral status of the "river of protest" rests not on the choice of any tactical behavior, but rather on the essential *nature* of the movement. The very continued existence of mankind as a genus on planet Earth—humanity's survival as such—depends urgently on the eradication of white racist world supremacy. That is what the Black struggle is all about. Hence the Black cause could not surrender the moral high ground as long as it aims to extinguish white supremacy, no matter how coldly calculating and seemingly ruthless its choice of means.

•

For Black folk living in the U.S. and Canada the aim is parity and the power to maintain that parity. The parity we seek means equal representation according to population percentage in all advantageous living conditions, and in all of society's decision-making power posts which enable enjoyment of the good things in life. At the present time all that we have is overrepresentation in all the disadvantageous living circumstances—an overrepresentation of powerlessness. As an "ultra-minority," Blacks in Canada need to learn and recognize that as a group their fate is connected with the large Black community south of the border. The racist political economy that aided in the development of the United States is not distinct from Canadian society. The "Great White North" has always nestled under the blanket of racism. African Americans and African Canadians, both, need remember that North American society is part of a civilization dominated by the principle of racial preference. We need to memorize the lesson of the social primer: this society values might over morality. North American civilization is hierarchical in a Social Darwinist sense that projects whites as the benchmark for what is the fittest and the best. Its talent for scientific and technological development is expressed in militaristic and staunchly individualistic fashion. Home to liberalism and occasionally to anti-racist forces, North America's dynamism makes it a larger home to racism and redneckism.

Since the really crucial avenues to economic parity and wealth are hogged by whites and blocked to African Americans as a rule, the quest for decisive political influence over the State, particularly at the federal level, will become even more of a life and death affair as we move into the twenty-first century. We have no other choice in the matter. We have to be *political*. Unfortunately we shall have to live with the fact that a lot of our people will continue to consider themselves as "non-political"—a costly illusion. As one prominent Black expert on public administration explains it, " fiscal policy—the public financial transactions of government—determines the state of the overall economy, and consequently, the state of Black America" (Henderson 1990:53). If for no other reason, we dare not let up in our efforts to regulate the three levels of government—federal, state, and local.

Data from Atlanta shows why the political path is the more accessible route to empowerment for the Black community than the path of entrepreneurial accumulation of wealth. In the Georgia capital in 1989, Black contractors got 92.7 percent of their revenue from public sector agreements. Atlanta's white contractors in contrast derived only 20 percent of their revenue from the public sector. The whites were privileged to do most of their business with private projects. The same pattern is repeated in every locality with a significant Black population. The overwhelming majority of American economic activity is generated from the private ownership sector. Afro-American entrepreneurs are much more dependent on government patronage than is white business enterprise, except perhaps for the great (white-owned) defense contractors whose sole domestic customer can only be the government. Atlanta shows clear evidence of continuing racial discrimination in the construction industry. Discrimination is rife too in most other sectors of privately-owned business, and not confined to the state of Georgia. African-Americans are in the main still locked out from the country's dominant corporate structures. Integration is inchmeal and tokenistic in North America's executive suites. "Glass ceilings" are everywhere.

Wagering all on infiltrating the private corporate sector therefore does not come across as the smartest strategy. The racist poliltial economy is set up to prevent Blacks from using economic means to become a significant force in white corporate capital. Consequently it makes more sense to concentrate instead on participation in and control of the state. We require strategies which enable us to manipulate the political process and the agencies of government as means to the accumulation of wealth and prosperity—a political path to economic development. Government is the main mover in human affairs. The state is a source of power and authority and of control over all the agencies of civil society—including the Church. The police and military establishments are the arms by which the state forces compliance. Although there are many autonomous institutions in this pluralistic society— everything from churches to charities to private schools and clubs—none is as potent as the United States Government. He who controls the government can steer the economy, set guidelines for scientific and technological development, set standards for public health, shape the laws, and referee litigation. He who controls the government burns the deepest mark on U.S. life in general.

The aim of Black liberation should therefore be the political one—power over human behavior grows out of control of the levers of government. The state is the final trump in the human tussle for advantage. Now some of our most brilliant and most well-meaning thinkers have opposed *total* dependency on the state to meet vital Black needs. I for one do not advocate *dependence* on the government; I advocate *control* of the state, and—since as a minority sole control is not possible for us in North America—then in conjunction with a coalition. I am adamantly against welfare dependency. Whether our influence is exerted directly (through elected officials for example) or indirectly does not matter all that much as long as our grasp on the government apparatus is firm. We must use the state as an agent of Black empowerment.

To those who wisely caution that disadvantage for Afro-Americans would continue to exist even if systemic discrimination were suddenly eliminated from social life, I say their objection is well grounded. There is very little prospect for the organic, non-political emergence, without forceful intervention by the state, of a racially-neutral society in which status and wealth would be awarded according to race-neutral character and contribution, or, to what is ironically called "merit." It is true that Black disadvantage would persist due to ingrained patterns created by prior racial discrimination. But, once again, this suggests the state as the only real remedy—its policies and interventions. Government authority can be manipulated to alter the social position of Black people, politically, economically, and socially -manipulated for better or for worse. There can be no "color-blind" society here *without* affirmative action, minority set-asides, and reparations. These are remedial measures impossible to enact without deliberate government action, and without them, ancient wrongs will never be redressed; new racial parities will never see light of day.

＊

The "game of power" is the ultimate game. It is the one that really matters when it comes to determining the direction in which society is to move. Other forms of people-binding activity take a back seat to the power game. Though other kinds of collective activity may be high in profile, compared to it they are froth on the totality of social life. The sticking point is that our folks seemed to be the only ones who did not know this. Blacks have rarely recognized the supreme value of sheer power, instead usually believing that either moral rearmament, religion, or improved personal behavior was the key to happiness. Or we have concentrated on praiseworthy but symptomatic endeavors. We have heaped up academic degrees, strived in small businesses, rehabilitated relations between Black men and women, reclaimed ex-convicts, dealt with crises of drug addiction, sheltered single-female headed families, and nurtured responsible youth in order to break the cycle of teenage pregnancies. These activities are worthy, but unlikely to give us the massive power required to break the cycle of oppression and poverty.

This has made it easier for the white man to monopolize the "only game in town," the one that ultimately molds all other areas of people activity. Power is the cause of which the above ills are symptoms. Taking the metaphor one step further, we can say that the prime objects of capture on the power chessboard—the criterion of victory—are the government "king" and the economy "queen." And the economic monarch stalked in the game of power is *not* any small businessman. She owns and controls the major means of production; society's large scale production assets. It does not matter how one obtains power—historically any means have been valid, fair ones or foul, as long as they provide real lasting power. Surely the means by which these United States became the greatest power on earth—genocide of Amerindians and enslavement of Africans— were sordid.

Thus in its function even a minimally post-racist America would have to be an America which would uphold *wealth parity*. It would have to ensure Black ownership of significant corporate production assets. Across-the-board economic parity would require that African Americans not exceed their population quotient in any *negative* indicator. No more overrepresentation among the poor, the unschooled and the unhealthy! A post-racist America would have a *human and constitutional rights system* which really imposed social equality and equal justice in place of the travesties we now endure. Black political empowerment proportionate to population percentage would become a principle enshrined in the Constitution. The Black community would finally get "equality of results" based initially on reparations.

We must move swiftly and be on guard, for there are those— articulate intellectuals even—who thirst for our blood. For example, Jared Taylor, author of *Paved with Good Intentions: The Failure of Race Relations in America*, and current darling of white conservative eggheads, urges his Aryan blood brothers to sharpen their race-weapons. He wants them ready for a soon-to-come racial Armageddon. A diatribe against African Americans, Taylor's book has quietly grown popular among white suburban semi-wits and in right-wing campus circles. He and his camp followers see us as a pernicious cancer in the U.S. body politic, a serious drag on white Americans' quality of life. His answer to the age-old political riddle, "What is to be done?" is to put Black people back in their "place." Taylor advocates that our numbers be reduced—by compulsory birth control if possible, by rougher methods if necessary. And by backing Taylor's call for a ban on affirmative action in a new book, *The Conscience of a Black Conservative*, Armstrong Williams, a wrong-headed Black man, has in effect applauded the racist agenda against his own people.

For those whose morality never surmounts cost accounting, white America can be presented with a bill it cannot refute. Blacks and other people of color have the potential to generate so much disruption and turmoil in the coming years that the 1992 Los Angeles uprising would seem like a backyard barbecue. Effective repression would be so costly it would bring near-total social collapse and anarchy. The monetary costs would be astronomical. Though also steep, the alternative of compensation, affirmative action, minority set-asides and reparations would prove much less expensive than social turmoil and repression—and certainly more socially healthy. There is no preclusive evidence that white America would choose the holocaustal alternative to the sane one if confronted with this situation. About 140 years ago it chose to recognize the Black victory over chattel slavery rather than submit to Confederate secession.

Fussing at people, admonishing folks to be good has never worked. Not once in the entire history of the human race. Ethical upbringing has severe limitations as the catalyst of real social transformation. The time has come to offer our people a less exalted alternative, a "less" moral and spiritual precept, but one with more potential clout. I would have us seek *power*. I would have us attain the means to defend ourselves as a people against any aggressors, shielding ourselves with lethal force where and when necessary. As Malcolm X put it, we can achieve these ends by any means necessary. Our place in history would then take care of itself.

We must have white supremacy down!

BIBLIOGRAPHY

America, Richard A., ed. (1990). *The Wealth of Races. The Present Value of Benefits from Past Injustice.* New York: Greenwood Press.

Aptheker, Herbert (1991). *Anti-Racism in U.S. History: The First Two Hundred Years.* Westport, Conn.: Greenwood Press.

Aptheker, Herbert (1975). "The History of Anti-Racism in the United States." *The Black Scholar*, Vol. 6. No. 5.

Aspen Institute Conferences (1989 and 1990). *A More Perfect Union: Achieving Hispanic Parity by the Year 2000.* Aspen, Colo.

Asante, Molefi K. (1988). *Afrocentricity.* Trenton, N.J.: Africa World Press.

Asante, Molefi K. (1980). *Afrocentricity: The Theory of Social Change.* Buffalo: Amulefi.

Asante, Molefi K. (1990). *Kemet, Afrocentricity and Knowledge.* Trenton, N.J.: Africa World Press.

Asante, Molefi K. (1993). *Malcolm X as Cultural Hero and Other Afrocentric Essays.* Trenton, N.J.: Africa World Press.

Asante, M.K. and K.W. Asante, eds. (1985). *African Culture: The Rhythms of Unity.* Westport, Conn.: Greenwood Press.

Baldwin, James (1963). *The Fire Next Time.* New York: Dial Press.

Baldwin, James (1972). *No Name in the Street.* New York: Dial Press.

Baldwin, James (1965). *Nobody Knows My Name: More Notes of a Native Son*. London: Corgi Books.

Batchelder, Alan B. (1964). "Decline in Relative Income of Negro Men." *Quarterly Journal of Economics*, Vol. 78.

Bell, Derrick (1987). *And We Are Not Saved: The Elusive Quest for Racial Justice*. New York: Basic Books.

Bell, Derrick (1992). *Faces at the Bottom of the Well: The Permanence of Racism*. New York: Basic Books.

Bell, Derrick (1980). *Race, Racism and American Law*. 2nd ed. Boston: Little, Brown and Company.

Bennett, Lerone Jr., (1984). *Before the Mayflower: A History of Black America*. 5th ed. New York: Penguin Books.

Berlowitz, M.J. and R.S. Edari, eds. (1984). *Racism and the Denial of Human Rights*. Minneapolis.

Berry, Mary Frances and John W. Blassingame (1982). *Long Memory: The Black Experience in America*. New York: Oxford University Press.

Billingsley, Andrew (1992). *Climbing Jacob's Ladder: The Enduring Legacy of African-American Families*. New York: Simon & Schuster.

Black Enterprise.

Block, F., R. Cloward, B. Ehenreich and F. Fox Piven (1987). *The Mean Season: The Attack on the Welfare State*. New York: Pantheon.

Boggs, James (1969). *Manifesto for a Black Revolutionary Party*. Philadelphia: Pacesetters Publishing House.

Bonachichff, E. (1976). "Advanced Capitalism and Black/White Relations in the United States: A Split Labor Market Interpretation." *American Sociological Review*. 41.

Bracey, Jr., Meier A. And E. Rudwick, eds. (1970). *Black Nationalism in America*. Indianapolis: Bobbs-Merrill Co.

Bradley, David (1981). *The Chaneysville Incident*. New York: Harper & Row.

Bradley, Michael (1991). *The Iceman Inheritance: Prehistoric Sources of Western Man's Racism, Sexism and Aggression*. New York: Kayode Publications.

Brenner, Lenni (1984). "The Misguided Search for Black/Jewish Unity." *Freedomways*, Vol. 24, No. 2.

Brown, Elaine (1992). *A Taste of Power: A Black Woman's Story*. New York: Pantheon Books.

Bullard, R.D., ed. (1993). *Confronting Environmental Racism: Voices from the Grassroots*. Boston: South End Press.

Bullard, R.D. (1992). "Urban Infrastructure: Social, Environmental and Health Risks to African Americans." *The State of Black America, 1992.* New York: National Urban League, Inc.

Busby, Margaret, ed. (1992). *Daughters of Africa: An International Anthology of Words and Writings by Women of African Descent from the Ancient Egyptians to the Present.* London: Jonathan Cape.

Campbell, Horace (1987). *Rasta and Resistance from Marcus Garvey to Walter Rodney.* Trenton, N.J.: Africa World Press.

Carmichael, Stokely and Charles V. Hamilton (1967). *Black Power: The Politics of Liberation.* New York: Penguin Books.

Carson, C., D.J. Garrow, G. Gill, V. Harding and Hine D. Clark, eds. (1991). *The Eyes on the Prize Civil Rights Reader: Documents, Speeches and First Hand Accounts from the Black Freedom Struggle 1954-1990.* New York: Penguin Books.

Carter, Stephen L. (1991). *Reflections of an Afrirmative Action Baby.* New York: Basic Books.

Casely-Hayford, Joseph (1911). *Africa Unbound.*

Cherry, Robert (1991). "Race and Gender Aspects of Marxian Macromodels: The Case of the Social Structure of the Accumulation School, 1948-68." *Science and Society.* Vol. 55, No. 1.

Chestnut, J.L. Jr. and Julia Cass (1991). *Black in Selma: The Uncommon Life of J.L. Chestnut, Jr..* New York: Anchor Books Doubleday.

Christman, Robert and Robert L. Allen (1991). *Court of Appeal: The Black Community Speaks Out on the Racial and Sexual Politics of Clarence Thomas vs. Anita Hill.* New York: Ballantine Books.

Clarke, John Henrik, ed. (1969). *Malcolm X: The Man and His Times.* New York: Macmillan Company.

Clarke, John Henrik (1974). *Marcus Garvey and the Vision of Africa.* New York: Random House.

Clarke, John H., ed. (1991). *New Dimensions in African History: The London Lectures of Dr. Yosef ben-Jochannen and Dr. John Henrik Clarke.* Trenton, N.J.: Africa World Press.

The Claude A. Barnett Papers. Part Three. Subject files on Black Americans, 1918-1967. Series I. Race Relations, 1923-1965. Bethesda, Maryland: University Publications of America.

Cole, Johnnetta B. (1993). *Conversations: Straight Talk with America's Sister President.* New York: Doubleday.

Colton, Elizabeth O. (1989). *The Jackson Phenomenon: The Man, the Power, the Message.* New York: Doubleday.

Cone, James H. (1969). *Black Theology and Black Power.* New York:

Seabury Press.

Cone, James H. (1991). *Martin and Malcolm and America: A Dream or a Nightmare*. Maryknoll, N.Y.: Orbis Books.

Cose, Ellis (1993). *The Rage of a Privileged Class*. New York: Harper Collins.

Cottingham, C. (1982). *Race, Poverty and the Urban Underclass*. Lexington, Mass.

Cox, Oliver KC. (1976). *Race Relations*. Detroit: Wayne State University Press.

Cress Welsing, Frances (1991). *The Isis Papers: The Keys to the Colors*. Chicago: Third World Press.

Cross, Theodore (1984). *The Black Power Imperative: Racial Inequality and the Politics of Nonviolence*. New York: Faulkner.

Crouch, Stanley (1990). *Notes of a Hanging Judge*. New York: Oxford University Press.

Darity, W. Jr., ed. (1984). *Labor Economics: Modern Views*. Boston.

Davis, Angela Y. (1981). *Women, Race and Class*. New York: Random House.

Diop, Cheikh Anta (1974). *The African Origin of Civilization*. New York: Lawrence Hill and Company.

Diop, Cheikh Anta (1991). *Civilization or Barbarism: An Authentic Anthropology*. Brooklyn: Lawrence Hill Books.

Diop, Cheikh Anta (1978). *The Cultural Unity of Black Africa*. Chicago: Third World Press.

Diop, Cheikh Anta (1987). *Precolonial Black Africa: A Comparative Study of the Political and Social Systems of Europe and Black Africa, from Antiquity to the Formation of Modern States*. Brooklyn: Lawrence Hill Books.

Drake, St. Clair (1987). *Black Folk Here and There: An Essay in History and Anthropology*. 2 volumes. Los Angeles: Center for Afro-American Studies, UCLA.

DuBois, W.E.B. (1969). *The Souls of Black Folks*. New York: The New American Library.

Duneier, Mitchell (1992). *Slim's Table: Race, Respectability, and Masculinity*. Chicago: University of Chicago Press.

Dyson, Michael Eric (1993). *Reflecting Black: African-American Cultural Criticism*. Minneapolis: University of Minnesota Press.

Edari, Ronald S. (1991). "Underclass: An Inquiry into its Theoretical Status and Ideological Dimensions." *NST: Nature, Society and Thought*. Vol. 4, No. 12.

Evanzz, Karl (1992). *The Judas Factor: The Plot to Kill Malcolm X*. New York: Thunder's Mouth Press.

Fabre, Michel (1991). *From Harlem to Paris: Black American Writers in France,1840-1980*. Urbana and Chicago: University of Illinois Press.

Fanon, Frantz (1967). *Black Skins, White Masks*. New York: Grove Press.

Fanon, Frantz (1970). *Toward the African Revolution*. Harmondsworth: Penguin Books.

Fanon, Frantz (1968). *The Wretched of the Earth*. New York: Grove Press.

Farley, R. And W.R. Allen, eds. (1987). *The Color Line and the Quality of Life in America: The Population of the United States in the 1980s*. New York: Russel Sage Foundation.

Farrakhan, Louis (1993). *A Torchlight for America*. Chicago: FCN Publishing Co.

Feagin, J.R. and M.P. Sikes (1994). *Living with Racism: The Black Middle-Class Experience*. Boston: Beacon Press.

Fichtenbaum, R. (1989). "A Critique of the Segmentation Theory of Racial Discrimination." *NST: Nature, Society and Thought*. Volume 3, No. 4.

Fiskus, Ronald J. (1992). *The Constitutional Logic of Affirmative Action*. Chapel Hill, N.C.: Duke University Press.

Fletcher, J., T. Jones and S. Lotringer, eds. (1993). *Still Black, Still Strong, Survivors of the U.S. War Against Black Revolutionaries: Dhoruba Bin Wahad, Mumia Abu-Jamal, Assata Shakur*. Brooklyn: Semiotext(e).

Foner, Philip S. (1976). *Organized Labor and the Black Worker, 1619-1973*. New York: International Publishers.

Forman, James (1972). *The Making of Black Revolutionaries*. New York: The Macmillan Company.

Foster, Cecil (1991). *Distorted Mirror: Canada's Racist Face*. Toronto: Harper Collins.

Franklin, John Hope (1993). *The Color Line: Legacy for the Twenty-First Century*. Columbia, Missouri: University of Missouri Press.

Franklin, John Hope and Alfred A. Moss Jr. (1994). *From Slavery to Freedom: A History of African Americans. Seventh Edition*. New York: McGraw-Hill.

Franklin, Raymond S. (1991). *Shadows of Race and Class*. Minneapolis: University of Minnesota Press.

Franklin, V.P. (1992). *Black Self-Determination: A Cultural History of*

Afro-American Resistance. Brooklyn: Lawrence Hill Books.

Frederickson, George M. (1971). *The Black Image in the White Mind.* New York.

Frederickson, George M. (1981). *White Supremacy: A Comparative Study in American and South African History.* Oxford and New York: Oxford University Press.

Galeano, Eduardo (1984, 1991). *Open Veins in Latin America: Five Centuries of the Pillage of a Continent.* New York: Monthly Review Press.

Garvey, Amy Jacques, ed. (1969). *Philosophy and Opinions of Marcus Garvey, Two Volumes in One.* New York: Arno Press and The New York Times.

Gibbs, Jewelle Taylor, ed. (1988). *Young, Black and Male in America: An Endangered Species.* New York and Westport, Conn.: Auburn House.

Glazer, Nathan (1975). *Affirmative Discrimination: Ethnic Inequality and Public Policy.* New York: Basic Books.

Glenn, E.N. (1985). "Racial Ethnic Women's Labor: The Intersection of Race, Gender and Class Oppression." *Review of Radical Political Economics.* 17.

The Globe and Mail.

Gomes, Ralph C. and Linda Faye Williams (1992). *From Exclusion to Inclusion: The Long Struggle for African American Political Power.* New York and Westport, Conn.: Greenwood Press.

Gordon, Diana (1990). *The Justice Juggernaut: Fighting Street Crime, Controlling Citizens.* Brunswick, N.J.: Rutgers University.

Guinier, Lani (1994). *The Tyranny of the Majority: Fundamental Fairness in Representative Democracy.* New York: The Free Press Macmillan.

Gwaltney, John Langston, ed. (1993). *Drylongso: A Self-Portrait of Black America.* New York: The New Press.

Hacker, Andrew (1992). *Two Nations: Black and White, Separate, Hostile, Unequal.* New York: Ballantine Books.

Hampton, Henry and Steve Fayer, eds. (1991). *Voices of Freedom: An Oral History of the Civil Rights Movement from the 1950s through the 1980s.* New York: Bantam Books.

Haney-Lopez, Ian (1991). "Community Ties, Race, and Faculty Hiring: The Case for Professors Who Don't Think White." *Reconstruction.* Vol. I, No. 3.

Harding, Vincent (1981). *There Is a River: The Black Struggle for Freedom in America.* San Diego: Harcourt Brace Jovanovich.

Harlan, Louis (1983). *Booker T. Washington: The Wizard of Tuskegee, 1901-1915.* New York: Oxford University Press.

Harris, William J., ed. (1991). *The LeRoi Jones / Amiri Baraka Reader.* New York: Thunder's Mouth Press.

Henderson, Lenneal, J. (1990). "Budget and Tax Strategy: Implications for Blacks." *The State of Black America, 1990.* New York: National Urban League, Inc.

Henry, Keith S. (1981). *Black Politics in Toronto Since World War I.* Toronto: The Multicultural History Society of Ontario.

Hernton, Calvin C. (1965). *Sex and Racism in America.* New York: Grove Press.

Hilliard, David and Lewis Cole (1993). *This Side of Glory: The Autobiography of David Hilliard and the Story of the Black Panther Party.* Boston: Little, Brown and Company.

Hoetink, Herman (1967). *Caribbean Race Relations: A Study of Two Variants.* London: Oxford University Press.

Howe, Louise Kapp, ed. (1970). *The White Majority Between Poverty and Affluence.* New York.

Huggins, Nathan Irvin (1990). *Black Odyssey: The African-American Ordeal in Slavery.* New York: Vintage Books.

Huggins, N.I., M. Kilson and D.M. Fox, eds. (1971). *Key Issures in the Afro-American Experience.* 2 volumes. New York: Harcourt Brace Jovanovich.

Hutchinson, Earl Ofari (1994). *The Assassination of the Black Male Image.* Los Angeles: Middle Passage Press.

Ice T. (1994). *The Ice Opinion.* New York: St. Martin's Press.

Jahn, Janheinz (1961). *The New African Culture.* New York: Grove Press.

Jaynes, G.D. and R.M. Williams, eds. (1989). *Common Destiny: Blacks and American Society.* Washington, D.C.: National Academy Press.

Jones, LeRoi (1963). *Blues People: Negro Music in White America.* New York: William Morrow and Company.

Jhally, Sut and Justin Lewis (1992). *Enlightened Racism: The Cosby Show, Audiences and the Myth of the American Dream.* Boulder City, Colorado: Westview Press.

Jordan, Winthrop D. (1974). *The White Man's Burden: Historical Origins of Racism in the United States.* London and New York: Oxford University Press.

Jordan, Winthrop D. (1968). *White Over Black: American Attitudes toward the Negro, 1550-1812.* Baltimore: Penguin Books.

Journal of African Civilizations.

Journal of Negro History.

Karenga, Maulana (1982). *Introduction to Black Studies*. Inglewood, Cal.: Kawaida.

Karim, Imam Benjamin, ed. (1971). *The End of White World Supremacy: Four Speeches by Malcolm X*. New York: Arcade Publishing.

Kelley, Robin D.G. (1994). *Race Rebels, Politics and the Black Working Class*. New York: The Free Press Macmillan.

Keto, C. Tschloane (1989). *The Africa Centered Perspective of History*. Blackwood, N.J.: K.A. Publications.

King, Martin Luther, Jr. (1963). *Why We Can't Wait*. New York and Toronto: The New American Library.

King, Patricia (1992). The Ongoing Struggle Over Clarence Thomas—Against Clarence Thomas." *Reconstruction*. Vol. I, No. 4.

Ki-Zerbo, J. (1963). *Le monde african noir*. Paris: Présence Africaine.

Kluger, Richard (1976). *Simple Justice: The History of Brown v. Board of Education and Black America's Struggle for Equality*. New York: Vintage Books Random House.

Kovel, Joel (1971). *White Racism: A Psychohistory*. New York: Vintage Books.

Kozol Jonathan (1991). *Savage Inequalities: Children in America's Schools*. New York: Crown Publishers.

Lee, Spike (1992). *By Any Means Necessary: The Trials and Tribulations of the Making of Malcolm X*. New York: Hyperion.

Lemann, Nicholas (1991). *The Promised Land: The Great Black Migration and How It Changed America*. New York: Vintage Books.

Lewis, David Levering (1993). *W.E.B. DuBois: Biography of a Race, 1868-1919*. New York: Henry Holt and Company.

Lincoln, C. Eric (1974). *The Black Church Since Frazier*. New York: Schocken Books.

Litwack, Leon (1961). *North of Slavery: The Negro in the Free States, 1790-1860*. Chicago.

MacGregor, Morris J. and Bernard C. Nalty, eds. (1977). *Blacks in the United States Armed Forces: Basic Documents*. 13 volumes. Wilmington, Del.: Scholarly Resources.

Madhubuti, Haki R. (1990). *Black Men: Obsolete, Single, Dangerous. Afrikan American Families in Transition*. Chicago: Third World Press.

Madhubuti, Haki R. (1994). *Claiming Earth: Race, Rage, Rape, Redemption; Blacks Seeking a Culture of Enlightened Empowerment*. Chicago: Third World Press.

Magubane, Bernard M. (1987). *The Ties That Bind: African-American Consciousness of Africa*. Trenton, N.J.: Africa World Press.

Maher, Lisa (1990). "Criminalizing Pregnancy—The Downside of a Kinder, Gentler Nation?" *Social Justice: A Journal of Crime, Conflict and World Order*. Fall 1990.

Majors, Richard and Janet Mancini Bilson (1992). *Cool Pose: The Dilemmas of Black Manhood in America*. New York: Simon & Schuster.

Malcolm X (1970). *By Any Means Necessary: Speeches, Interviews, and a Letter by Malcolm X*. New York: Pathfinder Press.

Malcolm X (1990). *On Afro-American History*. New York: Pathfinder Press.

Mandela, Nelson (1994). *Long Walk to Freedom: The Autobiography of Nelson Mandela*. Boston: Little Brown and Company.

Mao Tse-tung (1965). *Selected Works*. Peking.

Maquet, J.J. (1972). *Africanity: The Cultural Unity of Africa*. New York: Oxford University Press.

Marable, Manning (1992). *The Crisis of Color and Democracy: Essays on Race, Class and Power*. Monroe, Maine: Common Courage Press.

Marable, Manning (1984). *Race, Reform and Rebellion: The Second Reconstruction in Black America, 1945-1982*. London: Macmillan Press.

Massey, Douglas S. And Nancy A. Denton (1993). *American Apartheid: Segregation and the Making of the Underclass*. Cambridge, Mass.: Harvard University Press.

Martin, Tony (1993). *The Jewish Onslaught: Despatches from the Wellesley Battlefront*. Dover, Mass.: The Majority Press.

Martin, Tony (1976). *Race First: The Ideological and Organizational Struggles of Marcus Garvey and the Universal Negro Improvement Association*. Dover, Mass.: The Majority Press.

Maurer, Marc (1991). *Americans Behind Bars: A Comparison of International Rates of Incarceration*. Washington, D.C.: Sentencing Project.

Maurer, Marc (1990). *Young Black Men and the Criminal Justice System: A Growing National Problem*. Washington, D.C.: The Sentencing Project.

Mazrui, Ali (1990). "Dr. Schweitzer's Racism." *Transition: An International Review*. No. 53.

McCorkel, Mac (1991). "Gantt versus Helms: Toward the New Progressive Era?" *Reconstruction*. Volume 1, No. 3.

McKague, Ormond, ed. (1991). *Racism in Canada*. Saskatoon: Fifth House Publishers.

McKenzie, Floretta Dukes (with Patricia Evans) (1991). "Education Strategies for the '90s." *The State of Black America, 1991*. New York: National Urban League, Inc.

McMillan, Terry, ed. (1990). *Breaking Ice: An Anthology of Contemporary African-American Fiction*. New York: Penguin Books.

Meier, A., E. Rudwick and F.L. Broderick, eds. (1971). *Black Protest Thought in the Twentieth Century*. Second Edition. Indianapolis: Bobbs-Merrill Company.

Miller, Warren E. (1991). "Developing Untapped Talent: A National Call for African-American Technologists." *The State of Black America, 1991*. New York: National Urban League, Inc.

Mills, Kay (1991). *This Little Light of Mine: The Life of Fannie Lou Hamer*. New York: Dutton Books.

Money.

Monteiro, Tony (1991). "Criminalization of African-Americans: The Face of Racism." *Political Affairs*, April 1991.

Munford, Clarence J. (1991). *The Black Ordeal of Slavery and Slave Trading in the French West Indies, 1625-1715*. 3 volumes. Lewiston, N.Y.: The Edwin Mellen Press.

Munford, Clarence J. (1976). "Ideology, Racist Mystification and America." *Revolutionary World. An International Journal of Philosophy*. 17/18.

Munford, Clarence J. (1978). *Production Relations, Class and Black Liberation*. Amsterdam: B.R. Gruner.

Murphy, Joseph M. (1988). *Santería: An African Religion in America*. Boston: Beacon Press.

Myrdal, Gunnar (1964 edition). *An American Dilemma*. 2 volumes. New York: McGraw-Hill.

Naison, Mark (1991). "Outlaw Culture and Black Neighborhoods." *Reconstruction*. Vol. I, No. 4.

Nascimento, Abdias do (1989). *Brazil, Mixture or Massacre: Essays in the Genocide of a Black People*. Dover, Mass.: First Majority Press.

Nascimento, Abdias do (1979). *Mixture or Massacre: The Genocide of a Race*. Buffalo: Afrodiaspora.

Nascimento, Abdias do (1985). "Quilombismo: The African-Brazilian Road to Socialism." M.K. Asante, eds. *African Culture: The Rhythms of Unity*. Westport, Conn.: Greenwood Press.

Nascimento, Abdias do (1977). *Racial Democracy in Brazil*. Ibadan:

Sketch Publishing.

Nash, Gary B. And Richard Weiss, eds. (1970). *The Great Fear: Race in the Mind of America*. New York: Holt, Rinehart and Winston.

The New York Amsterdam News.

Nieman, Donald G. (1991). *Promises to Keep: African-Americans and the Cosntitutional Order, 1776 to the Present*. New York: Oxford University Press.

Obenga, Theophile (1973). *L'Afrique dans l'antiquité*. Paris: Présence Africaine.

Obenga, Theophile (1980). *Pour une nouvelle histoire*. Paris: Préscnce Africaine.

Omi, Michael and Howard Winant (1986). *Racial Formation in the United States: From 1960 to the 1980s*. New York and London: Routledge.

Pearson, Hugh (1994). *The Shadow of the Panther: Huey Newton and the Price of Black Power in America*. Reading, Mass.: Addison-Wesley Publishing.

People's Weekly World.

Perlo, V. (1988). *Super Profits and Crises: Modern U.S. Capitalism*. New York: International Publishers.

Perry, Bruce, ed. (1989). *Malcolm X: The Last Speeches*. New York: Pathfinder Press.

Population Reference Bureau, Inc. (1991). *African Americans in the 1990s*, compiled from data issued by the U.S. Bureau of the Census, *1990 Current Population Reports*. Washington, D.C.

Reed, Ishmael (1993). *Airing Dirty Laundry*. Reading, Mass.: Addison-Wesley Publishing Company.

Reider, Jonathan (1985). *Canarsie: The Jews and Italians of Brooklyn Against Liberalism*. Cambridge, Mass.: Harvard University Press.

Riley, Dorothy Winbush, ed. (1993). *My Soul Looks Back, 'Less I Forget: A Collection of Quotations by People of Color*. New York: Harper Collins.

Ringer, B.B. and E.R. Lawless (1989). *Race-Ethnicity and Society*. New York and London: Routledge.

Rodney, Walter (1975). "Africa in Europe and the Americas" and "The Guinea Coast." *The Cambridge History of Africa, Volume 4: From c. 1600 to c. 1790*. Cambridge: Cambridge University Press.

Rodney, Walter (1966). "African Slavery and Other Forms of Social Oppression of the Upper Guinea Coast in the Context of the Atlantic Slave Trade." *Journal of African History*. 7.

Rodney, Walter (1985). "The Colonial Economy." *General History of Africa. VII: Africa under Colonial Domination 1880-1935*. Paris: UNESCO.

Rodney, Walter (1972). *How Europe Underdeveloped Africa*. London and Dar-es-Salaam: Bogle-L'Ouverture Publications.

Ruch, E.A. and K.C. Anyanwu (1981). *African Philosophy*. Rome: Catholic Book Agency.

Russell, K., M. Wilson and R. Hall (1993). *The Color Complex: The Politics of Skin Color Among African Americans*. New York: Anchor Books Doubleday.

Shapiro, Herbert (1988). *White Violence and Black Response from Reconstruction to Montgomery*. Amherst, Mass.: University of Massachusetts Press.

Simone, Timothy Maligalim (1989). *About Face: Race in Postmodern America*. Brooklyn: Autonomedia.

Smith, Robert C. (1991). "Hammering at the Truth." *Transition: An International Review*. No. 54.

Smitherman, Geneva (1977). *Talkin and Testifyin: The Language of Black America*. Detroit: Wayne State University Press.

Sofala, J.A. (1973). *The African Culture and the African Personality*. Ibadan: African Resources Publishing Co.

Southern, Eileen (1971). *The Music of Black Americans: A History*. New York: W.W. Norton.

Staples, Robert (1987). "Black Male Genocide: A Final Solution to the Race Problem in America." *Black Scholar*. Vol. 18, No. 3.

Staples, Robert (1982). *Black Masculinity: The Black Male's Role in American Society*. San Francisco: The Black Scholar Press.

Steele, Shelby (1990). *The Content of Our Character: A New Vision of Race in America*. New York: St. Martin's Press.

Swain, Carol (1992). *Black Faces, Black Interests: The Representation of African American Interests in Congress*. Cambridge, Mass.: Harvard University Press.

Swinton, D.H. (1990). "The Economic Status of Black Americans during the 1980s: A Decade of Limited Progress." *The State of Black America, 1990*. New York: National Urban League, Inc.

Swinton, David H. (1993). "The Economic Status of African Americans during the Reagan-Bush Era: Withered Opportunities, Limited Outcomes, and Uncertain Outlook." *The State of Black America, 1993*. New York: National Urban League, Inc.

Swinton, David H. (1991). "The Economic Status of African Americans:

'Permanent' Poverty and Inequality." *The State of Black America, 1991*. New York: National Urban League, Inc.

Terry, Wallace (1992). *Bloods: An Oral History of the Vietnam War by Black Veterans*. New York: Ballantine Books.

Tidwell, Billy (1993). "African Americans and the 21st Century Labor Market: Improving the Fit." *The State of Black America, 1993*. New York: National Urban League, Inc.

Tidwell, Billy (1991). "Economic Costs of Racism." *The State of Black America, 1991*. New York: National Urban League, Inc.

Toll, William (1979). *The Resurgence of Race: Black Social Theory from Reconstruction to the Pan-African Conferences*. Philadelphia: Temple University Press.

Trouillot, Michel-Rolph (1990). *Haiti State Against Nation: The Origins and Legacy of Duvalierism*. New York: Monthly Review Press.

U.S. Bureau of the Census (March 1985). *Household and Family Characteristics* (Current Population Reports, Population Characteristics, Series P-20, No. 411). Washington, D.C.

U.S. Bureau of the Census (1987). *Survey of Minority-Owned Business Enterprises, 1987*. Washington, D.C.: U.S. Department of Commerce.

Urban Institute (1991). *Opportunities Denied, Opportunities Diminished: Discrimination in Hiring*. Washington, D.C.

USA Today.

Van Deburg, William L. (1992). *New Day in Babylon: The Black Power Movement and American Culture, 1965-1975*. Chicago and London: University of Chicago Press.

Van den Berghe, P.L. (1967). *Race and Racism: A Comparative Perspective*. New York.

Van Sertima, Ivan (1992). *African Presence in Early America*. New Brunswick and London: Transaction Publishers.

Van Sertima, Ivan (1986). *Great African Thinkers, Vol. 1: Cheikh Anta Diop*. New Brunswick, N.J.: Transaction Publishers.

Van Sertima, Ivan (1976). *They Came Before Columbus*. New York: Random House.

Walker, Clarence E. (1991). *Deromanticizing Black History: Critical Essays and Reappraisals*. Knoxville: The University of Tennessee Press.

Washington, James M., ed. (1991). *A Testament of Hope: The Essential Writings of Martin Luther King, Jr.*. San Francisco: Harper Collins.

Watkins, Mel (1994). *On the Real Side: Laughing, Lying, and Signifying -*

The Underground Tradition of African American Humor that Transformed American Culture from Slavery to Richard Pryor. New York: Simon & Schuster.

Wellman, David T. (1993). *Portraits of White Racism*. Second edition. New York: Cambridge University Press.

West, Cornell (1993). *Race Matters*. Boston: Beacon Press.

Wiley, Ralph (1993). *What Black People Should Do Now: Dispatches from Near the Vanguard*. New York: Ballantine Books.

Wiley, Ralph (1991). *Why Black People Tend to Shout: Cold Facts and Wry Views from a Black Man's World*. New York: Penguin Books.

Williams, Chancellor (1987). *The Destruction of Black Civilization: Great Issues of a Race from 4500 B.C. to 2000 A.D.* Chicago: Third World Press.

Williams, Eric (1944). *Capitalism & Slavery*. London: Andre Deutsch.

Williams, Evelyn (1993). *Inadmissible Evidence: The Story of the African-American Trial Lawyer Who Defended the Black Liberation Army*. Brooklyn: Lawrence Hill Books.

Williams, Juan (1988). *Eyes on the Prize: America's Civil Rights Years, 1954-1965*. New York: Penguin Books.

Williams, R. (1987). "A Reconsideration of Racial Earnings Inequality." *Review of Radical Political Economics*. 19.

Williams, T.A. and W. Kornblum (1991). "A Portrait of Youth: Coming of Age in Harlem Public Housing." *The State of Black America, 1991*. New York: National Urban League, Inc.

Wilmore, Gayraud S. and James H. Cone, eds. (1979). *Black Theology: A Documentary History, 1966-1979*. Maryknoll, N.Y.: Orbis Books.

Wilson, Edward (1975). *Sociobiology: The New Synthesis*. Cambridge, Mass.: Harvard University Press.

Wright, Bruce (1990). *Black Robes, White Justice*. New York: Carol Publishing Group.

Yeboah, S.K. (1988). *The Ideology of Racism*. London: Hansib Publishing.

Yerby, Frank (1979). *A Darkness at Ingraham's Crest*. New York: The Dial Press.

INDEX